TOURISM, TRAVEL AND
HOSPITALITY LAW

Thomson Reuters (Professional) Australia Limited
100 Harris Street Pyrmont NSW 2009
Tel: (02) 8587 7000 Fax: (02) 8587 7100
LTA.Service@thomsonreuters.com
www.thomsonreuters.com.au
For all customer inquiries please ring 1300 304 195
(for calls within Australia only)

INTERNATIONAL AGENTS & DISTRIBUTORS

NORTH AMERICA
Thomson Reuters
Eagan
United States of America

ASIA PACIFIC
Thomson Reuters
Sydney
Australia

LATIN AMERICA
Thomson Reuters
São Paulo
Brazil

EUROPE
Thomson Reuters
London
United Kingdom

TOURISM, TRAVEL AND HOSPITALITY LAW

TREVOR C ATHERTON

B Com; LLB (Hons) Qld; MSc Tourism Management (Dist) Surrey; LLM Tourism Law (Bond)
Solicitor: Australia, England, Wales
Visiting Professor: Bond and other Universities
Director: Atherton Advisory Pty Ltd, International Tourism Policy Law & Development Consultants
Partner: Atherton Legal
Contact: trevor@athertonadvisory.com

TRUDIE A ATHERTON

BA; LLB (Hons) Qld; LLM Tourism Law (Bond); Grad Dip Env. law (Syd)
Solicitor: Australia, England, Wales
Visiting Professor: Bond and other Universities
Director: Atherton Advisory Pty Ltd, International Tourism Policy Law & Development Consultants
Partner: Atherton Legal
Contact: trudie@athertonadvisory.com

SECOND EDITION

LAWBOOK CO.2011

Published in Sydney by

Thomson Reuters (Professional) Australia Limited ABN 64
058 914 668

100 Harris Street, Pyrmont, NSW

First edition 1998

National Library of Australia
Cataloguing-in-Publication entry
Atherton, Trevor, 1950-
  Tourism, travel and hospitality law/Trevor C Atherton
and Trudie-Ann Atherton.
2nd ed.

9780455228372 (pbk.)
Includes index.
 Tourism–Law and legislation–Australia. Travel
agents–Legal status, laws, etc.–Australia. Hospitality
industry–Law and legislation–Australia.
Atherton, Trudie-Ann, 1953-
343.940783384791

© 2011 Published in book form under licence to Thomson Reuters (Professional) Australia Ltd

This publication is copyright. Other than for the purposes of and subject to the conditions prescribed under the Copyright Act, no part of it may in any form or by any means (electronic, mechanical, microcopying, photocopying, recording or otherwise) be reproduced, stored in a retrieval system or transmitted without prior written permission. Inquiries should be addressed to the authors.

All legislative material herein is reproduced by permission but does not purport to be the official or authorised version. It is subject to Commonwealth of Australia copyright. The *Copyright Act 1968* permits certain reproduction and publication of Commonwealth legislation. In particular, s 182A of the Act enables a complete copy to be made by or on behalf of a particular person. For reproduction or publication beyond that permitted by the Act, permission should be sought in writing. Requests should be submitted online at www.ag.gov.au/cca, faxed to (02) 6250 5989 or mailed to Commonwealth Copyright Administration, Attorney-General's Department, Robert Garran Offices, National Circuit, Barton ACT 2600.

                     Publisher: Robert Wilson
                     Printed by Ligare Pty Ltd, Riverwood, NSW

This book has been printed on paper certified by the Programme for the Endorsement of Forest Certification (PEFC). PEFC is committed to sustainable forest management through third party forest certification of responsibly managed forests.

FOREWORD

Geoff Dixon
Chairman, Tourism Australia

Globally, tourism has become big business with many nations now enjoying the significant economic and social benefits that the industry brings.

It is a truly global industry which sees the flow on effects not only reach international cities but also underpinning many regional economies as well.

By its very nature as a service industry, tourism is also a significant employer of people – with up to one million people in Australia alone directly and indirectly involved in the industry. This could be in major corporations involved in tourism and hospitality or small family operated businesses.

Tourism is an industry too that continues to grow as people's appetite for travel needs to be satisfied, despite the many competing ways that they can spend their leisure time and dollars.

Over the next decade international arrivals globally are expected to increase by more than half a billion to 1.6 billion annually, and with this will come increased demand for a wide range of tourism related products and services.

There will be increased demands on investment, infrastructure, transport, tourism product and skilled people. It will also require those involved in the sector to have an understanding of the wide range of legal responsibilities. Whether it be national or international consumer laws, duties of care to passengers, guests and patrons.

For a truly global industry like tourism there is a definite need for a comprehensive text covering Tourism, Travel & Hospitality Law. It has been produced by two experienced tourism operators turned legal academics who fully understand the complexities of the sector.

This second edition of *Tourism, Travel & Hospitality Law* is a comprehensive and practical management tool for all those involved in the industry.

November 2010

PREFACE

When we commenced practice 30 years ago as solicitors and accountants at the little North Queensland town of Airlie Beach, tourism was displacing sugar as the main industry in the surrounding Whitsunday region. Inevitably, our boutique practice concentrated on the hotels, resorts, package holidays, shipping, aviation, diving and the associated property and commercial transactions taking place at an emerging destination. We found the work and the people involved so interesting that we have specialised in this field of the law ever since. It has taken us from practice through tourism development and operation to consulting work for industry on compliance and risk management through our law firm Atherton Legal and for government and international organisations on tourism policy, law and development through our consultancy Atherton Advisory Pty Ltd.

This book was conceived in the 1990s when Bond University provided us with the opportunity to build upon our experience and develop the academic side of the subject. The first edition published in 1998 evolved from the materials collected, developed and presented in Tourism Law and related courses and from our research and consulting work through this period and this has continued through this second edition of the book. And no doubt it will continue to evolve through future editions.

We are grateful to our publishers, Thomson Reuters and particularly to Robert Wilson, Commercial Manager for Books who, after many years of encouragement, persuaded us to take time out from our other commitments to write this second edition. We also thank Lara Weeks, who undertook the formidable task of turning the manuscript into this text.

As mentioned, the second edition is based on our further teaching, research and consulting in the subject areas. Trudie undertook the major task of incorporating all this material into the second edition of the book. Trevor wrote Chapters 1 and 9 and reviewed and refined the drafts of Chapters 11-15.

The scope and structure of this text are described in Chapter 1. We have endeavoured to present the law according to the information available to us generally at mid-2010, although some later developments have been incorporated. The law is continually changing and readers should not rely on this work without checking for the latest developments. We welcome readers' comments and references to further cases and materials of interest.

TREVOR C ATHERTON
TRUDIE-ANN ATHERTON
www.athertonadvisory.com
Atherton Legal

Sydney
November 2010

TABLE OF CONTENTS

Foreword v
Preface vii
Table of Cases xi
Table of Statutes xxiii

1: Introduction 1

2: Common law 9

3: Statute 41

4: Contract 63

5: Torts 95

6: Criminal Law 115

7: Insurance 137

8: Employment 157

9: Consumer Protection 183

10: Dispute resolution 231

11: Travel agency and distribution 247

12: Passenger Transport 317

13: Traveller Accommodation 399

14: Food and Beverage 433

15: Activities and attractions 471

Index 545

TABLE OF CASES

A

Adamopoulos v Olympic Airways SA (1991) 25 NSWLR 75 .... 11.650
Adams v Lindsell (1818) 106 ER 250 .... 4.100
Adeels Palace Pty Ltd v Moubarak; Adeels Palace Pty Ltd v Bou Najem [2009] JCA 48 .... 5.70
Air France v Saks 18 Avi 18,538 .... 12.590
Air France v Teichner (1988) ETL 187 .... 12.590
Airlines of NSW Case (No 2) (1965) 113 CLR 65 .... 12.475
Airlines of NSW P/L v NSW (No 1) (1964) 113 CLR 1 .... 12.475
Alcock v Chief Constable of South Yorkshire Police [1992] AC 310 .... 5.50
Alexander Pushkin: Gill v Charter Travel Co (unreported, Qld Sup Ct, De Jersey J, 16
    February 1996) 12.90, 12.360
Alldis v Huxley (1891) 8 WN (NSW) 23 .... 13.45
Allison v Hewitt (1974) 3 NSWDCR 193 .... 2.235
Amalgamated Society of Engineers v Adelaide Steamship Co Ltd (1920) 28 CLR 129 .... 3.170
American Airlines Inc v Georgeopoulos (unreported, NSW CA, Clarke and Sheller JJA, Simos
    AKJA, 26 September 1996, 40762/93) 12.590
Anglo-Continental Holidays Ltd v Typaldos Lines (London) Ltd [1967] 2 Lloyd's Rep 61 .... 11.290,
                                                                                                                                         11.645
Annetts v Australian Stations Pty Ltd; Tame v State of New South Wales (2002) 191 ALR 449 .... 5.50
Ansell Rubber Co Pty Ltd v Allied Rubber Industries Pty Ltd [1967] VR 37 .... 8.45
Antolovich v Sun Alliance Insurance Ltd (1989) 5 ANZ Ins Cas 60-915 .... 7.25
Ashburn Anstalt v Arnold [1989] 1 Ch 1 .... 15.30
Athens-Macdonald Travel Service Pty Ltd v Kazis [1970] SASR 264 ..... 2.225, 9.345, 11.130, 11.230,
                                                                                                                                         11.645
Attorney-General v Antrobus (1905) 2 Ch 188 .... 12.170
Australia and New Zealand Banking Group Ltd v Travel Agents Registration Board
    (unreported, Sup Crt NSW, Lee J, 21 November 1985, BC 8500407) 11.500
Australian Broadcasting Tribunal v Bond (1990) 94 ALR 11 .... 11.420
Australian Coastal Shipping v O'Reilly (1962) 107 CLR 46 .... 12.325
Australian Competition and Consumer Commission (ACCC) v Trading Post and Google Inc
    (2007) FCA 1419 .... 11.710
Australian Conservation Foundation v South Australia (1990) 53 SASR 349 .... 15.300
Australian Federation of Travel Agents Ltd v Trade Practices Commission (1976) ATPR (Com)
    15,553 .... 9.250, 9.275, 11.375
Australian Federation of Travel Agents Ltd, Re (1982) ATPR (Com) 50-047 .... 11.375
Australian National Airways Pty Ltd v Commonwealth (1945) 71 CLR 29 .... 12.475, 12.485
Australian National Railways Commission v Ranger Uranium Mines Pty Ltd (1989) 97 FLR
    134 .... 12.265
Australian Racing Drivers Club v Metcalf (1961) 106 CLR 177 .... 15.80
Australian Rugby Union v The Hospitality Group Pty Ltd (2000) 173 ALR 702 .... 15.45
Australian Safeway Stores v Zaluzna (1987) 162 CLR 479 .... 13.60, 15.70, 15.370
Australian Telecommunications Commission v Hart (1982) 43 ALR 165 .... 8.35

B

BP Refinery (Westernport) Pty Ltd v Shire of Hastings (1977) 52 ALJR 20 .... 4.215, 9.350
Baikie v Fullerton-Smith [1961] NZLR 901 .... 15.30
Baker v Landsell Protective Agency 590 F Supp 165 US District Court SDNY 12.595
Balmain New Ferry Co Ltd v Robertson (1906) 4 CLR 379 ..... 4.230, 4.235, 13.105, 15.100, 15.215
Baltic Shipping Company v Dillon (The Mikhail Lermontov) (1993) 176 CLR 344 .... 2.235, 4.410,
                                                                                                                        4.440, 11.290, 12.455
Banco de Portugal v Waterlow [1932] AC 453 .... 4.435
Barclays Bank Ltd v TOSG Trust Fund Ltd [1984] 2 WLR 49 .... 11.620
Barkway v South Wales Transport Co Ltd [1950] 1 All ER 392 .... 12.35

Barton v Westpac Banking Corp (1983) ATPR 40-338 .... 9.135
Bateman v Slatyer (1987) 71 ALR 553 .... 9.55
Baxter v British Airways Plc & Qantas Airways Ltd (1988) ATPR 40-877 .... 9.55, 9.295
Beaches & Bush Properties v Jennings [2003] NSWSC 798 .... 4.420
Belfast & Ballymena Railway v Keys (1861) 9 HLC 556 .... 12.45
Benjamins v BEA 14 Avi 18,370 (1979) 12.590
Bennett v Peninsular & Oriental Steamboat Co (1848) 6 CB 775 .... 12.15, 12.25, 12.355
Bernstein of Leigh (Baron) v Skyviews & General Ltd [1978] QB 479 .... 15.55
Berry v Da Costa (1866) LR 1 CP 331 .... 2.235
Beswick v Beswick (1968) AC 58 .... 12.745
Bolzan v Appolonio (unreported, NSW Sup Ct, Giles J, 25 July 1988, BC 8801704) 11.70
Boral Resources (Qld) Pty Ltd v Pyke [1992] 2 Qd R 25 .... 7.60
Bornier v Air Inter RFDA 340 .... 12.640
"Bowbelle", The [1990] 1 Lloyd's Reports 532 .... 12.425
Bowman v Durham Holdings Pty Ltd (1973) 47 ALJR 606 .... 4.100
Bowron v Lucock (unreported, District Court of NSW, 2002) 14.295
Boyd v Carah Coaches Pty Ltd (1979) 145 CLR 78 .... 11.410, 11.420, 14.195
Boyle v Ozden (1986) EOC 92-165 .... 8.150
Bratty v Attorney-General (Northern Ireland) [1963] AC 386 .... 6.150
Brinkibon Ltd v Stahag Stahl und Stahlwarenhandels-Gesellschaft mbH [1983] 2 AC 34 .... 4.100
British Airways Board v Taylor [1976] WLR 13 .... 3.230, 9.165
British Traders' Insurance Co Ltd v Monson (1964) 111 CLR 86 .... 7.40
Britten v Great Western Railway [1899] 1 QB 243 .... 12.40
Brodie v Singleton Shire Council (2001) 206 CLR 512 .... 5.125
Buckland v The King [1933] 1 KB 329 .... 12.40
Burnie Port Authority v General Jones Pty Ltd (1994) 179 CLR 520 .... 5.100, 11.25, 15.70
Burns v Royal Hotel (St Andrews) Ltd (1957) Scots Law Times 53 .... 13.10, 13.75, 13.110
Burrows v Rhodes (1899) 1 QB 516 .... 8.30
Burton v Pinkerton (1867) LR 2 Ex 340 .... 2.235
Butcher v South Western Railway Co (1855) 16 CB 13 .... 12.55
Byrne v Tienhoven (1880) 5 CPD 344 .... 4.75

C

Cambodia v Thailand ICJ 1962/16 .... 15.350
Cameron v Qantas Airways Ltd (1995) ATPR 51-417; (1995) 5 FCR 147 .... 9.60, 9.100, 9.165,
                                                                                                                        11.235
Canterbury Bankstown Rugby League Club v Rogers (1993) Aust Torts Reps 81-246 .... 5.120
Caras International Tours v Travel Agents Licensing Authority (unreported, Vic AAT, 16 May
    1994) 11.425
Carlill v Carbolic Smoke Ball Co [1892] 2 QB 484; [1893] 1 QB 256 .... 4.30, 4.50, 4.55, 4.90,
                                                                                          4.125, 9.10, 12.15, 15.120, 15.215
Carman v Smithfield Tavern FNQ Pty Limited t/as Palmer Kate's Saloon [2000] ACTSC 11 .... 14.55
Carpenter v Haymarket Hotel Limited [1930] TLR 11 .... 13.75, 13.80
Causer v Browne [1952] VLR 1 .... 4.250
Cementaid (NSW) Pty Ltd v Chambers (unreported, NSW Sup Ct, Spender AJ, No
    12295/94, 29 March 1995) 8.25
Chan Shui Ying v HYFCO Travel Agency Limited [2007] HKHC 1060/2005 .... 9.350
Chapman v Hearse (1961) 106 CLR 112 .... 5.35, 5.70
Chea Kam Wing Victor v Kwan Kin Travel Services Ltd [2007] 1 HKLRD 937 .... 9.350, 11.305
Chordas v Bryant [1988] 92 FLR 413 .... 13.60, 14.275, 14.285, 14.290
Clarke v West Ham Corp (1909) 2 KB 858 .... 12.15
Club Mediterranee SA v Sterling 283 SE2d 30 .... 9.165
Coggs v Barnard (1704) 2 Ld Raym 909 .... 13.115
Cohen v South Eastern Railway (1873) 2 Ex D 235 .... 12.50
Cole v PC 443A [1936] 3 All ER 107 .... 15.25
Cole v South Tweed Heads Rugby League Football Club Ltd and Anor (2004) 217 CLR 469 ..... 5.60,
                                                                                                            14.315, 14.320
Collen v Wright (1857) 120 ER 241 .... 11.170
Collier v Sunday Referee Publishing Co Ltd [1940] 2 KB 647 .... 8.50

Collins v Godefroy (1831) 109 ER 1040 .... 4.140
Colquhoun v Brooks (1886) 21 QBD 52 .... 3.210
Columbia Coffee & Tea v Churchill (1992) NSWLR 141 .... 5.90
Commercial Bank of Australia v Amadio [1983] 151 CLR 447 .... 2.35, 4.385, 9.70
Commonwealth v Amman Aviation Pty Ltd (1991) 174 CLR 64 .... 4.425
Commonwealth v Huon Channel and Peninsular Steamship Co Ltd (1917) 24 CLR 385 .... 12.380
Commonwealth v Tasmania (1983) 158 CLR 1 .... 15.270
Commonwealth of Australia v Yarmirr (2001) 208 CLR 1 .... 2.65, 15.320
Con-Stan Industries of Australia Pty Ltd v Norwich Winterthur Insurance (Australia) Ltd
   (1986) 160 CLR 226 .... 7.110
Conviction of Chamberlain, Re (1988) 93 FLR 239 .... 6.205
Cooke v Midland Railway (1892) 9 TLR 147 .... 12.605
Cooper Brooks v FCT (1981) ALR 151 .... 3.225
Coroner's Case No 621/01 .... 15.95
Cosgrove & Anor v Johns [1998] QCA 110 .... 14.310
Coulls v Bagot's Executor & Trustee Co Ltd (1967) 119 CLR 460 .... 4.395
Coulson, Ex parte; Re Jones (1947) 48 SR (NSW) 178 .... 13.40
Cowell v Rosehill Racecourse (1937) 56 CLR 605 .... 15.30, 15.35
Craven v Strand Holidays (1982) 142 DLR (3d) 31 .... 9.340, 11.250, 11.645
Croston v Vaughan [1938] 1 KB 540 .... 5.175, 12.35
Cullen v Trappell (1980) 146 CLR 1 .... 2.235
Curtis v Chemical Cleaning & Dyeing Co [1951] 1 KB 805 .... 4.240, 4.310

D

D, Re [1976] Fam 185 .... 2.25
DPP v Ray [1974] AC 370 .... 6.105
Dalgety Wine Estates Pty Ltd v Rizzon (1979) 141 CLR 552 .... 14.165
Daniel v Hotel Pacific [1953] VLR 447 .... 13.40
Darling Casino Ltd v New South Wales Casino Control Authority (unreported, High Court of
   Australia, 3 April 1997) 15.170
Dawson v World Travel Headquarters (1981) ATPR 40-240 .... 9.120, 9.130
Day v Trans World Airlines Inc 628 F2d 31 (1975) 12.590
Deatons Pty Ltd v Flew (1949) 79 CLR 370 .... 5.120, 14.300, 11.175
Defina v Kenny [1946] 72 CLR 164 .... 15.135
Dennis Hotels Pty Ltd v Victoria (1960) 104 CLR 529 .... 14.150
Derry v Peek (1889) 14 App Cas 337 .... 4.315
Devonald v Rosser & Sons [1906] 2 KB 728 .... 8.50
Dick Bentley Productions Ltd v Harold Smith (Motors) Ltd [1965] 1 WLR 623 .... 4.180, 4.185
Dickenson v Dodds (1876) 2 Ch D 463 .... 4.75
Digital Equipment Corporation (Australia) Pty Ltd v Jetset Tours (NSW) Pty Ltd (unreported,
   SC NSW Windeyer J, 4 September 1995, BC 9505370) 11.610
Dillon v Baltic Shipping Co "Mikhail Lermontov" (1993) 176 CLR 344; [1992] 22 NSWLR 1;
   (1990) ATPR 40-992 .... 4.390, 9.70, 9.185, 9.200, 12.15, 12.40, 12.65, 12.85, 12.90, 12.415,
                                                                                                                                          15.30
Director v Phoenician Club (1997) (unreported) 14.245
Distilled Spirits Industry Council of Australia Inc v National Food Authority (1994) No
   V94/85 AAT No 9685 .... 14.30
Dixon v Birch (1873) LR 8 Exch 135 .... 13.35
Dodd v Outrigger Hotel 501 P 2d 368 .... 9.165
Doe d Pitt v Laming (1814) 4 Camp 73 NP 13.30
Doherty v Traveland Pty Ltd; Doherty v Associated Travel (1982) ATPR 40-323 .... 9.120
Donoghue v Stevenson (1932) AC 562 .... 2.145, 5.30, 5.35, 8.65, 9.10, 14.05, 14.90
Doolan v Air New Zealand (1978) ATPR 40-082 .... 9.105
Doubleday v Kelly [2005] NSWCA 151 .... 15.450
Drysdale v New Era Steamship Co Ltd (1936) 55 Ll LR 45 .... 8.95
Dubai/ Emirates' Air Services Agreement [2005] ATS 8 .... 12.495
Ducret v Nissan Motor Co (Australia) Pty Ltd (1979) 38 FLR 126 .... 9.40
Dunlop v Selfridge [1915] AC 847 .... 4.125

E

EBay International AG v Creative Festival Entertainment Pty Limited (2006) 170 FCR 450 ...... 15.365
Eastwood v Kenyon [1840] 11 AD & El 348 .... 4.140
Egan v Ross (1928) 29 SR (NSW) 328 .... 11.70
Electric Supply Stores v Gaywood (1909) 100 LT 855 .... 12.50
Ellesmere v Wallace [1929] 2 Ch 1 .... 15.120
Elsis v Transworld Airlines 167 AD 2d 285; 562 NYS 2d 433; 1990 NY App Div LEXIS 1424 .... 11.105,
11.275, 11.645
Empirnall Holdings v Machon Paull (1966) 14 NSWLR 523 .... 4.95
Enright v Coolum Resort Pty Ltd & Anors [2002] QSC 394 .... 5.60, 5.65, 15.375, 15.385
Entores Ltd v Miles Far East Corporation [1955] 2 QB 327 .... 4.100
Esanda Finance Corporation Ltd v Peat Marwick Hungerfords [1997] ALJR 448 .... 5.90
Exchange Hotel Ltd v Murphy (1947) SASR 112 .... 5.120, 14.300

F

Fagan v Metropolitan Police Commissioner [1969] 1 QB 439 .... 6.80
Falko v James McEwan and Co (1977) VR 447 .... 2.235
Farley v Lums (1917) 19 WALR 117 .... 8.95
Felismina v TWA 13 Avi 17,145 (1974) 12.590
Felthouse v Bindley (1862) 142 ER 1037 .... 4.90
Fink v Fink (1946) 74 CLR 127 .... 2.235
Firebrasse v Brett (1687) 1 Vern 489; (1688) 2 Vern 71 .... 15.130
Flamingo Park Pty Ltd v Dolly Dolly Creation Pty Ltd (1986) 65 ALR 500 .... 8.50
Floyd v Eastern Airlines 23 Avi 17,367 (1992) 12.590
Forbes v NSW Trotting Club (1975) 25 ALR 1 .... 15.30
Foroughi v Star City Pty Ltd (2007) 163 FCR 131 .... 15.180, 15.190
Fox v Warde [1978] VR 362 .... 3.205
Friends of Hinchinbrook Society Inc v The Minister for the Environment and Ors [1997] 55
  FCA (Feb '97); [1997] 789 FCA (Aug '97) 15.270
Frugtniet v Secretary to the Department of Justice (unreported, Vic Court of Appeal, 24 April
  1996) 11.450, 11.470

G

Gacic v John Fairfax Publications Pty Ltd [2009] NSWSC 1198 .... 5.140
Gala v Preston (1991) 172 CLR 243 .... 5.55, 5.165
Garton v Bristol & Exeter Railway Co (1861) 121 ER 656 .... 12.25
Garzilli (Connie Francis) v Howard Johnson's Motor Lodges Inc (1976) 419 F Supp 1219;
  NY 1976 .... 13.65
Gateway Management Pty Ltd and Travel Compensation Fund, Re (1993) 5 VAR 613 .... 11.595
Gemmell v Goldsworthy [1942] SASR 55 .... 13.30, 13.55
Ghantous v Hawkesbury City Council (2001) 206 CLR 512 .... 5.125
Gifford v Strang Patrick Stevedoring (2003) 214 CLR 219 .... 5.50
Goldman v Thai Airways International (1983) TLR 7 .... 12.660, 12.665
Gordon v Silber (1890) 25 QBD 491 .... 13.85
"Goring", The [1988] 1 Lloyds Law Reports 397 .... 12.350
Graham Barclay Oysters Pty Ltd v Ryan (2002) 211 CLR 540 .... 14.105
Great Australian Bite Pty Ltd v Menmel Pty Ltd (1996) ATPR 410-506 .... 9.55
Great Lakes SC v Dederer [2006] NSWCA 101 .... 15.450
Great Northern Railway v LEP Transport [1922] 2 KB 742 .... 12.15, 12.265
Great Northern Railway v Swaffield (1874) LR 9 Ex 132 .... 11.60
Great Western Railway Co v Rimell (1856) 18 CB 575; 139 ER 1495 .... 12.150
Gregory v Commonwealth Railways Commissioner (1941) 66 CLR 50 .... 12.35, 12.265
Gresham v Lyon [1954] 2 All ER 786 .... 13.70, 13.110
Grey v Pearson (1857) 6 LC 61; 10 ER 1216 .... 3.175
Guthrun Pty Ltd v Harvey World Travel Franchise Holdings Pty Ltd (unreported, NSW Sup
  Ct, Hodgson J, 4 September 1989, BC 8901757) 11.130

H

Ha v New South Wales; Hammond & Associates v New South Wales (1997) 189 CLR 465 .... 14.150, 14.215
Hackshaw v Shaw (1985) 155 CLR 614 .... 13.60
Hadley v Baxendale (1854) 156 ER 145 .... 2.220, 4.430, 12.655
Hall v Brooklands Auto Racing Club (1933) 1 KB 205 .... 15.75
Halliday v Neville (1984) 155 CLR 1 .... 6.180
Hamilton v Lethbridge (1912) 14 CLR 236 .... 4.350
Hamlin v Great Northern Railway (1856) 1 H&N 408; 156 ER 1261 ...... 2.215, 2.220, 2.230, 2.235, 4.440, 12.30, 12.200, 12.280, 12.610
Hancock v Cunnain (1886) 12 VLR 9 .... 12.15
Hanson v Barwise [1930] St R Qd 285 .... 13.45, 13.85
Harmer v Cornelius (1858) 141 ER 94 .... 8.95
Harvey v Facey [1893] AC 552 .... 4.70
Harvey v RG O'Dell Ltd [1958] 2QB 78 .... 8.30
Hastie v Great Eastern Railway (1911) 46 LJ News 12.40
Hedley Byrne & Co Ltd v Heller & Partners [1964] AC 465 .... 2.90, 4.320, 5.90, 5.95
Henthorn v Fraser (1892) 2 Ch 27 .... 4.100
Hercules Motors Pty Ltd v Schubert (1953) 53 SR (NSW) 301 .... 4.140
Hernandez v Air France 14 Avi 17,421 .... 12.590
Heydon's Case (1584) 3 Co Rep 7a; 76 ER 637 .... 3.180
Hill v Van Erp (1997) 188 CLR 159 .... 5.90
Hill v Wnm Hill (Park Lane) [1949] AC 530 .... 15.135
Hinton v Dibbin (1842) 2 QB 646; 114 ER 253 .... 12.150
Hivac Ltd v Park Royal Scientific Instruments Ltd [1946] Ch 169 .... 8.25
Hobbs v London South West Railway (1875) LR 10 QB 11 ...... 2.230, 2.235, 12.30, 12.200, 12.280, 12.610
Hobbs v Petersham Transport Co Pty Ltd (1971) 124 CLR 220 .... 12.35, 13.115
Hodgkinson v London and North Western Railway Co (1884) 14 QBD 228 .... 12.55
Hogan v Rusty Rees Pty Ltd (Queensland Supreme Court Writ No 174/85 upheld on appeal No 82 of 1988 .... 14.280
Holt v Fynbout Pty Ltd (unreported, NSW Sup Ct, Cohen J, 28 May 1987, BC 8701344) 11.270, 11.145, 11.645
Holwell Securities Ltd v Hughes [1974] 1 WLR 155 .... 4.100
Hong Kong Fir Shipping v Kawasaki Kaisen Kaisher Ltd [1962] 2 QB 26 .... 12.360
Hospital Products Ltd v United States Surgical Corporation (1984-1985) 156 CLR 41 .... 11.115
Houghland v RR Low (Luxury Coaches) Ltd [1962] 1 QB 696 .... 13.115
Hudston v Midland Railway [1869] LR 4 QB 366 .... 12.40
Hughes & Vale v New South Wales (No 2) (1955) 93 CLR 127 .... 11.420, 14.195
Huntley v Bedford Hotel (1892) 56 JP 23 .... 13.80
Hurst v Picture Theatres Ltd [1915] 1 KB 1 .... 15.30
Husserl v Swiss Air Transport Co 351 F Supp 702 SDNY (affirmed 185 F2d 1210) 12.590
Hyde v Wrench (1840) 49 ER 132 .... 4.70

I

ILG Travel Ltd (in administration), Re [1995] 2 BCLC 128 .... 11.240, 11.645, 11.665
Ingham v Hie Lee (1912) 15 CLR 267 .... 3.215
Innkeepers case, The (1368) YB 42 Edw III 11 No 13 .... 13.15
Insight Vacations Pty Ltd v Young [2010] NSWCA 137 .... 9.200, 12.70, 15.430
Insurance Commissioner v Joyce (1948) 77 CLR 39 .... 5.150
International Air Transport Association v Alitalia Linea Aera Italiana SPA (1985) 7 ATPR 40-537 .... 9.250, 9.275
Ionides v Pender (1874) LR 9 QB 531 .... 7.25
Irving v Heferen [1995] 1 Qd R 255 .... 13.30, 13.55, 13.60, 13.70, 13.85, 13.90, 13.110
Italiano v Barbaro (1993) 114 ALR 21 .... 5.55

J

JM Allen (Merchandise) Ltd v Cloke [1963] 2 QB 340	15.135
Jack v Transworld Airlines Inc 854 F Supp 654 (1994)	12.590
Jackson v Chrysler Acceptances (1978) RTR 474	2.235
Jackson v Horizon Holidays (1975) 1 WLR 1468	2.235, 15.30
Jaensch v Coffey (1984) 155 CLR 549	5.50
James v Commonwealth (1939) 62 CLR 339	12.15, 12.25
Jarvis v Swan Tours [1973] 1 All ER 71; [1972] 3 WLR 954	2.230, 2.235, 9.10, 9.310, 9.345, 11.300, 11.645, 12.200, 12.280, 12.655, 15.30
John v Bacon (1870) LR CP 437	12.55
John Carter v Hanson Haulage [1965] 1 QB 495	12.190
John Fairfax Publications Pty Ltd v Gacic (2007) 230 CLR 291	5.140
Johns v Cosgrove & ors (1997) QSC 229	14.310, 14.325
Jones v Jackson Ltd (1873) 29 LT 399	13.75, 13.80

K

K&S Lake City Freighters Pty Ltd v Gordon & Gotch Ltd (1985) 157 CLR 309	12.205
Kabbani v International Total Services US District Court	12.595
Kakavas v Crown Ltd [2007] VSC 526	15.180, 15.195
Karfunkel v Singapore Airlines and Air France 14 Avi 17,674	12.590
Kaufman v Gerson [1904] 1 KB 591	4.380
Kellett v Cowan [1906] Qd St R 116	13.75
Kelly v Allard & Ors (1987) 4 ANZ Insurance Cases 60-798	8.30
Kemp v Intasun Holidays Ltd [1987] BTLC 353	11.235, 11.645
Kennison v Daire (1986) 160 CLR 129	6.65
Khedive, The (1880) 5 App Cas 876	12.645
Kirmani v Captain Cook Cruises Pty Ltd (1985) 159 CLR 351	12.365, 12.380, 12.415
Korean Airline Disaster case 23 Avi 17	12.590
Krell v Henry [1903] 2 KB 740	4.375
Kural v The Queen (1987) 162 CLR 502	6.50
Kylie v Lysfar Pty Ltd (1985) ATPR 40-614	9.100

L

L'Estrange v F Graucob Ltd [1934] 2 KB 394	4.240
Lambert v Monaghan (1917) 19 WAR 99	13.55
Lawrence v Fox 20 NY 268 (1859)	12.745
Leaf v International Galleries [1950] 2 KB 86	4.325
Lee v Knapp [1967] 2 QB 442	3.175
Legione v Hateley (1983) 152 CLR 406	4.415
Levy v Curran (1909) 9 SR (NSW) 725	13.75
Lewis, Ex parte (1888) 21 QBD 321	12.170
Liga Knitting Mills v Lombard Insurance Co Ltd (1983) 3 ANZ Ins Cas 60-551	7.25
London and Globe Finance Corp Ltd, Re [1903] 1 Ch 728	6.105
Lord Bernstein of Leigh v Skyviews & General Ltd [1978] QB 479	12.480, 15.105
Lord Guthrie in Burns v Royal Hotel (St Andrews) Limited (1957) Scotts Law Times 53	13.20
Lormine v Zenereb [2006] NSWCA 200	15.460
Lovett v Hobbs (1680) 2 Shaw KB 187	12.15
Lowden v The Queen (1982) 139 DLR 3d 257	11.675

M

Mabo v Queensland [No 2] (1992) 175 CLR 1	2.65, 2.75, 15.320
MacRobertson Miller Airlines v Commissioner of Taxation (WA) (1975) 133 CLR 125	4.110, 12.575
Macaura v Northern Assurance Co Ltd [1925] AC 619	7.20, 15.120
Mackie v Weinholt (1880) 5 QSCR 211	8.35

Macrow v Great Western Railway Co (1871) LR QB 612 .... 12.40, 12.45
Mantra Group Pty Ltd v Tailly Pty Ltd [2010] FCA 291 (26 March 2010) 11.715
March v Stramare (1991) 171 CLR 506 .... 5.70
Maxwell v Murphy (1957) 96 CLR 261 .... 3.75
Mayfield Holdings Ltd v Moana Reef Ltd [1973] 1 NZLR 309 .... 15.30
Mayne Nickless Ltd v Pegler [1974] 1 NSWLR 228 .... 7.25
McDonald's Systems Australia Pty Ltd v McWilliams Wines Pty Ltd (1979) 28 ALR 236 .... 9.55
McKenna v Avoir Pty Ltd (1981) WAR 255 .... 12.590
McNaughton (1843) 8 ER 718 .... 6.130
Medical Defence Union Ltd v Department of Trade [1980] Ch 82 .... 7.40
Mendonca and Santiago v South Sydney Junior Rugby League Club Ltd (unreported, Sup
    Ct NSW, Sully J, 16 December 1993, No 14099 of 1989) 15.135, 15.210, 15.215
Menow v Hosenberger 7 DLR (3d) 494 .... 14.270
Mercer v Commissioner for Road Transport and Tramways (NSW) (1937) 56 CLR 580 .... 5.175,
                                                                                                        12.35
Metrans Pty Ltd v Courtney-Smith (1983) 1 IPR 185 .... 8.45
Michael Edgley International Pty Ltd v Ashton's Nominees Pty Ltd (1979) 38 FLR 135 .... 9.45
Miller v Federal Coffee Palace (1889) 15 VLR 30 .... 13.30
Morgan v Ravey (1861) 158 ER 109 .... 13.75
Mount Isa Mines Ltd v Pusey (1970) 125 CLR 383 .... 2.235
Mulligan v Coffs Harbour City Council & Ors [2003] NSWSC 49 .... 5.60
Mundro Pty Ltd v Commissioner for Consumer Affairs (1988) 4 SR (WA) 3181 .... 11.425
Mutual Life & Citizen's Assurance Co Ltd v Evatt (1968) 122 CLR 556 .... 5.90

N

Nader v Allegheney Airlines Inc (1976) 426 US 290 .... 9.10, 9.15, 9.165
Nagel v Rottnest Island Authority (1993) 177 CLR 423 .... 5.45, 5.60
National Food Authority v Scotch Whisky Association (1995) 129 ALR 357; (1995) 21 AAR
    260; (1995) 38 ALD 1 .... 14.30
Naylor v Canterbury Park Racecourse (1935) 35 SR (NSW) 281 .... 15.30
New South Wales v Commonwealth (The Seas and Submerged Lands Act Case) (1975) 135
    CLR 337 .... 12.325
Newell v Canadian Pacific Airlines 74 DLR 3d 574 (1976) 12.590, 12.655
Newsholme Bros v Road Transport General Insurance Ltd [1929] 2 KB 356 .... 7.110
Nguyen v Nguyen (1990) 169 CLR 245 .... 2.160
Nordenfelt v Maxim-Nordenfelt Guns and Ammunition Co [1894] AC 535 .... 9.240
North Sydney MC v Sydney Serviced Apartments P/L (1990) 71 LGRA 432 .... 13.175
Northern Sandblasting Pty Ltd v Harris (1997) 188 CLR 313 .... 13.60, 5.100, 15.370
Norton v Kilduff [1974] Qd R 47 .... 14.160
Nott v Maclurcan (1903) 20 WN (NSW) 135 .... 13.60, 13.75, 13.95
Number Two Janminga Pty Ltd and Travel Agents Licensing Authority, Re (1991) 5 VAR 200 .... 11.400,
                                                                                                        11.420, 11.525

O

O'Connor v SP Bray (1936-1937) 56 CLR 464 .... 8.210
O'Dea v O'Hara, South Australian Advertiser 17 May 1895 .... 13.75
O'Shea v Permanent Trustee Co of NSW (1971) Qd R 1 .... 5.150
Oakford Executive Apartments v Van der Top (Unreported, Vic Sup Ct, O'Brien J, 23 January
    1992) 13.30, 13.35, 13.40, 13.45, 13.110
Oceanic Steam Navigation Co Ltd (the White Star Line) v Mellor (the "Titanic") (1914) 233
    US 718 .... 12.305, 12.455
Oceanic Sun Line Special Shipping v Fay (1988) 165 CLR 197 .... 4.270, 9.235, 12.450
Odgers v McMiken [1974] 8 SASR 119 .... 11.110, 11.170, 11.225, 11.245, 11.285
Ogwo v Taylor [1988] AC 431 .... 13.60
Olley v Marlborough Court [1949] 1 KB 532 .... 4.250, 4.270, 13.100, 13.105, 13.110, 15.365
Oscar Chess v Williams [1957] 1 WLR 370 .... 4.170, 4.185
Ottoman Bank v Chakarian [1930] AC 277 .... 8.35

Overseas Tankship (UK) Ltd v Morts Dock Engineering Co Ltd (1961) AC 388 .... 5.75
Overseas Tankships (UK) v Miller SS Co [1967] 1 AC 617 .... 5.75

P

P&O Steam Navigation Co & Ors v Youell & Ors [1997] 2 Lloyd's Rep 136 .... 12.435
Park v Berkley (1930) 25 Tas LR 67 .... 13.75, 13.85
Parker v South Eastern Railway Co (1877) 2 CPD 416 .... 4.260
Parkview (Keppel) Pty Ltd v Mytarc Pty Ltd (1984) ASC 55-351 .... 9.65
Payne v Cave (1789) 100 ER 502 .... 4.75
Pearce v Florenca (1976) 135 CLR 507 .... 12.325
Penn Plastic Co Pty Ltd v Sadliers Transport Co (Vic) Pty Ltd (1976) 136 CLR 28 .... 12.105
Perre v Apand Pty Ltd (1999) 198 CLR 180 .... 5.45
Peterson v Moloney (1951) 84 CLR 91 .... 11.70
Peterswald v Bartley (1904) 1 CLR 497 .... 14.150
Pharmaceutical Society of Great Britain v Boots Cash Chemists (Southern) Ltd [1953] 1 QB
  401 .... 4.60, 4.65
Phoenix Assurance Co of Australia Ltd v Liddy (unreported, NSW SC (CA), No 85 of 1983) 7.200
Pinetrees Lodge Pty Ltd v Atlas International Pty Ltd (1981) 59 FLR 244 .... 9.55
Pitt Son & Badgery v Proulefco SA (1984) 153 CLR 644 .... 13.115
Powell v Lee (1908) 99 LT 284 .... 4.85
Prast v the Town of Cottesloe [2000] WASCA 275 .... 5.60
Prebble v Reeves [1910] VLR 88 .... 11.125
Preston v Star City (1999) NSWSC 1273 .... 15.180, 15.185, 15.190
Preston v Star City Limited (No 3) [2005] NSWSC 1223 .... 14.295
Preti v Conservation Land Corp; Sahara Tours; Parks & NT Wildlife Commission [2007] 20
  NTLR 97 .... 15.395
Priestley v Fowler (1837) 3 M&W 1 .... 8.165
Prudential Insurance Co v Commissioners of Inland Revenue [1904] 2 KB 658 .... 7.15
Pupazzoni v Fremantle Fisherman's Co-operative Society Ltd (1981) 23 AILR 168 .... 8.70

Q

Quan Yick v Hinds (1905) 2 CLR 345 .... 15.130
Queensland v Commonwealth (1988) 62 ALJR 143 .... 15.270
Quilted Products Manufacturers' Association of Australia, Re (1988) ATPR (Com) 50-070 .... 9.40

R

R v Anderson; Ex parte IPEC Air P/L (1965) 113 CLR 177 .... 12.485
R v Bateman (1925) 19 Cr App R 8 .... 6.55
R v Byrne [1960] 2QB 396 .... 6.155
R v Burgess; Ex parte Henry (1936) 55 CLR 608 .... 12.475
R v Darling Island Stevedoring and Lighterage Co Ltd; ex parte Halliday and Sullivan (1938)
  60 CLR 601 .... 8.95
R v Davidson (1969) VR 667 .... 6.135
R v Dixon Ex parte Prince (1979) WAR 11 .... 10.45
R v Enright [1961] VR 663 .... 6.160
R v Fawkner (1669) 2 Keb 506 .... 14.135
R v Geoffrey Ian "Jack" Nairn (unreported, Supreme Court, Cairns 1999) 15.490
R v Gilmartin [1983] 1 All ER 829 .... 6.105
R v Hall [1972] 2 All ER 1009 .... 6.100, 11.675
R v Hyde Justices [1912] 1 KB 645 .... 14.195
R v Loughman [1981] VR 443 .... 6.135
R v Mark Wilhelm [2010] NSWSC 378 .... 12.460
R v Parsons [1983] 2 VR 499 .... 2.200
R v Police Magistrate at Hughenden and Reid; Ex parte John Cumming [1915] St R Qd 147 .... 10.120
R v Poole; Ex parte Henry (1939) 61 CLR 634 .... 12.475
R v Porter (1933) 55 CLR 182 .... 6.130

R v Sanby (Unreported, Court of Appeal NT, 1993) 6.55, 6.60, 15.95, 15.485
R v Specker; Ex parte Alvaro (1986) 44 SASR 60 .... 15.175
R v Ward (1938) 39 SR (NSW) 308 .... 6.90
R Lowe Lippman Figdor & Franck (a firm) v AGC (Advances) Ltd [1992] 2 VR 671 .... 5.90
Railways, Commissioner for v Halley (1978) 20 ALR 409 .... 5.155
Railways, Commissioner of v Ruprecht (1979) 142 CLR 563 .... 5.155
Re No ATPR 41-051 2 Janminga Pty Ltd v Travel Agents Licensing Authority (1991) 3 VAR
    200 .... 3.245
Ready Mix Concrete (South East) Ltd v Minister of Pensions and National Insurance (1968)
    2 QB 497 .... 8.15
Redhead v Midland Railway (1869) LR 4 QB 379 .... 12.270
Reed v Wiser 14 Avi 17 .... 12.625
Registrar of Titles v Keddell (1993) Q Conv R 54-455 .... 15.160
Resolution of the Judges (1624) Hut 99 .... 14.135
Revill v Newbery [1996] 2 WLR 239 .... 13.60
Richardson v Forestry Commission (1988) 164 CLR 261 .... 15.270
Robins v Gray [1895] 2 QB 501 .... 13.75, 13.85
Robinson v Balmain New Ferry Co [1910] AC 295 .... 4.235
Robinson v Harman (1848) 1 Exch 850 .... 4.440
Robinson v Western Australian Museum (1977) 138 CLR 283 .... 12.325
Rockard v Mexicoach (1982) 689 FR 2d 1257 .... 9.340
Rogers v Whittaker (1992) 175 CLR 479 .... 5.65
Roka v Collins (unreported, SA CCA, 10 January 1994) 11.475, 11.520
Romeo v Conservation Commission (NT) (1998) 192 CLR 431 .... 5.60
Rookard v Mexicoach 680 F 2d 1257 (1982) 11.250, 11.645
Roscorla v Thomas (1842) 3 QB 234 .... 4.135
Rose v Plenty (1976) 1 All ER 97 .... 5.120
Rose and Frank Co v Crompton Bros Ltd [1923] 2 KB 261 .... 4.155
Rosenthal v London County Council (1924) 131 LT 563 .... 12.60
Royal Brunei Airlines Sdn Bhd v Philip Tan Kok Ming [1995] 2 AC 378 .... 11.650, 11.655, 11.660
Rumsey v North Eastern Railway (1863) 14 CB (NS) 641 .... 12.50
Russell v London & South West Railway (1908) 24 TLR 548 .... 5.180
Ryan v Brain (1994) 1 Qd R 681 .... 14.160
Ryder v Wombwell (1868) LR 4 Exch 32 .... 4.345
Rylands v Fletcher (1868) LR 3 HL 330 .... 5.160
Rylands Bros (Aust) Ltd v Morgan (1927) 27 SR (NSW) 161 .... 3.210

S

SG White v The Ship "Mediterranean" (1966) Qd R 211 .... 12.350
SS Pharmaceutical Co Ltd v Qantas Airways (1988) 22 NSWLR 734; (1991) 1 LR 288 .... 12.665
Salt Union Ltd v Wood [1893] 1 QB 370 .... 12.380
San Sebastian Pty Ltd v The Minister (1986) 162 CLR 340 .... 5.90
Saunders v Anglia Building Society [1971] AC 1004 .... 4.370
Saunders v Spencer (1566) 73 ER 591 .... 13.80
Scrutons v Midland Silicones Ltd [1962] AC 446 .... 4.395
Searle v Wallbank [1947] AC 341 .... 2.120
Secretary of State for Trade v Booth (The "Boche") [1984] 1 All ER 464 .... 12.420
Sew Hoy & Sons Ltd v Stars Travel Ltd (unreported, High Court of New Zealand, Dunedin,
    5 September 1985, M186/84) 12.575
Shacklock v Ethorpe [1939] 3 All ER 372 .... 13.75
Shaddock & Associates Pty Ltd v Parramatta City Council (1981) 150 CLR 225 ...... 5.85, 5.90, 5.95,
                                                                                                                         7.130
Shaw v DPP (1962) AC 220 .... 2.25
Sigsworth, Re; Bedford v Bedford [1935] Ch 89 .... 3.170
Simpkins v Pays [1955] 1 WLR 975 .... 4.150
Singapore Airlines v Taprobane Tours (WA) Pty Ltd (1991) 33 FCR 158 .... 9.255
Slatter v Railway Commissioner of New South Wales (1931) 45 CLR 68 .... 14.165
Smith v Bond (1843) 11 M&W 549 .... 15.130
Smith v Charles Baker & Sons (1891) AC 325 .... 5.150

Smith v Hughes [1960] 1 WLR 830 .... 3.180
Smith v McDonnell (unreported, NSW Sup Ct, 30 March 1995) 4.150
Smitton v Orient Steam Navigation Co (1907) LT 848 .... 12.45
Soanes v London South Western Railway (1919) 88 LJKB 524 .... 12.55
Southern Pacific Hotel Services Inc v Southern Pacific Hotel Corporation Ltd (unreported,
    NSWSup Ct, Finlay J, 20 September 1985, Butterworths Unreported Cases 8500526) 3.215
Squires v Whisken (1811) 3 Camp 140 .... 15.125
Starks v RSM Security Pty Ltd [2004] NSWCA 351 .... 5.120
State Government Insurance Commission (SA) v Trigwell (1979) 142 CLR 617 .... 2.75, 2.120, 2.145
Steiner v Magic Carpet Tours Pty Ltd (1984) ATPR 40-490 .... 9.55, 9.360, 13.55
Stephens Travel Service International Pty Ltd (Receivers and Managers Appointed) v Qantas
    Airways Ltd (1988) 13 NSWLR 629 .... 11.295, 11.650, 11.655, 11.660
Stevens v Brodribb Sawmilling Co Pty Ltd (1986) 160 CLR 16 .... 5.115, 8.15
Stinchcombe v Thomas [1957] VR 509 .... 8.55
Subramaniam a/l Paramasivam v Lain-lain lwn Malaysian Airline System Bhd [1996] 3 MLJ
    64 .... 12.50
Suncorp General Insurance Ltd v Cheihk (1999) 10 ANZ Insurance Cases 61-442 .... 7.25
Sunshine Coast Regional Council; v Ebis Enterprises Pty Ltd [2010] QPEC 52 .... 13.175
Swain v Waverley Municipal Council (2005) 220 CLR 517 .... 5.60, 15.390

T

TNT (Melbourne) Pty Ltd v May & Baker (Aust) Pty Ltd (1966) 115 CLR 353 .... 13.115
Taco Co of Australia v Taco Bell Pty Ltd (1982) 42 ALR 177 .... 3.255, 9.55
Tallerman and Co Pty Ltd v Nathan's Merchandise (Vic) Pty Ltd (1957) 98 CLR 93 .... 4.100
Tashis v Lahaina Investment Corp 480 F2d 1019 (9th Circuit 1979) 15.375, 15.405
Tasmania v Commonwealth (1988) 164 CLR 1 .... 12.325
Taylor v Caldwell (1863) 3 B&S 826 .... 4.375
Tepko Pty Limited v Water Board (1999) Aust Torts Reports 81-525 .... 5.90
Theeman v Forte Properties Pty Ltd [1973] 1 NSWLR 418 .... 13.40
Thomas Cook Pty Ltd v Aviation and Tourism Services Pty Ltd (unreported, NSW Sup Ct,
    Yeldham J, 13 August 1985, BC 8500696) 11.295, 11.645
Thomas Nationwide Transport (Melbourne) Pty Ltd v May & Baker (Australia) Pty Ltd
    (1966) 115 CLR 353 .... 12.30
Thornton v Shoe Lane Parking (1971) 2 QB 163 .... 4.250, 4.265, 4.270
Timbrell v Waterhouse (1885) LR (NSW) 77 .... 12.55
Timm v Hoffman & Co (1873) 29 LT 271 .... 4.110
Timney v British Airways PLC (1992) 56 SASR 287 .... 12.700
Tonzo Pty Ltd v Amore (unreported NSW DC, Dunford J, 11 Dec 1987) 14.60
Trade Practices Commission v Autoways Pty Ltd (1990) ATPR 41-051 .... 3.250
Trade Practices Commission v Caravella (1994) ATPR 41-293 .... 9.250
Trade Practices Commission v GLO Juice Co Pty Ltd (1987) 73 ALR 407 .... 9.100, 9.110
Travel Compensation Fund v Digital Equipment Corporation (Australia) Pty Ltd (unreported
    Sup Crt NSW, Cole J, 18 February 1991, BC 9102336) 11.35, 11.40, 11.610
Travel Compensation Fund v Robert Tambree trading as Tambree and Associates & ors
    (2005) 224 CLR 627 .... 5.65, 11.620
Travel Compensation Fund v Travel Guide Pty Ltd (In Liquidation) (unreported, Federal
    Court, 13 February 1997) 11.620
Travel Compensation Fund, Dunn and Others, Re (unreported, Federal Court, Wilcox J, 2
    December 1992) 11.400, 11.435, 11.615, 11.620
Travel World Service Pty Ltd v Rose Grisbrook Pty Ltd (Sup Crt Vic 11.640
Trident Insurance Co v McNeice Bros (1988) 165 CLR 107 .... 4.395, 12.745, 15.30
Truth and Sportsman Ltd v Molesworth [1956] AR (NSW) 924 .... 8.35
Tucker v McCann [1948] VLR 22 .... 5.175, 12.35
Turner v Queensland Motels Pty Ltd [1968] Qd R 189 ...... 13.10, 13.20, 13.30, 13.40, 13.75, 13.80
Tweedle v Atkinson (1861) 121 ER 762 .... 4.395

U

Union Steamship Co of New Zealand Ltd v Commonwealth (1925) 36 CLR 130 .... 12.380

V

Vacations Pty Ltd v Young [2010] NSWCA 137 .... 11.300
Vairy v Wyong Shire Council (2005) 223 CLR 422 .... 5.60
Venning v Suburban Taxi Service Pty Ltd (1996) ATPR 41-468 .... 9.255
Victoria Park Racing & Recreation Grounds v Taylor (1937) 58 CLR 479 .... 15.60
Victrawl Pty Ltd v Telstra Corporation Ltd [1995] 131 ALR 465 .... 12.365
Viro v The Queen (1978) 141 CLR 88 .... 2.185

W

W D & H O Wills Ltd v Jamieson [1957] AR (NSW) 547 .... 8.95
Wacando v Commonwealth (1981) 148 CLR 1 .... 3.250
Wakim, Re; Ex parte McNally (1999) 198 CLR 511 .... 2.190, 10.85
Wall v Silver Wing Surface Arrangements Ltd (trading as Enterprise Holidays) (unreported,
  Hodgson J, 18 November 1981) 9.340, 9.350, 11.255, 11.260, 11.645
Wallis v Downard-Pickford (North Queensland) Pty Ltd (1994) 179 CLR 388 .... 9.185, 9.200, 12.85,
                                                12.110, 12.115, 12.120, 12.125, 12.150, 12.415
Watts v Morrow (1991) 1 WLR 1421 .... 15.30
Waverley, Municipality of v Bloom [1999] NSWCA 229 .... 5.60
Webber v Mutual Community Ltd (1991) 6 ANZ Ins Cas 61-079 .... 7.25
Webster v Orlitz [1917] VLR 107 .... 13.30
Western Australia v Ward (2002) 213 CLR 1 .... 2.65, 15.320
White v Bluett (1853) LJ Ex 36 .... 4.140
White v Chief Constable of South Yorkshire Police (1999) 2 AC 455 .... 5.50
White v John Warwick and Co Ltd [1953] 12 All ER 1021; 1 WLR 1285 .... 5.10, 9.185, 12.215,
                                                                                      12.420, 15.365
Whitehouse v Queensland (1960) 104 CLR 609 .... 14.150
Wik Peoples v Queensland (1996) 187 CLR 1 .... 2.65, 2.75, 15.320
Wilks v Cheltenham Cycle Club (1971) WLR 608 .... 15.75
Williams v African SS Co (1856) 1 HLN 300 .... 12.370
Williams v Linnitt [1951] 1 KB 565 .... 13.30, 13.70, 13.95, 13.100, 13.110, 13.145, 15.360
Williams v Owen [1956] ER 1 .... 13.75
Wilson v Best Travel Ltd [1993] 1 All ER 353 .... 9.340, 9.350, 11.260, 11.645
Wilsons & Clyde Coal Co v English [1938] AC 37 .... 8.65
Winkworth v Ravey [1931] 1 KB (1861) 652 .... 13.75
Winter Gardens Theatre (London) Ltd v Millennium Productions Ltd [1946] 1 All ER 678 .... 15.30
Wong Mee Wan v Kwan Kin Travel Services Ltd [1995] 4 All ER 745 .... 1.45, 9.335, 9.345, 9.350,
                                                9.365, 11.35, 11.245, 11.280, 11.305, 11.645, 12.630, 15.365
Wood v Leadbitter 153 Eng Rep 351 (1845) 15.30
Woodar Investments v Wimpey [1980] 1 All ER 571 .... 15.30
Woolworths Ltd v Crotty (1942) 66 CLR 603 .... 2.235
Wormald v Robertson (1992) Aust Torts Reports 81-180 .... 13.60, 14.275, 14.290
Wright v Embassy Hotel (1934) 39 SJ 12 .... 13.80
Wyong Shire Council v Shirt (1980) 146 CLR 40 .... 5.60, 15.380

Y

Yetton v Eastwoods Froy Ltd [1967] 1 WLR 104 .... 8.105
Young v Travel Agents Registration Board (1987) 18 IR 173 .... 11.515

Z

Zoneff v Elcom Credit Union Ltd (1990) 94 ALR 445 .... 9.185

TABLE OF STATUTES

COMMONWEALTH

Acts Interpretation Act 1901
s 5: 3.65
s 13(1): 3.130
s 13(3): 3.130, 3.140
s 15AA: 3.115, 3.185
s 15AB: 3.140, 3.215, 3.225
s 15AB(1): 3.225
s 46: 3.260

Administrative Decisions (Judicial Review) Act 1977: 2.165

Admiralty Act 1988: 12.350
s 3: 12.380

Age Discrimination Act 2004: 8.140

Air Navigation Act 1920: 12.475, 12.510
s 20: 12.480

Airlines Agreement Act 1981: 12.485

Airlines Agreement (Termination) Act 1990: 12.485

Australia Acts 1986: 2.45, 2.185

Australian Consumer Law – – see **Competition and Consumer Act 2010**, Schedule 2

Australian Land Transport Development Act 1988: 12.240

Australian Maritime Safety Authority Act 1990: 12.345

Australian National Airlines Act 1945: 12.475

Australian National Railways Commission Act 1983: 12.255

Australian National Railways Commission Sale Act 1997: 12.240, 12.255

Australian Passports Act 2005: 11.155
s 32: 11.155

Australian Workplace Safety Standards Act 2005: 8.175, 15.475

Civil Aviation Agreement Act 1952: 12.485

Civil Aviation (Carriers' Liability) Act 1959: 12.475, 12.550, 12.555, 12.560, 12.575, 12.580, 12.590, 12.595, 12.605, 12.625, 12.635, 12.640, 12.645, 12.650, 12.665, 12.700
s 8: 12.550
s 11: 12.550
s 11A: 12.550
s 12: 12.590
s 12(2): 12.590
s 13: 12.590
s 14: 12.590
s 15: 12.590
s 16: 12.645
s 21A: 12.550
s 28: 12.590
s 29(1): 12.595, 12.605
s 29(2)(b): 12.595
s 29(3): 12.595
s 29(4): 12.595
s 30(1): 12.690
s 30(2): 12.690
s 31: 12.575, 12.580
s 31(1): 12.555
s 32(2): 12.580
s 33: 12.625
s 34: 12.695
s 35: 12.590
s 35(2): 12.590
s 36: 12.590
s 37: 12.590
s 38: 12.590
s 39: 12.645
s 40: 12.575, 12.580
s 41: 12.575, 12.580
ss 41A to 41L: 12.550, 12.555

Civil Aviation (Civil Liability) Act 1959
s 5: 12.560
ss 10 to 11: 12.560
s 11A: 12.560
s 12: 12.560
s 12(2): 12.560
s 13: 12.560
s 14: 12.560

s 15: 12.560
s 16: 12.560
ss 17 to 18: 12.560
s 19: 12.560
s 20: 12.560
s 21A: 12.560
ss 21 to 22: 12.560
s 23: 12.560
ss 24 to 25: 12.560
s 25A: 12.560
s 25B: 12.560
s 26: 12.560
s 27: 12.560
s 28: 12.560
s 29: 12.560
s 30: 12.560
s 31: 12.560
s 32: 12.560
s 33: 12.560
s 34: 12.560
s 35: 12.560
s 35(2): 12.560
s 36: 12.560
s 37: 12.560
s 38: 12.560
s 39: 12.560
s 40: 12.560
s 42: 12.560
Pt IVA: 12.560

Coastal Waters (State Title) Act 1980: 12.325
s 98: 12.325

Commonwealth of Australia Constitution Act 1901: 2.45, 2.160, 15.265
s 9: 9.200
s 51(xxxiii): 12.240
s 51(xxxiv): 12.240
s 51(xxxii): 12.240
s 51(xxix): 12.325, 12.475
s 51(xxxix): 15.270
s 51(i): 9.25, 12.240, 12.325, 12.475
s 51(vi): 12.475
s 51(xx): 9.25
s 57: 3.55
s 71: 2.165, 2.170
s 73: 2.160
s 75: 2.160
s 76: 2.160
s 90: 14.150, 14.215
s 92: 11.410, 11.420, 12.475, 12.485

Commonwealth of Australia
Constitution Act 1901 — cont
    s 98: 12.240
    s 109: 8.140, 12.415,
        12.700

Competition Policy Reform Act
    1995: 12.250

Competition and Consumer
    Act 2010: 2.165, 9.30, 9.40,
        9.240, 9.290, 11.45
    s 35: 6.165
    s 44ZZRA: 9.245
    s 45: 9.40, 9.250
    s 46: 9.255
    s 47: 9.260
    s 47(6): 9.260
    s 47(7): 9.260
    s 48: 9.275
    s 50: 9.280
    s 51: 9.285
    s 76: 9.290
    s 79: 9.290
    s 84: 9.290
    s 85: 9.290
    Pt IIIA: 12.250
    Pt V: 9.290
    Pt IV: 9.240, 9.250, 9.270,
        9.285, 9.290
    Pt VII: 9.285
    Pt XIA: 9.240
    Schedule 2: Australian
        Consumer Law: 2.35,
        4.10, 6.165, 7.140,
        11.185, 11.260, 12.60
    s 3: 9.45
    s 4: 9.55, 9.185, 12.65
    s 7: 9.355, 14.100
    s 18: 9.165, 9.360, 9.365,
        12.75, 12.610,
        15.405
    ss 18 to 28: 9.50
    s 20: 9.365, 12.75
    s 21: 2.35, 9.70, 9.365
    s 21(2): 9.70
    s 22: 9.40, 9.70
    s 22(2): 9.70
    s 23: 9.80, 9.360
    s 23(2): 9.85
    s 23(3): 9.70
    s 24: 9.80, 9.360
    s 24(4): 9.80
    s 25: 9.80, 9.360
    s 26: 9.80
    s 27: 9.80
    s 28: 9.80
    s 29: 9.60, 9.100, 9.110,
        9.165, 9.360, 9.365,
        12.610, 15.405
    s 29(2): 9.100

s 29(3): 9.100
s 29(g): 9.105, 9.120,
    9.130, 9.200
ss 29 to 50: 9.90
s 32: 3.200, 9.145, 9.365
s 33: 9.110
s 34: 9.115, 9.120, 9.165,
    9.365
s 35: 9.150, 9.365
s 36: 9.125, 9.130, 9.135,
    9.165, 9.365
s 36(5): 9.125
s 40: 4.90
s 41: 4.90
s 48: 3.205, 9.155, 9.365
s 50: 9.160
s 51: 9.180
ss 51 to 65: 9.170
s 52: 9.65, 9.180
s 53: 9.180
s 54: 9.180, 9.355, 12.215,
    12.270, 12.360,
    12.420, 15.410,
    15.415
ss 54 to 56: 14.85
s 55: 9.180, 12.65, 12.270,
    12.360, 12.420
s 56: 9.180, 9.355
s 57: 9.180, 9.355
s 58: 9.180
s 59: 9.180
s 60: 9.185, 9.350, 9.360,
    9.365, 12.65, 12.90,
    12.215, 12.270,
    12.285, 12.360,
    12.390, 12.415,
    12.420, 12.600,
    12.610, 15.410,
    15.415
ss 60 to 61: 12.85
ss 60 to 62: 12.65, 12.80
ss 60 to 63: 12.90, 14.85
ss 60 to 64: 12.115
s 61: 9.350, 9.355, 9.360,
    12.215, 12.270,
    12.285, 12.360,
    12.390, 12.415,
    12.420, 12.600,
    12.610, 15.410,
    15.415
s 61(1): 9.185, 9.365, 12.65
s 61(2): 9.185, 9.365
s 62: 9.165, 9.185, 9.360,
    9.365, 12.65, 12.200,
    12.280, 12.605,
    12.610
s 63: 9.185, 12.65, 12.80,
    12.85, 12.115
s 64: 2.35, 4.275, 9.200,
    9.350, 9.360, 9.365,

12.75, 12.215,
12.285, 12.415,
12.420, 12.600,
15.415
s 64A: 9.200, 12.75, 12.80,
    12.115, 12.215,
    12.420, 15.415
s 67: 9.235, 9.355, 9.360
s 68: 9.230
s 100: 9.190
s 101: 9.190
s 103: 9.190
ss 104 to 133: 9.170
s 134: 9.360
ss 134 to 137: 9.170
ss 138 to 150: 9.170
s 139: 15.430
s 139A: 9.360, 9.365,
    12.75, 15.455
s 139A(2): 15.430
s 139A(4): 15.430
s 139B(2): 9.120
s 236: 5.175
ss 259 to 286: 9.195
s 275: 5.185, 9.200, 12.70,
    12.110, 12.125,
    12.150, 12.415,
    15.435
Ch 2: 3.250
Ch 3: 3.230, 3.250
Ch 5: 9.290
Pt 2-2: 4.390
Pt 3-1: 15.400
Pt 3-5: 9.355
Pt 3-5, Div 1: 9.335
Pt 3.1, Div 1: 9.140
Pt 3.3: 9.210
Pt 3.4: 9.215
Pt 3.5: 9.220
Pt 5-2, Div 3: 4.220
Pt IV: 9.240
Divs 3 to 5: 14.100, 14.105

Consumer Guarantees Act
    1993: 9.175

Copyright Act 1968
    s 31(3): 15.55

Corporations Act 2001: 7.10
    s 50AAA: 8.110
    ss 199A(2) to (4): 8.30
    s 761A: 7.110
    ss 792A to 792I: 7.110
    s 914A: 7.110
    s 941A: 7.110
    s 946A: 7.110
    s 985B: 7.110
    s 1012A: 7.110
    Ch 7: 7.110

Crimes Act 1914: 6.15, 6.85

Table of Statutes

Crimes Act 1914 — cont
s 50AD: 6.85
ss 50DA to 50DB: 6.85

Crimes (Child Sex Tourism)
Amendment Act 1994: 6.85
Pt IIIA: 6.85

Crimes at Sea Act 2000: 12.335

Criminal Code: 6.15, 11.340
s 6.1: 6.165
s 7: 11.615
s 10.3: 6.135
s 12: 11.615
s 22: 13.90
s 134.1: 6.105
s 232: 15.135
Pt 4: 15.135
Pts 7.3 to 7.7: 6.110
Div 134: 11.675
Div 135: 11.675
Div 272: 11.340

Criminal Code Amendment
(Theft, Bribery and related
Offences) Act 2000: 11.190

Customs (Prohibited Imports)
Regulations 1956
reg 4A: 12.485

Damage by Aircraft Act 1999:
12.480, 12.765

Disability Discrimination Act
1992
s 4: 8.140

Domicile Act 1982
s 10: 13.155

Electronic Transactions Act
1999: 4.105, 11.700
s 14(4): 4.105

Environmental Protection
(Impact of Proposals) Act
1974: 15.270

Environmental Protection and
Biodiversity Conservation
Act 1999: 15.265, 15.270,
15.340

Equal Opportunity for Women
in the Workplace Act 1999:
8.145
s 2A: 8.145

Fair Work Act 2009: 8.100,
8.110, 8.120, 8.125, 10.30,
10.45
s 3: 8.120
s 13: 8.100

s 14: 8.100
s 26: 8.110
s 27: 8.110
s 55: 8.125
s 61: 8.125
s 388: 8.100
s 391(1A): 8.110
s 392: 8.110
s 682: 10.45
Pt 2-3: 8.125
Pt 2-4: 8.130
Pt 5-2: 10.45

Family Law Act 1975: 2.165,
2.170
s 63B: 10.35
s 95: 2.160
Pt VIII: 10.65

Federal Court of Australia Act
1976: 2.165
s 33: 2.160
s 33C: 14.105
s 53A(1A): 10.35
s 53A(1): 10.35
Pt III, Div 2: 2.165
Pt IVA: 14.105

Federal Magistrates Act 1999:
2.175

Financial Services Reform Act
2001: 7.10, 7.110, 11.55

Financial Transaction Reports
Act 1988: 15.175

Food Standards Australia New
Zealand Act 1991: 14.20,
14.30
s 3: 14.35
s 5: 14.50
s 7: 14.30
s 9: 14.30
s 10: 14.30
ss 14 to 19: 14.30
s 20: 14.35
s 28: 14.35
s 32: 14.35
s 40: 14.30
Pt 3, Div 1: 14.30
Pt 3, Div 2: 14.30

Franchise Fee Windfall Tax
(Collection) Act 1997:
14.150

Franchise Fee Windfall Tax
(Imposition) Act 1997:
14.150

Great Barrier Reef Marine Park
Act 1975: 15.270

Hotel Proprietors Act 1956:
13.75

Human Rights and Equal
Opportunity Commission
Act 1986: 8.140
s 25Y: 8.140
s 25Z: 8.140
s 25ZA: 8.140

Income Tax Assessment Act
1936: 8.55

Insurance (Agents and Brokers)
Contracts Act 1984: 11.55

Insurance Contracts Act 1984:
7.10, 7.20, 7.60, 7.95,
7.100, 7.105, 7.145, 15.120
s 11(1): 7.75
s 13: 7.25
ss 16 to 17: 7.20
ss 16 to 18: 15.120
s 21: 7.25
s 21(2): 7.25
s 38(1): 7.95
s 44: 7.30, 7.45
s 45: 7.30, 7.55
s 48: 4.395
s 54: 7.130
s 58(2): 7.100
s 60(1): 7.105
s 65(1)(c)(i): 7.60
s 65(1)(c)(ii): 7.60
s 65(4): 7.60
s 66: 7.60, 8.30
s 66(b): 7.60
s 76: 7.55

Insurance Contracts
Regulations 1985: 7.200
regs 25 to 29: 7.200
reg 27: 7.200
Div 6: 7.205

International Air Services
Commission Act 1992:
12.490

International Arbitration Act
1974: 10.60

Interstate Road Transport Act
1985: 12.165

Judiciary Act 1903: 2.160
s 30: 2.160

Jurisdiction of Courts (Cross
Vesting) Act 1987: 10.85

Legislative Instruments Act
2003
s 3: 3.260

Licensing (Consolidation) Act
1910: 14.135

Limitation of Liability for
Maritime Claims Act 1989:
12.90, 12.365, 12.375,
12.415
s 5: 12.415

Maritime Legislation
Amendment Act 1994:
12.320

Marriage Act 1961: 2.170

Military Rehabilitation and
Compensation Act 2004:
8.155

Model Work Health and Safety
Act 2010: 8.180, 8.195,
8.200, 8.205, 8.210, 8.215,
8.220, 8.225, 8.230, 8.235
s 2: 8.180
ss 4 to 8: 8.185
s 5: 8.195
s 7(2): 8.195
s 8: 8.190
s 18(2): 8.200
s 18(3)(a): 8.215
s 18(3)(b): 8.215
s 18(3)(c): 8.215
s 18(3)(d): 8.215
s 18(5): 8.195
s 22: 8.215
s 27: 8.200
s 28: 8.200
s 74: 8.220
s 75: 8.220
s 190: 8.230
s 194: 8.230
s 196: 8.230
s 256: 8.235
s 257: 8.235
s 349: 8.210
Pt 2, Div 3: 8.195
Pt 3: 8.225
Pt 8: 8.230
Pt 9: 8.230
Div 2: 8.200, 8.205
Div 4: 8.220
subdiv 1: 8.185
subdiv 2: 8.185, 8.190,
8.195, 8.200

National Food Authority
Amendment Act 1995:
14.30, 14.35

National Road Transport
Commission Act 1992:
12.165

Native Title Act 1993: 2.65,
15.320
s 3: 2.65
s 21: 15.320
s 223: 15.320

Navigation Act 1912: 12.325,
12.345, 12.350, 12.415
s 2: 12.325, 12.370, 12.415
s 2(2): 12.325
s 5: 12.380
s 6: 12.325, 12.350, 12.380
s 6(5): 12.370
s 10: 12.370
s 189: 12.345
s 258A: 12.420
s 332: 12.415
s 338: 12.370, 12.405
s 338(b): 12.370
s 427: 12.325, 12.345

Navigation Amendment Act
1979: 12.365, 12.375
Pt VIII: 12.375

Northern Territory Acceptance
Act 1910: 12.105

Occupational Health and Safety
(Commonwealth
Employees) Act 1991:
8.175, 15.475

Occupational Health and Safety
(Maritime Industry) Act
1993: 8.175, 15.475

Passenger Movement Charge
Act 1978: 9.155

Passenger Movement Charges
Collection Act 1978: 9.155

Privy Council (Appeals from the
High Court Act) 1975:
2.185

Privy Council (Limitation of
Appeals) Act 1968: 2.185

Qantas Sale Act 1992: 12.510

Racial Discrimination Act 1975:
12.25, 15.320
s 9: 8.140

Railway Standardization (New
South Wales and Victoria)
Agreement Act 1958:
12.240

Railways Agreement (Western
Australia) Act 1961: 12.240

Registered Clubs Act 1976:
14.170

Safe Work Australia Act 2008:
8.155
s 3: 8.180
s 10: 8.175

Safety, Rehabilitation and
Compensation Act 1988:
8.15, 8.155

Seafarers Rehabilitation and
Compensation Act 1992:
8.155

Seas and Submerged Lands Act
1973: 12.320

Sex Discrimination Act 1984:
12.25
ss 5 to 7B: 8.140
s 28A: 8.150
ss 28A to 28L: 8.150
Div 3: 8.150

Shipping Registration Act 1981
s 3(1): 12.325
s 12(1): 12.335
s 13: 12.335
s 14(a): 12.335

Space Activities Act 1998:
12.525

Statute of Westminster Act
1942: 2.45

Telecommunications Act 1975:
8.35

Tourism Australia Act 2004:
3.85, 3.95, 3.105, 3.115,
3.130
s 1: 3.105
s 2: 3.105
s 3: 3.120
s 6: 3.115

Trade Practices Act 1974:
2.165, 9.15, 9.20, 9.25,
9.30, 9.35, 9.45, 9.50, 9.55,
9.70, 9.80, 9.90, 9.140,
9.175, 9.180, 9.185, 9.195,
9.200, 9.210, 9.220, 9.265,
11.375, 12.65, 12.105,
12.150, 14.85, 14.105,
15.410, 15.415, 15.430 —
see **Competition and
Consumer Act 2010**
s 4: 9.45
s 6: 9.25
s 6(3): 9.25
s 6(4): 9.25
s 18: 9.55, 9.60, 9.90,
9.100, 9.110, 9.115
s 20: 9.200

Trade Practices Act
1974 — cont
  s 23: 9.200
  s 29: 9.115
  s 51A: 9.55
  s 51AA: 9.70
  s 51AB: 9.70
  s 51AC: 9.70
  s 52: 9.55, 9.110, 9.295,
    11.710
  s 52(aa): 9.100
  s 53: 9.100, 9.110
  s 53(c): 9.105, 9.120,
    9.130, 9.295
  s 53(d): 11.710
  s 53C: 9.155
  s 54: 3.200, 9.145, 9.180
  s 55: 9.110, 9.185
  s 55A: 9.115, 9.120, 9.130
  s 56: 9.150
  s 58: 9.125, 9.135
  s 60: 9.160
  s 68: 9.200, 12.90
  s 68A: 9.200
  s 68B: 15.430
  s 69: 9.180
  s 70: 9.180, 14.85
  s 71: 14.85
  s 71(1): 9.180
  s 71(2): 9.180
  s 72: 9.180
  s 74: 9.185, 9.350, 12.65,
    12.85, 12.90, 12.110,
    12.115, 13.60, 14.85,
    15.430
  s 74(1): 9.185, 12.65
  s 74(2): 9.185, 12.65
  s 74(2)A: 12.70
  s 74(3): 9.185, 12.85,
    12.115
  s 74F: 9.180
  s 74G: 9.180
  s 82: 9.295
  s 84(2): 9.120
  s 139A: 9.200
  s 139A(4): 9.200
  Pt V: 3.250
  Pt V, Div 1: 9.20
  Pt V, Div 2: 9.20
  Pt IV: 9.20
  Pt IVA: 9.20

Trade Practices Amendment
  (Australian Consumer Law)
  Act (No 1) 2010: 9.30

Trade Practices Amendment
  (Australian Consumer Law)
  Act (No 2) 2010: 9.30
  s 2: 13.125
  s 29(m): 13.75, 13.135

  s 50: 13.125
  s 60: 13.60, 13.115
  s 61: 13.60, 13.115, 13.125
  s 64: 13.125
  s 64A: 13.125
  s 139A: 13.125
  s 157: 6.165
  s 275: 13.125
  Sch 5: 3.260

Transport Legislation
  Amendment Act 1995:
  7.155, 12.345, 12.550,
  12.555

Travel Agents Act 1973: 11.655

Vagrants Gaming and Other
  Offences Act 1931: 15.135
  s 19: 15.135
  s 20: 15.135
  s 21: 15.135
  s 21A: 15.135
  s 22: 15.135

Work Health and Safety Act
  2010: 8.05, 8.180

Workplace Relations Act 1996:
  8.100, 10.30

World Heritage Properties
  Conservation Act 1983:
  15.265, 15.270
  s 9: 15.270
  s 10: 15.270

*AUSTRALIAN CAPITAL
TERRITORY*

ACT Civil and Administrative
  Tribunal Act 2008: 10.125
  s 7: 10.155
  s 15: 10.135
  s 33: 10.150
  s 38: 10.150
  Pt 4: 10.155
  Pt 6: 10.155

Agents Act 2003: 11.385,
  11.545
  s 6: 11.400
  s 11: 11.395, 11.400
  s 12: 11.415
  s 13(d): 11.400
  s 15: 11.460
  s 21: 11.390
  s 21(2): 11.390
  s 23: 11.390
  s 24: 11.420
  s 26: 11.385, 11.420
  s 27: 11.390
  s 27(1): 11.470

  s 27(2): 11.470
  s 27(3): 11.470
  s 28: 11.410, 11.415
  s 29: 11.410, 11.415
  s 30: 11.415, 11.490
  s 31: 11.415
  s 32: 11.415
  s 34:
  s 42: 11.495, 11.530
  s 53: 11.415
  s 65: 11.505
  s 69: 11.465
  s 70: 11.465
  s 91: , 11.560, 11.580
  s 92: 11.495, 11.555
  s 94: 11.390, 11.600,
    11.615
  s 94(3): 11.615
  s 94(4): 11.615
  s 95: 11.390, 11.615
  s 97: 11.460
  ss 127 to 130: 11.480
  s 158: 11.590
  s 167: 11.445, 11.510,
    11.520, 11.530
  s 168: 11.510
  s 169: 11.495
  s 171: 11.460
  s 178: 11.460

Business Names Act 1963:
  11.460

Casino Control Act 2006:
  15.175
  s 107: 15.205
  Pt 2: 15.175
  Pt 4: 15.175
  Pt 5: 15.175
  Pt 8: 15.175
  Pt 10: 15.175

Civil Law (Wrongs) Act 2002:
  5.130, 5.155, 5.165, 5.185,
  15.435, 15.445
  s 4: 12.140
  s 9: 12.150
  s 10: 12.150
  s 11: 13.145
  s 95-86: 14.325
  s 144: 13.200
  s 145: 13.200
  s 146: 13.200
  s 148: 13.200
  s 149: 13.200
  s 152(1)(a): 13.200
  s 152(1)(b): 13.200
  s 153(5): 13.200
  s 154: 13.200
  Ch 11: 13.130, 13.200

Civil Law (Wrongs) Act
2002 — cont
  Pt 11.2: 12.130, 12.135,
    12.145

Competition Policy Reform
  (ACT) Act 1996: 9.20, 9.240

Criminal Code 2002: 6.15
  s 41: 6.135

Fair Trading Act 1992: 9.20

Food Act 2001: 14.45
  s 27: 14.40, 14.55

Gambling Regulation Act 2003:
    15.120, 15.135
  s 13: 15.135
  s 13A: 15.135

Gaming Machine Act 2004:
    15.210
  Pt 1: 15.210
  Pt 2: 15.210
  Pt 3: 15.210
  Pt 4: 15.210
  Pt 5: 15.210
  Pt 6: 15.210
  Pt 11: 15.210
  Pt 12: 15.210
  Pt 13: 15.210

Innkeepers Act 1968
  s 4: 13.145

Liquor Act 1975: 14.140
  s 33: 14.215
  s 45: 14.170
  s 46: 14.170
  s 48: 14.170
  s 49: 14.170
  s 52: 14.195
  s 64: 14.195
  s 138: 14.215, 14.245
  s 152: 14.215
  s 179: 14.215
  Pt 2: 14.220
  Pt 4, Div 2: 14.185
  Pt 4, Div 4.3: 14.185
  Pt 4, Div 4.5: 14.185
  Pt 4, Div 4.6: 14.185
  Pt 6: 14.215
  Pt 10: 14.215, 14.230

Liquor Ordinance
  s 79: 14.285

Magistrates Court Act 1930
  s 257: 2.210
  s 266A: 2.210

Residential Tenancies Act 1997:
    13.45

Road Transport (Third Party
  Insurance) Act 2008: 12.195

Sale of Goods Act 1954: 4.10,
  9.20

Trade Measurement Act 1991:
  14.65

Trade Measurement
  Administration Act 1991:
  14.65

Trustee Act 1925: 11.30

Work Safety Act 2008: 8.175,
  15.475

Workers' Compensation Act
  1951: 8.15, 8.155

NEW SOUTH WALES

Anti-Discrimination Act 1977
  s 122J: 8.145

Business Names Act 2002:
  11.460

Casino Control Act 1992:
    15.175
  s 163: 15.185
  Pt 2: 15.175
  Pt 3: 15.175
  Pt 3, Div 2: 15.175
  Pt 4: 15.175
  Pt 8: 15.175

Civil Liability Act 2002: 5.185,
    15.435, 15.445
  s 5I: 15.445
  ss 5J to N: 15.455
  s 5M: 15.455
  s 5R: 5.155
  s 43: 5.175
  s 46(2): 14.325
  ss 47 to 50: 14.325
  s 49: 14.325
  s 50: 5.100, 14.325, 15.370
  s 50(2): 14.325
  Pt 2: 15.445
  Pt 5: 15.465
  Pt 9: 15.465

Commercial Arbitration Act
  2010: 10.60

Common Carriers Act 1902:
    12.105, 12.130
  s 4: 12.140
  s 5(2): 12.145
  s 5(3): 12.145
  s 6(1): 12.145
  s 7(1): 12.145

  s 9: 12.150
  s 10: 12.150
  s 11: 12.145
  Sch 2: 12.135

Competition Policy Reform
  (NSW) Act 1995: 9.20,
  9.240

Consumer Claims Act 1998
  s 3: 10.140
  s 8: 10.155

Consumer, Trader and Tenancy
    Tribunal Act 2001: 10.125
  s 33: 10.150
  s 55: 10.150

Contracts Review Act 1980:
  2.235, 4.390, 9.70, 9.80

Control Act 1992: 15.155

Crimes Act 1900: 6.20
  s 23: 6.160
  s 23A: 6.155
  s 23A(3): 6.150
  s 59: 5.20
  s 61: 5.20
  s 192E: 6.105
  ss 192E to H: 6.105
  ss 249A to J: 6.110
  s 249B: 6.110
  s 249G: 6.110

Crimes Amendment (Fraud,
  Identity and Forgery
  Offences) Act 2009: 6.105

Criminal Procedure Act 1986
  Sch 1: 6.45

Damage by Aircraft Act 1952:
  12.480

Defamation Act 2005: 5.130
  s 21: 10.110

District Court Act 1973
  s 4: 2.205, 10.85

Employers' Liability Act 1991
  ss 3 to 5: 8.30

Environmental Planning and
  Assessment Act 1979:
  15.265

Fair Trading Act 1987: 9.20
  s 18: 11.495
  s 44: 11.495
  Pt 7: 9.40

Food Act 2003: 14.45
  s 8(2): 14.55
  s 9(2)(d): 14.55

Food Act 2003 — *cont*
  s 19: 14.55
  s 21: 14.40, 14.55
  s 22: 14.60
  s 108(e): 14.70
  s 133(2)(e): 14.75

Food Amendment (Food Safety Supervisors) Act 2009
  Pt 8, Div 3: 14.70

Gaming Act 1850: 15.135

Gaming Machines Act 2001: 15.210
  Pt 1: 15.210
  Pt 4: 15.210
  Pt 5: 15.210
  Pt 6: 15.210
  Pt 7: 15.210

Homebush Motor Racing (Sydney 400) Act 2008: 15.10, 15.115
  s 35: 15.55, 15.60

Industrial Relations Act 1996: 8.110

Innkeepers Act 1968: 13.130, 13.200
  s 3: 13.145, 13.200
  s 3(1): 13.145, 13.200
  s 4: 13.145, 13.200
  s 5: 13.145, 13.200
  s 6: 13.145, 13.200
  s 6(a): 13.145, 13.200
  s 7(1): 13.145
  s 7(2): 13.145, 13.200
  s 7(3)(a): 13.145, 13.200
  s 7(3)(b): 13.145, 13.200
  s 8: 13.145, 13.200

Jury Act 1977
  s 20: 10.110

Law Reform (Contributory Negligence and Apportionment of Liability) Act 1991
  s 5G: 15.445

Liquor Act 1912: 14.135

Liquor Act 1982
  s 100: 13.145

Liquor Act 2007: 14.135, 14.140
  s 3: 14.145, 14.215
  s 4: 14.155
  s 5: 14.215
  s 15: 14.170
  s 16: 14.170
  s 19: 14.170
  s 24: 14.170
  s 42: 14.190
  s 44: 14.190, 14.195
  s 47: 14.215
  s 48: 14.195
  s 52: 14.255
  s 59: 14.185
  s 60: 14.185
  s 68: 14.195
  s 73: 14.245
  s 77: 14.215, 14.245
  s 91: 14.215
  s 99: 14.245
  s 138: 14.225
  Pt 3, Divs 1 to 7: 14.170
  Pt 4, Div 1: 14.185
  Pt 5: 14.195, 14.220
  Pt 7, Div 2: 14.215
  Pt 9: 14.235
  Pt 10: 14.230

Local Court Act 2007
  s 29: 2.210

Major Events Act 2009: 15.10, 15.52, 15.115
  s 41(b): 15.52
  Div 4: 15.105
  Div 5: 15.100

Motor Accidents Compensation Act 1999: 12.195

Occupational Health and Safety Act 2000: 8.175, 15.475

Passenger Transport Act 1990: 12.180

Property, Stock and Business Agents Act 2002
  s 3: 13.165
  s 8: 13.165
  s 23: 13.165

Rail Safety Act 2008: 12.260, 12.270

Registered Clubs Act 1976: 14.245, 15.215
  s 45: 15.215

Residential Tenancies Act 1987: 13.45
  s 6: 13.160

Sale of Goods Act 1923: 4.10, 9.20

Sale of Goods (Vienna Convention) Act 1986: 9.230

The Gaming Act 1850: 15.135

Trade Measurement Act 1989: 14.65

Trade Measurement (Repeal) Act 2009: 14.65

Transport Administration Act 1988: 12.240
  s 91: 12.265
  s 99: 12.265
  s 102: 12.185

Travel Agents Act 1986: 11.385
  s 3(2): 11.400
  s 4: 11.395
  s 4(1): 11.400
  s 4(2): 11.400
  s 4(4)(a): 11.400
  s 5: 11.400, 11.435
  s 6(1): 11.390
  s 6(1)(b): 11.390
  s 6(2): 11.390
  s 7: 11.460
  s 8: 11.410
  s 9(1): 11.415
  s 9(2): 11.415
  s 10: 11.390, 11.420
  ss 10(3) to (5): 11.420
  s 10(8): 11.415
  s 11(1): 11.440
  s 11(2): 11.560, 11.580
  s 11(2)(a): 11.385,
  s 11(2)(b):
  s 12(2): 11.460
  s 20: 11.510
  s 20(1): 11.505
  s 20(1)(c): 11.545
  s 20(6): 11.495
  s 20(7): 11.495
  s 20(8): 11.520
  s 21: 11.520
  s 21(1): 11.510
  s 22: 11.445, 11.530
  s 22(3): 11.590
  s 24: 11.590
  s 25: 11.445, 11.530, 11.590
  s 26: 11.460
  s 27: 11.460
  s 28: 11.535
  ss 28 to 32: 11.535
  s 29: 11.540
  s 30: 11.540
  s 31: 11.545
  s 31(2): 11.540
  s 33: 11.460
  s 34: 11.460
  s 35: 11.460
  s 36: 11.465
  s 37(1): 11.470
  s 37(2): 11.470

Travel Agents Act 1986 — cont
s 38(3): 11.390, 11.555
s 40(3): 11.615
s 40(4): 11.615
s 40(5): 11.615
s 40(6): 11.390, 11.615
s 40(7): 11.390, 11.615
s 41: 11.480
s 43: 11.495
s 44(4): 11.495
s 45: 11.495
s 54: 11.495
s 57(2)(a): 11.600

Travel Agents Order 2005
cl 4: 11.400
cl 7: 11.465

Travel Agents Regulations 2006
reg 6: 11.410
reg 12: 11.465
Sch 2: 11.410

Trustee Act 1925: 11.30

Uniform Civil Procedure Rules 2005
Pt 20: 10.35

Unlawful Gambling Act 1998: 15.120, 15.135
s 16: 15.135

Workers' Compensation Act 1987: 8.15, 8.155
s 151A: 8.70

NORTHERN TERRITORY

Accommodation Providers Act: 13.130, 13.145
s 6(1): 13.145
s 10: 13.145
s 11: 13.145

Accommodation Providers Act : 13.200
s 3(1): 13.200
s 3(1)(c): 13.200
s 4: 13.200
s 5: 13.200
s 6(2): 13.200
s 6(3)(a): 13.200
s 6(3)(b): 13.200
s 6(3)(e): 13.200
s 7: 13.200
s 9: 13.200
s 11: 13.200
s 19: 13.200

AustralAsia Railway Corporation Act: 12.245

Business Names Act: 11.460

Commercial Passenger (Road) Transport Act: 12.180

Competition Policy Reform (NT) Act: 9.20, 9.240

Consumer Affairs and Fair Trading Act: 9.20
s 3(2): 11.400
s 18: 11.495
ss 20 to 22: 11.495
s 23: 11.495
s 24: 11.495
s 185: 11.400, 11.600
s 186: 11.395
s 186(1): 11.400
s 186(2)(a): 11.400
s 186(3): 11.400
s 187(1): 11.400
s 188: 11.390
s 188(1)(b): 11.390
s 188(2): 11.390, 11.555
s 188(3): 11.390, 11.555
s 188(4): 11.390
s 189: 11.390
s 190: 11.410
s 191(1)(a): 11.415
s 191(1)(b): 11.415
s 191(2): 11.415
s 191(3): 11.415
s 192: 11.415
s 193: 11.390, 11.420
ss 193(3) to (5): 11.420
s 193(9): 11.415
s 194(2): 11.460
s 195(1):
s 195(1)(b): 11.385, , 11.560
s 195(2): 11.440
s 195(3): 11.440
s 196: 11.460
s 203: 11.460
s 204: 11.510
s 204(1): 11.505
s 204(6): 11.495
s 204(7): 11.495
s 204(8): 11.520
s 205: 11.520
s 205(1): 11.510
s 206: 11.445, 11.530
s 206(3): 11.590
s 207: 11.520, 11.530
s 208: 11.590
s 209: 11.460
s 210: 11.460
s 211: 11.460
s 212: 11.480
s 213: 11.465
s 214(1): 11.470
s 214(2): 11.470
s 215: 11.535

ss 215 to 219: 11.535
s 216: 11.540
s 217: 11.540
s 218: 11.545
s 218(2): 11.540
s 220: 11.600
ss 220 to 223: 11.625
s 221: 11.385, , 11.560, 11.580, 11.625
s 222(1): 11.615
s 222(2): 11.615
s 222(3): 11.615
s 222(4): 11.390, 11.615
s 337: 11.625
Pt XI: 11.385

Consumer Affairs and Fair Trading Amendment Act: 5.185, 14.325, 15.435

Criminal Code
s 12: 11.390
s 33: 6.135
s 37: 6.155
s 186: 5.20
s 187: 5.20
s 188: 5.20
s 226A: 6.125
s 226B: 6.125

Criminal Code Act: 6.15

Defamation Act: 5.130

Food Act : 14.45
s 20: 14.40, 14.55

Gaming Control Act: 15.120, 15.135, 15.175
s 13: 15.175
s 26: 15.175
s 46H: 15.175
ss 46J to N: 15.175
s 135: 15.135

Gaming Machine Act: 15.210
s 3: 15.210
s 17: 15.210
ss 28 to 34: 15.210
ss 45 to 51: 15.210
ss 98 to 115: 15.210
ss 116 to 120: 15.210
ss 143 to 157: 15.210
s 165: 15.210

Land Rights Act: 15.320

Liquor Act: 14.140
s 19: 14.220
s 24: 14.170
s 26: 14.185
s 27: 14.190
s 28: 14.190
s 29: 14.190

Liquor Act — cont
  s 31: 14.195, 14.215
  s 32A: 14.185
  s 33: 14.185
  s 39: 14.185
  ss 40 to 41: 14.185
  s 46F: 14.190
  s 48A: 14.235
  s 59: 14.200
  s 101AN: 14.235
  s 102: 14.215, 14.245
  s 105: 14.215, 14.245
  s 106: 14.215
  ss 106A to 106E: 14.215
  s 107: 14.215
  s 108: 14.215
  s 110: 14.215
  ss 111 to 113: 14.215
  ss 116A to 118: 14.215
  s 124: 14.230, 14.235

Local Court Act
  s 3: 2.210

Motor Accidents (Compensation) Act: 12.195

Northern Territory Criminal Code
  s 154: 6.60

Proportionate Liability Act: 15.445

Residential Tenancies Act: 13.45

Sale of Goods Act: 9.20

Small Claims Act: 10.125
  s 9: 10.150
  s 18: 10.150

Trade Measurement Act: 14.65

Trade Measurement Administration Act: 14.65

Trade Measurement Legislation Repeal Act: 14.65

Trustee Act: 11.30

Workers Rehabilitation and Compensation Act: 8.15, 8.155

Workplace Health and Safety Act 2009: 8.175, 15.475

QUEENSLAND

Acts Interpretation Act 1954
  s 14(2): 3.130
  s 14(4): 3.140
  s 14(5): 3.135
  s 14A: 3.115, 3.185
  s 14B: 3.140, 3.215, 3.225
  s 15A: 3.65
  s 20(1)(a): 12.120
  s 20(2): 12.120

Anti-Discrimination Act 1991
  s 119: 8.150

Business Names Act 1962: 11.460

Carriage of Goods by Land (Carriers' Liability) Act 1967: 12.110
  s 5(1): 12.120

Carriage of Goods by Land (Carriers' Liability) Repeal Act 1993: 12.120

Casino Control Act 1982: 15.155, 15.175
  Pt 2: 15.175
  Pt 3: 15.175
  Pt 4: 15.175
  Pt 5: 15.175
  Pt 8: 15.175

Civil Liability Act 2003: 5.185, 15.435, 15.445, 15.465
  s 15: 15.445
  s 16: 15.445
  s 17: 15.455
  s 18: 15.455
  s 19: 15.455
  s 34: 15.465
  s 38: 15.465
  s 46: 14.325
  ss 46 to 49: 14.325
  s 47: 14.325
  s 73: 10.110
  Div 6: 5.155

Competition Policy Reform (Qld) Act 1996: 9.20, 9.240

Criminal Code: 5.20, 6.15
  s 25: 6.135
  s 245: 6.80
  ss 268 to 269: 6.160
  s 304A: 6.155
  s 391(a): 6.65
  s 408C: 6.105
  ss 442A to M: 6.110
  ss 442A to 442M: 11.190
  s 245: 5.20
  s 246: 5.20
  s 288: 15.95
  s 289: 15.95
  s 355: 5.20
  s 408C: 11.675
  s 546: 6.190
  s 552B: 6.45

Defamation Act 2005: 5.130

District Court Act 1967
  s 68: 2.205, 10.85

Dividing Fences Act 1953: 10.135

Drugs Misuse Act 1986: 6.15

Fair Trading Act 1989: 9.20

Food Act 2006: 14.45
  s 8: 14.65
  s 39: 14.40, 14.55

Gaming Machine Act 1991: 15.135, 15.210
  Pt 1: 15.210
  Pt 2: 15.210
  Pt 3: 15.210
  Pt 4: 15.210
  Pt 5: 15.210
  Pt 6: 15.210
  Pt 7: 15.210
  Pt 8: 15.210
  Pt 9: 15.210
  Pt 10: 15.210
  Sch 2: 15.210

Gold Coast Motor Racing Events Act 1990: 15.10, 15.55, 15.60, 15.100, 15.115

Industrial Relations Act 1999: 8.110

Jurisdiction of Courts (Cross Vesting) Act 1987: 10.85

Jury Act 1995: 6.200
  s 32: 10.110

Law Reform Act 1995: 4.340

Law Reform (Tortfeasors Contribution, Contributory Negligence, and Division of Chattels) Act 1952: 13.75

Liquor Act 1912: 14.135
  s 78: 14.290

Liquor Act 1992: 14.135, 14.140, 14.250
  s 3(a): 14.145
  s 3(d)(i): 14.145
  s 3(d)(ii): 14.145
  s 3(e): 14.145
  s 4: 14.155
  s 4B: 14.155
  s 44: 14.215

Liquor Act 1992 — cont
s 67A: 14.170
s 67AA: 14.170
s 76: 14.170
s 105: 14.185
s 107(1): 14.195
s 111: 14.185, 14.200
s 113: 14.185
s 116: 14.195
s 117: 14.190
s 117A: 14.190
s 118: 14.190
s 118A: 14.190
s 119: 14.190, 14.195
ss 143 to 144: 14.215
s 145B: 14.215
s 154: 14.215
s 155: 14.215
s 155AA: 14.215
s 156: 14.215, 14.245
s 156(1): 14.270
s 164: 14.215
Pt 4, Div 2: 14.170
Pt 5, Div 3: 14.185
Pt 7: 14.220, 14.225
Pt 9: 14.215
Pt 10: 14.220, 14.230

Magistrates Court Act 1921
s 4: 2.210

Major Sports Facilities Act 2001: 15.10, 15.52, 15.115
Pt 4A: 15.52
Pt 4B: 15.105

Maritime Safety Queensland Act 2002: 12.345

Motor Accident Insurance Act 1994: 12.195

Mutual Recognition (Queensland) Act 1992: 11.410

Property Agents and Motor Dealers Act 2000
ss 111 to 127: 13.165
s 114: 11.55
s 128: 11.400, 13.165
s 160: 13.165

Property Law Act 1974
s 11: 4.05
s 11(1)(a): 4.05
s 55: 4.395, 12.745, 15.30
s 59: 4.285

Queensland Civil and Administrative Tribunal Act 2009: 10.125
s 12: 10.135

s 28: 10.155
s 46: 10.145
s 50: 10.150
s 126: 10.155
Pt 7: 10.155
Sch 3: 10.140

Recreational Services (Limitation of Liability) Act 2002: 15.455

Regulatory Offences Act 1985
s 6: 6.15, 6.65, 6.105
s 6(1): 6.65
s 6(2): 6.65, 6.165
s 7: 6.65

Residential Tenancies Act 1994: 13.40, 13.45
s 21: 13.40, 13.45, 13.160
s 22: 13.40, 13.45
s 26: 13.40, 13.45

Residential Tenancies and Rooming Accommodation Act 2008: 10.135

Sale of Goods Act 1896: 4.10, 9.20
s 56: 9.20

Succession Act 1981
s 66: 5.20

The Gaming Act 1850: 15.135

Tourism Services Act 2003: 3.15

Trade Measurement Act 1990: 14.65

Trade Measurement Administration Act 1990: 14.65

Trade Measurement Legislation Repeal Act 2009: 14.65

Transport Operations (Marine Safety) Act 1994: 12.345

Transport Operations (Passenger Transport) Act 1994: 12.180

Transport Operations (Translink Transit Authority) Act 2008: 12.240

Travel Agents Act 1988: 11.385, 11.545
s 6: 11.400
s 8: 11.400
s 9: 11.395
s 9(1): 11.400

s 9(2)(a): 11.400
s 9(3): 11.400
s 11:
s 12: 11.390
s 12(1): 11.390
s 12(1)(b): 11.390
s 12(3): 11.390, 11.555
s 12(4): 11.390, 11.555
s 12(5): 11.390
s 13: 11.390
s 14: 11.410
s 14(3): 11.415
s 15(1): 11.415
s 15(2): 11.415
s 16: 11.415
s 17: 11.415
s 18: 11.420
s 18(1)(c)(a): 11.420
s 18(5): 11.415
s 20: 11.440
s 20(1)(a):
s 20(1)(b): 11.385, , 11.560, 11.580
s 21: 11.460
s 24: 11.510
s 24(1): 11.505
s 24(6): 11.495
s 24(7): 11.495
s 24(8): 11.520
s 25: 11.520
s 25(1): 11.510
s 25(2): 11.615
s 25(3): 11.615
s 26: 11.445, 11.530
s 26(7): 11.590, 11.605
s 29: 11.460
s 30: 11.460
s 31: 11.460
s 32(1): 11.460
s 32(2)(a): 11.460
s 32(2)(b): 11.460
s 33: 11.480
s 34: 11.465
s 35(1): 11.470
s 35(2): 11.470
s 37: 11.385, , 11.560, 11.580
s 40: 11.600
s 41: 11.605
s 41(2): 11.555
s 42(3): 11.615
s 42(4): 11.615
s 42(5): 11.615
s 42(6): 11.390, 11.615
s 42(7): 11.390, 11.615
s 44: 11.495
s 45: 11.495
s 45(3): 11.495
s 45(4): 11.495
ss 45A to C: 11.495

Travel Agents Act 1988 — cont
  s 46: 11.495
  s 47: 11.495

Travel Agents Regulations 1998
  reg 6(1)(b): 11.400
  Sch 1: 11.465
  Sch 3, reg 1: 11.465
  Sch 3, reg 2: 11.465

Traveller Accommodation Providers (Liability) Act 2001: 13.130, 13.145, 13.200
  s 6: 13.200
  s 7: 13.200
  s 8(2): 13.200
  s 8(3): 13.200
  s 8(4)(a): 13.35
  s 9: 13.200
  s 10: 13.200
  s 13(1)(a): 13.200
  s 14(4): 13.145
  s 14(7): 13.200

Trusts Act 1973: 11.30

Uniform Civil Procedure Rules 1999
  Div 3: 10.35

Wagering Act 1998: 15.120, 15.135
  s 248: 15.135
  Sch 2: 15.120, 15.135

Wild Rivers Act 2005: 2.65

Workers' Compensation and Rehabilitation Act 2003: 8.15, 8.155

Workplace Health and Safety Act 1995: 8.175, 15.475
  s 28(2): 14.255

SOUTH AUSTRALIA

Age of Majority (Reduction Act) 1971: 4.340

AustralAsia Railway Corporation Act 1996: 12.245

Business Names Act 1996: 11.460

Carriers Act 1891: 12.105

Casino Act 1997: 15.155, 15.175
  Pt 4: 15.175
  Pt 5: 15.175
  Pt 6: 15.175

Civil Liability Act 1936
  s 59: 8.30

Competition Policy Reform (SA) Act 1996: 9.20, 9.240

Consumer Transactions Act 1972: 9.200

Criminal Law Consolidation Act 1935: 6.20
  s 15C: 6.125
  ss 130 to 133: 6.105
  ss 145 to 150: 6.110
  s 271: 6.190
  s 285BB: 6.160

Defamation Act 2005: 5.130

District Court Act 1991
  s 8: 2.205, 10.85

Equal Opportunity Act 1984: 8.145
  s 87: 8.150

Fair Trading Act 1987: 9.20

Fair Work Act 1994: 8.110

Food Act 2001: 14.45
  s 21: 14.40, 14.55

Gaming Machines Act 1992: 15.210
  Pt 1: 15.210
  Pt 2: 15.210
  Pt 3: 15.210
  Pt 4: 15.210
  Pt 4A: 15.210
  Pt 5: 15.210
  Pt 7: 15.210
  Pt 8: 15.210

Juries Act 1927
  s 5: 10.110

Law Reform (Contributory Negligence and Apportionment of Liability) Act 1991: 15.445
  s 38: 15.445
  s 39: 15.445
  s 42: 15.465
  s 74: 15.465
  Pt 8: 15.445

Licensing Act 1967-1975
  s 120: 13.135
  ss 120 to 121: 13.135

Liquor Licensing Act 1985: 13.135

Liquor Licensing Act 1997: 14.140

  s 3(a): 14.145
  s 3(b): 14.145
  s 4: 14.155
  s 28A: 14.190
  s 32: 14.170
  s 34: 14.170
  s 35: 14.170
  s 36: 14.170
  s 38: 14.215
  s 52: 14.190
  s 55: 14.195
  s 56: 14.195
  s 57: 14.195
  s 58: 14.195
  s 59: 14.195
  s 63: 14.195
  s 71: 14.215
  s 75A: 14.190
  s 76: 14.190
  ss 77 to 79: 14.190
  s 97: 14.215
  ss 100 to 101: 14.215
  s 101: 14.215
  s 109: 14.215
  s 123: 14.235
  s 124: 14.215
  s 131A: 14.215
  s 132: 14.235
  s 133: 14.235
  Pt 4, Div 1: 14.185
  Pt 4, Div 3: 14.185
  Pt 4, Div 4: 14.185
  Pt 4, Div 5: 14.185
  Pt 4, Div 6: 14.185
  Pt 4, Div 9: 14.185, 14.200
  Pt 6, Div 2: 14.215
  Pt 6, Div 6: 14.215
  Pt 6, Div 8: 14.215, 14.245
  Pt 7: 14.215
  Pt 8: 14.230
  Pts 8 to 11: 14.220
  Pt 9, Div 1: 14.225
  Divs 7 to 8A: 14.215

Lottery & Gaming Act 1936: 15.120, 15.135
  s 50: 15.135
  s 50A: 15.135

Magistrates Court Act 1991: 10.125
  s 3: 2.210
  s 8: 2.210
  s 38(5): 10.150
  s 38(6): 10.155
  Pt V, Div II: 10.155

Motor Vehicles Act 1959
  s 133: 12.195
  Pt IV: 12.195

Occupational Health, Safety
and Welfare Act 1986:
8.175, 15.475

Passenger Transport Act 1994:
12.180, 12.240

Rail Safety Act 2007: 12.260,
12.270

Railways (Transfer Agreement)
Act 1975: 12.240

Recreational Services
(Limitation of Liability) Act
2002: 5.165, 5.185, 14.325,
15.435, 15.455

Residential Tenancies Act 1995:
13.45

Sale of Goods Act 1895: 4.10,
9.20

Supreme Court Act 1935
s 65: 10.35

Survival of Causes of Action Act
1940: 5.20

Trade Measurement Act 1993:
14.65

Trade Measurement
Administration Act 1993:
14.65

Travel Agents Act 1986:
11.385, 11.545
s 3: 11.400, 11.600
s 4: 11.395
s 4(2)(a): 11.400
s 4(3): 11.400
s 5(2): 11.400
s 7: 11.390
s 7(1)(b): 11.400
s 7(2): 11.390, 11.555
s 7(3): 11.390, 11.555
s 7(4): 11.390
s 8: 11.410
s 8(2): 11.415
s 9: 11.420
s 10(1):
s 10(2): 11.440
s 11: 11.445
s 13: 11.465
s 14: 11.460
s 16(1): 11.505
s 17: 11.490
s 18: 11.510
s 18B: 11.470, 11.520
s 18B(1): 11.510
s 18B(1)(b): 11.520
s 18C: 11.470

s 19: 11.600
s 20: 11.385, , 11.560,
 11.580
s 21: 11.590
s 25(1): 11.615
s 27: 11.495
s 32: 11.495
s 33: 11.460
s 34(1): 11.460
s 34(2)(a): 11.460
s 34(2)(b): 11.460
s 35: 11.480
s 36: 11.495
s 37: 11.415, 11.495

Trustee Act 1936: 11.30

Workers' Rehabilitation and
Compensation Act 1986:
8.15, 8.155

Wrongs (Liability and Damages
for Personal Injury)
Amendment Act 2002: 5.50,
5.155

TASMANIA

Age of Majority Act 1973:
4.340

Business Names Act 1962:
11.460

Civil Liability Act 2002: 5.155,
5.165, 5.185, 15.435,
15.445
ss 4A to 5: 14.325
s 49A(1): 13.200
s 49A(3): 13.200
s 49A(3)(a): 13.200
s 49A(3)(b): 13.200
s 49A(3)(c): 13.200
s 158A(3): 13.145
Pt 10A: 13.130, 13.145,
 13.200

Common Carriers Act 1874:
12.105, 12.130
s 3: 12.135, 12.140
s 4: 12.145
s 4(2): 12.145
s 5: 12.145
s 6: 12.145
s 9: 12.145
s 10: 12.150
s 11: 12.145
s 14: 12.150

Criminal Code Act 1924: 6.15
s 252A: 6.105
ss 266 to 266B: 6.110

Defamation Act 2005: 5.130

Fair Trading Act 1990: 9.20

Food Act 2003: 14.45
s 21: 14.40, 14.55

Gaming Control Act 1993:
15.120, 15.135, 15.175,
15.210
ss 4A to C: 15.210
s 114: 15.135
Pt 1: 15.210
Pt 3: 15.175, 15.210
Pt 4: 15.175, 15.210
Pts 4A to C: 15.210
Pt 5: 15.210
Pt 6: 15.210
Pt 7: 15.175, 15.210
Pt 8: 15.210
Pt 9: 15.175, 15.210

Industrial Relations Act 1984:
8.110

Liquor Licensing Act Act 1990:
14.140
s 7: 14.170
s 8: 14.170
s 10: 14.170
s 11: 14.170
s 22: 14.195
s 23: 14.185, 14.190
ss 27 to 29: 14.185
s 30: 14.185
ss 37 to 38: 14.200
s 47: 14.215
ss 53 to 55: 14.215
ss 60 to 61: 14.215
s 62: 14.215, 14.245
ss 95 to 97: 14.235
s 221: 14.195
Pt 2, Div 4: 14.235
Pt 2, Div 5: 14.215
Pt 2, Div 6: 14.230
Pt 2, Div 7: 14.220, 14.225
Pt 2, Divs 4 to 5: 14.220

Magistrates Court (Civil
Division) Act 1992: 10.125
s 3: 2.210
s 31AA: 10.150
s 31AF: 10.150
Pt 3: 10.155
Pt 5: 10.155
Div 4: 10.155

Motor Accidents (Liabilities and
Compensation) Act 1973:
12.195

Passenger Transport Act 1997:
12.180

Table of Statutes

Racing and Gaming Act 1952: 15.210

Rail Company Act 2009: 12.240

Railways (Transfer to Commonwealth) Act 1974: 12.240

Residential Tenancies Act 1997: 13.45

Sale of Goods Act 1896: 4.10, 9.20

Supreme Court Rules 2000
Pt 20: 10.35

Trade Measurement Act 1999: 14.65

Trade Measurement (Tasmania) Administration Act 1999: 14.65

Travel Agents Act 1987: 11.385, 11.545
s 3(2): 11.400
s 3(5): 11.400
s 4: 11.400
s 4(1): 11.400
s 4(2): 11.400
s 4(5): 11.400
s 5: 11.395
s 18: 11.390
s 18(1)(b): 11.390
s 18(2): 11.390
s 18(3): 11.390
s 19: 11.410
s 19(d):
s 19(e):
s 20(1): 11.415
s 20(2): 11.385, 11.415
s 21: 11.390, 11.420
ss 21(3) to (5): 11.420
s 21(8): 11.415
s 22(1): 11.440
s 22(2): , 11.560, 11.580
s 23: 11.460
s 24(2): 11.460
s 26:
s 32: 11.510
s 32(1): 11.505
s 32(8): 11.520
s 33: 11.520
s 33(1): 11.510
s 34: 11.445, 11.530
s 34(3): 11.590
s 35: 11.460
s 36: 11.460
s 36(6): 11.495
s 36(7): 11.495
s 37: 11.460
s 38: 11.460
s 39: 11.460
s 40: , 11.465
s 41(1): 11.470
s 41(3): 11.470
s 42(3): 11.615
s 42(4): 11.615
s 42(5): 11.615
s 42(6): 11.390, 11.615
s 42(7): 11.390, 11.615
s 42(8): 11.390, 11.615
s 43: 11.480
s 44: 11.390, 11.615
s 45(2): 11.390, 11.555
s 45(10): 11.390, 11.555
s 48: 11.495
s 48(4): 11.495
s 48(5): 11.495
s 49: 11.495
s 55(2)(m): 11.600

Trustee Act 1898: 11.30

Unordered Goods and Services Act 1973
s 6: 4.90
s 7: 4.90

Workers' Rehabilitation and Compensation Act 1988: 8.15, 8.155

Workplace Health and Safety Ac 1995: 8.175, 15.475

VICTORIA

Age of Majority Act 1977: 4.340

Australian Grand Prix Act 1994: 3.215, 15.10, 15.55, 15.60, 15.100, 15.115

Business Names Act 1962: 11.460

Carriers and Innkeepers Liability Act 1958: 12.105, 12.130, 13.130, 13.200
s 3: 12.135, 12.140
s 4: 12.145
s 5: 12.145
s 6: 12.145
s 8: 12.150
s 9: 12.145
s 10: 12.150
s 11: 12.145
s 26(1): 13.145, 13.200
s 27(1): 13.145, 13.200
s 27(2): 13.145, 13.200
s 28: 13.145, 13.200
s 29(a): 13.145, 13.200
s 30(1)(a): 13.145, 13.200
s 30(1)(a)(i): 13.145, 13.200
s 30(1)(a)(ii): 13.145, 13.200
s 30(1)(b): 13.145, 13.200
s 30(4): 13.145, 13.200
s 30(5): 13.145, 13.200
s 31: 13.145, 13.200

Casino Control Act 1991: 15.155, 15.175
s 78B: 15.195
Pt 2: 15.175
Pt 4: 15.175
Pt 8: 15.175
Pt 10: 15.175

Competition Policy Reform (Victoria) Act 1995: 9.20, 9.240

Courts Legislation (Jurisdiction) Act 2006
s 3: 2.205, 10.85

Crimes Act 1958: 6.20
ss 81 to 82: 6.105
ss 175 to 180: 6.110
ss 457 to 458: 6.190

Crimes (Consolidation of Offences) Act 1981
ss 458 to 459A: 6.180

Defamation Act 2005: 5.130

Equal Opportunity Act 1995: 8.145

Fair Trading Act 1985: 9.20, 9.50

Fair Trading Act 1999
Pt 2B: 9.80

Food Act 1984: 14.45
s 16: 14.40, 14.55

Gambling Regulation Act 2003: 15.210
Ch 3: 15.210
Pt 1: 15.210
Pt 3: 15.210
Pt 4: 15.210
Pt 4A: 15.210
Pt 5: 15.210
Pt 7: 15.210
Pt 8: 15.210
Pt 9: 15.210

Goods Act 1958: 9.20

Juries Act 2000

Juries Act 2000 — *cont*
s 22: 10.110

Liquor Control Reform Act 1998: 14.140, 14.195, 15.120, 15.135
s 3: 14.155
s 3AB: 14.215
s 8: 14.170
s 9: 14.170
s 9A: 14.170
s 10: 14.170
s 11A: 14.170
s 15: 14.170, 15.135
s 16: 15.135
s 30: 14.185
s 35: 14.190
s 38: 14.190
s 39: 14.190
s 40: 14.190
ss 44 to 47: 14.195
s 46: 14.195
s 69: 14.185
s 96: 14.235
s 108: 14.215,]14.275]
Pt 2, Div 3: 14.200
Pt 2, Div 4: 14.185, 14.215
Pt 2, Div 8: 14.185
Pt 2, Div 9: 14.185
Pts 6 to 7: 14.220
Pt 7: 14.215, 14.225
Pt 8: 14.230, 14.235
Pt 8, Div 2: 14.215
Pt 49: 14.215

Magistrates Court Act 1989
s 3: 2.210
s 25: 6.45

Major Sporting Events Act 2009: 15.10, 15.52, 15.115
Pt 4: 15.100
Pt 7: 15.105
Pt 8: 15.105
Pt 9: 15.52
Div 3: 15.60

Occupational Health and Safety Act 2004: 8.175, 15.475

Rail Safety Act 2006: 12.260, 12.270

Residential Tenancies Act 1997: 13.45

Sale of Goods (Vienna Convention) Act 1987: 4.10

Small Claims Tribunals Act 1973
s 2(1): 10.135

Supreme Court (General Civil Procedure) Rules 1996
r 50.07: 10.35

Trade Measurement Act 1995: 14.65

Trade Measurement Administration Act 1995: 14.65

Transport Accident Act 1986: 12.195

Transport Act 1983: 12.180, 12.240

Travel Agents Act 1986: 11.385
s 3: 11.600
s 3(2): 11.400
s 4: 11.395
s 4(1): 11.400
s 4(2): 11.400
s 4(5): 11.400
s 6: 11.390
s 6(1): 11.390
s 6(1)(b): 11.390
s 6(2): 11.390
s 7: 11.460
s 8: 11.410
s 9(2): 11.415
s 9(3): 11.415
s 10: 11.390, 11.420
ss 10(3) to (5): 11.420
s 11(1): 11.440
s 11(2): 11.385, , 11.560, 11.580
s 12(2): 11.460
s 20: 11.495, 11.510
s 20(1): 11.490, 11.505
s 20(1)(c): 11.545
s 20(2) to (8): 11.520
s 21: 11.520
s 21(1): 11.510
s 22: 11.445, 11.530
s 23: 11.460
s 24: 11.460
s 25: 11.535
ss 25 to 29: 11.535
s 28: 11.545
s 28(3): 11.540
s 30: 11.460
s 31: 11.460
s 32: 11.460
s 33: 11.465
s 34(1): 11.470
s 34(2): 11.470
s 35(2): 11.390, 11.555
s 35(10): 11.390, 11.555
s 37(3): 11.615
s 37(4): 11.615
s 37(5): 11.615

s 37(6): 11.390, 11.615
s 37(7): 11.390, 11.615
s 38: 11.390
s 39: 11.480
s 41: 11.495
s 42A: 11.495
s 46: 11.590, 11.600

Trustee Act 1958: 11.30

Victorian Civil and Administrative Tribunal Act 1998: 10.125
s 74: 10.145
s 101: 10.150
Pt 3: 10.155

Workers' Compensation Act 1958: 8.15, 8.155

Wrongs Act 1958: 15.445
ss 14F to 14H: 14.325
s 14G: 14.325
s 55: 15.445
s 56: 15.445
Pt 12: 15.465
Pt VB: 15.445

Wrongs and Other Acts (Public Liability Insurance Reform) Act 2002: 5.165, 5.185, 15.435

WESTERN AUSTRALIA

Age of Majority Act 1972: 4.340

Business Names Act 1962: 11.460

Carriers Act 1920: 12.105

Casino Control Act 1984: 15.175
Pt 2: 15.175
Pt 3: 15.175
Pt 4: 15.175
Pt 5: 15.175

Civil Liability Act 2002: 5.185, 15.435, 15.445
s 5L: 14.325
s 5AE: 14.325

Competition Policy Reform (WA) Act 1996: 9.20, 9.240

Criminal Code Act 1913: 6.15
s 25: 6.135
s 222: 5.20
s 244: 6.125
s 409: 6.105
ss 529 to 546: 6.110

Defamation Act 2005: 5.130

District Court of Western
   Australia Act 1969
   s 6: 2.205, 10.85

Equal Opportunity Act 1984:
   8.145
   s 24: 8.150
   s 140: 8.145
   s 145: 8.145

Fair Trading Act 1987: 9.20

Food Act 2008: 14.45
   s 22: 14.55

Gaming and Wagering
   Commission Act 1987:
   15.120, 15.135, 15.210
   s 2: 15.125
   s 3: 15.120, 15.125
   s 4: 15.135
   Pt 1: 15.210
   Pt 2: 15.210
   Pt 4: 15.210
   Pt 5: 15.210
   Pt 5, Div 5: 15.210

Industrial Relations Act 1979:
   8.110

Innkeepers Act 1920: 13.140

Juries Act 1957
   s 19: 10.110

Liquor Act 1970: 13.140
   s 173: 13.140

Liquor Control Act 1988:
   13.75, 13.130, 13.200,
   14.140
   s 3A: 14.215
   s 37: 14.195
   s 41: 14.170
   s 42: 14.170
   s 48: 14.170
   s 50: 14.170
   s 66: 14.195
   s 67: 14.190
   s 68: 14.190
   s 72: 14.195
   ss 73 to 74: 14.190
   ss 95 to 96: 14.235
   s 99: 14.215
   s 105: 13.145, 13.200
   s 107: 13.140, 13.145,
        13.200
   s 107(b): 13.145, 13.200
   s 107(c): 13.145, 13.200
   s 117: 14.215
   s 176: 13.140
   Pt 3, Div 7: 14.185

Pt 3, Div 8: 14.185
Pt 3, Div 9: 14.185
Pt 3, Div 12: 14.185
Pt 4, Div 2: 14.215
Pt 4, Div 4: 14.215
Pt 4, Div 5: 14.215
Pt 4, Div 6: 14.215, 14.245
Pt 4, Div 9: 14.215
Pt 5: 14.215
Pt 6: 14.220, 14.225,
   14.230

Magistrates Court (Civil
   Proceedings) Act 2004:
   10.125, 10.135
   s 4: 2.210
   s 29: 10.150
   s 32: 10.155
   Pt 4: 10.155

Motor Vehicle (Third Party
   Insurance) Act 1943: 12.195

Occupational Safety and Health
   Act 1984: 8.175, 13.60,
   15.475

Public Transport Authority Act
   2003: 12.180

Railways (Access) Amendment
   Act 2000: 12.240

Residential Tenancies Act 1987:
   13.45

Sale of Goods Act 1895: 4.10,
   9.20

Supreme Court Act 1935
   s 69: 10.35

Trade Measurement Act 2006:
   14.65

Trade Measurement
   Administration Act 2006:
   14.65

Travel Agents Act 1985: 11.385
   s 4: 11.395, 11.400
   s 4(1)(e): 11.400
   s 4(2): 11.400
   s 4(4): 11.400
   s 5: 11.400
   s 6(1): 11.390, 11.400
   s 7: 11.390
   s 7(2): 11.390
   s 8: 11.460
   s 9: 11.410
   s 10(1): 11.415
   s 10(2): 11.415
   s 10(3): 11.415
   s 10(4): 11.415

s 11: 11.415
s 12: 11.420
s 12(3): 11.420
s 12(4): 11.420
s 12(5): 11.415
s 13: 11.440
s 13(2): 11.385, , 11.560,
   11.580
s 21: 11.490, 11.510
s 21(4): 11.505
s 21(4)(b): 11.545
s 21(4)(f): 11.505
s 22: 11.520
s 22(1): 11.510
s 22(1)(b): 11.520
s 23: 11.445, 11.530
s 23(2): 11.590
s 24: 11.590
s 25: 11.445, 11.530,
   11.590
s 26: 11.460
s 27: 11.460
s 28: 11.460
s 29: 11.465
s 30(1): 11.470
s 30(2): 11.470
s 31: 11.390
s 32: 11.390, 11.555
ss 33 to 35: 11.460
s 36: 11.535
ss 36 to 40: 11.535
s 37: 11.540
s 38: 11.540
s 39: 11.545
s 39(2): 11.540
s 41: 11.480
s 49(1): 11.615
s 49(2): 11.615
s 49(3): 11.615
s 49(4): 11.390, 11.615
s 49(5): 11.390
s 50: 11.495
s 52: 11.495
s 59(2)(h): 11.600

Trustee Act 1962: 11.30

Western Australian Marine Act
   1982: 12.415

Workers' Compensation and
   Injury Management Act
   1981: 8.15, 8.155

IMPERIAL

5 & 6 Will 4 c 41 (1835):
   15.130

Assize of Bread and Ale 1266:
   14.10, 14.65

Australian Courts Act 1828:
2.45
s 24: 2.45

Colonial Laws Validity Act 1865: 2.45

Commonwealth of Australia Constitution Act 1901: 2.45, 2.160, 15.265
s 9: 9.200
s 51(xxxiii): 12.240
s 51(xxxiv): 12.240
s 51(xxxii): 12.240
s 51(xxix): 12.325, 12.475
s 51(xxxix): 15.270
s 51(i): 9.25, 12.240, 12.325, 12.475
s 51(vi): 12.475
s 51(xx): 9.25
s 57: 3.55
s 71: 2.165, 2.170
s 73: 2.160
s 75: 2.160
s 76: 2.160
s 90: 14.150, 14.215
s 92: 11.410, 11.420, 12.475, 12.485
s 98: 12.240
s 109: 8.140, 12.415, 12.700

Gaming Act 1845: 15.130, 15.135
s 18: 15.130

Imperial Acts of 1664: 15.130

Merchant Shipping Act 1894
s 504: 12.380

Statute 8 Anne c 14 (1710): 15.125, 15.130
s 1: 15.130
s 2: 15.130

Statute 16 Car II c 7: 15.125
s 2: 15.130
s 3: 15.130

Statute 12 Rich II c 6 (1388): 15.125

Statute of Westminster 1931: 2.45

ONTARIO

Travel Industry Act 1974: 3.215, 11.675

FRANCE

Napoleonic Code 1804: 2.70

NEW ZEALAND

Consumer Guarantees Act 1993
s 7: 9.180

UNITED KINGDOM

Administration of Estates Act 1925: 3.170

Betting and Lotteries Act 1963: 15.140

Carriers Act 1830: 12.105

Employers' Liability Act 1877: 8.70

Gaming Act 1968: 15.140

Hotel Proprietors Act 1956: 13.200
s 1(3): 13.200
s 2(1)(a): 13.200
s 2(2): 13.145, 13.200
s 2(3): 13.200
s 2(3)(a): 13.200
s 2(3)(b): 13.200
s 2(3)(c): 13.200

Innkeepers Liability Act 1863: 13.75, 13.105, 13.110, 13.130
s 3: 13.105

Judicature Acts 1873: 2.60

Merchant Shipping Act 1894: 12.365

Pharmacy Poisons Act 1933: 4.65

Railway Clauses Consolidation Act 1848: 12.250

Road Traffic Act 1960: 3.175

Sale of Goods Act 1893: 9.20

Sale of Goods and Services Act 1982
s 13: 9.350

Street Offences Act 1959
s 1: 3.180

Supply of Goods and Services Act 1982
s 13: 11.260

Theft Act 1968: 6.100
s 1: 11.675
s 5(3): 6.100, 11.675

Trade Descriptions Act 1968: 3.230

TREATIES AND CONVENTIONS

Athens Convention 1974 — *see* **International Convention relating to the Carriage of Passengers and their Luggage by Sea**

Brussels Convention 1957 — *see* **International Convention relating to Limitation of Liability of Owners of Sea-going Ships**

Convention Concerning the Protection of the World Cultural and Natural Heritage 1972 (World Heritage Convention): 15.235, 15.265, 15.340
Art 1: 15.245, 15.295
Art 2: 15.250, 15.295
Art 3: 15.255
Art 4: 15.235, 15.255, 15.260
Art 5: 15.255, 15.295, 15.300, 15.320
Art 5(a): 15.295, 15.315
Art 5(e): 15.310
Art 6: 15.255
Art 11(1): 15.235, 15.255
Art 11(2): 15.235, 15.255
Art 11(3): 15.235, 15.255
Art 11(4): 15.235, 15.255
Art 15: 15.235
Art 27: 15.295, 15.310

Convention against the Taking of Hostages 1979: 12.675

Convention concerning International Carriage by Rail: 12.235

Convention for the Suppression of Unlawful Acts against the Safety of Civil Aviation 1971: 12.675

Convention for the Unification of Certain Rules for International Carriage 1999 (Montreal Convention): 12.620, 12.775
Art 1: 12.560
Art 2: 12.560
Art 3: 12.560, 12.580
Art 3(1): 12.745
Art 17: 12.560, 12.640, 12.680

Convention for the Unification of Certain Rules for International Carriage 1999 (Montreal Convention) — cont
  Art 17(2): 12.595, 12.600, 12.720
  Art 17(3): 12.595
  Art 18: 12.595
  Art 19: 12.560, 12.640
  Art 20: 12.560, 12.645, 12.650
  Art 21: 12.715
  Art 21(2): 12.680, 12.715, 12.720, 12.725, 12.730
  Art 22: 12.560
  Art 24: 12.620, 12.685, 12.715
  Art 25: 12.715, 12.745
  Art 26: 12.560
  Art 28: 12.685, 12.745
  Art 29: 12.560
  Art 30: 12.560
  Art 31: 12.560
  Art 31(1): 12.690
  Art 31(2): 12.690
  Art 31(3): 12.690
  Art 33: 12.560, 12.705, 12.715, 12.740, 12.745
  Art 34: 12.755
  Art 35: 12.560, 12.695
  Art 36: 12.560
  Art 38: 12.560
  Art 43: 12.625
  Art 50: 12.685
  Art 51: 12.560

Convention for the Unification of Certain Rules Relating to International Transportation by Air 1929 (Warsaw Convention): 12.390, 12.535, 12.545
  Art 1: 12.665
  Art 1(2): 12.745
  Art 1(3): 12.630
  Art 3: 12.580
  Art 3(2): 4.110
  Art 3(5): 12.575
  Art 4: 12.580
  Art 5: 12.580
  Art 17: 12.590, 12.595, 12.650, 12.720, 12.730, 12.735
  Art 17(2): 12.580
  Art 17(2)(3): 12.580
  Art 18: 12.580, 12.600, 12.605, 12.650, 12.720
  Art 18(2): 12.580
  Art 18(4): 12.595
  Art 19: 12.580, 12.605, 12.615, 12.645, 12.650, 12.720
  Art 20: 12.590, 12.595, 12.640, 12.715, 12.720, 12.735
  Art 21: 12.620
  Art 21(2)(a): 12.650
  Art 22: 12.575, 12.665, 12.715, 12.730, 12.735
  Art 22(1): 12.550, 12.745
  Art 22(2): 12.580, 12.665
  Art 24: 12.605, 12.745
  Art 25: 12.410, 12.660, 12.665, 12.720
  Art 25A: 12.625
  Art 26: 12.615
  Art 26(1): 12.690
  Art 26(2): 12.690
  Art 26(3): 12.690
  Art 28: 12.700, 12.705, 12.715
  Art 29: 12.695, 12.700
  Art 30: 12.625
  Art 32: 12.745
  Art 36: 12.630
  Art 36(2): 12.630
  Art 36(3): 12.630
  Art 47: 12.615
  Art 49: 12.615
  Art VI: 12.540

Convention on Biological Diversity 1992: 15.340

Convention on Conservation of Nature in the South Pacific 1976: 15.340

Convention on International Civil Aviation 1944 (Chicago Convention): 12.470
  Art 1: 12.470, 12.480
  Art 6: 12.480
  Art 7: 12.480
  Art 44: 12.470
  Pt II: 12.470

Convention on International Railway Transport 1980 (COTIF): 12.295
  Art 6(1): 12.295
  Art 26(2): 12.295
  Arts 30 to 31: 12.295
  Art 32: 12.295
  Art 35(2): 12.295
  Arts 38 to 41: 12.295
  Art 46: 12.295
  Art 53: 12.295
  Art 55: 12.295

Convention on International Trade in Endangered Species 1973: 15.340

Convention on Offences and Certain Other Acts Committed on Board Aircraft 1963: 12.675

Convention on the Conservation of Migratory Species of Wild Animals 1979: 15.340

Convention on the Limitation of Liability for Maritime Claims 1976 (London Convention): 12.90, 12.365, 12.375, 12.520
  Art 1.1: 12.385
  Art 1.2: 12.380, 12.385
  Art 1.4: 12.385
  Art 1.5: 12.385
  Art 1.6: 12.385
  Art 2: 12.390
  Art 3: 12.390
  Art 4: 12.410, 12.650
  Art 5: 12.410
  Art 6: 12.405
  Art 6(b): 12.405
  Art 8: 12.395
  Art 9: 12.395
  Art 11: 12.400
  Arts 12 to 14: 12.400
  Art 13: 12.400
  Art 15: 12.380
  Art 15(2): 12.415
  Art 15.5: 12.380

Convention on the Prevention and Punishment of Crimes against Internationally Protected Persons, including Diplomatic Agents 1973: 12.675

General Risks Convention 2009: 12.765, 12.775

Guadalajara Convention 1963 and Guadalajara Supplementary Convention 1961: 12.630
  Art 32: 12.755
  Art I(b): 12.630
  Art I(c): 12.630
  Art I: 12.750
  Art II: 12.750
  Art III: 12.750
  Art III(1): 12.630, 12.750
  Art III(2): 12.630, 12.750

Guadalajara Convention 1963 and Guadalajara Supplementary Convention 1961 — cont
  Art VII: 12.750
  Art IX: 12.750
  Art X: 12.750

Hague Protocol 1955: 4.110
  Art 1: 12.560
  Art 2: 12.560
  Art 3: 12.560
  Art 4: 12.560, 12.655
  Art 17: 12.560
  Art 18: 12.560
  Art 18(1): 12.655
  Art 19: 12.560
  Art 20: 12.560
  Art 21: 12.560
  Art 22: 12.560, 12.655
  Art 22(2): 12.655
  Art 23: 12.560
  Art 24: 12.560
  Art 25: 12.560, 12.650, 12.655
  Art 25A: 12.560
  Art 26: 12.560
  Art 28: 12.560
  Art 29: 12.560
  Art 31: 12.560
  Art 32: 12.560
  Art 33: 12.560
  Art 34: 12.560

International Convention relating to the Carriage of Passengers and their Luggage by Sea 1974 (Athens Convention): 12.425, 12.445, 12.450
  Art 1.9: 12.425
  Art 2: 12.425
  Art 5: 12.425
  Arts 7 to 10: 12.425
  Art 8: 12.425
  Art 9: 12.425
  Art 10: 12.425
  Art 13: 12.425
  Art 15: 12.425
  Art 16: 12.425
  Art 18: 12.425

International Convention on the Safety of Life at Sea 1974 (SOLAS): 12.305, 12.345

Interational Convention for the Protection of Performers, Producers of Phonograms and Breadcasting Organisations (Rome Convention) 1952: 12.765

International Convention for the Suppression of Terrorist Bombings 1997: 12.675

International Convention relating to Limitation of Liability of Owners of Sea-going Ships: 12.375

International Labour Organisation (ILO) Convention on the Elimination of all Forms of Discrimination (Employment and Occupation) 1966
  Art 1: 8.140

LLMC Protocol 1996
  Art 3: 12.405
  Art 7.1: 12.395

Paris Convention on Intellectual Property: 9.110

Protocol on the Contract for the International Carriage of Passengers and Luggage by Inland Waterways: 12.430

Protocol on the Contract for the International Carriage of Passengers and Luggage by Road: 12.220

Protocol relating to the Limitation of Liability of Owners of Inland Navigation Vessels: 12.430

Ramsar Convention 1971: 15.340

Registration Convention: 12.520

Rescue Agreement Treaty: 12.520

Treaty on Principles Governing the Activities of States in the Exploration and Use of Outer Space, including the Moon and Other Celestial Bodies, 1967 (Outer Spact Treaty): 12.520
  Art I: 12.520
  Art V: 12.520
  Art II: 12.520
  Art IV: 12.520
  Art IX: 12.520
  Art VI: 12.520
  Art III: 12.520

United Nations Convention on the International Sale of Goods 1980: 9.230

United Nations Convention on the Law of the Sea 1982 (LOS): 12.310, 12.315, 12.320

United Nations Universal Declaration of Human Rights
  Art 10: 6.200

Unlawful Interferences Convention 2009: 12.765, 12.770

Vienna Convention on International Sale of Goods 1980: 9.230

Warsaw Convention — see **Convention for the Unification of Certain Rules relating to International Transportation by Air**

CHAPTER 1

Introduction

    [1.10]   Structure of the book 2
    [1.25]   Definitions and concepts 4

[1.05] Tourism, travel and hospitality can be traced back to the Seven Wonders of the ancient world. However it is only in more recent times that we have begun to recognise this industry and to appreciate its size and importance. It is now regarded by many as the world's largest and fastest growing industry. In Australia, as in many other countries, it arguably offers some of the best prospects for future employment and economic prosperity.

The law regulating this industry can also be traced back to antiquity. Tourism, travel and hospitality feature in some of the earliest recorded statutes and cases. However it is only very recently that the systematic collection and study of these laws has begun. This study reveals a history of crude and often counter-productive approaches to the regulation of the industry. It also shows that in many cases current laws cast onerous and often unexpected responsibilities upon the industry. In these circumstances corporate compliance and reform require a better knowledge and understanding of tourism, travel and hospitality law. This text is designed to assist government, industry and their advisers in this task. In particular, it is designed to serve the needs of each of the following groups:

- *Students of tourism, travel and hospitality*: There are a multitude of tertiary courses in tourism, travel and hospitality offered by TAFE and university institutions around the country. This text is primarily designed to meet the needs of these courses with a particular focus on the development of the skills and knowledge required to ensure business compliance with the law governing tourism, travel and hospitality.

- *Law students*: The text is designed so that tourism, travel and hospitality law can be introduced more widely into the law curriculum at both the undergraduate and graduate level.

- *Industry*: The law now governs almost every aspect of an enterprise, so to manage a business successfully requires sufficient knowledge and understanding of the legal framework to avoid the pitfalls and take advantage of any opportunities. This text is also designed to provide an outline of the legal framework for managers in the tourism, travel and hospitality industry.

- *Government*: Effective regulation is a complex task, particularly with a multifaceted transnational service industry such as tourism, travel and hospitality. The comparative approach of the text, the policy discussion and suggestions for reform are designed to assist regulators in this task.

- *Advisers*: This text provides legal and other advisers in tourism, travel and hospitality with a useful synthesis of the subject together with footnotes providing full references and sources of additional materials on most topics.

- *Researchers*: Tourism, travel and hospitality attracts researchers from many disciplines and the outline of the legal framework provided in the text together with extensive references and materials is designed to assist researchers from all disciplines.

Structure of the book

[1.10] Tourism, travel and hospitality law is eclectic, drawing upon almost every branch of the law. Nevertheless the industry does have distinctive characteristics which are reflected both in recurring themes and the general law subjects most relevant to the industry. There is also a substantial body of specialised law which has been developed specifically for the industry at international, national and State level. Given the diversity of the law and the particular needs of each of the identified user groups, this text has been structured so that the contents can be packaged into modules. Each user group can select those modules and chapters most relevant to its specific needs. The modular structure is presented in the diagram below.

Modular structure

	Chapters	Modules
1.	Introduction	
2.	Common law	A. Introduction to law
3.	Statute	
4.	Contract	
5.	Torts	B. Core law subjects
6.	Criminal law	
7.	Insurance	
8.	Employment	C. Other relevant law subjects
9.	Consumer Protection	
10.	Dispute resolution	D. Practice
11.	Travel agency and distribution	E. Distribution
12.	Passenger transport	
13.	Traveller accommodation	F. Components or operating sectors of the industry
14.	Food and beverage	
15.	Activities and attractions	

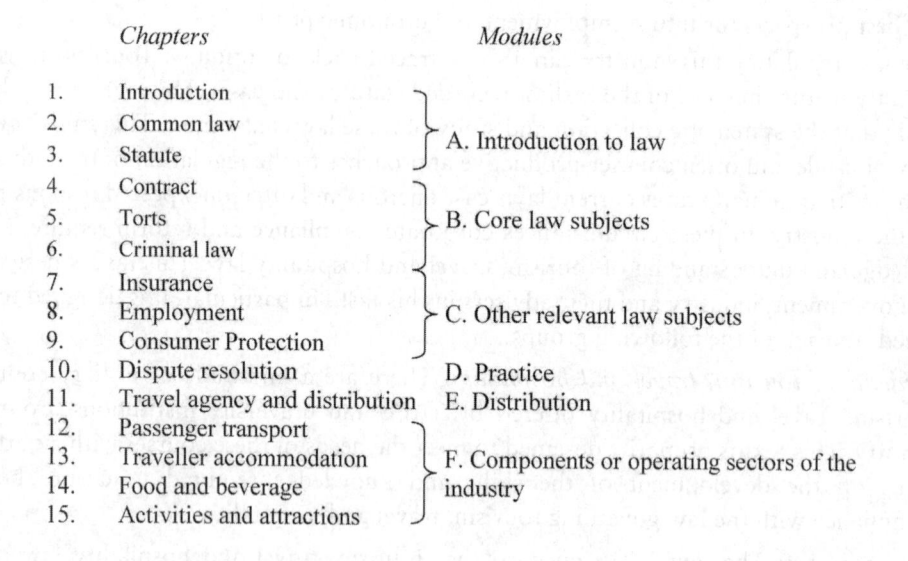

[1.15]

The purpose and approach of each module is as follows.

- A. Introduction to law

This module provides non-lawyers with an outline of the main sources and methods of the law. Chapter 2 discusses the common law and the fundamental principles of the doctrine of precedent illustrated by examining the development of the common law on damages for disappointment in tourism, travel and hospitality cases. Chapter 3 discusses statute law and the techniques of statutory interpretation illustrated by selected consumer protection provisions of the *Australian Consumer Law*. These chapters provide non-lawyers with the basic skills required to move on to Module B.

- B. Core law subjects

This module covers the key principles of the three core subjects of the general law. Chapter 4 deals with contract law, which is the foundation of all commercial law. Chapter 5 deals with the law of torts, which is the other main source of civil liability at common law. Chapter 6 discusses the criminal law, which is the public law dimension of the legal framework. These chapters complete the "pure" law subjects and provide non-lawyers with the more advanced legal skills "applied" in the subsequent modules.

- C. Other relevant law subjects

    This module deals with three more advanced legal subjects which apply the principles covered in the first two modules. Because the content focuses on issues in the tourism, travel and hospitality industry this module may also be of interest to lawyers and other groups with legal skills. Chapter 7 deals with insurance law with an exercise based on a travel policy. Chapter 8 discusses employment law and covers the employment contract, awards, discrimination and occupational health and safety. Chapter 9 is concerned with consumer protection, and competition law, illustrated by the law applicable to package holidays.
- D. Practice

    Chapter 10 covers the range of methods available to resolve legal disputes, including negotiation, mediation, arbitration and court proceedings. It includes a DIY exercise involving making a claim in the Consumer Claims Tribunal.
- E. Distribution

    Chapter 11 discusses the law of agency and covers travel agent licensing and the travel compensation fund. It includes a detailed comparison of the legislation in each State under the Uniform Licensing Scheme and an examination of the key legal issues and challenges facing travel agents and those who deal with them. It also covers the developing laws and issues arising in distribution of the tourism and travel product over the internet.
- F. Components or operating sectors of the industry

    This module deals with the main components of the tourism product, each of which is a major sector of the industry. It is expected that groups will be able to select their areas of most interest from these chapters. Each chapter provides an historical perspective, analysis of the common law, comparative study of the legislation in all States and a discussion of the key international codes, customs and conventions. Chapter 12 covers passenger transport laws, including the rights and duties of common carriers as amended by statute and also the particular laws governing transport by road, rail, sea and air. Chapter 13 discusses traveller accommodation and covers the rights and duties of common innkeepers as amended by statute and also the particular laws which govern each type of accommodation. Food and beverage law is covered in Chapter 14, which considers the responsibility of those involved in food and beverage handling at common law and under statute, including issues involved in food and liquor licensing. Chapter 15 is concerned with activities and attractions and considers the rights and duties of proprietors and occupiers of venues and the particular laws and issues involved in gambling, World Heritage areas, adventure tourism, theme parks and sporting events.

Structure of each chapter

[1.20] Each chapter has been designed to provide a succinct analysis of the law along with the references and other materials required for further study or analysis. So far as practicable, the authors have endeavoured to incorporate the following features.

History–The law evolves continually and where possible the authors have tried to provide a brief history of its development. This assists with the understanding of the policy issues involved and gives an insight into where the law is headed in the future.

Organisations: websites–Key organisations involved in making or administering relevant law or policy are described and where available the authors have provided website references. This will assist readers to access wider research materials and to keep abreast of developments.

International/national–Tourism, travel and hospitality are by definition transborder and transnational activities. This makes the lawyer's task more complex. Nevertheless the authors have endeavoured to provide a comparative analysis of the key laws in all States of Australia together with international codes, customs and conventions where relevant.

Industry examples–In keeping with the title and subject matter, wherever possible the authors have tried to use cases and examples from the tourism, travel and hospitality industry.

Case studies–Case studies have been presented on the most important case decisions and on decisions which the authors regard as good illustrations or examples of the issues or the reasoning involved in each of the chapters.

Paragraph numbering–While every effort has been made to structure and present the material in its most logical and convenient format, extensive interlinking and cross referencing is still required and this has been facilitated by paragraph numbering. This also assists the search for key issues and concepts.

Footnotes for further research–As the text is designed for various groups with differing levels of legal skills, the authors have endeavoured to provide a plain English text, putting as much of the complexity and references as possible into the footnotes.

Comparative tables of legislation–The object has been to provide an Australian text and this requires coverage of the Commonwealth and of its six States and two Territories. Readers may share the authors' exasperation with the complexity which this generates, but hopefully the comparative tables of legislation which are provided in some of the relevant chapters will simplify the task for readers and researchers.

Exercises–Finally, the authors have designed practical exercises for each chapter to illustrate the key principles discussed and to provide practice in identifying the issues and applying the law.

Definitions and concepts

Definitions

[1.25] There have been many attempts to define "tourism". Two definitions which are most useful for the purposes of this book are as follows

> Tourism denotes the temporary, short term *movement of people* to destinations outside the places where they normally live and work and their *activities* during their *stay* at these destinations. [1]
> "Tourism" means the activities of persons travelling to and staying in countries outside their country of residence for not more than one consecutive year for leisure, business and other purposes. [2]

The elements emphasised in the first definition highlight the main components of the tourism industry namely "movement of people" (ie, *passenger transport*), "stay" (ie, *traveller accommodation*) and "activities" (ie, the *activities and attractions* at the destination which motivate the visit). *Travel agency and distribution* deal with the distribution of the tourism product. The title of this book includes the word "travel" to capture passenger transport and distribution for all purposes (including eg travel to work), not only that relating to tourism, it also includes the word "hospitality" to capture all *food and beverage* services, not only those provided in tourism. The law on each of the components or subjects italicised is collected, analysed and presented in a specific chapter in the book.

---

1   AK Burkart and S Medlik, *Tourism: Past Present and Future* (Heinemann, London, 1974).
2   World Trade Organisation, *GATS Draft Annex on Tourism 2001*. See http://www.wto.org.

Law and regulation

[1.30] In many senses "regulate" is a broader term than "law". The *Oxford English Dictionary* provides the following definition:

"Regulate" : control by rule, subject to restrictions, moderate, adapt to requirements.

So regulations include:

1. conventions, statutes, case law; and
2. agreements, customs, codes and practices.

The regulatory framework for tourism, particularly at the international level includes many regulations of the second type and so wherever relevant these are also examined in this book. The industry prefers self regulation to black letter law and if the common objective is compliance the regulator needs to consider all means and use the most effective available

Why regulate? The following diagram illustrates the traditional economic theory that regulation is necessary to cure market failure and that the regulatory process is a continual course of action and reaction to changing rules and circumstances. Of course regulation is also required to deal with a wider range of political, ethical, social, cultural and environmental challenges many of which are "externalities" in economic terms. This is particularly important in a dynamic industry like tourism.

Figure 1: Methods of regulation

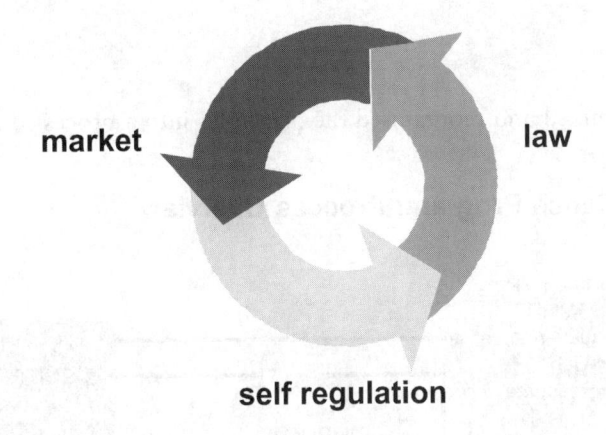

market — law — self regulation

Unlike any other industry, tourism affects and is affected by almost everything else that happens in the economy, society and environment. Tourism authorities need to ensure that laws and regulations are carefully designed and monitored to ensure tourism is sustainable and properly harnessed for all the potential social, cultural, economic and environmental benefits which it can potentially deliver.[3] The authors hope that this book will make a useful contribution to this process.[4]

---

[3] TC Atherton, *The Regulation of Tourism Destination Planning, Development and Management* (MSc thesis, University of Surrey, 1991).

[4] Through http://www.athertonadvisory.com the authors provide international advisory services to government and international aid and development agencies on this subject.

Regulatory compliance

[1.35] Readers of this book will appreciate that tourism is subjected to some complex and onerous legal and regulatory obligations which may have serious consequences if ignored. Breaches can lead to:

- organisation, directors, managers and advisers held responsible;
- litigation;
- compensation payments;
- injunctions;
- prosecutions;
- bad publicity and damage to brand;
- insurance difficulties; and
- avoidance of the organisation, destination and country.

The Australian Standard

[1.40] The rational approach for any organisation handling regulatory risks is a proactive Compliance Program. The world's first regulatory compliance standard is the Australian Standard Compliance Program.[5] The Standard describes the principles involved in an effective compliance Program in three steps which are:

- commit;
- implement;
- monitor.

The authors have refined and reorganised the principles into a process diagram as illustrated below.

Figure 2: Compliance Program: Process Overview

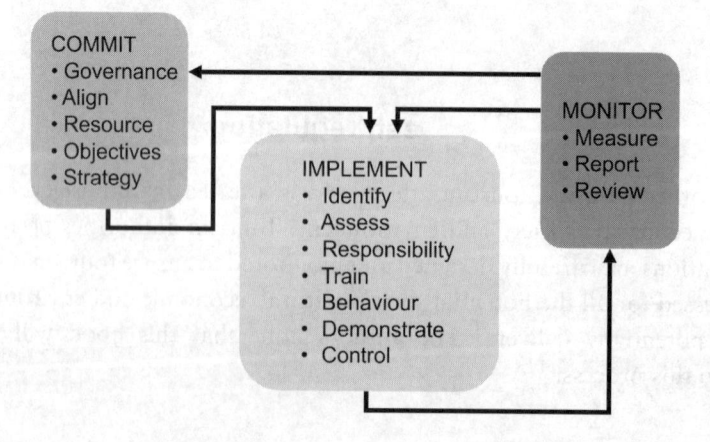

```
        COMMIT                                    MONITOR
      • Governance ◄─────────────────────────   • Measure
      • Align                                    • Report
      • Resource                                 • Review
      • Objectives        IMPLEMENT
      • Strategy          • Identify
                          • Assess
                          • Responsibility
                          • Train
                          • Behaviour
                          • Demonstrate
                          • Control
```

---

5   AS 3806 1998-2006.

Applying the Australian Standard to the tourism industry

[1.45] Regulatory compliance programs for the tourism industry are still in an early stage of development. However they will become increasingly important, not just in more litigious developed countries but also in the developing world for a number of reasons, including:

- the peculiar characteristics of the industry–travel by definition mixes peoples and their legal systems;
- globalisation and advances in transport and communications technology;
- established international conventions on passenger transport, world heritage and new issues such as child sex tourism;
- legal developments on extraterritorial responsibility including the EC Directive and the *Wong Mee Wan case* [6] discussed in Chapter 9;
- the targeting of tourists and their vulnerability when things go wrong;
- instant global publicity to adverse incidents and their impact on travel advisories, the withdrawal of insurance and permission to travel.

The first step in implementing a regulatory compliance program in an organisation is, of course, to identify the relevant laws, regulations, codes and standards which apply. Then these need to be assessed, compliance systems designed, responsibilities allocated, staff trained and monitored etc as shown in the process diagram above. The authors trust that this book will make a useful contribution to the process. [7]

---

[6] *Wong Mee Wan v Kwan Kin Travel* (1995) 4 All ER 745.

[7] Through http://www.athertonadvisory.com the authors provide international advisory services to industry on this subject.

CHAPTER 2

Common law

[2.05] HISTORICAL BACKGROUND 10
    [2.05]   Origins and Sources of Australian Law 10
        [2.05]   What is the law? 10
        [2.20]   Theories of law 11
        [2.40]   Rule of law 13
        [2.45]   Sources of law 14

[2.75] BASIC PROPOSITIONS AND DEFINITIONS 17
    [2.75]   Judges as law-makers 17
    [2.80]   Ratio decidendi, obiter dicta and other terms 18
        [2.85]   Ratio decidendi 18
        [2.90]   Obiter dicta 19
        [2.95]   Case law 19
        [2.100]   Original and appellate jurisdiction of the courts 19

[2.105] DOCTRINE OF PRECEDENT 20
    [2.110]   The Practice of precedent 20
        [2.115]   Philosophy 20
        [2.120]   Rules of precedent 20
        [2.125]   Methodology 21
        [2.130]   Avoiding the doctrine of precedent 21

[2.155] COURT HIERARCHY 23
    [2.160]   Australian Federal Court Hierarchy 23
        [2.160]   High Court of Australia 23
        [2.165]   Federal Court of Australia 24
        [2.170]   Family Court of Australia 24
        [2.175]   Federal Magistrates Court 25
    [2.195]   Australian State Court Hierarchy 27
        [2.200]   Supreme Court 27
        [2.205]   District or County courts 28
        [2.210]   Magistrates or Local courts 28

[2.215] THE COMMON LAW AT WORK 29
    [2.215]   Evolution of the principle of damages for disappointment in contract 29
        [2.220]   *Hamlin v Great Northern Railway* 29
        [2.225]   *Athens-Macdonald Travel Service Pty Ltd v Kazis* 31
        [2.230]   *Jarvis v Swans Tours Ltd* 33
        [2.235]   *Baltic Shipping Co v Dillon* 35

HISTORICAL BACKGROUND

Origins and Sources of Australian Law

What is the law?

[2.05] Law has been described as "the cement of society and an essential medium of change".[1] What are the characteristics of laws which bind communities together and are they really necessary for regulating and controlling behaviour within a given community?

Characteristics

> "Rights without remedies, philosophical theories incapable of enforcement and laws without meaning are of no assistance to the citizen."[2]

[2.10] There are a number of characteristics which differentiate the laws of a democratic society from, say, the "laws" of science or even the "laws" of fashion. These include the fact that:

- these rules are enforceable by sanctions such as fines or jail sentences;
- most people are willing to obey the majority of the rules set down; and
- the rules do not offend principles of fundamental justice.

Underpinning these characteristics is the notion that the law is certain and accessible to all. Sometimes, there is a perception within the community that particular laws are harsh or unfair or unjust. When sufficient people feel strongly enough about such a law, they may refuse to obey it, demonstrating their opposition to the law either by peaceful civil disobedience protests or by noisy demonstrations and riots.

If those persons charged with the responsibility of making the rules within a society lose sight of the fact that all laws must satisfy the test of fundamental justice,[3] they run the risk that eventually a majority of people will refuse to obey those laws.[4] When this occurs, the fabric of organised society begins to crumble.[5] The concepts of law, justice and morality should always coincide.

Origin and role of law

> "What then is this law business about? It is about the fact that our society is honeycombed with disputes. Disputes actual and potential; disputes to be settled and disputes to be prevented; both appealing to law, both making up the business of law. But obviously those which most violently call for attention are the actual disputes.
>
> ...First, so that there may be peace, for the disputants; for other persons...disputants are disturbing. And secondly, so that the dispute may really be put to rest, which means, so that a solution may be

---

1   G Williams, *Learning the Law* (Stevens, London, 1982), p 1.
2   GW Keeton, *The Elementary Principles of Jurisprudence* (Pitman, London, 1949).
3   Some laws have the appearance of laws validly made but they fail the test of fundamental justice and are therefore really invalid in society, for example, the Nazi regime denying Jews nationality and the more recent atrocities committed within Cambodia and Romania and against the Bosniaks by the Bosnian Serb forces.
4   An example of this occurred some years ago in the United States of America following the acquittal of police officers accused of bashing an Afro-American man, Rodney King. The black community in Los Angeles was not satisfied that the rules of fundamental justice had been followed.
5   KN Llewellyn, *The Brambelbush: On our Law and its Study* (Oceana Publications, New York, 1930), p 33.

achieved which, at least in the main, is bearable to the parties and not disgusting to the lookers-on. This doing of something about disputes, this doing of it reasonably, is the business of law." [6]

[2.15] Throughout history, people have chosen to live in communities because they have had common interests in:

- defending themselves against aggressors;
- sharing the workload; and
- fulfilling certain religious or cultural ideals.

Inevitably, the community would need to set guidelines or rules for the conduct of its members in their daily life. The person or persons who emerged to fulfill this role of law maker – a king, chieftain or group of tribal elders – enjoyed the respect of the rest of the community, who would therefore obey the new rules. Such respect was forthcoming either because the people believed that the authority figure could be trusted to create a peaceful and ordered society, or because they feared his power to enforce the new rules through the might of his army, or perhaps a combination of the two.

In any event, those rules or laws served a dual function in the community. They acted as both *peace keeper* and *peace maker* within that society.

The same is true today. Everyone is presumed to know the law and is expected to obey it. Provided that the law is fundamentally just and fair, it plays an important peacekeeping function. In democratic societies, people are elected to the role of law maker (the Parliament). The Parliament then appoints administrators to oversee the smooth functioning of the law (the Executive arm of government), including the police force, whose task it is to enforce the criminal laws. This is part of the peacemaking function of law. Similarly, when disagreements arise between members of a community a third group of people, the judiciary, apply the community's rules to settle those disputes.

The role of the law is to hold society together peacefully. This happens only if a majority of people believe that the rules of law should be obeyed because they are right.

Theories of law

[2.20] There are a number of different theories of law. This section will examine two of the dominant theories which reflect opposing views. They are *natural law* and *legal positivism*.

Natural law

[2.25] Natural law is closely linked to concepts of morality and justice. Originally associated with the expression of God's divine reason, [7] the theory is based on the premise that only those laws which reflect principles of community morality, universally applicable, deserve our obedience. In other words, law must demonstrate some "intrinsic moral quality" [8] in order to be valid. To this extent, natural law is said to be superior to the rules laid down by political leaders. [9]

---

6   KN Llewellyn, *The Brambelbush: On our Law and its Study* (Oceana Publications, New York, 1930), p 33.
7   Saint Thomas Aquinas.
8   Jean Jacques Rousseau, *The Social Contract* (1762).
9   For example, although "laws" were passed validly by the Parliament in Nazi Germany for the purpose of exterminating the Jewish population living there, a natural lawyer would argue that those laws were fundamentally unjust and therefore invalid because they offend basic morality.

It is also related to the social nature of man. The writer-philosopher John Locke referred to a "social contract" between the government and its people whereby the citizens surrendered their political power to the ruler in exchange for assurances of having their personal and property rights protected. The government breached that social contract if it failed in its duty of protecting those natural rights, thus entitling the people to revolt. [10]

The idea that the people living in a community should have fundamental human rights which no government could validly remove is one of the most important tenets of natural law. In fact, the *American Bill of Rights* is based on this natural law theory of "the inalienable natural rights of man". [11]

Legal positivism

[2.30] Legal positivism is not so concerned with morals, ethics or justice. It does not seek any religious or humane basis for its validity. Nor does it recognise that there is a universal natural law which overrides the laws of political superiors. It is based on the notion that law is "the command of him that have the legislative power". [12]

The theory was largely developed and moulded by the legal philosopher John Austen, [13] who asserted that the command of a political superior was the source of all law. This political superior or sovereign power could be identified as one:

- whom the bulk of all society habitually obeyed; and
- who was not in the habit of obeying any other person or body; and
- whose power could not be legally limited.

The difficulty with this theory is that exceptions abound. For example, sources of law in Australia emanate from three levels of sovereign power – federal, State and local government – so that there is no one body to which all persons owe their obedience. At the international level, the reverse is true. The United Nations which is responsible for the introduction of many international conventions, treaties and protocols is not a law-making body superior to the sovereignty of its member states. Member states adopt these conventions not because they are bound to obey a politically superior body but because they respect it. As a consequence, there is a growing body of "soft laws" developing at the international level in the form of declarations, resolutions, framework convention principles, agendas and other non treaty obligations which contrast with the traditional binding force of "hard laws". The United Nations survives and flourishes because of the important diplomatic role it plays in international relations. Similarly, in primitive societies, customary rules evolve in the absence of any sovereign will.

---

10 See more generally P Parkinson, *Tradition and Change in Australian Law* (4th ed, Lawbook Co, Sydney, 2009), Chapter 1.

11 For examples of natural law being applied by the courts see:
   (1) a case of public morality, the *Ladies Directory case* (*Shaw v DPP* (1962) AC 220), in which Shaw published a booklet giving information as to the addresses, telephone numbers and other particulars of various prostitutes. He was found guilty of conspiring to corrupt public morals. The decision was upheld by the House of Lords, which made approving reference to the role of the court as the custodian of public morals and its duty to preserve the moral welfare of the state;
   (2) a case of protecting individual natural rights: *Re D* [1976] Fam 185 (UK) in which a judge refused to allow the parents of a mentally disabled girl to have her sterilised. To do so would have interfered with her "natural right to bear children".

12 Thomas Hobbes (1681).

13 Austen gave a series of lectures on jurisprudence at University College, London, during the years 1827-1832.

The tension between law, justice and morality

[2.35] Until World War II, the theory of legal positivism and the will of the political superior prevailed in society.[14] Subsequently, its popularity has waned in favour of the natural law concepts of fairness and justice. People are more willing now to challenge laws which they perceive to be unjust or immoral. For example, many young people refused to obey the conscription laws introduced into federal Parliament during the Vietnam War. Others within the community who opposed the law organised public protest rallies encouraging civil disobedience of it. Eventually, the Parliament responded by abolishing conscription.[15]

This is a recurring theme in a democratic society based on political checks and balances. After all, in our system of government, politicians rely on their popularity to stay in office. If the government's laws are unpopular and lack sufficient public support, the politicians will be voted out of office. They must constantly reassess social morality. The introduction in 1996 of uniform gun laws throughout Australia highlighted this political dilemma.[16]

Even judges are sensitive to ensuring that justice is done between parties, particularly where a power imbalance exists. For example, banks must now ensure that they have not taken unfair and improper advantage of a special disability of their client in order to obtain some gain or benefit which they would not have obtained otherwise. If they have, the agreement may be set aside because of that "unconscionable conduct".[17] Exemption clauses in contractual agreements are enforced at common law under the principles of freedom of contract, subject to the "ticket case" principles (see [4.240]). Now principles of consumer protection prevail and the use of these so called "waiver" clauses is more restricted. Indeed, s 64 of the *Australian Consumer Law*[18] declares void any term of a contract which purports to exclude, restrict or modify the consumer guarantees provided under this legislation. Historically this did lead to problems for the tourism industry which had relied on such exclusion clauses to limit exposure to litigation from risks often associated with adventure tourism activities. For more detailed discussion on this point, see Chapter 15 [15.355].

When law, justice and morality fall out of step with each other, people in contemporary society may resort to a public demonstration of their dissatisfaction with the rules, either peacefully (civil disobedience) or violently (riots). When this happens, the government has a choice. It can impose even harsher penalties to deter more offenders or it can review the offending legislation to better reflect society's changing moral values.[19]

Rule of law

[2.40] Through an evolutionary process, the rule of law in society reflects the various theories of law to a greater and lesser extent. Most laws are positive laws. They are made by the sovereign authority, Parliament, which can enforce those laws in the community through its

---

14 It lost popularity after it was revealed that the German government had undertaken a mass extermination program against its own people.
15 One of the first acts of the newly elected Whitlam Labor government was to abolish the law in 1972. Similarly, the prohibition laws in the United States failed because they lacked sufficient public support.
16 For example, during the heated debate preceding the passing of the legislation, the gun lobby posed the question: Was it "right" that people should have their guns taken away from them – even if they were to be compensated? Wasn't that a breach of fundamental justice – even if the law was validly passed?
17 See *Commercial Bank of Australia v Amadio* [1983] 151 CLR 447. See also *Australian Consumer Law*, s 20-22.
18 See *Competition and Consumer Act 2010*, Schedule 2.
19 See more generally A Terry and D Giugni, *Business, Society & the Law* (3rd ed, 2002, Harcourt Brace, Sydney), Chapter 1.

law enforcement agencies (for example, the police force) which bring those who disobey the rules before the courts to be punished. Underlying this view, however, is the belief that the law must be fundamentally just and fair to all.

The rule of law [20] is a recognition of certain basic human rights, including the five "freedoms" of the individual. These are:

- freedom of the person [21]
- freedom of opinion [22]
- freedom of property [23]
- freedom of public assembly [24]
- freedom of contract. [25]

Its philosophy is that all people should be treated equally under the law and that a person should not be punished except for a breach of the law established in the ordinary legal manner. In other words, governments should not behave arbitrarily in the exercise of justice but should always act according to law. In developing countries, where the rule of law is weak and respect for individual freedoms is poor, breaches of these basic human rights occur more frequently. [26]

Sources of law

[2.45] Australia was settled by Europeans in 1788 with the landing of the First Fleet at Botany Bay and the establishment of the colony of New South Wales. All the laws of England, both common law and statute, were "received" into the colony at that time. Between then and 1828, there was much confusion about which laws should apply in the colony – the laws which were continuing to be passed by Westminster Parliament in England or the ones being passed by the colonial legislature. With the passing of the *Australian Courts Act 1828* (IMP), the matter was supposed to be resolved. Section 24 of that Act said:

> All laws and statutes in force within the realm of England at the time of the passing of this Act…shall be applied in the administration of justice in the courts of New South Wales and Van Diemen's land respectively so far as the same can be applied within the said colonies.

From that point forward, the colonial legislatures became the predominant sources of law-making within the colonies with power to make, amend and repeal the existing body of law. [27]

In Australia today, there are two principal sources of law. These are *common law* and *statute*. However, additional sources include *equity* and *customary law*.

---

20 Propounded by A V Dicey, a 19th century English constitutional lawyer, in his lectures on the relations between law and public opinion in England (MacMillan, London, 1930).
21 For example, from assault or false imprisonment.
22 That is, everyone should be able to express their opinion without fear, within limits (such as without defaming others or using obscene language in public places).
23 For example, from trespass or nuisance. Of course, now with zoning restrictions and other restrictive trade practices it is no longer true that a "man's home is his castle" to do with as he pleases!
24 Subject to local government authority approval.
25 That is, individuals should be able to enter into contracts with persons of choice without interference.
26 For example, there are cases of political prisoners held in jails for long periods of time without a trial in China.
27 Exceptions existed. Paramount force legislation still prevailed over local laws in the colony. Over time, the passing of a number of Acts, both Commonwealth and Imperial, have entrenched the local Parliaments as the only source of statute law in Australia. They include: *Colonial Laws Validity Act 1865* (IMP); *Commonwealth of Australia Constitution Act 1900* (IMP); *Statute of Westminster 1931* (IMP); *Statute of Westminster Act 1942* (Cth); *Australia Acts 1986* (Cth).

Common law

[2.50] Our legal system is based on the English common law model. We have borrowed the same legal institutions, system of government and even some laws. Historically in England, the common law originated in custom, but with the development of the King's Court, a more sophisticated legal system emerged. The King's justices travelled around the kingdom hearing cases and over time developed a common set of principles for resolving particular disputes of a similar kind.

This law is not found in Acts of Parliament, but comes from judicial decisions on actual cases decided in court. The body of case law which has grown through this process is contained in the law reports. Indeed, the rules of precedent encourage consistency and predictability in the common law by declaring that previous decisions are binding on the courts as case law unless and until they are upset by decisions of a superior court or by an Act of Parliament. The doctrine of precedent is discussed in [2.105].

One other distinguishing feature of the common law is the manner in which the trial process is conducted. It is based on an adversarial system, in which the parties each tell their story in turn. The judge generally acts as umpire of proceedings. He or she does not seek the absolute truth but relies on the parties themselves to define the issues for the court in documents called "the pleadings". This approach must be contrasted with civil law jurisdictions such as Thailand or France, where the role of judges is to investigate the circumstances of the case and to find out the truth. This is an inquisitorial process.

Statute

[2.55] Acts of Parliament are the other very important source of Australian law. There are several levels of government in Australia from which they emanate.[28] These laws differ from the judge-made common law in a number of respects. First, there is a presumption that the Parliament enacts legislation prospectively unless it is expressly stated that the Act is to apply retrospectively. By contrast, all judgments have retrospective effect.

Secondly, unlike the role of the courts whose task it is to resolve particular disputes between individuals as they arise, Parliament is concerned to legislate on matters of policy which affect the wider community rather than individual members of it. Thirdly, whereas judges are restricted by the doctrine of precedent in shaping the law, Parliament may enact laws on a broad range of topics subject only to constitutional limits. It does not matter to the Parliament whether there is a dispute in existence on a particular matter before enacting such legislation.

Parliament is the supreme law-making body and thus has the power to repeal and amend its previous legislation. More importantly for judges, it means that Parliament can legislate to overturn the impact of a particular judgment.

Equity

[2.60] In one sense, the development of equity was an example of natural law requiring the King to exercise his prerogative to see that justice was done between parties. The rigidity of common law rules and procedures led to the development of the Court of Chancery, originally presided over by the King's religious adviser, the Bishop. The Chancellor, as he was called, was given discretionary powers to "do justice" between parties where the common law had failed, so long as the party seeking relief came to the court in "good conscience". Over time, the court developed a body of rules which became known as the law of equity.

---

28   Federal, State and Territory Parliaments. Another level of rule making is that of local government.

The courts of law and equity have now been fused, [29] but many of these principles survive today and continue to influence the resolution of disputes. For example, concepts of unconscionable conduct or breach of confidence or unjust enrichment were developed in the Equity courts. The common law remedy of monetary compensation did not always properly compensate a successful plaintiff who may have been a business person wanting to stop the unfair practices of her or his competitor. The Equity courts developed remedies such as injunction and specific performance to meet these needs.

Customary law

[2.65] Until 1992, it was presumed that Australia was *terra nullius* until the arrival of the First Fleet and white settlement and so traditional Aboriginal rights to use land for hunting, fishing, gathering, spiritual and other purposes had not been recognised by the courts in Australia. Then, in the case of *Mabo v Queensland [No 2]*, a majority of the High Court held: [30]

> In the result, six members of the court (Dawson J dissenting) are in agreement that the common law of this country recognises a form of native title which, in the cases where it has not been extinguished, reflects the entitlement of the indigenous inhabitants, in accordance with laws and customs, to their traditional lands and that, subject to the effect of some particular Crown leases, the land entitlement of the Murray Islanders in accordance with their laws or customs is preserved, as native title, under the law of Queensland.

This was a rejection of the theory of *terra nullius* and a partial recognition of native title land rights by its indigenous people. The federal Parliament shortly after enacted the *Native Title Act 1993* (Cth) which purported to establish mechanisms for recognising, protecting and processing future native title claims, amongst other things. [31] Subsequent court cases have sought to further define and refine the scope of the native title legislation, including that:

- certain types of pastoral leases can extinguish native title; [32]
- any native title in relation to the territorial sea is subject to the common law public rights of fishing and navigation and the public international law right of innocent passage; [33]
- any exclusive right to fish in tidal waters is extinguished and that there are no native title rights to or interest in any mineral or petroleum. However, the *Native Titles Act 1993* (Cth) does protect hunting, gathering and fishing rights in relation to land or waters where the indigenous peoples concerned have a connection with the land or waters by tradition. [34]

Queensland enacted the *Wild Rivers Act 2005* with the stated object to "preserve the natural values of rivers that have not been significantly affected by development and thus have all, or almost all, of their natural values intact". [35] This has brought the Queensland government into conflict with the indigenous people of the Cape York Peninsula because most of the rivers now protected by the new legislation are in fact on lands claimed by traditional indigenous owners within the Cape. These traditional owners argue that they have always cared for this pristine wilderness area and that they will now be effectively prohibited from commencing any small scale sustainable tourism and other developments and thus denied the opportunity to provide

---

29 *Judicature Acts 1873* (UK).
30 *Mabo v Queensland [No 2]* (1992) 175 CLR 1 (per Mason CJ and McHugh J at 15).
31 *Native Title Act 1993* (Cth), s 3 Main Objects.
32 *Wik Peoples v Queensland* (1996) 187 CLR 1.
33 *Commonwealth of Australia v Yarmirr; Yarmirr v Northern Territory* (2001) 208 CLR 1.
34 *Western Australia v Ward* (2002) 213 CLR 1.
35 Queensland Government, http://www.derm.qld.gov.au/wildrivers/legislation.html (sourced 2/2/10).

an independent economy for the local community there. At the same time the legislation is silent on the commencement of mining activities which could destroy its natural heritage values.

In April 2009, Australia endorsed the *United Nations Declaration on the Rights of Indigenous Peoples* The Declaration greatly strengthens the rights of indigenous people globally and, in Article 3, recognises their right "...to freely pursue their economic, social and cultural development." Although non-binding, the Declaration will undoubtedly play an important role in future negotiations between governments at both federal and State levels and indigenous peoples in Australia and the Torres Strait Islands.

Other Systems of Law

[2.70] The three most common systems of law worldwide are common law, civil law and islamic law. The civil law system originated from Roman law (*Justinian's Code* 529 AD) and was later developed in France (*Napoleonic Code 1804*). Its distinguishing feature is that the laws are wholly contained in civil codes. It is the system of law widely used throughout Continental Europe, South East Asia and elsewhere.

Islamic or Shar'iah law (law of God) is the third of the most common legal systems. It is the predominant system of law in Middle Eastern and other Muslim countries like Pakistan and Malaysia. It is a religious law combining "both faith and practice. It embraces worship, individual attitude and conduct as well as social norms and laws, whether political, economic, familial, criminal or civil".[36] This is in sharp contrast with the other two systems of law which strictly separate the functions of religious belief, law and policy.

BASIC PROPOSITIONS AND DEFINITIONS

Judges as law-makers

[2.75] If the business of the law is to resolve disputes, then that task falls largely on the courts and in particular on the judges who administer justice. Their primary function is to apply and declare the law and to restore the social order which may have been threatened or disrupted by the dispute.

They do this by adopting certain techniques and procedures. These include:

- the process of statutory interpretation, that is, deciding the meaning of a particular statute. They may rely on common law rules of construction or on statutory interventions such as those set out in Acts Interpretation Acts. (See also Chapter 3.)

- application of the doctrine of precedent, that is, referring to previous judgments or precedents to help resolve the present dispute. The special rules of the doctrine of precedent are discussed in detail in [2.120].

Pursuant to the rules of precedent, judges are bound to follow the existing law. In this way, everyone can be assured of certainty and predictability in the judicial process. Judges do not have power to arbitrarily change the law. However, every time a judge listens to a case and finds an established legal principle and applies or modifies it according to the rules of precedent or statutory interpretation, he or she is developing and creating new common law to a greater or lesser extent.

---

36   See Dr. Mohammad Omar Farooq, *What is Shariah? Definition/Description potpourri* website at www.globalwebpost.com/farooqm/study_res/islam/fiqh/farooq_shariah.html (sourced: 23/08/2010).

This is a subtle process, because judges may act only to resolve existing disputes brought before them even if the principles arising from the case have a more general application within the wider community. [37] The other important feature of judges as law makers is that their judgments always have retrospective effect, focusing as they do on an event which took place sometime in the past.

In *State Government Insurance Commission (SA) v Trigwell*, [38] Mason J said:

> The court is neither a legislature nor a law reform agency. Its responsibility is to decide cases by applying the law to the facts as found. The court's facilities, techniques and procedures are adapted to that responsibility, they are not adapted to legislative functions or to law reform activities.
>
> ...These considerations must deter a court from departing too readily from a settled rule of the common law and from replacing it with a new rule.

Judges must therefore be careful not to retrospectively change the law and thus undermine those principles of uniformity and consistency on which the rules of precedent are based. If judges do depart too dramatically from settled principles of law, it is for the legislature to decide whether to limit the impact of the judgment through statutory interventions. [39]

Ratio decidendi, obiter dicta and other terms

[2.80] When a matter goes to court, the judge listens to all the evidence and after hearing submissions from Counsel (barristers), he or she finds the facts (material or legally relevant facts). Based on the findings of fact, the judge will analyse the issues arising from those facts (the legal rights and duties of the respective parties) and apply the relevant legal rules. He or she then reaches a conclusion and gives reasons for that decision (or judgment). A copy of the judge's reasons will be handed to the parties in the action.

Ratio decidendi

[2.85] The *ratio decidendi* [40] of the case is:

> any rule of law expressly or impliedly treated by a judge as a necessary step in reaching his conclusion, having regard to the line of reasoning adopted by him. [41]

The importance of identifying the ratio of a case is crucial. In terms of the rules of precedent, it is the ratio of a case which is binding on subsequent courts lower in the same court hierarchy. If there is more than one judgment, then it is the majority ratio of the court which is binding and not the ratio found in the dissenting judgment(s). If the case is authority for several different propositions of law there may be "multiple ratios". The fact is that some judges always express their reasons for decision concisely and simply and others use a more verbose and complex style. In either case it is left to the reader to find the ratio of the case, a skill which can only be mastered through practice (see [2.210]ff).

---

37 For example, the potential implications of *Mabo v Queensland [No 2]* (1992) 175 CLR 1 on native title rights.
38 *State Government Insurance Commission (SA) v Trigwell* (1979) 142 CLR 617 at 633.
39 For example, at the time of the Native Title legislative solution of 1993 there was consensus that any native title rights over present or former pastoral and other Crown leases had been extinguished. However, the later High Court *Wik* decision (1996) then held otherwise. Its effect was that pastoralists' interests co-existed with native title rights and interests and may revive upon expiry or termination of the lease. Further federal legislation was then required to deal with the problems created by the decision.
40 The plural is *rationes decidendi*.
41 R Cross, *Precedent in English Law* (3rd ed, Clarendon Press, Oxford, 1979), p 76.

Obiter dicta

[2.90] The judgment may refer, by way of illustration, to alternative fact situations which would give rise to the application of different legal principles and conclusions. These things said in passing are obiter dicta [42] and do not form part of the reasons for decision or ratio of the case. The relevance of obiter dicta varies according to the authority of the court in which some new principle of law is explored and to the importance of the issues discussed. For example, some 50 pages of the judgment of the House of Lords in *Hedley Byrne & Co Ltd v Heller & Partners Ltd* [43] was devoted to a discussion of the emerging principle of negligent misstatement in the law of torts, although on the facts of that case the court held that the rule was not applicable.

Case law

[2.95] The common law is based on a systematic law reporting scheme. Case law is the record of reported judges' decisions which are to be found in the various series of Law Reports. This allows judges to refer readily to previously decided cases which raise similar legal issues to the one presently before the court. These previously decided cases which are close in facts or legal principles to the one under consideration are called *precedents*. The existence of a body of case law promotes consistency, uniformity and predictability in the judicial law-making process.

Original and appellate jurisdiction of the courts

[2.100] Within the court hierarchy there are both "courts of first instance" and "appeal courts". The court in which a matter is first heard is the court of first instance. If one of the parties to the dispute is unhappy with that court's judgment, that party may take the matter on appeal. The appeal court, after hearing the appeal, usually has several choices open to it. It can:

- dismiss the appeal (thus *affirming* the judgment of the court below); or
- allow the appeal (thus *reversing* the judgment of the court below); or
- vary the judgment appealed from in part; or
- send the matter back for retrial.

Some courts in the hierarchy may have:

- only original jurisdiction; or
- both original and appellate jurisdiction; or
- only appellate jurisdiction.

See [2.155] and following for further discussion.

---

[42] The singular is obiter dictum.
[43] *Hedley Byrne & Co Ltd v Heller & Partners Ltd* [1964] AC 465.

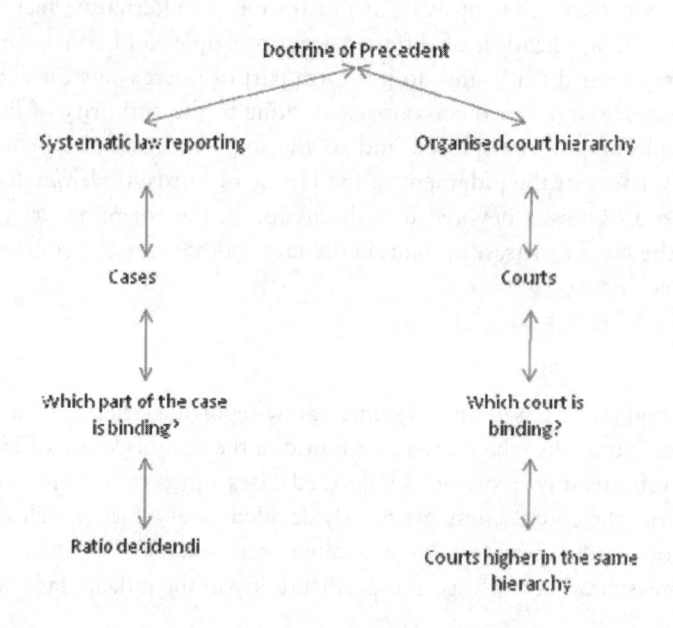

DOCTRINE OF PRECEDENT

```
                    Doctrine of Precedent
                    ↙              ↘
        Systematic law reporting    Organised court hierarchy
                ↕                          ↕
              Cases                      Courts
                ↕                          ↕
        Which part of the case      Which court is
           is binding?                 binding?
                ↕                          ↕
           Ratio decidendi          Courts higher in the same
                                         hierarchy
```

[2.105]

The Practice of precedent

[2.110] The process of extracting the relevant rule from a previous case and applying it in a later dispute is called the doctrine of precedent or *stare decisis*.[44]

Philosophy

[2.115] The doctrine of precedent promotes concepts of reliability, impartiality and equality for all under the law. The underlying philosophy is that:

- similar cases raising similar issues should be treated the same; and
- the law should be easily accessible – quickly and efficiently.

To achieve these objectives, the doctrine depends upon two factors:

1. a systematic form of law reporting or case law;[45] and
2. a structured court hierarchy.[46]

The case law enables judges to access conveniently and quickly the relevant principles of the common law contained in the ratio of previously decided cases. The structured court hierarchy assists the judges in determining which courts and which cases are of greatest authority.

Rules of precedent

[2.120] Not all precedents carry the same judicial authority or weight. Some are of greater significance than others. Judges must be able to recognise which previous cases are binding precedents to be followed by them if applicable and which prior cases carry persuasive authority only to be applied if suitable.

---

44   This means "to stand by previous decisions".
45   This began on a regular basis in England in 1865.
46   This came in 1873 with the passing of the Judicature Acts and the amalgamation of the courts.

The rules which have evolved include:

1. only the ratio decidendi of a case is binding.
2. each court is bound by decisions of courts higher in the same judicial hierarchy.
3. courts at the top of the hierarchy are not bound by the decisions of lower courts in the same judicial hierarchy although these decisions may have persuasive authority.
4. a decision of a court in a different judicial hierarchy is not binding but may have persuasive authority.
5. judges on one level do not have to follow the decisions of other judges on the same level but may choose to do so, in the interests of consistency.
6. superior appellate courts can refuse to follow their own previous decisions but are reluctant to do so.
7. precedents do not necessarily lapse by the passage of time.

The rules rely heavily on an understanding of the structured court hierarchy (which is examined in [2.155]ff). The rules also place a great emphasis on consistency of judicial approach, which may lead to inflexibility and a failure to decide some cases on their merit.[47] When Parliament decides that the common law through the courts no longer reflects the norms of society, it will step in and remedy the situation by legislation.

Methodology

[2.125] How does the doctrine of precedent work in practice? What if the legal principles arising from an otherwise binding precedent no longer enjoy judicial support? Are there ways to avoid an apparently binding decision?

Avoiding the doctrine of precedent

[2.130] To overcome some of the rigidity of the rules of precedent, courts have developed several strategies to allow judicial law-making to remain more flexible. If the previous case is an apparently binding precedent, some of these techniques include:

- distinguishing the case on the facts;
- strictly or narrowly interpreting the case;
- declaring that social conditions have changed;
- pronouncing that the case was wrongly decided.

Distinguishing cases on the facts

[2.135] It is unlikely that two identical fact scenarios will ever present before the courts. However, many different fact scenarios give rise to the same legally relevant facts and issues.

---

47   For example, in *State Government Insurance Commission (SA) v Trigwell* (1979) 142 CLR 617, the High Court felt bound to follow the House of Lords' decision in *Searle v Wallbank* [1947] AC 341, which held that an adjoining landowner owed no duty to road users for damage caused by his straying animals. This rule developed over a long period of time before cars were ever heard of and during the period when England was largely an agrarian nation.
In fact, the common law in the United Kingdom had been subsequently changed by legislation to provide for liability for animals. But the common law rule still prevailed here. Why didn't the Australian Parliaments also bring in corresponding legislation? Obviously conditions in the United Kingdom were different from those in Australia. It was up to the various State Parliaments to change the law and not all of them were prepared to do so, thus favouring landowners who would otherwise be faced with huge bills for fencing and other modifications. These would have to be political decisions.

For example, there is no difference in the legal issues or relevant facts arising out of an accident involving a drink driver who loses control of her or his vehicle and causes injury to a passenger whether he or she hits a parked car or drives through a fence. Different principles of fact and law apply, however, if the driver was not drunk but instead suffered an epileptic fit or was stung by a bee at the time he or she lost control of the vehicle.

If there are legally relevant differences between the facts of the two cases, the judges have some flexibility in determining whether a previous decision should be applied or distinguished on its facts.

Strictly or narrowly interpreting a case

[2.140] Occasionally, judges must reject a precedent on the basis that its ratio is not just a general summary of existing law but rather an expansion of those legal principles which effectively creates a new law. When the law is expressed too broadly in a precedent case, subsequent judges will strictly or narrowly interpret it or confine the case to its own facts so as to avoid an inappropriate application of the common law.

Declaring that social conditions have changed

[2.145] In *Trigwell's case*,[48] the question was whether a landowner should be responsible for her or his animals straying onto the road and causing harm. At the time when the rule was formulated in England, there were no vehicles or roads as we know them today, animals could roam freely on the common and landowners enjoyed considerable political influence. Those social conditions have changed today, but in the result the judges were reluctant to depart from an old precedent which no longer expressed principles appropriate for the present day.

On the other hand, the case of *Donaghue v Stevenson*[49] is an excellent example of how the judges were prepared to recognise a change in social conditions. During the time leading up to the decision, the sale and distribution of products had become a complex process usually involving a manufacturer, a wholesaler and a retailer. The existing privity of contract rules excluded liability in contract between a manufacturer and the ultimate consumer of goods. In this landmark case, the judges developed the law of negligence which effectively gave consumers a right of action against the manufacturer, making it responsible for its products in tort as well as in contract.

Pronouncing that the case was wrongly decided

[2.150] In exceptional cases, a judge may declare that the precedent was wrongly decided.[50] This may have happened because a relevant statute or case was overlooked by the previous court, and if it had been taken into account the ultimate decision would have been different. In other words, the decision was given in ignorance of an inconsistent legislative provision or existing case law. Generally, only superior courts in the hierarchy will use this argument.

Other arguments include:

- the particular legal principle has only the status of obiter dicta;
- the case is from a different court hierarchy and is therefore only persuasive; or
- the case has subsequently been overruled by a higher court.

---

48 *State Government Insurance Commission (SA) v Trigwell* (1979) 142 CLR 617 at 633.
49 *Donaghue v Stevenson* [1932] AC 562 (House of Lords).
50 Latin phrase *per incuriam*, meaning literally, "through want of care".

COURT HIERARCHY

[2.155] Since the doctrine of precedent depends in part upon a structured court hierarchy, it is necessary to examine this aspect within the context of the Australian courts system. There are in fact two distinct court systems in Australia – federal and State – which must be understood.

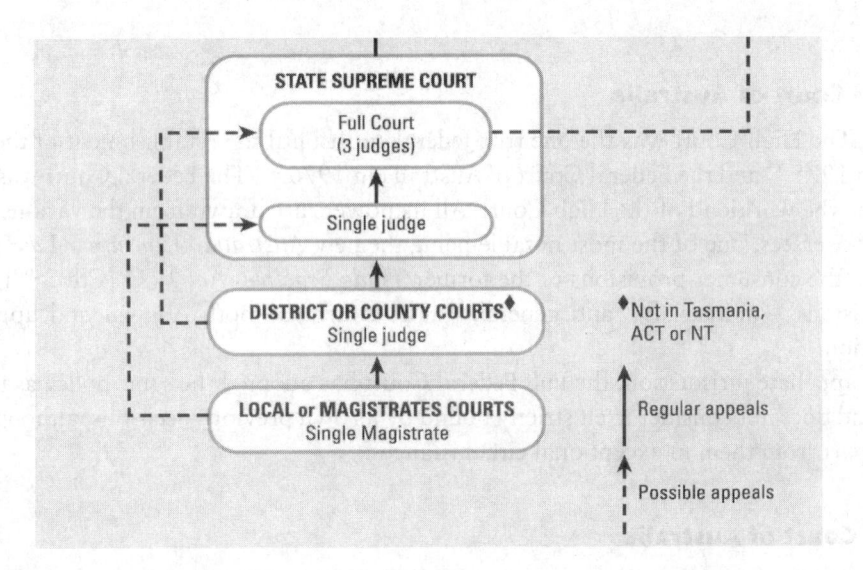

```
                    STATE SUPREME COURT
                      Full Court
                      (3 judges)

                      Single judge

              DISTRICT OR COUNTY COURTS♦       ♦Not in Tasmania,
                      Single judge              ACT or NT

              LOCAL or MAGISTRATES COURTS       Regular appeals
                    Single Magistrate
                                                 Possible appeals
```

Australian Federal Court Hierarchy

High Court of Australia

[2.160] The High Court is the highest judicial tribunal in Australia for both federal and State court hierarchies. Its power is drawn from the:

- *Commonwealth of Australia Constitution Act 1900* (IMP);
- *Judiciary Act 1903* (Cth).

The primary function of the High Court is the interpretation of the Commonwealth Constitution. It has both original [51] and appellate [52] jurisdiction, although the bulk of its work is in hearing appeals. Since 1986, it has been the final court of appeal for both Australian court systems.

---

51   Under s 75 of the Commonwealth Constitution it has original (inherent) jurisdiction in a number of important matters, including cases which affect: foreign affairs, constitutional questions and cases concerning the legislative powers of the federal Parliament, in particular matters arising under any treaty; affecting consulates or other representatives of other countries; in which the Commonwealth or a person suing or being sued on behalf of the Commonwealth is a party; between States or between residents of different States or between a State and a resident of a different State; or in which a case is brought against the Commonwealth government and its officers. Additionally, pursuant to s 76 of the Commonwealth Constitution and s 30 of the *Judiciary Act 1903*, the High Court also has vested jurisdiction in all matters arising under the Constitution or involving its interpretation; or trials of indictable offences against the laws of the Commonwealth. The difference is that the federal Parliament has vested these powers in the High Court by Act of Parliament and therefore can remove them by Act of Parliament. The inherent powers of the High Court under the Commonwealth Constitution cannot be removed by Act of Parliament.

Being the ultimate court of appeal in both federal and State matters, the High Court does not consider itself strictly bound by its own previous decisions. However, the court has remarked that:

> The occasions upon which the departure from previous authority is warranted are infrequent and exceptional and pose no real threat to the doctrine of precedent and the predictability of the law. [53]

Federal Court of Australia

[2.165] The High Court was the one true federal court until the establishment of the Family Court in 1975 [54] and the Federal Court of Australia in 1976. [55] The Federal Court was created to lighten the workload of the High Court. All its powers are drawn from the various statutes which it oversees, one of the most notable being the new *Australian Consumer Law* which is based on the consumer provisions of the former *Trade Practices Act 1974* (Cth). [56] There are two divisions – industrial [57] and general. [58] The court has both original and appellate [59] jurisdiction.

In its appellate jurisdiction, the Full Federal Court has adopted the same policy as the High Court and does not consider itself strictly bound by its own previous decisions, although it will only depart from them in exceptional circumstances.

Family Court of Australia

[2.170] The Family Court of Australia was established in 1976 pursuant to the *Family Law Act 1975* (Cth). [60] Its main aim is to be a "helping court" in family matters, so the emphasis is on conciliation in resolving disputes about:

- children;
- property; and
- extricating the parties from an unsatisfactory marriage, leaving them with as much dignity as possible.

---

52 Commonwealth Constitution, s 73. It hears appeals from decisions of: single judges of the High Court in its original jurisdiction; the Full Court of the Federal Court by special leave: *Federal Court Act 1976* (Cth), s 33; or from other courts exercising federal jurisdiction (for example, Family Court with leave): *Family Law Act 1975* (Cth), s 95.
53 *Nguyen v Nguyen* (1990) 169 CLR 245 at 269.
54 *Family Law Act 1975* (Cth).
55 The *Federal Court of Australia Act 1976* (Cth). Federal Parliament created the Federal Court pursuant to its powers under s 71 of the Commonwealth Constitution, which provides that the judicial power of the Commonwealth shall be vested in the High Court and such other federal courts as Parliament creates.
56 See also *Administrative Decisions (Judicial Review) Act 1977* (Cth).
57 This replaces the jurisdiction of the former Australian Industrial Court.
58 This replaces the former Federal Court of Bankruptcy. It has exclusive jurisdiction over federal tax disputes and oversees enforcement of such legislation as the *Competition and Consumer Act 2010* (Cth) and *Administrative Decisions (Judicial Review) Act 1977* (Cth).
59 *Federal Court of Australia Act 1976* (Cth), Div 2 Pt III. Subject to the provision of other Acts, the Full Court of the Federal Court hears appeals from single judges of the court and State and Territory Supreme Courts in their exercise of federal jurisdiction.
60 Federal Parliament created the Family Court pursuant to its powers under s 71 of the Commonwealth Constitution, which provides that the judicial power of the Commonwealth shall be vested in the High Court and such other federal courts as Parliament creates.

It also oversees proceedings under the *Marriage Act 1961* (Cth). It has both original and appellate [61] jurisdiction in all such matters.

Federal Magistrates Court

[2.175] In 1999, the Federal Magistrates Court of Australia [62] with jurisdiction conferred by the *Federal Magistrates (Consequential Amendments) Act 1999* (Cth) was established specifically to lighten the workload on the Federal and Family Courts in particular. Appeals lie direct from the Federal Magistrates Courts to the Federal or Family Courts and the decisions of single judges and the Full Court are generally binding on federal magistrates. During 2004, the Federal Magistrates Court commenced a Combined Registry initiative with the Family Court reflecting the community's desire for a more streamlined and simplified access to the family law system. [63]

Federal tribunals and commissions

[2.180] There are several federal tribunals, including:

- the Administrative Appeals Tribunal which reviews a broad range of administrative decisions including its taxation appeals division; and
- the Australian Competition Tribunal which hears applications for review from the Australian Competition and Consumer Commission and which together work to regulate anti-competitive business practices and provide protection for consumers.

Tribunals are quasi-judicial bodies, so their procedures are often less formal. Because the tribunal deals in specialist matters, the hearing may be a faster, cheaper process than going through the ordinary courts.

The Privy Council

[2.185] The Privy Council was once the ultimate court of appeal within the Australian court structure. Until 1975, appeals lay from the High Court to the Judicial Committee of the Privy Council (UK). [64] Then, with the passing of the *Privy Council (Appeals from the High Court Act) 1975* (Cth), that right of appeal from the High Court to the Privy Council was abolished.

However, between 1976 and 1986, an avenue of appeal still lay to the Privy Council from State courts in matters of State jurisdiction. This right of appeal was also abolished in 1986 with the passing of the *Australia Acts*, [65] so that now all appeals from State courts must go to the High Court. There is no longer a right of appeal to the Privy Council from any Australian courts.

---

61 The Full Family Court hears appeals from single judge decisions of the Family Court. Appeal also lies to a single judge of the Family Court from the Federal Magistrates Courts.
62 *Federal Magistrates Act 1999* (Cth).
63 The Australian Government is presently taking submissions and is consulting with interested parties on a better framework for federal courts, particularly focussing on the federal family system. In her submission dated 6 June 2008, Chief Justice Bryant of the Family Court suggested that the Federal Magistrates Court and the Family Court of Australia should merge creating a new federal court with a new name. For further information, see Australian Government Attorney General's Department website at http://www.ag.gov.au.
64 In 1968, with the passing of the *Privy Council (Limitation of Appeals) Act 1968* (Cth), leave to appeal from the High Court to the Privy Council could be sought in limited circumstances only.
65 The *Australia Act 1986* (Cth) and corresponding legislation in the Australian States and United Kingdom.

Since the Privy Council is no longer part of the Australian court hierarchy, the High Court has indicated that it no longer considers itself bound by decisions of the Privy Council, although those decisions still have considerable persuasive authority. [66]

Cross-vesting legislation

[2.190] With the introduction of the Family Court and the Federal Court of Australia, Australia effectively had two separate court hierarchies – State and federal – with the High Court at the apex of each court system.

Sometimes this caused problems for litigants whose disputes may have involved issues which straddled both State and federal jurisdiction. When this happened, litigants suffered the frustration and expense of choosing one court over another, only to find the matter being transferred back to the first court.

In his second reading speech, introducing this cross-vesting legislation, the then Attorney-General, Mr Lionel Bowen, said:

> The reasons for the proposed scheme are that litigants have occasionally experienced inconvenience and have been put to unnecessary expense as a result of, first, uncertainties as to the jurisdictional nature of federal, state and territory courts, particularly in the areas of trade practice and family law; and, second, the lack of powers in those courts to ensure that proceedings which are instituted in different courts, but which ought to be tried together, are tried in one court. [67]

The cross-vesting legislation was initially introduced in 1987 so enabling all matters to be heard in the more appropriate court rather than separately as before, thus saving time and expense and the risk of the dispute "falling between two stools". However, following a High Court decision in *Re Wakim* [68] declaring the legislation unconstitutional, the Commonwealth and States in the spirit of co-operative federalism made an agreement in 2001 on national uniform legislation effectively settling the matter. For further discussion see [10.85].

---

66 *Viro v The Queen* (1978) 141 CLR 88.
67 *Parliamentary Debates,* House of Representatives, 1986, No 151, p 2555.
68 *Re Wakim; Ex parte McNally* (1999) 198 CLR 511.

Australian State Court Hierarchy

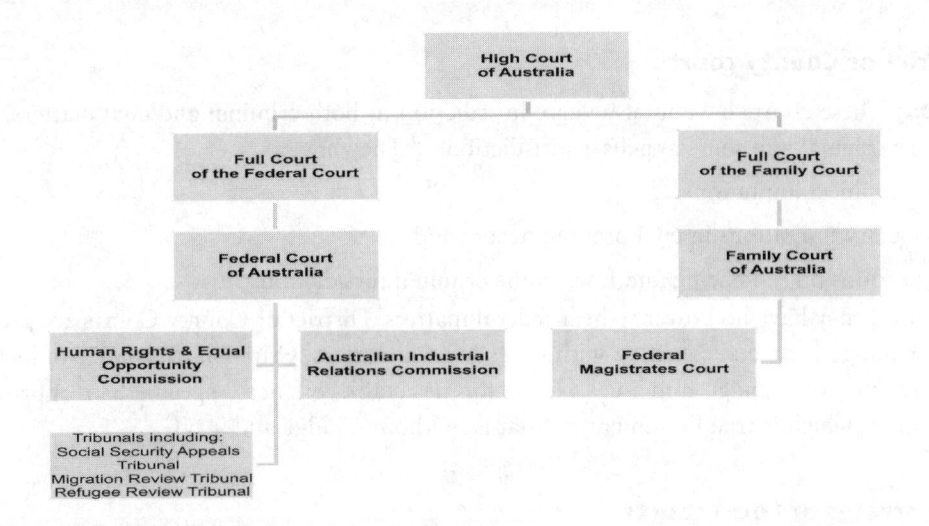

```
                    High Court
                    of Australia
                   /            \
         Full Court              Full Court
    of the Federal Court      of the Family Court
              |                        |
        Federal Court             Family Court
         of Australia              of Australia
       /      |      \                  
Human Rights  Australian    Federal
& Equal       Industrial    Magistrates
Opportunity   Relations     Court
Commission    Commission    

Tribunals including:
Social Security Appeals Tribunal
Migration Review Tribunal
Refugee Review Tribunal
```

[2.195] Each of the Australian States and Territories has its own separate court system and hierarchy of courts. The basic structure comprises:

- Supreme Court;
- District or County courts;
- Local or Magistrates' Courts.

Different court procedures exist for civil and criminal trials (see Chapter 6 [6.170]ff describing the criminal trial process). Chapter 10 examines the civil trial. Within the State court hierarchies, all courts to a greater or lesser extent enjoy both civil and criminal jurisdiction.

Supreme Court

[2.200] This is the highest court in each State and exercises both criminal and civil jurisdiction. The Supreme Court is a superior court of record whose geographical jurisdiction extends to the border of the State or Territory. It has:

- no monetary limitations in civil proceedings; and
- greater sentencing powers and can impose heavy fines in its criminal jurisdiction.

It has original and appellate jurisdiction. Since appeals lie to the High Court only by "special leave" in limited circumstances, State Supreme Courts of Appeal are effectively final courts of appeal in many matters. For this reason, the High Court has suggested that it is now inappropriate for State Supreme Courts of Appeal to consider themselves bound by their own previous decisions, although they have shown a reluctance to depart from those previous decisions unless they were clearly wrong.

State Supreme Courts are also invested with federal jurisdiction in certain matters, which places them within the federal court hierarchy as well (see Federal Court diagram above). In the application of federal law, the view is that State courts exercising federal jurisdiction should act uniformly and that it is undesirable for them to reach different decisions. [69]

District or County courts

[2.205] These courts have intermediate jurisdiction in both criminal and civil matters. They exercise original and some appellate jurisdiction. [70] They have:

- geographical limitations; [71]
- monetary limitations in civil proceedings; [72] and
- limitations on sentencing and fines in the criminal jurisdiction. [73]

Generally, they have no power to hear federal matters. District or County Courts are presided over by judges, sometimes sitting with juries in civil matters. Criminal trials are conducted in the presence of a judge and jury except for indictable offences, specified in appropriate legislation, which is triable summarily (that is, without a judge and jury).

Magistrates or Local courts

[2.210] Magistrates courts have limited original jurisdiction in all criminal and civil matters. They are inferior courts of record with:

- geographical limitations; [74]
- monetary limitations in civil proceedings; [75] and
- limitations on sentencing and fines in criminal jurisdiction.

They have original but no appellate jurisdiction. Appeals lie to higher courts in civil and criminal matters.

These courts are presided over not by judges but by "stipendiary magistrates", that is, paid public officials, usually with a professional legal background.

---

69 *R v Parsons* [1983] 2 VR 499.
70 That is, they hear appeals from Magistrates' Courts in civil and minor criminal matters.
71 That is, actions must be commenced in districts which have nexus (connection) with the claim.
72 For example, *District Court Act 1967* (Qld), s 68, $250,000; *District Court Act 1973* (NSW), s 4, $750,000; *Courts Legislation (Jurisdiction) Act 2006* (Vic), s 3, county courts in Victoria to have an unlimited civil jurisdiction; *District Court Act 1991* (SA), s 8, subject to some qualifications, South Australian district courts have the same unlimited civil jurisdiction as Supreme Courts; *District Court of Western Australia Act 1969* (WA), s 6, $750,000 and unlimited jurisdiction in claims for damages for personal injuries.
73 The District or County Court has jurisdiction in respect of most indictable offences except murder, treason, piracy and the most serious drug offences.
74 That is, actions must be commenced in districts which have a nexus (connection) with the claim.
75 This varies from jurisdiction to jurisdiction. For example, see *Magistrates Court (Civil Division) Act 1992* (Tas), s 3 claims up to $50,000 and $5,000 in minor civil claims; *Magistrates Court (Civil Proceedings) Act 2004* (WA), s 4 claims up to $75,000; *Magistrates Court Act 1991* (SA), s 8 claims involving personal injuries and property $80,000 and for other civil claims $40,000, s 3 small claims up to $6,000 are dealt with more informally; *Magistrates Court Act 1921* (Qld), s 4 claims up to $50,000 and small debts up to $7,500; *Magistrates Court Act 1989* (Vic), s 3 claims up to $100,000; *Local Court Act 2007* (NSW), s 29 claims up to $60,000 and small claims up to $10,000; *Local Court Act* (NT), s 3 claims up to $100,000 with claims less than $10,000 dealt with as small claims; *Magistrates Court Act 1930* (ACT), s 257 claims up to $50,000 but not civil disputes less than $410,000 (s 266A).

THE COMMON LAW AT WORK

Evolution of the principle of damages for disappointment in contract

[2.215] The object of this section is to trace the development of a principle through the case law. The section highlights the techniques and reasoning that judges use in applying or finding ways around the rules of precedent to develop new principles. The particular cases chosen govern civil compensation with respect to damages for injured feelings, inconvenience or anxiety – generally referred to as "damages for disappointment". Originally, the courts did not recognise compensation for such heads of damage except in cases such as breach of promise to marry or where the mental distress was consequential upon the suffering of some physical injury or physical inconvenience. Damages for "disappointment of mind" alone were not recognised.[76]

Hamlin v Great Northern Railway

[2.220] *Hamlin v Great Northern Railway* (1856) 1 H&N 408; 156 ER 1261

[Facts are as set out in the report.]

The declaration stated that the defendants were the owners of a railway and of carriages for the conveyance of passengers; that the plaintiff was received by the defendants as a passenger to be carried from London to Hull by a train which the defendants advertised and represented to the plaintiff, by a published train bill, to be a train arriving at Hull at nine hours and thirty minutes in the afternoon, and that by reason of the negligence and default of the defendants, the train did not arrive at Hull at that time or within a reasonable time afterwards, whereby the plaintiff was unable to carry on his necessary affairs and business as a tailor, and was deprived of the profits which otherwise would have accrued to him by reason of his business, and was put to great trouble, inconvenience, and expense by reason of the delay.

The defendants pleaded several pleas upon which issues were joined.

At the trial before Martin B, at the Middlesex sittings in the present term, it appeared that the plaintiff was a master tailor going to Yorkshire to see his customers, having previously made arrangements to meet them at particular times and places. On the 25th October, 1855, he took a ticket for Hull by the two o'clock train from Kings Cross, which was advertised to arrive at Hull at half past nine o'clock. On reaching Great Grimsby he found that there was no train to take him on to Hull. It appeared that the ferry boats from New Holland to Hull only run in connection with the trains. The plaintiff stated that there was no possibility of his getting to Hull that night, and that he therefore remained at Great Grimsby, and paid 2s for his bed and some refreshment. In the morning he presented his ticket for Hull, but the Company refused to recognise it, and he paid 1s4d as the fare from Great Grimsby to Hull. He arrived at Hull at half past eight o'clock on Friday the 26th, and being too late for the seven o'clock train from Hull to Driffield, was unable to keep his appointments at Driffield and other places, which were generally on the market days. He stated that he incurred considerable expense, and lost much time, in going to the houses of his customers, having been eight days longer on his journey than he would have been if he had been able to have kept his appointments.

The learned Judge directed the jury that the defendants had broken the contract and that the plaintiff was entitled to recover for the direct consequences of that breach of contract; that he would have been entitled to charge the Company with the expenses of getting to Hull, but that he had no right to cast upon the Company the remote consequences of remaining the night at Grimsby; that,

---

76 See in particular *Hamlin v Great Northern Railway Co* (1856) 1 H&N 408; 156 ER 1261.

Hamlin v Great Northern Railway cont.

not having communicated to the Company his intention of proceeding from Hull to Driffield he could not recover damages from having been prevented from doing so; that he was entitled to the fare paid from Great Grimsby, and perhaps the 2s for his bed and refreshment. He ruled that the damages ought not to exceed 5s. Verdict for the plaintiff, with 5s damages.

Wilde moved (Nov 10) for a new trial on the ground of misdirection. According to the rule laid down in *Hadley v Baxendale* (9 Exch 341) it must be admitted that the plaintiff, not having communicated to the defendants the special injury likely to result from the breach of contract, cannot charge them with the specific damage he incurred. But he is entitled to some damages, and, as a matter of law, the Judge could not tell the jury that they could give no substantial damages beyond 5s. The damages are in the hands of the jury, with certain limited exceptions. It is said that there is a distinction between actions of tort and actions founded upon contract, and that with the exception of the case of a contract to marry, in actions for breaches of contract the inconvenience or injury to the feelings of the plaintiff cannot be taken into consideration in assessing the damage. But the reason why the contract to marry is said to be an exception is that it is a contract affecting the person. The contract, the breach of which is complained of here, is of a similar character. In a case recently tried before Martin, B, the plaintiff had been a passenger on board an emigrant ship, and complained of not having been supplied with sugar during the voyage, and it was held that he was entitled to recover substantial damages. [Martin, B. That was a different case. Here the plaintiff could have got to Hull in time if he had chosen to do so.] He referred to the distinction made in the code of Louisiana, art. 1928-3, cited *Sedgwick on Damages*, 209, – between actions for the breach of ordinary contracts and such as have for their object some intellectual enjoyment or other legal gratification not appreciable in money.

Cur adv vult.

Pollock, CB, now said – We are all of opinion that the rule must be refused. The action is brought to recover damages for a breach of contract. A contract to marry has always been considered an exceptional case, in which the injury to the feelings of the party may be taken into consideration. So in the case of wrongs not founded on contract, the damages are entirely a question for the jury, who may consider the injury to the feelings, and many other matters which have no place in questions of contract. In actions for breaches of contract the damages must be such as are capable of being appreciated or estimated. Mr Wilde was invited at the trial to state what were the damages to which the plaintiff was entitled. He said, general damages. The plaintiff is entitled to nominal damages, at all events, and such other damages of a pecuniary kind as he may have really sustained as a direct consequence of the breach of contract. Each case of this description must be decided with reference to the circumstances peculiar to it; but it may be laid down as a rule, that generally in actions upon contracts no damages can be given which cannot be stated specifically, and that the plaintiff is entitled to recover whatever damages naturally result from the breach of contract, but not damages for disappointment of mind occasioned by the breach of contract.

Rule refused.

Note: What was the *ratio* of this case?

Athens-Macdonald Travel Service Pty Ltd v Kazis

[2.225] *Athens-Macdonald Travel Service Pty Ltd v Kazis* (1970) SASR 264

[Facts are set out in the report.]

Zelling J: The plaintiff-respondent's claim was for breach of his contract with the defendant-appellant, a travel agency, to provide him and his family with the travel facilities for a three months' holiday in Cyprus. The defendant admitted liability and the case proceeded as an assessment of damages only.

...The plaintiff desired to take his family back to Cyprus so that he and his wife could meet their parents and close relatives and the children could meet and be met by their grandparents and in order to do this the respondent and his wife worked long hours in their fish and chip shop to save enough money to finance a trip to Cyprus. They entered into a contract with the appellant company through its principal agent in Australia, a man named Josephides. The contract consisted of a series of letters passing between the parties which were proved in evidence. The basic essentials of the contract were that the appellant contracted to supply the respondent with an air travel itinerary for the respondent and his wife and children which would provide them with a stay of three months certain in Cyprus. The appellant was also told by the respondent what arrangements he was making and was obliged to make with regard to the carrying on of his business whilst he was absent overseas. Shortly before going overseas the appellant informed the respondent through the appellant's Adelaide office that the arrangements that it had made would necessitate the respondent leaving Cyprus with his family to return to Australia three weeks before the time he had stipulated. The respondent expostulated both with the Adelaide agent and with Josephides and was told that if he went to Melbourne on the Saturday morning ie, the day on which he was to leave to go overseas, everything would be fixed up. He went to Melbourne on the day of the flight and was then told that the matter would be fixed up in Athens.

[Quoting Special Magistrate's judgment]

The plaintiff was deliberately deceived...There is, in my view, no question but that the plaintiff has established beyond doubt that he suffered the most serious physical discomfort and hardship and a very substantial inconvenience and that all these things were a direct result of the plaintiff...literally being forced to get on the plane in Cyprus for the return; journey to his home in this State, twenty-one days before he wanted to...

[at page 269]

...Mr Mansfield for the Appellant, contended that if the respondent suffered any discomfort at all, which counsel disputed, the respondent could only be compensated for purely physical discomfort and that the proper measure of damages was in effect 9/182 (ie four and a half out of ninety-one) of the fare – a figure which I have not troubled to compute exactly but which is of the order of $150 and not $650 as given by the learned Special Magistrate.

This raises the general question of how one computes damages for inconvenience and loss of comfort, a matter which does not seem to have been the subject of discussion in the textbooks and decided cases.

There is no doubt that the general principle in assessing damages in contract is that, so far as money will do it, the wronged party is to be put in the same position as if the contract had been properly performed.

This is, however, an unreal notion in a contract for an overseas tour by air as this was. As Mr Boylan, for the respondent, said, the object of this tour was an enjoyable holiday and what the plaintiff got

Athens-Macdonald Travel Service Pty Ltd v Kazis cont.

after years of hard work was anything but an enjoyable holiday. No amount of money by way of damages will ever turn that holiday into the sort of holiday the plaintiff contracted for and reasonably expected to get...

I turn now to a consideration of the cases in chronological order. They are as follows:

1. *Hamlin v Great Northern Railway Company.* [Facts repeated]. Pollock CB in giving the judgment of the Court, said:

The plaintiff is entitled to nominal damages, at all events, and such other damages of a pecuniary kind as he may have really sustained as a direct consequence of the breach of contract. Each case of this description must be decided with reference to the circumstances peculiar to it; but it may be laid down as a rule, that generally in actions upon contracts no damages can be given which cannot be stated specifically, and that the plaintiff is entitled to recover whatever damages naturally result from the breach of contract, but not damages for disappointment of mind occasioned by the breach of contract.

Clearly the Court excluded all consideration of any mental element in the computation of damages...

3. *Hobbs and Wife v London and South Western Railway Company* (1875) LR 10 QB 111

[Plaintiff and wife and children caught defendant's train at midnight for a particular destination but in fact it terminated at a different station. Forced to walk four or five miles home in the drizzling rain carrying their children. Wife caught cold and was unable to help husband in his business.]

...All the judges held that the plaintiff could recover for physical inconvenience. Archibald J said, at p 124:

The case is not one of mere vexation, but it is one of physical inconvenience, which can in a sense be measured by money value, and the parties here had the fair measure of that inconvenience in the damages given by the jury.

Again the emphasis is on physical inconvenience, but Cockburn CJ in his judgment at p 116 refers to "physical inconvenience or *suffering.*"...

5. *Stedman v Swan's Tours* (1951) 95 Sol Jo 727

[Plaintiff contracted with defendant to arrange superior rooms with a sea view in some first class hotel in Jersey. When the plaintiff and his guests arrived, they discovered they had been given inferior rooms with no sea views. Holiday was completely spoilt.]

Singleton LJ, who gave the main judgment, said:

Damages could be recovered for appreciable inconvenience and discomfort caused by breach of contract. It might be difficult to assess the amount to be awarded, but no more difficult than to assess the amount to be given for pain and suffering in a case of personal injuries...

Again a "spoilt" holiday must mean a holiday marred by discomfort...

The difficulty which I find in assessing what is physical discomfort and inconvenience in a case such as this is that all inconvenience has to include some mental element. I agree immediately that as to mere disappointment, regret or other feelings of the mind simpliciter the law has not progressed so far yet that I can say, sitting as a single Judge of this Court, that damages can be awarded under this head, although I think that the law on this topic is in fact lagging badly behind other fields in the law of damages in this respect. But in assessing what is discomfort and what is inconvenience as elements in damages, one cannot do so without taking into account the circumstances in which the plaintiff in each case found himself. What is inconvenience and discomfort to one person is not to another, and what is inconvenience and discomfort in one contractual situation is not in another. This was a contract by a travel agency to provide a tour of a certain kind and the type of inconvenience and

Athens-Macdonald Travel Service Pty Ltd v Kazis cont.

discomfort which is proper to be considered in relation to such a contract is in my opinion the inconvenience and discomfort of the type which I have detailed above and which must of necessity have a mental element in it. In addition, it is in my opinion a fallacy to say that "physical inconvenience" includes only what one is compelled to do and not what one is not compelled to do, because a number of the things complained of by the plaintiff, the respondent before me, were of the second kind, but in a contract of this type the second is just as much a physical inconvenience if one has to subsume it under the old labels as the first, and the respondent is equally entitled to be compensated for it. It is just as much discomfort and inconvenience on a tour to spend a day doing nothing staying in a hotel or seeing something for the second time when one has planned something new and different for that day – when one has only limited days at one's disposal – as to be forced to do something actively to try and retrieve a situation brought about by the contract being broken...

―――― ❧☙ ――――

Note: What did the judge think of *Hamlin's case*? Did he apply that case to the present facts? What limitations did the judge place on the concept of damages for disappointment?

Jarvis v Swans Tours Ltd

[2.230] *Jarvis v Swans Tours Ltd* (1972) 3 WLR 954

[Facts are as set out in the report.]

Lord Denning MR. Mr Jarvis is a solicitor, employed by a local authority at Barking. In 1969 he was minded to go for Christmas to Switzerland. He was looking forward to a skiing holiday. It is his one fortnight's holiday for the year. He prefers it in the winter rather than in the summer.

Mr Jarvis read a brochure issued by Swans Tours Ltd. He was much attracted by the description of Mörlialp, Giswil, Central Switzerland. I will not read the whole of it, but just pick out some of the principal attractions:

"House Party Centre with special resident host...Mörlialp is a most wonderful little resort on a sunny plateau...Up there you will find yourself in the midst of beautiful alpine scenery, which in winter becomes a wonderland of sun, snow and ice, with a wide variety of fine ski-runs, a skating rink and exhilarating toboggan run...Why did we choose the Hotel Krone... mainly and most of all because of the 'Gemütlichkeit' and friendly welcome you will receive from Herr and Frau Weibel...The Hotel Krone has its own Alphütte Bar which will be open several evenings a week...No doubt you will be in for a great time, when you book this house-party holiday...Mr Weibel, the charming owner, speaks English."

On the same page, in a special yellow box it was said:

Swans House Party in Mörlialp. All these House Party arrangements are included in the price of your holiday. Welcome party on arrival. Afternoon tea and cake for 7 days. Swiss dinner by candlelight. Fondue party. Yodler evening. Chali farewell party in the "Alphütte Bar". Service of representative.

Alongside on the same page there was a special note about ski-packs. "Hire of Skis, Sticks and Boots...Ski Tuition...12 days £11.10."

In August 1969, on the faith of that brochure, Mr Jarvis booked a 15-day holiday, with ski-pack. The total charge was £63.45, including Christmas supplement. He was to fly from Gatwick to Zurich on December 20, 1969, and return on January 3, 1970.

The plaintiff went on the holiday, but he was very disappointed. He was a man of about 35 and he expected to be one of house party of some 30 or so people. Instead, he found there were only 13 during the first week. In the second week there was no house party at all. He was the only person the second week, in this hotel with no house party at all, and no one could speak English, except himself.

Jarvis v Swans Tours Ltd cont.

He was very disappointed, too, with the skiing. It was some distance away at Giswil. There were no ordinary length skis. There were only mini-skis, about 3 ft. long. So he did not get his skiing as he wanted to. In the second week he did get some longer skis for a couple of days, but then, because of the boots, his feet got rubbed and he could not continue even with the long skis. So his skiing holiday, from his point of view, was pretty well ruined.

There were many other matters, too. They appear trivial when they are set down in writing, but I have no doubt they loomed large in Mr Jarvis's mind, when coupled with the other disappointments. He did not have the nice Swiss cakes which he was hoping for. The only cakes for tea were potato crisps and little dry nut cakes. The yodeller evening consisted of one man from the locality who came in his working clothes for a little while, and sang four or five songs very quickly. The "Alphütte Bar" was an unoccupied annexe which was only open one evening. There was a representative, Mrs Storr, there during the first week, but she was not there during the second week.

The matter was summed up by the judge:

> During the first week he got a holiday in Switzerland which was to some extent inferior…and, as to the second week, he got a holiday which was largely inferior to what he was led to expect.

What is the legal position? I think that the statements in the brochure were representations or warranties. The breaches of them give Mr Jarvis a right to damages. It is not necessary to decide whether they were representations or warranties: because since the *Misrepresentation Act 1967* (Cth), there is a remedy in damages for misrepresentation as well as for breach of warranty.

The one question in the case is: What is the amount of damages? The judge seems to have taken the difference in value between what he paid for and what he got. He said that he intended to give "the difference between the two values and no other damages" under any other head. He thought that Mr Jarvis had got half of what he paid for. So the judge gave him half the amount which he had paid, namely, £31.72. Mr Jarvis appeals to this court. He says that the damages ought to have been much more.

…

What is the right way of assessing damages? It has often been said that on a breach of contract damages cannot be given for mental distress. Thus in *Hamlin v Great Northern Railway Co* [1959] 1 H & N 408, 411 Pollock CB said that damages cannot be given "for the disappointment of mind occasioned by the breach of contract." And in *Hobbs v London & South Western Railway Co* (1875) LR 10 QB 111, 122, Mellor J said that

> for the mere inconvenience, such as annoyance and loss of temper, or vexation, or for being disappointed in a particular thing which you have set your mind upon, without real physical inconvenience resulting, you cannot recover damages.

The courts in those days only allowed the plaintiff to recover damages if he suffered physical inconvenience, such as having to walk five miles home, as in *Hobbs' case*; or to live in an over-crowded house, *Bailey v Bullock* [1950] 2 All ER 1167.

I think that those limitations are out of date. In a proper case damages for mental distress can be recovered in contract, just as damages for shock can be recovered in tort. One such case is a contract for a holiday, or any other contract to provide entertainment and enjoyment. If the contracting party breaks his contract, damages can be given for the disappointment, the distress, the upset and frustration caused by the breach. I know that it is difficult to assess in terms of money, but it is no more difficult than the assessment which the courts have to make every day in personal injury cases for loss of amenities. Take the present case. Mr Jarvis has only a fortnight's holiday in the year. He books it far ahead, and looks forward to it all that time. He ought to be compensated for the loss of it.

Jarvis v Swans Tours Ltd cont.

A good illustration was given by Edmund Davies LJ in the course of the argument. He put the case of a man who has taken a ticket for Glyndbourne. It is the only night on which he can get there. He hires a car to take him. The car does not turn up. His damages are not limited to the mere cost of the ticket. He is entitled to general damages for the disappointment he has suffered and the loss of the entertainment which he should have had. Here, Mr Jarvis's fortnight's winter holiday has been a grave disappointment. It is true that he was conveyed to Switzerland and back and had meals and bed in the hotel. But that is not what he went for. He went to enjoy himself with all the facilities which the defendants said he would have. He is entitled to damages for the lack of those facilities, and for his loss of enjoyment.

...

I think the judge was in error in taking the sum paid for the holiday £63.45 and halving it. The right measure of damages is to compensate him for the loss of entertainment and enjoyment which he was promised, and which he did not get.

Looking at the matter quite broadly, I think the damages in this case should be the sum of £125. I would allow the appeal, accordingly.

Note: What is the reason, do you think, for Lord Denning not referring to *Athens-MacDonald v Kazis*? What factors did he take into account in determining the amount of damages for disappointment?

Baltic Shipping Co v Dillon

[2.235] *Baltic Shipping Co v Dillon* (1993) 176 CLR 344

[Facts are as set out in the report. Footnotes have been renumbered.]

McHugh J. Baltic Shipping Company ("Baltic") appeals against an order of the Supreme Court of New South Wales (Court of Appeal). The order in question dismissed an appeal by Baltic against so much of an order made in the Admiralty Division of the Supreme Court as awarded damages to the respondent, Mrs Joan Norma Dillon, for breach of contract by Baltic. The action for breach of contract arose out of the sinking of the *Mikhail Lermontov*, a cruise ship owned by Baltic.

2. Sometime prior to 7 February 1986, Baltic agreed in consideration of the sum of $2,205, payable in advance, to carry Mrs Dillon on the *Mikhail Lermontov* on a fourteen day cruise in the South Pacific. At about 5.30 pm on 16 February 1986, the tenth day of the cruise, the ship struck a rock. It sank later that evening. Mrs Dillon was taken off the ship, shortly before it sank. Subsequently, she commenced an action against Baltic in the Admiralty Division of the Supreme Court of New South Wales for breach of contract. After the hearing of the action had commenced, Baltic admitted liability. Pursuant to the powers conferred by the *Contracts Review Act 1980* (NSW), Carruthers J, who heard the action,[77] set aside a deed under which Mrs Dillon released Baltic from liability in consideration of the payment of

---

77 *Baltic Shipping Co "The Mikhail Lermontov" v Dillon* (1989) 21 NSWLR 614.

Baltic Shipping Co v Dillon cont.

certain moneys including a partial repayment of her fare. His Honour awarded Mrs Dillon the following damages:

Restitution of the balance of fare	$ 1,417
Loss of valuables	4,265
Compensation for disappointment and distress	5,000
Damages for personal injury	35,000
	$45,682

An appeal to the Court of Appeal (Gleeson CJ and Kirby P, Mahoney JA dissenting) against the award of damages failed. [78]

The questions for determination in this Court are whether Mrs Dillon was entitled to have her fare refunded and whether she was entitled to claim damages for distress and disappointment because the cruise was not completed.

...

The claim for damages for distress and disappointment

The appeal against the award of damages for distress and disappointment should be dismissed. Under the common law, damages are not recoverable for distress or disappointment arising from a breach of contract unless the distress or disappointment arises from breach of an express or implied term that the promisor will provide the promisee with pleasure, enjoyment or personal protection or unless the distress or disappointment is consequent upon the suffering of physical injury or physical inconvenience. In the present case, it was an implied term of the contract that the fourteen day cruise in the South Pacific would be an enjoyable experience. The sinking of the *Mikhail Lermontov* resulted in a breach of that term. Consequently, the trial judge was correct in awarding damages to Mrs Dillon for the disappointment which she suffered when the cruise failed to provide the enjoyment which Baltic had promised.

The general rule relating to damages for distress and disappointment

Damages for breach of contract cannot ordinarily be awarded for distress or disappointment arising from that breach. In *Hamlin v The Great Northern Railway Company*, [79] Pollock CB said:

> In actions for breaches of contract the damages must be such as are capable of being appreciated or estimated...but it may be laid down as a rule, that generally in actions upon contracts no damages can be given which cannot be stated specifically, and that the plaintiff is entitled to recover whatever damages naturally result from the breach of contract, but not damages for the disappointment of mind occasioned by the breach of contract. [80]

In *Hamlin*, the defendant, in breach of contract, failed to carry the plaintiff to his destination in accordance with the advertised timetable, forcing the plaintiff to obtain overnight accommodation in the course of his journey and to buy a new ticket to resume his journey. The plaintiff sued for breach of contract alleging that, in consequence of the delay, he failed to keep appointments with customers and was detained for longer than he should have been. The Court of Exchequer held that he was entitled only to nominal damages "and such other damages of a pecuniary kind as he may have really sustained as a direct consequence of the breach of contract". [81]

...

The exceptions

---

78   *Baltic Shipping Co v Dillon* (1991) 22 NSWLR 1.
79   *Hamlin v Great Northern Railway Co* (1856) 1 H & N 408; 156 ER 1261 at 411 (H & N), 1262 (ER).
80   This passage was cited with approval by Dixon and McTiernan JJ in *Fink v Fink* (1946) 74 CLR 127 at 142-143.
81   *Hamlin v Great Northern Railway Co* (1856) 1 H and N 408 (156 ER 1261 at 411 (H and N), 1262 (ER)).

Baltic Shipping Co v Dillon cont.

From an early period, the common law allowed damages for injured feelings and wounded pride consequent upon a breach of a promise of marriage. [82] Moreover, soon after the decision in Hamlin, the Court of Exchequer held that damages for "inconveniences and annoyances" could be awarded for breach of contract. In *Burton v Pinkerton*, [83] the plaintiff had agreed to serve as a seaman on a ship "upon an ordinary commercial voyage" ((200) ibid, at p 348.). However, in breach of contract, the defendant placed the ship under the control of a foreign government which was at war, causing the plaintiff to leave the ship at a foreign port. The Court held that the plaintiff was entitled to damages for the inconveniences and annoyances arising from the defendant's breach of contract.

29. Nine years after *Burton*, the Queens Bench held that a plaintiff was entitled to damages for the inconvenience of having to walk home in the early hours of the morning when a train failed to stop at the station for which he had bought a ticket. [84] Cockburn CJ said [85] that:

> if the jury are satisfied that in the particular instance personal inconvenience or suffering has been occasioned, and that it has been occasioned as the immediate effect of the breach of the contract, I can see no reasonable principle why that should not be compensated for.

His Lordship said that *Hamlin* did not decide that personal inconvenience, however serious, was not to be taken into account as a subject-matter of damages. Blackburn J asserted [86] that in *Hamlin* there was no inconvenience at all, saying [87] that "sleeping at Grimsby instead of Hull seems really to be nothing". Mellor J said: [88]

> that for the mere inconvenience, such as annoyance and loss of temper, or vexation, or for being disappointed in a particular thing which you have set your mind upon, without real physical inconvenience resulting, you cannot recover damages. That is purely sentimental, and not a case where the word inconvenience, as I here use it, would apply.

But his Lordship went on to say [89] that:

> where the inconvenience is real and substantial arising from being obliged to walk home, I cannot see why that should not be capable of being assessed as damages in respect of inconvenience.

...

In *Jarvis v Swans Tours Ltd*, [90] the Court of Appeal made...an award of damages for "loss of enjoyment" where the plaintiff's skiing holiday did not measure up to the promises in the defendant's brochure. Lord Denning MR thought that *Hamlin* and *Hobbs* no longer stated the law accurately. His Lordship said: [91]

> In a proper case damages for mental distress can be recovered in contract, just as damages for shock can be recovered in tort. One such case is a contract for a holiday, or any other

---

82	*Berry v Da Costa* (1866) LR 1 CP 331 at 333.
83	*Burton v Pinkerton* (1867) LR 2 Ex 340.
84	*Hobbs v London and South Western Railway Co* (1875) LR 10 QB 111.
85	*Hobbs v London and South Western Railway Co* (1875) LR 10 QB 111 at 116.
86	*Hobbs v London and South Western Railway Co* (1875) LR 10 QB 111 120.
87	*Hobbs v London and South Western Railway Co* (1875) LR 10 QB 111 120-121.
88	*Hobbs v London and South Western Railway Co* (1875) LR 10 QB 111 122.
89	*Hobbs v London and South Western Railway Co* (1875) LR 10 QB 111 123.
90	*Jarvis v Swans Tours Ltd* (1973) QB 233.
91	*Jarvis v Swans Tours Ltd* (1973) QB 233 237-238.

Baltic Shipping Co v Dillon cont.

contract to provide entertainment and enjoyment. If the contracting party breaks his contract, damages can be given for the disappointment, the distress, the upset and frustration caused by the breach.

He did not further elucidate the meaning of "a proper case". Edmund Davies LJ said [92] that where a person has paid for:

> an invigorating and amusing holiday and...returns home dejected because his expectations have been largely unfulfilled...it would be quite wrong to say that his disappointment must find no reflection in the damages to be awarded

Stephenson LJ said [93] that:

> there may be contracts in which the parties contemplate inconvenience on breach which may be described as mental: frustration, annoyance, disappointment; and, as...this is such a contract, the damages for breach of it should take such wider inconvenience or discomfort into account.

Damages for disappointment have been awarded in other "holiday" cases. [94]

...

Apart from the decision of Zelling J in *Athens-McDonald Travel Services Pty Ltd* and the decision of the Court of Appeal in the present case, Australian courts have paid little attention to the developments in England in the last 40 years concerning the award of damages for distress arising from breach of contract. In *Allison v Hewitt* [95] and *Falko v James McEwan and Co*, [96] Jarvis was distinguished on the basis that it applied to holiday situations and not to ordinary commercial contracts.

...

The applicable rule

...

The application of basic principle concerning the awarding of damages for breach of contract requires an award of damages for distress or disappointment where it is an express or implied term of the contract that the promisor will provide pleasure or enjoyment or personal protection for the promisee. Unless this Court were to refuse to follow *Burton*, *Hobbs* and *Bailey* as well as the decisions in *Stedman* and *Athens-McDonald Travel Services Pty Ltd*, damages must also be recoverable for distress or disappointment consequent upon the suffering of physical inconvenience as the consequence of a breach of contract. Furthermore, because damages for personal injury may be recovered in an action for breach of contract [97] and because psychiatric illness constitutes personal injury, [98] damages for mental distress associated with a psychiatric illness or physical injury must also be recoverable in an action for breach of contract.

In the result, the Court should not presently reject the general rule enunciated in *Hamlin*. At the same time, it should recognise that damages for distress or disappointment are recoverable in an action for breach of contract if it arises from breach of an express or implied term that the promisor will

---

92   *Jarvis v Swans Tours Ltd* (1973) QB 233 239.
93   *Jarvis v Swans Tours Ltd* (1973) QB 233 240-241.
94   *Jackson v Horizon Holidays* (1975) 1 WLR 1468; *Jackson v Chrysler Acceptances* (1978) RTR 474.
95   *Allison v Hewitt* (1974) 3 NSWDCR 193.
96   *Falko v James McEwan and Co* (1977) VR 447.
97   *Woolworths Ltd v Crotty* (1942) 66 CLR 603; *Cullen v Trappell* (1980) 146 CLR 1.
98   *Mount Isa Mines Ltd v Pusey* (1970) 125 CLR 383.

Baltic Shipping Co v Dillon cont.

provide the promisee with pleasure or enjoyment or personal protection or if it is consequent upon the suffering or physical injury or physical inconvenience. The question whether the general rule enunciated in *Hamlin* should be overruled can be considered when the Court has heard full argument on the question.

Mrs Dillon's right to damages for distress and disappointment

The contract between Mrs Dillon and Baltic was one in which Baltic impliedly promised to provide a pleasurable and enjoyable cruise for fourteen days. Its failure to do so means that it must pay damages for the distress and disappointment suffered by Mrs Dillon. [99] However, the sum awarded to her was more than twice the sum paid as the price of the fare. When combined with the return of the fare, it was much too high a figure. I agree with the comment of Kirby (p 94) [100] in the Court of Appeal that in the absence of "some exceptional circumstance increasing the sting of the failure to provide the enjoyment and pleasure promised…no more than half the sum awarded in this case should be the norm for the ordinary passenger". This sum is, of course, in addition to any damages awarded for the financial loss suffered by a plaintiff in paying for a promise which has not been fulfilled.

…

[ORDER:] Appeal allowed.

———— ☙❦ ————

Note: How do you think *Hamlin's case* would be decided today if it were to come before an Australian court? Is there still a distinction between business travel (*Hamlin's case*) and leisure travel (*Jarvis' case*) in determining whether damages for disappointment are recoverable?

Exercise

Turmoil in the Top End

Leanora and Liam were very excited about their upcoming four week holiday. They had planned to combine an adventure safari bus tour in the Top End with a more relaxing cruise in the Timor Sea to finish. They booked each component of the holiday separately over the internet and paid for each in advance amounting in total to AUD$15,000.00.

The bus tour was scheduled to last two weeks ending in Darwin on the day before their cruise of the Timor Sea was to commence. The online brochure promised: "…*transportation by luxury air-conditioned coach, comprehensive sightseeing, experienced driver, in-depth commentary from your Tour Guide plus much more…*". The reality of the holiday experience was somewhat different from the expectation. Their assigned bus for the safari tour was old and draughty and there were no seat belts on board. The driver appeared young and nervous and gave little visitor interpretation of all the major sites along the way. There was no independent tour guide.

By the end of the first week, Leanora and Liam were really looking forward to the next phase of the holiday, the Timor Sea cruise, which they imagined would be much more relaxing than the bus trip was proving to be. There had already been too many early morning rises, long days on bumpy roads and hot dusty conditions on board the bus. Three days later, disaster struck when the bus, travelling at speed, missed a corner, slid across the road and landed on its

---

99 See *Jarvis v Swan Tours* (1973) QB 233.
100 *Baltic Shipping Co v Dillon* (1991) 22 NSWLR 1 at 31.

Turmoil in the Top End cont.

side in a ditch. Without seat belts, Leanora and Liam were thrown out of their seats and each of them suffered minor injuries requiring their hospitalisation in Jabiru for the next four days.

When they were discharged from hospital, they headed straight back to Darwin to join the next phase of their holiday, the Timor Sea cruise, only to find that the ship had sailed out of port the afternoon before. They were naturally upset and frustrated but decided to fly to the next port of call, Broome, at their own expense, in five days' time, to meet the ship and join the rest of the cruise there. In the meantime, they knew no-one else in Darwin and needed to find temporary accommodation in a hotel in the city.

Leanora and Liam have calculated that their out-of-pocket expenses alone amounted to $5,000. They missed out on six of the fourteen days of the cruise that they had paid for (which was not refundable) and because of everything else that had happened, they felt that the rest of the holiday was spoilt anyway.

Discuss the issues. Using *Baltic Shipping Company v Dillon* as your precedent, answer the following questions.

(a) Advise Leanora and Liam whether they can make a claim for the inconvenience and distress that they have suffered and against whom? Give reasons.

(b) What other compensation could Leanora and Liam claim according to the authorities?

(c) What difference would it make (if any) if Leanora and Liam had informed the adventure safari tour operator of their total travel itinerary before booking their holiday?

(d) Rank the cases in this section in order of binding or persuasive authority.

CHAPTER 3

Statute

[3.05] THE PROCESS OF LEGISLATION		41
[3.10]	The Parliamentary Process	42
[3.15]	The original ideas	42
[3.20]	Drafting the Bill	42
[3.25]	Getting before the Parliament	42
[3.30]	Passage through Parliament	43
[3.60]	Royal assent	43
[3.65]	Proclamation/commencement	44
[3.70]	Regulations and administration	44
[3.75]	Retrospectivity	44
[3.80]	Parliamentary Sovereignty	45
[3.85] PHYSICAL APPEARANCE OF A STATUTE		45
[3.90]	Crest	47
[3.95]	Year and number of the Act	47
[3.100]	Words of enactment	47
[3.105]	Royal assent	47
[3.110]	Title	47
[3.115]	Statement of objects and purposes	48
[3.120]	Definitions/interpretation section	48
[3.125]	Schedules	48
[3.130]	Headings	48
[3.135]	Punctuation	48
[3.140]	Marginal notes	49
[3.145] SOURCES FOR STATUTORY INTERPRETATION		49
[3.150]	Intrinsic Material	50
[3.155]	Text of the statute	50
[3.160]	Rules of statutory interpretation	50
[3.195]	Presumptions	53
[3.220]	Extrinsic Material	55
[3.225]	Statutory intervention	55
[3.230]	Other statutes of relevance	57
[3.235]	Doctrine of precedent	57
[3.240] OVERALL APPROACH TO STATUTORY INTERPRETATION		57
[3.245]	Read the Act as a Whole	57
[3.250]	Legislative Intent	58
[3.255]	Target Audience	58
[3.260] DELEGATED LEGISLATION		59

THE PROCESS OF LEGISLATION

[3.05] The previous chapter concentrated on the role the courts play in the law-making process and focused on the strengths and weaknesses of that system. This chapter turns its attention to that other important law-maker – the Parliament.

The first section of this chapter looks at:

- the parliamentary process;
- the presumption against retrospectivity; and
- parliamentary sovereignty.

The Parliamentary Process

[3.10] The Parliamentary process is directed towards making statutes. The steps involved in the making of these laws include:
- the original idea;
- drafting the Bill;
- getting the Bill before the Parliament;
- passage through Parliament;
- Royal assent;
- proclamation/commencement; and
- regulations and administration.

The original ideas

[3.15] How can a good idea be turned into law? There are a number of ways for this to occur. For example, members of the travel, hospitality or tourism-related industries can band together as a group and make recommendations for the introduction of new laws or the amendment of existing laws to the relevant government department.[1] This is called "lobbying" and it is a very effective means of initiating changes to the law. Alternatively, ideas for change could be circulated in the media, which might generate public debate on the issues raised.

Drafting the Bill

[3.20] If these methods are successful, they will lead to a presentation of the proposal to Cabinet by the relevant Minister. If Cabinet adopts the proposal, it then passes through various stages to become legislation. One of the most important stages is the point at which the proposal is drafted into legislative form. This is done by the Office of the Parliamentary Draftsperson, whose job it is to make legislation that works properly, using clear, simple, unambiguous language that accurately translates policy into law. To this end, the Parliamentary draftsperson will refer to the standard set of provisions for legislation in the relevant Acts Interpretation Act.[2]

Getting before the Parliament

[3.25] Once the Bill is adopted by the Cabinet, it is included in the government's legislative program. The Leader of the House, in consultation with the Premier (or Prime Minister in

---

[1] This is what happened in Queensland when the tourism product in that State was being undermined by the unscrupulous behaviour of some inbound tour operators and tour guides towards tourists. This unscrupulous behaviour included controlled shopping, misrepresentations, overcharging for goods and services and unconscionable conduct leaving tourists with a negative and distorted view of Queensland. It led to the introduction of the *Tourism Services Act 2003* (Qld), the intention of which is: "... to provide protection for tourists in dealings with inbound tour operators and tour guides, and for related purposes".

[2] C Enright, *Studying Law* (The Federation Press, Sydney, 1995), p 263.

federal Parliament) and the Cabinet office, will oversee its preparation and presentation to the Parliament at a time convenient to the government.

Passage through Parliament

[3.30] This does vary between Parliaments, depending on Standing Orders, but generally speaking the Bill passes through the following stages before emerging as legislation.

First reading (title only)

[3.35] The first reading is a formality. The motion "that this Bill be now read a first time" is put by the Speaker immediately after the Bill has been received, and it is immediately voted upon without amendment or debate. By agreeing to read a Bill for the first time, the House is merely authorising its printing.

Second reading

[3.40] This is followed by the Minister's speech (and explanatory notes are usually distributed). This is the time when the Minister explains the policy behind the Bill. For example, in 2009, the then Minister for Small Business, Independent Contractors and the Service Economy, Dr Craig Emerson, introduced the *Trade Practices Amendment (Australian Consumer Law) Bill* into federal Parliament. In his second reading of the Bill the Minister explained that, amongst other things, it would become a single, national consumer law to be called the Australian Consumer Law.[3]

Committee stages

[3.45] The debate on the Bill is then adjourned to allow the members of the House an opportunity to study the explanation offered by the Minister, to present reasoned arguments for and against the proposed legislation and to suggest amendments.

Third reading

[3.50] Once the Bill has passed the second reading and amendments have been approved in Committee stages, the motion for the third reading is normally carried. If it is, the Bill is deemed to have been passed by the House and becomes an Act.

Transmission to the Upper House (where relevant)

[3.55] The procedure for consideration in the second House is much the same as in the first.

There are special procedures for resolving deadlocks (for example, recommendations for amendments) but if there is continuing disagreement, the deadlock provisions of the Constitution[4] may provide the basis for a double dissolution.[5]

Royal assent

[3.60] Although for all practical purposes, Parliament consists of the two Houses (in Queensland just one), the Crown is formally part of the Parliament. So after the passage of a Bill through Parliament, to complete parliamentary approval it is necessary for the Royal

---

3   House of Representatives, *Hansard*, 2009-06-24/0078.
4   *Commonwealth of Australia Constitution Act 1900* (Cth), s 57 ("Commonwealth Constitution").
5   C Enright, *Studying Law* (The Federation Press, Sydney, 1995), p 264.

assent to be given. The Act is presented to the Governor or Governor-General for Royal assent. This may not be withheld under the conventions of the Constitutions of the Australian States.

Proclamation/commencement

[3.65] Pursuant to the *Acts Interpretation Act 1901* (Cth), s 5, Acts are deemed to come into operation 28 days after Royal assent unless otherwise provided for in the Act. Acts amending the Constitution operate from the date of Royal assent.[6]

In most cases, Acts provide that they are to come into operation on "a date to be proclaimed". This allows regulations to be drafted and machinery arrangements to be made for the administration of the Act before it comes into operation. Subsequently, the date will be published in the *Government Gazette*. Acts may be proclaimed in whole or in part and some are never proclaimed.

If Acts form part of a legislative scheme, it may be that the dates for commencement of all the Acts will be interdependent on each other.

Regulations and administration

[3.70] Acts, in general, contain broad powers and policy while the regulations are designed to fill in the details which can be changed without the need for new legislation (for example, speed limits, fines, administrative details). When these legal rules are made, they are known as subordinate or delegated legislation and take the form of regulations, rules, orders or by-laws.

Retrospectivity

[3.75] Parliament is presumed to legislate prospectively. Otherwise, clear words are needed to make an Act operate from before the date on which it was passed. Dixon CJ in *Maxwell v Murphy*[7] said:

> The general rule of the common law is that a statute changing the law ought not, unless the intention appears with reasonable certainty, to be understood as applying to facts or events that have already occurred in such a way as to confer or impose or otherwise affect rights or liabilities which the law had defined by reference to the past events.

This presumption can be rebutted by:
- express provision;
- necessary implication/intendment;
- declaratory Acts;
- validating Acts; and
- procedural Acts.

In 1982, the then federal Treasurer, John Howard, introduced the retrospective *"bottom of the harbour"* legislation into federal Parliament and in his second reading speech of the Bill he explained:

---

6   The rule varies from jurisdiction to jurisdiction, for example, see the *Acts Interpretation Act 1954* (Qld), s 15A – Acts are deemed to come into operation on the date of Royal assent unless otherwise expressly provided for in the Act.

7   *Maxwell v Murphy* (1957) 96 CLR 261.

Our normal and general reluctance to introduce legislation having any retrospective element has, on this occasion, been tempered by the competing consideration of overall perceptions as to the equity and fairness of our taxation system and the distribution of the tax burden.[8]

Parliamentary Sovereignty

[3.80] Legal rules made by Parliament are known as enacted law or statute law or legislation. The fact is that Parliament can make or unmake whatever laws it likes on any topic that it might choose, subject to the Parliament acting within its constitutional power to make those laws. This has allowed the various Australian governments to regulate all kinds of human endeavour and to adopt a more interventionist role in the life of the Australian community as a whole.

What follows from this doctrine of parliamentary sovereignty is that statute law prevails over common law. However, if the words of a statute are unclear or inconsistent, it is the judges who must interpret their meaning. The prominent role of the courts in statutory interpretation provides the link between the courts and the Parliament in the legislative process.

PHYSICAL APPEARANCE OF A STATUTE

[3.85] It is important to examine the parts of a statute which together make up its physical appearance. These include:

- crest;
- year and number of the Act;
- enacting words;
- Royal assent;
- title;
- statement of objects and purposes;
- date on which the Act comes into force;
- parts and divisions;
- sections, subsections and paragraphs;
- headings;
- definitions;
- schedules;
- marginal notes;
- punctuation.

Examples of most of these physical features can be found in the extract from the *Tourism Australia Act 2004* (Cth) reproduced below.

---

8   House of Representatives, Commonwealth Parliamentary *Debates* (Vol HR129, 1982), p 1866.

Tourism Australia Act 2004
No 74 of 2004 as amended

An Act to establish Tourism Australia, and for related purposes

Part 1–Preliminary

1 Short title [*see* Note 1]

This Act may be cited as the *Tourism Australia Act 2004*.

2 Commencement

(1) Each provision of this Act specified in column 1 of the table commences, or is taken to have commenced, in accordance with column 2 of the table. Any other statement in column 2 has effect according to its terms.

3 Definitions

In this Act, unless the contrary intention appears:
"appointed member" means a member other than the Managing Director.
"Australia," when used in a geographical sense, includes the external Territories.
"Board" means the Board of Directors of Tourism Australia.
"Chair" means the Chair of the Board.
"Deputy Chair" means the Deputy Chair of the Board.
"Managing Director" means the Managing Director of Tourism Australia.
"member" means a member of the Board (including the Chair and Deputy Chair).

4 Extended geographical application of this Act

(1) This Act extends to every external Territory.

(2) This Act applies both within and outside Australia.

Part 2–Tourism Australia

5 Establishment

(1) Tourism Australia is established by this section.

(2) Tourism Australia:

    (a) is a body corporate; and

    (b) must have a seal; and

    (c) may sue and be sued.

    Note: The *Commonwealth Authorities and Companies Act 1997* applies to Tourism Australia. That Act deals with matters relating to Commonwealth authorities, including reporting and accountability, banking and investment, and conduct of executive officers.

(3) The seal of Tourism Australia is to be kept in such custody as the Board directs, and is not to be used except as authorised by the Board.

(4) All courts, judges and persons acting judicially must:

    (a) take judicial notice of the imprint of the seal of Tourism Australia appearing on a document; and

    (b) presume that the document was duly sealed.

6 Objects

Tourism Australia's objects are:

(a) to influence people to travel to Australia, including for events; and

(b) to influence people travelling to Australia to also travel throughout Australia; and

(c) to influence Australians to travel throughout Australia, including for events; and

(d) to help foster a sustainable tourism industry in Australia; and

(e) to help increase the economic benefits to Australia from tourism.

Part 3–The Board of Directors of Tourism Australia
Division 1–The Board
9 Establishment
The Board of Directors of Tourism Australia is established by this section.
10 Functions
The Board has the following functions:

(a) to ensure the proper and efficient performance of Tourism Australia's functions;

(b) to determine Tourism Australia's policy in relation to any matter.

11 Powers
The Board has power to do all things necessary or convenient to be done for or in connection with the performance of its functions.
12 Membership
The Board consists of the following members:

(a) the Chair;

(b) the Deputy Chair;

(d) the Managing Director;

(e) 6 other members.

Note: Section 18B of the *Acts Interpretation Act 1901* deals with the title of the Chair.

The following discussion focuses on the significance of each of these parts of the Act.

Crest

[3.90] Some jurisdictions print their crest on statutes. Despite its strong visual appearance, the crest has no effect on the operation or interpretation of a statute.

Year and number of the Act

[3.95] The year and number of the statute appears below the crest and are used for citation purposes only. They have no interpretive significance. So, in the case of the *Tourism Australia Act 2004* it was the 74th Act passed in 2004.

Words of enactment

[3.100] The enacting words are "BE IT ENACTED by the Queen, and the Senate and House of Representatives of the Commonwealth of Australia, as follows". This is a formal statement that Parliament is exercising its statute making powers. These words usually appear at the beginning of the statute before the first section. They have no effect on the Act's interpretation.

Royal assent

[3.105] This is the final step in the statute making process. See [3.60]. In the case of the *Tourism Australia Act 2004*, the Royal assent was given to Sections 1 and 2 on 23 June, 2004.

Title

[3.110] Acts have two titles, a short title and a long title. In the given example, the long title is "An Act to establish Tourism Australia, and for related purposes."

Statement of objects and purposes

[3.115] Once, the practice was to commence an Act with a "preamble" which gave some background to it. Today the function of the preamble has been largely replaced by a "statement of objects and purposes" section which appears within the statute itself. This is in fact a statutory recognition [9] of a common law rule known as the "mischief rule". Courts are now directed towards an interpretation which promotes the original object and purpose of the Act. The statement of objects and purposes is a specific provision in the Act which uses plain words to express as succinctly as possible the policy behind the legislation. In the current example, the objects of the the *Tourism Australia Act 2004* (Cth), are quite clear in s 6.

Definitions/interpretation section

[3.120] These sections are placed near the beginning of the Act and are extremely helpful in understanding the meanings of words within the context of the Act. In the present example, s 3 is the Definitions section.

Schedules

[3.125] Often information which is complementary to some section(s) of the Act and which needs to be displayed in tabular form, for example, will appear in the schedule. Nevertheless, it is still part of the Act.

Headings

[3.130] The *Tourism Australia Act 2004* (Cth), like many other Acts, is divided into parts, divisions and sections and each section has a heading. However, headings of Parts, Divisions and Subdivisions only are deemed to be part of federal statutes but not headings to sections, [10] although these may be used to assist interpretation of some State legislation when the wording of the section is ambiguous. [11]

Punctuation

[3.135] Punctuation is part of the Act [12] and may therefore prove useful in resolving potential ambiguities within the wording of a section.

---

9   See for example *Acts Interpretation Act 1901* (Cth), s 15AA; *Acts Interpretation Act 1954* (Qld), s 14A.
10 *Acts Interpretation Act 1901* (Cth), s 13(1) and (3).
11 For example, *Acts Interpretation Act 1954* (Qld), s 14(2) – headings are part of the Act itself and therefore may be taken into account in interpreting an Act if the Act was enacted after 30 June 1991 or if the heading to the section was amended after 30 June 1991.
12 For example, see *Acts Interpretation Act 1954* (Qld), s 14(5).

Marginal notes

[3.140] Strictly speaking, marginal notes do not form part of the Act itself but are put alongside different sections of the Act by the parliamentary draftsperson to provide a short summary of them. In some States,[13] Parliament has abandoned the use of marginal notes altogether but where they do appear in statutes, they form part of the extrinsic materials to which courts may properly refer for the purpose of statutory interpretation.[14]

SOURCES FOR STATUTORY INTERPRETATION

```
                    SOURCES FOR STATUTORY INTERPRETATION
                           /                    \
                  Intrinsic Materials        Extrinsic Materials
                  /      |       \            /       |        \
            Text of   Rules of              Precedent  Other    Statutory
            the Act   Statutory  Presumptions       Legislation Interventions
                      Interpretation
```

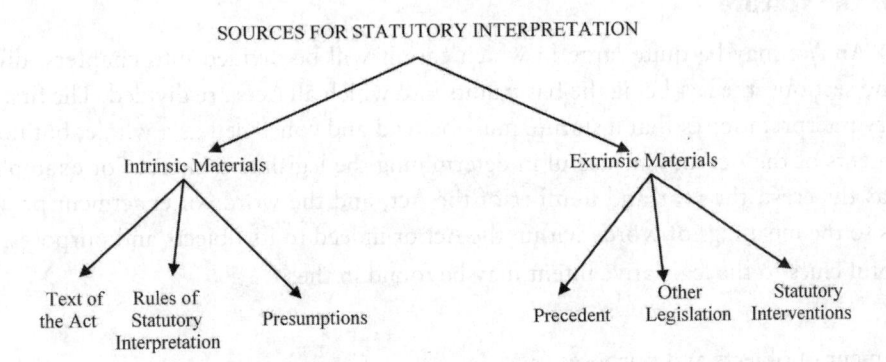

[3.145] The process by which a good idea may become part of the law has already been discussed in [3.10]ff. However, converting policy into law is not a simple process and what began as a good idea might well be unrecognisable once it has been reduced to the words of a section in an Act.

Sometimes, the words of the section have more than one meaning and it is not clear which meaning is intended. On other occasions, there is a discrepancy between the plain meaning of the words of the statute and the object or purpose which the Act was intending to address.

How can these problems be resolved? To answer this question, it is necessary to review the sources of statutory interpretation which are available to the court in its search for a construction of the Act which best reflects its legislative intent.

There are two sources of statutory interpretation: *intrinsic* and *extrinsic* materials. Intrinsic materials are those which are located within the Act itself and which provide assistance in interpreting the legislative intent. Extrinsic materials are those which do not form part of the Act itself but which amount to legitimate aids in the construction of the legislative intent.

---

13 The Queensland Parliament does not use marginal notes as such. But see *Acts Interpretation Act 1954* (Qld), s 14(4) which states "A note in an Act to the Act or to a provision of the Act, as opposed to a footnote, an editor's note or an endnote mentioned in subsection (7) is part of the Act." Footnotes, editor's notes and endnotes are not part of an Act.

14 See *Acts Interpretation Act 1901* (Cth), 15AB, which allows material which does not form part of the Act to be used in interpretation. This would include marginal notes: cf *Acts Interpretation Act 1954* (Qld), s 14B. See also *Acts Interpretation Act 1901* (Cth), s 13(3), which states "... No marginal note, footnote or endnote to an Act, and no heading to a section of an Act, shall be taken to be part of the Act."

Intrinsic Material

[3.150] An example of a typical statute appears in [3.85]. It is important to be able to identify those parts of the Act (intrinsic materials) which are used as legitimate tools of statutory interpretation. These include:
- text of the Act;
- rules of statutory interpretation; and
- presumptions.

Text of the statute

[3.155] An Act may be quite large in which case it will be divided into chapters, divisions, parts and sections, the last being the basic units into which all Acts are divided. The first rule of statutory interpretation is that a statute must be read and construed as a whole, but not all of the elements of the Act may be useful in determining the legislative intent. For example, such things as the crest, the year and number of the Act, and the words of enactment provide no clues as to the meanings of words within the Act or indeed to its objects and purposes.

Helpful clues to the legislative intent may be found in the:
- title;
- statement of objects and purposes;
- definitions/interpretation sections;
- punctuation; and
- marginal notes.

Rules of statutory interpretation

[3.160] Over time, the courts developed their own rules of statutory interpretation. The use of the word "rules" was somewhat of a misnomer, however, as there never was any obligation on the part of the judges to use them. It was simply a matter of practical expediency.

More recently, Parliaments (both Commonwealth and State) have introduced statutory rules in the form of the various Acts Interpretation Acts. Together these common law and statutory rules provide a comprehensive approach to statutory interpretation.

Traditional common law rules

[3.165] At common law, the courts developed a number of traditional "rules" for the interpretation of statutes, known as:
- the literal rule;
- the golden rule; and
- the mischief or "purpose" rule.

Literal rule

"The fundamental rule of interpretation...is that a statute is to be expounded according to the intent of the parliament that made it; and that intention has to be formed by an examination of the language used in the statute as a whole. The question is, what does the language mean; and when we find what

the language means, in its ordinary and natural sense, it is our duty to obey that meaning, even if we think that result to be inconvenient or impolite or improbable." [15]

[3.170] This approach requires the courts to look for the plain, ordinary meaning of the words as understood in their context. It assumes that Parliament's intention is fully and clearly contained in the words of the statute and that there will be no disagreement as to what the ordinary meaning of those words is.

The underlying philosophy is that courts should not be called upon to question the wisdom or fairness of a provision. These are political issues and should be resolved by the policy makers. The court's role is simply to interpret Parliament's intention as conveyed by the words of the statute. If this reveals a gap in the legislative intent, then the courts will invite the Parliament to amend the Act.

Sometimes, however, this approach may lead to an absurd, inconsistent or unreasonable outcome, in which case the rule will need to be modified so as to achieve a just result. [16]

Golden rule

"*The grammatical and ordinary sense of the words is to be adhered to, unless this would lead to some absurdity, or some repugnance or inconsistency with the rest of the instrument, in which case the grammatical and ordinary sense of the words may be modified so as to avoid that absurdity and inconsistency, but no further.*" [17]

[3.175] The golden rule is a more commonsense approach to statutory interpretation which takes over where the literal rule leaves off. This rule allows courts to modify the words of an Act where their ordinary meaning creates an absurdity or inconsistency. [18]

Mischief rule

[3.180] If neither the literal rule nor the golden rule provides any meaningful explanation of the legislative intent, then the court may adopt the approach set down in an early English decision called *Heydon's Case*. [19] There the court stated that the

sure and true interpretation of all statutes requires consideration of four factors:

1. what was the common law before the making of the Act?
2. what was the mischief and defect for which the common law did not provide?
3. what remedy the Parliament resolved and appointed to cure the problem?
4. the true reason of the remedy. [20]

---

15   *Amalgamated Society of Engineers v Adelaide Steamship Co Ltd* (1920) 28 CLR 129 at 161-162.
16   For example, in the case of *Re Sigsworth; Bedford v Bedford* [1935] Ch 89, a son murdered his mother. There was a well settled principle that a sane murderer could not then claim under his victim's will, but as it happened in this case the victim (his mother) died intestate. A literal interpretation of the *Administration of Estates Act 1925* (UK) would have allowed the son to share in his mother's estate. However, Clauson J at 92 said that "general words which might include cases obnoxious to the principle must be read and construed as subject to it".
17   *Grey v Pearson* (1857) 6 LC 61; 10 ER 1216, (61) at 106.
18   For example, the *Road Traffic Act 1960* (UK) requires drivers to "stop" after an accident. In *Lee v Knapp* [1967] 2 QB 442 the defendant driver stopped momentarily before leaving the scene of the accident and argued that this satisfied his legal obligations. The court held that on a proper interpretation of the Act, the section required the motorist to stop "for such a period as may be reasonable" to allow for names, addresses and other details to be exchanged.
19   *Heydon's Case* (1584) 3 Co Rep 7a; 76 ER 637.
20   For example, the *Street Offences Act 1959* (UK) provided in s 1 that: "It shall be an offence for a common prostitute to loiter or solicit in a street or public place for the purpose of prostitution." In *Smith v Hughes*

In this approach, the court looks for the true *purpose* of the Act and that is why it is sometimes referred to as a purposive approach [21] to statutory interpretation. This common law rule now has a statutory equivalent in the form of the statement of objects and purposes section which appears in more recent legislation.

The once popular literal approach favoured by courts is now giving way to the purposive approach to statutory interpretation. Courts are showing a greater preparedness to examine the policy behind the Act so as to better understand its legislative intent. They have been encouraged to take this approach by some recent important statutory interventions. This trend also coincides with the various Parliaments' policy to make legislation easier to understand by making it more general and by using plain legal language. [22]

Statutory rules

[3.185] Statutory intervention in the form of the various Acts Interpretation Acts (Commonwealth and State) has introduced statutory rules which encourage courts to adopt an interpretation that will positively promote the purpose or object of the Act or one that will best achieve its purpose, that is, a purposive approach to statutory interpretation.

Note the wording of s 15AA of the *Acts Interpretation Act 1901* (Cth):

> In the interpretation of a provision of an Act, *a construction that would promote the purpose or object underlying the Act* (whether that purpose or object is expressly stated in the Act or not) shall be preferred to a construction that would not promote that purpose or object (emphasis added). [23]

Dictionaries

[3.190] Dictionaries are a further aid to interpretation and may be used as a guide to the popular meanings of words. However, there are several qualifications to this including:

- if a phrase consists of two or more words then the meaning of the phrase may be different from the meaning of each of the individual words of which the phrase consists. This is called "compounding"; [24]
- common law countries (USA, UK, Australia and the like) may have slight variations in the meanings of words so a dictionary from the relevant jurisdiction should be used; and

---

[1960] 1 WLR 830, several prostitutes were charged with offences under this Act when in fact they had been standing on a balcony or behind windows in their house and had solicited men passing in the street below by tapping on the balcony rail or window pane and calling out to them. Lord Parker CJ said (at 832): "For my part, I approach this matter by considering what is the mischief aimed at by this Act. Everybody knows that this was an Act intended to clean up the streets ... Viewed in that way, it can matter little whether the prostitute is soliciting while in the street or is standing in a doorway or on a balcony ...."

21 Some commentators also refer to this as the "purpose approach". See J Carvan, *Understanding the Australian Legal System* (6th ed, Lawbook Co. 2010), p 129.

22 See more generally P Parkinson, *Tradition and Change in Australian Law* (4th ed, Law Book Co, 2009), on Interpreting Statutes.

23 Cf *Acts Interpretation Act 1954* (Qld), s 14A, which in a sense permits the court to legislate by redrafting the Act in order to achieve its purpose.
>   (1) In the interpretation of a provision of an Act, *the interpretation that will best achieve the purpose of the Act is to be preferred* to any other interpretation.
>   (2) subsection (1) ... applies whether or not the purpose is expressly stated in the Act. (Emphasis added.)

24 For example, "unfair competition" (undercutting, bribery, monopoly) has acquired a meaning separate from the sum of each of the words which go to make it up.

- words and not their synonyms must be interpreted.

Presumptions

[3.195] The courts have also crafted some other "tools" of statutory interpretation in the form of a number of presumptions about the meanings of words. The effect of these presumptions is to state a likely or plausible view of Parliament's intention. Three of the more common ones will be examined.

Ejusdem generis

[3.200] This Latin maxim means literally "of the same kind". The maxim applies when an Act lists words of a particular meaning which are followed by words of more general meaning. Take, for example, s 32 of the *Australian Consumer Law*, which refers to a person who in trade or commerce "offer[s] any rebate, gift, prize or other free item."[25]

What do the words "other free item" mean in this context? They are general words and at first reading appear to have a wide operation which would allow the offer of any items for which the consumer has not paid.

However, the words "offers any rebate, gift, prize" are specific words and if they can be fitted into one family of words, *ejusdem generis*, it might be possible to narrow the meaning of the general phrase. Do the words form part of the same group? Yes: they are words connoting some kind of specific windfall to the recipient, in this case the consumer. Therefore, "other free item" should be taken to mean "and other similar windfalls as those offered to the consumer". However they would probably not include windfalls which are materially different from those being offered, such as a "cash prize" which turns out to be a store credit, or where the cost of the "free gift" has already been factored into the selling price of the advertised goods.[26]

Noscitur a sociis

[3.205] This Latin maxim in effect means "words of a feather flock together". The maxim is used to restrict the scope of words by reference to other words in their immediate context. Take, for example, s 48 of the *Australian Consumer Law*[27] which provides in part "...the supply, or possible supply, to another person of goods or services of a kind ordinarily acquired for *personal, domestic or household use or consumption*."

---

25 *Australian Consumer Law*, s 32 (similar to the former *Trade Practices Act 1974* (Cth) s 54) states:
   Offering rebates, gifts, prizes etc.
   (1) A person must not, in trade or commerce, offer any rebate, gift, prize or other free item with the intention of not providing it, or of not providing it as offered, in connection with:
       (a) the supply or possible supply of goods or services; or
       (b) the promotion by any means of the supply or use of goods or services; or
       (c) the sale or grant, or the possible sale or grant, of an interest in land; or
       (d) the promotion by any means of the sale or grant of an interest in land.

26 Australian Corporation and Consumer Commission booklet, *Advertising and Selling – a business guide to consumer protection under The Trade Practices Act* (1997), p 46.

27 Section 48 states:
   (1) A person must not, in trade or commerce, in connection with:
       (a) the supply, or possible supply, to another person of goods or services of a kind ordinarily acquired for personal, domestic or household use or consumption; or
       (b) the promotion by any means of the supply to another person, or of the use by another person, of goods or services of a kind ordinarily acquired for personal, domestic or household use or consumption; make a representation with respect to an amount that, if

The ejusdem generis rule is inapplicable here because there is no combination of specific words followed by more general words. The noscitur a sociis rule is more appropriate [28] because of the association of words with similar meaning such as "personal, domestic or household use". These words clearly indicate that the target audiences [29] are private consumers and not commercial or business enterprises. In the context of tourism, travel and hospitality, the bulk of services are supplied for private consumption.

Expressio unius est exclusio alterius

[3.210] Literally, this Latin maxim means that the *express* mention of one or more things of a particular class excludes all other members of the same class. This presumption is used with great caution especially where an Act, has undergone substantial revisions over a number of years. The parliamentary draftsperson may not have applied the same degree of precision as to what was to be included or excluded in the subsequent amendments or additions.

Lopes LJ in *Colquhoun v Brooks* [30] stated that the maxim:

> is often a valuable servant, but a dangerous master to follow in the construction of statutes or documents. The exclusio is often the result of inadvertence or accident, and the maxim ought not to be applied, when its application, having regard to the subject-matter to which it is to be applied, leads to inconsistency or injustice.

Value presumptions

[3.215] Value presumptions apply *in* the statutory interpretation of particular type of statute, namely:

- criminal;
- fiscal or taxing; or
- remedial.

For example, a court will construe that a person who is charged with an offence under a section of a criminal Act is entitled to the benefit of any doubt as to the meaning of the Act. In *Ingham v Hie Lee*, [31] Barton J said:

> in construing a penal provision we are bound to remember that we ought not to adopt a construction adverse to an accused person unless he is brought clearly within the words of the Act.

---

paid, would constitute a part of the consideration for the supply of the goods or services unless the person also specifies, in a prominent way and as a single figure, the single price for the goods or services.

28 See *Fox v Warde* [1978] VR 362, was a prostitute an "occupier" of premises in the context of a section which read "tenant, lessee, occupier or person in charge"?
    The court held:
    > If one looks at the associated words, a tenant has lawful possession and the power of excluding everyone including the landlord from the premises. So also has the lessee. The person in charge of premises is, by the very words used, a person with power to take control and exercise control over the premises. In association with those three other words I think "occupier" means something more than a person who simply uses a particular room... .

29 For further discussion on this point, see [3.255].
30 *Colquhoun v Brooks* (1886) 21 QBD 52 at 65; followed in *Rylands Bros (Aust) Ltd v Morgan* (1927) 27 SR (NSW) 161.
31 *Ingham v Hie Lee* (1912) 15 CLR 267 at 271.

This rule applies equally to fiscal or taxing statutes. Express words in the Act itself are needed to impose taxes, rates and charges on individuals.[32]

In contrast, courts construe remedial acts liberally and beneficially in favour of the individual so as to give the fullest relief which the fair meaning of its language will allow. Furthermore, courts generally construe a statute in conformity with the common law, which protects rights to property and the right to remain silent, that is, the privilege against self-incrimination amongst others.[33] However, if the language of the Act is plain in its intention, then courts have no alternative but to acknowledge that those rights have been abrogated by statute.[34]

Extrinsic Material

[3.220] Having looked at the possible sources for statutory interpretation from within an Act itself, attention must now be focused on extrinsic materials – those sources for statutory interpretation which are located outside the Act. There are three main sources:

- statutory intervention;
- other statutes of relevance; and
- the doctrine of precedent.

Statutory intervention

[3.225] Under common law principles of statutory interpretation, courts were reluctant to look at extrinsic material to ascertain Parliament's intention. Judges had recourse to extrinsic aids of construction to uncover the legislative intent only when there was ambiguity or when an absurd result would follow. The dilemma that the courts faced was that by interpreting the words of the Act to fit the parliamentary intent, they were in fact becoming part of the law-making process and thus potentially compromising the independent function of the judiciary. Would it not be preferable to let the words of the Act speak for themselves?

The position has been made clearer for courts through the statutory intervention of the various State and Commonwealth Acts Interpretation Acts.[35] Provisions in these Acts have identified, in a non-exhaustive way, materials which courts may access and which will assist them in finding the objects and purposes of statutes. Nonetheless, the circumstances in which these extrinsic materials may be accessed are still quite limited. These include cases where it is necessary:

---

32 See also *Southern Pacific Hotel Services Inc v Southern Pacific Hotel Corporation Ltd* (unreported, NSWSup Ct, Finlay J, 20 September 1985, Butterworths Unreported Cases 8500526). *Facts*: S, a company based in Canada, entered an agreement to provide promotion and marketing services to a related company, C, the operator of the Southern Pacific (formerly Travelodge) hotel chain in Australasia. When C was sold to a Singapore investor the companies ceased to be related and C sought to avoid the agreement because, among other reasons, S did not have a licence to carry on business as a travel agent under the *Travel Industry Act 1974* (Ontario). *Held*: The definition was extremely wide and if read literally would include every newspaper and television station which ran tourism advertisements. The purpose of the Act was to protect travellers and it should be *interpreted narrowly so as not to make illegal this promotion and marketing contract.* Note that the problem would not arise in Australia because merely arranging for accommodation is outside our definition of carrying on business as a travel agent.

33 Other rules include the presumption against ousting jurisdiction of or limiting access to courts since public policy dictates that they should always be available for resolving disputes between subjects.

34 See, for example, *Acts Interpretation Act 1901* (Cth), s 15AB and the *Acts Interpretation Act 1954* (Qld), s 14B. See, for example, *Australian Grands Prix Act 1994* (Vic) which temporarily removes access to public spaces.

35 See, for example, *Acts Interpretation Act 1901* (Cth), 15AB and *Acts Interpretation Act 1954* (Qld), s 14B.

(a) to confirm that the meaning of the provision is the ordinary meaning conveyed by the text of the provision taking into account its context in the Act and the purpose or object underlying the Act; or

(b) to determine the meaning of the provision when –

   (i) the provision is ambiguous or obscure; or

   (ii) the ordinary meaning conveyed by the text of the provision taking into account its context in the Act and the purpose or object underlying the Act leads to a result that is manifestly absurd or is unreasonable. [36]

As part of the legislative process, a draft Bill passes through a number of stages before it becomes enacted legislation. During these stages, various documents such as an Explanatory Memorandum for the Bill, working papers, and the draft Bill itself, are created. Other reports of committees and commissions leading up to the passing of the Act may be referred to. Policy statements are made and, of course, parliamentary debates discussing the proposed law take place in Parliament. All of these are potential – but external – sources for understanding better the parliamentary intent behind the new Act. What use, if any, can be made of these materials?

Section 15AB of the *Acts Interpretation Act 1901* (Cth), sets out a non-exhaustive list of materials which courts may use to help them interpret legislation. These include:

(a) all matters not forming part of the Act that are set out in the document containing the text of the Act as printed by the Government Printer;

(b) any relevant report of a Royal Commission, Law Reform Commission, committee of inquiry or other similar body that was laid before either House of the Parliament before the time when the provision was enacted;

(c) any relevant report of a committee of the Parliament or of either House of the Parliament that was made to the Parliament or that House of the Parliament before the time when the provision was enacted;

(d) any treaty or other international agreement that is referred to in the Act;

(e) any explanatory memorandum relating to the Bill containing the provision, or any other relevant document, that was laid before, or furnished to the members of, either House of the Parliament by a Minister before the time when the provision was enacted;

(f) the speech made to a House of the Parliament by a Minister on the occasion of the moving by that Minister of a motion that the Bill containing the provision be read a second time in that House;

(g) any document (whether or not a document to which a preceding paragraph applies) that is declared by the Act to be a relevant document for the purposes of this section; and

(h) any relevant material in the Journals of the Senate, in the Votes and Proceedings of the House of Representatives or in any official record of debates in the Parliament or either House of the Parliament. [37]

However, extrinsic materials cannot be substituted for the text of the statute. The fundamental rule of statutory interpretation has not changed. The meaning of an Act is construed from reading the words of the Act as a whole and

---

36   *Acts Interpretation Act 1901* (Cth), s 15AB(1).
37   See also *Acts Interpretation Act 1954* (Qld), s 14B.

the fundamental object of statutory construction in every case is to ascertain the legislative intention by reference to the language of the instrument viewed as a whole. In performing this task the courts look to the operation of the statute according to its terms and to legitimate aids of construction...[38]

Other statutes of relevance

[3.230] Where similar legislation deals with the same subject matter (even when it is from another jurisdiction) then those Acts may be consulted. For example, the *Trade Descriptions Act 1968* (UK) contained provisions of similar effect to Chapter 3 of the *Australian Consumer Law*. In the case of *British Airways Board v Taylor*[39] the House of Lords had to consider the effect of a statement on the persons who were likely to read that advertisement. They said:

> indeed it is an essential feature of the Act that, when it had to be considered whether descriptions or statements are misleading, it is the meaning which they are likely to bear to the person or persons to whom they are addressed that matters, and not the meaning which they might, on analysis, bear to a trained legal mind.

Similar observations have been made by Australian courts in interpreting domestic legislation.[40] The *Australian Consumer Law* forms part of a consumer protection legislative scheme which involves all States and Territories. In those circumstances, it is usually possible to refer to any of the Acts within the scheme in order to assist in the interpretation of a particular Act.

Doctrine of precedent

[3.235] As has been illustrated throughout this chapter, cases are also a source of judicial interpretation of provisions of an Act. See Chapter 2 [2.105]ff.

OVERALL APPROACH TO STATUTORY INTERPRETATION

[3.240] The best approach to statutory interpretation is to:
- read the Act as a whole;
- determine the legislative intent; and
- identify the target audience.

Read the Act as a Whole

[3.245] In one travel agency case,[41] the Administrative Review Tribunal demonstrated the overall approach to statutory interpretation as follows:

> This is an application to review the decision of the Travel Agents Licensing Authority. That Authority was established by the *Travel Agents Act 1986*, which came into force on 1 February, 1987
> ...The long title of the Act states that its purpose "is to provide for the licensing of travel agents and the regulation of their operation". It is an important piece of consumer legislation. In the words of the Minister for Consumer Affairs in his Second Reading Speech it is based

---

38 *Cooper Brooks v FCT* (1981) ALR 151 at 169-170.
39 *British Airways Board v Taylor* [1976] WLR 13 at 18.
40 See [3.250] below.
41 *Re No ATPR 41-051 2 Janminga Pty Ltd v Travel Agents Licensing Authority* (1991) 3 VAR 200 at 201.

upon the recognition "that the incompetence or dishonesty of a travel agent can destroy a trip for which ordinary people have saved for a long time and which they may never have the chance to repeat" and that "in the past, agency failures have caused consumers to lose hundreds of dollars, mostly with no chance of recovering their money." (*Hansard*, 27 March 1986)

Legislative Intent

[3.250] Courts frequently look at Parliamentary Debates (*Hansard*) and other parliamentary papers to see the problem with which Parliament is trying to deal. As Mason J pointed out in *Wacando v Commonwealth*:[42]

> there is a case for treating the Minister's statement, particularly when it is not contested, as cogent evidence of the mischief aimed at.

For example, in his second reading speech on the *Trade Practices Amendment (Australian Consumer Law) Bill* in 2009, the then Minister for Small Business, Independent Contractors and the Service Economy, Dr Craig Emerson, noted that

> In accordance with the intergovernmental agreement, the Australian Consumer Law incorporates the current consumer protection and unconscionable conduct provisions of the *Trade Practices Act*. It creates national laws for consumer product safety and for statutory consumer guarantees, to reform and replace existing Commonwealth, State and Territory laws.
> The Australian Consumer Law enhances the consumer provisions of the Trade Practices Act by drawing on existing legislative approaches to these matters in the states and territories.[43]

Those consumer protections are now provided by Chapters 2 and 3 of the *Australian Consumer Law*. In *Trade Practices Commission v Autoways Pty Ltd*,[44] Pincus J explained that the legislative policy behind such consumer protection legislation is to cause advertisers to tell the whole story:

> This is likely to be of assistance, particularly to the less sophisticated buyers, in determining whether a purchase is desirable, and also in comparing the desirability of one product against that of another.[45]

Target Audience

[3.255] It is always necessary to identify the particular class of persons to whom the legislation is addressed. For example, retail advertisements are now regulated by the *Australian Consumer Law* and complementary State legislation, but who is the target audience? The court said in *Taco Co of Australia v Taco Bell Pty Ltd*[46] that it includes "the astute and the gullible, the intelligent and the not so intelligent, the well educated as well as the poorly educated, men and women of all ages pursuing a variety of vocations".

The court then looks at the effect of the advertisement on an average member of that class of persons who are likely to read and consider the advertisement.

---

42 *Wacando v Commonwealth* (1981) 148 CLR 1.
43 House of Representatives, *Hansard*, 2009-06-24/0078.
44 *Trade Practices Commission v Autoways Pty Ltd* (1990) ATPR 41-051.
45 This observation was made in reference to Part V of the *Trade Practices Act 1974* (Cth) which is similar to *Australian Consumer Law*, Chapter 3.
46 *Taco Co of Australia v Taco Bell Pty Ltd* (1982) 42 ALR 177.

DELEGATED LEGISLATION

[3.260] Sometimes referred to as subordinate legislation,[47] delegated legislation is law which is made by a body or person to whom Parliament has, by statute,[48] delegated law-making authority. Most often this is the Minister whose department has administrative responsibility for the Act. For example, *Trade Practices Amendment (Australian Consumer Law) Act (No 2) 2010* (Cth), Schedule 5 reads in part as follows:

(1) The Commission may, by resolution, delegate

  (a) any of its functions and powers under or in relation to Parts VI and XI and the Australian Consumer Law; and

  (b) any of its powers under Part XII that relate to those Parts or the Australian Consumer Law;

  to a staff member of the Australian Securities and Investments Commission within the meaning of section 5 of the *Australian Securities and Investments Commission Act 2001*.

Pursuant to the *Acts Interpretation Act 1901* (Cth), s 46 all regulations and other legislative instruments which includes delegated laws or quasi legislation must be published in the *Government Gazette*. Nevertheless, because delegated legislation is not made directly by Parliament, and, therefore not subject to the same scrutiny that other legislation must endure, there is a commonly held view in the community that it is somehow "less democratic".

The alternative point of view is that if Parliaments did not have power to delegate law-making authority, the democratic processes would slow down considerably because:

- first, it saves parliamentary time and enables the decision makers to respond to changing circumstances in society more quickly than Parliament could.

- secondly, delegated legislators must act within the terms and for the purposes prescribed by the parent Act or their regulations will be declared ultra vires (beyond power). In fact, parliamentary committees are established to scrutinise delegated legislation after it is made.[49]

- thirdly, Parliament does not always have the particular technical expertise required to deal with detailed or intricate subject matters and so delegating the task to an expert body is the only practical solution.

Now try the statutory interpretation exercises based on sections of the *Australian Consumer Law* extracted below.

Chapter 1: Introduction
2. Definitions
4.(1) In this Schedule,
"goods" includes –
(a) ships, aircraft and other vehicles; and

---

47 Other terms include by-laws, orders in council, ordinances, regulations, rules.
48 This is often referred to as the parent, enabling, empowering or delegating Act.
49 See *Legislative Instruments Act 2003* (Cth), s 3:
  (1) The object of this Act is to provide a comprehensive regime for the management of Commonwealth legislative instruments by: ...
    (e) establishing improved mechanisms for Parliamentary scrutiny of legislative instruments; and
    (f) establishing mechanisms to ensure that legislative instruments are periodically reviewed and, if they no longer have a continuing purpose, repealed.

(b) animals, including fish; and

(c) minerals, trees and crops, whether on, under or attached to land or not; and

(d) gas and electricity; and

(e) computer software; and

(f) second-hand goods; and

(g) any component part of, or accessory to, goods.

"services" includes:

(a) any rights (including rights in relation to, and interests in, real or personal property), benefits, privileges or facilities that are, or are to be, provided, granted or conferred in trade or commerce, and

(b) without limiting paragraph (a), the rights, benefits, privileges or facilities that are, or are to be, provided, granted or conferred under:

  (i) a contract for or in relation to the performance of work (including work of a professional nature), whether with or without the supply of goods; or

  (ii) a contract for or in relation to the provision of, or the use or enjoyment of facilities for, amusement, entertainment, recreation or instruction; or

  (iii) a contract for or in relation to the conferring of rights, benefits or privileges for which remuneration is payable in the form of a royalty, tribute, levy or similar exaction; or

  (iv) a contract of insurance; or

  (v) a contract between a banker and a customer of the banker entered into in the course of the carrying on by the banker of the business of banking; or

  (vi) any contract for or in relation to the lending of money;

but does not include rights or benefits being the supply of goods or the performance of work under a contract of service.

Chapter 3: Specific Protections

Part 3 – 1 Unfair practices

Division 1 – False and misleading representations etc

32 **Offering Rebates, gifts prizes etc**

(1) A person must not, in trade or commerce, offer any rebate, gift, prize or other free item with the intention of not providing it, or of not providing it as offered, in connection with:

  (a) the supply or possible supply of goods or services; or

  (b) the promotion by any means of the supply or use of goods or services; or

  (c) the sale or grant, or the possible sale or grant, of an interest in land; or

  (d) the promotion by any means of the sale or grant of an interest in land.

35. Bait Advertising

(1) A person must not, in trade or commerce, advertise goods or services for supply at a specified price if:

  (a) there are reasonable grounds for believing that the person will not be able to offer for supply those goods or services at that price for a period that is, and in quantities that are, reasonable, having regard to:

    (i) the nature of the market in which the person carries on business; and

    (ii) the nature of the advertisement; and

  (b) the person is aware or ought reasonably to be aware of those grounds.

36 Wrongly accepting payment

(1) A person must not, in trade or commerce, accept payment or other consideration for goods or services if, at the time of the acceptance, the person intends not to supply the goods or services.

(2) A person must not, in trade or commerce, accept payment or other consideration for goods or services if, at the time of the acceptance, the person intends to supply goods or services materially different from the goods or services in respect of which the payment or other consideration is accepted.

(3) A person must not, in trade or commerce, accept payment or other consideration for goods or services if, at the time of the acceptance:

   (a) there are reasonable grounds for believing that the person will not be able to supply the goods or services:

      (i) within the period specified by or on behalf of the person at or before the time the payment or other consideration was accepted; or

      (ii) if no period is specified at or before that time–within a reasonable time; and

   (b) the person is aware or ought reasonably to be aware of those grounds.

Division 4 - Pricing
48. Single Price to be specified in certain circumstances

(1) A person must not, in trade or commerce, in connection with:

   (a) the supply, or possible supply, to another person of goods or services of a kind ordinarily acquired for personal, domestic or household use or consumption; or

   (b) the promotion by any means of the supply to another person, or of the use by another person, of goods or services of a kind ordinarily acquired for personal, domestic or household use or consumption;

make a representation with respect to an amount that, if paid, would constitute a part of the consideration for the supply of the goods or services unless the person also specifies, in a prominent way and as a single figure, the single price for the goods or services.

Note: A pecuniary penalty may be imposed for a contravention of any of these ssctions.

Chapter 4: Offences
Part 4-6 Defences
207 Reasonable mistake of fact
208 Act or default of another person etc.
209 Publication of advertisements in the ordinary course of business
210 Supplying goods acquired for the purpose of re-supply
211 Supplying services acquired for the purpose of re-supply

Chapter 5: Enforcement and remedies
Part 5 – 2 Remedies
Division 3–Damages
236 Actions for damages

(1) If:

   (a) a person (the *claimant*) suffers loss or damage because of the conduct of another person; and

   (b) the conduct contravened a provision of Chapter 2 or 3;

the claimant may recover the amount of the loss or damage by action against that other person, or against any person involved in the contravention.

(2) An action under subsection (1) may be commenced at any time within 6 years after the day on which the cause of action that relates to the conduct accrued.

Exercise

A sprat to catch a mackerel

Kwikbucks Pty Ltd trading as "*Beachfront Holiday Resort*":

(1). has noticed a slowdown in its forward bookings. To boost its sales along, the resort manager, Bob Brown, has placed the following advertisement in the local newspaper:

A sprat to catch a mackerel cont.

> Stay for 7 nights and you get one night free!

Harry and Sally are interested in taking up the offer, especially as the nightly rates at *Beachfront Holiday Resort* are usually well beyond their budget. However, upon checking out, they are given an invoice for the whole 7 nights. When they queried the bill expecting one night free, the manager explained that they had misunderstood the promotion and that they would have to stay an extra night in order to take advantage of the offer.

(2) provides the following information on the Resort's official website:

> Enjoy peace and relaxation in the serenity of your own seaside chalet interrupted only by the gentle lapping of the waves against the sand. Hurry and book now so you don't miss out!

The reality is that there is only one "beachside chalet" that remotely fits this description and it is presently disposed as the water sports activity centre. However, management surveys conducted informally with guests demonstrates that the statement attracts a lot of enquiry. Of course, management's response is always that the "beachside chalet" is already booked but that other accommodation of similar or better standard is available.

(3) has distributed an e-flyer to all travel agencies marketing its Resort which announces:

> Hot summer specials on all accommodation packages. For the low, low price of $550 guests can stay in 5 star luxury and then pay for their holiday later in one of Australia's finest resorts. Offer closes soon.

In fact, company policy relating to the *Beachside Holiday Resort* clearly states that:

(a) rooms are let for a minimum of 2 nights; and

(b) the price of a standard room for two people is $550.00 plus GST;

(c) the six deluxe suites (normally $850 per night) are not to be offered in accommodation packages; and

(d) staff are required to obtain a credit card imprint from guests on arrival.

In each of these cases, has Kwikbucks Pty Ltd trading as "*Beachfront Holiday Resort*", or any other person, committed an offence and, if so, under which provisions of the *Australian Consumer Law*?

(i) What defences are available in case of an alleged offence?

(ii) What penalties or damages may be available to the courts or consumers in the event of a successful prosecution?

Give your reasons, referring to the various sources of statutory interpretation available to the court in each case.

CHAPTER 4

Contract

[4.05] CHARACTERISTICS OF A CONTRACT		64
[4.05]	Definition	64
[4.10]	Sources of Contract Law	64
[4.15]	Types of Contracts	65
[4.20]	Formal or simple contracts	65
[4.30]	Unilateral or bilateral contracts	66
[4.40] FORMATION OF A CONTRACT		66
[4.45]	Offer	66
[4.50]	Offers to the world at large	67
[4.55]	*Carlill v Carbolic Smoke Ball Co*	67
[4.60]	Offers and invitations to treat	68
[4.65]	*Pharmaceutical Society of Great Britain v Boots Cash Chemists*	68
[4.70]	Cross offers, counter offers and mere supply of information	69
[4.75]	Termination of offers	69
[4.80]	Acceptance	70
[4.85]	Communication of acceptance	70
[4.110]	Unqualified acceptance	72
[4.115]	Revocation of acceptance	73
[4.120]	Consideration	73
[4.125]	Definition	73
[4.130]	Principles	73
[4.145]	Intention to Create Legal Relations	74
[4.150]	Domestic and social agreements	75
[4.155]	Commercial agreements	75
[4.165] TERMS OF A CONTRACT		76
[4.170]	Representations	76
[4.175]	Statute	76
[4.180]	Representations and terms	76
[4.185]	*Dick Bentley Productions v Harold Smith (Motors)*	77
[4.190]	Express or Implied Terms	77
[4.195]	Express terms	77
[4.210]	Implied terms	78
[4.225]	Exclusion Clauses	79
[4.230]	Previous dealings	80
[4.235]	*Balmain New Ferry Co Ltd v Robertson*	80
[4.240]	Reasonable notice – the ticket cases	80
[4.260]	*Parker v South Eastern Railway Co*	81
[4.265]	*Thornton v Shoe Lane Parking Ltd*	82
[4.280]	Factors affecting validity	82
[4.305]	Misrepresentation	83
[4.310]	Innocent misrepresentation	84
[4.315]	Fraudulent misrepresentation	84
[4.320]	Negligent misrepresentation	84
[4.340]	Minors	85
[4.355]	Mentally ill persons	86

63

	[4.360]	Mistake and Frustration	86
	[4.365]	Unilateral mistake	87
	[4.375]	Frustration	87
	[4.380]	Duress, undue influence, unconscionability	87
	[4.385]	Equity and unconscionability	88
	[4.390]	Statute	88
	[4.395]	Privity of Contract	88
[4.400]	REMEDIES FOR BREACH OF CONTRACT		90
	[4.405]	Rescission	90
	[4.410]	Restitution	90
	[4.415]	Specific Performance	90
	[4.420]	Injunction	91
	[4.425]	Damages	91

CHARACTERISTICS OF A CONTRACT

Definition

[4.05] A contract is an agreement or a bargain made between two or more persons which creates obligations that are enforceable at law. In everyday language, the term "contract" is used to refer to both:

- the agreement of the parties; and (if there is one)
- the document which expresses that agreement;

although strictly speaking, it is the agreement of the parties which is the contract.

However, the existence of a contract does not necessarily mean that it is enforceable. For example, contracts for the sale of land will generally not be enforceable unless they are also in writing and signed.[1]

Sources of Contract Law

[4.10] There are three main sources of contract law. They are:

- case law;
- statute;
- the agreement between the parties.

The primary source of contract law is case law. In addition, contract law has been greatly modified by the operation of a number of statutes, for example the *Australian Consumer Law*[2] and the various State *Sale of Goods* Acts.[3] These statutes mark the trend away from freedom of contract and "buyer beware" towards legislative protection of consumers and others in weaker bargaining positions. See further Chapter 9, [9.20].

---

[1] This applies under the old Statute of Frauds and current equivalents such as s 11 of the *Property Law Act 1974* (Qld) which states in s 11(1)(a) that: "no interest in land can be created or disposed of except by writing signed by the person creating or conveying the same, or by the person's agent lawfully authorised in writing, or by will, or by operation of law".

[2] *Competition and Consumer Act 2010* (Cth), Schedule 2.

[3] *Sale of Goods Act 1923* (NSW); *Sale of Goods (Vienna Convention) Act 1987* (Vic); *Sale of Goods Act 1896* (Qld); *Sale of Goods Act 1895* (WA); *Sale of Goods Act 1895* (SA); *Sale of Goods Act 1896* (Tas); *Sale of Goods Act 1954* (ACT).

The other source of contract law is the agreement itself. Ideally this should cover the rights and liabilities of the parties in all likely circumstances. Unfortunately, parties do not always agree in detail on what is to happen in particular circumstances. When things go wrong, the dispute may be settled by:

- direct or facilitated negotiation between the parties; or
- arbitration, if there is provision for it in the contract; or
- litigation, if all else fails.

See Chapter 10 for further discussion of these issues.

Types of Contracts

[4.15] In the commercial world, there are many different types of contracts, for example insurance contracts, contracts for sale of goods or services and contracts for sale of land. There are several ways of categorising contracts depending upon the manner in which they have come into existence. This section examines the distinction between contracts described as:

- formal or simple; and
- unilateral or bilateral.

Formal or simple contracts

Formal contracts

[4.20] These agreements are in writing contained in a deed often referred to as a contract under seal. They must be "signed, sealed and delivered" by the party or parties to be bound. Some deeds must be witnessed by an independent person or a Justice of the Peace or authenticated by a Notary Public. The degree of formality is greater than that required for creating simple contracts.

Simple contracts

[4.25] Simple contracts require little formality. They may be:

- oral contracts;
- written contracts; or
- partly oral and partly written contracts.

The difference between formal and simple contracts is, whereas a formal contract is enforceable if all the formal requirements have been satisfied, a simple contract is enforceable only if something of value, called "consideration", has been exchanged between the parties to the agreement. This concept is explained further in [4.115] and following.

Unilateral or bilateral contracts

Unilateral contracts

[4.30] In unilateral agreements only one party, the promisor, is obliged to do anything. The promisor promises something in exchange for the doing of a specified act. The unusual feature of such an agreement is that the promise is made by one promisor, usually to the world at large. [4]

For example, if a person loses something and places an advertisement in the paper promising a reward of $100 to whomsoever finds it, a unilateral contract is formed between that person and the finder of the lost property provided that the finder saw the advertisement first and then acted upon it.

Bilateral contracts

[4.35] In bilateral agreements, there are two promisors and both parties are obliged to do something. In other words, there is a promise in exchange for a promise.

If, in the previous example, the person promised to pay the $100 to a particular person if they agreed to endeavour to find the lost property during the period of one week, a bilateral contract is formed between those two parties, that is, a promise of $100 in exchange for a promise to try and find the lost property.

Multilateral contracts are simply those contracts which involve more than two parties, such as a partnership agreement or an international convention.

FORMATION OF A CONTRACT

[4.40] The key elements of a contract are:
- offer;
- acceptance;
- consideration; and
- intention to be legally bound.

In simple terms:

$$\text{Agreement (offer and acceptance) + intention + consideration = CONTRACT}$$

Offer

[4.45] An agreement is the meeting of two minds or a consensus ad idem. This is the concept of offer and acceptance. An offer may be defined as an "indication by one person to another of his willingness to enter into a contract with him on certain terms". [5] It has also been described as a definite promise. [6] An offer indicates willingness by the offeror to be bound without further negotiation. A statement amounts to an offer if the person to whom it is addressed reasonably interprets it as such. The test is objective.

---

4   See *Carlill v Carbolic Smoke Ball Co* (1893) 1 QB 256 in [4.55].
5   J W Carter and D J Harland, *Contract Law in Australia* (4th ed, Butterworths, Sydney, 2002).
6   W R Anson, *Anson's Law of Contract* (27th ed, Clarendon Press, Oxford, 1998).

Offers to the world at large

[4.50] Offers can be made to:

- one person;
- a class of persons; or
- the world at large.

It is up to the offeror to decide the persons to whom the offer will be made. Only those persons to whom the offer is addressed may accept. Therefore, even when offers are made to the world at large, they are capable of acceptance only by the person (or persons) who complies with the terms of the offer. The classic case which highlights this principle is *Carlill v Carbolic Smoke Ball Co*.

Carlill v Carbolic Smoke Ball Co

[4.55] *Carlill v Carbolic Smoke Ball Co* (1893) 1 QB 256

Facts: The Carbolic Smoke Ball Co ("the company") placed an advertisement in a London newspaper claiming that its product, the Carbolic Smoke Ball, could cure influenza. The company offered £100 if the product did not have the desired effect. To show its good faith in the matter, the company declared that it had deposited £1,000 with its bankers. Mrs Carlill read the advertisement and decided to put the claim to the test. She bought the product and used it in the manner prescribed in the advertisement. She did not recover from influenza as promised so she advised the company of the failure of its product and claimed the £100 reward. The company refused to pay Mrs Carlill so she commenced legal proceedings against the company for breach of contract.

Mrs Carlill argued that the advertisement constituted an offer which she had accepted by buying the product. This was her "consideration" for the contract. When the company refused to pay the £100, it had breached its promise. The company claimed, on the other hand, that the advertisement did not amount to an offer because there was no intention on its part to be bound without further

Carlill v Carbolic Smoke Ball Co cont.

negotiation. The court had to decide whether it was possible for the company to make an offer to the world at large and, if so, whether the offer was capable of being accepted by an individual who did not communicate her intention to accept it.

Decision: The English Court of Appeal held that there was a contract and Mrs Carlill was entitled to recover the £100. Even where an offer is made to the public at large, provided it is capable of being accepted by a specific individual, it will be binding on the offeror.

This case is authority for the principle that once there is an offer, supported by an intention to create legal relations, acceptance and consideration, a contract is made. These other elements of a contract are discussed below.

Offers and invitations to treat

[4.60] An invitation to treat is an invitation to others to make offers. It does not indicate willingness on the part of the person who makes the invitation to treat to enter into any contractual obligations.

Sometimes it is difficult to decide whether a statement is an offer or an invitation to treat. It really depends on whether the person making the statement intends to make a binding offer or not. Again, this is an objective test. The distinction between the two was clearly defined in the celebrated case of *Pharmaceutical Society of Great Britain v Boots Cash Chemists (Southern) Ltd*.[7]

Pharmaceutical Society of Great Britain v Boots Cash Chemists

[4.65] *Pharmaceutical Society of Great Britain v Boots Cash Chemists (Southern) Ltd* [1953] 1 QB 401

Facts: The *Pharmacy Poisons Act 1933* (UK) prohibited the sale of certain drugs unless sold "under the supervision of a registered pharmacist". Boots Cash Chemists had set up their pharmacies as supermarkets with checkout operators near the front door. They were prosecuted under the Act. The prosecution alleged that putting the goods on the shelves with prices marked was an offer and that the customer accepted the offer by taking the goods from the shelf. The contract of sale was formed at this point and thus the sale of the prohibited drugs took place without supervision.

Decision: The English Court of Appeal rejected this approach and held that the display of goods on the shelves, even with prices marked, was an invitation to treat and not an offer. The offer took place when the customer selected the goods and expressed a desire to buy them, normally by taking them to the cash register. The shopkeeper could then accept the offer or reject it. A registered pharmacist was present at the cash register and therefore the sale took place under his or her supervision.

Besides displays of goods in shops, other examples of invitations to treat include:
- advertisements and catalogues;
- restaurant menus; and
- travel brochures.

The philosophy underlying the distinction is quite simple. If the situation were otherwise, a restaurant proprietor might be regarded as making an offer by displaying a menu with marked

---

7   *Pharmaceutical Society of Great Britain v Boots Cash Chemists (Southern) Ltd* [1953] 1 QB 401.

prices. If the number of orders (that is, binding acceptances) for lobster thermidor, for example, exceeded the total stock for the day, he or she would not be able to actually perform the contract if more lobsters could not be procured. This would make the proprietor liable for breach of contract to each customer whose order could not be filled – an absurd result.

However, in the case of advertisements there is certainly no definite rule, and sometimes an advertisement is capable of taking effect as an offer, as *Carlill v Carbolic Smoke Ball Co* illustrates. If the statement contained in the advertisement is "mere puff", an obvious advertising gimmick designed simply to induce a contract but not intended to form part of the contractual obligation, then the advertiser may not be expected to honour it.[8] As a precaution, an advertiser/seller should avoid the problem by stating that stock is limited or, in the case of a poster displayed, by removing the poster altogether when the stock is exhausted.

Cross offers, counter offers and mere supply of information

[4.70] When two parties communicate their offers to one another simultaneously and in substantially similar terms, there are two offers (cross offers) but no acceptances and therefore no agreement. Similarly, a response supplying information to an enquiry regarding the price of property does not amount to an offer.[9]

A counter offer, which is more common, occurs when one party (the offeree) rejects the former offer made by the offeror and substitutes a new offer for it.[10] Unless this new offer is accepted by the former offeror, there is no agreement and no contract.

Termination of offers

[4.75] Offers do not usually remain open indefinitely but often impose a time limit for acceptance. Alternatively, if no time limit is set, then once a reasonable time for acceptance has expired, the offer may lapse.

Naturally, the offeror may revoke or withdraw the offer at any time before acceptance,[11] but the rule is that revocation of an offer is ineffective until communicated to the offeree.[12]

---

8   Subject to the *Australian Consumer Law*, s 18 Misleading or deceptive conduct and following. See Chapter 9.
9   See *Harvey v Facey* [1893] AC 552. *Facts:* the plaintiff sent a telegram to the defendant (the vendor of a farm) asking "Will you sell us Bumper Hall Pen? [a farm] Telegraph lowest cash price." The vendor replied by telegram, stating "Lowest cash price for Bumper Hall Pen £900". *Held:* The statement was not an offer. The mere statement of the lowest price the vendor would accept contained no implied promise to sell at that price.
10 See *Hyde v Wrench* (1840) 49 ER 132. *Facts:* The defendant offered to sell his farm for £1000. The plaintiff replied, offering £950 which the defendant refused. The plaintiff then agreed to pay £1000. The defendant, though he had not withdrawn his offer at that stage, neither assented to nor rejected the proposal but subsequently refused to go through with the sale. The plaintiff sued. *Held:* The plaintiff had made a counter offer which effectively rejected the defendant's original offer which ceased to exist at that point. Consequently when the plaintiff agreed to pay the asked price the agreement was not an acceptance of the defendant's now defunct offer to sell, but a fresh offer to buy. As the offer was never accepted, there was no contract.
11 See *Payne v Cave* (1789) 100 ER 502. *Facts:* The defendant bid £40 for goods being auctioned, but before they were knocked down to him, he withdrew the bid. *Held:* A bid is merely an offer and it may be revoked at any time prior to acceptance. Acceptance at auction occurs on the fall of the hammer and as the defendant had withdrawn his bid before that happened, the offer had terminated and the auctioneer could not accept it.
12 The postal rule (see [4.100]) does not apply to revocation and revocation by post will be ineffective until it actually reaches the offeree: *Byrne v Tienhoven* (1880) 5 CPD 344.

However, if the offeree knows, either directly from the offeror or indirectly through a third party, that the offer has been revoked, he or she cannot accept it.[13] Of course, once the offer has been accepted it is irrevocable.

Acceptance

[4.80] Acceptance of an offer may be by words or conduct. It must be:

- communicated to the offeror; and
- an unqualified acceptance of the terms of the offer.

Of course, only those persons to whom the offer is made may accept it. In the case of unilateral contracts or offers made to the world at large, only those persons who have the offer in mind when they perform the act specified will be deemed to have accepted the offer.

Communication of acceptance

[4.85] The general rule is that an acceptance has no effect until it is communicated to the offeror. The offeree or her or his agent[14] may communicate their acceptance of the offer by either words or action. Mental assent coupled with silence is not enough.

On the other hand, exceptions to the rule regarding communication abound including:

- waiver of communication;
- previous dealings; and
- acceptance by post.

Waiver of communication

[4.90] An offeror may waive her or his right to communication of acceptance. This was illustrated in *Carlill v Carbolic Smoke Ball Co*[15] and in other unilateral contracts such as the "reward" cases, where the offeror offers to pay money for the return of lost property. In other words, the offeror stipulates that the method of acceptance is the performance of the terms of the offer in the prescribed manner, that is, actions rather than words.

Although the offeror may waive his or her rights to communication of acceptance, he or she cannot impose contractual liability on the offeree by insisting that silence will be taken as acceptance of the offer.[16] Consumer protection legislation also prevents a failure to reply or silence from satisfying the requirements of acceptance.[17]

Previous course of dealings

[4.95] If the parties have had a course of business dealings over a period of time based on the terms contained in an agreement which has never been signed by the offeree, the agreement is

---

13   *Dickenson v Dodds* (1876) 2 Ch D 463.
14   *Powell v Lee* (1908) 99 LT 284.
15   *Carlill v Carbolic Smoke Ball Co* (1893) 1 QB 256.
16   See *Felthouse v Bindley* (1862) 142 ER 1037 where the offeror stated: "If I hear no more about him, I consider the horse mine at that price." There was no contract.
17   See ss 40 and 41 of the *Australian Consumer Law* which provide that a person in trade or commerce may not assert a right to payment from another person for unsolicited goods unless the person has reason to believe it has a right to payment. If a recipient receives unordered goods, those goods shall upon the expiration of the relevant period (either one or three months) become the property of the recipient and that the recipient shall not be liable for damage to the goods other than wilful damage caused within the relevant period. For further examples, see *Unordered Goods and Services Act 1973* (Tas), ss 6 and 7.

nevertheless binding because the parties have conducted their dealings as if they were bound by it. The conduct of the parties is the basis of acceptance.

McHugh J A said in the case of *Empirnall Holdings v Machon Paull*:[18]

> where an offeree with a reasonable opportunity to reject the offer of goods or services takes the benefit of them under circumstances which indicate that they were to be paid for in accordance with the offer, it is open to the tribunal of fact to hold that the offer was accepted according to its terms.

The postal rule

[4.100] Acceptance by post is effective communication when the post or telegraph is used as the means of communicating acceptance. The acceptance is complete when the letter is posted or the telegram (now obsolete in Australia) is sent, even if it is never actually received! This is known as the postal rule.[19]

The rule evolved during a time when the post was the most likely mode of communication. It does not apply to instantaneous modes of communication (telephone, telex,[20] facsimile machine,[21] and so on), where actual receipt of the communication is required. Nevertheless the postal rule remains an archaic exception to the general rule regarding effective communication. To narrow the scope and effect of the rule, the courts have developed a number of exceptions to it. For example:

- the postal rule applies only if it is clear that it was within the contemplation of the parties that, according to the ordinary usages of mankind, the post would be used as a means of communicating the acceptance of an offer (or that the post was prescribed by the offeror as the method of communication of acceptance);[22]
- the offeror may exclude the postal rule and insist that even if the post is used as the method of communication, he or she requires actual notification of acceptance before the contract will be complete;[23]
- actual communication is to be regarded as essential to the conclusion of any agreement where the parties' dealings are protracted and contentious.[24]

Electronic Communication

[4.105] Electronic mail or email is transmitted via the internet *"where it may bounce from a minimum of one computer to an infinite number before reaching the ISP of the receiver. The message will then be retrieved by the recipient by logging into their ISP and downloading the message"*.[25] This type of communication is not just an electronic version of the postal

---

18 *Empirnall Holdings v Machon Paull* (1966) 14 NSWLR 523 at 535.
19 *Adams v Lindsell* (1818) 106 ER 250.
20 *Entores Ltd v Miles Far East Corporation* [1955] 2 QB 327.
21 *Brinkibon Ltd v Stahag Stahl und Stahlwarenhandels-Gesellschaft mbH* [1983] 2 AC 34.
22 *Henthorn v Fraser* (1892) 2 Ch 27.
23 *Holwell Securities Ltd v Hughes* [1974] 1 WLR 155 (CA), where the court held than an agreement which provided that an option "shall be exercised by notice in writing to the defendant at any time within 6 months from the date of the agreement" indicated that acceptance must actually be communicated to the offeror. See also *Bowman v Durham Holdings Pty Ltd* (1973) 47 ALJR 606.
24 *Tallerman and Co Pty Ltd v Nathan's Merchandise (Vic) Pty Ltd* (1957) 98 CLR 93.
25 S Christensen, "Formation of Contracts by Email – Is it Just the Same as the Post?" (2001) QUT Law and Justice Journal 3 at para 6.24.

system.[26] It is yet another mode of modern communication which should be excepted from the application of the postal rule although no Australian court has yet definitively ruled on this point.

In March 2000, the *Electronic Transactions Act 1999* (Cth) became law. It basically follows the UNCITRAL Model Law on Electronic Commerce and is part of a proposed national uniform scheme for all States and Territories as well.[27] Its objects include:

- the removal of legal obstacles to conducting e-commerce and electronic transactions in general; and
- default rules for time and place of sending and receipt.

For example, parties to an electronic communication must stipulate the information system for receipt of correspondence otherwise receipt will occur at "the time when it comes to the attention of the addressee".[28] In other words, this would be when the recipient opens the mailbox on their computer.

Unqualified acceptance

[4.110] Since an offer is an expression of willingness to contract on certain terms, acceptance of the offer must be an unqualified acceptance of the terms stated in the offer without any deletions, additions or conditions. The last section highlighted the fact that the offeror may prescribe both the manner and form of acceptance.[29]

Counter offers,[30] cross offers[31] and conditional acceptances[32] do not constitute good acceptance. On the other hand, clauses such as "subject to finance" or "subject to satisfactory approval by the surveyor" are called conditions (precedent or subsequent) to the performance of the contract. In these cases, there is a binding agreement but both parties anticipate that if the conditions stipulated are not satisfied, then the contract will be void or voidable.

However in some cases it may be difficult to work out when a contract has been entered using traditional offer and acceptance analysis. Consider airline ticketing. In *MacRobertson Miller Airlines v Commissioner of Taxation (WA)*,[33] the High Court held that for stamp duty purposes a domestic airline ticket was not a contract and that the contract was not entered into until the passenger checked in or perhaps even until the passenger boarded the plane. The court was split on what the ticket actually was. Barwick CJ found the ticket to be a mere receipt, Stephen J found the ticket to be an offer and Jacobs J found the ticket to be a voucher.

---

26 S Christensen, "Formation of Contracts by Email – Is it Just the Same as the Post?" (2001) QUT Law and Justice Journal 3 at para 6.2.3.
27 To date, New South Wales, Victoria and the Australian Capital Territory.
28 *Electronic Transactions Act 1999* (Cth), s 14(4) which basically followed the UNCITRAL *Model Law on Electronic Commerce*, Article 15.
29 For example, acceptance may be the exchange of promises resulting in a bilateral contract, or a promise for an act resulting in a unilateral contract.
30 A counter offer is a rejection of the original offer so as to cause the original offer to terminate. See [4.70].
31 In *Timm v Hoffman & Co* (1873) 29 LT 271, the defendant wrote a letter to the plaintiff offering to sell iron to the plaintiff. The plaintiff, however, also wrote a letter offering to buy iron from the defendant. Their terms, however, were not identical. Therefore the court said there was no "agreement" here, that is, no offer and acceptance. This was an example of cross offers.
32 There is no such thing as a "conditional acceptance".
33 *MacRobertson Miller Airlines v Commissioner of Taxation (WA)* (1975) 133 CLR 125.

An international passenger ticket constitutes prima facie [34] (not conclusive) evidence of the entry into a contract of carriage and of its conditions, [35] whereas the contractual status of a domestic ticket remains in doubt. See Chapter 12.

Revocation of acceptance

[4.115] Just as an offer may be terminated by notice to the offeree, so too an acceptance may be revoked provided that the revocation comes to the offeror's attention before he or she receives the acceptance.

Consideration

[4.120] It has already been noted that a simple contract must be supported by consideration otherwise it will not be enforceable by the promisee. The promisee must be able to point to evidence of the fact that they have provided consideration for the other party's promise. Consideration is the price paid for the promisor's promise. The "price" may take the form of a counter promise or it may involve the doing of an act.

Definition

[4.125] Sometimes consideration is defined in terms of a bargain. For example: "An act or forbearance of one party, or the promise thereof, is the price for which the promise of the other is bought, and the promise thus given for value is enforceable". [36]

At other times it is defined in terms of a benefit and a detriment. In the *Carbolic Smoke Ball case*, Mrs Carlill put herself to the inconvenience of administering the smoke ball treatment in the prescribed manner for some weeks. The court held that this was good consideration in the circumstances. Lord Justice Bowen said:

> Any act of the plaintiff from which the defendant derives a benefit or advantage or any labour detriment or inconvenience sustained by the plaintiff provided such an act is performed or such inconvenience suffered by the plaintiff, with consent, either express or implied of the defendant is enough to create consideration. [37]

Principles

[4.130] Some rules for consideration include that it must be:

- executory or executed but not past; and
- something of value.

Consideration must be executory or executed

[4.135] Executory consideration usually arises in bilateral contracts where mutual promises have been exchanged but have yet to be performed. The making of binding promises may be regarded as consideration.

Executed consideration, on the other hand, usually arises in unilateral contracts where there is a promise in exchange for the performance of an act, for example the return of lost property for which a reward has been promised. In these cases, the immediate performance of the act is executed consideration.

---

34 That is, the onus is on the party alleging otherwise to prove the claim.
35 Article 3(2) of the *Warsaw Convention 1929*, as amended by the *Hague Protocol 1955*.
36 Per Lord Dunedin in *Dunlop v Selfridge* [1915] AC 847.
37 *Carlill v Carbolic Smoke Ball Co* (1893) 1 QB 256 at 271.

The timing of consideration is important. There is a general rule that past consideration is no consideration. In other words, if an act or promise which is relied on as constituting consideration is done or given before the promisor's promise, then the consideration is said to be past consideration. It cannot be said to be the price for the promise.[38]

Consideration must be something of value

[4.140] Consideration must be adequate and something of real value, although it need not be of an equivalent value to the promisor's promise. For example, promises made in consideration of "love and affection"[39] are not sufficient. Similarly, promises made pursuant to moral obligations on the part of the promisor are not legally binding unless supported by good consideration.[40]

However, a promise to refrain from taking legal action (that is, forbearance to sue) against another in circumstances in which the promisor genuinely believes in her or his chances of success may be good consideration provided that the original claim was reasonable and neither vexatious nor frivolous.[41]

Of course, a promise to do or refrain from doing something is generally good consideration only if the promisor does not already have an existing obligation in that respect. For example, the performance of existing contractual obligations or public duties, such as attending court under subpoena,[42] is not sufficient consideration. To constitute good consideration, the promisee must do something over and above their existing legal obligations.

Intention to Create Legal Relations

[4.145] One of the essential elements of a contract is the requirement of an intention to create legal relations. Even if other elements of a contract are present, for example offer, acceptance and consideration, but there was no intention by the parties at the relevant time to enter into legal relations, then the contract will not be enforceable at law.

In practice, it is unusual for a court to be presented with a problem about intention. This is because of the presumptions relating to:

- domestic and social agreements; and
- commercial agreements.

---

38   *Roscorla v Thomas* (1842) 3 QB 234. Consider the situation where an act looks like past consideration but is in fact executed consideration, for example, where services have been rendered without any express agreement on the price to be paid. Courts will allow "a reasonable sum" as part of the original agreement.

39   See also *White v Bluett* (1853) LJ Ex 36. *Facts*: A son alleged that his father had agreed to discharge his liability under a promissory note (that is, to let him off a debt) if the son agreed "not to bore his father" by complaining that he, the son, had not received as many advantages and benefits as his other brothers. *Held*: This promise "not to bore his father" was not good consideration for the father's promise to discharge his liability under the promissory note.

40   *Eastwood v Kenyon* [1840] 11 AD & El 348. *Facts*: Eastwood was a guardian of an infant called Miss S. He had incurred, voluntarily, considerable expense on her education and other expenses. When Miss S came of age, she promised to repay her guardian. Indeed, after her marriage, her husband also promised to repay E. However, neither of them paid E and he sued for payments. *Held*: There was only a moral obligation to perform: no legal obligation existed because their promises of repayment were not supported by consideration.

41   *Hercules Motors Pty Ltd v Schubert* (1953) 53 SR (NSW) 301.

42   *Collins v Godefroy* (1831) 109 ER 1040.

Domestic and social agreements

[4.150] There is a presumption that parties to social or domestic agreements do not intend their promises to be legally binding. It is possible to rebut this presumption by evidence to the contrary. In the absence of express words, the test which the court applies is "would reasonable people think that the agreement was intended to be legally binding?" This is an objective test.

Sometimes social arrangements occur in which family and friends who regularly purchase lottery or other competition tickets under one name agree to share the winnings if successful.[43] The courts' attitude to such arrangements is that they are legally enforceable, thus rebutting the presumption. In the New South Wales Supreme Court, Hodgson J said:

> [I] think the law should not be over-reluctant to give effect to agreements or intentions which in the event affect very large sums of money, and which are not between family members who might be expected to rely on family obligations rather than legal obligations.[44]

Commercial agreements

[4.155] There is a strong presumption that commercial agreements are to be legally binding and enforceable. Once again it may be rebutted by appropriate evidence. For example, the parties may expressly state in the agreement that it is to be binding in "honour only".

This was the case in *Rose and Frank Co v Crompton Bros Ltd* where a clause appeared in a commercial agreement to the effect that: "This document does not give rise to any legal relationship, nor is it intended by the parties that any legal consequences shall flow from this agreement."[45]

The court held that this amounted to an acceptable honour clause which rebutted the presumption in favour of a legally binding agreement. In other words, the agreement was not enforceable at law.[46]

Key features of intention to be bound

[4.160] Unless there is an intention to be legally bound:

- there is no contract; and
- a party cannot seek remedies for breach of the other party's promises.

The consequences that flow from this can sometimes be quite serious. For example, ownership of property cannot pass under a contract which never existed (void ab initio). In the absence of an express intention, therefore, the courts apply an objective test in determining whether the intention to be bound existed. To do this, they will examine the subject matter of the agreement and the surrounding discussions and negotiations that took place.

---

43 *Simpkins v Pays* [1955] 1 WLR975. *Facts*: A grandmother, granddaughter and friend regularly entered a newspaper competition under the grandmother's name. All contributed to incidental expenses and made an agreement to share winnings. Their entry was successful but the defendant refused to share the prize and her friend sued. The grandmother claimed there was no contract, merely a friendly arrangement with no legal obligation. *Held*: The agreement was enforceable. The friend (plaintiff) was contractually entitled to her share of the prize because the parties must have contemplated the legal consequences.

44 *Smith v McDonnell* (unreported, NSW Sup Ct, 30 March 1995).

45 *Rose and Frank Co v Crompton Bros Ltd* [1923] 2 KB 261.

46 Compare this honour clause with the following clause: "No court of law shall have jurisdiction over or power to adjudicate in respect of any matter arising out of this agreement or any breach thereof." Such a clause is unacceptable, as it is an attempt to oust the jurisdiction of the court.

TERMS OF A CONTRACT

[4.165] Assuming that the parties have reached agreement and a valid contract exists, the next matters to consider are the terms of that agreement and what they mean.

In determining what the parties have agreed, courts must distinguish between statements that are not enforceable, such as invitations to treat, sales talk or mere "puffs", and those that are. A further distinction must be drawn between:

- representations;
- express or implied terms of the contract;
- exclusion clauses.

These matters have been extensively modified by consumer protection legislation, which even provides remedies for mere "puffs" if they are deceptive or misleading: see Chapter 9.

Representations

[4.170] Mere representations are statements which may induce the formation of a contract but are not intended to be terms of the contract. Consequently, they are not enforceable at law. However the law confers certain rights on a party who has been induced into a contract by a false statement of fact.

Such false representations of fact may be classified as either:

- innocent misrepresentations;[47]
- negligent misrepresentations; or
- fraudulent misrepresentations.

The importance of the distinction lies in the remedies available. For example, in the case of an innocent misrepresentation the remedy is only rescission (which means treating the contract as at an end). However, in the case of fraudulent misrepresentation, the remedy is rescission and damages. The party may also sue in tort for deceit. If the representation was negligent, then not only may the party rescind the contract but they may also claim damages in tort for negligent misstatement (see Chapter 5, [5.85]).

Statute

[4.175] Under consumer protection legislation, misrepresentations – whether innocent, negligent or fraudulent – are likely to be deceptive and misleading conduct or unfair trading. This legislation provides a wide range of civil remedies, including damages and rescission, and the offender may be prosecuted and fined. See Chapter 9, [9.60]ff.

Representations and terms

[4.180] Whether an oral statement is a mere representation or a term of the contract is a question of fact to be determined objectively; for example by analysing "what would a reasonable bystander infer from the conduct of the parties?" The courts try to give effect to the parties' intention. The significance of the distinction is that, if the statement is a term of the

---

[47] For example *Oscar Chess v Williams* [1957] 1 WLR 370, in which a car was described as a "1948 Model Morris Minor" by Williams in the belief that it was true. This seemed to be confirmed by the registration book. In fact it was a 1939 model worth much less. The court held that the statement was not a binding promise but rather an innocent misrepresentation.

contract, then the breach of that term will entitle the innocent party to damages in any event, whether that party elects to rescind or proceed with the contract. The difference is illustrated by the case of *Dick Bentley Productions Ltd v Harold Smith (Motors) Ltd*.

Dick Bentley Productions v Harold Smith (Motors)

[4.185] *Dick Bentley Productions Ltd v Harold Smith (Motors) Ltd* [1965] 1 WLR 623

Facts: The plaintiff bought a motor car from the defendant. During the negotiations, the defendant said that the car had travelled only 20,000 miles since the fitting of a replacement engine and gearbox. The plaintiff paid £1850 for the car. It was later discovered that the car had travelled nearly 100,000 miles. The plaintiff sued the defendant for damages for breach of contract.

The English Court of Appeal had to decide whether the statement by the defendant was a term of the contract entitling the plaintiff to damages.

Decision: The statement made was intended to be relied upon and was in fact relied on. The defendant car dealer was in a position to know, or at least to find out, the history of the car before making the statement. The statement was therefore held to be a term of the contract. In fact, the court classified this term as a warranty. The decision is contrasted with *Oscar Chess v Williams* [48] where the facts were similar, but this time the statement was made by a customer selling a motor car to a dealer and the Court of Appeal found the statement was a mere representation because the buyer rather than the seller was the expert.

──── ଛେଉ ────

Express or Implied Terms

[4.190] Contractual terms may be either "express" or "implied". Express terms are those which the parties have expressly agreed to incorporate in their agreement. Implied terms are those which the parties have not expressly agreed upon but which may nevertheless be implied into the contract by law.

Express terms

[4.195] A contract may be:
- an oral agreement; or
- in writing; or
- partly in writing and partly oral.

The agreement may contain essential and non-essential terms.

---

48   *Oscar Chess v Williams* [1957] 1 WLR 370.

Parol evidence rule

[4.200] When the terms of a contract have been reduced to writing, the courts are very reluctant to admit into evidence oral statements made during negotiations which may contradict the terms contained in the written document. This is called the *parol (oral) evidence rule*.[49] Generally, the parties are bound by the express terms of the written document once they have signed it.[50]

Conditions and warranties

[4.205] Contractual terms are also categorised as being either:

- a warranty; or
- a condition.

Again, the relevance of the distinction rests with the remedies available for breach in either case. Conditions are essential or major terms of the contract. A breach of condition entitles the innocent party to a choice of remedies, including:

- to proceed with the contract; or
- to terminate the contract; and/or
- to sue for breach of contract.

On the other hand, a warranty is a non-essential or minor term of a contract so that the innocent party must proceed with the contract but may seek damages for breach. To illustrate the difference between the two, take the example of a flight from Sydney to Los Angeles. If the flight were redirected to Buenos Aires instead, that would probably constitute a breach of condition. However, if the same flight's departure was delayed by two hours that would more likely be a breach of warranty.

Implied terms

[4.210] The sources of implied terms include:

- common law; and
- statute.

Common law

[4.215] The courts will always try to give effect to the parties' intention without rewriting their contract for them. However, there are occasions where certain terms which have not been expressly included in the agreement may nevertheless be implied by the courts. Such implied terms must:

- be reasonable and equitable;
- be necessary to give the contract business efficacy;
- be so obvious that it goes without saying;
- be capable of clear expression;

---

49 This is often important in written contracts where the issues involve: (i) determining what the terms are; and (ii) what those terms mean.
50 But see exceptions in [4.280] and following.

- not contradict any express term of the contract.[51]

Statute

[4.220] Historically, under consumer protection legislation, there have been extensive terms and conditions implied into contracts for the sale or supply of goods and services. In the supply of goods these terms include conditions that goods will conform with description, be fit for the purpose and be of merchantable quality. In the supply of services the warranty is that the services will be supplied with all due care and skill and will be reasonably fit for the purpose.

The *Australian Consumer Law* now replaces the State and Territory Fair Trading, Sale of Goods and other legislation on implied conditions and warranties in the supply of goods and services in consumer transactions. It introduces a system of statutory guarantees which are independent of contract law. Breaches of statutory consumer guarantees are directly enforceable under the *Australian Consumer Law* rather than in contract law. Remedies, including damages,[52] are available to all consumers who are not confined by privity of contract principles, See Chapter 9, [9.290]ff.

Exclusion Clauses

[4.225] Sometimes an express term in the written document purports to exclude or limit one party's liability for breach of contract or for negligence. These exemption clauses, as they are called, may be either:

- exclusion clauses; or
- limitation clauses.

Exclusion clauses exclude liability completely and are commonly found in standard form contracts, for example, in many train, bus or ferry tickets and in dry cleaning, car parking and other similar kinds of dockets. Limitation clauses do not exclude liability entirely but purport to restrict liability to a certain monetary amount or to limit the time in which a claim may be made.

Since the consumer has no freedom to negotiate the details of these standard form contracts and may have limited choice of companies with whom to deal,[53] courts have traditionally tried to protect consumers as much as possible by adopting a strict approach to exemption clauses. First, courts require a high standard of proof that the exclusion clause is actually incorporated into the contract. Secondly, if it is a term of the contract, then courts try to construe the clause in favour of the consumer in determining whether on a true construction of the clause it is wide enough to cover the conduct complained of.

Subject to these stringent tests, courts have enforced exemption clauses in contracts where there is evidence of:

- previous dealings; or
- reasonable notice ("ticket" cases).

---

51   A statement of principle by the Privy Council in *BP Refinery (Westernport) Pty Ltd v Shire of Hastings* (1977) 52 ALJR 20.

52   *Australian Consumer Law*, Part 5-2 Remedies, Division 3, Damages.

53   For example, a consumer must travel on one of only a few domestic air carriers in Australia, all of whose air tickets contain exclusion clauses.

Previous dealings

[4.230] An exemption clause may be inferred as a term of a contract without specific reference to it because of a previous consistent course of dealings between the parties. Generally, this will be the case only if the party against whom the exclusion clause is being used actually knew from previous dealings that the party relying on the exemption clause [54] contracted only on that basis. This is an objective test and will depend on such factors as the frequency of the previous dealings and whether the affected party had been given reasonable notice of the clause so as to allow the other party to rely upon it. The classic case is *Balmain New Ferry Co Ltd v Robertson*.

Balmain New Ferry Co Ltd v Robertson

[4.235] *Balmain New Ferry Co Ltd v Robertson* (1906) 4 CLR 379

Facts: The company operated a ferry service from Circular Quay to Balmain. Fares were collected at the turnstile near the Circular Quay entrance. Robertson (who was a lawyer) paid to get through the turnstile to catch a ferry but missed it. When he attempted to leave through the turnstile, he was asked for another penny, which he refused to pay. He was restrained from going through the turnstile without paying and he sued the company for false imprisonment. In its defence, the company relied on a notice near its turnstiles which read: "Notice. A fare of one penny must be paid on entering or leaving the wharf. No exception will be made to this rule, whether the passenger has travelled by ferry or not."

Decision: The High Court held the company was not liable. The company had done all that was reasonably necessary to bring the exemption clause to Robertson's attention. He had taken frequent similar journeys with the ferry company. Whether he knew of the clause or not, he should reasonably have known of it.

Postscript: Mr Robertson appealed to the Privy Council, which confirmed the High Court's decision. [55] Although Mr Robertson was a lawyer he reputedly incurred legal expenses of £10,000 (in an argument over one penny) and this and the embarrassment of the outcome ultimately caused his ruin. This reinforces the old lawyers' saying that a lawyer who acts for himself has a fool for a client!

Reasonable notice – the "ticket" cases

[4.240] The general rule is that when a party has signed a contractual document, they are bound by the terms of that document. Thus, in the absence of any fraud or misrepresentation, if an exclusion clause is included as one of the terms, the person is bound by that clause irrespective of whether or not he or she has read or understood it. [56] It follows that in cases involving tickets or dockets containing exclusion clauses, where one party signs an acknowledgment, then the ordinary rules of contract apply.

However, in this regard it is now important to consider unconscionability at common law and under the consumer protection legislation. See Chapter 9, [9.70]ff.

---

54   That is, the *proferens*.
55   Sub nom *Robinson v Balmain New Ferry Co* [1910] AC 295.
56   See *L'Estrange v F Graucob Ltd* [1934] 2 KB 394. *Curtis v Chemical Cleaning Co* (1951) 1 KB 805 is an example of a case where one party could not rely on a signed document due to misrepresentation.

Terms displayed or delivered

[4.245] However, what if the exclusion clause is not contained in a document signed by the customer but is displayed via a sign or delivered in a ticket? The courts have held that the customer will be bound by such clauses only if they have either:

- actual notice of the existence of the term; or
- constructive notice of its existence

before they enter into the contract. Notice which is given after the making of a contract will not be effective.

Notice

[4.250] Few problems arise with actual notice because the clause is specifically brought to the party's attention. In the case of constructive notice, however, the party is not actually aware of the existence of the clause. The party relying on the clause must therefore establish that reasonable notice has been given to the customer. This is established if:

- a reasonable person would consider the document to have contractual force rather then a mere receipt or acknowledgment; [57]
- reasonable steps were taken to draw the customer's attention to it; [58]
- the notice was given prior to or at the time of the contract. [59]

Reasonable steps

[4.255] This may be done by delivering the document containing the clause to the customer or by the display of signs or notices. What will be considered "reasonable steps" is a question of fact which the following cases illustrate.

Parker v South Eastern Railway Co

[4.260] *Parker v South Eastern Railway Co* (1877) 2 CPD 416

Facts: A docket was given to the plaintiff when he deposited his luggage at a railway station cloakroom. The docket contained the words "see back" and on the back of the docket were printed a number of conditions, one of which was a clause which limited the defendant's liability for loss of any package to £10 only. The plaintiff's bag was lost and he claimed for its value of £24 10 shillings.

Decision: The court held that sufficient notice was given regarding the limiting clause and thus the defendant's liability to the plaintiff was limited to £10.

───── ೪ටಙ ─────

Compare this case with the approach in the following famous case.

---

[57] See *Causer v Browne* [1952] VLR 1. *Facts*: A dry-cleaning docket was given by the defendant to the plaintiff containing a term which said: "No responsibility is accepted for loss or injuries to articles through any cause whatsoever". *Held*: The docket could only be reasonably viewed by a customer as a voucher for the customer to produce when collecting the goods. Therefore that document could not be regarded as part of the dry-cleaning contract, thus exempting the defendant from liability for negligence.

[58] *Thornton v Shoe Lane Parking* (1971) 2 QB 163.

[59] *Olley v Marlborough Court Ltd* (1949) 1 KB 532.

Thornton v Shoe Lane Parking Ltd

[4.265] *Thornton v Shoe Lane Parking Ltd* (1971) 2 QB 163

Facts: Mr Thornton drove his car into a new automatic car park which he had not visited before. There was a notice displayed outside the car park which said "parked at owner's risk". At the entrance, Thornton was required to stop and pick up a ticket from a machine. At the bottom of the ticket there was a statement that the ticket was issued "subject to conditions displayed on the premises". The conditions included exemption from liability for injury to the customer. Thornton suffered personal injuries when he returned to the garage to collect his car.

Decision: The English Court of Appeal had to decide whether the defendant garage owner could rely on the exemption clause. In order for the plaintiff to read the conditions which were posted on a pillar opposite the machine, he would have had to drive his car into the garage and to have walked around to find them. Thus it was held that the defendant had not taken reasonably sufficient steps to draw the plaintiff's attention to the exemption clause.

In that case, Lord Denning pointed out that the contract was made as soon as the customer put the money into the machine and a ticket was issued. Since the exemption clause would only be brought to the customer's attention after the contract was made, it could not be incorporated as one of the terms of the contract.

―――― ഌ ――――

Timing

[4.270] As Lord Denning indicated in *Thornton v Shoe Lane Parking Ltd*,[60] the third requirement is that notice must be given prior to or at the time of the contract. Notice given after the contract is made has no effect. Thus in *Oceanic Sun Line Special Shipping v Fay*[61] the limitation clause on the back of the cruise ticket did not apply because Mr Fay received it only on boarding the ship in the Mediterranean, long after the contract for the Mediterranean cruise had been completed in Sydney: see Chapter 12. Similarly in *Olley v Marlborough Court*,[62] a hotel could not rely on a limitation clause on the inside of a guest bedroom door as the contract for the accommodation was completed at reception before the guest went to the room: see Chapter 13.

Statute

[4.275] As mentioned in the discussion on implied terms ([4.210]ff) there are extensive statutory guarantees imposed on the supply of goods and services in consumer transactions. Section 64 of the *Australian Consumer Law* declares void any term of a contract which purports to exclude, restrict or modify the consumer guarantees which it provides. For more detailed discussion, see Chapter 9, [9.200]ff).

Factors affecting validity

[4.280] Not all simple contracts are enforceable. They may be either:
- unenforceable;
- voidable;

---

60   *Thornton v Shoe Lane Parking* (1971) 2 QB 163.
61   *Oceanic Sun Line Special Shipping v Fay* (1988) 165 CLR 197.
62   *Olley v Marlborough Court* [1949] 1 KB 532.

- void; or
- illegal.

Unenforceable contracts

[4.285] Unenforceable contracts are those simple contracts which have all the essential elements of a contract, for example agreement, consideration and an intention to create legal relations, but which the law will not enforce, perhaps because one party lacks capacity to contract or because the law requires the agreement to be in a certain written form to be enforceable [63] or because the agreement is unconscionable.

Voidable contracts

[4.290] A voidable contract is one which is initially valid but which one party has an option to avoid or affirm on the basis that it was induced by the other party's misrepresentation or undue influence. The innocent party may sue for the equitable remedy of rescission which allows them to recover property transferred by them under the contract provided that such property has not already been transferred to an innocent third party for value.

Void contracts

[4.295] A void contract is one which never existed (a nullity) so that money paid or property transferred under it generally can be recovered by the transferor. No title to the money or property passes and so the transferee cannot pass title to a third party. A contract may be void for uncertainty or because the agreement was induced by a mistake on the part of one or both of the parties.

Illegal contracts

[4.300] An illegal contract is one prohibited by law. It may be forbidden by statute or by the common law on grounds of public policy. [64] Generally, property transferred pursuant to an illegal contract cannot be recovered.

In summary, some of the factors which affect validity and enforceability of a contract include:

- misrepresentation;
- capacity;
- mistake and frustration;
- duress; and
- privity.

Misrepresentation

[4.305] In [4.170] three types of misrepresentation were identified. They were:

- innocent misrepresentation.

---

63   For example see *Property Law Act 1974* (Qld), s 59 – "No action may be brought upon any contract for the sale or other disposition of land or any interest in land unless the contract upon which such action is brought, or some memorandum or note of the contract, is in writing, and signed by the party to be charged, or by some person by the party lawfully authorised."

64   Examples include agreements to commit crimes, torts or fraud or which promote sexual immorality or corruption in public life.

- fraudulent misrepresentation;
- negligent misrepresentation.

The common elements of these types of misrepresentation are the false statements of fact which are intended to and actually do induce the contract with the party who is misled. How do the courts distinguish between the different types?

Innocent misrepresentation

[4.310] If all the common elements for misrepresentation are present but it is not possible to establish any fraud or negligence, then the statement is an innocent misrepresentation.[65] In that case, the remedy is rescission of contract; that is, a right to reject the defective goods and to seek repayment of the price.

Fraudulent misrepresentation

[4.315] Where there is evidence that the statement was made knowing that it was false or recklessly as to whether it was true or false, then this is a fraudulent misrepresentation. There is also an action at common law for the tort of deceit.[66] The remedy is damages and/or rescission of the contract.

Negligent misrepresentation

[4.320] Sometimes, an innocent misrepresentation may also be negligent. Negligent misrepresentations or misstatements are an aspect of negligence in the law of torts.[67] Again, the remedy is damages in torts and/or rescission of the contract. See [5.85] for further discussion on this topic.

---

65   See, for example, *Curtis v Chemical Cleaning & Dyeing Co* [1951] 1 KB 805 (concerning damage to beads and sequins on a wedding dress) where it was held that there was innocent misrepresentation by the shop assistant about the contents of a docket.

66   See *Derry v Peek* (1889) 14 App Cas 337. *Facts*: In 1889, a certain Act of Parliament was enacted which provided that, with the consent of the Board of Trade, companies could apply for a right to use steam or mechanical power for trams rather than animal power. Derry fraudulently advertised and represented that its company had a right to use steam or mechanical power for trams and that this would be beneficial to the company. Peek, relying on the representation that the company had this right, bought shares in the company. As it turned out, the company had only *applied* for the requisite consent, which was later given only upon certain conditions. In the end, the company was wound up. Peek sued Derry under the tort of deceit, claiming damages for fraudulent misrepresentation. *Held*: Derry finally lost when the case went up to the House of Lords. The court found that no fraudulent misrepresentation was established on the facts. However, the principle that comes out of this case is that there must be a representation knowing it is false or reckless as to its truth or falsity.

67   See, for example, *Hedley Byrne & Co v Heller & Partners* [1964] AC 465 where the House of Lords held that a bank which had gratuitously but negligently given advice as to the solvency of one of its clients to a person to whom it had no contractual relationship might be liable to a person who had acted upon that advice and who had suffered injury or damage as a result.

The right to rescind

[4.325] The right to rescind is a common remedy in all these types of misrepresentation cases. However, that right to rescind does not last forever and may be lost if:

- restitution of the goods is impossible;[68]
- an innocent third party has bought the goods in good faith for value;
- the buyer has expressly affirmed the contract after discovering the misrepresentation; or
- more than a reasonable time has elapsed for the buyer to have discovered the misrepresentation.[69]

Statute

[4.330] As mentioned before in [4.175], under consumer protection legislation, misrepresentations (whether innocent, negligent or fraudulent) are likely to be deceptive and misleading conduct or unfair trading. The remedies available under this legislation include damages and rescission and the offender may be prosecuted and fined. See Chapter 9, [9.290]ff.

Capacity

[4.335] Some classes of people lack full legal capacity and need the law's protection. These include:

- minors;
- mentally ill persons.

Other classes of individuals have restrictions placed on their ability to contract to protect society's interests. These include:

- bankrupts;
- corporations;
- aliens.

Minors

[4.340] A minor or infant at common law is a person under the age of 21 years. Statutory interventions have redefined a minor as a person under 18 years of age.[70] Since the law seeks to protect minors against persons who would take advantage of their youth and inexperience, a contract made by infants is generally enforceable by them but cannot be enforced against them. In other words, the contract is voidable at the option of the infant.

Two exceptions to this rule are:

- contracts for necessaries; or
- beneficial contracts of service.

---

68   A plaintiff can only rescind the contract if both parties can be restored to their original position. This is virtually impossible in the case of a holiday experience which has gone wrong because there are no tangible goods to be returned for a refund.

69   See *Leaf v International Galleries* [1950] 2 KB 86. The plaintiff tried to rescind the purchase of a painting some five years later, when he discovered that it had been painted by a different artist. The court held that this was not a reasonable time.

70   See for example the *Law Reform Act 1995* (Qld); *Age of Majority (Reduction Act) 1971* (SA); *Age of Majority Act 1977* (Vic); *Age of Majority Act 1972* (WA); *Age of Majority Act 1973* (Tas).

Contracts for necessaries

[4.345] Like the rest of us, minors need food, clothing, shelter and medical supplies. If the item contracted for, by the particular minor, can be classified as a "necessary" then the agreement is enforceable against her or him. Minors must pay a reasonable price for the necessaries supplied to them. What amounts to a "necessary" in any given case depends upon such factors as the type of goods purchased and the living standards to which the infant is generally accustomed.

For example, in the case of *Ryder v Wombwell*[71] the defendant infant, who had a substantial annual income, bought on credit a pair of shirt sleeve studs made of crystals adorned with diamonds and rubies and an antique goblet in silver as a gift for a friend at whose house he had been staying. He failed to pay for them and the shopkeeper sued. The court held that the shopkeeper bore the onus of proving that the items purchased were "necessaries" and in the event he had produced no such evidence.

Beneficial contracts of service

[4.350] Infants usually enter into contracts of service for the purpose of:

- earning an income; and/or
- learning some trade or skill, for example a cadetship or apprenticeship.

Although such contracts cannot be specifically enforced in the sense that the infant cannot be required to stay with the employer, nevertheless he or she may be liable for any breach resulting from her or his premature departure. The contract will be enforceable, if, on the whole, the contract is for the infant's benefit. Thus in the case of *Hamilton v Lethbridge*[72] a minor argued that a restraint of trade clause in his articles of clerkship with his employer was not beneficial and therefore not enforceable. The High Court held that although the contract contained some clauses which may have appeared prejudicial to the minor, on balance the contract as a whole was beneficial and therefore enforceable.

Mentally ill persons

[4.355] Contracts entered into with mentally ill persons will be voidable by them if at the time when they contracted, they were unable to understand the nature of what they were agreeing to and this was or should have been apparent to the other party.

Mistake and Frustration

[4.360] There are three types of mistake:

- common mistake;[73]
- mutual mistake;[74] and
- unilateral mistake.

---

71   *Ryder v Wombwell* (1868) LR 4 Exch 32.
72   *Hamilton v Lethbridge* (1912) 14 CLR 236.
73   That is, where both parties make the same mistake.
74   That is, where the parties are both mistaken but their mistakes are not the same – they are at "cross purposes".

Unilateral mistake

[4.365] A unilateral mistake occurs when only one party is mistaken as to either:

- the identity of the other party; or
- the terms of the contract; or
- the nature of the document signed

and the other party tries to take advantage of that mistake.

Non est factum

[4.370] When the contract signed by the party is entirely different in nature from the one they thought they were signing, the party may raise the defence of *non est factum* (this is not my deed). In the case of *Saunders v Anglia Building Society*,[75] the House of Lords said that to succeed, the plaintiff must show that:

- the document signed was fundamentally, radically, or totally different in character from the one which he or she thought it to be;
- he or she was not careless or unduly negligent in checking the contents of the document; or
- he or she had to rely on others for advice, for example because of blindness or illiteracy or inability to understand the particular document.

Generally a contract is void if there has been a sufficiently fundamental mistake of fact.

Frustration

[4.375] The doctrine of frustration applies if, due to unforeseeable and unavoidable circumstances, one of the parties will lose all the benefit of the contract. When this happens, the party is entitled to be discharged from the contract and to recover all moneys paid under it.

For example, in one English case, the plaintiff rented a room for one day in June 1902 at a special rate specifically for the purpose of watching the Coronation procession. Unfortunately, King Edward VII fell ill and the procession did not take place after all. The plaintiff sued for recovery of his rent. The court held that he was entitled to be discharged from the contract because the entire purpose of the contract had been frustrated from his point of view.[76]

In another example of the principle, a music hall which had been hired out for a series of concerts was destroyed by fire before the opening night. The defendants were held not liable in damages to the plaintiff because the performance of the contract depended upon the continuing existence of something which had since perished, thus excusing performance.[77]

Duress, undue influence, unconscionability

[4.380] When there is a power imbalance between the bargaining parties, the stronger party may be tempted to exert some form of pressure on the weaker party to enter into the agreement. This may take the form of actual violence or intimidation, in which case it is referred to as duress (for example, threatening to criminally prosecute a woman's husband if the woman does not sign the contract).[78]

---

75 *Saunders v Anglia Building Society* [1971] AC 1004.
76 *Krell v Henry* [1903] 2 KB 740.
77 *Taylor v Caldwell* (1863) 3 B&S 826.
78 *Kaufman v Gerson* [1904] 1 KB 591.

Undue influence is the exertion of some kind of moral pressure. It arises whenever one party abuses the influence that he or she has over the decisions of another for the purpose of obtaining some undue benefit, either personally or for some third party. There is a presumption in favour of undue influence where the contracting parties are in a special relationship, for example parent and child, religious adviser and devotee, doctor and patient. This presumption may be rebutted by proving that the weaker party had access to independent advice or by showing that the weaker party exercised independent judgment.

When there is evidence of duress or undue influence, the contract is voidable at the option of the weaker party provided that he or she acts within a reasonable length of time after the pressure has ceased.

Equity and unconscionability

[4.385] At common law, the courts would not necessarily set aside contracts that appeared harsh or oppressive. However, in the leading Australian case of *Commercial Bank of Australia v Amadio*,[79] the High Court said that in exercising its equitable jurisdiction it was prepared to set aside a transaction as unconscionable where there is evidence that:

- the weaker party is under a special disability vis-à-vis the stronger;
- the stronger is aware of that special disability;
- it is unfair for the stronger to procure the agreement in those circumstances.

Again, unconscionable contracts are voidable at the option of the weaker party. In other words, the whole transaction will be set aside and the parties restored to their original position. However, the right to relief may be lost through ratification, affirmation, acquiescence, intervention of a third party or even by the weaker party also being guilty of unconscionable conduct.

Statute

[4.390] Unconscionable conduct is also prohibited under consumer protection legislation[80] and one consequence is that the contract or the unconscionable terms are unenforceable. This is illustrated by *Dillon v Baltic Shipping Co "Mikhail Lermontov"*[81] (see the case note at [12.90] below) where the New South Wales Court of Appeal upheld the trial judge's finding that the full release signed by Mrs Dillon for $4,786, when her claim against the shipping company was worth $51,396, was void for unconscionability[82] and she was entitled to recover the full amount. The court relied on the insufficiency of the sum paid, the inequality of bargaining power and the diminished capacity of Mrs Dillon at the time. The High Court refused leave to appeal on this ground. See Chapter 9, [9.70].

Privity of Contract

[4.395] As a general rule, only the original parties to a contract acquire rights or incur liabilities under it. A contract cannot normally impose obligations or confer rights on third

---

79   *Commercial Bank of Australia v Amadio* (1983) 151 CLR 447.
80   See, for example, *Australian Consumer Law*, Part 2-2 Unconscionable conduct.
81   *Dillon v Baltic Shipping Co "Mikhail Lermontov"* [1992] 22 NSWLR 1.
82   Under the *Contracts Review Act 1980* (NSW).

parties.[83] Barwick CJ has expressed the principle thus: "It must be accepted that, according to our law, a person not a party to a contract may not himself sue upon it so as directly to enforce its obligations."[84]

Exceptions to the general rule include:

- agency, because the third party would be a party to the contract;
- trustee for the third party, so long as there is evidence of clear intention to create a trust;
- statutory provisions relating to insurance contracts;[85]
- other statutory exceptions;[86] and,
- exclusion clauses intended to benefit an agent or employee.

In *Trident Insurance Co v McNeice Bros*,[87] the High Court enforced an insurance contract at the suit of a third party beneficiary. Some authors have argued that this case marks the beginning of a general relaxation of the privity of contract rule at common law. However clarification of this awaits further decisions.

The position is clearer with exemption clauses. In *Scrutons v Midland Silicones Ltd*[88] the court set out the conditions in which third parties might take advantage of exemption or limitation clauses. In particular, Lord Reid stipulated that:

- the contract must make it clear that the clause was intended to benefit the third party;
- the principal must have been contracting on his own behalf and as agent for the third party;
- the principal must have had authority to contract on behalf of the third party; and
- the third party must have provided consideration for the exemption from liability.

Sometimes referred to as "Himalaya" clauses,[89] these standard exclusion clauses are frequently found in contracts limiting shipowners' liability. The exemption is extended to cover their servants, agents and independent contractors such as the stevedoring companies.

However, unless the third party can bring themselves within one of the exceptions to the general rule, they will generally not be able to enforce any of the rights or obligations of the contract.

---

83 See, for example, *Tweedle v Atkinson* (1861) 121 ER 762. *Facts*: Tweedle was engaged to Guy's daughter. To provide for the young couple after their marriage, Guy and Tweedle's father, John, agreed between them that each would pay Tweedle £100. It was further agreed that Tweedle could sue for their sums. When he died, Guy had still not paid the promised sum and Tweedle sued the executor, Atkinson, for the money. *Held*: His action failed. He was "a stranger to the consideration" and, not having paid for the promise, could not enforce it. The fact that Guy had made no promise to him would also have debarred him from recovery on the grounds of privity of contract.

84 *Coulls v Bagot's Executor & Trustee Co Ltd* (1967) 119 CLR 460.

85 The *Insurance Contracts Act 1984* (Cth), s 48 abrogates common law doctrine of privity of contract with respect to insurance contracts to which that Act applies.

86 See, for example, *Property Law Act 1974* (Qld), s 55 *Contracts for the benefit of third parties*. Under the *Australian Consumer Law*, statutory consumer guarantees are available to all consumers who are not confined by privity of contract principles, see Chapter 9 ([9.185]ff).

87 *Trident Insurance Co v McNeice Bros* (1988) 165 CLR 107.

88 *Scrutons v Midland Silicones Ltd* [1962] AC 446.

89 These are named after the ship at the centre of one such dispute.

REMEDIES FOR BREACH OF CONTRACT

[4.400] The previous section examined the circumstances which affect the enforceability or validity of a contract. It touched on some of the kinds of remedies that are available for breach of contract. It also highlighted the fact that the type of remedy available is dependent on the type of breach which has occurred; for example, compare the different remedies available for innocent, negligent or fraudulent misrepresentation.

This section looks at the possible remedies for breach of contract including:

- rescission;
- restitution;
- specific performance;
- injunction; and
- damages.

Rescission

[4.405] When an innocent party treats the contract as discharged because of the breach, he or she may take proceedings for the equitable remedy of rescission of the contract. It usually involves an election by the innocent party to proceed with or to terminate the contract. Rescission is often available in cases where a contract is voidable, for example, in cases of fraudulent, negligent or innocent misrepresentation (see [4.305]ff).

Restitution

[4.410] Rescission treats the contract as at an end, but often the innocent party may have paid money in error or may have provided some benefit to the defendant in the form of goods supplied or services rendered. Naturally, they will want to be restored to the position they occupied before the contract was made and it may be unjust for the other party to retain those benefits.

Restitution is thus based on the equitable principle of unjust enrichment. It arises most often in contract law when the innocent party is claiming either for the return of money paid in error or for a reasonable remuneration for goods or services provided. In other words where there has been a total failure of consideration. In these cases, the court may compel the other party to restore the money or other benefit received where they have clearly been unjustly enriched at the innocent party's expense. [90]

Specific Performance

[4.415] Specific performance is an equitable remedy and therefore discretionary, requiring the performance of a specified act imposed by the contract. It will usually only be granted if the common law remedy of damages for breach would be inadequate in the circumstances. For example, it is unlikely to be granted in sale of goods contracts because the consumer may purchase similar goods elsewhere. However, in cases involving the sale of land, for example,

---

[90] In *Baltic Shipping Company v Dillon* (1993) 176 CLR 344 (facts available in [2.225]) the High Court had to consider the circumstances in which restitution would apply. It held that so far as the contract between Mrs Dillon and Baltic Shipping Company was concerned, Mrs Dillon was only entitled to restitution of the purchase price corresponding to the period of the trip that she missed.

where the land cannot be conveyed without the vendor's signature on the transfer, the court may require the guilty party to carry out their contractual obligations by forcing them to execute the instrument. [91]

Injunction

[4.420] Like specific performance, injunction is also a discretionary equitable remedy. However, it operates to prohibit or prevent the performance of some specified act, for example, a restraint of trade clause contained in a personal service contract. If the person should attempt to set up in business within a certain radius of the former employer within the time limit specified, the other party may seek injunctive relief to prevent that person from doing so. To succeed, the person seeking the injunction must show that they are not also in breach of the contract and that they are ready, willing and able to perform the balance of it. [92]

Damages

[4.425] Damages is a common law remedy which is an award of monetary compensation to the innocent party for the loss caused to her or him by the breach of contract. The innocent party may recover either a substantial sum of money for a serious breach or a nominal sum for a minor breach. In the more serious cases, the innocent party usually also has an option to rescind the contract, that is, to treat it as discharged because of the breach.

Damages are designed to put the innocent party in the same position, so far as money can do it, as if the contract had been performed. [93] In other words, damages are a substitute for the performance of the contract. It follows then that they are not intended as a punishment for the party breaching the contract but as a genuine estimate of the loss caused by the breach. The guiding principles in assessment of damages include:

- remoteness of damage;
- mitigation of loss; and
- heads of damage.

Remoteness of Damage

[4.430] Damages are assessed on the basis of loss naturally flowing from the breach and actually contemplated as a probable result of it. The courts apply an objective and a subjective test in determining the extent of the losses covered.

---

[91] See *Legione v Hateley* (1983) 152 CLR 406 where the High Court reconsidered the grant of specific performance to a purchaser of land who fails to complete on time, time being of the essence of the contract.

[92] See *Beaches & Bush Properties v Jennings* [2003] NSWSC 798. *Facts*: The plaintiff was a real estate agency in Ulladulla NSW and defendant was employed as a salesperson. The employment agreement between the parties included provisions prohibiting the defendant from being employed by or providing services of a real estate agent for a period of 6 months post employment termination. The restraint applied to the area surrounding Ulladulla. The defendant resigned and almost immediately commenced employment with another real estate agency operating in Milton and Mollymook, two towns very close to Ulladulla and within the area described in the restraint of trade clause. *Held*: In the light of the personal nature of the defendant's role within the business, the restraint period of 6 months was considered to be reasonable. As to the extent of the territorial restriction, the Court recognised that there were a significant number of real estate agencies outside the restricted territory which could potentially employ him. Austin J granted a final injunction enforcing the terms of the restraint of trade clause.

[93] *Commonwealth v Amman Aviation Pty Ltd* (1991) 174 CLR 64.

The leading case is *Hadley v Baxendale*,[94] where the delay of a carrier in transporting a mill crank shaft for repair caused substantial losses of production at the mill. The court identified two types of loss for which damagers are recoverable:

- loss reasonably contemplated in the ordinary course of events (that is, objective contemplation). This did not apply here as the carrier may reasonably have expected the mill to hold a spare shaft.
- loss naturally flowing from special or exceptional circumstances made known to both parties at the time they made the contract (that is, subjective contemplation). Nor did this apply here as the carrier was not told that the mill would be idle during the delay.

In contract, the rationale for the limits is called remoteness of damage. Compare the similar concept of foreseeability in tort. See [5.40].

Mitigation of Loss

[4.435] Each party to a contract has a duty to mitigate her or his losses. As an incentive, a plaintiff may not recover losses which she or he could have avoided through her or his reasonable efforts. All that is required is that each party act reasonably. Neither party has to put themselves out unduly or to accept something less so as to reduce the damages which the other party may otherwise be required to pay.[95]

The principle is succinctly put by Lord Macmillan in *Banco de Portugal v Waterlow*[96] when he said:

> The law is satisfied if the party placed in a difficult situation by reason of the breach ... has acted reasonably in the adoption of remedial measures, and he will not be held disentitled to recover the cost of such measures merely because the party in breach can suggest that other measures less burdensome to him might have been taken.

Sometimes parties to a contract agree on the pre-estimate of damages (otherwise referred to as liquidated damages) in the event of a breach. For example, it is the practice among many holiday accommodation providers to require full payment of the accommodation in advance of the arrival of guests. In the event of a cancellation, the guests will forfeit their accommodation monies unless and until the owner re-lets the premises. This is simply a reflection of the losses which the owner would otherwise have suffered and has been developed in response to industry concerns associated with guest "no shows".

Heads of damage

[4.440] The same principle applies to the measure of damages as to the award of damages itself. That is, all those losses flowing from the breach are recoverable so far as money can do it.[97] Assessment of the measure of damages for breach of contract may therefore reflect (amongst other things):

- liquidated damages being an amount agreed upon by the parties and contained in the contract which is awarded in lieu of actual damages;

---

94   *Hadley v Baxendale* (1854) 156 ER 145.
95   S Graw, *An Introduction to the Law of Contract* (6th ed, Lawbook Co, Sydney, 2008), p 453
96   *Banco de Portugal v Waterlow* [1932] AC 453 at 506.
97   *Robinson v Harman* (1848) 1 Exch 850.

- diminution in the value of property before and after the causative act or omission creating the lost value; [98]
- out of pocket expenses incurred as a result of the breach; [99]
- personal injuries [100] which can be "attached" to the breach; [101] and
- non economic loss such as damages for disappointment and distress in travel contracts. [102]

Exercise

A Lost Opportunity

Paul and Linda and their three young children live in Melbourne. Last week, they booked a holiday to the Whitsundays in North Queensland commencing next week. They had looked at some online properties and finally chose the *Whitsunday Wilderness Retreat*, a holiday house situated on an isolated beach location not far from the town of Whitsunday. They spoke to the owner, Harry Hardhead, and confirmed its availability and then went ahead and booked the house for two weeks at a cost of $2500.00 per week. They arranged with Harry to pay the $5000.00 accommodation monies into his bank account because he insisted that under the booking conditions he required payment in full for Paul and Linda to secure confirmation of their booking. Based on their confirmed accommodation, they proceeded to purchase their airline tickets and looked forward to their upcoming holiday.

This week disaster has struck the family. The youngest child, Scarlet, has developed whooping cough. The child must be quarantined for three weeks. Paul and Linda have contacted the airline which has advised them of its policy to refuse to carry passengers with a contagious disease. However, the airline has assured them that it would reschedule their flights when Scarlet is cleared by her doctor to travel. Paul and Linda have considered driving to Queensland but with three small children this does not seem very practical especially as they would have to allow 8 of the 14 days in travel time alone. Finally they have decided to postpone the holiday for three months.

When Paul and Linda rang to advise Harry of their decision, his response was unexpected. He told them that unless he could relet the *Whitsunday Wilderness Retreat* for the two weeks they have already booked commencing next week that they would forfeit the whole $5000.00 paid for their present accommodation. Worse still, they would have to pay again for more accommodation later on! Harry added that as he relies on the internet for all his booking enquiry, it was most unlikely at this late stage that he would be able to find another person

---

98 *Black's Law Dictionary* (6th ed, West Publishing Co 1990), pp 390-392.
99 See *Hamlin v Great Northern Railway Co* (1856) 1 H&N 408; 156 ER 1261 at [2.220]. Mr. Hamlin spent extra days on the road as a result of the breach and his out of pocket expenses included unbudgeted accommodation and food for which he was ultimately compensated.
100 The majority of personal injuries claims are based in the Law of Tort (see Chapter 5) but the same principles apply to actions for breach of contract, subject only to the different rules about causation and remoteness of damage.
101 See *Baltic Shipping Company v Dillon* (1993) 176 CLR 344 (facts at [2.235]). Mrs. Dillon suffered a broken leg as she was escaping the sinking ship for which she was compensated because it was caused by the breach and was not too remote.
102 See *Baltic Shipping Company v Dillon* (1993) 176 CLR 344 (facts at [2.235]). The contract had the object of providing enjoyment or relaxation. Mrs. Dillon was entitled to recover damages for anxiety flowing from the breach of contract.

A Lost Opportunity cont.

willing to book the *Whitsunday Wilderness Retreat* at such short notice. Paul and Linda have tried to negotiate with Harry to refund their accommodation money and have even suggested that he should keep a reasonable sum to cover the loss of the first night's accommodation, say, $500.00.

Harry is relying on a term in the booking conditions which reads:

16. Cancellation of Booking. If the booking is cancelled 2 months or less prior to commencement date, no refund shall be made unless and until the premises are re-booked for the total period of the proposed occupancy in which case a service fee of 12% shall be charged. Cancellations must be forwarded to management in writing.

This and other booking conditions relating to the *Whitsunday Wilderness Retreat* are posted on the website and Harry always sends a printed copy of them to customers with their booking confirmation and accommodation receipt. Paul and Linda have a copy of the conditions in their possession.

Advise Paul and Linda and Harry of their respective rights and obligations under the contract.

CHAPTER 5

Torts

[5.05] INTRODUCTION TO TORTS		95
[5.05]	Definition	95
[5.10]	Civil Liability	95
[5.15]	Elements of a Tort	96
[5.20]	Distinction between Intentional and Unintentional Torts	96
[5.25]	Elements of the Tort of Negligence	97
[5.30]	The duty of care	97
[5.35]	Donoghue v Stevenson	98
[5.60]	Breach of the duty	101
[5.70]	Damage	103
[5.80]	Other Specific Torts	104
[5.85]	Negligent misstatement	104
[5.100]	Vicarious liability	105
[5.125]	Public authorities	107
[5.130]	Defamation	108
[5.145]	General Defences to Negligence	109
[5.150]	Voluntary assumption of risk	109
[5.155]	Contributory negligence	110
[5.160]	Inevitable accident	111
[5.165]	Illegal enterprise	111
[5.170]	Evidential Matters	112
[5.175]	Breach of statutory duty	112
[5.180]	Res ipsa loquitur	113
[5.185]	Tort Reform in Australia	113

INTRODUCTION TO TORTS

Definition

[5.05] A tort is a civil wrong. It has been described as: "An injury other than a breach of contract which the law will redress with damages".[1]

Civil Liability

[5.10] Torts law comes predominantly from the common law (cases), although in recent years there has been statutory intervention creating duties which may give rise to breach of statutory duty.

There is an overlap between torts, contract and criminal law. In the case of the torts/criminal law overlap, however, the parties and the outcomes are different. For example, in the criminal law, the state prosecutes and the penalty is a fine or imprisonment. So, if a person is assaulted by another, the state will prosecute the offender on behalf of the community as a whole. However, the victim may also commence independent civil proceedings seeking compensation for her or his injuries.

---

[1] JG Fleming, *The Law of Torts* (8th ed, LBC Information Services, Sydney, 1998), p 1.

In the case of the torts/contract law overlap, the outcomes and the parties may indeed be the same. For example, a tourist who hires a defective bicycle and is injured may sue on the contract for breach of warranty and in tort for negligence.[2] The remedy usually sought in either case is damages.

Elements of a Tort

[5.15] There must be some element of fault, either intentional or careless. With few exceptions at common law, courts have traditionally adopted a policy of "letting the loss lie where it falls" unless there is fault. In other words, there can be no liability without fault. Under statute law, it is more common to find torts of strict liability where the defendant is responsible for the damage caused even in the absence of fault. In those cases, it is enough that the defendant did the act that caused the damage. These "no fault" provisions are often to be found in public health and safety legislation and in the various State regulatory offences Acts.

Distinction between Intentional and Unintentional Torts

[5.20] Historically, torts were characterised as either direct (intentional) or indirect (unintentional). The major distinction between the two categories was that intentional torts were actionable without proof of damage whereas unintentional torts required proof of damage. Intentional torts were based on actions in trespass. All that the plaintiff had to show was that the defendant intended to do the harmful act, not that he or she intended to cause harm.

For example, the tort of trespass against land is the direct result of a voluntary act. Hence if a person is thrown or pushed onto someone's land they have not committed a trespass, but it may be enough if that person simply walks on someone's land or enters it for the purpose of collecting something. Of course, a reasonable defence would be that the person entered the property for the purpose of collecting a straying child or animal.

The actions of assault and battery are examples of "trespass to the person". At common law, the distinction between the two is that in assault a person intentionally creates in another person an immediate fear of unlawful force. Battery is the actual application of such force. In both cases the threat and/or application of force takes place without the consent of the victim. Consequently bouncers in nightclubs and security officers in other crowd control situations must be careful not to exercise "unlawful force" in the conduct of their duties or they may find themselves in court defending a charge of trespass to the person. Worse still, because of the tort/criminal law overlap, they may also find themselves being prosecuted for "assault". In the criminal law in most Australian States no distinction is made between threats of force and the actual application of such force. "Assault" covers both meanings.[3]

Other examples of intentional torts include:

---

2   *White v John Warwick & Co Ltd* [1953] 1 WLR 1285.

3   The *Criminal Code* (Qld) contains a number of provisions of relevance including s 245 (definition of assault), s 246 (assaults unlawful), s 355 (common assault); s 222 of the *Criminal Code* (WA) provides that any application of force to the person of another without that person's consent is assault and any assault (unless authorised, justified or excused by law) is unlawful and constitutes an offense; assault is dealt with in ss 186, 187 and 188 of the *Criminal Code* (NT); s 61 (common assault), s 59 (assault occasioning actual bodily harm) of the *Crimes Act 1900* (NSW) is also relevant.

- conversion;[4] and
- false imprisonment.[5]

Unintentional torts were based on actions in case, such as negligence. Here, of course, the plaintiff had to show not only that the defendant's conduct was blameworthy but also that it had caused her or him some harm.

At common law, actions ended with the death of one of the parties. That has been changed by statute.[6]

Elements of the Tort of Negligence

[5.25] Negligence is the most common form of civil action today. It is based on the notion that the defendant's reckless, careless or blameworthy conduct caused the plaintiff harm in circumstances in which the defendant should have taken more care.

The plaintiff must prove that:

- the defendant owed the plaintiff a duty of care;
- the defendant breached that duty of care;
- the defendant's breach caused the plaintiff to suffer damage;
- the damage suffered was reasonably foreseeable.

The duty of care

[5.30] The first element of negligence is establishing that the defendant owes a duty of care to the plaintiff. Unless the plaintiff can establish that such a relationship exists, the law will not allow the plaintiff to recover any losses he or she may have suffered, no matter how negligent the defendant may have been. Several relationships have already been recognised. For example, the duty owed by road users to each other, the duty owed by those giving paid professional advice, the duty owed by employers to employees and the duty owed by bailees to ensure the safety of property entrusted to their care by bailors.[7]

What is the test which establishes whether the duty of care exists? The famous "snail-in-the-bottle" case of *Donoghue v Stevenson* lays down the key "good neighbour" principles which have been applied in duty of case cases ever since.

---

4   That is, unauthorised possession by one person which is inconsistent with the ownership rights of another. For example, if a chattel is lost and then found by another who appropriates it to his/her own use without legal authority that is known as conversion.

5   That is, restraining a person in a bounded area without justification or consent. For example, if nursing staff at a hospital, fearing for the physical health of an inpatient, restrain that patient in a locked room, it may be a case of false imprisonment.

6   For example, see *Succession Act 1981* (Qld), s 66; *Survival of Causes of Action Act 1940* (SA).

7   The essence of bailment is that whilst the bailee has temporary physical possession of the personal property, the bailor has no intention of parting with the bailor's legal title. A good example of bailment is the valet service provided by larger hotels and accommodation providers for the parking of guests' vehicles. The owner has an expectation the vehicle will be returned in the same condition as it was in when he or she handed over the keys to the valet.

Donoghue v Stevenson

[5.35] *Donoghue v Stevenson* (1932) AC 562

Facts: The plaintiff's friend bought from a local shop a bottle of ginger beer for her to drink. Because the bottle was made of dark opaque glass, the plaintiff could not see inside the bottle. She proceeded to consume the contents until she detected the presence of a decomposing snail in the bottle. She felt ill immediately and alleged subsequently that she had contracted a serious illness from consuming the contaminated contents of the bottle. The plaintiff sued the soft drink manufacturer.

Decision: Lord Atkin explained the existence of the duty in this way:

> The rule that you are to love your neighbour becomes in law you must not injure your neighbour, and the lawyer's question, who is my neighbour, receives a restricted reply. You must take reasonable care to avoid acts or omissions which you can reasonably foresee would be likely to injure your neighbour. Who, then, in law, is my neighbour? The answer seems to be – persons who are so closely and directly affected by my act that I ought to have them in contemplation as being so affected when I am directing my mind to the acts or omissions which are called in question.

In other words, all that the plaintiff must show was that he or she was one of a class of persons who would foreseeably be at risk of injury in some way if the defendant failed to take reasonable care. It was not necessary to show that the precise manner in which the injuries were sustained was reasonably foreseeable.[8]

Reasonable foreseeability

[5.40] For a long time following this case, courts applied the reasonable foreseeability test alone to establish the existence of a duty of care. If the consequences of the defendant's conduct were not reasonably foreseeable, then there was no duty of care and no liability on the part of the defendant. However, because of the undemanding nature of the reasonable foreseeability test, it was becoming increasingly easy in any given situation to identify a class of persons who would foreseeably be at risk of injury in some way if the defendant failed to take reasonable care.

Therefore, for fear of opening the floodgates to a rash of claims, particularly in complex cases involving purely economic loss and in the nervous shock cases, courts tried to limit its potential scope by applying the "proximity test".

Proximity

[5.45] So what does "proximity" mean? According to the cases, the proximity may be either:

- physical;[9] or
- circumstantial;[10] or
- causal.[11]

The High Court examined the concept of proximity in *Nagel v Rottnest Island Authority*.[12] In that case, the plaintiff hit his head on a submerged rock as he dived into a natural swimming

---

8 See *Chapman v Hearse* (1961) 106 CLR 112.
9 For example, in motor vehicle collision cases.
10 That is, arising out of the relationship between the parties, such as employer/employee or professional adviser/client.
11 Where there is some other close connection between the negligent act and the damage suffered.
12 *Nagel v Rottnest Island Authority* (1993) 177 CLR 423.

pool called "The Basin" on Rottnest Island near Perth. He suffered quadriplegia. He sued the statutory authority in charge of the island claiming negligence on the defendant's part in failing to put up any signs warning that it was unsafe to dive into "The Basin". In finding that the defendant did owe a duty of care, a majority of the court said:

> this is a case in which it is possible to ascertain the existence of a generalised duty of care ... to take reasonable steps to avoid a foreseeable risk of injury ... owed to members of the public who resort to the Basin to swim, without looking to foreseeability, a concept which in many other situations is the influential, if not decisive, determinant of the existence of a relationship of proximity.

However, in *Perre v Apand Pty Ltd*,[13] the High Court now appears to be moving away from a reliance on questions of proximity as determinative of the existence of a duty of care.

Nervous shock (psychiatric injury)

[5.50] In recent years, everyone has witnessed the aftermath of a number of serious accidents, even massacres, on television.[14] There is almost an unlimited class of persons who might conceivably be affected psychologically by viewing such incidents and the reasonable foreseeability test is inadequate in defining the exclusive class of persons to whom the duty should be owed. Thus courts faced with these "nervous shock" cases used the proximity test to prevent "opening the floodgates" to such potentially unlimited claims. The cases limited the duty of care to persons who:

- fear for their own safety or that of some other person (not necessarily a close relative); or
- see or hear the death of or injury to another (not including the defendant) or the immediate aftermath.

In other words the proximity must exist both in time and space.[15] Additionally, the plaintiff must have suffered "nervous shock", defined as an immediate or sudden onslaught to the senses.

However in the case of *Annetts v Australian Stations Pty Ltd; Tame v State of New South Wales*,[16] the High Court ruled that liability for psychiatric injury should not be limited to cases where the injury is caused by a sudden shock to a plaintiff who has directly perceived a distressing phenomenon or its immediate aftermath. The question to be asked is whether it is

---

13 *Perre v Apand Pty Ltd* (1999) 198 CLR 180. *Facts*: The claim was brought by the Perre family, potato growers in the Riverland whose major sources of profit were lucrative contracts to supply potatoes to Western Australia. Seed potatoes supplied by Apand to a farm owned by the Sparnons near the Perre's land introduced a potato disease, bacterial wilt, onto the Sparnons' property. The disease did not spread to the Perres' land, but because Western Australian regulations prohibited the importation of potatoes grown within 20 kilometres of an outbreak of bacterial wilt for five years after the outbreak, the Perres lost all of their lucrative potato supply contracts to Western Australia. *Held* (on the issue if a duty of care): the Perres' loss was not caused by Apand's legitimate pursuit of its own commercial goals. Apand already had a duty not to infect the Sparnons with potato diseases and hence suffered no additional restriction on its freedom by the addition of a duty of care to the Perres'.
14 Such as the Port Arthur (Tasmania) massacre in April 1997, the terrorist attack on World Trade Centre (New York) September 11, 2001 and numerous train or bus disasters.
15 See *Jaensch v Coffey* (1984) 155 CLR 549: "the class of persons whose claims should be recognised, the proximity [in time and space] of such persons to the accident, and the means by which the shock is caused."
16 *Annetts v Australian Stations Pty Ltd; Tame v State of New South Wales* (2002) 191 ALR 449. *Facts*: The High Court was ruling on a preliminary issue as to whether an employer of a teenage boy working alone as a caretaker on a station in a remote part of the Kimberley owed a duty of care to the boy's parents. The boy left the station in a defective vehicle and was found several days later dead from dehydration, exhaustion

reasonable to require one person to have in contemplation injury of the kind that has been suffered by another and to take care to guard against such injury. [17]

Whether or not "aftermath" includes witnessing live television coverage of the tragedy has not been finally decided for Australia. [18] Since the introduction of the civil liability legislation, some States [19] now restrict recovery for pure mental harm to persons who directly witnessed a person being killed or injured or put in peril or were a close family member of the victim. For further discussion, see [5.185].

Illegality

[5.55] Do co-conspirators engaged in an illegal enterprise owe each other a duty of care? Must a bank robber in the course of blowing up a safe do so carefully so as to avoid injuring his accomplice and thus risk being sued for negligence? The High Court has said where the only relationship between the parties was one based on an illegal enterprise, the plaintiff cannot sue for damages because of an insufficient relationship of proximity between the parties. [20] Of course, public policy considerations cannot be ignored in the courts' reaching this conclusion especially since there is usually a physical as well as a causal proximity between the parties.

In *Italiano v Barbaro*, [21] the court said:

> The difficulty ... about fixing the standard and defining the duty is fundamental to the nature of law ... the law cannot regulate the incidents of crime, as if it were a lawful activity. To attempt to do so would be "grotesque"...

However, just because a person is engaged in illegal activity, he or she will not necessarily be debarred from recovering damages. Much depends on the seriousness of the joint criminal activity. For example, when someone acts in breach of statutory provisions designed to promote health, safety or workplace practices, it is both possible and proper for the court to determine an appropriate standard of care. An example could be co-workers in the hospitality industry, such as cooks, who flout safety regulations until one of them is burnt or injured.

---

and hypothermia. The parents alleged they had suffered pure psychiatric injury after learning of the circumstances. "Pure" psychiatric or psychological injury is the expression used to refer to a recognisable psychiatric illness which is neither caused by, nor related to, a physical injury sustained by the person concerned.

17 See also *Gifford v Strang Patrick Stevedoring* (2003) 214 CLR 219 where the High Court made a second attempt to adequately define the appropriate approach.

18 See the House of Lords decision in *Alcock v Chief Constable of South Yorkshire Police* [1992] AC 310 which did not rule out a situation where the close relative views the death of a loved one for the first time on live television, although that did not apply on the facts before it. *Alcock* was followed in *White v Chief Constable of South Yorkshire Police* (1999) 2 AC 455 where police officers claimed compensation for psychiatric injury against the police service. *Held*: That such a duty does not place a police officer in any better position than a bystander, and since a bystander could not claim, a duty-bound policeman's claim is liable to be rejected since he was a professional rescuer not intimately participating in the incident itself, or in the immediate aftermath.

19 For example, see *Wrongs (Liability and Damages for Personal Injury) Amendment Act 2002* (SA).

20 See *Gala v Preston* (1991) 172 CLR 243 where the majority of the court said: "When attention is given to the circumstances of the present case it is difficult to see how they can sustain a relationship of proximity which would generate a duty of care ... it would not be possible or feasible for a court to determine what was an appropriate standard of care to be expected of the first appellant as driver of the vehicle."

21 *Italiano v Barbaro* (1993) 114 ALR 21 at 48.

Breach of the duty

[5.60] If it can be established that the defendant does owe a duty of care to the plaintiff, then the next enquiry must be whether there has been a breach of that duty. In other words, has the defendant acted negligently? To answer this question, the courts compare the behaviour of the defendant with that expected of the "reasonable person" in similar circumstances to those of the defendant.

In the case of *Wyong Shire Council v Shirt*,[22] the defendant council had dredged a deep channel in a shallow lake and marked its existence by signs which read simply, "Deep Water". The plaintiff, an inexperienced water skier, believing that the signs meant deep water all around, fell in shallow water and suffered serious injuries.

The High Court said that:

> In deciding whether there has been a breach of duty of care the tribunal of fact must first ask itself whether a reasonable man in the defendant's position would have foreseen that his conduct involved a risk of injury to ... a class of persons that included the plaintiff. [If the answer to this is yes] it is then for the tribunal of fact to determine what a reasonable man would do by way of response to the risk.
>
> The fact finding tribunal must balance the magnitude of the risk, and the likelihood of it occurring, against the expense and difficulty of taking preventive action, along with any other "conflicting responsibilities".

The elements of breach of duty of care are thus:

- risk of harm;
- seriousness of harm;
- burden of eliminating the risk;
- social utility of the conduct.

To be reasonably foreseeable, the risk must not be far-fetched or fanciful but a real risk. In a series of beach-related injury cases,[23] plaintiffs have argued that local authorities have breached their duty of care to beach goers with (amongst other things) inadequate supervision of patrolled beaches[24] and lack of proper signage warning of hidden or natural dangers such as rips, "dumper" waves and sandbars.[25] However, Gleeson CJ and Kirby J in *Vairy v Wyong Shire Council*[26] said that:

---

22 *Wyong Shire Council v Shirt* (1980) 146 CLR 40.

23 In Australia, most of the cases on beach safety are against the relevant public authorities having the care, control and management of the beach starting with *Wyong Shire Council v Shirt* (1980) 146 CLR 40 and *Nagle v Rottnest Island Authority* (1992) 177 CLR 423. Then *Romeo v Conservation Commission (NT)* (1998) 192 CLR 431 (cliff fall – not liable as obvious risk, unreasonable to fence or erect warning signs); *Prast v Town of Cottesloe* [2000] WASCA 274 (body surfer dumped – not liable, obvious risk no duty to warn); *Mulligan v Coffs Harbour City Council & Ors* [2003] NSWSC 49 (swimmer diving in creek – not liable as obvious risk, unreasonable to sign); *Swain v Waverley Municipal Council* (2005) 220 CLR 517 (swimmer diving at Bondi Beach – liable as could have taken preventative measures).

24 *Municipality of Waverley v Bloom* [1999] NSWCA 229.

25 In *Prast v the Town of Cottesloe* [2000] WASCA 275 at [42]-[43], Justice Ipp said "to suggest that signs should be placed on all beaches in Australia indicating that swimming in the sea could lead to serious injury or death would, I suggest, be absurd. The absurdity lies in the obviousness of the danger that attaches to the common, everyday, activity of swimming in the sea ... Of course, where there are dangerous currents, or rips or surges or rocks or the possibility of the occasional king waves or other dangers that are peculiar to a particular beach, or part of a beach, special warnings may be called for, but that is not this case".

26 *Vairy v Wyong Shire Council* (2005) 223 CLR 422.

warning signs only serve a purpose if they are likely to inform a person of something that a person does not already know, or to draw attention to something that the person might have overlooked or forgotten.

In the case of *Enright v Coolum Resort Pty Ltd & Anors*,[27] the plaintiff, a widow, claimed compensation from the resort hotel where her deceased husband (a US citizen visiting Australia for a conference) had been staying as a guest and from the local Maroochy Shire Council which was the local authority in charge of Yaroomba Beach. Her husband drowned in the surf while swimming away from the resort's beach clubhouse and after it had closed for the day. The plaintiff alleged that the lack of signage warning of the dangers of the surf on the pathways leading to the beach adjacent to the resort contributed to her husband's death.

His Honour, Justice Moynihan, referred to the case law and noted that:

> the defendants are under an obligation to exercise a reasonable care to protect a person from the reasonably foreseeable consequences of the risks of water based recreational activities in general and of surfing at Yaroomba Beach in particular.
>
> In imposing a duty of care and more importantly in determining whether or not a duty has been breached the common law recognises individual autonomy and responsibility.[28]

The facts established that the deceased had a background of participation in water sports and that the resort had also developed its own risk management strategies to guide and assist their guests with regard to swimming and surfing activities. However the deceased had made no effort to acquire this information. In the result, the court was satisfied that there had been no breach of duty and the case was dismissed.[29]

Standard of care

[5.65] In determining whether the duty of care has been breached in any given situation, the court will ask itself whether the defendant failed to exercise the standard of care that was reasonable in all the circumstances. This is an objective test. In *Enright v Coolum Resort Pty Ltd & Anors*,[30] the court was satisfied that the defendant had acted reasonably and discharged its obligations to the plaintiff's husband through its risk management strategies (brochures and information sheets, private beach facilities and bus shuttle service for guests).

The standard of care varies according to the circumstances. It is measured against that required of the ordinary skilled person exercising and professing to have special skills.[31] Accordingly, a travel agent doing the work of a normal travel agent will be judged against the accepted standards of that profession. He or she has a special skill which others rely upon.

Similarly, an accountant engaged by a travel agent to prepare and audit the financial statements of the travel agency in accordance with a national scheme for the regulation of

---

27   *Enright v Coolum Resort Pty Ltd & Anors* [2002] QSC 394.
28   *Enright v Coolum Resort Pty Ltd & Anors* [2002] QSC 394 at [14]-[15].
29   See also *Cole v South Tweed Heads Rugby League Football Club Ltd* (2004) 217 CLR 469 where the court held that the defendant had discharged its duty to the female plaintiff who had been drinking at the defendant's club most of the day when its duty manager offered her a taxi home. She refused and was subsequently seriously injured when struck by a car near the defendant's premises.
30   *Enright v Coolum Resort Pty Ltd & Anors* [2002] QSC 394.
31   See *Rogers v Whittaker* (1992) 175 CLR 479, where the High Court imposed a requirement on medical professionals to disclose risks of particular concern to the individual patient rather than just the reasonably likely risks.

travel agents (the Travel Compensation Fund) must meet the standard of care required of an accountant or face professional liability. This is so even if the travel agent has acted illegally. [32]

Damage

Causation

[5.70] Damage is an essential part of the tort of negligence. Unless the plaintiff can show damage, her or his action will fail. However, the plaintiff must also establish that it was the defendant's negligence which caused the damage, and that it was not too remote. There are times when the defendant's actions are *the* cause of the damage and times when it is only *a* cause of the damage. Courts sometimes resolve this problem by using the *but for* test. That is, the plaintiff may only recover where the damage would not have occurred *but for* the defendant's negligent acts and omissions. [33]

However, what happens when later events have some effect on the situation created by the defendant's negligence? Then, the court must determine whether each subsequent event is a link in the chain of causation between the defendant's negligence and the plaintiff's injuries, or whether it has broken the chain of causation. [34]

Apart from the *but for* test, courts also determine causation by using a "common sense" approach. In *March v Stramare*, Deane J said: [35]

> For the purposes of the law of negligence, the question of causation arises in the context of the attribution of fault or responsibility whether an identified negligent act or omission of the defendant was so connected with the plaintiff's loss or injury that as a matter of ordinary common sense and experience, it should be regarded as a cause of it.

Remoteness of damage

[5.75] Where does a court draw the line when determining causation, remoteness of damage and assessment of damages? Policy, social values, discretion as to what is "fair" may play a part. However, in the end it must come down to a question of fact and reasonable foreseeability of the kind or type of damage suffered.

The principle of remoteness of damage is best illustrated by the *Wagon Mound* cases. In *Wagon Mound No 1* [36] the plaintiff owned a dockyard where welding work was under way.

---

32 See *Travel Compensation Fund v Robert Tambree trading as Tambree and Associates & ors* (2005) 224 CLR 627 where the facts established that the accountant and the auditor had engaged in misleading and deceptive conduct in preparing financial statements which failed to disclose substantial liabilities and instead reported a net profit.

33 *Chapman v Hearse* (1961) 106 CLR 112. The defendant drove his car negligently causing an accident. *Facts*: The plaintiff, a medical doctor stopped to administer medical assistance and was in turn run over by another car while doing so. *Held*: The defendant was primarily responsible for the plaintiff's injuries which would not have occurred "but for" the defendant's careless driving.

34 For example, see *Adeels Palace Pty Ltd v Moubarak; Adeels Palace Pty Ltd v Bou Najem* [2009] JCA 48. *Facts*: A dispute broke out between two women on the defendant's licensed premises during a New year's party in 2003. A third person left the premises and returned a short time later with a gun and shot the plaintiffs. *Held*: (in part) that the absence of security personnel at the licensed premises on the night the plaintiffs were shot was not a necessary condition of their being shot, and thus the "but for" test of causation was not satisfied.

35 *March v Stramare* (1991) 171 CLR 506 at 522. *Facts*: The defendant's truck was parked in the middle of the road with its hazard lights flashing. The plaintiff was drunk and speeding and collided with the rear of the truck seriously injuring himself. *Held*: The injuries were caused or materially contributed to by the wrongful conduct of the truck driver.

36 *Overseas Tankship (UK) Ltd v Morts Dock Engineering Co Ltd* (1961) AC 388.

The defendant was the owner of a tanker called *The Wagon Mound* moored in Sydney Harbour. Oil was spilled negligently from the tanker and it spread to the plaintiff's wharf. Molten metal from work being carried out on the wharf dropped onto floating cotton waste which ignited and set fire to the oil. The fire damaged the plaintiff's wharf.

The matter went on appeal to the Privy Council, which held that the damage was too remote. The evidence did not support a finding that the defendant knew and could have been expected to know that it's negligent conduct – spilling oil on water – would result in the kind of damage that the plaintiff suffered, that is, damage caused by fire. Their Lordships said (at 426) that:

> it would be wrong that a man should be held liable for damage unpredictable by a reasonable man because it was "direct" or "natural"; equally it would be wrong that he should escape liability, however "indirect" the damage, if he foresaw or could reasonably foresee the intervening events which led to its being done ... Thus foreseeability becomes the effective test.

However, in *Wagon Mound No 2*,[37] the plaintiff was the owner of one of the ships damaged in the fire. Evidence presented this time led the court to conclude that the defendant should have known that oil spilled on water was capable of ignition. Although the risk of fire was remote, it was not impossible. To satisfy the test, the Privy Council said there had to be "[a] real risk, one which would occur to the mind of a reasonable man in the defendant's position and which he would not brush aside as far-fetched".[38]

Other Specific Torts

[5.80] There are a number of special types of liability[39] in negligence, in particular:

- negligent misstatement;
- vicarious liability;
- public authorities; and
- defamation.

Negligent misstatement

When does the duty arise?

[5.85] It is now settled law that the duty arises when a person with special skills or knowledge gives advice to another in circumstances in which the person knows, or ought to realise, that the other person has placed reasonable reliance on that advice. In such circumstances, the person giving advice accepts the consequent responsibility for taking care in making the statement.

Gibbs CJ in *Shaddock & Associates Pty Ltd v Parramatta City Council*[40] said that the duty should:

> extend to persons who, on a serious occasion, give considered advice or information concerning a business or professional transaction.

---

37   *Overseas Tankships (UK) v Miller SS Co* [1967] 1 AC 617.
38   *Overseas Tankships (UK) v Miller SS Co* [1967] 1 AC 617 at 643.
39   Another special category was "occupier's liability" based on a distinction drawn between paying and non-paying visitors. However, now the test is based on general principles of negligence, reasonable foreseeability and proximity. Similarly the tort of "passing off" is now largely governed by consumer protection legislation: See Chapter 9.
40   *Shaddock & Associates Pty Ltd v Parramatta City Council* (1981) 150 CLR 225 at 234.

Whenever a person, with special skills or with access to information not otherwise readily available, responds to a request for information or advice and knows (or must reasonably contemplate) that the request is made on behalf of a limited class of persons for a particular purpose, the duty is likely to arise.

To whom is the duty owed?

[5.90] The fact that advice may be given gratuitously is irrelevant, but ordinary principles of proximity and foreseeability apply. Nor is it limited to a particular type of transaction or to a particular class of persons.

As Gibbs CJ said:

> I can see no reason in principle why a person who being possessed of special knowledge, undertakes to impart information to another and is aware that the other will act in reliance on the information, should be in a different position from a person who, being possessed of special skill, undertakes to advise another, knowing that the other will act on his advice. [41]

Any person who indicates their willingness to assume responsibility [42] for the advice they give or who induces reliance in another on their advice [43] will owe that other person a duty. Recent decisions in Australia confirm that the ambit of duty of care for negligent misstatement now extends to a known but unintended users of such a statement [44] and may even encompass a third party passive sufferer of that misstatement. [45]

Disclaimer of liability

[5.95] In *Hedley Byrne v Heller*, the defendants had prefaced their advice with a disclaimer of liability. In the end this proved fatal to the plaintiff's claim. However, in *Shaddock v Parramatta City Council*, [46] the High Court indicated that a disclaimer may not be effective to avoid liability in circumstances, for example, where the defendant is the only source of information such that the plaintiff and the defendant both know that the plaintiff has no choice but to rely on it. The effectiveness of disclaimers may also be challenged now under the consumer protection legislation (see [9.200]).

Vicarious liability

[5.100] What if the negligent defendant is "a man of straw" but has an employer with "deep pockets"? Can the plaintiff sue the employer instead? In some circumstances, it may be possible to impute the negligence of the servant to the master. This is the principle of vicarious liability and it is based on the philosophy that the master should be responsible for particular acts which she or he had ordered or later ratified her or his servant to do. There is no suggestion, however, that the master's conduct is blameworthy or that she or he is in breach of her or his own duty to take care.

---

41   *Shaddock & Associates Pty Ltd v Parramatta City Council* (1981) 150 CLR 225 at 233-234. See also *Hedley Byrne & Co Ltd v Heller & Partners* [1964] AC 465 and *Mutual Life & Citizen's Assurance Co Ltd v Evatt* (1968) 122 CLR 556 for further discussion of this principle.
42   *Columbia Coffee & Tea v Churchill* (1992) NSWLR 141.
43   *R Lowe Lippman Figdor & Franck (a firm) v AGC (Advances) Ltd* [1992] 2 VR 671.
44   See *Esanda Finance Corporation Ltd v Peat Marwick Hungerfords* [1997] ALJR 448 at 452-453; *Tepko Pty Limited v Water Board* (1999) Aust Torts Reports 81-525 although the earlier case of *San Sebastian Pty Ltd v The Minister* (1986) 162 CLR 340 seemed to limit liability of public authorities unless they intended the plaintiff (or a class of persons like the plaintiff) to act upon the policy the subject of the negligent misstatement.
45   *Hill v Van Erp* (1997) 188 CLR 159.
46   *Shaddock & Associates Pty Ltd v Parramatta City Council* (1981) 150 CLR 225.

Contrast this liability with "non-delegable" personal liability, such as that owed by hospitals to patients, schools to their pupils, employers to employees. It even extends to persons who have control of premises and who bring onto those premises dangerous substances, [47] or in some circumstances, to landlords to ensure that rental premises are safe for their tenants. [48] However, since the introduction of the civil liability legislation, it seems that this distinction at common law does not apply under statute. Pursuant to the legislation, a person sued for breach of a non delegable duty will have their liability determined as if they were vicariously liable for the negligence of the person in connection with the performance of the work or task. [49]

Threshold questions

[5.105] It is necessary to ask whether the tortfeasor was:
- the defendant's employee or an independent contractor; and
- acting in the normal course of her or his employment at the time the tort was committed.

Identifying the master/servant relationship

[5.110] It may be that the tortfeasor is not an employee but an independent contractor, that is, under a contract for services (independent contractor) not a contract of service (servant) (see [8.15]). The test is one of the degree of control which the employer exercises over the manner in which the work is to be performed.

What is the practical distinction between a contract of service and a contract for services?

[5.115] A contract for services is more likely in work involving a profession, trade or distinct calling on the part of the person engaged. It usually involves provision by the worker of their own place of work or of their own equipment and payment by them of business expenses. The worker's remuneration is generally paid without deduction for income tax. [50]

On the other hand, under a contract of service a person is employed as an integral part of the business, which means that he or she has defined duties and limited powers of delegation. Often, the worker's hours of work are set and instalments of tax are deducted from her or his pay cheque.

For further discussion, see [8.15].

Acts done in the course of employment

[5.120] Even if the existence of the master/servant relationship can be established, not all activities are covered. The test is that the employer is responsible for only those acts which can be regarded as a wrongful and an unauthorised mode of performing an authorised task done in the course of employment. In *Deatons Pty Ltd v Flew*, [51] for example, a bar attendant threw a glass of beer in the face of a difficult customer as she was trying to evict him from the premises. He suffered serious injury to his eye and sued her employer who argued, successfully,

---

47 *Burnie Port Authority v General Jones Pty Ltd* (1994) 179 CLR 520.
48 *Northern Sandblasting Pty. Ltd. v Harris* (1997) 188 CLR 313.
49 For example, see *Civil Liability Act 2002* (NSW), s 50.
50 See *Stevens v Brodribb Sawmilling Co Pty Ltd* (1986) 160 CLR 16.
51 *Deatons Pty Ltd v Flew* (1949) 79 CLR 370.

that the employee was acting outside the scope of her employment at the time. She was employed to serve drinks, not to act in the role of bouncer.

By contrast, in *Starks v RSM Security Pty Ltd* [52] the plaintiff, a patron at the Bondi Hotel, was asked to leave by a security officer. The plaintiff was not acting aggressively and questioned the request at which point the security officer head butted him causing personal injury. The plaintiff claimed damages against the security officer, his employer, the hotel owner and licensee of the premises. The court dismissed the claims against the last two defendants but allowed the first two claims to proceed. It held that the employer was vicariously liable for the actions of its security officer even though there had been unnecessary violence. However, if other factors were present, such as personal animosity, the result might have been different. In that event, the court would have concluded that the attack was an independent act directed against the victim even though the employee was carrying out duties at the time. [53]

In *Canterbury Bankstown Rugby League Club v Rogers*, [54] the plaintiff, a footballer, sued the defendant football club following injuries he received at the hands of one of its players. The club argued that the player, in inflicting such injuries, was "on a frolic of his own" at the time, but the court disagreed and said that the injury occurred while the player was doing what he was employed to do – that is, play football – albeit in an unauthorised manner. If the player had shot his opponent rather than punched him, perhaps the court would have viewed his behaviour differently.

There are public policy considerations which courts consider in determining vicarious liability. Generally, the defendant (employer) benefits from the acts of the tortfeasor (employee), so it is only fair that the employer should compensate for wrongs done in the course of obtaining those benefits. [55]

Public authorities

[5.125] Public authorities such as government instrumentalities and municipal councils are responsible for maintaining public utilities and spaces like national parks, beaches, waterways, highways and footpaths to name but a few. In determining their liability in the event of loss or injury, the courts must now take into account the financial and other resources that are reasonably available to the authority for the purpose of exercising those functions. [56] This approach is clearly demonstrated in the line of recreational swimming and surf related injury cases against municipal councils outlined in [5.60].

However, in the past, a road authority could escape liability for injuries or damage caused by its neglect or failure to act in respect of construction, repair and maintenance of its roads, footpaths, bridges and pathways unless at the time of the alleged failure the authority had actual knowledge of the particular risk that materialised and resulted in the harm.

---

52   *Starks v RSM Security Pty Ltd* [2004] NSWCA 351.
53   See also *Exchange Hotel Limited v Murphy* (1947) SASR 112.
54   *Canterbury Bankstown Rugby League Club v Rogers* (1993) Aust Torts Reps 81-246.
55   See Scarman J in *Rose v Plenty* (1976) 1 All ER 97.
56   This policy defence is enshrined in the civil liability legislation. See [5.185].

However, in *Brodie v Singleton Shire Council*,[57] the High Court appears to have moved away from this concept of "nonfeasance"[58] immunity for road authorities preferring instead that they be subject to the ordinary principles of negligence and statutory interpretation like other public authorities.[59]

Defamation

[5.130] A defamatory statement is one "which tends to lower a person in the estimation of his fellow men by making them think less of him".[60] Each State and Territory has now passed uniform defamation legislation which basically adopts the common law approach to most matters in defamation.[61]

Elements of the tort

[5.135] Elements of the tort include:

- defamatory matter;
- identification of the plaintiff;
- publication of the defamatory statement by words, signs or other form of communication; and
- no valid defences.

Defences to defamation

[5.140] Defences include:

- absolute privilege;
- truth (and public interest);
- qualified privilege or protection;
- honest opinion.

---

57 *Brodie v Singleton Shire Council* (2001) 206 CLR 512. *Facts*: Plaintiff drove his laden cement truck over an aged timber bridge which collapsed under its weight injuring him. *Held* The defendant Council successfully relied on nonfeasance in the NSW Court of Appeal.I The High Cort did not finally determine the matter between the parties but instead remitted the matter to the Court of Appeal for determination in accordance wth the ordinary principles of negligence and statutory construction.

58 That is, failure to carry out an obligation. Contrast this with *misfeasance* which is the improper performance of a lawful act.

59 See also *Ghantous v Hawkesbury City Council* (2001) 206 CLR 512 (leave granted at same time as in *Brodie v Singleton Shire Council*) *Facts*: Plaintiff fell and injured herself while walking on a footpath. The defect complained of was a depression at the side of a concrete footpath where grass and soil had been scoured out and eroded. *Held*: Plaintiff had not established negligence on the part of the defendant regardless of whether or not nonfeasance was available as a defence.

60 JG Fleming, *The Law of Torts* (8th ed, LBC Information Services, Sydney, 1998), p 525.

61 *Defamation Act 2005* (NSW); *Defamation Act 2005* (Vic); *Defamation Act 2005* (Qld); *Defamation Act 2005* (SA); *Defamation Act 2005* (WA); *Defamation Act 2005* (Tas); *Defamation Act* (NT); and *Civil Law (Wrongs) Act 2002* (ACT).

Truth or justification is a complete defence at common law [62] and also under the uniform defamation laws. Absolute privilege is also a complete defence, regardless of truth. [63]

Similarly, publishers of judicial or parliamentary proceedings or public meetings regarding matters of public interest or concern may enjoy qualified privilege so long as their reports of those proceedings are honestly broadcast for the information of the public and are reasonable in the circumstances. This allows statements to be published in the broader community without any legal right of redress on the part of the person so named and/or defamed.

A person relying on the defence of honest opinion does not need to prove truth of the published material but must, rather, satisfy the judge and jury that it was an honestly held opinion that was:

- clearly a matter of opinion and not a statement of fact;
- related to a matter of public interest; and
- based on "proper material". [64]

If the plaintiff can prove that the opinion was not honestly held then the defence fails.

In *John Fairfax Publications Pty Ltd v Gacic*, [65] a review was published in *The Sydney Morning Herald* of the *Coco Roco* restaurant by one of its food critics in September 2003. The review was extremely critical of the restaurant including that it was expensive, the food was unpalatable, the service was bad and the owners were incompetent for employing a chef who prepared such poor quality food. Subsequently, the restaurant closed in March 2004. The plaintiffs sued for defamation and the defendants relied on the defences of truth and fair comment (under the former legislation). In 2009, the matter returned to the Supreme Court of New South Wales where the court found that the defence of truth was established with respect to some bad service and that the defence of fair comment had been established with respect to the other parts of the review. The judge observed that the ordinary, reasonable reader would understand the review was the opinion of the food critic. [66]

General Defences to Negligence

[5.145] General defences to negligence are:

- voluntary assumption of risk;
- contributory negligence;
- inevitable accident; and,
- illegal enterprise.

Voluntary assumption of risk

[5.150] Voluntary assumption of risk is a total defence to an action for negligence at common law. In order to succeed, the defendant must show that the plaintiff was fully aware of the

---

62   Previous State legislation had modified this common law defence requiring a defendant to establish public benefit in order to mount a defence based on truth.
63   For example, a politician using parliamentary privilege to name a retired Supreme Court Judge in connection with paedophilia or reports or judgments in judicial proceedings or statutory enquiries; communications between high officers of state; and statements between lawyers and clients relevant to that relationship.
64   That is, material which is substantially true or privileged material.
65   *John Fairfax Publications Pty Ltd v Gacic* (2007) 230 CLR 291.
66   *Gacic v John Fairfax Publications Pty Ltd* [2009] NSWSC 1198.

extent of the risk posed by the defendant's negligence and that the plaintiff consented to that particular risk. [67] In other words, there must be:

- awareness of the risk posed by the defendant's negligence;
- a full appreciation of the extent of the risk; and
- a voluntary acceptance of that risk;

by the plaintiff.

It is not enough that he or she perceived the existence of danger but also that he or she fully appreciated it and voluntarily accepted the risk. [68] It applies particularly to sporting activities and those activities classified as "adventure tourism", such as skydiving, whitewater rafting, bungy jumping, rock climbing and indeed attempts at reaching the summit of Mount Everest! For more discussion; see Chapter 15.

The civil liability legislation has impacted the law regarding voluntary assumption of risk. [69] See [5.185] for further discussion.

Contributory negligence

[5.155] Contributory negligence used to be a complete defence to a plaintiff's claim and often led to a very harsh result, especially where the plaintiff had contributed in only small measure to her or his subsequent injuries and/or damages.

In recent years, contributory negligence has become entirely regulated by legislation in all States and Territories. [70] What the legislation does is to apportion damages according to each party's respective blame for the accident. For example, if the court finds that the plaintiff's contributory negligence is 20 per cent and that the proper amount of damages is $20,000, then the plaintiff will be awarded $16,000.

Because of the statutory intervention, contributory negligence is now only a partial defence. The law requires the plaintiff to take steps that a reasonable person would take for her or his own safety. Courts will often examine the plaintiff's own negligence to see if it contributed to her or his injuries, for example, in cases involving motor vehicle accidents where the plaintiff has failed to wear a seatbelt or a helmet, etc.

Traditionally, courts have been reluctant to find contributory negligence on the part of employees for "mere inattention or inadvertence" whilst they were engaged in their

---

67 Smith v Charles Baker & Sons (1891) AC 325; Insurance Commissioner v Joyce (1948) 77 CLR 39.
68 See O'Shea v Permanent Trustee Co of NSW (1971) Qd R 1, where the evidence was that the plaintiff knew that the defendant had been drinking but was unaware of how much, because they had not spent the whole evening together. The plaintiff was found contributorily negligent by impairing his own ability to judge the defendant's ability to drive.
69 For example, an intoxicated person in New South Wales is now deemed to have contributed 25 per cent to their injury. There is no liability in Queensland for personal injury suffered from obvious risks of dangerous recreational activities which would include some of those activities mentioned earlier.
70 For example Civil Liability Act 2002 (NSW), s 5R which states: "The principles that are applicable in determining whether a person has been negligent also apply in determining whether the person who suffered harm has been contributorily negligent in failing to take precautions against the risk of that harm." See also Civil Liability Act 2003 (Qld), Div 6.

employers' business.[71] Similarly, even in cases where employees have "knowingly" exposed themselves to the risk of injury, the High Court has said:[72]

> A finding that the plaintiff knew or ought to have known that what he was doing was highly dangerous does not necessarily establish that he was guilty of a lack of reasonable care for his own safety in the circumstances of his employment. It would also need to be established by the defendant that the plaintiff knew or ought to have known that what he did, even though it was highly dangerous, was not required of him in the performance of his duties.

In some States [73] the civil liability legislation now provides that where a person is injured while intoxicated, they are presumed to be contributorily negligent. The injured person then bears the evidential onus to rebut this presumption.

Inevitable accident

[5.160] Throughout history, there have been Acts of God, forces majeure, calamities and disasters which occur in nature that interrupt the expected course of events. Tsunamis, earthquakes, land slides and storms wreak havoc and may cause horrific personal injuries and damage to property. They could not possibly be prevented by the exercise of ordinary care, caution or skill.

Given exceptional conditions, public authorities and private citizens alike who owe a duty of care to plaintiffs either at common law or under statute may avoid liability if they can prove that the conditions were beyond their control and that an accident could not have been avoided, even with great skill and care. Lord Blackburn in the famous case of *Rylands v Fletcher*[74] put it this way:

> [The defendant] can excuse himself by showing that the escape was owing to the plaintiff's default; or perhaps that the escape was the consequence of vis major, or the act of God.

Illegal enterprise

[5.165] This topic has already been examined in the context of the discussion on the duty of care. In *Gala v Preston*,[75] joy riders in a stolen car were involved in a car accident. A passenger in the car was injured and sued the driver. The court found that by the very nature of the joint enterprise, the plaintiff would not be relying on the defendant to exercise any standard of care and the plaintiff voluntarily and enthusiastically accepted the risks of the enterprise.

The civil liability legislation impacts on illegal enterprises. Some States simply deny liability for damages if a court is satisfied that

- the accident occurred while the injured person was engaged in conduct constituting an indictable offence [76] or a serious offence;[77] and

---

71 See *Commissioner of Railways v Ruprecht* (1979) 142 CLR 563: "The plaintiff's inadvertence was not such as to amount to a failure to take reasonable care for his own safety ... I particularly rely on the circumstances that the employment demanded, and obtained, the plaintiff's concentration upon it, and involved a risk of danger to which the plaintiff had become habituated ..."
72 *Commissioner for Railways v Halley* (1978) 20 ALR 409 at 415.
73 See *Wrongs (Liability and Damages for Personal Injury) Amendment Act 2002* (SA); *Civil Liability Act 2002* (Tas); *Civil Law (Wrongs) Act 2002* (ACT).
74 *Rylands v Fletcher* (1868) LR 3 HL 330.
75 *Gala v Preston* (1991) 172 CLR 243.
76 *Recreational Services (Limitation of Liability) Act 2002* (SA); *Civil Law (Wrongs) Act 2002* (ACT).

- the injured person's conduct contributed materially to the risk of injury. Courts do have a discretion to award damages in exceptional circumstances.

In some other States, the court must consider whether the plaintiff was engaged in an illegal activity in determining whether a defendant's duty of care has been discharged. [78]

Evidential Matters

[5.170] It is the plaintiff's responsibility to prove that the defendant was at fault. In other words, the plaintiff bears the evidential onus of establishing proof of negligence. This can sometimes cause difficulties for plaintiffs, especially if it is not clear how or why the accident occurred. Fortunately, there are two legal principles which may assist the plaintiff in this task.

Breach of statutory duty

[5.175] Very often, when a plaintiff suffers personal injuries at the hands of a defendant, there is an allegation that he or she has breached some duty imposed by statute. A common example is the case of the drink driver involved in a motor vehicle collision, injuring others. Generally, the statute imposes only a penalty (fine or imprisonment) for the defendant's breach of the road traffic rules. The plaintiff must pursue their common law action for personal injuries alleging the defendant's negligent driving.

In producing evidence to support that claim of negligent driving, however, the plaintiff may refer to the fact of the defendant having consumed a quantity of alcohol and of having breached a particular statutory provision. In other words, the defendant's failure to comply with the relevant statute or regulatory standard establishes prima facie evidence of negligence. [79]

In rare cases, a statute may *specifically* provide that a plaintiff who has suffered injury following a defendant's breach of statutory duty may sue that person pursuant to the Act. For example, see the *Australian Consumer Law*, s 236:

(1) If:
   (a) a person (the *claimant*) suffers loss or damage because of the conduct of another person; and
   (b) the conduct contravened a provision of Chapter 2 or 3;
   the claimant may recover the amount of the loss or damage by action against that other person, or against any person involved in the contravention.

With the introduction of the civil liability legislation, in proceedings against public authorities based on breach of statutory duty, the plaintiff will now have to prove that the act or omission was in the circumstances so unreasonable that no authority having those sorts of functions would properly consider the act or omission to be a reasonable exercise of its role. [80]

More frequently, however, the two actions (common law negligence and breach of statutory duty) are quite distinct from each other.

---

77 *Civil Liability Act 2002* (Tas).
78 *Wrongs and Other Acts (Public Liability Insurance Reform) Act 2002* (Vic).
79 See for example the traffic law cases: *Mercer v Commissioner for Road Transport and Tramways (NSW)* (1937) 56 CLR 580; *Tucker v McCann* [1948] VLR 22; *Croston v Vaughan* [1938] 1 KB 540 at 551-552.
80 For example, see *Civil Liability Act 2002* (NSW), s 43.

Res ipsa loquitur

[5.180] This is an evidential principle that literally means "the act speaks for itself", that is, where negligence is the most probable cause of the plaintiff's injuries. For example, a pedestrian while walking along a footpath who was injured by falling debris from a nearby building site, would ask a court to draw an inference of negligence from the proved facts giving rise to the injuries he or she sustained.

The defendant would then need to rebut that inference of negligence by pointing to an explanation of the plaintiff's injuries consistent with the defendant's maintenance of reasonable safety standards. If that explanation were successful, the court would then have to consider whether or not the plaintiff had established their case on the balance of probabilities.

In the case of *Russell v London & South West Railway*,[81] Kennedy LJ explained the principle this way:

> *Res ipsa loquitur* does not mean, as I understand it, that merely because at the end of a journey a horse is found hurt, or somebody is hurt in the streets, the mere fact that he is hurt implies negligence. This is absurd. It means that the circumstances are, so to speak, eloquent of the negligence of somebody who brought about the state of things which is complained of.

Tort Reform in Australia

[5.185] In 2002, the Law Council of Australia made a submission[82] to the Negligence Review Panel chaired by Justice Ipp. It recognised that the principal functions of negligence law are:

- the compensation function;[83]
- the deterrent function; and,[84]
- the coercive justice or responsibility function.[85]

In our society, these functions are generally achieved through insurance which "spreads the risk" within the community so that victims receive a fair and just compensation and that wrongdoers have responsibility allocated proportionately. In the tourism industry, in particular, risk management is vital especially as recreational activities necessarily involve a degree of obvious and sometimes inherent danger which could expose the operator to large compensation claims in the event of a person suffering personal injuries or death during such an activity. Of course, the more claims that are made, the higher the premiums become industry wide and eventually some recreational activities are considered so "risky" that they are almost uninsurable. At this point, many operators will consider closing their businesses down.

The civil liability legislation (State and Territory)[86] now limits liability for dangerous recreational activities which particularly affects adventure tourism operators as well as addressing issues of foreseeability, breach of duty, voluntary assumption of risk, and

---

81   *Russell v London & South West Railway* (1908) 24 TLR 548 at 551.
82   Submission by the Law Council of Australia to the Negligence Review Panel on the *Review of the Law of Negligence* (2 August 2002), pp 7-9.
83   Fair and just recompense for persons injured through fault.
84   Encouragement of safety and risk management.
85   A just allocation among wrongdoers of responsibility for compensation.
86   *Civil Liability Act 2002* (NSW); *Civil Liability Act 2003* (Qld); *Recreational Services (Limitation of Liability) Act 2002* (SA); *Wrongs and Other Acts (Public Liability Insurance Reform) Act 2002* (Vic); *Civil Liability Act 2002* (WA); *Civil Liability Act 2002* (Tas); *Civil Law (Wrongs) Act 2002* (ACT); *Consumer Affairs and Fair Trading Amendment Act* (NT).

contributory negligence, amongst others. For its part, the *Australian Consumer Law* whose federal provisions normally prevail over State legislation deems in s 275 that if the State is the proper law of the contract, then its laws will apply to limit or preclude liability for failure to comply with a guarantee in the supply of services. This illustrates how the law is continuing to evolve to deal with the needs and issues arising in the tourism, travel and hospitality industry. For further discussion, see Chapter 15.

Exercise

A walk on the wild side

Three teenage friends, Larry, Mo and Curly, decided to go camping for the weekend at the Crocodile Creek National Park. The access to the Park is by a dirt road. On arrival at the campground, there is a self registration booth where campers are required to register. There is also a Visitor Information billboard in the precinct of the campground which sets out all the walking tracks and scenic features and other points of interest within the Park. When the boys arrived at the campsite, they registered and then headed off for a swim in the creek. Next morning, the boys had another swim and then Curly suggested that they should all go to a rock pool known as the "Tear Drop". He had been there once before and it had been a lot of fun jumping from a height into the deep water below. The Tear Drop was listed on the billboard as a place of scenic interest and the map showed its location. However, there was no proper path to the rock pool so Larry and his mates climbed over rocks along the side of the creek and walked through the bush to get there.

The Tear Drop, as its name suggests, is a part of the creek where a partial oval-shaped pool has been formed by the surrounding rock. There is a steep drop off from the overhanging rocks to the deep creek waters below just perfect for swimming and diving. However, a rock ledge which is almost invisible beneath the waterline runs along one edge of the rock pool wall. Curly was the first to jump off the overhanging rock encouraging his friends to follow. Mo jumped next. Larry hesitated, inspected the rock pool without noticing the submerged rock ledge and then dived into the water. He immediately struck his head on this ledge suffering serious head and spinal injuries.

There is evidence that the park is always manned by a park ranger and that he is aware that people use the rock pool for swimming and diving. If he sees people heading off for the Tear Drop, he usually warns them of the hazards associated with diving or jumping into the rock pool below. On this occasion, he did not see Larry and his friends. There are no signs anywhere in the Park warning of the dangers of swimming or diving at the Tear Drop.

Does Larry have a cause of action against the National Parks authority? What (if any) defence(s) could be raised? Discuss whether the issues are different:

(1)   at common law; and

(2)   under *Civil Liability* legislation.

For further discussion of issues, see *Reardon v State of Queensland* [2007] QSA 436.

CHAPTER 6

Criminal Law

[6.05] THE CRIMINAL LAW IN CONTEXT		115
[6.10] SOURCES OF THE CRIMINAL LAW		116
[6.15]	Coded Jurisdictions	116
[6.20]	Common Law Jurisdictions	116
[6.25]	Advantages of codifying the criminal law	117
[6.30] CLASSIFICATION OF OFFENCES		117
[6.35]	Indictable Offences	117
[6.40]	Summary Offences	117
[6.45]	Indictable offences tried summarily	117
[6.50] ELEMENTS OF CRIMINAL LIABILITY		118
[6.55]	Gross Negligence	119
[6.60]	*R v Sanby*	119
[6.65]	Strict Liability	120
[6.70] PARTICULAR OFFENCES		121
[6.75]	Offences against the Person	121
[6.75]	Homicide	121
[6.80]	Assault	122
[6.85]	Child sex tourism	122
[6.90]	Offences against Property	123
[6.90]	Stealing	123
[6.100]	*R v Hall*	124
[6.110]	Secret commissions	125
[6.115]	Defences	126
[6.120]	Complete defences	126
[6.145]	Partial defences	128
[6.165]	Statutory defences	130
[6.170] THE CRIMINAL PROCEDURE		131
[6.175]	Arrest	131
[6.180]	Entry on private property	132
[6.185]	Warrants	132
[6.190]	Citizens' arrests	132
[6.195]	The Preliminary Hearing	133
[6.200]	The Trial	133
[6.205]	Standard of Proof	134

THE CRIMINAL LAW IN CONTEXT

[6.05] A crime is an offence against the state or the community at large. In most developed countries where the rule of law is strong, it is the task of the police force to maintain law and order in the community and to bring offenders to justice. When a crime is committed, the police will prosecute the offender in a court hearing open to the public. If the wrongdoer is found guilty, he or she will be punished either by a term of imprisonment or by some lesser penalty such as a fine.

In some developing countries where the rule of law is not so strong, there may be no effective police force to oversee criminal behaviour within the community. This is often associated with a court structure inadequately equipped to deal consistently with public prosecution of wrongdoers. When this occurs, it is left to the aggrieved parties (victims/plaintiffs) to "take the law into their own hands" and to commence private prosecutions. At this stage, the distinction between crimes which are prosecuted by the state and torts which are prosecuted by private individuals becomes blurred.

In fact there is often an overlap between criminal acts and civil wrongs because the commission of a crime usually involves some offence against another individual and/or their property which will also attract civil liability.

SOURCES OF THE CRIMINAL LAW

[6.10] The sources of criminal law are the same as for all other laws. They emanate from the Parliament and the courts. The two sources are *common law* (cases) and *Statute* or *Code*.

Different jurisdictions within Australia have adopted either a common law or a codified approach to criminal law, or a combination of both.

"Coded" Jurisdictions

[6.15] The Commonwealth,[1] Queensland,[2] Western Australia,[3] Tasmania,[4] Northern Territory[5] and more recently the Australian Capital Territory[6] have codified their criminal laws. The various codes have attempted to both restate common law principles and to incorporate other statutory rules. However, the common law element of the guilty mind ("mens rea") is absent from most Codes. The mental elements of offences (if any) are expressly provided for in the sections relating to those offences.

With time, new offences have been created so that the Codes no longer contain the whole of the substantive criminal law in these jurisdictions, for example, serious drug offences[7] and summary offences such as leaving hotels or restaurants without paying are also dealt with in other legislation.[8]

Common Law Jurisdictions

[6.20] In the other jurisdictions of New South Wales, Victoria and South Australia, common law principles remain the primary source of criminal law, but even in these jurisdictions there have been substantial statutory interventions.[9]

---

1 Criminal Code attached as a schedule to *Criminal Code Act 1995* (Cth); but also see *Crimes Act 1914* (Cth).
2 Criminal Code attached as a schedule to *Criminal Code Act 1899* (Qld).
3 Criminal Code attached as a schedule to *Criminal Code Act 1913* (WA).
4 Criminal Code attached as a schedule to *Criminal Code Act 1924* (Tas), although it leaves much of the common law intact.
5 Criminal Code attached as a schedule to *Criminal Code Act* (NT).
6 *Criminal Code 2002* (ACT) (enacted directly).
7 For example the *Drugs Misuse Act 1986* (Qld).
8 For example, the *Regulatory Offences Act 1985* (Qld), s 6: "Any person who with respect to food, drink, accommodation, or like goods and services, of the value of $150 or less obtained from any restaurant or hotel, motel, boarding house or like premises ... leaves such premises without discharging ... his or her lawful indebtedness ... is guilty of a regulatory offence...."
9 For example, *Crimes Act 1900* (NSW); *Crimes Act 1958* (Vic); *Criminal Law Consolidation Act 1935* (SA).

Advantages of codifying the criminal law

[6.25] It makes sense to codify laws which are referred to often. The law thus becomes easier to find and to understand. Remember also that "ignorance of the law is no excuse". That is why a Parliamentary Counsel's Committee has now produced a Model Criminal Code prepared as a law for any State or Territory to adapt if it so desires. [10]

Offences in the Model Criminal Code are presented in a systematic fashion and the terminology used is mainly consistent throughout. The Model Code endeavours to be comprehensive in dealing with all criminal issues so that it represents an exhaustive statement of the law on that topic. [11] A codified criminal law is the product of a democratic process, unlike the common law (which is judge-made), so that although it may be less flexible than the common law, it compensates for that by being more certain, predictable and responsive to changes in community values.

CLASSIFICATION OF OFFENCES

[6.30] The classification of crimes varies from jurisdiction to jurisdiction but there are three broad categories into which most offences fall. They are:
- wrongs against morality (for example, murder);
- threats to the peace and order of the community (for example, theft); and
- statutory offences directed to maintaining minimum standards of public health, safety and consumer protection in the community.

Indictable Offences

[6.35] In all Australian jurisdictions, criminal offences are categorised as either indictable or summary offences. The more serious offences such as murder, manslaughter, burglary and theft are triable on indictment. An indictment is the form of charge which commences proceedings before a court above the Magistrates Court level. In other words, indictable offences are generally heard before a judge and jury.

Summary Offences

[6.40] Less serious offences, such as common assault and various breaches of statutory regulations, are triable summarily, which means that they are normally heard and determined by a single magistrate in the absence of a jury. [12]

Indictable offences tried summarily

[6.45] In the common law jurisdictions, magistrates have been given statutory powers [13] to deal with some indictable, or more serious offences, summarily. [14] For example, in cases involving loss or damage to property, if that loss or damage is minimal or falls below a certain

---

10 It is a collation of draft provisions in various separate reports and submissions and finally published as a first edition on 28 May 2009.
11 For example, serious drug offences and computer offences are now included in the model code as well as the pre-existing serious offences to property and person.
12 B Fisse, *Howard's Criminal Law* (5th ed, Law Book Co, 1990), p 9.
13 For example, *Magistrates Court Act 1989* (Vic), s 25.
14 For example, see *Criminal Procedure Act 1986* (NSW), Schedule 1 for examples of such offences.

value, then the magistrate may decide to try the matter. However, before determining to do this, the magistrate must be satisfied that there are no serious issues involved and that he or she could impose an appropriate sentence on the accused person in the event of conviction.[15]

The "coded" jurisdictions make express provision for the summary trial of indictable offences, if appropriate.[16] Sometimes, the accused person must consent to the summary hearing before it can proceed in the lower court. In all cases, the magistrate has a discretion to require the accused person to stand trial in the higher court.

There are a number of advantages for the defendant in proceeding with a summary trial of the issues. First, it avoids the necessity for a costly and time-consuming trial in one of the higher courts. Secondly, the penalties which might attach to the offence in the higher court are generally significantly greater than those which the magistrate has power to impose. Thirdly, the process is much quicker even if the result is more likely to be a conviction.

ELEMENTS OF CRIMINAL LIABILITY

[6.50] The generally accepted view at common law has always been that a person should not be convicted of a criminal offence unless that person is coincidentally morally blameworthy for the crime. That is why children[17] and mentally insane persons are excused from criminal responsibility. However, there is a growing debate as to whether corporations can commit crimes which, of course, requires an examination of the state of mind of the corporation as an entity.[18] Even so, once charged with a criminal offence, a corporation must still be represented by a person standing for the company.[19]

This is reflected in the Latin maxim, *actus non facit reum nisi mens sit rea*.[20] The High Court in *Kural v The Queen*[21] discussed the mental element in crime and said that:

> Depending upon the nature of the particular offence, the requirement of a guilty mind may involve intention, foresight, knowledge or awareness with respect to some act, circumstance or consequence.

For a person to be morally blameworthy, two elements must be present. They are the wrongful act (actus reus); and the guilty mind (mens rea).

The intent (mens rea) to commit the crime and the wrongful act (actus reus) must coincide to constitute the crime. Sometimes, the prosecutor's task is made easy. For example, take the case of a person discovered in someone else's dwelling house without permission, at night, with goods belonging to that other person in his or her possession. The person would almost certainly be charged with the offence of burglary, one of the elements of which is the intent to commit a crime, in this case, stealing.

---

15 See generally L Waller and CR Williams, *Criminal Law Text and Cases* (11th ed, Butterworths, 2009).
16 For example, see Criminal Code (Qld), s 552B – Charges of indictable offences that may be dealt with summarily.
17 Under the age of ten years in most jurisdictions and under the age of seven years in Tasmania.
18 See S Bronitt & B McSherry, *Principles of Criminal Law* (3rd ed, Lawbook Co, 2010), Chapter 3 *Principles of Criminal Responsibility*.
19 A Gibson, *Commercial Law in Principle* (3rd ed, Lawbook Co, 2005), p 648.
20 That is, an act does not render a person guilty unless accompanied by a guilty mind.
21 *Kural v The Queen* (1987) 162 CLR 502 at 504 per Mason CJ, Deane and Dawson JJ.

Gross Negligence

[6.55] However, sometimes there is no intention on the part of the offender to cause harm to others – just a reckless disregard for the consequences of their actions. For example, is a drunk driver who runs down and kills a pedestrian morally blameworthy and therefore guilty of manslaughter (the unlawful killing) of that other person? Presumably, he or she neither intended nor foresaw the consequences of his or her impaired driving abilities.

As discussed in [5.25], negligence in the civil law is based on the notion that the defendant's reckless or careless conduct caused the plaintiff harm in circumstances in which the defendant should have taken more care. The standard of care to be applied is that of the reasonable person engaged in that activity.

The criminal law imposes a much higher standard of care. In order to establish criminal liability, the accused person must be guilty of "gross negligence". The English Court of Appeal in *R v Bateman* [22] explained that what had to be proved was that:

> the negligence of the accused went beyond a mere matter of compensation between subjects and showed such disregard for the life and safety of others as to amount to a crime against the State and conduct deserving punishment.

A more recent tourism case touching on this issue is that of *R v Sanby*.

R v Sanby

[6.60] *R v Sanby* (Unreported, Court of Criminal Appeal Northern Territory, No CA8 of 1992)

Facts: Two hot-air balloons collided some 2,000 feet above ground level when the basket of the first balloon being operated by the defendant came into contact with the top of the second balloon in which there were 12 tourists and an operator. The basket of the defendant's balloon penetrated the fabric of the second balloon and a large vent opened. The second balloon deflated rapidly and the basket and its occupants plummeted to their deaths.

The defendant was charged (amongst other things) with manslaughter. The prosecution suggested that the defendant had so departed from the standard expected of the reasonable hot air balloon pilot that "it was a gross deviation from what ordinary, reasonable people would expect". He went on to say that the defendant "showed a callous and reckless and totally unacceptable disregard for the life and safety of people who were up there, fellow balloonists".

Decision: The defendant was eventually acquitted on all counts of manslaughter and found guilty of a lesser crime. [23] This finding was also subsequently quashed on appeal. In considering the defendant's appeal, Mildren J examined the comments made by the prosecutor in his opening speech and concluded that:

> He was, after all, opening a case for manslaughter, an essential ingredient of which was that the Crown had to prove actual foresight by the appellant of the possibility of death to his passengers as a consequence of his actions, which were of such a kind that no reasonable person similarly circumstanced to the appellant and having such foresight would have proceeded with that conduct: Criminal Code s 31(2).

In other words, gross negligence in this case would have been established if:

- there was evidence that the defendant actually saw the second balloon before the collision; and
- that he foresaw the possibility of danger; and

---

22   *R v Bateman* (1925) 19 Cr App R 8 at 11-12 per Salter LCJ.
23   Pursuant to s 154 of the *Northern Territory Criminal Code*.

R v Sanby cont.

- that he failed to take the steps that a reasonable balloonist would have taken to avoid the collision or the possibility of it. [24]

On the evidence presented, the jury remained unconvinced that the elements of "gross negligence" had been satisfied. [25]

Strict Liability

[6.65] A further complication arises when the source of the criminal offence is statute law. In many instances, the legislative provision may simply refer to the doing of the act itself as constituting the crime without there being any reference to intent or moral blameworthiness ("the guilty mind"). In those cases, the courts must decide whether the Parliament required proof of the guilty mind or not. This is, of course, a departure from the general principles of criminal liability and it is often attributable to public policy considerations, such as making the task of the law enforcement agencies (the police) in obtaining convictions a little easier.

What the courts look for are words such as "with intent", "knowingly", or "wilfully" in the statute. When these words are present, the prosecution must establish evidence of the guilty mind as well as the doing of the unlawful act. For example, both in the common law and "coded" jurisdictions, larceny or stealing requires evidence of a fraudulent intent to permanently deprive the owner of the thing taken. [26]

However, when those words are absent, the prosecution need only prove the doing of the unlawful act(s) without reference to the defendant's state of mind – a much simpler matter. This means the defendant may be punished for an act over which he or she had no control or for which he or she could not be morally blamed. For this reason, most offences of strict liability are for commonly occurring or regulatory infractions of the law such as those concerning workplace health and safety, food safety, consumer protection and environmental protective measures. [27]

To illustrate the difference in approach between offences of strict liability and those requiring proof of criminal intent, take the example of a person renting a holiday flat who

---

24   *R v Sanby* (Unreported, Court of Criminal Appeal Northern Territory, No CA8 of 1992), at 39 per Mildren J.

25   In 1995, two directors of Garibaldi Smallgoods Pty Ltd, South Australia, were charged with manslaughter over the death of a young girl who suffered serious complications after eating some Garibaldi mettwurst. The charges were later dropped in favour of lesser charges to which the directors pleaded guilty. In 1998, Kack Nairn, skipper of the Outer Edge, was charged with manslaughter over the disappearance of two divers, Tom and Eileen Lonergan, who were left behind on a dive trip. He was subsequently acquitted at trial of all charges in 1999. These two cases illustrate the degree of difficulty courts face in proving "gross negligence".

26   For example s 391(a) of the *Criminal Code Act 1899* (Qld) states in part: "A person who fraudulently takes anything capable of being stolen, or fraudulently converts to the person's own use or to the use of any other person anything capable of being stolen, is said to steal that thing." The section goes on to talk about what amounts to a "fraudulent intent", including an intent to permanently deprive the owner of the thing of it. Compare this with the elements of the offence of larceny at common law which include that (a) a person must without the consent of the owner; (b) fraudulently and without claim of right made in good faith; (c) take and carry away; (d) anything capable of being stolen; with intent at the time of such taking permanently to deprive the owner of that property. See, for example, *Kennison v Daire* (1986) 160 CLR 129.

27   A Gibson, *Commercial Law in Principle* (3 rd ed, Lawbook Co, 2005), p 645.

leaves without paying for their stay. Stealing is a serious offence both in the "coded" jurisdictions and at common law, requiring proof of intent.[28]

Alternatively, the person could be charged pursuant to s 6 of the *Regulatory Offences Act 1985* (Qld) which creates offences analogous to stealing but which may be summarily determined. Section 6(1) provides:

> (1) Any person who, with respect to food, drink, accommodation, or like goods and services, of the value of $150 or less obtained from any restaurant or hotel, motel, boarding house or like premises–
>
> (a) leaves such premises without discharging, or attempting honestly, or making proper arrangements, to discharge, his or her lawful indebtedness therefore; or
>
> (b) purports to pay for them with a cheque that is not met on presentation or a credit card or similar document the person is not authorised to use;
>
> is guilty of a regulatory offence.

The effect of this section is to remove the element of "intent" from the offence. There is no mention of the words "wilfully", "knowingly" or "with intent" and so the prosecution need establish only the fact that the person has left the premises without lawfully paying their bill. It does not need to prove "the guilty mind" as well. Section 6(2) goes on to provide that:

> It is a defence to a charge of an offence defined in subsection (1)(b) to prove the defendant believed on reasonable grounds the cheque would be paid in full on presentation or the defendant was authorised to use the credit card or similar document.

In the situation where the defendant has offered to pay for the accommodation with a cheque that bounces or with an unauthorised credit card, the onus of proof then shifts to the defendant to establish their defence. The defendant must satisfy the magistrate "on the balance of probabilities" that the defendant believed on reasonable grounds that they had discharged their obligations by paying as they did. The overall result is that more people are likely to be convicted of stealing offences under this provision than under the provisions requiring proof of intent.[29]

PARTICULAR OFFENCES

[6.70] It has already been noted in [6.30] that the criminal law is directed to maintaining standards of morality, protecting individuals and their property and regulating certain activities for reasons of public policy. This section will examine in more detail:

- offences against the person; and
- offences against property.

Offences against the Person

Homicide

[6.75] Homicide is the killing of another human being. It may be either:

- murder – intention to kill;

---

28   See previous discussion on elements of stealing.
29   Compare with *Regulatory Offences Act 1985* (Qld), s 7 *Unauthorised damage to property* –which does require the prosecution to prove that a person "wilfully" destroyed or damaged property – an element of intent.

- manslaughter – no intention to kill; or
- excusable – self-defence or a police officer acting to prevent a crime.

One of the elements of the crime of murder is the guilty mind (mens rea) which may be evidenced by motive to kill, for example. At [6.55] we discussed the elements of the crime of manslaughter in some detail. It is different from murder in that there is no element of intent to kill. For example, a motorist who is grossly negligent in driving a car which kills another may be guilty of manslaughter. The degree of neglect ("gross negligence") which attracts criminal responsibility is much greater than that which would suffice in a civil proceeding and it is therefore often difficult to get convictions.

Assault

[6.80] Assaults fall into two categories – non-sexual and sexual. There is an overlap between torts and the criminal law with respect to assault, which has already been discussed in [5.20]. The only real difference in the definition of assault between the common law and "coded" jurisdictions is in the dropping of the term "battery" in the statutory definitions.[30] Battery is the actual application of force. No such distinction of "assault and battery" exists in the statutory definitions so that both the threat and/or application of force amount to an assault.

The common law definition of assault (including battery) may be described as "the actual intended use of ... force to another person without his consent".[31] The statutory position is reasonably encapsulated in s 245 of the Criminal Code (Qld) "Definition of Assault". It states:

> A person who strikes, touches, or moves, or otherwise applies force of any kind to, the person of another, either directly or indirectly, without the other person's consent, or with the other person's consent if the consent is obtained by fraud, or who by any bodily act or gesture attempts or threatens to apply force of any kind to the person of another without the other person's consent, under such circumstances that the person making the attempt or threat has actually or apparently a present ability to effect a person's purpose, is said to assault that other person, and the act is called an assault...

The offence is committed if there is a threat or the application of force to another without their consent in circumstances in which the victim fears that the other person has an actual or apparent ability to carry out their threat. Security officers, bouncers in nightclubs and persons in charge of crowd control situations must be careful in the conduct of their duties to exercise discretion in handling difficult or rowdy people or they may find themselves in court defending a charge of assault.

Rape and indecent assault are examples of sexual assaults which require additional elements of proof.

Child sex tourism

[6.85] There has been growing evidence over the past decade that many people from economically developed countries travel to developing countries specifically for the purpose of engaging in sexual activities with children under 16 years of age. This has become known as "child sex tourism". Ironically, most developed countries like Australia have domestic laws which prohibit such activities between children and adults and offenders suffer severe

---

30   B Fisse, *Howard's Criminal Law* (5th ed, Law Book Co, 1990), p 138.
31   *Fagan v Metropolitan Police Commissioner* [1969] 1 QB 439 at 444.

penalties. However, in those countries where the rule of law is weaker [32] no such criminal laws may exist, or if they do, they are not properly enforced.

In an effort to discourage their citizens from participating in child sex tourism, many developed countries including Australia, the United States of America, New Zealand and the European Union have now established extra-territorial laws to prosecute and punish offenders even though the crime took place overseas

In Australia, the federal government amended the *Crimes Act 1914* (Cth) introducing a new Part IIIA entitled Child Sex Tourism.[33] It provides for the prosecution of Australians[34] in Australia for engaging in, profiting from or encouraging sexual activities with children anywhere in the world. Penalties range from 12 to 17 years in prison and/or substantial fines.

The Act also targets those within the tourism industry, particularly travel agents, who may arrange, supply or profit from child sex tourism both within Australia and overseas.[35] For a further discussion, see [11.340].

Offences against Property

Stealing

[6.90] The best known property offences are those involving theft. The elements of theft are:

> the taking away of a chattel belonging to another person, coupled with a purpose on the part of the taker to permanently deprive the owner of the property in the thing taken.
>
> If such a taking occurs without the consent of the owner and not under a genuine claim of right, the crime of larceny is committed.[36]

For further discussion of theft see [6.65]. Some of the other more important property offences include:

- conversion/misappropriation; and
- obtaining goods or services by deception.

Conversion or misappropriation

[6.95] A person converts or appropriates property if he or she deals with it in a way which is inconsistent with the rights of the owner of the property. Conversion is a form of stealing, but here the offender initially comes into possession of the goods quite lawfully. The intention to permanently deprive the owner of the property in the thing taken does not take place until some time later. The elements of the offence include:

- transfer of possession but not ownership of property from victim to defendant;
- instructions from victim to deal with the property in a certain way;
- honest receipt of property by the defendant; and

---

32   Such places as Cambodia, Thailand, the Philippines, and Eastern Europe.
33   See *Crimes (Child Sex Tourism) Amendment Act 1994* (Cth).
34   Section 50AD of the *Crimes Act 1914* (Cth). For example, a Fijian born Australian citizen was charged with a number of child sex offences in Vanuatu and New Caledonia by the federal police who arrested him at the Brisbane International airport in December in 2007. The charges were later dropped.
35   See ss 50DA – 50DB of the *Crimes Act 1914* (Cth).
36   Sir Frederick Jordan CJ in *R v Ward* (1938) 39 SR (NSW) 308 at 311.

- subsequent dishonest misappropriation by defendant of entrusted property.[37]

An example would be the valet parking attendant (bailee) who receives a guest's vehicle and car keys in accordance with their bailment and who subsequently refuses to deliver up the vehicle to the owner on demand. The following case illustrates the point in travel agency.

R v Hall

[6.100] *R v Hall* [1972] 2 All ER 1009

Facts: The defendant was a partner in a firm of travel agents who received money from clients as deposits and payments for charter flights to America. The funds were paid into the firm's general account. The flights were never scheduled and the money was not refunded. The defendant was convicted on seven counts of theft in respect of the money received from clients. He appealed.

Decision: Theft is defined in the *Theft Act 1968* (UK) as "the dishonest appropriation of property belonging to another". Section 5(3) provides that:

> Where a person receives property from or on account of another, and is under an obligation to the other to retain and deal with that property or the proceeds in a particular way, the property or proceeds shall be regarded (as against him) as belonging to the other.

On the special facts of the case, the court ruled that the convictions should be quashed. However, their Lordships (Edmund-Davies and Stephenson LJJ and Boreham J) went on to say that:

> Nevertheless when a client goes to a firm carrying on the business of travel agents and pays them money, he expects that in return he will, in due course, receive the tickets and other documents necessary for him to accomplish the trip for which he is paying, and the firm are "under an obligation" to perform their part to fulfil this expectation and are liable to pay him damages if they do not. But in our judgment, what was not here established was that these clients expected them "to retain and deal with that property or its proceeds in a particular way" and that an "obligation" to do so was undertaken by the appellant.

Interestingly, the court referred to the overlap which also exists between the criminal law and another area of civil liability – contract law. Counsel for the defendant conceded throughout that "the travel agent undertakes a contractual obligation in relation to arranging flights and at the proper time paying the airline and any other expenses".

———— ∞⊙⋈ ————

The criminal law may have been unsuccessful in delivering a verdict for the victims, but disgruntled travellers may, in certain circumstances, be able to sue their travel agent for breach of contract. For further discussion on the role of the travel agent, see [11.220]ff.

Obtaining goods or services by deception

[6.105] Business proprietors often have to deal with customers who obtain some financial advantage by deception. This deception may take the form of a direct evasion of a debt, for example leaving a restaurant without paying for a meal or leaving a hotel without paying for accommodation. Alternatively, it may be an indirect evasion, such as the passing of a valueless or "bouncing" cheque in payment for goods and services. The elements of the offence of obtaining goods by false pretences (as it sometimes referred to) are:

- a false misrepresentation of fact;
- past or present;
- which induces the victim;

---

37   B Fisse, *Howard's Criminal Law* (5th ed, Law Book Company, 1990), p 205.

- to part with his property.[38]

Deception (that is, an intention to defraud) is an essential ingredient of the offence. It requires something positive on the part of the offender. In *Re London and Globe Finance Corp Ltd*[39] Buckley J said:

> To deceive is, I apprehend, to induce a man to believe that a thing is true which is false, and which the person practising the deceit knows or believes to be false.

Consequently, it may be difficult to prove that a person who orders a meal in a restaurant intending to pay for it at the time and who then subsequently changes her or his mind and leaves without paying has committed a deception as opposed to a "dishonest evasion of his obligation to pay".[40]

Similarly, when a person writes a cheque for a sum in excess of her or his bank account, this is not necessarily a deception because the person is representing that sufficient funds will be in the account when the cheque is presented, not that the money is there when he or she writes the cheque.[41] The other view is that by handing over of the cheque, "the drawer... impliedly represent[s] that the existing facts at the date when he delivers the cheque to the payee or to his agent are such that in the ordinary course the cheque will, on presentation, on or after the date specified on the cheque, be met".[42]

Some jurisdictions have introduced specific legislation which removes the necessity for proof of intent for these sorts of offences where the value is below certain limits and makes it incumbent upon the defendant to show that they were not dishonest.[43]

Much of the complexity of the common law relating to the more serious offences in the area of fraud, forgery and identity crime has been modernised by statutory reforms in almost all jurisdictions.[44] For example, following recent amendments to the *Crimes Act 1900* (NSW), s 192E[45] states that.

(1) A person who, by any deception, dishonestly:

(a) obtains property belonging to another, or

(b) obtains any financial advantage or causes any financial disadvantage,

is guilty of the offence of fraud.

Secret commissions

[6.110] This is not, strictly speaking, a "property offence". This offence arises when an agent is conducting business on behalf of her or his principal and corruptly receives some inducement or reward (a bribe) from a third person which would tend to influence the way, favourably or otherwise, the agent treats that third person with respect to the principal's business.

---

38 B Fisse, *Howard's Criminal Law* (5th ed, Law Book Company, 1990), pp 229-230.
39 *Re London and Globe Finance Corp Ltd* [1903] 1 Ch 728 at 732.
40 See Lord Reid (dissenting) in *DPP v Ray* [1974] AC 370 at 380 (House of Lords).
41 KG Kenny, *An Introduction to Criminal Law in Queensland and Western Australia* (7th ed, Butterworths, 2003), Chapter 14 *Offences relating to Property*.
42 *R v Gilmartin* [1983] 1 All ER 829 at 835 per Robert Goff LJ.
43 See discussion in [6.65] and in particular the *Regulatory Offences Act 1985* (Qld), s 6.
44 For example, *Criminal Code Act 1995* (Cth), s 134.1; *Crimes Act 1900* (NSW), ss 192E – H; *Criminal Law Consolidation Act 1935* (SA), P 5, ss 130 – 133; *Criminal Code Act 1899* (Qld), s 408C, *Criminal Code Act 1913* (WA), s 409; Criminal Code (Tas), s 252A; *Crimes) Act 1959* (Vic), ss 81 – 82.
45 *Crimes Amendment (Fraud, Identity and Forgery Offences) Act 2009* (NSW).

The relationship of principal and agent often exists between travel agents and wholesale tour operators (see [11.245]) or real estate agents and property management agents and their clients, for example. Those agents must ensure that they do not receive any secret gifts or offers from another person without the knowledge of their client (principal). To do so is to receive a secret commission which may be punishable under either Commonwealth [46] or State [47] legislation. The federal legislation applies whenever the parties to a transaction reside in different States or one of them resides outside Australia.

The new s 249B of the *Crimes Act 1900* (NSW) sets out the general position. It provides that it is an offence:

(1) If any agent corruptly receives or solicits (or corruptly agrees to receive or solicit) from another person for the agent or for anyone else any benefit:

   (a) as an inducement or reward for or otherwise on account of:

      (i) doing or not doing something, or having done or not having done something, or

      (ii) showing or not showing, or having shown or not having shown, favour or disfavour to any person,

   in relation to the affairs or business of the agent's principal, or

   (b) the receipt or any expectation of which would in any way tend to influence the agent to show, or not to show, favour or disfavour to any person in relation to the affairs or business of the agent's principal,

the agent is liable to imprisonment for 7 years.

The Act goes further and provides for the recovery of the bribe from the agent and the principal may also recover the value of the gift from both the agent and the person offering the bribe. [48]

Defences

[6.115] In every criminal trial, an accused person has a choice. He or she may choose to say nothing and simply require the prosecution to prove the allegations against the accused beyond reasonable doubt. On the other hand, the accused may put forward a positive defence to the charge(s). The effect of a defence is to suggest an alternative version of the facts consistent with the defendant's innocence. If successful, it establishes the absence of intent ("the guilty mind") which is one of the essential elements of criminality. [49] For example, in a trial of murder an accused, whilst not denying that he or she killed the deceased, may assert that he or she was acting in self-defence.

Complete defences

[6.120] Some defences, if established, may entitle the defendant to an acquittal of the charge because they demonstrate a complete justification or excuse for the actions complained of. These include:

- self-defence;

---

46   *Criminal Code Act 1995* (Cth), Pts 7.3 – 7.7 deal with theft, fraud, bribery and related offences.
47   *Crimes Act 1900* (NSW), Pt 4A, ss 249A – J; Criminal Code (Qld), Ch 42A, ss 442A – M; *Criminal Law Consolidation Act 1935* (SA), Pt 6, ss 145 – 150; Criminal Code (WA), Ch LV, ss 529 – 546; Criminal Code (Tas), ss 266 – 266B, *Crimes Act 1958* (Vic), ss 175 – 180.
48   *Crimes Act 1900* (NSW), s 249G.
49   See for discussion, [6.50].

- insanity;
- necessity; and
- mistake.

Self-defence

[6.125] The accused must satisfy the court that the use of force was both reasonable and proportional to the threatened violence in the circumstances. Coincidentally, the use of force in defence of property is much more limited than in the defence of persons. Therefore, whether a jury would consider it to be excessive force or not for a home owner to use a gun to shoot at an unarmed intruder on her or his premises is a question of fact. Some States have responded to so-called "home invasions" with legislation. [50]

Insanity

[6.130] Should a defendant decide to plead mental impairment or insanity, the onus switches to the defendant to establish that defence on the balance of probabilities. The accused must establish that he or she was unable to understand the nature and quality of the act done or that it was "wrong". Dixon CJ in *R v Porter* [51] described the term as meaning:

> What is meant by wrong, is wrong having regard to the everyday standards of reasonable people ... [T]he main question ... is whether ... [the accused] was disabled from knowing that it was a wrong act to commit in the sense that ordinary reasonable [people] understand right and wrong and that he [or she] was disabled from considering with some degree of composure and reason what he [or she] was doing and its wrongness.

There was some speculation in the press at the time of the impending trial of Martin Bryant, the person responsible for the Port Arthur massacres in April 1996, that he might plead not guilty but insane to all counts of murder. He was examined by several psychiatrists, some of whom must have expressed doubt that "he was suffering such a defect of reason (caused by mental disease) that he did not know the nature and quality of the act, or, knowing its nature and quality, did not know that what he was doing was wrong". [52] In the result, Bryant pleaded guilty to all charges.

The criminal law applies only to persons who have the ability or capacity to reason about the significance of their conduct. [53]

Necessity

[6.135] Sometimes it is necessary to kill one life in order to preserve another. The classic example is that of termination of pregnancy by a doctor in circumstances in which he or she believes that the mother's life or health would be seriously threatened by the continuation of

---

50 Criminal Code (NT), ss 226A and 226B; Criminal Code (WA), s 244; *Criminal Law Consolidation Act 1935* (SA), s 15C.
51 *R v Porter* (1933) 55 CLR 182 at 190.
52 The test for insanity was set out in the case of *McNaughton* (1843) 8 ER 718 and is known as the *McNaughton Rules*.
53 S Bronitt and B McSherry, *Principles of Criminal Law* (3rd ed, Lawbook Co, 2010), Chapter 4 *Mental State Defences*.

the pregnancy. To succeed, the defendant must show that on the balance of competing harm, the decision to terminate the pregnancy was the lesser of two evils.[54]

It will also apply in cases of extraordinary emergency where the defendant acts intuitively in response to the surrounding drama. In *R v Loughman*,[55] Young CJ and King J identified the elements at common law as follows:

> [T]he criminal act must have been done only in order to avoid certain consequences which would have inflicted irreparable evil upon the accused or upon others who he was bound to protect ... the accused must honestly believe on reasonable grounds that he was placed in a situation of imminent peril ... the acts done to avoid the imminent peril must not be out of proportion to the peril to be avoided ...

The Criminal Codes, and federal and State legislation, contain defences of sudden extraordinary emergency and closely follow the common law definition.[56]

Mistake

[6.140] The old adage "ignorance of the law is no excuse" still applies. A person relying on this defence must have made a mistake of fact and not of law, because everyone is presumed to know the law.

However, this must be balanced against another basic common law principle of criminal responsibility which is that a person is not criminally liable for an act or omission if he or she holds an honest and reasonable belief in a state of facts, which, if true, would make the act or omission innocent. The defence may be raised whenever mens rea ("the guilty mind") is an element of the offence.

The mistake must only be genuine and if the prosecution is unable to prove otherwise, the conclusion will be that the defendant did not have the requisite intent to commit the crime and so should not be held criminally responsible for the act(s). For example, if a person removed property belonging to another, mistakenly believing it to be her or his own, this would not be theft because intent is an element of that offence. See [6.90].

The defence of honest and reasonable mistake is available in cases in which mens rea is not an element of the offence. However, if this defence is pleaded, the defendant bears the evidential onus and must point to evidence both that the mistake was an honest one and that it was also reasonable in the circumstances.

Partial defences

[6.145] Some defences operate to reduce the seriousness of the offence charged. For example, the crime of murder may be reduced to manslaughter where there is evidence of:

- intoxication; or
- diminished responsibility; or
- provocation.

---

54 *R v Davidson* (1969) VR 667 where the defendant claimed that a therapeutic abortion was necessary to save the woman from serious danger to her life or her physical or mental health and that it was not disproportionate to the danger averted.
55 *R v Loughman* [1981] VR 443 at 448.
56 *Criminal Code 1995* (Cth), s 10.3; Criminal Code (ACT), s 41; Criminal Code (NT), s 33; Criminal Code (Qld), s 25; Criminal Code (WA), s 25.

Intoxication

[6.150] For public policy reasons, intoxication is not often a justifiable excuse for behaving in an otherwise unlawful manner. However, in crimes such as murder where intent is at issue, the defendant may argue that because of her or his ingestion of alcohol or drugs, he or she was incapable of forming the necessary intent. The defendant may also argue that because of that intoxication, the conduct was involuntary. In other words, the defendant was unaware of the acts he or she was performing. [57]

Of course, if the defendant consumes the alcohol or drugs expressly for the purpose of providing the necessary "courage" to commit the crime, it is difficult to see how the defence would succeed. [58] The intention would already have been formed and the subsequent acting out of the crime could scarcely be called "involuntary".

Diminished responsibility

[6.155] A plea of insanity is only available where the defendant "did not know the nature and quality of the act, or, knowing its nature and quality, did not know that what he was doing was wrong". [59] However, a plea of diminished responsibility to a murder charge is available if the accused knew that what he or she was doing was morally wrong but "at the time of the acts or omissions causing the death concerned, the person's capacity to understand events or to judge whether the person's actions were right or wrong, to control himself or herself was substantially impaired by an abnormality of mind arising from an underlying condition". [60] The test at common law is outlined in *R v Byrne* [61] by Lord Parker CJ who said:

> [A] state of mind so different from that of ordinary human beings that the reasonable [person] would term it abnormal. It appears ... to be wide enough to cover the mind's activities in all its aspects, not only the perception of physical acts and matters and the ability to form a rational judgment as to whether an act is right or wrong, but also the ability to exercise will power to control physical acts in accordance with that rational judgment.

The onus rests with the defendant to prove the defence and, if successful, will reduce liability for murder to manslaughter. The defence is sometimes raised in cases involving murder of a spouse where there has been a long history of domestic violence. It is otherwise referred to as the "battered women's syndrome".

Provocation

[6.160] When provocation is pleaded successfully, its effect is to negate the element of intent and it will thus reduce murder to manslaughter. The underlying philosophy is that the defendant should not be convicted of murder in circumstances where the deceased may have been partly responsible for her or his own death (for example, where this was induced by taunts or insulting gestures) or where the defendant has acted from "blind passion". [62] Conversely, there is a movement towards removing this partial defence because it is open to

---

57 This is a reference to another defence of automatism – "an act which is done by the muscles without any control of the mind": *Bratty v Attorney-General (Northern Ireland)* [1963] AC 386 at 409 per Lord Denning. An example is a motor vehicle accident in which the driver injures another as a result of being attached by a swarm of bees or having a sudden epileptic fit.
58 See, for example, *Crimes Act 1900* (NSW), s 23A(3).
59 See [6.130].
60 *Crimes Act 1900* (NSW), s 23A. See also, Criminal Code (NT), s 37; Criminal Code (Qld), s 304A.
61 *R v Byrne* [1960] 2QB 396 at 403.
62 B Fisse, *Howard's Criminal Law* (5th ed, Law Book Company, 1990), pp 84-85.

abuse. For example, it is often difficult to gauge from the facts whether the accused simply lost their temper without provocation or whether they truly lost self control after provocation.[63]

First, the provocative words or acts of the deceased must have caused in the defendant a sudden and temporary loss of self-control. This is a subjective test demanding an enquiry into the defendant's actual state of mind. Secondly, the provocation must be of such a character as to cause an ordinary person to lose control. This is an objective test which assesses whether the defendant's lack of self control fell "outside the ordinary or common range of human temperaments".[64] Tasmania abolished the defence of provocation in 2003 but it remains a defence in other State jurisdictions.[65]

Statutory defences

[6.165] It has already been noted in [6.65] that there are a number of offences which have been created by statute which contain no element of intention, recklessness or negligence. These are offences of strict liability and they form a general exception to the rule that a person should not be criminally liable unless he or she is also morally blameworthy. So ingrained is this principle in our criminal law that most offences of strict liability are of a minor or regulatory nature.

The other feature of statutory interventions into the criminal law is that the same piece of legislation creating the offence generally provides its own statutory defence(s).[66] For example, the *Australian Consumer Law*[67] Chapter 3 identifies a number of specific activities which attract *criminal* liability under Chapter 4 and which generally replicate the civil provisions dealing with unfair trading practices. Because of this replication, the consumer protection enforcement agency[68] therefore has a discretion whether to institute civil or criminal proceedings, or indeed both, where there has been a specific breach of the law. However, criminal and civil proceedings will be pursued through separate court proceedings and by different agencies.[69]

Bait advertising is one such unfair trading practice which attracts both civil[70] and criminal[71] liability under the *Australian Consumer Law*. Section 157 illustrates both the criminal nature of the offence and outlines the defence(s) available. It provides (in part) as follows:

> (2) A person commits an **offence** if:
>
> > (a) the person, in trade or commerce, advertises goods or services for supply at a specified price; and

---

63   S Bronitt & B McSherry, *Principles of Criminal Law* (3rd ed, Lawbook Co, 2010), Chapter 5 *Partial Defences*.
64   *Rv Enright* [1961] VR 663 at 669.
65   For example, *Crimes Act 1900* (NSW), s 23; Criminal Code (Qld), ss 268 – 269; *Criminal Law Consolidation Act 1935* (SA), s 285BB.
66   Refer again to the *Regulatory Offences Act 1985* (Qld), s 6(2) which provides that: "It is a defence to a charge of an offence ... to prove the defendant believed on reasonable grounds the cheque would be paid in full on presentation or the defendant was authorised to use the credit card or similar document."
67   *Competition and Consumer Act 2010* (Cth), Schedule 2.
68   Chapter 5: The Australian Competition and Consumer Commission (ACCC) or relevant State and Territory consumer agencies.
69   In the case of criminal proceedings, the Commonwealth Director of Public Prosecutions will investigate breaches of the *Australian Consumer Law*.
70   *Australian Consumer Law*, s 35.
71   *Australian Consumer Law*, s 157.

(b) the person fails to offer such goods or services for supply at that price for a period that is, and in quantities that are, reasonable having regard to:
  (i) the nature of the market in which the person carries on business; and
  (ii) the nature of the advertisement.
Penalty:
(a) if the person is a body corporate–$1,100,000; or
(b) if the person is not a body corporate–$220,000.
The section clarifies that:
(3) Subsections (1) and (2) are **offences** of strict liability. [72]
Finally, the section goes on to state that:
(4) In a prosecution of a person (the *defendant*) under subsection (2), for failing to offer goods or services to another person (the *customer*), it is a defence if:
  (a) the defendant proves that:
    (i) he or she offered to supply, or to procure a third person to supply, goods or services of the kind advertised to the customer within a reasonable time, in a reasonable quantity and at the advertised price; or
    (ii) he or she offered to supply immediately, or to procure a third person to supply within a reasonable time, equivalent goods or services to the customer in a reasonable quantity and at the price at which the first-mentioned goods or services were advertised; and
  (b) in either case, if the offer was accepted by the customer, the defendant proves that he or she has so supplied, or procured a third person to supply, the goods or services.

This last subsection lists a number of possible scenarios which, if established, would relieve the defendant of culpability. In such cases, the burden of proof rests with the defendant to establish the defence on the balance of probabilities. This is the civil standard of proof, see [6.205] for further discussion of this issue.

THE CRIMINAL PROCEDURE

[6.170] The most important presumption of the criminal law is that a person is innocent until proven guilty. Another oft-quoted phrase is that "justice must be done and must be seen to be done." As a result, the courts have developed a special set of procedures to handle criminal matters.

Arrest

[6.175] The police force is at the front line of criminal investigation. There are a number of issues involving the authority of police officers and other people in enforcing the criminal law which must be addressed. For example:
- in what circumstances is it justifiable for police officers to enter upon private premises to make arrests?
- when do police officers require warrants for the arrest of offenders?
- is a citizen's arrest lawful or unlawful?

---

72 Strict Liability is defined in the Criminal Code (Cth), s 6.1.

Entry on private property

[6.180] In the leading High Court case of *Halliday v Neville*,[73] police officers entered the driveway of someone else's home for the purpose of effecting the arrest of a third party, Halliday. The question arose whether the police officers had acted lawfully in making the arrest or whether at the time they were trespassers on private property.

This issue of trespass straddles the boundary with the law of torts (see [5.20]). The court had to decide whether the police officers had an implied licence to enter upon the premises. This was a question of fact evidenced by the means of access leading to the entrance of the premises. For example, if the entrance was obstructed by locked gates, or signs which generally or particularly designated which visitors were prohibited or unauthorised, then no licence could be implied.

The court held that in general a police officer has no implied licence to enter upon and remain on private property to transact business where that business is of no benefit to the person in possession of that property, such as in the case in point. Statutory powers restricted the right of entry and search for the purposes of arrest to specific circumstances[74] and the police officers' actions in this case infringed upon the privacy of the individual and went beyond their statutory powers.

Warrants

[6.185] At common law, there was a general power of arrest without warrant for crimes (for example, treason, murder, arson, serious theft) or for breaches of the peace. All States have introduced statutory provisions which augment the common law position so that there are many exceptions to this rule.

Alternatively, if the offence is not one which permits immediate arrest, then the police officer must lay a complaint before a magistrate or judge seeking a warrant for the arrest of the offender. The magistrate or judge must first be satisfied that there is sufficient cause for its issue and may refrain from doing so if a summons to appear would be as effective in guaranteeing the appearance of the defendant before the court.

Citizens' arrests

[6.190] The common law position was that any person could make arrests in the circumstances outlined above. It is still possible for members of the public to assist the police by apprehending, for example, any person they find:

- committing any offence; or
- loitering at night in circumstances giving reasonable grounds for believing that the other person is committing an offence; or
- escaping from custody or avoiding lawful arrest.

---

73   *Halliday v Neville* (1984) 155 CLR 1.
74   For example see the *Crimes (Consolidation of Offences) Act 1981* (Vic), ss 458 – 459A, restricting entry to cases of "serious indictable offences".

Following the arrest without warrant, the citizen must either take the person to the nearest courthouse or to a member of the police force so that the offender can be dealt with according to law.[75]

The Preliminary Hearing

[6.195] A Magistrates' Court operates without a jury. It hears all simple offences, those of a regulatory nature and it has power to try some indictable offences summarily. When the magistrate is empowered by statute to deal "summarily" with an indictable offence, he or she must fulfil the function of the judge and jury. The magistrate becomes both the tribunal of law and of fact. Generally, the penalties imposed in a summary trial are lighter than the sentences and fines which are handed down in the higher courts.

The other very important function of the Magistrates' Court is that it conducts a preliminary inquiry (otherwise referred to as a "committal proceeding") for indictable offences to determine whether the accused should be committed to stand trial in the higher courts. This involves an examination of the prosecution witnesses. If, after hearing the prosecution's case, the magistrate is satisfied that there is a prima facie (literally "on the face of it") case to answer, then he or she will commit the defendant to stand trial in either one or other of the higher courts depending on the seriousness of the charge.

The Trial

[6.200] Article 10 of the *Universal Declaration of Human Rights* provides that "everyone is entitled to a fair and public hearing by an independent and impartial tribunal, in the determination of his rights and obligations and of any criminal charge against him".

When a person is committed for trial in one of the higher courts,[76] their case will be heard before a judge and jury. The judge is the arbiter of law and the jury is the tribunal of fact. The prosecution will lead its evidence first by calling witnesses, often the police officers involved in the arrest of the defendant, who will be examined in chief. The defendant's barrister has a right to cross-examine these witnesses to test their credibility. At the end of the prosecution case, the judge must decide whether there is a sufficient case to answer. If not, the judge will direct the jury to find the accused "not guilty".

If there is a sufficient case to answer, then the defendant will be asked if he or she intends to call evidence in his or her defence. The defendant may decide to call no witnesses, in which case the Crown prosecutor will address the jury first. This gives the defence barrister the tactical advantage of addressing the jury last. However, if the defendant decides to call evidence in defence of the charge, the Crown prosecutor will have the last address to the jury. Finally, after all the addresses, the judge will "sum up" for the jury, who must then retire to consider their verdict. In most jurisdictions, majority verdicts are now allowed for all but the

---

75   See for example, Criminal Code (Qld), s 546, *Crimes Act 1958* (Vic), ss 457 – 458; *Criminal Law Consolidation Act 1935* (SA), s 271.
76   Generally referred to as Local or District or Supreme Courts, depending on the jurisdiction.

most serious criminal offences.[77] A unanimous jury verdict is still required for offences such as murder, or where the offender is liable (if found guilty) to a mandatory life sentence, or for offences against the Commonwealth.[78]

If the verdict is "not guilty", the defendant will be immediately discharged from the court. If the verdict is "guilty", then the defendant is likely to be remanded into custody while the judge decides on the appropriate sentence.

Standard of Proof

[6.205] The standard of proof in a criminal trial is generally "beyond a reasonable doubt". In the celebrated case of *Re Conviction of Chamberlain*,[79] Nader J explained the prosecution's onus of proof in this way:

> The task of a criminal court is to ask and answer the question whether it is satisfied beyond reasonable doubt that the accused is *guilty* of the crime charged. ... [U]nder the criminal law a person is *presumed innocent* until the contrary is proved. It is not the Court's function to establish innocence because, in the absence of a conviction, innocence is presumed: no finding is required (emphasis added).

It is a high standard of proof, much higher than the standard of proof ("on the balance of probabilities") required in civil proceedings. Indeed, the prosecution's task of establishing the guilt of the defendant beyond a reasonable doubt has often proved too hard. The O J Simpson trials in the United States of America – criminal and civil – highlighted the problem. Although the prosecution in the criminal trial was unable to satisfy the jury beyond reasonable doubt of Simpson's involvement in the death of his wife and her lover, the civil trial produced the opposite result, which may well be attributed at least partly to the different standards of proof.

In their defence, accused persons may point to evidence which they hope will raise some doubt in the minds of the jurors, whilst the onus remains with the Crown to prove its case to the satisfaction of the jury beyond reasonable doubt.

Exercise

The Holidaymakers from Hell

Bert and Ernie and five mates from Melbourne are celebrating Schoolies Week at the Gold Coast Penthouse, a property they found and booked online. They paid a deposit by direct debit from Ernie's parents' bank account to confirm the booking with the balance due on arrival. However, the boys' flight from Melbourne was delayed and they arrived late in the evening at the holiday apartment building. The onsite manager had kindly left them a note with the keys to the Penthouse inside.

During the next six days, the boys partied hard all night and slept most of the day. One evening, they invited some girls back to the Penthouse for a "bubble" party which consisted of filling the dishwasher with bubble bath liquid, turning the machine on and waiting for the bubbles to spill out all over the apartment. It was great fun.

On the morning of their departure, however, after too little sleep, hangovers and with their tempers frayed, Bert and Ernie had a terrible fight. Bert knocked Ernie to the floor, punched

---

[77] South Australia, Victoria, Western Australia, Tasmania, the Northern Territory, and recently New South Wales (2005) and Queensland (2009).
[78] See *Jury Act 1995* (Qld).
[79] *Re Conviction of Chamberlain* (1988) 93 FLR 239 at 26.

The Holidaymakers from Hell cont.

him and then kicked a hole in the wall. He then left in a hurry. The other friends came to Ernie's rescue and took him off to a local doctor to make sure he was okay before heading out to the airport.

When the cleaners arrived, the door to the Penthouse was wide open and the evidence of the fight and the "bubble" party were quite clear. They called in the onsite manager who had been busy all week with a building full of young guests and who had not had time to catch up with the boys. It suddenly occurred to her that they had not paid for the balance of their accommodation before leaving.

Nearly all the paintwork in the apartment had been affected by the bubbles settling on the walls and ceiling and the whole apartment would require repainting. To fix the hole in the wall, a builder needed to replace the entire hallway wall with a new sheet of masonite. Apart from these major problems, the cleaners spent twice as long as the Penthouse usually took to clean because of the rubbish and the general messy state in which the boys had left it.

The onsite manager has called in the police. She has given them the names of all the boys. The police are investigating the possibility of laying charges against:

(i) Bert,

(ii) Ernie,

(iii) the other boys,

with respect to the property damage, assault and leaving the premises without paying for their accommodation. What defences, if any, are available to each of them?

CHAPTER 7

Insurance

[7.05] INTRODUCTION		137
[7.10]	Nature of Insurance Contracts	138
[7.10]	Sources of law	138
[7.15]	Definitions	138
[7.20]	Insurable interest	138
[7.25]	Duty of disclosure	139
[7.30]	Indemnity principle	140
[7.60]	Subrogation	141
[7.65] GENERAL PRINCIPLES		142
[7.70]	Formation of Contract	142
[7.75]	The elements of contract	143
[7.90]	Timing	143
[7.95]	Cover notes	144
[7.100]	Renewal and cancellation of policies	144
[7.110]	Insurance Intermediaries	145
[7.115]	Travel agents	146
[7.120]	Specific Types of Insurance	147
[7.125]	Liability insurance	147
[7.160]	Property insurance	149
[7.185]	Commercial insurance	150
[7.200] TRAVEL INSURANCE		150
[7.205]	Travel Insurance Regulations	151

INTRODUCTION

[7.05] The tourism, travel and hospitality industry involves transporting, accommodating and entertaining people and in doing so there is always a risk to the traveller that something may go wrong. For example, a holidaymaker's baggage may go missing, their flights may be delayed, or their accommodation may be cancelled. A tourist may be robbed of their possessions or a visitor may require medical treatment or evacuation home following illness or accident.

On the other hand, the tourism, travel and hospitality industry is also like any other business – there are risks for the operator associated with employing staff and giving customers professional advice. There is always a risk that the premises could be damaged by fire or flood. The contents of the business could be stolen or the equipment may simply break down.

In each of these situations, the prudent traveller or business operator insures against such risks. This chapter discusses the general principles involved in an insurance contract and examines specifically a contract of travel insurance.

Nature of Insurance Contracts

Sources of law

[7.10] The two sources of law with respect to contracts of insurance are *common law* and *statute*.

The most important legislative interventions in the area of insurance law are the *Insurance Contracts Act 1984* (Cth) and the *Financial Services Reform Act 2001* (Cth) with flow on effects to other legislation, such as the *Corporations Act 2001* (Cth). Their impact on common law principles will be discussed.

Definitions

[7.15] A contract of insurance is a contract in which a person (called the insurer) in return for some consideration agrees to pay a sum of money or to provide some other benefit to another party (called the insured) on the happening of a specified event.[1] There must be some uncertainty about if or when the specified event will occur.[2] The consideration here is the payment of a sum of money called a premium. The benefit which the insurer agrees to provide is either money or its equivalent on the happening of the specified event, for example, replacing stolen baggage or rebuilding fire-damaged premises.

Distinguishing features of a contract of insurance include:

- the insurable interest;
- the duty of disclosure;
- the doctrine of indemnity; and
- the subrogation principle.

Insurable interest

[7.20] The person entitled to the benefit (the insured) must have an insurable interest in the subject matter of the insurance. Obviously, a business proprietor has an insurable interest in their premises and contents, such as office equipment and vehicles. They also have an insurable interest in the safety of those who enter their premises and those to whom they provide advice.

Transport providers such as airlines, rail and bus companies are responsible for the care and safety of travellers and their belongings, so they also have an insurable interest. Similarly, accommodation houses have an insurable interest in the protection of their property from damage caused by guests or in damage caused to guests, for example, falling down stairs or tripping over obstacles.

At common law under contracts of general insurance, the insurable interest must be of a legal or equitable kind. However, that has changed since the introduction of the *Insurance*

---

1 *Prudential Insurance Co v Commissioners of Inland Revenue* [1904] 2 KB 658 at 663 per Channell J.
2 *Prudential Insurance Co v Commissioners of Inland Revenue* [1904] 2 KB 658 at 663 per Channell J. In cases of general insurance, for example against theft, loss, flood, fire etc, there is always an amount of speculation as to whether the event will occur. In policies of life insurance, however, the uncertainty is in *when* the event will occur, not *whether* it will.

Contracts Act 1984 (Cth) which requires a "pecuniary or financial loss". [3] It is the insurable interest against loss, theft or destruction of the subject matter which distinguishes a contract of insurance from a gambling or wagering contract where there is no real interest in the preservation of the "event" which results in either a gain or a loss for the person betting on it. For further discussion of this see [15.120].

Duty of disclosure

[7.25] The nature of the contract is one of mutual [4] utmost good faith (*uberrimae fidei*) both at common law and under statute, [5] which means in practical terms that the insured is under a duty to disclose all material facts and not to misrepresent material facts associated with the risk to the insurer. Only then can the insurer properly assess and accept the risk.

To misrepresent or fail to disclose a material or relevant [6] fact during negotiations entitles the insurer to avoid the contract. A fact is material if "it would have reasonably affected the mind of a prudent insurer in determining whether he will accept the insurance, and if so, at what premium and on what conditions". [7]

It is vitally important that the person seeking to be insured should disclose all relevant information when completing the proposal form. This includes providing additional information on the form if it is material. Courts have held such matters as the following to be material facts which should have been disclosed:

- prior claims had led to a previous insurance policy being cancelled; [8]
- explosives were being stored on the premises thus increasing the physical risk of fire;
- the person seeking medical cover has a pre-existing injury; [9]
- the person seeking the insurance has a criminal record increasing the moral risk; [10]
- the property is over-insured creating, a temptation to destroy it and make a claim. [11]

On the other hand, there are a number of matters which the insured is not required to disclose to the insurer, including: [12]

- matters of common notoriety; [13]
- matters which diminish the risk;
- matters which the insurer in the ordinary course of business ought reasonably to know;
- matters in which compliance with the duty to disclose has been waived by the insurer.

---

3   See, for example, *Macaura v Northern Assurance Co Ltd* [1925] AC 619 where the major shareholder and creditor of a company could not recover under a policy he had effected over timber which lay on his land but was owned by the company. See also *Insurance Contracts Act 1984* (Cth), ss 16 – 17.
4   For example, see *Suncorp General Insurance Ltd v Cheihk* (1999) 10 ANZ Insurance Cases 61-442 where the court found that the insurer had failed in its obligation to advise the insured of his duty of disclosure therefore the insurer could not exercise any of its rights stemming from the alleged non-disclosure.
5   *Insurance Contracts Act 1984* (Cth), s 13.
6   *Insurance Contracts Act 1984* (Cth), s 21.
7   *Mayne Nickless Ltd v Pegler* [1974] 1 NSWLR 228 at 239 per Samuels J.
8   *Liga Knitting Mills v Lombard Insurance Co Ltd* (1983) 3 ANZ Ins Cas 60-551, SC (Vic).
9   *Webber v Mutual Community Ltd* (1991) 6 ANZ Ins Cas 61-079.
10 *Antolovich v Sun Alliance Insurance Ltd* (1989) 5 ANZ Ins Cas 60-915.
11 *Ionides v Pender* (1874) LR 9 QB 531.
12 *Insurance Contracts Act 1984* (Cth), s 21(2).
13 For example, "Smoking is a health hazard".

Of course, the insurer may also expressly require that the insured person disclose any changed circumstances during the term of the policy.

Indemnity principle

[7.30] Contracts of insurance provide different types of benefits which may be classified as either *indemnity* or *non-indemnity (contingency)* insurance. The starting point is that the insured should not profit from the loss.[14]

Indemnity insurance

[7.35] In most cases the insurer agrees to reimburse the insured for the actual loss suffered from the accepted risk, for example, property or liability insurance. In other words, the insured is entitled to be restored to the financial position they enjoyed prior to the happening of the specified event such as the burglary or the fire or the loss of profits. This is the principle of indemnity.

Unless specified, however, general indemnity insurance guarantees only compensation for current market value of the insured property at the time of the claim. In the case of a second-hand motor vehicle, for example, this would mean replacing the wrecked or stolen car with one of similar vintage and value. A better alternative is indemnity insurance which guarantees replacement value of the insured property thus enabling the insured to purchase a new car. Of course, the premium will reflect the insurer's increased financial exposure under the risk covered.

Contingency insurance

[7.40] Not all contracts of insurance provide indemnity for the loss suffered. Contingency insurance:

> provides no indemnity but instead a payment upon a contingent event, as in a life policy or a personal injury policy ... The contractual sum is paid if the life ends or the limb is lost, irrespective of the value of the life or the limb.[15]

Examples of contingency insurance include policies of life, sickness or personal accident insurance. The insurer agrees to pay a certain sum of money on the happening of the specified event whether or not it represents the actual loss suffered. For example, when travellers take out insurance for medical expenses incurred overseas, the insurer will usually impose an upper monetary limit on the claim.

Of course, the insured is not entitled to make a profit at the expense of the insurer.[16] Associated with this principle are rules relating to:

- under-insurance;
- over-insurance; and
- double insurance.

Under-insurance

[7.45] If the insured is tempted to under-insure their property to avoid a more expensive premium, they may be in for a rude shock. Many insurance policies contain "averaging"

---

14   For example, double insurance s 45 or underinsurance s 44 of the *Insurance Contracts Act 1984* (Cth).
15   *Medical Defence Union Ltd v Department of Trade* [1980] Ch 82 at 89 per Sir Robert Megarry VC.
16   *British Traders' Insurance Co Ltd v Monson* (1964) 111 CLR 86 at 92-94.

clauses which effectively make the insured person their own insurer for the amount under-insured. Thus, for example, if the property is insured for half its real value, and the insured makes a claim on her or his insurer, the insurer is likely to apply the averaging clause and pay only half the claim, expecting the insured to meet the other half of the claim.

Section 44 of the *Insurance Contracts Act 1984* (Cth) has modified the application of the averaging rule with respect to residential properties. If the property is insured to 80 per cent or more of its value, then the averaging clause will be ineffective. Even where the property is insured to a lesser value, the Act provides its own formula for calculating the parties' respective contributions.[17]

Over-insurance

[7.50] If the insured decides to over value their property and pay premiums based on the over value, they will still only be entitled to claim for the actual loss suffered if the property is destroyed or damaged. They are not entitled to make a profit and the insurer is not required to compensate for more than the actual loss.

Double insurance

[7.55] Similarly, if the insured takes out two contracts of insurance covering the one risk, for example, fire insurance over property, this is called double insurance. Again, the insured stands to make a profit if he or she were entitled to make a full claim against each company on the happening of the specified event.

The rule is that if the sum total of the two policies does not exceed the insured risk, then the insured may claim from each company the whole of the amount insured with each of them. However, if the amount insured under separate contracts does exceed the actual loss, the insured may elect which insurer should pay the claim. That insurer is then entitled, under the doctrine of contribution, to seek an adjustment from any other insurer who may also be liable for the loss.[18]

Subrogation

[7.60] Once a claim is made and paid under a contract of indemnity the insurer is entitled to exercise all the legal rights of the insured against any third parties who may have been responsible for causing the injury, loss or damage. This includes the right of ownership and the right to take legal action. The insurer will be seeking to recover some of the insured's losses caused by the third party's negligence. This is called the principle of subrogation. It does not apply to non-indemnity insurance, for example, life, sickness or personal accident insurance.

In other words, subrogation gives the insurer the right to:

- commence proceedings against third parties in the name of the insured;
- recover the amount of the insured's losses from third parties even though the insured has been indemnified for such loss by the insurer.

It must be remembered that pursuant to the subrogation principle, the insurer is entitled to exercise only rights which the insured already enjoys. For example, if there is a contract

---

17 The formula is AS/P, where A = amount of loss or damage in dollars; S = sum insured for property under the contract; P = 80% of dollar value of the property.

18 See *Insurance Contracts Act 1984* (Cth), s 76. Section 45 of the Act provides that a term in a contract of general insurance limiting or excluding the insurer's liability because the insured entered into some other contract of insurance is void.

between the insured and a third party containing an exclusion clause preventing claims against the third party in the event of loss or damage, then both the insured and the insurer are bound by that provision.

Conversely, the insured must not waive or limit their legal rights against a third party when a claim arises, for example property damage caused by a motor vehicle accident. Admissions made by the insured driver at the scene of the accident either to the police or to the third party driver may result in the insurer either avoiding the claim altogether or limiting the amount payable under the policy.

Under the *Insurance Contracts Act 1984* (Cth), these rights are modified and in fact the insurer is not entitled to be subrogated to the rights of the insured against third parties in the following circumstances:

- if the insured has not exercised the relevant rights and might reasonably be expected not to exercise those rights because of a family relationship or other personal relationship between the insured and the third party;[19]
- in the case of a third party who drove the insured vehicle with the insured's consent if the insured has not exercised those rights and might reasonably be expected not to exercise those rights;[20] and
- in the case of an employee of the insured in respect of conduct which occurred during the course of or arose out of the employee's employment.[21]

In the first two cases, if the third party is uninsured, the insurer is prevented from exercising its rights of subrogation altogether. However, if the third party happens to be insured for the risk which caused the insured's loss or damage, then the insurer in exercising its rights of subrogation against the third party may recover no more than the third party would recover from his or her insurance company for the loss.[22] In each case, if there is evidence of serious or wilful misconduct on the part of the third party, the insurer may exercise its rights of subrogation in any event.[23]

Subrogation is also important in travel agency where the Travel Compensation Fund pays a claimant and then has rights of subrogation against the defaulting travel agent (see [11.615]).

GENERAL PRINCIPLES

[7.65] This section analyses an insurance contract, comparing and contrasting it with other kinds of contracts. There are some special features which set an insurance contract apart from other types of contract and these are highlighted. Finally, descriptions of some specific types of insurance are provided.

Formation of Contract

[7.70] A contract of general insurance, like all other contracts, contains:

- the elements of contract:

19　*Insurance Contracts Act 1984* (Cth), s 65(1)(c)(i).
20　*Insurance Contracts Act 1984* (Cth), s 65(1)(c)(ii).
21　*Insurance Contracts Act 1984* (Cth), s 66.
22　*Insurance Contracts Act 1984* (Cth), s 65(4).
23　*Insurance Contracts Act 1984* (Cth), s 66(b). See also *Boral Resources (Qld) Pty Ltd v Pyke* [1992] 2 Qd R 25, for a description of what actions amount to "serious or wilful misconduct".

- offer;
- acceptance;
- consideration; and
- intention to create legal relations.

In addition, there are other special features of an insurance contract, including:

- the time when the policy commences;
- rules relating to cover notes; and
- cancellation and renewal of policies.

The elements of contract

Offer and acceptance

[7.75] The offer is made by the insured on completion of the proposal form. This form is described as:

> a document containing questions to which a person is asked to give answers (whether in the document or not), where the answers are intended (whether by the person who answered them, by the insurer or by some other person) to be used in connection with a proposed contract of insurance... [24]

Once the completed proposal form has been submitted to the insurer, it has the option of accepting or rejecting the offer. If the insurer accepts the offer, it will issue a policy and receive payment of a premium. The policy contains the terms of the agreement between the insured and the insurer.

Consideration

[7.80] The price paid for the promise by the insurer to indemnify the insured against the happening of the specified event is called the premium. It is usually a monetary payment specified in the contract. The premium will vary according to the risk which is covered.

Intention to create legal relations

[7.85] A contract of insurance is not in the nature of a social or domestic arrangement but rather an agreement struck in an "arm's length" business context. The rights and obligations of the respective parties may be set out in the policy of insurance or they may arise from statute. In either case, they are enforceable at law. For further discussion on this topic see [4.145]ff.

Timing

[7.90] Usually, the insurance cover commences from the date that the proposal is accepted by the insurer regardless of the fact that the premium may not yet have been paid by the insured. On the other hand, the parties may structure their agreement so that the cover is either backdated [25] or commences at some time in the future. The period of cover will normally be specified in the policy.

---

24   *Insurance Contracts Act 1984* (Cth), s 11(1).
25   For example, policies which replace cover notes are often backdated to the date on which the interim cover commenced.

Cover notes

[7.95] A cover note is simply an interim contract while the insurer considers the written proposal. It usually expires after a limited period of time (for example, 28 days). It incorporates terms similar to or the same as those contained in the insurer's general insurance policy for that type of insurance. At common law, the insurer would often include the proviso that the cover note was subject to a "satisfactory proposal" for a contract of insurance which would replace the interim contract. The *Insurance Contracts Act 1984* (Cth) makes such provisions void.[26]

Cover notes are useful in the purchase of property, either residential or commercial. In such cases, it is always wise to consider the terms of the contract of sale. Sometimes the risk associated with the property passes to the purchaser on signing the contract[27] and at other times it remains with the vendor until completion.[28] In the former case, the purchaser should quickly arrange a cover note over the premises pending settlement. Otherwise, if the premises should be damaged or destroyed by fire, for example, the purchaser may still be required to settle even though the building no longer exists.

Renewal and cancellation of policies

Renewal

[7.100] Once the period of cover specified in the policy expires, the insurance contract will lapse unless renewed. Renewal takes place either:

(a)   when the insured tenders the next premium to the insurer who may accept or reject it; or

(b)   when the insured pays the next premium in response to a notice of renewal sent by the insurer.

Pursuant to the *Insurance Contracts Act 1984* (Cth), the insurer is bound to send a notice of renewal to the insured no later than 14 days before the original insurance contract is about to expire.[29]

Cancellation

[7.105] Alternatively, the insured may cancel the contract of insurance by notice to the insurer. In that event, the insurer is generally entitled to retain a proportion of the premium relating to the expired period of the insurance together with an amount to cover administrative costs.

Under the provisions of the *Insurance Contracts Act 1984* (Cth), the insurer may cancel contracts of general insurance only if the insured:

- failed to comply with the duty of utmost good faith or with the duty of disclosure;
- made a misrepresentation to the insurer during the negotiations for the contract but before it was entered into;

---

26   *Insurance Contracts Act 1984* (Cth), s 38(1).
27   For example, contracts over residential properties in Queensland.
28   For example, contracts over strata title properties in New South Wales. There is some debate on who bears the risk over residential property although it is clear that the vendor is the trustee of the property.
29   *Insurance Contracts Act 1984* (Cth), s 58(2).

- failed to comply with a provision of the contract, including a provision with respect to payment of the premium; or
- made a fraudulent claim under the contract. [30]

Insurance Intermediaries

[7.110] Brokers and insurance agents may also be referred to as "insurance intermediaries". They each arrange for contracts of insurance between insurance companies and persons seeking to become insured.

Insurance brokers do business independently with a number of different insurers. Their aim is to "shop around" to try to get the best insurance policy for their clients, the insured. For their part, the persons seeking insurance through a broker will pay a brokerage fee. Insurance agents, on the other hand, usually act for one particular insurance company. They earn a commission from the insurer upon the successful negotiation of a contract with the insured.

Sometimes the distinction between brokers and insurance agents becomes blurred. This happens when a broker has entered into a delegated authority binder scheme with a specific insurance company. The binder [31] scheme enables the broker to underwrite risks within agreed parameters, issue their own branded policy documentation and generally to provide better client management services.

Insurance brokers are one category of financial service professionals regulated by the Australian Securities and Investments Commission (ASIC). [32] ASIC's priority is to safeguard the money of policy holders. The *Financial Services Reform Act 2001* (Cth) [33] and Chapter 7 of the *Corporations Act 2001* (Cth) and regulations, govern the licensing, conduct and delivery of financial services provided by brokers and other agents. [34]

Insurance intermediaries require a financial services licence, either as brokers or agents, if they:

- deal in a financial product; [35] or
- provide financial product advice. [36]

There are also stringent disclosure provisions requiring financial services licensees to provide retail clients with a:

- Financial Services Guide; [37]
- Statement of Advice; [38] and

---

30   *Insurance Contracts Act 1984* (Cth), s 60(1).
31   See *Corporations Act 2001* (Cth), Ch 7, s 761A, Definitions.
32   For example, brokers must be registered and, amongst other things, must provide financial services efficiently, honestly and fairly. They must have risk management and dispute resolution systems and must maintain separate "broking accounts". There are penalties for non-compliance. See also *Corporations Act 2001* (Cth), s 914A.
33   This Act came into full effect 11 March, 2004.
34   *Corporations Act 2001* (Cth), ss 792A – 792I.
35   That is, if they issue and/or arrange insurance for their clients.
36   That is, if they make recommendations or statements designed to influence a prospective insured's decision in relation to a particular insurance product.
37   *Corporations Act 2001* (Cth), s 941A.
38   *Corporations Act 2001* (Cth), s 946A.

- Product Disclosure Statement.[39]

The *Corporations Act 2001* (Cth), s 985B states that:

(1) If:

(a) a contract of insurance is arranged or effected by a financial services licensee; and

(b) the licensee is not the insurer;

payment to the licensee of money payable (whether in respect of a premium or otherwise) by the insured under or in relation to the contract is a discharge, as between the insured and the insurer, of the liability of the insured to the insurer in respect of that money.

This section overcomes some of the problems that insured persons faced at common law when dealing with agents[40] or brokers.[41] Insurance intermediaries are deemed to be agents of the insurer and not the insured and so premiums paid by clients to intermediaries in respect of an existing liability must be honoured by the insurer.

Travel agents

[7.115] At first glance, travel agents may appear to be "insurance intermediaries" requiring a financial services licence. After all, travel agents often provide advertising materials (brochures and other literature) to customers which may contain recommendations for particular travel insurance or may suggest that particular travel insurance is appropriate in the customer's circumstances. Similarly, they often arrange for travel insurance with an insurer on behalf of the customer. These activities could be construed as giving financial product advice and/or dealing in a financial product, respectively.

Although travel agents are the logical distributors of travel insurance, the onerous regulatory licensing requirements for insurance brokers and agents dealing in and selling financial products would be too burdensome for travel agencies.[42] In recognition of this dilemma, ASIC[43] now allows Australian financial services licensees (for example, insurers) the option to appoint people to deal in general insurance products like travel insurance[44] on their behalf, without having to appoint them as authorised representatives and thus avoiding the authorisation requirements of brokers and agents.

Pursuant to this relief, the insurer (financial services licensee) will be responsible for the activities of the travel agents (distributors). For their part, the travel agents so appointed must:

- tell retail clients which insurer they act for;
- reveal what remuneration they receive; and
- demonstrate how retail clients can access the insurer's dispute resolution system.

---

39   *Corporations Act 2001* (Cth), s 1012A where personal advice is given to the retail client.

40   See *Newsholme Bros v Road Transport General Insurance Ltd* [1929] 2 KB 356, where the court held that an agent who completes a proposal form does so as the insured's agent and not as the agent of the insurance company.

41   See *Con-Stan Industries of Australia Pty Ltd v Norwich Winterthur Insurance (Australia) Ltd* (1986) 160 CLR 226, where the High Court held that payment of a premium to a broker who did not pass it on to the insurer for whatever reason does not discharge the obligation to pay the premium to the insurer.

42   For further discussion on licensing requirements for travel agents, see [11.220]ff.

43   See ASIC Media Release IR 05-59 (Thursday 27 October, 2005) entitled *ASIC offers general insurance dealers a choice on how to appoint their distributors*.

44   For example, general insurance products are also distributed by car dealers and real estate agents.

On the other hand, as distributors, travel agents may only deal in financial products but must not offer product advice. They may, however, distribute travel insurance for more than one insurer.

Travel agents operate under a written agreement with the insurer. As the distributor of the insurer, the travel agent is liable to record accurately the answers given by the customer in response to questions in the proposal form. In relation to the insurance policy, the travel agent may also be liable to the customer for:

- negligent misrepresentations as to the policy benefits or obligations under the contract or the amount of the premium; [45]
- failure to arrange insurance on behalf of an insured as agreed; [46]
- misleading or deceptive conduct (under consumer protection legislation). [47]

Specific Types of Insurance

[7.120] There are a number of different types of general insurance policies. This section will examine those insurable risks which affect the travel and hospitality business community, including:

- liability insurance;
- property insurance; and
- commercial insurance.

Liability insurance

[7.125] Legal liability for personal injuries or property damage caused to third parties may arise in several ways. Areas of concern include:

- professional indemnity insurance;
- public liability insurance;
- product liability insurance;
- workers' compensation insurance;
- third party motor vehicle insurance; and
- air carriers' liability insurance.

These are described below.

Professional indemnity insurance

[7.130] Whenever advice is sought and given in a serious business context with the insured or their agent apparently having some special skill or expertise to provide that information, there is a risk that they will be exposed to a claim for professional negligence if the advice

---

45   See Torts [5.85]ff.
46   See Contract Law Chapter 4 generally.
47   See Consumer Protection [9.140].

subsequently turns out to be unreliable.[48] Travel agents in particular should be aware of the conduct which constitutes negligent misstatement.[49] See [11.325] for further discussion of this issue.

Public liability insurance

[7.135] If a person entering upon business premises should accidentally injure themselves, the occupier of those premises may be liable. Although the risk is relatively small (which is reflected in the low premiums), the damages awarded for personal injuries claims can run quite high, so a generous cover is recommended.[50]

Product liability insurance

[7.140] Consumers today are far more willing to sue a manufacturer or a designer for losses or injuries caused by the use, sale or consumption of defective products. They may choose to bring an action in tort or pursuant to the consumer protection provisions of the *Australian Consumer Law*[51] or its State and Territory counterparts. In any event, all service providers should carry adequate cover. The legal risks involved are discussed in [9.205]ff.

Workers' compensation insurance

[7.145] All employers are responsible for work-related injuries caused to their employees.[52] They must insure compulsorily through their own State or Territory workers' compensation scheme. These schemes require employers to pay a premium based on the estimated annual earnings of employees. Injuries sustained in the course of employment include those which occur while travelling to or from work. Once a claim is made by an employee, he or she is usually paid a weekly sum until they return to work. However, in the case of serious injury or permanent disability it is more usual for the employee to receive a lump sum payment based on a statutory schedule.

This is "no fault" insurance, which means that it does not matter that the worker acted negligently, thus contributing to or causing her or his own injuries. However, if the accident occurred because of the employer's negligence in failing to provide a safe system of work, for example, then the employee may also have a common law claim. The employer should take out additional cover for this risk. These matters are discussed further in [8.155]ff.

Third party motor vehicle insurance

[7.150] People are injured in motor vehicle accidents daily through the negligent driving of others. To spread the cost of this risk in the community, in each State and Territory motorists pay an annual registration fee on their vehicle, which includes a premium for compulsory third party insurance. This is discussed further in [12.185].

---

48   See *Shaddock and Associates Pty Ltd v Parramatta City Council* (1981) 150 CLR 225.
49   See also *Insurance Contracts Act 1984* (Cth), s 54 regarding insurer's refusal to pay claims in certain circumstances.
50   Between AUD$10 million and AUD$20 million.
51   *Competition and Consumer Act 2010* (Cth), Schedule 2, Part 3.5.
52   The *Insurance Contracts Act 1984* (Cth) does not apply to workers' compensation.

Air carriers' liability insurance

[7.155] Under international conventions and federal and State legislation, air carriers are presumed liable up to certain limits for the death or injury to passengers. Since 1995 [53] Australia has increased the limits for domestic aviation to $500,000 per passenger [54] and now requires international and domestic air carriers to maintain insurance to cover compensation up to the limit for the full capacity of the aircraft. See [12.535]ff.

Property insurance

[7.160] Liability insurance is concerned with injury suffered by or damage caused to others. Property insurance, on the other hand, is concerned with covering the risk of damage to one's own premises or physical assets. It includes:

- dwellings, buildings, contents insurance;
- comprehensive car insurance;
- plate glass insurance;
- cash in transit insurance.

These topics are discussed below.

Dwellings, buildings, contents insurance

[7.165] Just as home owners will insure against the risk of fire, earthquake, flood or tempest destroying their property, so too should business operators insure against such risks damaging their premises. Similarly, the home owner will insure the contents of their house against the loss or damage to contents caused by theft, accident or the careless acts of the insured or a third party. So too should the business operator.

Comprehensive motor vehicle insurance

[7.170] Apart from personal injury claims arising out of motor vehicle accidents, there is always the risk of property damage to the vehicles involved. Comprehensive insurance provides cover for property damage to or loss of the insured's own vehicle through theft or accident. It also indemnifies the insured against claims by third parties for property damage caused by the insured's negligence. [55]

Plate glass insurance

[7.175] Most businesses have a shopfront plate glass window which, if broken and left unrepaired for any length of time, would expose the business to a security risk. Plate glass insurance policies may cover a range of events from hailstorm to explosion and usually provide for temporary measures (such as boarding up the broken panes) to secure the premises until the new plate glass is installed. Under the terms of many commercial leases, such insurance is mandatory on the part of the tenant.

---

53   *Transport Legislation Amendment Act 1995* (Cth) and equivalent State legislation.
54   There is currently a proposal before the Department of Infrastructure, Transport, Regional Development and Local Government to increase the limit of domestic air carriers' liability to $725,000 to reflect rises in the cost of living since the last review.
55   See *Insurance Contract Regulations 1985* (Cth), regs 5 – 8, which prescribe standard cover.

Cash in transit insurance

[7.180] If the business is one which generates large sums of money that require daily banking or if the cash required for the wages payroll is a substantial sum, then it may be worthwhile considering this type of insurance. It provides cover against loss through theft or accident on the way to and from the bank.

Commercial insurance

[7.185] Apart from the risks of personal injury and property damage caused by negligence, theft or the weather, business operators are exposed to additional risks associated with the running of their businesses. For example, the location of the commercial premises may be critical to the success of a business activity.

Alternatively, one of the employees may have particular trade skills or knowledge which are central to the financial viability of the business. In either case, it is possible to insure against the risk of something happening either to the key location of the premises or to the key personnel.

Key person insurance

[7.190] As the name suggests, this insurance covers persons whose knowledge and experience are pivotal to the success of the business. Their death or permanent disability would have a disruptive effect on the continuing operation of the business while a replacement person is found and/or trained. The proceeds of the policy can be used towards defraying the costs of this lengthy process.

Business interruption

[7.195] A business operation can be disrupted for a number of reasons. For example, fire, water damage or explosion may render the key premises uninhabitable for a period of time. The owners may have to relocate their business to temporary premises elsewhere in a less satisfactory location. Alternatively, if the business relies on the use of machinery, then a serious machinery breakdown requiring parts to be flown in from overseas, may lead to a temporary loss of production.

Finally, if the suppliers to the business fail to meet their contractual obligations to the firm, this could result in a shortage of product for sale and thus a partial cessation of the business operation. Each of these risks, the associated loss of profits and/or re-establishment expenses, may be insured against.

These days, too, most businesses depend on high-tech computer equipment to store vital business information. This equipment should be covered by service or maintenance agreements against the possibility of breakdown which would also cause major disruption to business.

TRAVEL INSURANCE

A good travel insurance policy can be as valuable as a parachute on a plummeting plane or a life-boat on a sinking ship. [56]

[7.200] There are so many things which can and do go wrong for travellers. They may lose their baggage or have their money stolen, their travel plans may be disrupted or cancelled,

---

56   *Choice* Magazine (November 1991), p 24.

causing losses, or they may suffer injury or illness while away, thus incurring medical expenses. Although it is not compulsory for travellers to take out travel insurance, it is certainly advisable.

Travel agents and others selling travel insurance need to be familiar with the provisions of the *Insurance Contracts Regulations 1985* (Cth), relating to travel insurance.[57] Their professional advice will be sought and relied upon by members of the travelling public so they must be careful not to make misrepresentations about the cover actually provided and, indeed, should not give product advice unless they hold a financial services licence (see [7.115]).

To keep premiums lower, insurers generally impose monetary limits on compensation payable on a claim by travellers. Typical cover for overseas travel includes:

- overseas medical, dental and additional expenses;
- travel delay, cancellation and associated expenses;
- accidental death, disability and loss of income;
- loss of or damage to personal baggage and effects;
- personal liability.

In addition, the policy usually expressly excludes liability in the kinds of circumstances outlined in reg 27. For example, a pre-existing medical condition or disability which causes the insured to cancel their travel plans is not covered by travel insurance.[58]

The *Insurance Contracts Regulations 1985* make special provisions for travel insurance and these are reproduced below in [7.205]. The regulations contain the standard clauses which will appear in all such travel insurance policies

Travel Insurance Regulations

[7.205] Prescribed contracts [59]

25. The following class of contracts of insurance is declared to be a class of contracts in relation to which Division 1 of Part V of the Act applies, namely, contracts that provide insurance cover (whether or not the cover is limited or restricted in any way) in respect of one or more of the following:

(a) financial loss in respect of:

   (i) fares for any form of transport to be used; or

   (ii) accommodation to be used;

   in the course of the specified journey in the event that the insured person does not commence or complete the specified journey;

(b) loss of or damage to personal belongings that occurs while the insured person is on the specified journey;

(c) a sickness or disease contracted or an injury sustained by the insured person while on the specified journey;

where the insured or one of the insureds is a natural person.

---

57 In particular, *Insurance Contracts Regulations 1985* (Cth), Div 6, regs 25 – 29.

58 *Phoenix Assurance Co of Australia Ltd v Liddy* (unreported, NSW SC (CA), No 85 of 1983). *Facts:* There was a claim under an insurance policy by Mrs Liddy, who was disabled by an operation on congenital bunions. She was unable to proceed with travel arrangements as planned, and sought a refund of $2,000. The insurance company refused to pay. *Held:* On appeal, by majority, in favour of the insurer. Mrs Liddy's "illness" was traceable to her congenital bunion problem, which was pre-existing.

59 *Insurance Contracts Regulations 1985* (Cth), Div 6 – Travel insurance.

Prescribed events

26. The following, except in so far as they are excluded by regulation 27, are declared to be prescribed events in relation to a contract referred to in regulation 25:

(a) financial loss on account of:
   (i) fares for any form of transport to be used; or
   (ii) accommodation to be used;
   in the course of the specified journey in the event that the insured person or a member of the insured person's travelling party, through unforeseen circumstances beyond the control of the insured person or member, respectively, cannot reasonably be expected to commence or complete the journey;

(b) loss of or damage occurring to personal belongings of the insured person during the course of the specified journey;

(c) the death of the insured person or a member of the insured's travelling party while on the specified journey;

(d) the insured person or a member of the insured's travelling party contracting a sickness or disease or sustaining an injury while on the specified journey.

Exclusions

27. The following are excluded:

(a) financial loss, loss of or damage to personal belongings or death, sickness or injury, occurring as a result of:
   (i) war or warlike activities;
   (ii) expropriation of any thing;
   (iii) the use, existence or escape of nuclear weapons material, or ionizing radiation from, or contamination by radioactivity from, any nuclear fuel or nuclear waste from the combustion of nuclear fuel; or
   (iv) the insured person or a member of the insured person's travelling party:
      (A) being under the influence of intoxicating liquor or of a drug, other than a drug taken or administered by or in accordance with the advice of a duly qualified medical practitioner;
      (B) being addicted to intoxicating liquor or to a drug;
      (C) taking part in a riot or civil commotion;
      (D) acting maliciously; or
      (E) engaging in professional sporting activities;

(b) financial loss, loss of or damage to personal belongings or death, sickness or injury, intentionally caused by:
   (i) the insured person; or
   (ii) a member of the insured person's travelling party;
   or by a person acting with the express or implied consent of any of them;

(c) financial loss as a result of:
   (i) the insured person failing to commence or complete the journey:
      (A) for financial, business or contractual reasons, being reasons related to the insured person or to a member of the insured person's travelling party; or

(B) because of a sickness, disease or disability to which a person was subject at any time during the period of six months before the contract was entered into and continues to be subject to after that time;

(ii) the insured person or a member of the insured person's travelling party being disinclined to travel; or

(iii) contravention of, or failure to comply with, a law (including the law of a foreign country) by the insured person or a member of the insured person's travelling party;

(d) loss of or damage occurring to personal belongings as a result of:
  (i) depreciation;
  (ii) wear and tear, mildew, rust or corrosion;
  (iii) the action of insects or vermin;
  (iv) mechanical or electrical breakdown or failure of the personal belongings;
  (v) the personal belongings being cleaned, dyed, altered or repaired; or
  (vi) in the case of personal belongings that are fragile or brittle – the negligence of the insured;

(e) death occurring or injury sustained as a result of a sickness or disability to which the person concerned was subject at any time during the period of 6 months before the contract was entered into and continues to be subject to after that time;

(f) death occurring or injury sustained at a time when the person concerned is flying, or engaging in aerial activities, otherwise than as a passenger in an aircraft that is authorised to fly under a law that relates to the safety of aircraft;

(g) the insured person or a member of the insured's travelling party sustaining a deliberately self-inflicted injury.

Minimum amounts

28.

(1) Subject to these Regulations, for the purposes of section 34 of the Act, the minimum amount in respect of a claim made under a contract referred to in regulation 25, being a claim that arises out of an event referred to in paragraph 26(a) or (b), is declared to be the amount sufficient to indemnify the person who made the claim in respect of his or her loss or damage.

(2) Subject to these Regulations, for the purposes of section 34 of the Act, the minimum amount in respect of a claim made under a contract referred to in regulation 25, being a claim that arises out of an event referred to in paragraph 26(c), is declared to be the amount sufficient to indemnify the person who made the claim in respect of the reasonable cost of:
  (a) the funeral or cremation; or
  (b) transporting the remains of the deceased person to the deceased's former place of residence.

(3)   Subject to these Regulations, for the purposes of section 34 of the Act, the minimum amount in respect of a claim made under a contract referred to in regulation 25, being a claim that arises out of an event referred to in paragraph 26(d), is declared to be the amount sufficient to indemnify the person who made the claim in respect of the reasonable cost of:

(a)   medical, surgical, hospital, ambulance and nursing home charges; and

(b)   other medical treatment;

incurred during the specified journey as a result of the sickness, disease or injury.

Limits on minimum amounts

29. Where the insured knew, or a reasonable person in the circumstances would have known, that a particular amount is the maximum amount that would be payable by the insurer under the contract of insurance whatever the circumstances, then, in relation to a claim under that contract, the minimum amount for the purposes of section 34 of the Act shall be the first-mentioned amount or the amount declared by the relevant provision of these Regulations to be the minimum amount inrespect of the claim, whichever is the less.

Exercise

We've got you covered

Obtain a copy of a travel insurance policy from any travel agency. Check to see that the terms and conditions set out in the brochure and/or policy accord with regs 25-29 (reproduced above). Then read and answer the following problem.

Bill and Betty Blunder are travelling to Thailand for their honeymoon. Bill spoke with Sally Smart, his local travel agent, about the potential risks, and she advised him that she could arrange the most comprehensive travel insurance for their trip through an insurance company called *Travelpack*, one of three travel insurers whose brochures appeared in Sally's travel shop. The premium cost $550.00 but Sally assured Bill that this would cover Betty and him for all the major travel problems such as sickness, loss of baggage, travel delays, cancellation of accommodation and so on. Bill gave Sally all of his and Betty's personal details so that she could complete the proposal form but failed to divulge that Betty was a diabetic requiring daily medication.

While Bill and Betty were staying in Bangkok at the Klongside Hotel and dining at its restaurant, they each became ill, suffering from nausea and diarrhoea after eating undercooked chicken. Betty fell into a coma after her body failed to absorb her medication with the loss of so much fluid and she required hospitalisation in Bangkok. As soon as Betty was well enough to travel, Bill returned home with her. He still had symptoms and was admitted to his local hospital where he was diagnosed with a more persistent form of dysentery requiring treatment with intravenous drugs and antibiotics.

When the hospital and other medical bills started arriving, Bill, believing he was covered, sent them all to the insurer, *Travelpack*. He also claimed for the extra time that he spent at the Klongside Hotel while waiting for Betty to recover.

The insurer has rejected Betty's claim for medical expenses in Bangkok based on the fact that Bill failed to disclose that Betty was a diabetic (a material fact) in the proposal form. It has also rejected Bill's claim for the additional accommodation expenses associated with Betty's illness. It has agreed to pay Bill's medical expenses and has advised Bill that he will be required

We've got you covered cont.

as a witness in any legal proceedings which it may commence against the hotel in Bangkok. Bill is uncertain whether to co-operate in the circumstances.

Betty's medical expenses amount to $20,000. Bill argues that his travel agent, Sally Smart, should have been more diligent. He says that his failure to reveal that Betty was a diabetic was an oversight on his part and that in any event her sudden illness was more to do with the food poisoning than with the fact that she was a diabetic. He also argues that by paying the premium to Sally, the insurer has accepted liability

Bill has decided to take legal action against Sally, the travel agent, for providing him with poor advice on travel insurance and the insurer, *Travelpack*, for failing to meet its obligations under the policy of insurance. Advise Bill of his likely chances of success. Advise Sally and *Travelpack* of their respective rights and obligations.

CHAPTER 8

Employment

[8.05] INTRODUCTION 157
[8.10] CONTRACT OF EMPLOYMENT 158
    [8.15]   Definition 158
    [8.20]   Rights and Duties 159
        [8.25]   Employee's duties 160
        [8.50]   Employer's duties 162
    [8.75]   Termination of Contracts of Service 165
        [8.80]   Deliberate or consequential termination 165
        [8.90]   Breach of contract of employment 166
        [8.100]   Unfair dismissal 167
[8.115] STATUTORY INTERVENTION 168
[8.120] FAIR WORK LEGISLATION, AWARDS AND AGREEMENTS 169
    [8.125]   Modern Awards and Agreements 169
    [8.130]   Agreements in the workplace 170
[8.135] HUMAN RIGHTS ISSUES 171
    [8.140]   Discrimination 171
        [8.145]   Equal opportunity 172
        [8.150]   Sexual harassment 173
[8.155] WORKERS COMPENSATION 173
[8.160] OCCUPATIONAL HEALTH AND SAFETY 174
    [8.160]   History 174
        [8.165]   *Priestley v Fowler* 174
    [8.170]   Organisations 176
        [8.170]   International 176
        [8.175]   National and State 176
    [8.180]   OHS Legislation 177
        [8.185]   Definitions 177
        [8.205]   OHS duties 178
        [8.220]   Workplace arrangements 180
        [8.230]   Inspections and enforcement 180
        [8.235]   Codes and standards 181

INTRODUCTION

[8.05] Employment involves both public and private law. Individuals may enter into contracts of employment which are governed by the rules of contract, an area of private law. However, many of the terms of that employment contract affecting such matters as minimum wage rates, hours of work, holiday leave and the like, have already been set and regulated by an industrial agreement or an award.

Freedom of contract has had to yield to pressures of public policy. The philosophy is that unless workers receive a fair day's pay for a fair day's work and reasonable working conditions, then economic and social welfare as a whole will suffer. Consequently, the federal

Parliament and each State and Territory have passed legislation giving force and effect to these awards and agreements through a system of industrial tribunals, thus bringing employment into the public law arena.

Similarly, the community has an interest in the health and safety of the workplace. Just as the motoring public must share the high cost of personal injury claims arising out of motor vehicle accidents,[1] so too should employers cover the risk of work-related injuries and accidents so that those disabled or sick employees do not become a heavy financial burden on society. Compulsory workers' compensation legislation in all States and Territories addresses this public concern. Also, because prevention is better than cure, all States and Territories have workplace health and safety legislation which develops and enforces minimum standards and codes of practice to improve workplace health and safety.[2]

This chapter examines the contract of employment focusing on the rights and obligations of the respective parties in the workplace at common law and under statute. It addresses some of the human rights issues such as discrimination, sexual harassment and equal opportunity in the workplace. It outlines particular awards affecting the tourism, travel and hospitality industry and finally, it considers the workplace health and safety aspects of employment law.

CONTRACT OF EMPLOYMENT

[8.10] The essential elements of a contract must exist (that is, offer, acceptance, consideration and intention to create legal relations). The parties must have legal capacity to enter into the agreement and the contract must not be for an illegal purpose. For further discussion see [4.40].

Definition

"A contract of employment comes about through the engagement of one person to perform work for and under the direction and control of another. The relationship is known as the employer-employee (previously master-servant) relationship."[3]

[8.15] It is not always clear whether a person has been engaged as an employee of the business enterprise or as an independent contractor. In other words, the law draws a distinction between:

- a contract of service (employer/employee); and
- a contract for services (independent contractor).

First, it is the former type of contract which usually incorporates the terms and conditions imposed by the relevant industrial award. Secondly, the employer is responsible to third parties for all negligent acts of her or his employees engaged under a contract of services

---

1 See [7.150] on compulsory third party motor vehicle insurance.
2 Safe Work Australia has now developed a model *Work Health and Safety Act 2010* which all State Ministers endorsed in December 2009. This will require each State and Territory to pass their own laws which mirror the model law and adopt them by December 2011. The model law is supported by work health and safety regulations. Model Codes of Practice are available that can also be adopted.
3 *Australian Employment Law Guide* (looseleaf service, CCH Australia Ltd), 15-300.

pursuant to the principle of vicarious liability discussed in [5.100]. Finally, statutory requirements such as those imposed by the workers' compensation legislation [4] apply only to workers under contracts of service. [5]

The definition highlights the method used to differentiate between the two types of contract. It often comes down to a question of how much control the employer exercises over the work performed by the so-called employee. For example, a contract of service will probably exhibit the following key features:

- a particular person does the work in exchange for periodic remuneration;
- the employer has the right to suspend or dismiss the person engaged;
- the employer has the right to the exclusive services of the person engaged;
- the employer has the right to dictate the place, hours and method of work;
- the employer provides the workplace, materials, tools and equipment required for the work; and
- other provisions in the contract are not inconsistent with it being a contract of service. [6]

On the other hand, a contract for services is more likely to exhibit key features including:

- the payment of remuneration for the work without deduction for income tax;
- the payment of business expenses by the person engaged;
- the provision by that person of their own place of work, tools or equipment;
- the person engaged selects the method of work; and
- the work involves a profession, trade or distinct calling on the part of the person engaged. [7]

For further discussion, see [5.110] and following.

Rights and Duties

[8.20] Once it is clear that a contract of employment exists, it is necessary to determine the respective rights and duties of the employer and employee under that agreement. The contract may be oral or written and will usually contain express terms. Both at common law and under relevant statute law, even in the absence of express agreement, some terms will be implied in any event.

These include the employee's duties:

- to provide faithful service;
- to exercise skill and care;
- to obey reasonable directions;
- to give reasonable attendance at the workplace; and

---

[4] *Safety, Rehabilitation and Compensation Act 1988* (Cth); *Workers' Compensation Act 1951* (ACT); *Workers Rehabilitation and Compensation Act* (NT); *Workers' Compensation Act 1987* (NSW); *Workers' Compensation and Rehabilitation Act 2003* (Qld); *Workers' Rehabilitation and Compensation Act 1986* (SA); *Workers' Rehabilitation and Compensation Act 1988* (Tas); *Workers' Compensation Act 1958* (Vic); *Workers' Compensation and Injury Management Act 1981* (WA).

[5] Consider, for example, whether a dive instructor is an employee or an independent contractor: see J Wilks and T C Atherton, "The lifestyle factor: Employment practices in the Queensland recreational diving industry" (1995) *Australian Journal of Hospitality Management* 2(1).

[6] *Stevens v Brodribb Sawmilling Co Pty Ltd* (1986) 160 CLR 16 at 36-37. See also *Ready Mix Concrete (South East) Ltd v Minister of Pensions and National Insurance* (1968) 2 QB 497.

[7] *Stevens v Brodribb Sawmilling Co Pty Ltd* (1986) 160 CLR 16 at 36-37.

- not to disclose confidential information after termination.

For its part, the employer's duties are

- to provide work;
- to pay wages;
- to provide paid leave;
- to provide a reasonably safe system of work; and
- to indemnify employees.

At the outset it can be seen that each party's duties are the other party's rights. For this reason the rights and duties of the parties will be discussed in terms of the duties of each party.

Employee's duties

Faithful service

[8.25] As the topic suggests, an employee is required to give good and faithful service to her or his employer under the terms of their agreement. This means that the employee should not harm the employer's enterprise either by sharing trade secrets with the employer's competitors or by withholding important information from the employer.

Similarly, the employer's best interests are not served by employees who work for competitors in their spare time [8] or who solicit customers to transfer their business to the employee when they leave their current workplace. [9] Additionally, an employee is accountable for any secret profits he or she makes from third parties at the employer's expense.

Skill and care

[8.30] The employee gives an implied warranty that he or she possesses the required skills for the job together with an implied promise that he or she will exercise reasonable care in carrying out the work. If the employee fails to honour these terms and a third party suffers loss or injury as a result, it will usually be the employer who is held responsible because of their "deep pockets".

If, however, the employee is sued successfully by a third party, then the employee may turn to the employer seeking reimbursement. This is one of the implied terms of the contract of employment that the employer will indemnify the employee for their civil or criminal liability arising out of their conduct in the workplace. If the employee knew or must be presumed to have known that their conduct (either civil or criminal), which gave rise to the liability was unlawful, then they may not be able to rely on the implied indemnity provision. [10] On the other hand, if they were directed by their employer to engage in such unlawful activity, then the implied indemnity continues to apply [11] unless expressly prohibited by statute. [12]

Sometimes the employer may sue the employee for their lack of skill and care, seeking damages for breach of contract (including reimbursement for any sums which the employer

---

[8] *Cementaid (NSW) Pty Ltd v Chambers* (unreported, NSW Sup Ct, Spender AJ, No 12295/94, 29 March 1995).
[9] *Hivac Ltd v Park Royal Scientific Instruments Ltd* [1946] Ch 169 at 177 per Lord Green MR and Morton LJ.
[10] *Burrows v Rhodes* (1899) 1 QB 516.
[11] *Kelly v Allard & Ors* (1987) 4 ANZ Insurance Cases 60-798.
[12] For example, *Corporations Act 2001* (Cth), s 199A(2) – (4) which specifically prohibits indemnity of persons who incur liabilities while acting as officers or auditors of a company.

may have been required to pay to third parties as a result of the employee's negligence).[13] In some jurisdictions, this common law right is prohibited by statute.[14]

In any case, all employees must co-operate with employers in taking reasonable care for their own health and safety and for that of their fellow workers and others at the workplace.

Duty to obey reasonable directions

[8.35] It is the duty of the employee to obey the lawful and reasonable directions of the employer incidental to the contract of employment. However, employees are not bound to obey orders to perform work which is outside the scope of their contractual obligations and inappropriate to their level of skills and social status. For example, it was held that a cook was not bound by an order to work in a dairy [15] but that a B-grade journalist was bound by an order to work at a lower grade.[16]

The orders must be reasonable in the circumstances. Thus orders which put an employee in fear of her or his life need not be obeyed.[17] However, where the employer imposes a particular dress code and the employee persistently disobeys an order to conform to it, that may give rise to an actionable breach of contract.[18]

A typical clause in a contract of employment in the hospitality industry might read:

> I agree to conform to the following dress code standards in the workplace and during training:
> My uniform will be clean and pressed ... Excessive jewellery and/ or piercings are generally not accepted in the front of house environment as it may present hygiene implications.[19]

Attendance at the workplace

[8.40] There is nothing more frustrating than an employee who stays away from work for substantial periods of time without good cause or who, by their behaviour, indicates an unwillingness to be bound by the obligation to be present at work during all office hours. Such behaviour may give rise to dismissal of the employee if the absence is one which causes some identifiable loss to the business and is not just an isolated incident. However, the employer is required in these circumstances to give a warning to the employee to improve their conduct or

---

13   *Harvey v RG O'Dell Ltd* [1958] 2QB 78. *Facts*: The employer injured a fellow worker while driving him to work negligently on his motorcycle. *Held*: The court held that the employer was not entitled to the indemnity because the employee was employed as a storeman and not a driver and the implied term in the contract to exercise reasonable skill and care did not extend to his driving skills.

14   *Employers' Liability Act 1991* (NSW), ss 3 – 5; *Civil Liability Act 1936* (SA), s 59. Only if the employee's negligence amounts to serious or wilful misconduct is the action permitted. This is similar to the rules of subrogation under the *Insurance Contracts Act 1984* (Cth), s 66: see [7.60].

15   *Mackie v Weinholt* (1880) 5 QSCR 211.

16   *Truth and Sportsman Ltd v Molesworth* [1956] AR (NSW) 924.

17   *Ottoman Bank v Chakarian* [1930] AC 277. *Facts*: A bank employee was ordered to transfer to an overseas branch in a country where he feared for his life because of his ethnic origins. He refused to go and the bank dismissed him. *Held*: The employee was entitled to damages for wrongful dismissal. His personal safety was in real danger.

18   *Australian Telecommunications Commission v Hart* (1982) 43 ALR 165. *Facts*: A male employee persistently disobeyed directions not to wear a caftan and thongs to work. *Held*: The employee was under a duty to obey reasonable directions, of which this was one. He was fined under the *Telecommunications Act 1975* (Cth). See also *Woolworths Limited (t/as Safeway) v Cameron Brown* (Australian Industrial Relations Commission, 26 September 2005, PR 963023).

19   Hospitality Group, *Training Conditions of Employment* (Food and Beverage Traineeship).

performance or risk dismissal and then allow a reasonable amount of time for that improvement in performance or conduct to take place.[20]

Confidentiality after termination

[8.45] Even when the employment contract comes to an end, the employee is not free to disclose their former employer's trade secrets. Their obligation of confidentiality (discussed in [8.25] above) continues. Should the employee attempt to use such information in a subsequent business venture of their own or for the benefit of a new employer, the former employer may apply to the courts for an injunction either to prevent the continuance of the business or to demand delivery up of the offensive material[21] and/or machinery[22] for the purpose of destroying it.

This is not to say that an employee can never set up in business in competition with a former employer. They can, so long as they use their own skill and knowledge and so long as they have not covenanted otherwise. For example, if the original contract of employment contained valid restrictive trade covenants, then the employee may be prevented contractually from setting up their business within a certain geographical area for a period of time, the particular terms of which will vary from agreement to agreement.

Employer's duties

Work

[8.50] So long as the employer continues to pay wages, he or she is not obliged to find work for the employee, with the following exceptions:

- if the employee works in the entertainment industry and has an existing reputation as a singer or actor, for example, then the employer must provide work which will maintain and enhance that reputation;[23]
- if the employee has been appointed to a certain office with attendant powers and privileges attached to it, the employer's failure to permit the employer to take up that position or to destroy the position amounts to a failure to give the full remuneration contracted for;[24]
- if the employee is paid by commission or at piece rates, then the employer has an obligation to provide enough work for the employee to make a reasonable wage even if this is unprofitable for the employer's business.[25]

Wages

[8.55] From the employees' perspective, one of the most important aspects of their employment contract is receiving a wage. The wage is paid by the employer in consideration of the promise by the employee to perform work. As a general rule, the employer is not required to pay the worker in advance of the performance of that work. Usually, the employment

---

20   Australian Government, *Small business Fair Dismissal Code*, Checklist (commenced 1 July 2009).
21   *Metrans Pty Ltd v Courtney-Smith* (1983) 1 IPR 185 where an order was made to destroy copies of customer lists.
22   *Ansell Rubber Co Pty Ltd v Allied Rubber Industries Pty Ltd* [1967] VR 37 where orders were made to dismantle machinery and deliver it up to the plaintiff for destruction.
23   *Flamingo Park Pty Ltd v Dolly Dolly Creation Pty Ltd* (1986) 65 ALR 500.
24   *Collier v Sunday Referee Publishing Co Ltd* [1940] 2 KB 647.
25   *Devonald v Rosser & Sons* [1906] 2 KB 728.

contract and/or the award will stipulate the obligation of the employer to pay wages to the employee on a regular periodic basis (for example, each week or fortnight).[26]

Just how much the employee is entitled to receive may be governed by an industrial award or agreement. Furthermore, if deductions are to be made from the wage for taxation purposes[27] or because of the existence of a garnishee order,[28] then these matters are governed by statute. In the absence of an express agreement, the worker is entitled to a reasonable remuneration.[29]

Paid leave

[8.60] This seems to be a creature of statute or workplace award or agreement. The Australian Government's *National Employment Standards* and the *Hospitality Industry (General) Awards 2010* combine to contain the minimum conditions of employment for employees. The different types of paid leave in the tourism, travel and hospitality industry are set out in Part 6 and they include, for example:

- annual leave;[30]
- personal carers' (sick) leave and compassionate leave;[31]
- community service leave;[32] and
- public holidays.[33]

In addition, most awards now provide for parental leave, whether paid or unpaid.[34]

Health and safety

[8.65] Originally at common law, employers' responsibility for the health and safety of employees was very limited. Gradually, through the industrial revolution, this position was reformed by statute and, shortly after *Donoghue v Stevenson*[35] established the general duty of care in tort, employers were held[36] to owe a common law duty of care to employees to provide:

- safe premises;

---

26 For example, see *Hospitality Industry (General) Award 2010*, Clause 26 which stipulates payment of wages on a weekly or fortnightly basis.
27 *Income Tax Assessment Act 1936* (Cth).
28 Supreme, District and Magistrates' Courts Acts of each of the States and Territories.
29 *Stinchcombe v Thomas* [1957] VR 509. *Facts*: The plaintiff was promised by the deceased that he would "well reward" her if she worked for him as housekeeper until he died. *Held*: In an action against the executor that the promise to "well reward" her was too vague to create legal relations, the plaintiff was able to recover on a quantum meruit for services rendered.
30 See Australian Government *National Employment Standards*, Division 5. The entitlement is four weeks on completion of every 12 months of continuous service. See also *Hospitality Industry (General) Award 2010*, Clause 34 for variations and exceptions.
31 See Australian Government *National Employment Standards*, Division 6. See also *Hospitality Industry (General) Award 2010*, Clause 35.
32 See Australian Government *National Employment Standards*, Division 7. See also *Hospitality Industry (General) Award 2010*, Clause 36.
33 See Australian Government *National Employment Standards*, Division 9. See also *Hospitality Industry (General) Award 2010*, Clause 37.
34 See Australian Government *National Employment Standards*, Division 4. See also *Hospitality Industry (General) Award 2010*, Clause 37.
35 *Donoghue v Stevenson* [1932] AC 562.
36 *Wilsons & Clyde Coal Co v English* [1938] AC 37.

- safe plant and equipment; and
- a safe system of work.

This duty of care arises in tort and also as an implied term in the contract of employment. It has been augmented by a similar public duty under workplace health and safety legislation so that breach of the duty is also a quasi-criminal offence. These matters are discussed in more detail later in [8.180]ff.

Indemnity

[8.70] There is an implied term in the contract of employment that the employer will indemnify employees for any liability, loss or expense incurred by them in the course of their employment.[37] There are two aspects to this indemnity:

- claims by employees who suffer injury, loss or damage in the workplace; and
- claims by third parties against employees who through their negligence cause injury, loss or damage.

In the first instance, the workers' compensation legislation entitles employees to all proper expenses and loss of earnings related to the disability or sickness which has occurred in the course of their employment.[38] Apart from these rights, the employer has both a common law and statutory duty to provide a safe system of work as mentioned above. Breach of this condition may result in an action for breach of statutory duty and/or common law negligence (see [8.210]). In most jurisdictions, the recovery of damages at common law and under statute have been restricted.[39]

The main defences that employers would raise to these claims were:

- voluntary assumption of risk;
- contributory negligence; and
- illegal purpose.

For a more detailed discussion of these defences see [5.150]ff.

In any event, the courts now recognise that employees are in a considerably weaker bargaining position than employers as they may need their job no matter how dangerous or difficult it is to perform. As a matter of public policy, therefore, courts now view such defences sceptically.[40]

In the second case, an employer is vicariously liable to third parties for the negligent acts of her or his employees. This is based on the philosophy that the employee is simply following the lawful orders of her or his employer. Thus, if the employer could point to evidence of serious or wilful misconduct on the part of the employee such that they were said to be "on a frolic of

---

37   *Pupazzoni v Fremantle Fisherman's Co-operative Society Ltd* (1981) 23 AILR 168.

38   See *Hospitality Industry (General) Award 2010*, Clause 21.5 Accident Pay sets out employees' current entitlements. Note that the operation of this clause ceases on 31 December 2014 (Clause 21.5(d)).

39   See for example the *Workers' Compensation Act 1987* (NSW), s 151A. Queensland and the Australian Capital Territory apart, all other States impose a threshold that workers must meet before they can sue their employer at common law for damages.

40   Compare this attitude with that expressed by Bramwell LJ to a parliamentary select committee in 1877 which was considering the introduction of the *Employers' Liability Act 1877* (UK). He said "Why does he not leave the employment if he knows that it is dangerous? To my mind, it is a sad thing to hear men come into court, as I have heard them, and excuse themselves for not having done that on the ground that their bread depended on it, or something of that sort" (quoted in A H Manchester, *Modern Legal History* (Butterworths, London, 1985), p 296).

their own" (that is, acting outside the scope of their employment), then the employer would have a successful defence to a claim by a third party.[41] See also the discussion on indemnity in [8.30].

Termination of Contracts of Service

[8.75] The contract of employment may provide that the employment is for a fixed term (for example, two years) or that it will come to an end on the completion of the specified task, in which case no notice is required. However, what are the rights and obligations of the respective parties if one of them decides to terminate the contract early and in what circumstances is this lawful?

There are three different situations which this section will explore:

- deliberate or consequential termination of employment;
- breach of contract of employment; and
- unfair or wrongful dismissal.

Deliberate or consequential termination

Deliberate termination

[8.80] There are a number of ways in which a contract of employment may be deliberately terminated, including:

- retirement;
- resignation; or
- mutual agreement.

In the absence of express terms, a contract of employment is terminable upon either party giving reasonable notice to the other to bring the employment to an end. What is considered "reasonable notice" will vary according to the circumstances. The awards generally set out the minimum period of notice required to be given to employees or payment in lieu thereof.[42]

Consequential termination

[8.85] Obviously, if the employer, being a natural person, or an employee, dies, the contract of employment between the two is terminated. On the other hand, if the employer is a separate legal entity such as a company, the death of a director does not bring the contract of employment with staff to an end.

However, if the employer is declared bankrupt or the employer company is put into liquidation, this will terminate the employment contract. If there are outstanding wages and salaries due, the employees will be given preferred creditors' status in the winding up of the estate.

Other examples of consequential termination include illness or permanent incapacity, and takeovers and mergers. In the latter case, the employer company may not assign the contract of employment to the new business entity but must terminate the contract of employment with its

---

41 Refer to [5.95]ff for further discussion.
42 See for example Australian Government, *National Employment Standards,* Division 10. Note that redundancy pay (subdiv B) for permanent employees may also be applicable to businesses with more than 15 staff. See also *Hospitality Industry (General) Award 2010,* Part 3 Clauses 16-17.

existing employees. They are entitled to proper notice of the transfer of business. The new employer has the option of continuing or terminating those existing contracts with employees on the same terms and conditions as they previously enjoyed. [43]

Breach of contract of employment

[8.90] Once the bargain is struck, the parties to the contract of employment are expected to perform their respective duties. If it appears from the behaviour of one of the parties that they no longer wish to be bound by the terms of the agreement, then the other party may accept the repudiation and terminate the contract. [44]

Alternatively, if it becomes apparent that an essential term of the contract has been breached, this also entitles the innocent party to terminate the contract. In the case of employment contracts, one of the essential terms is that the employer will pay a proper wage. Another is that employees must not engage in misconduct.

Summary dismissal

[8.95] An employer had the right to dismiss an employee "on the spot" for misconduct. To justify dismissing an employee without notice or warning, an employer must believe on reasonable grounds that the conduct complained of is extremely serious. In the past, such misconduct included the following behaviour:

- drunkenness; [45]
- dishonesty or fraud; [46]
- abusive or bad language; [47]
- incompetence of a skilled employee or of a person claiming to have those skills; [48]
- wilful disobedience of the employer's orders so long as those orders were reasonable and lawful. [49]

With the introduction of the *Fair Work 2009* legislation (see [8.100]) and associated regulations and codes of conduct, [50] misconduct warranting immediate summary dismissal may be limited to theft, fraud, violence and serious breaches of workplace health and safety. [51]

The right to summarily dismiss is not mandatory and the employer may decide to waive her or his rights to terminate the contract. That being the case, he or she cannot later attempt to reopen the matter.

---

43 For example, accrued leave, superannuation entitlements, and redundancy benefits. See Australian Government, *National Employment Standards*, Division 10.
44 For example, in the case of an employee, abandonment of work; in the case of an employer, exclusion from the workplace.
45 *Drysdale v New Era Steamship Co Ltd* (1936) 55 Ll LR 45.
46 *W D & H O Wills Ltd v Jamieson* [1957] AR (NSW) 547.
47 *Farley v Lums* (1917) 19 WALR 117. In that case the language used by the employee to his employer was: "It's a bit bloody hot keeping a man waiting so damn long." Things have changed a lot since 1917!
48 See for example *Harmer v Cornelius* (1858) 141 ER 94.
49 *R v Darling Island Stevedoring and Lighterage Co Ltd; ex parte Halliday and Sullivan* (1938) 60 CLR 601 at 621-622 per Dixon J.
50 For example, the *Small Business Fair Dismissal Code*, which was operational from 1 July 2009.
51 In the case of theft, fraud and violence in the workplace, it is sufficient though not essential that the employer report the matter to the police.

Unfair dismissal

[8.100] The concept of unfair dismissal is a creature of statute The *Fair Work Act 2009* (Cth)[52] replaced the *Workplace Relations Act 1996* (Cth) completely on 1 January 2010, bringing into existence the *National Employment Standards* and the modern awards such as the *Hospitality Industry (General) Award*. The *Fair Work* legislation covers all National System employers and their employees.[53] Under the Act, the test to be applied by *Fair Work Australia* in unfair dismissal actions is whether:

- the employee was dismissed;
- the dismissal was harsh, unjust or unreasonable;
- the dismissal was not consistent with the *Small Business Fair Dismissal Code*;[54]
- The dismissal was not for a genuine redundancy.

The steps to resolution of the dispute include:

- *Fair Work Australia* will hold a conciliation which is an informal, private and confidential process; and
- if not resolved by the conciliator, then a Conference or Hearing will be commenced.

Frivolous and malicious claims will be discouraged.

In order to avoid unnecessary complaints, the *Fair Work Act 2009* incorporates the *Small Businesses Fair Dismissal Code* which sets out the procedure for terminating someone's employment. It includes a checklist for small business employers[55] to follow to ensure a fair process. When a small business follows the checklist, this action is a protection or defence against an unfair dismissal application. The scheme is not available for use by larger employers who are expected to have more formal Human Resources processes of their own.

Unfair dismissal must be distinguished from unlawful dismissal which is not excusable, even for small employers. Examples include dismissing employees on the basis of race, sex, colour, sexual preference, age, physical or mental disability, marital status, family or carer's responsibilities, pregnancy, religion, political opinion, national extraction or social origin. It is also unlawful to terminate an employee's employment if they are temporarily absent from work because of illness or injury, because of union involvement or non-involvement or because of absence from work during parental leave.[56] For further discussion, see [8.135]ff.

Wrongful dismissal

[8.105] At common law, employees may claim damages (monetary compensation) for wrongful dismissal; that is, dismissal without proper notice or summary dismissal without good cause. Usually, it is restricted to the wages that the employee would have earned if proper notice had been given. In some cases, where the employee has been entitled to additional benefits such as share of profits, board and lodging, tips and the like, then her or his damages

---

52   Sections of the Act commenced progressively and came fully into effect from 1 January 2010.
53   The terms National System employee and National System employer are defined in the *Fair Work Act 2009* (Cth) in ss 13 and 14 respectively and include employees of corporations, the Commonwealth government, and a Commonwealth authority amongst others.
54   *Fair Work Act 2009* (Cth), s 388.
55   This is currently applicable to small businesses employing fewer than 15 full time employees but from 1 January 2011, the number of employees used to define a small business will be based on a headcount of less than 15 employees regardless of whether they are full-time equivalent employees.
56   For further information, see Australian Government Fair Work Ombudsman 07, *Best Practice Guide Small Business & the Fair Work Act*.

may be more substantial. In either case, the employee must demonstrate that he or she has tried to mitigate any losses by seeking alternative employment.[57]

Reinstatement and compensation

[8.110] Pursuant to the *Fair Work* legislation, if a *Fair Work Australia* conference hearing process decides in favour of the employee, an appropriate remedy must be awarded which takes into account all of the circumstances, including the viability of the employer's business. The primary remedy is reinstatement[58] or compensation where reinstatement is inappropriate. *Fair Work Australia* may also order reinstatement of an employee to an associated entity of the employer where the employee's position no longer exists with the original employer but that position or an equivalent position is available in the associated entity.[59]

Alternatively, if reinstatement is inappropriate, then *Fair Work Australia* may order compensation in lieu of it. There are a number of factors which will affect the amount of compensation granted, including:

- the effect on the viability of the employer's business;
- the length of the employee's service;
- the remuneration the employee would have received but for the dismissal;
- efforts by the employee to mitigate their loss; and
- the amount of any pay earned by the employee since dismissal.

No compensation will be granted for shock, distress or humiliation caused by the manner of the employee's dismissal.[60] There is also a cap on the amount of compensation which may be awarded.[61]

The *Fair Work Act 2009* (Cth) excludes State and Territory industrial laws[62] from applying to National System employers and their employees. These employees are still, however, subject to State and Territory laws which regulate key aspects of employment like workplace health and safety, workers compensation and discrimination laws.[63] Modern awards are also subject to these State and Territory laws but prevail over industry specific employment laws to the extent that they are inconsistent with them.

STATUTORY INTERVENTION

[8.115] In summary, the main legislative interventions in the area of employment law at both State and federal level include:

- industrial relations legislation;

---

57 *Yetton v Eastwoods Froy Ltd* [1967] 1 WLR 104.
58 That is, as the name suggests, the employee is put back in the same position he or she enjoyed as if the dismissal had never occurred, including all their former rights and privileges.
59 *Fair Work Act 2009* (Cth), s 391(1A). An associated entity is defined in *Corporations Act 2001* (Cth), s 50AAA.
60 *Fair Work Act 2009* (Cth), s 392.
61 The formula is based on the following: (1) half the amount of the high income threshold ($100,000 for full-time employees, indexed; (2) the amount of remuneration received by the person, or that they were entitled to receive (whichever is higher) in the 26 weeks before the dismissal from 27 August 2007 and annually each year after that on 1 July.
62 See, for example, *Industrial Relations Act 1999* (Qld); *Fair Work Act 1994* (SA); *Industrial Relations Act 1984* (Tas); *Industrial Relations Act 1979* (WA); *Industrial Relations Act 1996* (NSW).
63 See *Fair Work Act 2009* (Cth), ss 26 and 27.

- anti-discrimination legislation;
- workers' compensation legislation; and
- occupational health and safety legislation.

The following sections examine these statutory interventions in more detail.

FAIR WORK LEGISLATION, AWARDS AND AGREEMENTS

[8.120] The new *Fair Work Act 2009* (Cth) will have a marked effect on the future development of federal awards and agreements in employment law. Its key initiatives are fairness and flexibility. It aims to provide a balanced framework for co-operative and productive workplace relations with:

- workplace relations laws that are fair to workers, flexible for business, and promote economic prosperity;
- a guaranteed minimum safety net of employment terms and conditions;
- work and family balance, the prevention of discrimination, freedom of association and effective processes for resolving workplace disputes and grievances; and
- minimum conditions in enterprise bargaining processes.[64]

The next section examines the new framework for workplace relations which the Act establishes and its impact on the making of awards and agreements.

Modern Awards and Agreements

[8.125] The purpose of awards and agreements is to set minimum rates of pay and conditions of work for employees in the workplace. The industrial agreement is usually negotiated between a particular employer group (for example, the Australian Hotels' Association) and the corresponding employees' collective representative which is the particular union interested in that field of activity.[65]

The *Fair Work Act 2009* (Cth) establishes a framework for developing modern awards[66] which streamline and consolidate existing awards so that they are industry or occupation-based and easier for employers and employees to use and understand. For example, the modern *Hospitality Industry (General) Award 2010* applies throughout Australia to employers engaged in the hospitality industry.[67] The modern award system is administered by *Fair Work Australia*, the new "one stop shop" industrial umpire which replaces many of the former entities.[68]

The modern *Hospitality Industry (General) Award 2010* reflects existing award conditions as well as building on the *National Employment Standards* legislated in the *Fair Work Act*

---

64   See *Fair Work Act 2009* (Cth), s 3.
65   In the present example, the Australian Liquor, Hospitality and Miscellaneous Workers' Union (LHMU).
66   See *Fair Work Act 2009* (Cth), Part 2-3.
67   It includes hotels, motor inns, motels, serviced apartments, ski lodges, holiday flats and units, wine saloons and wine bars, taverns, resorts, casinos, function areas and convention centres but not registered or licensed clubs or restaurants and catering or higher earning employees.
68   These include the Australian Industrial Relations Commission, Workplace Australia, Workplace Ombudsman, Australian Building and Construction Commission amongst others.

2009.[69] The *National Employment Standards* represent 10 minimum standards for employment particularly pertaining to minimum rates of pay and working conditions. They are:

- Hours of Work
- Flexible working arrangements
- Parental Leave
- Annual Leave
- Personal Carer's Leave
- Community Service Leave
- Long Service Leave
- Public Holidays
- Notice of Termination and Redundancy
- Fair Work Information Statement.[70]

A modern award will not apply where there is an enterprise agreement between employers and employees except to the extent that the base rate of pay for an enterprise agreement cannot be less than the modern award or the national minimum wage. As noted in [8.110], a modern award, like the *Hospitality Industry (General) Award*, will prevail over State and Territory industry specific employment laws to the extent of any inconsistency with them

Agreements in the workplace

[8.130] Enterprise agreements[71] allow employers and employees to tailor their accord on wages and conditions to meet the specific needs of their workplace environment. These agreements benefit small businesses in particular. In order to be approved by *Fair Work Australia*, an enterprise agreement must address the following issues:

- nominal expiry date (up to 4 years);
- dispute settlement clause allowing for an external party such as *Fair Work Australia* to settle disputes;
- flexibility term to allow for variation on an individual basis;
- consultation clause for negotiating on any major change with employees;
- pay rates – must be at least the rates in the relevant modern award or national minimum wage;
- other matters pertaining to the employment relationship including deductions from wages.

Following negotiations between the bargaining representatives,[72] the employer must circulate copies of the proposed agreement amongst employees and the majority of employees must vote in favour of the agreement. The enterprise agreement is then submitted to *Fair Work Australia* which must be satisfied that it:

---

69   *Fair Work Act 2009* (Cth), s 55. For example, the modern award will provide an extra week of annual leave for shift workers.
70   *Fair Work Act 2009* (Cth), s 61.
71   *Fair Work Act 2009* (Cth), Parts 2-4.
72   These include the employer's appointed bargaining representative, and a union representative if there is one or more members at the workplace unless the member appoints another bargaining representative.

- represents a genuine agreement between the parties;
- meets the minimum conditions set out in the *National Employment Standards*;
- guarantees that each class of employee will be better off overall than they would have been under a modern award; and
- does not undermine good faith bargaining;

before approving it.[73]

Like modern awards, an enterprise agreement will prevail over State and Territory industry specific employment laws to the extent of any inconsistency with them.

HUMAN RIGHTS ISSUES

[8.135] Issues such as equal opportunity, discrimination and sexual harassment arise most frequently in the context of the workplace. They are closely linked with the conditions of employment. This section examines each of the issues and the measures which Parliament has taken to overcome some of the problems.

Discrimination

[8.140] Discrimination has been defined as:

> Any distinction, exclusion or preference made on the basis of race, colour, sex, political opinion, national extraction or social origin, which has the effect of nullifying or impairing equality of opportunity or treatment in employment or occupation; and such other distinction, exclusion or preference which has the effect of nullifying or impairing equality of opportunity or treatment in employment or occupation as may be determined after consultation with representative employers' and workers' organisations and other appropriate bodies.[74]

There are numerous ways in which discrimination in the workplace may occur but federal Parliament[75] has identified four areas to target:

- sex discrimination;[76]
- racial discrimination;[77] and
- disability discrimination;[78] and

---

73 A summary of the new Fair Work requirements are set out in the Australian government Fair Work Ombudsman 07, *Best Practice Guide Small Business & the Fair Work Act*.

74 Article 1 of the International Labour Organisation (ILO), *Convention on the Elimination of all Forms of Discrimination (Employment and Occupation) 1966*.

75 Most of the Australian States and Territories have passed anti-discrimination legislation as well. Any provisions which are inconsistent with the federal legislation will be rendered inoperative pursuant to s 109 of the Commonwealth Constitution.

76 The *Sex Discrimination Act 1984* (Cth), ss 5 – 7B prohibits discrimination (direct or indirect) on the grounds of sex, marital status or pregnancy in a number of areas, including employment.

77 The *Racial Discrimination Act 1975* (Cth), s 9 prohibits any act involving a distinction, exclusion, restriction or preference made on the basis of race, colour, national extraction or social origin, which has the effect of nullifying or impairing the recognition, enjoyment or exercise (on an equal footing) of any human right or fundamental freedom in the political, economic, social, cultural or any other field of public life.

78 The *Disability Discrimination Act 1992* (Cth), s 4 defines "Disability" to include total or partial loss of the person's bodily or mental functions; total or partial loss of a part of the body; the presence in the body of organisms causing disease or illness; malfunction, malformation or disfigurement of a part of the person's body (inter alia).

- age discrimination.[79]

In each case, the complainant or a person acting on their behalf must lodge a written complaint with the Human Rights and Equal Opportunity Commission[80] setting out the particular acts of discrimination complained of. The matter is then referred to a Commissioner appointed under each Act who has power to investigate the circumstances of the complaint with the aim of settling the dispute by conciliation. If that fails, the case is referred to the Commission for a determination.

The Commission has power,[81] amongst other things, to

- dismiss the complaint; or

if the complaint is substantiated, declare that the respondent should:

- apologise;
- not repeat the unlawful conduct;
- employ, re-employ or promote the complainant;
- pay damages by way of compensation to the complainant.

Such determinations are not binding or conclusive between any of the parties and either the Commission or the complainant may institute proceedings in the Federal Court for their enforcement.[82]

Equal opportunity

[8.145] In a sense, "equal opportunity" is the antidote to discrimination. It is a declaration by the employer that he or she is making an objective assessment of the individual employee's abilities, rights and privileges putting aside any natural prejudice the employer may have. It is not defined in the legislation.[83] Indeed, even in those States which have passed "equal opportunity" legislation, the focus is still on the type of behaviour which is discriminatory.

Perhaps the most positive move towards real equal opportunity for women, members of racial minorities and persons with physical or intellectual disabilities has been the introduction of affirmative action legislation.[84] This legislation aims to remove some of the barriers to employment traditionally experienced by these groups. For example, the federal legislation requires employers with 100 or more employees to develop workplace programs to appoint and promote women on the basis of merit – quite simply giving them a "fair go" – and to report annually on the progress made.[85]

---

79   *Age Discrimination Act 2004* (Cth).
80   Established under the *Human Rights and Equal Opportunity Commission Act 1986* (Cth).
81   *Human Rights and equal Opportunity Commission Act 1986* (Cth), ss 25Y and 25Z.
82   *Human Rights and equal Opportunity Commission Act 1986* (Cth), s 25ZA.
83   See, for example, *Equal Opportunity Act 1984* (SA); *Equal Opportunity Act 1995* (Vic); *Equal Opportunity Act 1984* (WA).
84   *Equal Opportunity for Women in the Workplace Act 1999* (Cth); *Anti-Discrimination Act 1977* (NSW), s 122J; *Equal Opportunity Act 1984* (WA), ss 140, 145.
85   *Equal Opportunity for Women in the Workplace Act 1999* (Cth), s 2A.

Sexual harassment

[8.150] One particularly insidious form of discrimination is that based on sexual harassment. Sexual harassment, either by an employer of an employee or by a fellow employee, is prohibited.[86] It occurs where, for example, a person

(a) ... makes an unwelcome sexual advance, or an unwelcome request for sexual favours, to the person harassed; or

(b) engages in other unwelcome conduct of a sexual nature in relation to the person harassed;

in circumstances in which a reasonable person, having regard to all the circumstances, would have anticipated that the person harassed would be offended, humiliated or intimidated.[87]

In some jurisdictions, the legislation adds a further proviso that the person who is the subject of these attentions must believe on reasonable grounds that a rejection of the advance, a refusal of the request or the taking of objection to the conduct may disadvantage their employment or possible employment.[88]

WORKERS COMPENSATION

[8.155] Workers compensation is a compulsory insurance scheme for all employers designed to rehabilitate and compensate workers who suffer injury and/or contract disease in the course of their employment, regardless of who is at fault. If an employee can prove that their injuries were caused by the negligence of another person at the workplace, either a fellow employee or the employer, then they may also have a common law claim. Entitlements may include:

- payment of medical expenses;
- loss of earnings;
- rehabilitation;
- long term care;
- reasonable funeral expenses in the event of fatal injuries;
- lump sum compensation.

Each of the Australian States and Territories[89] has its own scheme and the Commonwealth has three such schemes.[90] The schemes are administered in each jurisdiction by an agency which is responsible for determining the entitlement an employee injured in the workplace

---

86   See for example *Boyle v Ozden* (1986) EOC 92-165 (CCH) where the owners of a food shop who were absent overseas at the time of the incidents were held vicariously liable for the harassment of one employee by another because they had not done anything active to prevent the harassment from happening.

87   *Sex Discrimination Act 1984* (Cth), s 28A; see also *Anti-Discrimination Act 1991* (Qld), s 119.

88   See for example, *Sex Discrimination Act 1984* (Cth), Div 3, ss 28A – 28L; *Equal Opportunity Act 1984* (SA), s 87; *Equal Opportunity Act 1984* (WA), s 24.

89   *Workers' Compensation Act 1951* (ACT); *Workers Rehabilitation and Compensation Act* (NT); *Workers' Compensation Act 1987* (NSW); *Workers' Compensation and Rehabilitation Act 2003* (Qld); *Workers' Rehabilitation and Compensation Act 1986* (SA); *Workers' Rehabilitation and Compensation Act 1988* (Tas); *Workers' Compensation Act 1958* (Vic); *Workers' Compensation and Injury Management Act 1981* (WA).

90   *Safety, Rehabilitation and Compensation Act 1988* (Cth) which covers Australian government employees, Australian Defence Force personnel with service before 1 July 2004 and employees of licensed self insurers; *Seafarers Rehabilitation and Compensation Act 1992* (Cth); *Military Rehabilitation and Compensation Act 2004* (Cth) which covers Australian Defence Force personnel since 1 July 2004.

may receive.[91] However, the claims process and the daily management of injured workers is run by private insurance companies who are paid a fee by the government to do so. The aim is to rehabilitate the worker, if that is appropriate, so that they may return safely to the workplace as quickly as possible.

For their part, employers must not only ensure that they participate in the workers compensation scheme but must also ensure that they are providing a safe and healthy workplace for their employees in accordance with the relevant legislation and their particular insurance policy. If they fail to fulfil these obligations, then they face significant fines and penalties. Employers' responsibilities for workers compensation and workplace health and safety go hand in hand. To this end, the federal Parliament has enacted the *Safe Work Australia Act 2008* (Cth) which creates *Safe Work Australia*, a body whose objective is to improve occupational health and safety outcomes and workers' compensation arrangements in Australia. The next section discusses workplace, health and safety in more detail.

OCCUPATIONAL HEALTH AND SAFETY

History

[8.160] In 1837, when the first occupational health and safety (OHS) case came before the courts, it was already well accepted that an employer was vicariously liable to a third party injured by the tortious acts of an employee (see [5.100]ff). However, rather than extend that protection to an employee injured by a fellow employee, the court made an exception to vicarious liability and laid down the notorious doctrine of "common employment" which provided employers with a very effective defence in OHS cases at common law. This reflected the laissez-faire "employee beware" attitude of the times.

Priestley v Fowler

[8.165] *Priestley v Fowler* (1837) 3 M&W 1

Facts: Priestley was a butcher's assistant who was injured in the course of employment when he fell from an overloaded van. He claimed damages from his employer.

Decision: Lord Arbinger held that the employer could not be held liable. The decision was thereafter interpreted as authority for the defence of "common employment" which was rationalised on the volenti non fit injuria principle; that is, an employee knew and accepted the risk of working with fellow employees. However it was not clear from the report that the van was overloaded by a fellow employee. Also, Lord Arbinger's reasoning is confused and in the examples he used to illustrate how absurd it would be to hold the employer liable there were independent contractors as well as employees responsible. Lord Arbinger's examples of absurdity concerned domestic servant situations, many of which have a tourism, travel or hospitality dimension:

> The footman, therefore, who rides behind the carriage, may have an action against his master for a defect in the carriage owing to the negligence of the coachmaker, or for the defect in the harness arising from the negligence of the harnessmaker, or for drunkenness, neglect or want of skill in the coachman...The master...would be liable to the servant for the negligence of the chambermaid, for putting him into a damp bed; for that of the upholsterer,

---

91   For example, WorkCover NSW, WA, SA, WorkSafe Victoria, Department of Justice and WorkCover Tasmania, Department of Justice NT, Chief Minister's Department – Office of Industrial Relations, Departmet of Justice and Attorney General Qld.

Priestley v Fowler cont.

for sending him a crazy bedstead whereby he was made to fall down while asleep and injure himself; for the negligence of the cook, in not properly cleaning the copper vessels used in the kitchen, of the butcher, in supplying the family with meat of a quality injurious to health...

Postscript: To add insult to injury, on losing the case Priestley was unable to pay the legal costs and was thrown into debtors' prison, where he spent the next 33 years! However the wheel has turned and now the employer would probably be found liable in each of the examples of absurdity cited above in rejection of Priestley's claim.

———— ଛଠାର ————

It took the legislature and the courts almost 100 years to overcome the doctrine of common employment and provide employees with OHS protection. Reform began with the *Employer's Liability Act 1880* (Eng) which restricted the scope of *volenti non fit injuria* in employment cases and was soon followed in the Australian colonies.[92] It was followed by the first major *Factory Act 1833* in 1833.

The modern approach at common law was established in 1938[93] by the House of Lords in *Wilsons & Clyde Coal Co v English*[94] which held that an employer owes a general duty of care to employees to take reasonable care to provide:

- safe premises;
- safe plant and equipment; and
- a safe system of work.[95]

The House of Lords further held that this general duty is the personal responsibility of the employer and could not be delegated to other employees and thus was not subject to the defence of common employment. This general duty of care in tort is discussed in Chapter 5. A similar duty of care is usually implied into the contract of employment and this is discussed in Chapter 4.

The doctrine of common employment has been abolished altogether by statute in England and Australia.[96] Occupational health and safety is now governed by international conventions and extensive Commonwealth and State legislation designed to ensure that workplaces are safe and healthy.

---

92 See for example New South Wales: 46 Vic No 6 (1882); Queensland: 50 Vic No 24 (1886).
93 Following *Donoghue v Stevenson* [1932] AC 562.
94 *Wilsons & Clyde Coal Co v English* [1938] AC 37.
95 *Wilsons & Clyde Coal Co v English* [1938] AC 37 at 78 per Lord Wright.
96 See for example England 1948: *Law Reform (Personal Injuries) Act* 116 12 Geo VI Ch 41; NSW: *Workers Compensation Act 1926*, s 65(1); Qld: *Law Reform (Abolition of the Rule of Common Employment) Act 1951*, 15 Geo VI No 41 of 1951.

Organisations

International

[8.170] The International Labour Organization (ILO)[97] was created in 1919 and is now a United Nations Agency dedicated to the promotion of social justice for working people everywhere. It has 183 member countries[98] and gives employers' and employees' organisations equal representation in the formulation of policies. The ILO's activities on OHS comprise:

- ILO Conventions, Recommendations and Codes of Practice which set international standards on OHS;
- research, collection and dissemination of information including the activities conducted through its International Labour Office and the International Occupational Safety and Health Information Centre (CIS);[99]
- technical assistance on OHS to member countries.

National and State

[8.175] Under the Constitution the Commonwealth powers over this field are limited and so OHS legislation comprises the Commonwealth's Act for its own employees and corresponding State and Territory legislation. The principal OHS legislation[100] is administered by an OHS authority in each jurisdiction.[101]

Safe Work Australia,[102] through its National OHS Strategy, provides a forum for all governments, employer organisations and employee organisations to develop uniform approaches to OHS on particular issues.[103] For this purpose SafeWork Australia has power to declare National OHS Standards and Codes of Practice which States or Territories may adopt as regulations or codes of practice under their OHS legislation. If adopted as regulations they become legally enforceable. If adopted as codes of practice they merely provide advice on how to meet regulatory requirements and are not legally enforceable although they can be used in court as evidence that legal requirements have or have not been met. National OHS Standards and Codes of Practice have been developed on matters of particular relevance to tourism,

---

97 International Labour Organization (ILO), see http://www.ilo.org.
98 As at April 2010. See ILO at http://www.ilo.org.
99 International Occupational Safety and Health Information Centre (CIS), http://www.ilocis.org/en/abcisilo2.html.
100 OHS legislation comprises: *Australian Workplace Safety Standards Act 2005* (Cth); *Occupational Health and Safety (Commonwealth Employees) Act 1991* (Cth); *Occupational Health and Safety (Maritime Industry) Act 1993* (Cth); *Work Safety Act 2008* (ACT); *Occupational Health and Safety Act 2000* (NSW); *Workplace Health and Safety Act* (NT); *Workplace Health and Safety Act 1995* (Qld); *Occupational Health, Safety and Welfare Act 1986* (SA); *Workplace Health and Safety Ac 1995* (Tas); *Occupational Health and Safety Act 2004* (Vic); *Occupational Safety and Health Act 1984* (WA).
101 OHS Authorities comprise: Commonwealth: Comcare and Australian Safety and Compensation Council ACT Workcover; WorkCover NSW; NT WorkSafe; Queensland Workplace Health and Safety Board; SafeWork SA: WorkCover Tasmania; Victorian WorkCover Authority; WorkCover WA.
102 See SafeWork Australia at http://www.safeworkaustralia.gov.au/swa.
103 *Safe Work Australia Act 2008* (Cth), s 10.

travel and hospitality such as management and protection of hearing at work, occupational overuse syndrome and passive smoking in the workplace amongst others. [104]

OHS Legislation

[8.180] As foreshadowed above, the OHS regulatory system uses the full range of legal measures from legislation to self-regulation. [105] The OHS principal legislation provides the general regulatory framework and requires all persons involved (including employers, employees and suppliers of plant) to take responsibility for OHS. This is enforced by inspectors. However a more self-regulatory approach is required for the detailed OHS requirements at particular workplaces and these are developed through standards and codes of practice administered by on-site committees. In any OHS issue it is important to understand this structure and to consider all four types of regulation:

- legislation;
- regulations;
- standards; and
- codes of practice.

Safe Work Australia [106] has now prepared a model *Work Health and Safety Act 2010* [107] designed to provide a balanced and nationally consistent regulatory framework for adoption by the Commonwealth and each of the States and Territories. It is described in more detail in the following discussion. [108]

Definitions

[8.185] To ensure that workplaces are safe and healthy the model law imposes duties upon employers and others to protect employees and others. Workplaces and the persons responsible and persons protected are defined in wide terms. [109]

Workplace

[8.190] "Workplace" is generally defined to include almost any "place where work is carried out for a business or undertaking and includes any place where a worker goes, or is likely to be, while at work". It includes vehicles, ships and other mobile structures on either land or sea. [110] This definition is broad enough to include most places where tourism, travel and hospitality products are produced and consumed.

---

104 For more detail, see SafeWork Australia website Index of National Standards Codes of Practice and related Guidance Notes at http://www.safeworkaustralia.gov.au/swa/HealthSafety/OHSstandards.
105 The Australian regulatory system for OHS follows the recommendations of the UK Robens Committee.
106 *Safe Work Australia Act 2008* (Cth), s 3. To access the *Model Work Health and Safety Act 2010* see *Safe Work Australia* at http://www.safeworkaustralia.gov.au/swa/Model+Legislation/Model+Work+Health+and+Safety+Act.
107 Prepared by the Parliamentary Counsel's Committee and approved by the Workplace Relations Ministers' Council on 21 December 2009.
108 The Act commences on 1 January 2012. See *Model Work Health and Safety Act 2010* (Cth), s 2.
109 *Model Work Health and Safety Act 2010*, subdivisions 1 and 2, ss 4 – 8.
110 *Model Work Health and Safety Act 2010*, subdivision 2, s 8.

Persons responsible

[8.195] The principal duties under the *Model Work Health and Safety* legislation are imposed upon the *"person who is conducting a business or undertaking at the workplace"*.[111] "Employer" has been defined previously ([8.15]). The occupier is usually the proprietor or the person who has the management and control of the workplace. This would usually include the travel agent in Chapter 11 ([11.395]); the carrier in Chapter 12 ([12.535]ff); the innkeeper in Chapter 13; the licensee in Chapter 14 ([14.245]ff; and, the proprietor, owner and operator in Chapter 15 ([15.15]). The occupier will also usually be the employer. If the employer is an individual and self-employed, they may also be a worker if they carry out the work in that business or undertaking (see [8.200]).[112]

However, the *Model Work Health and Safety Act 2010* also imposes some duties on other groups, including manufacturers, suppliers or importers of plant and equipment.[113]

Persons protected

[8.200] The principal persons protected under the *Model Work Health and Safety Act 2010* are employees and this term has also been defined previously (see [8.15], [5.110]ff). However, for the purposes of the *Model Work Health and Safety Act 2010*, these persons are referred to as "workers" and include subcontractors, outworkers, volunteers and self employed persons.[114]

Does the *Model Work Health and Safety Act 2010* cover *any* person present at the workplace, such as tourists?[115] This is particularly important in tourism, travel and hospitality because the customer usually travels to the workplace where the product is produced and consumed.[116] Consider for example theme parks, restaurants and farm tourism. If it extends to protect tourists in adventure tourism the responsibility upon the employer and occupier becomes quite onerous.[117] It is also an especially important consideration for national parks.[118]

OHS duties

[8.205] The *Model Work Health and Safety Act 2010* creates a wide range of duties on employers, occupiers, employees and other persons responsible for workplaces.[119] Many of these are similar to those imposed under the duty of care at common law. However, unlike those common law duties, the *Model Work Health and Safety Act 2010* imposes public law duties and breach has quasi-criminal consequences, such as notice to improve, prohibitions, prosecutions and fines.

---

111 *Model Work Health and Safety Act 2010*, subdivision 2, s 5.
112 *Model Work Health and Safety Act 2010*, subdivision 2, ss 7(2) and 18(5).
113 For example, see *Model Work Health and Safety Act 2010*, Part 2: Health and Safety Duties, Division 3.
114 *Model Work Health and Safety Act 2010*, subdivision 2. See also s 27: the Duties of Workers.
115 *Model Work Health and Safety Act 2010*, Division 2: Primary Duty of Care, s 18(2). See also s 28, Duties of other persons at the workplace.
116 See J Wilks and T C Atherton, "Workplace health and safety: An emerging issue for the Queensland tourism and hospitality industry" (1994) 4(3) *Australian Journal of Leisure and Recreation* 37-41.
117 See T C Atherton, *Regulating adventure tour operators*. Proceedings of the World Adventure Travel & Ecotourism Conference (Hobart, November 1994); T C Atherton, "Adventure insurance: a new industry minefield", *The Travel Reporter* October 1994 at 12.
118 T C Atherton, *Licensed to thrill: regulating adventure tourism in World Heritage areas* (12 pages, paper presented at the Australian Tourism Research conference, Griffith University, 10-11 February 1994).
119 *Model Work Health and Safety Act 2010*, Division 2: Primary Duty of Care.

Breach of statutory duty

[8.210] Although the *Model Work Health and Safety Act 2010* does not create an express right of compensation in civil action by the person protected against the person responsible, such a right usually arises under the common law doctrine of breach of statutory duty. The claim is based in tort and is similar to an action in negligence except that it is easier to prove. Mere failure to comply with the relevant statute or regulatory standard is prima facie evidence of negligence. See also [5.175].

As in other circumstances where this argument arises, the legislation must be construed to determine whether or not the intention was to create a civil right of action for damages for breach of statutory duty or whether the intention was to create purely penalty provisions. In *O'Connor v SP Bray* [120] Dixon J outlined the principle as follows:

> [with a statutory] provision prescribing a specific precaution for the safety of others in a manner where the person upon whom the duty is laid is, under the general law of negligence, bound to exercise due care, the duty will give rise to a correlative private right, unless from the nature of the provision or from the scope of the legislation of which it forms part a contrary intention appears. The effect of such a provision is to define specifically what must be done in furtherance of the general duty to protect the safety of those affected by the operations carried on.

The *Model Work Health and Safety Act 2010* makes the legislative intent not to interfere with a civil right of action very clear. Section 349 states:

> Nothing in this Act is to be construed as:
> ... (c) affecting the extent (if any) to which a right of action arises, or civil proceedings may be taken, with respect to breaches of duties or obligations imposed by the regulations.

Duties

[8.215] The *Model Work Health and Safety Act 2010* prescribes a list of duties which are similar to the common law duties which an employer owes to an employee and they are discussed below under similar headings. So far as is reasonably practicable, persons a business or undertaking must ensure:

- **Safe premises**

  This is the duty to provide and maintain safe and healthy workplace premises and locations. Standards are usually set for specific aspects such as access, egress, fire safety, lighting, ventilation, repair, cleanliness and amenities. Special standards are also usually set for specific types of workplaces such as construction sites, breweries, bakeries etc. [121]

- **Safe plant and equipment**

  This is the duty on employers and suppliers, repairers and importers to ensure the safety of plant and equipment. Special standards are usually set for specified high-risk plant, which includes escalators, ski lifts, cable cars and amusement devices. [122]

- **Safe system of work**

  The system of work is the usual method adopted for carrying out the work and includes the layout, tools, machines, number of employees, protective clothing, communications and supervision of the work process. The duty on employers, occupiers and employees is to

---

120   *O'Connor v SP Bray* (1936-1937) 56 CLR 464 at 478.
121   *Model Work Health and Safety Act 2010*, s 18(3)(a).
122   *Model Work Health and Safety Act 2010*, s 18(3)(b).

ensure the health and safety of employees and others at the workplace. Again, there are special standards for specified work processes. [123]

- **Materials and substances**

   Advances in knowledge and technology have led to increased regulation of the use of dangerous materials and substances. Obligations include precautionary measures for handling, atmospheric testing, protective clothing and equipment and first aid facilities. [124]

- **Particular health problems, industries**

   Regulations, standards and codes are introduced from time to time to deal with particular health problems such as HIV/AIDS and passive smoking. Particular industries may also warrant special regulations such as in the case of mining, construction, and maritime operations.

While the principal duties are imposed upon employers and occupiers, the *Model Work Health and Safety Act 2010* also makes manufacturers, suppliers or importers of plant and equipment and employees responsible for their part of the work. [125]

Workplace arrangements

Committees

[8.220] The *Model Work Health and Safety Act 2010* provides for the use of committees at the workplace as a self-regulatory mechanism for investigation, discussion and making recommendations about OHS matters. [126] These committees usually comprise representatives of both the employer and the employees. Committees promote flexibility, responsiveness, awareness of OHS, participation in policy and planning, communication between management and shop floor and a preventative rather than a reactive approach to OHS. There is also provision for the inclusion of a health and safety representative on the committee if there is one at the workplace. [127]

Accident prevention programs

[8.225] Accidents and near accidents provide valuable lessons and warnings and the *Model Work Health and Safety Act 2010* requires records of these events to be kept and reports of more serious accidents to be made to the jurisdictional OHS regulator. [128]

Inspections and enforcement

[8.230] The provisions of the *Model Work Health and Safety Act 2010* are to be enforced by inspectors appointed by the jurisdictional OHS regulator. [129] Inspectors have wide powers to enter workplaces, obtain information, take possession of plant and equipment and direct that a workplace not be disturbed. They may take the following steps in enforcement:

- give employers advice either on specific work practices or applicable codes of conduct;

---

123   *Model Work Health and Safety Act 2010*, s 18(3)(c).
124   *Model Work Health and Safety Act 2010*, s 18(3)(d).
125   See, for example, *Model Work Health and Safety Act 2010*, s 22.
126   *Model Work Health and Safety Act 2010*, Division 4: Health and Safety Committees, s 74.
127   *Model Work Health and Safety Act 2010*, s 75.
128   *Model Work Health and Safety Act 2010*, Part 3: Incident Notification.
129   *Model Work Health and Safety Act 2010*, Parts 8 and 9.

- issue an improvement notice;[130] or
- issue a prohibition notice;[131]

Failure to comply with the directions of an inspector attracts substantial fines.[132]

Codes and standards

[8.235] As discussed above, codes and standards form an important part of the regulatory system for OHS and the *Model Work Health and Safety Act 2010* provides for their development and adoption.[133] Compliance with standards is usually compulsory. Codes of practice are usually merely advisory, but although not legally enforceable they can be used in court as evidence that legal requirements have or have not been met.[134] Thus it is very important for both employers and employees to be continually informed and educated on the developing codes and standards applicable to their industry.

Exercise

Your fired!

The Pink Lilly is a restaurant in your town famous for its fabulous desserts. *Flambé Bombe Alaska* is its most popular sweet with its meringue covered ice cream doused all over in brandy liqueur and served with the lights turned down low while the chef flames it up. The restaurant owner, Harry Hustler, has given his 10 employees strict instructions on fire safety in the preparation and presentation of this and other flaming desserts and drinks in conformity with the OHS regulations relevant to restaurants and cafes. These regulations recommend that alcohol should never be added to a pan or burner and that the cook should always use long fireplace matches in contact with flammable substances.

Freddy Fumble has been a part time chef at the *Pink Lilly* for nearly two years. Last Saturday night, Freddy was ridiculously busy preparing one *Flambé Bombe Alaska* after another. Finally he used up the last of the matches in the kitchen and all of the usual brandy liqueur. Undeterred, Freddy improvised. Being a smoker, he had a cigarette lighter in his jacket pocket and he also managed to find some rum which he knew was also a highly flammable spirit.

He received a request to flame up the dessert at the table of a special birthday guest, Ruby, whose hair colour matched her name. He put the *Bombe Alaska* in the middle of the table, drenched it in the rum and using his lighter, set fire to the alcohol. With an almighty roar, the dessert exploded in flames and the blast hit Freddy on the face and arms. The blast also set fire to Ruby's hair as she leaned forward in anticipation of the spectacle.

Freddy and Ruby were taken to hospital for treatment. The doctors have indicated that Freddy will need several months of rehabilitation following some reconstructive surgery to his face and skin grafts on his arms. Ruby has lost most of her hair and will need to wear a wig for the time being.

---

130 *Model Work Health and Safety Act 2010*, s 190.
131 *Model Work Health and Safety Act 2010*, s 194.
132 For example, for failure to comply with a prohibition notice the penalty is $100,000 in the case of an individual or $500,000 in the case of a body corporate. See *Model Work Health and Safety Act 2010*, s 196.
133 *Model Work Health and Safety Act 2010*, s 256: Codes of Practice.
134 *Model Work Health and Safety Act 2010*, s 257.

Your fired! cont.

Harry is furious over the incident and the bad publicity it has generated for his restaurant. He has issued Freddy with a dismissal notice effective immediately citing his violation of the fire safety regulations as his reason for sacking him. He has also told Freddy that he was on a frolic of his own and should never have set fire to the *Flambé Bombe Alaska* at Ruby's table. Freddy believes he has been treated unfairly and harshly in the circumstances and that not only should he be reinstated immediately but that he is entitled to receive his weekly wage while he is away from work. In the past, on special occasions Freddy has flamed up desserts at patrons' tables as part of his duties as a chef. With respect to her injuries, Ruby is considering bringing an action against Freddy for common law negligence. She is also considering an action based on breach of statutory duty because although she was not an employee of the *Pink Lilly*, she was a person present at the workplace (the restaurant dining room) pursuant to OHS legislation.

Advise each of the parties of the merits of their claims and/or defences and where they should commence their cause(s) of action, if any.

CHAPTER 9

Consumer Protection

[9.10] ORIGIN OF CONSUMER PROTECTION		184
[9.10]	Common Law: Buyer Beware	184
[9.15]	Consumer Protection Legislation: Seller Beware	185
[9.20]	Overview of Legislation to 2010	186
[9.25]	Jurisdiction	187
[9.30]	2010 Reforms: The Australian Consumer Law	188
[9.35]	Administration	189
[9.40]	Codes of Conduct	190
[9.45]	Definitions	191
[9.50] GENERAL CONDUCT		192
[9.55]	Misleading or Deceptive Conduct	193
[9.60]	Remedies and enforcement	194
[9.65]	*Parkview (Keppel) Pty Ltd v Mytarc Pty Ltd*	194
[9.70]	Unconscionable Conduct	195
[9.75]	Remedies and enforcement	197
[9.80]	Unfair Contract Terms	198
[9.85]	Remedies and enforcement	199
[9.90] SPECIFIC UNFAIR PRACTICES		200
[9.95]	Remedies and enforcement	200
[9.100]	False or misleading representations (s 29)	200
[9.105]	*Doolan v Air New Zealand*	201
[9.110]	Misleading conduct re goods (s 33)	202
[9.115]	Misleading conduct re services (s 34)	202
[9.120]	*Doherty v Traveland Pty Ltd; Doherty v Associated Travel*	202
[9.125]	Accepting payment without supply (s 36)	203
[9.130]	*Dawson v World Travel Headquarters*	203
[9.135]	*Barton v Westpac Banking Corp*	204
[9.140]	Other specific types of misleading and deceptive conduct	204
[9.165]	Overbooking	205
[9.170] OTHER CONSUMER PROTECTION MEASURES		206
[9.175] CONSUMER GUARANTEES		206
[9.180]	Consumer Guarantees in the Supply of Goods	207
[9.185]	Consumer Guarantees in the Supply of Services	209
[9.190]	Miscellaneous requirements	211
[9.195]	Remedies and enforcement	211
[9.200]	Exclusion and limitation	211
[9.205]	Product liability	213
[9.210]	Safety of Consumer Goods and Product Related Services	213
[9.215]	Information Standards	214
[9.220]	Liability of Manufacturers and Importers for Defective Goods	214
[9.225]	International Contracts	214
[9.230]	International sale of goods: Vienna Convention	214
[9.235]	Conflict of laws	215
[9.240] COMPETITION		215

[9.245]	Cartel Conduct (Division 1)	215
[9.250]	Anti-Competitive Contracts and Arrangements (s 45)	216
[9.255]	Misuse of Market Power (s 46)	216
[9.260]	Exclusive Dealing (s 47)	217
[9.265]	Warning to travel industry on advertising, third line forcing	217
[9.270]	Other Types of Anti-Competitive Conduct	218
[9.275]	Price fixing (s 48)	218
[9.280]	Mergers and acquisitions (s 50)	219
[9.285]	Authorisations and Exemptions	219
[9.290] ENFORCEMENT AND REMEDIES		219
[9.295]	Baxter v British Airways Plc & Qantas Airways Ltd	220
[9.300] PACKAGE HOLIDAYS		221
[9.305]	Definition	221
[9.310]	Damages for Disappointment	221
[9.315]	Who is Responsible?	222
[9.320]	Agency	223
[9.325]	Common law	224
[9.340]	First category cases	224
[9.345]	Second category cases	225
[9.350]	Wong Mee Wan v Kwan Kin Travel Services Ltd	225
[9.355]	EC Directive on Package Holidays	227
[9.365]	Unpackaging holidays	229

[9.05] This chapter examines the consumer protection and competition laws as they affect the tourism, travel and hospitality industry. It also considers the recent developments in the law on package holidays and the EC Directive.

ORIGIN OF CONSUMER PROTECTION

Common Law: Buyer Beware

[9.10] The guiding principle of common law is the maxim *caveat emptor*: let the buyer beware. It reflects medieval practices where goods were simple and usually produced locally and placed on display in markets and fairs. It was up to the buyer to look, see, touch, feel and often sample them before purchase. The seller took no responsibility for quality and suitability. With the Industrial Revolution, goods became more diverse and complex and retailers and intermediaries entered the markets. Nevertheless the maxim prevailed, fortified by the laissez-faire doctrine of freedom of contract which allowed manufacturers and sellers to avoid responsibility for their products by agreement![1]

The 20th century witnessed tremendous development of products and trade, the emergence of services products and the entry of mass marketing and advertising. Advertisers now "push" products to consumers. Manufacturers rarely deal directly with consumers and the products pass through layers of wholesalers, retailers, agents and other intermediaries.

---

1   Even the warranties and conditions implied by the *Sales of Goods Acts* in the 1890s could be excluded expressly or impliedly by the contract.

Despite some milestones such as *Carlill v Carbolic Smokeball Co*[2] ([4.55]), *Donoghue v Stevenson*[3] ([5.35]), *Jarvis v Swan Tours*[4] ([2.230]), and *Nader v Allegheney Airlines Inc*[5] ([9.165]), the common law could not keep up with these developments.

In tourism, travel and hospitality, consumers are particularly vulnerable under the old common law rules. The product is usually intangible (consider, for example, a package holiday) and often distributed through intermediaries. There is usually no opportunity to look, see, touch, feel or sample the product before purchase or consumption. The industry and its customers must rely heavily on representations and information about the product in brochures, videos, Computerised Reservation Systems (CRS), and now the internet. The product is usually delivered, used and consumed all at the same time. These features mean that traditional common law remedies are usually ineffectual for the following reasons:[6]

- privity of contract means that travel agents and tour operators, while acting as mere agents, have no responsibility on the contract between the travel supplier and the client ([4.395]).

- rescission (returning the product for a refund), the only common law remedy for misrepresentation, is usually impossible because the product is consumed as the defect is discovered: you cannot return time occupying a hotel, plane or cruise ship; nor can you return food or beverage after it has been consumed ([4.405]).

- liability for damages in contract and tort can be avoided by carefully wording the terms of standard contract documentation ([4.195]ff).[7]

The result is that consumers are often left without a remedy for defective tourism and travel goods and services at common law.

Consumer Protection Legislation: Seller Beware

[9.15] In the 1960s and 1970s the consumer rights movement forced a radical change towards the other extreme of *caveat venditor*: let the seller beware. One of the key activists was the consumer lawyer Ralph Nader in the USA (see Overbooking, *Nader v Allegheney Airlines* at [9.165]. The movement highlighted the inadequacies of the old laws and successfully lobbied for the introduction of consumer protection legislation to shift the responsibility from the buyers of products to the sellers and manufacturers. This approach now has international endorsement through the United Nations Guidelines for Consumer Protection[8] and has been adopted throughout much of the developed western world.

The philosophy behind consumer protection legislation was described in the Australian Attorney-General's second reading speech on the Trade Practices Bill:[9]

> In consumer transactions unfair practices are widespread. The existing law is still founded on the principle of *caveat emptor*: meaning "let the buyer beware". That principle may have been appropriate for transactions conducted in village markets. It has ceased to be appropriate as a general

---

2   *Carlill v Carbolic Smokeball Co* [1892] 2 QB 484.
3   *Donoghue v Stevenson* [1932] AC 562.
4   *Jarvis v Swan Tours* [1973] 2 QB 233.
5   *Nader v Allegheney Airlines Inc* (1976) 426 US 290.
6   See T C Atherton, "Package holidays: legal aspects" (1994) *Tourism Management* 15(3) at 193-199.
7   The warranties and conditions implied by the *Sales of Goods Acts* in the 1890s did not apply to services and in any event could be excluded.
8   See United Nations General Assembly Resolution 39/248: *Guidelines for Consumer Protection*.
9   Senator the Hon L K Murphy QC, Senate Parliamentary Debates, 30 July 1974, *Hansard*, Vol 60, pp 540-541.

rule. Now the marketing of goods and services is conducted on an organised basis and by trained business executives. The untrained consumer is no match for the businessman who attempts to persuade the consumer to buy goods or services on terms and conditions suitable to the vendor. The consumer needs protection by the law and this Bill will provide such protection.

The *Trade Practices Act 1974* (Cth) also introduced comprehensive provisions on competition law, as common law rules on restraint of trade had similarly not kept up with the complexity and sophistication of modern trade and business. Competition laws and consumer protection laws are complementary: [10]

> If we are thinking about price, quality and service (three fundamentals for consumers) then competition may often be the best way to secure them. If we are thinking more broadly about general standards of living, then the forces that can maintain or improve industry efficiency are vital. Competition is one such force. Consumers not only benefit from competition, they activate it, and one of the purposes of consumer protection law is to ensure they are in a position to do so.

Overview of Legislation to 2010

[9.20] Consumer protection and competition law has been a complex mix of State and federal law. The dominant statute was the *Trade Practices Act 1974* (Cth), but because of constitutional limitations on federal jurisdiction [9.25], State legislation was also important. The subject matter and the relevant legislation up to 2010 can be divided into three parts as follows:

Subject	Federal legislation	State legislation
Supply of products	*Trade Practices Act 1974* Part V Division 2	Sale of Goods legislation [11]
Fair trading	*Trade Practices Act 1974* Part IVA; Part V Division 1	Fair Trading legislation [12]
Competition law	*Trade Practices Act 1974* Part IV and Competition Code	Competition Policy Reform Legislation [13]

The Sale of Goods legislation has its origins in the customary practices developed by merchants over many centuries. This "law merchant" was gradually incorporated into the common law and this in turn was codified by the *Sale of Goods Act 1893* (UK). This legislation was adopted by all Australian States and indeed throughout most of the common law world. Under this law various warranties and conditions are implied into every contract for the sale of goods. At the time it was hailed as consumer law although it contained a fundamental weakness: the conditions and warranties could be excluded expressly or

---

10   TPC Annual Report 1983-1984, at para A 5.6.
11   The Sale of Goods legislation comprises: ACT: *Sale of Goods Act 1954*; NSW: *Sale of Goods Act 1923*; NT: *Sale of Goods Act*; Qld: *Sale of Goods Act 1896*; SA: *Sale of Goods Act 1895*; Tas: *Sale of Goods Act 1896*; Vic: *Goods Act 1958*; WA: *Sale of Goods Act 1895*.
12   The Fair Trading legislation comprises: ACT: *Fair Trading Act 1992*; NSW: *Fair Trading Act 1987*; NT: *Consumer Affairs and Fair Trading Act*; Qld: *Fair Trading Act 1989*; SA: *Fair Trading Act 1987*; Tas: *Fair Trading Act 1990*; Vic: *Fair Trading Act 1985*; WA: *Fair Trading Act 1987*.
13   The Competition Policy Reform legislation comprises: ACT: *Competition Policy Reform (ACT) Act 1996*; NSW: *Competition Policy Reform (NSW) Act 1995*; NT: *Competition Policy Reform (NT) Act*; Qld: *Competition Policy Reform (Qld) Act 1996*; SA: *Competition Policy Reform (SA) Act 1996*; Vic: *Competition Policy Reform (Victoria) Act 1995*; WA: *Competition Policy Reform (WA) Act 1996*.

impliedly by the terms of the contract.[14] Sellers soon discovered the loophole and this resulted in the widespread use of standard form contracts with wide exclusion and limitation clauses (see [4.225]). Nevertheless, where exclusion or limitation was impractical, the Sale of Goods legislation formed an important part of the regulatory system. In tourism, travel and hospitality it has been particularly important in the sale of food and beverage.

The *Trade Practices Act 1974* built on the principles of the Sales of Goods legislation and broadened the coverage to include supply as well as sale, and services as well as goods. It also overcame the main weakness by generally prohibiting exclusion of the implied conditions and warranties. The inclusion of services and the prohibition on exclusion in consumer transactions was particularly important for tourism, travel and hospitality because it caught the vast bulk of transactions in this industry.[15]

The Fair Trading legislation has regulated trading practices in many ways so as to protect consumers' interests. Unlike the Sale of Goods legislation it was not confined to the parties to a contract of sale but covered all those who were involved in the conduct of trade and commerce with consumers. Thus it also covered servants, agents, independent contractors and other intermediaries who made representations, advertised, promoted or otherwise provided information to consumers. This has provided the main regulatory system for the marketing and promotion of tourism, travel and hospitality. As it cast personal responsibility on agents and intermediaries it has been particularly important for travel agents and tour operators.[16]

Finally, the Competition legislation promoted consumer interests indirectly by ensuring that suppliers of goods and services operated competitively and efficiently. The *Trade Practices Act 1974* provisions were much wider than the narrow restrictions on restraint of trade at common law and sought to achieve the wider economic objectives of a competitive market. Originally confined by the limits of federal jurisdiction and sovereign immunity, legislation implementing the national competition policy now extended the provisions to most commercial and professional activities including State authorities and instrumentalities. There have been many competition law cases involving the tourism, travel and hospitality industry.

Jurisdiction

[9.25] Although many of the provisions of the *Trade Practices Act 1974* now have corresponding State legislation, there were numerous differences and it has been important to determine whether the federal or State legislation applied. The application of federal government legislation like the *Trade Practices Act 1974* is limited to those matters over which it has constitutional power. Thus the Act covers conduct by corporations [17] with extensions to cover individuals or unincorporated firms [18] where they:

- engage in interstate or international trade and commerce; [19]

- use the mail or telephone or advertise on radio or television in connection with the transaction; [20]

---

14 See for example s 56 of the *Sale of Goods Act 1896* (Qld).
15 See T C Atherton, "Changes to *Trade Practices Act* increase liability" (1992) 1(3) *Tourism and Travel Review* 7.
16 See T C Atherton, "Package holidays: tourists' trial buy or deal becomes operators' trial by ordeal" (1993) 1(3) *Current Commercial Law* 100-109.
17 Constitution, s 51(xx): Foreign corporations, and trading and financial corporations formed within the limits of the Commonwealth.
18 Section 6.
19 Constitution, s 51(i): Trade and commerce with other countries and among the States.
20 Section 6(3).

- trade with the Commonwealth or one of its instrumentalities;
- are professional persons (which would include travel agents) engaged in deceptive or misleading conduct "in the course of promotional activities". [21]

Otherwise the *Trade Practices Act 1974* generally does not apply to individuals or unincorporated firms dealing within a State. Those dealings are usually covered by the corresponding State legislation.

2010 Reforms: The Australian Consumer Law

[9.30] Fortunately, the legislative maze described in [9.20] has now been replaced by a single national consumer law. The objectives of this major reform were described in the Minister's second reading speech on the *Trade Practices Amendment (Australian Consumer Law) Bill (No 2) 2010* as follows: [22]

> The complex array of 17 national, state and territory generic consumer laws, along with other provisions scattered throughout many other laws, must be rationalised. While these laws may work well for many purposes, each of them differs and that is to the cost of consumers and business.
>
> Australian consumers deserve laws which make their rights clear and consistent, and which protect them equally wherever they live. At the same time, Australian businesses deserve simple, national consumer laws that make compliance easier.
>
> A single national consumer law is the best means of achieving these results. Rather than relying on nine parliaments making piecemeal changes, the Australian Consumer Law will ensure responsive consumer laws with a truly national reach. [23]

The legislative arrangements to enact and implement the *Australian Consumer Law* were agreed among the States, Territories and the Commonwealth at the Council of Australian Governments on 2 October 2008 and procedures for administration and amendments through time to maintain a single national law are set out in the *Inter-Governmental Agreement for the Australian Consumer Law* dated 2 July 2009.

The text of the *Australian Consumer Law* has been agreed based on the *Trade Practices Act 1974* but drawing on best practice from the States and Territories.

The ACL will:

- replace a wide range of existing national and State and Territory consumer laws and will clarify understanding of the law for both Australian consumers and businesses;
- be a schedule to the *Competition and Consumer Act 2010*, which will be the new name of the *Trade Practices Act 1974* (*Trade Practices Act*);
- be applied as a law of the Commonwealth. Each State and Territory will also make the ACL a law of its respective jurisdiction. This means that the same provisions will apply across Australia;
- be enforced by all Australian courts and tribunals, including the courts and tribunals of the States and Territories; and
- be administered by the Australian Competition and Consumer Commission and each State and Territory's consumer law agency. [24]

---

21 Section 6(4).
22 The Hon Dr Craig Emerson, House of Representative Debates, 17 March 2010, *Hansard*, p 2718.
23 The authors have long advocated a similar approach to many of the other laws and regulations on tourism, travel and hospitality.
24 Attorney-General's Department, Commonwealth of Australia, *The Australian Consumer Law A Guide to Provisions*, (Barton, ACT April 2010), p ix.

The timetable and progress on enactment and implementation are as follows:[25]
- *Trade Practices Amendment (Australian Consumer Law) Act (No 1) 2010* ("No 1"): enacted and commenced 15 April 2010. It:
  (a) Establishes the ACL and the administration and amendment arrangements
  (b) Introduces new unfair contract terms regime
  (c) Provides new penalties and enforcement powers (expected to be effective after 1 July 2010).
- *Trade Practices Amendment (Australian Consumer Law) Act (No 2) 2010* ("No 2"): enacted and progressively introduced from 1 July, 2010. It:
  (d) Implements the remainder of the *Australian Consumer Law* provisions drawn from the *Trade Practices Act 1974*;
  (e) Implements reforms drawing on best practice state and territory laws;
  (f) Introduces a new national product safety system; and
  (g) Introduces new consumer guarantee provisions replacing existing laws on conditions and warranties and state legislation
  (h) Changes the name of the *Trade Practices Act 1974* to the *Competition and Consumer Act 2010* (Cth).
- State and Territory legislation to be enacted to cover matters within their jurisdictions and this was expected by the end of 2010 so the *Australian Consumer Law* could be fully implemented by 1 January 2011.
- The *Competition and Consumer Legislation Amendment Bill 2010*, when passed by Parliament, will amend the law on the competition treatment of creeping acquisitions, in the context of mergers, and clarify customer and business rights in respect of unconscionable conduct

As these reforms are so far reaching and the implementation process is agreed and well advanced this Chapter discusses the *Australian Consumer Law* with cross references to the *Trade Practices Act 1974* but without further reference to the current State and Territory legislation discussed in [9.20] because it has been replaced by the *Australian Consumer Law*. However the established jurisprudence on the corresponding provisions of the *Trade Practices Act 1974* and State and Territory legislation ("FTAs") remains relevant to interpretation of the ACL.

The references to the *Australian Consumer Law* in following parts of this Chapter are based on the Acts No 1 and No 2 at the stage of implementation outlined above. It is likely there will be amendments to the *Australian Consumer Law* subsequent to enactment and the reader is cautioned to always check the current position.

Administration

[9.35] The *Trade Practices Act 1974* is administered by the Australian Competition and Consumer Commission (ACCC)[26] which comprises a Chairman, deputy Chairman and other members. The ACCC's main responsibilities are to:
- institute prosecutions for offences under the consumer protection provisions, subject to ministerial consent;

---

25 See http://www.treasury.gov.au/consumerlaw/content/legislation.asp (accessed 25 April 2010).
26 Australian Competition and Consumer Commission (ACCC) at http://www.accc.gov.au.

- provide public information and guidance on consumer protection issues;
- bring proceedings for contravention of the competition law provisions;
- issue or revoke authorisations for conduct which might otherwise contravene the competition law provisions.

One very useful publication for the tourism, travel and hospitality industry, which was issued by the ACCC in 1976 under its former name, is *Trade Practices Commission Information Circular No 18: Consumer Protection Travel Advertising Guidelines*. They provide a practical review of the application of the consumer protection laws discussed in the following parts of this chapter to particular types of conduct in travel advertising and promotion.

ACCC decisions to issue or revoke authorisations may be appealed to an administrative body known as the Australian Competition Tribunal. However prosecutions for consumer protection offences and proceedings to enforce the competition laws are brought by actions in the Federal Court.

Each State's Fair Trading legislation establishes a Consumer Affairs Agency to administer its Act. Most States have also established Consumer Claims Tribunals to resolve small claims particularly between consumers and traders. See Consumer Claims Courts [10.125]ff.

Codes of Conduct

[9.40] The development of consumer protection laws has been matched by a more consumer-oriented approach from suppliers. This is exemplified by the switch in management paradigms from a production-oriented approach (that is, trying to sell what we can produce) to the modern market-oriented approach (that is, trying to produce what we can sell).

The most interesting outcome from this from a legal point of view has been the growth in self-regulatory practices using codes of conduct or ethics for particular industries or practices within industries. Trade associations and other organisations have a key role in formulating, co-ordinating and administering these codes.

Industry much prefers self-regulation to formal laws. Self-regulatory codes of conduct are seen to have these advantages:
- flexibility;
- speed of introduction;
- speed of modification to changes in circumstances;
- reflects practical realities;
- industry "ownership" of the solution may reduce enforcement problems;
- avoids bureaucracy.

Self-regulation may offend s 45 of the *Competition and Consumer Act 2010* (Cth) as it may have the effect of lessening competition and variation in practices among competitors on the matters covered. However it is also recognised that they have offsetting public benefits and the ACCC has indicated in *Re Quilted Products Manufacturers' Association of Australia*[27] that acceptable self-regulatory schemes will have the following features:
- coverage of a substantial proportion of the members of the industry (where coverage is not substantial, standards are not to be sacrificed to increase coverage);
- commercially significant incentives to comply with the code of practice;

---

[27] *Re Quilted Products Manufacturers' Association of Australia* (1988) ATPR (Com) 50-070.

- industry-based forums for complaint resolution; and
- public participation.

The ACCC has now issued formal guidelines for implementing codes of conduct.[28] There are many successful examples in the tourism, travel and hospitality industries, including the codes implemented by the Australian Federation of Australia (AFTA) Code of Ethics ([11.380]), International Air Transport Association (IATA) Passenger Liability Agreements ([12.710]ff), and the Ecotourism Association of Australia Accreditation scheme (Chapter 15). A general code of conduct for the tourism industry has now been introduced by the Tourism Council of Australia. There is also specific provision for such codes under the Fair Trading legislation.[29]

This approach has considerable scope for further use in conjunction with a proactive approach by industry organisations to the challenges and opportunities of regulation. Ignorance of the law is no excuse. If anything the penalties imposed under the consumer protection legislation are increased if the operator has not taken care to be and remain familiar with regulatory requirements and to properly train and instruct staff on their responsibilities.[30]

The ACCC, under the *Competition and Consumer Act 2010* (Cth) may prescribe a code of practice (or a part or provision) as an industry code of practice and categorised as either voluntary or mandatory. Such codes have been prescribed for franchising and certain other sectors but so far none in tourism, travel and hospitality. Corporations must comply with mandatory codes of practice. The ACCC also encourages industries to develop non-prescribed voluntary codes of conduct to promote compliance with the *Competition and Consumer Act 2010*. Codes of conduct are also relevant in determining whether conduct is unconscionable under *Australian Consumer Law*, s 22.

Definitions

[9.45] The *Australian Consumer Law* defines a number of key terms largely based on the *Trade Practices Act 1974* (Cth) and so the jurisprudence on these aspects of the *Trade Practices Act 1974* and Fair Trading Acts remains relevant for interpretation of the *Australian Consumer Law*. Key terms defined in s 3 of the *Australian Consumer Law* include:

- **Consumer:** A person is a "consumer" if he or she acquires goods that are "of a kind ordinarily acquired for personal, domestic or household use or consumption".[31]

  This is relevant for consumer guarantees and certain other provisions but most consumer protection provisions apply to all individuals and businesses where the conduct is in trade and commerce.

- **Services:** Like the *Trade Practices Act 1974* and FTAs, the *Australian Consumer Law* covers services as well as goods and this overcomes one of the major weaknesses in the Sale of Goods legislation. Services, which were insignificant when the Sales of Goods legislation was conceived, now account for more than half of world trade. Most of the products supplied to consumers in travel and tourism are services. They are defined by s 3 as follows:

  "services" includes [32]

---

28 See ACCC, *Guidelines for Implementing Codes, Checklist for Fair Trading Codes of Conduct* (1995) and related publications.
29 See for example Part 7 of the *Fair Trading Act 1987* (NSW).
30 See for example *Ducret v Nissan Motor Co (Australia) Pty Ltd* (1979) 38 FLR 126 at 133 per Northrop J.
31 The maximum monetary threshold of $40,000 under the *Trade Practices Act 1974* (Cth) has been deleted.
32 Similar to *Trade Practices Act 1974* (Cth), s 4.

[9.45] **191**

(a) any rights (including rights in relation to, and interests in, real or personal property), benefits, privileges or facilities that are, or are to be, provided, granted or conferred in trade or commerce, and

(b) without limiting paragraph (a), the rights, benefits, privileges or facilities that are, or are to be, provided, granted or conferred under

    (i) a contract for or in relation to the performance of work (including work of a professional nature), whether with or without the supply of goods; or

    (ii) *a contract for or in relation to the provision of, or the use or enjoyment of facilities for, amusement, entertainment, recreation or instruction; or* [emphasis added]

    (iii) a contract for or in relation to the conferring of rights, benefits or privileges for which remuneration is payable in the form of a royalty, tribute, levy or similar exaction; or

    (iv) a contract of insurance; or

    (v) a contract between a banker and a customer of the banker entered into in the course of the carrying on by the banker of the business of banking; or

(d) any contract for or in relation to the lending of moneys;
but does not include rights or benefits being the supply of goods or the performance of work under a contract of service.

Subparagraph (b)(ii) is particularly important for the tourism, travel and hospitality industry and would appear to cover most of its products, including travel agency, passenger transport, accommodation, activities and attractions [33] and the service component of food and beverage.

- **Trade and commerce** includes any business or professional activity whether or not carried out for profit.

Other key defined terms are discussed in the context of the parts to which they are most relevant.

GENERAL CONDUCT

[9.50] The *Australian Consumer Law* prohibits the following general types of conduct which are discussed in more detail in the following parts: [34]

- Misleading and Deceptive Conduct;
- Unconscionable Conduct; and
- Unfair Contract Terms.

The first two are based on similar provisions in the *Trade Practices Act 1974* and the State Fair Trading Acts which, as stated in the overview, have protected consumers' interests by regulating trading practices in various ways. Unlike the Sale of Goods legislation this did not depend on contract and it is not confined to the parties to a contract of sale. It has covered all those who are involved in the conduct of trade and commerce with consumers, including servants, agents, independent contractors and other intermediaries who make representations, advertise, promote or otherwise provide information to consumers. This has provided the

---

33 In *Michael Edgley International Pty Ltd v Ashton's Nominees Pty Ltd* (1979) 38 FLR 135 the court assumed that presentation of a circus was a "service".

34 *Australian Consumer Law*, Chapter 2, ss 18 – 28.

main regulatory system for the marketing and promotion of tourism, travel and hospitality. As it casts personal responsibility on agents and intermediaries it is particularly important for travel agents and tour operators.[35]

The third general type of conduct prohibited is drawn from the Victorian *Fair Trading Act 1985* and is confined to parties to a contract but because it focuses on standard contracts it is particularly important for the tourism, travel and hospitality industry.

Misleading or Deceptive Conduct

[9.55] The most important consumer protection provision in the *Australian Consumer Law* is, fortunately, also the briefest and simplest.

> **18. Misleading or deceptive conduct**
>
> (1) A person must not, in trade or commerce, engage in conduct that is misleading or deceptive or is likely to mislead or deceive.

This is identical to s 52 of the *Trade Practices Act 1974* except that "person" has now replaced "corporation". It establishes a "broad economy-wide norm of conduct"[36] and has been the cornerstone of consumer protection under the *Trade Practices Act 1974* and the Fair Trading Acts. A number of points need to be made about this provision:

- The intent of the defendant is not relevant. All that is relevant is the effect of the conduct. Thus s 18 imposes a strict civil liability.

- Evidence that someone has been misled is persuasive.[37] However no particular person need be misled. Where someone has been misled they are likely to bring an action for damages not only under this section but also under one of the following sections which spell out specific types of misleading or deceptive conduct.

- If it is alleged that the public is misled then the relevant section of the public must be identified, that is a class of consumers including the astute and the gullible, the intelligent and the not-so-intelligent, the well educated and the poorly educated.[38] See *Parkview (Keppell) Pty Ltd v Mytarc Pty Ltd* ([9.65]) and *Baxter v British Airways PLC & Qantas Airways Ltd*[39] ([9.295], casenote).

- With predictions or projections the defendant bears the onus of proving that it had reasonable grounds for making them.[40] This is important for travel agents to consider in answering client questions such as "Will it rain?", "Will it snow?", "Will it shine?" and the like.

---

35 See T C Atherton, "Package holidays: tourists' trial buy or deal becomes operators' trial by ordeal" (1993) 1(3) *Current Commercial Law* 100-109.

36 Attorney- General's Department, Commonwealth of Australia, *The Australian Consumer Law – A Guide to Provisions* (Barton, ACT, April 2010), p 4.

37 But see *Steiner v Magic Carpet Tours Pty Ltd* (1984) ATPR 40-490 where the Federal Court found that there was no misleading and deceptive conduct on the part of the tour operator or travel agent. The booking arrangements had actually been made for the Steiners but the Bali Bungalows had properly rejected the Steiners as guests because of Mr Steiner's intoxicated and obnoxious behaviour.

38 *Taco Co of Australia v Taco Bell Pty Ltd* (1982) 42 ALR 177.

39 *Parkview (Keppell) Pty Ltd v Mytarc Pty Ltd* ([9.145]) and *Baxter v British Airways PLC & Qantas Airways Ltd* (1988) ATPR 40-877.

40 *Australian Consumer Law*, s 4 (*Trade Practices Act 1974* (Cth), s 51A).

- Opinions by professionals or experts may convey that they are honestly held on rational grounds.[41] This is potentially very important for travel agents who daily recommend destinations, carriers, hotels and attractions.
- Originally designed for consumers, this provision has also been used extensively in a wide range of commercial situations, such as passing off and defamation actions. For example, in *McDonald's Systems Australia Pty Ltd v McWilliams Wines Pty Ltd*,[42] McDonalds tried to use it to prevent McWilliams Wines from using "Big Mac" to market their wines in large bottles, but the court found that wine was so different from food that this was confusing rather than misleading.[43]

Remedies and enforcement

[9.60] Upon a breach of s 18 any person suffering loss or damage may seek damages and the ACCC (or the relevant State and Territory consumer affairs agency) and any person may seek an injunction. Thus in *Cameron v Qantas*[44] a number of passengers successfully sued Qantas under this general provision and also under the relevant specific provision (equivalent to the *Australian Consumer Law*, s 29) for deceptive and misleading conduct in representing directly or through its agents that passengers who requested them would be given non-smoking seats.

Criminal sanctions and civil penalties do not apply to s 18. However breach of s 18 may also constitute breach of one of the subsequent sections which define specific types of misleading and deceptive conduct where these sanctions and penalties will apply.

Parkview (Keppel) Pty Ltd v Mytarc Pty Ltd

[9.65] *Parkview (Keppel) Pty Ltd v Mytarc Pty Ltd* (1984) ASC 55-351

Facts: Former executives of Great Keppel Island left and took over Happy Bay on Whitsunday Island, renaming it "Whitsunday 100". They revamped and promoted it to travel agents in the following terms:

> Happy Bay was a nice little resort but it wasn't exactly jumping...Beautiful. But no fun. Enter those wonderful people who brought you Great Keppel Island...Whitsunday 100...a full 100 per cent tropical, not sub-tropical, island resort...complete with state of the art disco...
>
> Whitsunday 100, The tropical island that makes Great Keppel look like a vicarage tea party...

Great Keppel sought an injunction to restrain the conduct, which they alleged was deceptive and misleading under s 52.

Decision: The Federal Court of Australia (McGregor J) held that the conduct was not deceptive and misleading. The promotional claims were literally correct but that was not decisive because even literally correct statements can be deceptive and misleading in some circumstances. Here the

---

41 *Bateman v Slatyer* (1987) 71 ALR 553 at 559.
42 *McDonald's Systems Australia Pty Ltd v McWilliams Wines Pty Ltd* (1979) 28 ALR 236.
43 See other relevant cases on passing off: (island resort) *Pinetrees Lodge Pty Ltd v Atlas International Pty Ltd* (1981) 59 FLR 244; (tacos) *Taco Co of Australia v Taco Bell Pty Ltd* (1982) 42 ALR 177; (night club) *Great Australian Bite Pty Ltd v Menmel Pty Ltd* (1996) ATPR 410-506.
44 *Cameron v Qantas* (1995) 55 FCR 147.

Parkview (Keppel) Pty Ltd v Mytarc Pty Ltd cont.

brochures had been sent only to travel agents who were a relatively educated and informed group who were not likely to have been misled.

―――― ∞)⊙⊰ ――――

Unconscionable Conduct

[9.70] Even at common law the courts have interfered with the freedom of contract and have declared unenforceable contractual provisions that are found to be grossly unfair.[45] In *Dillon v Baltic Shipping Co "Mikhail Lermontov"*[46] (see casenote at [12.90]) the New South Wales Court of Appeal upheld the trial judge's finding that the full release signed by Mrs Dillon for $4,786 when her claim against the shipping company was worth $51,396 was void for unconscionability[47] and that she was entitled to recover the full amount. The court relied on the insufficiency of the sum paid, the inequality of bargaining power and the diminished capacity of Mrs Dillon at the time. The High Court refused leave to appeal on this ground.

Similar provisions were incorporated into the *Trade Practices Act 1974* (Cth) and Fair Trading Acts and the provisions have been adopted into the *Australian Consumer Law* as an initial basis for future development.[48] They provide as follows:

20 Unconscionable conduct within the meaning of the unwritten law

(1) A person must not, in trade or commerce, engage in conduct that is unconscionable, within the meaning of the unwritten law from time to time…[49]

This makes it a breach of the *Australian Consumer Law* for a person to engage in unconscionable conduct at common law so that the wide remedies available under the *Australian Consumer Law* apply.

21 Unconscionable conduct

(1) A person must not, in trade or commerce, in connection with the supply or possible supply of goods or services [of a kind ordinarily acquired for personal, domestic or household use or consumption] to another person [the "consumer"], engage in conduct that is, in all the circumstances, unconscionable…[50]

This provides a general duty to trade fairly in consumer transactions.

22 Unconscionable conduct in business transactions

(1) A person ["the supplier"] must not, in trade or commerce, in connection with:

(a) the supply or possible supply of goods or services to another person (other than a listed public company) ["the business consumer"]; or

---

45   The principles at common law were laid down in *Commonwealth Bank v Amadio* (1983) 151 CLR 447 where the High Court held that it was unconscionable for the bank to enforce a guarantee from the debtor's parents, who were elderly, had little command of the English language and no independent advice.
46   *Dillon v Baltic Shipping Co "Mikhail Lermontov"* [1992] 22 NSWLR 1.
47   Under the *Contracts Review Act 1980* (NSW).
48   Attorney-General's Department, Commonwealth of Australia, *The Australian Consumer Law–A Guide to Provisions* (Barton, ACT, April 2010), p 5.
49   Similar to *Trade Practices Act 1974* (Cth), s 51AA.
50   Similar to *Trade Practices Act 1974* (Cth), s 51AB.

(b) the acquisition or possible acquisition of goods or services from another person (other than a listed public company);

engage in conduct that is, in all the circumstances, unconscionable. [51]

This provides a general duty to trade fairly in business transactions.

In both ss 21 [52] and 22 [53] courts are not constrained by equitable or common law concepts in determining whether the conduct was unconscionable in the circumstances. However the *Australian Consumer Law* provides a list of factors which courts may consider for guidance in determining whether or not a contravention has occurred. For ease of reference the parties have been termed "the consumer" (ie, the consumer or acquirer or person acting on their behalf) and "the offending party" (ie, the supplier or person acting on its behalf in the case of an acquisition by a small business). The following factors are included in the list for both sections.

a) the relative strengths of the bargaining positions of the parties;

b) whether, as a result of conduct engaged in by the offending party, the consumer was required to comply with conditions that were not reasonably necessary for the protection of the legitimate interests of the offending party;

c) whether the consumer was able to understand any documents relating to the supply or possible supply of the goods or services;

d) whether any undue influence or pressure was exerted on, or any unfair tactics were used against, the consumer by the offending party in relation to the supply or possible supply of the goods or services; and

e) the amount for which, and the circumstances under which, the consumer could have acquired identical or equivalent goods or services from a person other than the offending party.

The following additional factors are included in the list for s 22 business transactions:

f) the extent to which the offending party's conduct towards the business consumer was consistent with the offending party's conduct in similar transactions; and

g) the requirements of any applicable industry code (see [9.80]); and

h) the requirements of any other industry code, if the business consumer acted on the reasonable belief that the offending party would comply with that code; and

i) the extent to which the offending party unreasonably failed to disclose to the business consumer:

   (i) any intended conduct of the supplier that might affect the interests of the business consumer; and

   (ii) any risks to the business consumer arising from the offending party intended conduct (being risks that the offending party should have foreseen would not be apparent to the business consumer); and

j) if there is a contract between the offending party and the business consumer for the supply of the goods or services:

---

51 Similar to *Trade Practices Act 1974* (Cth), s 51AC.
52 *Australian Consumer Law*, s 21(2).
53 *Australian Consumer Law*, s 22(2).

(i) the extent to which the offending party was willing to negotiate the terms and conditions of the contract with the business consumer; and

(ii) the terms and conditions of the contract; and

(iii) the conduct of the offending party and the business consumer in complying with the terms and conditions of the contract; and

(iv) any conduct that the offending party or the business consumer engaged in, in connection with their commercial relationship, after they entered into the contract; and

k) without limiting paragraph (j), whether the offending party has a contractual right to vary unilaterally a term or condition of a contract between the offending party and the business consumer for the supply of the goods or services; and

l) the extent to which the offending party and the business consumer acted in good faith.

Section 23(3) of the *Australian Consumer Law* makes similar provisions to protect small business acquirers of goods and services and for this purpose provides a similar list of factors with the roles of the parties reversed to those outlined above.

These provisions are of enormous importance for the tourism, travel and hospitality industry especially considering:

- the peculiar uncertainties and exigencies of the industry;
- the usual imbalance in bargaining strength;
- the great variations in terms and pricing of its products;
- widespread use and commercial necessity for standard contract terms and booking conditions;
- the practical impossibility of negotiation in many cases;
- the widespread use and commercial necessity for reserving unilateral rights to cancel or vary the contract terms; and'
- the remedies available to consumers and the severe penalties which may be imposed on offenders.

These matters are yet to be properly addressed by the regulators or the industry and pose significant risk management and compliance challenges for the industry.

Remedies and enforcement

[9.75] Remedies for unconscionable conduct include injunctions, damages, compensatory orders and other remedies including adverse publicity orders.

Penalties also apply including civil pecuniary penalties up to a maximum of $1.1 million for a body corporate and $220,000 for a person other than a body corporate as well as disqualification orders and public warning notices.

Unfair Contract Terms

[9.80] The *Australian Consumer Law* introduces new provisions on unfair contract terms which were not in the *Trade Practices Act 1974* (Cth).[54] They came into effect at the Commonwealth level on 1 July 2010.[55]

Section 23 of the *Australian Consumer Law* provides that unfair terms in standard form consumer contracts are void. A "consumer contract" is a contract for the supply of goods or services to an individual for wholly or predominantly personal, domestic or household use or consumption.[56] This would include most tourism, travel and hospitality consumer goods and services except business entertainment and travel. Insurance contracts and certain shipping contracts are expressly excluded.[57]

It does not apply to terms defining the main subject matter of the contract or setting the upfront price. However changes to price or charges for contingencies are covered.[58]

Section 24 of the *Australian Consumer Law* provides that a term is "unfair" if

(a) it would cause a significant imbalance in the parties' rights and obligations arising under the contract; and

(b) it is not reasonably necessary in order to protect the legitimate interests of the party who would be advantaged by the term [the presumption is that it is not unless the party advantaged by the term proves otherwise[59]];

(c) it would cause detriment (whether financial or otherwise) to a party if it were to be applied or relied on.

In determining whether a term is unfair courts must consider the transparency of the term and the contract as a whole. To be transparent a term must be expressed in reasonably plain language, legible, presented clearly and readily available to the party affected by the term. This goes well beyond what is required to validly incorporate a term into a contract under the ticket case principles discussed in [4.240]ff.

Under s 27 of the *Australian Consumer Law*, if a contract is alleged to be "standard form" it is presumed to be so unless the other party proves otherwise. In making a determination a court must consider:

(a) whether one of the parties has all or most of the bargaining power…;

(b) whether the contract was prepared by one party before any discussion relating to the transaction occurred…;

(c) whether another party was, in effect, required either to accept or reject the terms of the contract … in the form in which they were presented;

(d) whether another party was given an effective opportunity to negotiate the terms of the contract that …;

(e) whether the terms of the contract … take into account the specific characteristics of another party or the particular transaction;

(f) any other matter prescribed by the regulations.

---

54 Unfair contract terms have been regulated in some States for some time: *Contracts Review Act 1980* (NSW) and the *Fair Trading Act 1999* (Vic), Part 2B.

55 Attorney-General's Department, Commonwealth of Australia, *The Australian Consumer Law— A Guide to Provisions* (Barton, ACT, April 2010), p 8.

56 Australian Consumer Law, s 23.

57 Australian Consumer Law, s 28.

58 Australian Consumer Law, s 26.

59 Australian Consumer Law, s 24(4).

By these criteria most tourism, travel and hospitality consumer contracts will be found to be "standard form".

Section 25 of the *Australian Consumer Law* provides examples of terms that may be unfair and these types of terms are often found in tourism, travel and hospitality consumer contracts:

Terms that permit, or have the effect of permitting, one party (but not another party) to

(a) ... avoid or limit performance of the contract;

(b) ... terminate the contract;...

(d) ...vary the terms of the contract;

(e) ...renew or not renew the contract;

(f) ... vary the upfront price payable under the contract without the right of another party to terminate the contract;

(g) ...vary the characteristics of the goods or services to be supplied,...or;

(h) ...determine whether the contract has been breached or to interpret its meaning;...

(j) assign the contract to the detriment of another party without that other party's consent;

A term that

(c) ...penalises, or has the effect of penalising, one party (but not another party) for a breach or termination of the contract;...

(i) ... limits, or has the effect of limiting, one party's vicarious liability for its agents;

(k) ... limits, or has the effect of limiting, one party's right to sue another party;

(l) ... limits, or has the effect of limiting, the evidence one party can adduce in proceedings relating to the contract;

(m) ... imposes, or has the effect of imposing, the evidential burden on one party in proceedings relating to the contract;

Further examples may be prescribed by regulations.

Like the provisions on unconscionable conduct, the unfair contract terms provisions are of enormous importance for the tourism, travel and hospitality industry especially considering:

- the peculiar uncertainties and exigencies of the industry;
- the usual imbalance in bargaining strength;
- widespread use and commercial necessity for standard contract terms and booking conditions;
- the practical impossibility of negotiation in many cases;
- the widespread use and commercial necessity for reserving unilateral rights to cancel or vary contract; and
- the remedies available to consumers and the penalties which may be imposed on offenders.

These matters are yet to be properly addressed by the regulators or the industry and pose significant risk management and compliance challenges for the industry.

Remedies and enforcement

[9.85] The offending term is void. However the contract continues to bind the parties if it is capable of operating without the offending term.[60]

---

60   *Australian Consumer Law*, s 23(2).

Other remedies available for unfair contract terms include injunctions, compensatory orders and redress for non-parties.

Unfair contract terms may also constitute unconscionable conduct in which case more severe remedies and enforcement mechanisms apply (see [9.70]).

SPECIFIC UNFAIR PRACTICES

[9.90] The *Australian Consumer Law* also prohibits specific types of conduct based on similar provisions in the *Trade Practices Act 1974* and best practices from the States Fair Trading Acts.[61] The specific sections collectively cover a wide range of matters so that a breach of s 18 or one of the other general provisions may also constitute a breach of one of the specific sections and vice versa.

The specific unfair practices most relevant to the tourism, travel and hospitality industry include the following which are discussed in more detail in the following parts:[62]

- False or misleading representations;
- Misleading conduct re goods;
- Misleading conduct re services;
- Accepting payment without supply; and
- Other.

Remedies and enforcement

[9.95] Remedies include injunctions, damages, compensatory orders and other remedies including adverse publicity orders.

Penalties also apply including criminal and civil pecuniary penalties up to a maximum of $1.1 million for a body corporate and $220,000 for a person other than a body corporate as well as disqualification orders and public warning notices.

False or misleading representations (s 29)

[9.100] Section 29 of the *Australian Consumer Law* is similar to s 53 of the *Trade Practices Act 1974* with new categories added which are drawn from Fair Trading Act best practices as noted below. It is the most important of the sections dealing with specific types of misleading and deceptive conduct as it sets out a detailed list of false representations in connection with the promotion and supply of goods and services. Invariably, breach of s 29 will also constitute breach of s 18 but s 29 provides severe penalties not available under s 18. It also provides a useful checklist for the type of conduct which the tourism, travel and hospitality industry must avoid.

> 29. False or misleading representations about goods or services
> A person must not, in trade or commerce, in connexion with the supply or possible supply of goods or services or in connexion with the promotion by any means of the supply or use of goods or services ... make a false or misleading representation that...: or

---

61 Attorney- General's Department, Commonwealth of Australia, *The Australian Consumer Law–A Guide to Provisions* (Barton, ACT, April 2010), p 10.
62 *Australian Consumer Law*, Chapter 3, Part 3.1, ss 29 – 50.

(a) ... that goods are of a particular standard, quality, value, grade, composition, style or model or have had a particular history or particular previous use;[63] or

(b) ... that services are of a particular standard, quality, value or grade;[64] or

(c) ... that goods are new; or

(d) ... that a particular person has agreed to acquire goods or services; or

(e) ... that purports to be a testimonial by any person relating to goods or services [new]; or

(f) ... concerning:

   (i) a testimonial by any person; or

   (ii) ... that purports to be such a testimonial;
   relating to goods or services [new]; or

(g) ...that goods or services have sponsorship, approval, performance characteristics, accessories, uses or benefits;[65] or

(h) ...that the person making the representation has a sponsorship, approval or affiliation; or

(i) .... with respect to the price of goods or services; or

(j) ... concerning the availability of facilities for the repair of goods or of spare parts for goods; or

(k) ... the place of origin of goods; or

(l) ... concerning the need for any goods or services; or

(m) ... concerning the existence, exclusion or effect of any condition, warranty, guarantee, right or remedy...

(n) ... concerning a requirement to pay for a contractual right that:

   (i) is wholly or partly equivalent to any condition, warranty, guarantee, right or remedy ...and

   (ii) a person has under a law of the Commonwealth a State or a Territory (other than an unwritten law). [new]

In relation to (e) or (f) a representation is taken to be misleading unless evidence is adduced to the contrary.[66]

Doolan v Air New Zealand

[9.105] *Doolan v Air New Zealand* (1978) ATPR 40-082

Facts: Doolan booked an 18-day US West Coast and Honolulu holiday through Jetset Tours as tour operator and travel agent with Air New Zealand as carrier. The return leg from Honolulu to Sydney was marked OK but in fact it was wait-listed. Air New Zealand could not confirm so the tour group had to depart Honolulu one day early and spend four hours in Nadi at a first class hotel and one day in Auckland, again at a first class hotel, without extra expense. Some passengers preferred the variations. Air New Zealand and Jetset were prosecuted for this conduct to four passengers under the equivalent of *Australian Consumer Law*, s 29(g) (*Trade Practices Act 1974* (Cth), s 53(c)) and pleaded guilty.

---

63 For example, see *Trade Practices Commission v GLO Juice Co Pty Ltd* (1987) 73 ALR 407 where an injunction was granted to restrain statements in the marketing of GLO juice that it "Contains 35% fruit juice" when in fact it contained not more than 17%.

64 For example, see *Kylie v Lysfar Pty Ltd* (1985) ATPR 40-614 where promoters were found to have breached equivalent *Trade Practices Act 1974* (Cth), s 52(aa) by advertising that certain players would be playing on all three days of a tennis tournament when in fact they would not.

65 See *Cameron v Qantas* (1995) 55 FCR 147 which concerned false representations that passengers would be allocated non-smoking seats.

66 *Australian Consumer Law*, s 29(2), (3).

Doolan v Air New Zealand cont.

Decision: The Federal Court of Australia (Franki J) accepted that the incident had occurred as the result of a misunderstanding between Air New Zealand and Jetset and that it was not a deliberate overbooking; that is, it was due to mistake or carelessness rather than dishonesty. Each was convicted and fined $1,000 ($250 for the conduct to each passenger on which the prosecution was based). Note the implications for yield management and overbooking as discussed below, [9.165].

―――― ဢဢ ――――

Misleading conduct re goods (s 33)

[9.110] Section 33 of the *Australian Consumer Law* (equivalent to *Trade Practices Act 1974*, s 55) concerns unfair practices in relation to goods. Although it covers similar ground to s 18 it provides the additional penalties not available under s 18. It is also wider than s 52 because it relates to misleading conduct to which the *Paris Convention on Intellectual Property* applies, relying on the broader Commonwealth external affairs power. It provides:

> s 33 Misleading conduct as to the nature etc. of goods
>
> A person must not, in trade or commerce, engage in conduct that is liable to mislead the public as to the nature, the manufacturing process, the characteristics, the suitability for their purpose or the quantity of any goods.

Thus in *Trade Practices Commission v GLO Juice Co Pty Ltd*[67] an injunction was granted to restrain statements in the marketing of GLO juice that it "contains 35% fruit juice" when in fact it contained not more than 17% in breach of the equivalent of *Australian Consumer Law*, ss 29 and 33 (*Trade Practices Act 1974*, ss 53 and 55).

Misleading conduct re services (s 34)

[9.115] Section 34 of the *Australian Consumer Law* (equivalent to *Trade Practices Act 1974*, s 55A) concerns unfair practices in relation to services. It also covers similar ground to s 18 and provides the additional penalties not available under s 18. It is also wider than s 18 because it applies to conduct which is *liable to mislead the public* whereas s 18 applies to conduct *likely to mislead and deceive*. Section 34 also overlaps s 29 to some extent. Section 34 provides:

> A person must not, in trade or commerce, engage in conduct that is liable to mislead the public as to the nature, the characteristics, the suitability for their purpose or the quantity of any services.

Doherty v Traveland Pty Ltd; Doherty v Associated Travel

[9.120] *Doherty v Traveland Pty Ltd; Doherty v Associated Travel* (1982) ATPR 40-323

Facts: A travel agent (AT) displayed a Traveland International Pty Ltd brochure which stated a tour was 13 days when, because of a change in Qantas schedules, it had been reduced to 11 days. On learning of the change the travel agent notified those who had booked the tour but took no steps to amend or withdraw the brochure which remained on display. Traveland and AT were prosecuted under the equivalent of *Australian Consumer Law*, ss 29(g) and 34 (*Trade Practices Act 1974*, ss 53(c) and 55A). The charges under the equivalent of s 29(g) were dismissed in other proceedings because of the failure to allege that the conduct was done in connection with the promotion of services as that section required. AT was a 50% owned subsidiary and Traveland Pty Ltd was a wholly owned subsidiary of Traveland International Pty Ltd.

---

67   *Trade Practices Commission v GLO Juice Co Pty Ltd* (1987) 73 ALR 407.

Doherty v Traveland Pty Ltd; Doherty v Associated Travel cont.

Decision: The Federal Court of Australia (Fisher J) held that the charges against Traveland Pty Ltd should be dismissed as it was not its brochure but that of another company in the group Traveland International and that it was not proved that the travel agent AT was acting on behalf of Traveland Pty Ltd in displaying the brochure within the equivalent of s 139B(2) of the *Australian Consumer Law* (*Trade Practices Act 1974*, s 84(2)). However AT was convicted of the charges under the equivalent of s 34 of the *Australian Consumer Law* (*Trade Practices Act 1974*, s 55A) and fined $2,000. The case illustrates that it is easier to prove a breach of s 34 than of s 29(g). It also should be noted that if a defendant is convicted under both ss 29(g) and 34 for the same conduct only one penalty is imposed. [68]

Accepting payment without supply (s 36)

[9.125] Section 36 of the *Australian Consumer Law* (equivalent to *Trade Practices Act 1974*, s 58) concerns another aspect often involved in transactions where there has been misleading or deceptive conduct in relation to the supply of goods and services. It makes the act of accepting payment itself a specific type of deceptive and misleading conduct for which the defendant may be liable for civil remedies as well as penalties.

> **Wrongly accepting payment**
> 36. ...A person must not, in trade or commerce, accept payment or other consideration for goods or services if, at the time of the acceptance:
>
> [1] the person intends not to supply the goods or services; [or]
>
> (2) ... the person intends to supply goods or services materially different from the goods or services in respect of which the payment or other consideration is accepted; [or]
>
> (b) ... there are reasonable grounds [of which the corporation is aware or ought reasonably to be aware] for believing that the person will not be able to supply the goods or services ... within the period specified by or on behalf of the person ... or ... if no period is specified ... within a reasonable time ...

Unfortunately much of the case law on this section has been generated in the travel industry.

If the supplier has exercised due diligence and the failure to supply is beyond their control they will not be liable under s 36. However this does not relieve a supplier from any specific contractual liabilities for failure to supply. [69]

Dawson v World Travel Headquarters

[9.130] *Dawson v World Travel Headquarters* (1981) ATPR 40-240; (1981) FL 455

Facts: World Travel was the travel agent and tour operator. Its brochure promoted a 16-day "Swingaway Asia" holiday but because of an airline schedule change it was only 15 days. This meant that instead of the advertised two days in Singapore there was only one. The brochure had been reprinted but the error was not corrected. Complaints were made to World Travel and to the Trade Practices Commission and World Travel was prosecuted under the equivalent of ss 29(g) and 36 of the *Australian Consumer Law* (*Trade Practices Act 1974*, ss 53(c) and 55A) and pleaded guilty. In the other case referred to above, World Travel was prosecuted under the equivalent of s 36 in respect of two other clients who had paid for their tours based on the incorrect brochures.

Decision: The Federal Court of Australia (Fisher J) accepted the evidence that it was difficult to correct tour details in brochures but nevertheless found that there had been a failure to withdraw,

---

68   *Dawson v World Travel Headquarters* (1981) ATPR 40-240.
69   *Australian Consumer Law*, s 36(5).

Dawson v World Travel Headquarters cont.

amend or correct the misleading statement. In the first matter it was held that where there are convictions under two sections for exactly the same conduct only one penalty, a fine of $1,000, should be imposed. In the second matter World Travel was convicted under the equivalent of s 36 and fined $3,000.

Barton v Westpac Banking Corp

[9.135] *Barton v Westpac Banking Corp* (1983) ATPR 40-338

Facts: Westpac was acting as both travel agent and tour operator. Its brochure included a 16-day "Discovery" tour via Singapore. After the brochure was distributed Qantas changed its schedule so that the tour became 15 days. Westpac made strong representations and thought it had convinced Qantas to honour the old schedule. It continued to take bookings and accepted advance payments through other agents for the tour without informing clients. It was prosecuted under the equivalent of s 36 of the *Australian Consumer Law* (*Trade Practices Act 1974*, s 58).

Decision: The Federal Court of Australia (Shepherd J) accepted that the reduced tour was materially different from that offered. However the charge was dismissed because the prosecutor failed to prove that Westpac had the requisite intent under the equivalent of s 36. This is not *mens rea* or guilty intent.

> it is not sufficient, in my opinion, to establish, as the evidence here clearly does establish, no more than that at the time the money was accepted the defendant by its agents intended to provide a 13 day tour. What must be established additionally is that the defendant by the same agents, or by other agents privy to the knowledge that the tour to be supplied was intended to be a 13 day tour, accepted the customer's money knowing it was paid for a 14 day tour. Otherwise the corporation is not shown to have intended to supply something which was materially different from that for which the money was paid. In order that a corporation may be shown to have had the requisite intention, those acting for it must be shown to have been in a position to apply their minds to the question of whether what was to be supplied would be something materially different from that for which the customer's money was accepted. How can one intend to supply something different from that for which one accepts a customer's money, if one does not appreciate what it is for which the customer's money is being paid?

Other specific types of misleading and deceptive conduct

[9.140] Part 3.1, Division 1 of the *Australian Consumer Law* also covers various other specific types of misleading and deceptive conduct. There are several types which are the most relevant to tourism, travel and hospitality. They concern particular advertising and promotional techniques which, if misused, can be deceptive and misleading giving rise to civil liability and possible penalties under the Division. The offences under some of the equivalent sections from the *Trade Practices Act 1974* have been set out in Chapter 3 and the reader is referred there for the detail.

Offering gifts and prizes (s 32)

[9.145] Section 32 of the *Australian Consumer Law* (equivalent to *Trade Practices Act 1974*, s 54) prohibits the offering of gifts, prizes or other free items in promotions for the supply of goods and services if there is no intention to provide the free items or to supply them as offered.

Bait advertising (s 35)

[9.150] Section 35 of the *Australian Consumer Law* (equivalent to *Trade Practices Act 1974*, s 56) prohibits bait advertising. The goods and services promoted must be available in reasonable quantities within a reasonable time on the terms offered.

Full price to be stated (s 48)

[9.155] Section 48 of the *Australian Consumer Law* (similar to *Trade Practices Act 1974*, 53C but wider) requires that in promotions for the supply of goods and services, prices quoted must be inclusive of all quantifiable, compulsory fees and charges. In the case of air fares this includes charges under the *Passenger Movement Charge Act 1978* (Cth) which airlines may pay and collect from the passenger under the *Passenger Movement Charges Collection Act 1978* (Cth).[70]

Harassment and coercion (s 50)

[9.160] Section 50 of the *Australian Consumer Law* (equivalent to *Trade Practices Act 1974*, s 60) prohibits the use of harassment or coercion in connection with the supply or possible supply of goods or services to a consumer or to recover payment. Touts and unscrupulous tour guides may offend this provision.

Overbooking

[9.165] Overbooking is common in tourism, travel and hospitality because production capacity is usually fixed, the product is perishable and is often sold in advance. Although reservations are contracts, they are often breached by guests who cancel late or simply never show up ("no shows"). Similarly operators also breach reservations contracts by overbooking with the result being that guests must be turned away ("bumped"). Overbooking is a breach of contract and the guest has a remedy in damages which can include substantial damages for disappointment. If the overbooking is not accidental but deliberate then it can constitute fraudulent misrepresentation.

This raises serious issues for the industry particularly with the advent of yield management techniques which involve a policy of deliberate overbooking to allow for expected late cancellations and no shows and still achieve full occupancy.

While not specifically mentioned as a type of deceptive and misleading conduct, overbooking clearly offends ss 18, 29 and 34 of the *Australian Consumer Law* and may also offend s 36. The operator is liable whether the overbooking is accidental or deliberate but if it is deliberate, then very severe penalties may be imposed.

These issues have been clearly canvassed in cases on airlines,[71] hotels[72] and resorts[73] and the principles also apply to other means of transport and to restaurants and theme parks. Overbooking often involves delay waiting for an alternative supply to become available. See now the guarantee of timeliness in the provision of services under *Australian Consumer Law*, s 62 (see [9.185]). This most often happens in passenger transport where the "bumped" passengers must wait for a later carrier (see Chapter 12 on liability for delay). The aviation

---

70 *Australian Consumer Law*, s 48–Example 3.
71 *Nader v Allegheney Airlines* (1976) 426 US 290; *British Airways Board v Taylor* (1976) WLR 13; *Cameron v Qantas* (1995) 55 FCR 147.
72 *Dodd v Outrigger Hotel* 501 P 2d 368 (Hawaii 1972).
73 *Club Mediterranee SA v Sterling* 283 SE2d 30.

industry has negotiated denied boarding compensation schemes to satisfy the main regulatory objections and these are mandated by the consumer protection authorities in Europe and the USA. Hotels, restaurants and other components should develop similar approaches through their trade associations to address the legal problems of the current practices.

OTHER CONSUMER PROTECTION MEASURES

[9.170] Other specific consumer protection measures covered are:

- Consumer Guarantees;[74]
- Product Safety;[75]
- Information Standards;[76] and
- Manufacturers' Liability.[77]

These are discussed in more detail in the following.

CONSUMER GUARANTEES

[9.175] The *Australian Consumer Law* introduces a single national system of statutory consumer guarantees which replaces existing State and Territory Fair Trading Acts, Sale of Goods and other legislation on implied conditions and warranties in the supply of goods and services.[78] These go beyond equivalent *Trade Practices Act 1974* provisions and are aligned with the New Zealand *Consumer Guarantees Act 1993*. Key features include:

- Breaches of statutory consumer guarantees are directly enforceable under the *Australian Consumer Law* rather than in contract law and *Australian Consumer Law* remedies apply.
- Contract law distinctions between "conditions" (entitling an aggrieved party to rescind as well as seek damages) and "warranties" (confining an aggrieved party to damages) are eliminated.[79]
- *Australian Consumer Law* consumer guarantees protect "consumers"[80] who acquire goods and services from Australian suppliers, importers or manufacturers.[81]
- Restrictions on exclusion and limitation apply.

Because these guarantees apply to supply of products (some in relation to "goods" some in relation to "services") "in trade or commerce" they:[82]

- do not apply to sales by individuals to other individuals or businesses;
- do apply to sales made by traditional auction;

---

74 *Australian Consumer Law*, Chapter 3, Part 3.2, ss 51 – 65.
75 *Australian Consumer Law*, Chapter 3, Part 3.3, ss 104 – 133.
76 *Australian Consumer Law*, Chapter 3, Part 3.4, ss 134 – 137.
77 *Australian Consumer Law*, Chapter 3, Part 3.5, ss 138 – 150.
78 Attorney- General's Department, Commonwealth of Australia, *The Australian Consumer Law–A Guide to Provisions* (Barton, ACT, April 2010), p 17.
79 The *Trade Practices Act 1974* and Sale of Goods legislation achieved a similar result by implying conditions and warranties on these matters into the contract for sale or supply. See Chapter 4, Contract.
80 See definition at [9.45].
81 So they are extended beyond the parties to the contract to also cover manufacturers where appropriate.
82 Attorney- General's Department, Commonwealth of Australia, *The Australian Consumer Law–A Guide to Provisions* (Barton, ACT, April 2010), p 17.

- do apply to online "auction" websites where the website operator does not operate as agent for the seller;
- do apply to second hand goods.

The guarantees applied to the supply of products are listed in the following table and each is discussed in the relevant parts below.

PRODUCT	
Goods	Services
s 51 Title	s 60 Due care and skill
s 52 Undisturbed possession	s 61(1) Fit for any disclosed purpose
s 53 No undisclosed securities	s 61(2) Achieve the result
s 54 Acceptable quality	s 62 Time of supply
s 55 Fit for any disclosed purpose	
s 56 Compliance with description	
s 57 Compliance with sample or demonstration model	
s 58 Repairs and spare parts available	
s 59 Express warranties	

It should be noted that in the tourism travel and hospitality industry the product is sometimes a hybrid of goods and services, in which case both sets of guarantees will apply. Examples include:

- Food and beverage (see Chapter 14);
- Supply of equipment in tourism activities (see Chapter 15).

Consumer Guarantees in the Supply of Goods

[9.180] The guarantees applied to the sale or supply [83] of goods to consumers in trade and commerce under the *Australian Consumer Law* are as follows. [84]

- **Title (s 51):** Consumers are guaranteed that the supplier has the right to sell or supply the goods to the consumer (similar to *Trade Practices Act 1974*, s 69).
- **Undisturbed possession (s 52):** Consumers are guaranteed of undisturbed possession (though limited in the case of a lease or hire or the like) except for disclosed securities or encumbrances (similar to *Trade Practices Act 1974*, s 69).
- **No undisclosed securities (s 53):** Goods must be free of any undisclosed security, charge or encumbrance (similar to *Trade Practices Act 1974*, s 69).
- **Acceptable quality (s 54):** Goods must be of "acceptable quality" to a reasonable consumer which means they must be (modified *Trade Practices Act 1974*, s 71(1) [85] incorporating NZ [86] best practice):
    - fit for all the purposes for which goods of that kind are commonly supplied;
    - acceptable in appearance and finish;
    - free from defects;

---

83   The Sale of Goods legislation is limited to sales.
84   Attorney-General's Department, Commonwealth of Australia, *The Australian Consumer Law—A Guide to Provisions* (Barton, ACT, April 2010), pp 18-19.
85   The *Trade Practices Act 1974* was based upon "merchantable quality" a concept derived from the original law merchant which was sometimes difficult to apply to more sophisticated contemporary goods.
86   *Consumer Guarantees Act 1993* (NZ), s 7.

- safe; and
- durable.

Matters to be considered in determining whether goods are of "acceptable quality" include:
- the nature of the goods;
- the price of the goods (if relevant);
- any statements made about the goods on any packaging or label;
- any representation made about the goods by the supplier or manufacturer; and
- any other relevant circumstances relating to the supply of the goods.

- Fit for any disclosed purpose (s 55): Goods must be reasonably fit for any purpose disclosed by the consumer to the supplier unless it is shown that the consumer did not reply or that it was unreasonable for the consumer to reply on the skill and judgment of the supplier (similar to *Trade Practices Act 1974*, s 71(2)). This guarantee ensures that goods meet the *subjective* standards required by the *consumer* and made known to the supplier in contrast with the *objective* standard of fitness for purpose which goods must also meet under the guarantee of acceptable quality under s 54.

In tourism, travel and hospitality the requirement that goods be "fit for the purpose" is often encountered in the following situations:

- in relation to the hire of equipment and vehicles, it requires road worthiness, rail worthiness and sea worthiness (see Chapter 12, [12.160], [12.230], [12.300]); and
- in relation to the supply of food and beverage, it requires that they be fit for human consumption (see Chapter 14, [14.50]).

Compliance with description (s 56): Goods must correspond with their description even where the goods are displayed and selected by the consumer (similar to *Trade Practices Act 1974*, s 70). This is particularly relevant in the following circumstances in tourism, travel and hospitality:

- where goods are purchased from a catalogue or brochure or over the internet;
- in labelling food and beverage (see also Chapter 14, [14.60]);
- where food and beverage are ordered from a restaurant menu.
- **Compliance with sample or demonstration model** (s 57): Where goods are supplied by reference to a sample (similar to *Trade Practices Act 1974*, s 72):
    - the goods must correspond with the sample in quality, state and condition;
    - the consumer must have a reasonable opportunity of comparing the goods with the sample; and
    - that the goods must be free from any defect not apparent on reasonable examination of the sample rendering them not of acceptable quality.
- **Repairs and spare parts available** (s 58): The manufacturer must take reasonable steps to make repairs and parts reasonably available for a reasonable period after goods are supplied (similar to *Trade Practices Act 1974*, s 74F).
- **Express warranties** (s 59): The *supplier* and *manufacturer* must comply with any express warranty which they give in relation to goods (similar to *Trade Practices Act 1974*, s 74G).

Consumer Guarantees in the Supply of Services

[9.185] As discussed above, most tourism, travel and hospitality products are services rather than goods and so the guarantees discussed above and the corresponding Sale of Goods Act conditions do not apply to much of the industry's production. The *Trade Practices Act 1974*, s 74 [87] introduced statutory warranties [88] in relation to the supply of services and these have been refined in the *Australian Consumer Law* and now apply nationally. While it is arguable that similar warranties are implied in contract [89] at common law, the restrictions on exclusion and limitation and the wider remedies available under the *Australian Consumer Law* mean these guarantees are of fundamental importance to consumer protection and risk management in the industry.

The guarantees applied to the supply [90] of services to consumers in trade and commerce under the *Australian Consumer Law* are as follows. [91]

- **Due care and skill (s 60):** Services must be rendered with due care and skill (similar to *Trade Practices Act 1974* s 74(1)). A similar *Trade Practices Act 1974* provision was held to apply to the luggage of a cruise ship passenger [92] by the Supreme Court in *Dillon v Baltic Shipping Co "Mikhail Lermontov"* [93] (see casenote at [12.90]) when the definition of services was quite narrow. Compare the duty of care in the tort of negligence (see [5.30]) which will also apply to the facts in many cases.

- **Fit for the purpose (s 61(1)):** Services (and any product resulting from the services) must be reasonably fit for any purpose disclosed by the consumer to the supplier unless it is shown that the consumer did not reply or that it was unreasonable for the consumer to reply on the skill and judgement of the supplier (similar to part of *Trade Practices Act 1974*, s 74(2)).

This guarantee ensures that services meet the *subjective* standards required by the consumer and made known to the supplier. It corresponds with the somewhat similar guarantee in relation to goods (s 55).

It has widespread application in the tourism, travel and hospitality industry including in:

- Passenger transport where the vehicle is "supplied" where it reinforces the general requirement that it be roadworthy, seaworthy, airworthy and the like (see Chapter 12);

- Traveller accommodation where it reinforces the general requirement that accommodation be habitable and have the standards and features required (see Chapter 13);

- Food and beverage where it reinforces the general requirements that they be fit for consumption (see Chapter 14); and

---

87 Some State Fair Trading Acts introduced similar warranties.

88 They were "warranties" rather than "conditions" because the contractual remedy of rescission and return of the goods was not available for services which are usually consumed as they are supplied and used. See Chapter 4.

89 See *White v John Warwick & Co Ltd* [1953] 1 WLR 1285 where it was held that hire of a defective bicycle was actionable in tort and contract under an implied warranty.

90 The Sale of Goods legislation is limited to sales.

91 Attorney-General's Department, Commonwealth of Australia, *The Australian Consumer Law–A Guide to Provisions* (Barton, ACT, April 2010), pp 18-19.

92 It would also now apply to the carriage of the passenger, following amendments to *Trade Practices Act 1974*, s 74 in 1986 which came into force shortly after the sinking of the ship. See now definition of "services" in *Australian Consumer Law*, s 4.

93 *Dillon v Baltic Shipping Co "Mikhail Lermontov"* (1990) ATPR 40-992.

- Activities and attractions where it reinforces basic requirements for safety and amenity and also in relation to special experiences which tourists may expect (see Chapter 15).
- **Achieve the result (s 61(2))**: Services (and any product resulting from the services) must be of such a nature, quality, state or condition that they might reasonably be expected to achieve the required result disclosed to the supplier (*or to a person by whom any prior negotiations or arrangements relating to the acquisition were made*) unless it is shown that the consumer did not reply or that it was unreasonable for the consumer to rely on the skill and judgment of the supplier (similar to part of *Trade Practices Act 1974*, s 74(2)).

    This provision focuses on the end result which the consumer wishes to achieve. Key issues arising from this provision include:
    - The substance of the *Trade Practices Act 1974* provision has been extended by the portion italicised in the paragraph above and this greatly extends the ambit to include the full range of intermediaries (travel agents, tour operators etc) who are often involved in the transaction. Disclosure to any one will make the supplier responsible for delivery whether or not the information was passed on and without restrictions under the law of agency (see Chapter 11);
    - In tourism, travel and hospitality the result sought by the consumer is often individual, intangible and experiential which might be difficult to define or cater for generally (see Chapter 15); and
    - Where this provision applies, one or more of the specific unfair practises provisions discussed above is also likely to apply to the facts and circumstances of the case.
- **Time for supply (s 62)**: Services must be supplied within a reasonable time if the time of supply has not been otherwise fixed in a contract or agreed. (This is a new requirement.)

    This has significant implications for tourism, travel and hospitality, particularly in relation to the intrinsic practices of overbooking and problems of delay (see Chapter 12 and Overbooking [9.165]). Key issues include:
    - standard contract provisions designed to avoid responsibility for delay may offend the unconscionable conduct and unfair contract terms provisions discussed above; and
    - there will be a contest between express mention of times or dates to accommodate guests or carry passengers (including convention obligations) and provisions seeking to relieve suppliers from responsibility and these may fall foul of the provisions restricting the right to limit or contract out of s 62 of the *Australian Consumer Law*.
- **Specified services not covered (s 63)**: The guarantees on services do not apply to contracts for (similar to *Trade Practices Act 1974*, s 74(3)):
    - *Transportation or storage of goods for business purposes*. The meaning of the equivalent *Trade Practices Act 1974* provision was considered in *Wallis v Downard-Pickford (North Queensland) Pty Ltd* [94] where the High Court held it did not exclude a removalist's liability for the belongings of a policemen who was being transferred (see casenote at [12.110]). However in tourism, travel and hospitality it may cover luggage and goods in business travel (see Chapter 12).

---

94   *Wallis v Downard-Pickford (North Queensland) Pty Ltd* (1994) 68 ALJR 395.

– Insurance. This covers the insurance policy itself and does not exclude the negligent advice and services provided by an insurance agent (or travel agent) in selling the policy: *Zoneff v Elcom Credit Union Ltd* [95] (see Chapter 7).

Miscellaneous requirements

[9.190] In the supply of goods and services to a consumer the supplier must also:

- provide the consumer with a proof of transaction if requested if the value is $75 or more. A GST invoice meets these requirements; [96]
- provide an itemised bill if the consumer so requests in the supply of services; [97]
- meet the prescribed requirements for a warranty against defects. [98]

Remedies and enforcement

[9.195] Consumers may take action under the *Australian Consumer Law* [99] to obtain a range of remedies against suppliers who fail to comply with the guarantees discussed above including: [100]

- requiring the supplier to remedy the defect;
- if the suppler does not remedy the defect or if it is a major defect the consumer may reject the goods or services;
- terminating the contract and obtaining a refund; and
- obtaining compensation for loss and damage.

Exclusion and limitation

[9.200] One of the innovations of the *Trade Practices Act 1974* was to restrict common law rights in contract to limit or exclude liability for implied warranties and conditions thus overcoming another major weakness in the Sale of Goods legislation. [101] The initial *Trade Practices Act 1974* provisions were harsh on suppliers especially on the tourism industry and there have been a series of amendments to try and refine their scope and application. This has been refined somewhat in the *Australian Consumer Law* in respect of consumer guarantees. Unfortunately the evolving exceptions, exceptions to exceptions and so forth structure has been retained leaving this important subject matter unduly complicated and confusing for consumers and suppliers alike.

Section 64 (*Trade Practices Act 1974*, s 68) declares void any term of a contract which purports to exclude, restrict or modify the consumer guarantees provided under the *Australian*

---

95   *Zoneff v Elcom Credit Union Ltd* (1990) 94 ALR 445.
96   *Australian Consumer Law*, s 100.
97   *Australian Consumer Law*, s 101.
98   *Australian Consumer Law*, s 103.
99   *Australian Consumer Law*, Part 5-4, ss 259 – 286.
100 In contrast, the *Trade Practices Act 1974* implied warranties and conditions into the contract between supplier and consumer and the only remedies available were those available under the general law of contract.
101 Most States also amended their Sale of Goods legislation (NSW, Vic) or amended their Fair Trading legislation (WA, NT) or passed other legislation (SA: *Consumer Transactions Act 1972*) to prevent the implied terms being excluded in consumer contracts.

Consumer Law. A similar section in the *Trade Practices Act 1974* was invoked in *Dillon v Baltic Shipping Co "Mikhail Lermontov"* [102] (see casenote at [12.90]) to invalidate an exclusion clause in a cruise ship passenger contract and it was also applied by the High Court in *Wallis v Downard-Pickford (North Queensland) Pty Ltd* [103] (see casenote at [12.110]) to override State legislation purporting to limit the liability of carriers as it prevails over State law under s 109 of the Constitution.

The exception is that Section 64A (*Trade Practices Act 1974*, s 68A) permits limitation of liability to repair or replacement in the case of goods or supplying again in the case of services (or the cost thereof) and this itself applies except where:

(a) The goods or services are "of a kind ordinarily acquired for personal, domestic or household use" (Trade Practices Act 1974, s 68A); or

(b) The consumer establishes it would not be fair or reasonable for the supplier to rely on the limitation having regard for factors such as the relative strength of bargaining position of the parties and the like. This reinforces the general provisions under s 23ff declaring unfair contract terms in consumer contracts void and under s 20ff prohibiting unconscionable conduct.

The provision of s 64A listed in (a) above is an exception to the exception and so it reinstates the generally harsh provision s 64 which prevents suppliers of those products from limiting or restricting liability. Any attempt to do so is void and may itself constitute a false representation under s 29(g), running the risk of civil liability and prosecution for a criminal offence. Unfortunately "personal, domestic or household use" covers most tourism, travel and hospitality products, except perhaps products designed and specially designated for business customers, for example business class air transport (see Chapter 12, [12.80]). This was criticised by this author and others as it placed Australian operators in this industry at a disadvantage compared with foreign competitors and with other industries. [104]

For some time it caused considerable problems in tourism particularly in adventure or recreational activities where risk is an integral part of the experience.

As part of the Australian tort law reforms specific provisions were enacted under the *Trade Practices Act 1974* and state Civil Liability legislation to overcome some of these problems (see Chapter 5). These have been refined in the *Australian Consumer Law*. Unfortunately they are presented as a series of further exceptions to the exceptions as follows.

Section 139A permits a supplier of "recreational services" to exclude, restrict or modify in contract liability in respect of death or personal injury.

Recreational services are services that consist of participation in:

(a) a sporting activity or a similar leisure time pursuit; or

(b) any other activity that:

(i) involves a significant degree of physical exertion or physical risk; and

(ii) is undertaken for the purposes of recreation, enjoyment or leisure.

This would include most adventure tourism activities. However there is an exception to the exception.

---

102 *Dillon v Baltic Shipping Co "Mikhail Lermontov"* (1990) ATPR 40-992.
103 *Wallis v Downard-Pickford (North Queensland) Pty Ltd* (1994) 68 ALJR 395.
104 See T C Atherton, "Changes to Trade Practices Act increase liability" *Tourism and Travel Review* 1992 1(3) at 7.

This exclusion, restriction or modification is not permitted for a significant personal injury caused by the reckless conduct of the supplier (s 139A(4) of the former *Trade Practices Act 1974*).

The supplier's conduct is *reckless conduct* if the supplier:
(a) is aware, or should reasonably have been aware, of a significant risk that the conduct could result in personal injury to another person; and
(b) engages in the conduct.

So for many adventure tourism operators where risk is an integral part of the experience, considerable risk of unlimited liability remains.

See further in relation to Adventure Tourism in [15.355]ff.

The supply of gas, electricity, telecommunications and other sectors specified by regulations are exempt from s 64. Section 275 of the *Australian Consumer Law* also permits limitation or exclusion of liability for failure to comply with a consumer guarantee in respect of the supply of services where the law of a State or Territory is the proper law of the contract and that law permits limitation or exclusion. [105]

Product liability

[9.205] The *Australian Consumer Law* provides several important measures on product liability which apply nationally including:

- Safety of Consumer Goods and Product Related Services;
- Information Standards;
- Liability of Manufacturers and Importers for Defective Goods.

These are discussed briefly below.

Safety of Consumer Goods and Product Related Services

[9.210] The *Australian Consumer Law* introduces a national regulatory framework for consumer product safety. [106] This builds upon the *Trade Practices Act 1974* provisions on the safety of consumer goods and extends to product related services.

The framework provides for the making and enforcement of:

- safety standards;
- safety bans;
- product recalls;
- safety warning notices; and
- mandatory reporting of accidents.

It applies also to product related services which means only services related to the supply, installation repair etc of goods. So the framework does not cover tourism services except for the supply of goods and equipment, for example, in recreational and adventure tourism. Thus it does not tackle the regulatory problems involved in more complex package holidays (see [9.300]ff).

The details are outside the scope of this book.

---

105 This was considered in the case of *Insight Vacations Pty Ltd v Young* [2010] NSWCA 137.
106 *Australian Consumer Law*, Part 3.3.

Information Standards

[9.215] Under the *Australian Consumer Law* the responsible Commonwealth Minister has power to prescribe information standards for particular goods and services which suppliers must meet.[107] It is an offence for a supplier not to meet the standard prescribed.

This has potential for use in the regulation of package holidays where international regulation has sought to provide better protection for consumers partly through prescribing the information which suppliers must provide (see [9.300]ff). However nothing has been done on this at this stage.

Liability of Manufacturers and Importers for Defective Goods

[9.220] Building upon the *Trade Practices Act 1974*, the *Australian Consumer Law* also creates national rules governing the liability of manufacturers and importers for safety defects in goods.[108] Any person who has suffered loss or injury as a result of the supply of a good with a safety defect may commence an action against the manufacturer for compensation. If a foreign manufacturer does not have a place of business in Australia action may be brought against the importer.

The approach is similar to that developed in the European Union. The only defences to liability are:

- safety defect did not exist at time of supply;
- safety defect arose only because of compliance with a mandatory standards;
- defect not discoverable because of state of scientific and technical knowledge;
- good was part of another defective good.

The provisions apply only to goods and so do not apply to international package holidays (see [9.300]ff). The details of these provisions is outside the scope of this book.

International Contracts

[9.225] There are two other provisions of the *Australian Consumer Law* which are important for international transactions.

International sale of goods: Vienna Convention

[9.230] The *United Nations Convention on the International Sale of Goods 1980* (the Vienna Convention) provides a set of uniform rules for the international trade in goods. The Convention has been signed by more than 20 states, including most of Australia's major trading partners, and has been enacted into Australian federal and State law.[109] Section 68 of the *Australian Consumer Law* provides that where there is an inconsistency between the Convention and the *Australian Consumer Law* provisions on consumer transactions, the Convention prevails. International sale of goods is also facilitated by the use of Incoterms developed by the international Chamber of Commerce (ICC). There is a need, but as yet there is no equivalent Convention, on the sale or services or standard contracts or terms for the international distribution of tourism services.

---

107 *Australian Consumer Law*, Part 3.4.
108 *Australian Consumer Law*, Part 3.5.
109 Each State also has legislation which enacts into law the *Vienna Convention on International Sale of Goods 1980*: see for example *Sale of Goods (Vienna Convention) Act 1986* (NSW).

Conflict of laws

[9.235] International transactions and travel always involve the laws of more than one legal system. These laws often provide different conclusions on questions of procedure, liability and the amount of damages to be awarded. To resolve these conflicts a complex set of principles of international law known as conflict of laws [110] has been developed. The parties to a contract also have considerable freedom to choose the law and courts of the country they wish to have settle their disputes. Nevertheless there are many uncertainties and difficulties which remain in international litigation and these frequently arise in tourism and travel cases. [111]

To ensure that the provisions of the *Australian Consumer Law* on consumer transactions are not unreasonably avoided by simply stipulating a foreign law, *Australian Consumer Law* s 67 provides that they apply wherever the law of Australia is the proper law of the contract regardless of any contrary stipulation in the contract.

COMPETITION

[9.240] As outlined in the overview, consumer interests are also promoted indirectly by the competition laws which are aimed directly at ensuring that suppliers of goods and services operate competitively and efficiently. The common law provided some regulation of this under the doctrine of restraint of trade, under which certain anti-competitive contractual provisions were made void. [112] Many of these cases concerned the old "tied house" arrangements between breweries and hotels. However the doctrine was limited by the competing theory of freedom of contract.

The provisions of the *Competition and Consumer Act 2010* are much wider than the common law restraint of trade doctrine and seek to achieve the wider economic objectives of a competitive market. They are contained in Part IV, "Restrictive Trade Practices". They were originally confined by the limits of federal jurisdiction and sovereign immunity. However under the National Competition Policy implemented by Competition Policy Reform legislation [113] a modified version of Part IV and Part XIA ("The Competition Code") now applies to most commercial and professional activities, including State authorities and instrumentalities. A detailed consideration of these matters is outside the scope of this text. [114]

There have been many competition law cases involving the tourism, travel and hospitality industry and the main sections involved are outlined below.

Cartel Conduct (Division 1)

[9.245] Section 44ZZRA of the *Competition and Consumer Act 2010* (Cth) provides a simplified outline of this as follows:

---

110 Or private international law.
111 See *Oceanic Sun Line Special Shipping Co v Fay* (1988) 165 CLR 197.
112 The principles, which still apply today, were formulated by the House of Lords in *Nordenfelt v Maxim-Nordenfelt Guns and Ammunition Co* [1894] AC 535.
113 The Competition Policy Reform legislation comprises: ACT: *Competition Policy Reform (ACT) Act 1996*; NSW: *Competition Policy Reform (NSW) Act 1995*; NT: *Competition Policy Reform (NT) Act*; Qld: *Competition Policy Reform (Qld) Act 1996*; SA: *Competition Policy Reform (SA) Act 1996*; Vic: *Competition Policy Reform (Victoria) Act 1995*; WA: *Competition Policy Reform (WA) Act 1996*.
114 See W Pengilley, *The Law of Travel and Tourism* (Blackstone Press, 1990) for an interesting analysis of the subject in terms of consumer protection and competition law.

This Division sets out parallel offences and civil penalty provisions relating to cartel conduct. A corporation must not make, or give effect to, a contract, arrangement or understanding that contains a cartel provision. A cartel provision is a provision relating to:

(a) price-fixing; or

(b) restricting outputs in the production and supply chain; or

(c) allocating customers, suppliers or territories; or

(d) bid-rigging;

by parties that are, or would otherwise be, in competition with each other.

The detail is beyond the scope of this book.

Anti-Competitive Contracts and Arrangements (s 45)

[9.250] Section 45 of the *Competition and Consumer Act 2010* (Cth) is the main provision of Part IV. It establishes the general prohibition on contracts, arrangements and understandings that are exclusionary or that have the effect of substantially lessening competition. Significant travel and tourism cases have included the following:

- *Australian Federation of Travel Agents (AFTA) case* [115] involving the activities of the trade association (see casenote at [11.375]).
- *International Air Transport Association (IATA) cases* [116] involving its trade association activities (see [12.710]).

In *Trade Practices Commission v Caravella*, [117] the tour operator was prosecuted and fined $5,500 under the section after admitting that it tried to organise a ban on a booking agent who was discounting tour prices in Cairns by rebating part of its commission.

Misuse of Market Power (s 46)

[9.255] Section 46 of the *Competition and Consumer Act 2010* (Cth) prohibits a corporation which has a substantial degree of power in a market from taking advantage of that power for certain anti-competitive purposes. There have been numerous tourism and travel industry cases on this section, including: [118]

- Regional airport development arrangements between Shire Councils and air carriers, particularly in the Whitsundays and Broome. These raise interesting questions as to whether these destinations are a "market" in the relevant sense.

- Long-term lease of available airport space to Ansett and Australian Airlines (now Qantas) on the eve of deregulation so that new entrants Compass I and Compass II were left with inadequate and unsuitable ground facilities. Aussie Airlines also complained of similar difficulties in gaining access. Car rental companies have also fought a similar battle to obtain access to airports.

---

115 *Australian Federation of Travel Agents Ltd v Trade Practices Commission* (1976) ATPR (Com) 15,553.

116 See the approval of IATA's Passenger Liability Agreements and also see *International Air Transport Association v Alitalia Linea Aera Italiana SPA* (1985) 7 ATPR 40-537.

117 *Trade Practices Commission v Caravella* (1994) ATPR 41-293.

118 For a review of the cases up to 1990 see W Pengilley, *The Law of Travel and Tourism* (Blackstone Press, 1990), pp 35-45.

- Carrier withdrawing from supply arrangements with tour operator. In *Singapore Airlines v Taprobane Tours (WA) Pty Ltd* [119] the carrier was found not to have breached s 46 because it did not have the necessary "market power" over flights from Australia to the Maldives.
- Hoteliers successfully lobbied Queensland Travel and Tourism Corporation to maintain its Sunlover package holiday program to prevent misuse of market power by the air carriers and their vertically integrated tour operations.
- Taxi owners' and prospective taxi owners' licences and relations with base operators. In *Venning v Suburban Taxi Service Pty Ltd* [120] a base operator was found not to have breached s 46 in cancelling a taxi owner's contract because the base operator was not shown to have a substantial degree of power in any one market.
- There have also been numerous cases involving air carrier operations, including predatory pricing, misuse of Computerised Reservation Systems (CRS) and review of hub and spoke arrangements used to increase carrier control at international airports.

Exclusive Dealing (s 47)

[9.260] Section 47 of the *Competition and Consumer Act 2010* (Cth) prohibits exclusive dealing. This takes many forms, including many of the old brewer/hotelier "tied house" arrangements which are now prohibited by the section. One of the more subtle and interesting forms is third line forcing. This is defined in s 47(6) and (7) to mean supplying goods or services only on condition that the customer acquires other goods and services from a nominated supplier. This section raises some immediate practical issues in the travel industry:

- The requirement that travel agents be members of the Travel Compensation Fund scheme as a condition of State licensing would appear to offend s 47 if, as in the Northern Territory, a competitive private insurance scheme is available (see [11.625]). It is likely that this will be reviewed under the National Competition Policy.
- Travel agents may recommend and even perhaps insist that clients take out travel insurance as a condition of travel but they cannot insist upon a particular insurer. The client must be allowed choice among a number of insurers even if the travel agent has an insurance agency with one of them. See the media release from the Australian Competition and Consumer Commission referred to below. [121]

Warning to travel industry on advertising, third line forcing

[9.265] Australian Competition and Consumer Commission Media Release 154/96 (14 November 1996): *Warning to travel industry on advertising, third line forcing*

A clear warning has been sent to travel agents against third-line forcing products on customers after Australian Competition and Consumer Commission action against a WA travel company. Travel agents must ensure their advertising is accurate, ACCC Chairman Professor Allan Fels said today. Cannon Investments Pty Ltd, trading as Travelshop, has acknowledged that it may have breached the third line forcing and consumer protection provisions of the *Trade Practices Act 1974*.

"Travelshop advertised that prospective passengers had to take out travel insurance from nominated insurance companies, and omitted the cost of insurance from the advertised price of

---

119 *Singapore Airlines v Taprobane Tours (WA) Pty Ltd* (1991) 33 FCR 158.
120 *Venning v Suburban Taxi Service Pty Ltd* (1996) ATPR 41-468.
121 Australian Competition and Consumer Commission (ACCC) at http://www.accc.gov.au.

Warning to travel industry on advertising, third line forcing cont.

flights," Professor Fels said. "Travelshop has agreed also to undertake remedial action to stop the conduct and ensure its future advertising meets accepted standards."

ACCC investigations showed Travelshop offered flights to London on condition that prospective passengers also acquired travel insurance from nominated insurance companies. This practice, known as third-line forcing, is prohibited under the Act. Additionally, the prices at which the flights were advertised did not include the additional costs associated with the travel insurance.

Travelshop has acknowledged that the conduct may have breached the Act and have co-operated fully with the ACCC to resolve the matter by offering a legally enforceable undertaking that it will:

x cease applying conditions to its travel services which may constitute third line forcing and, in future refrain from representing, in advertising or by any other means, that consumers are required to obtain travel insurance from another supplier in relation to any flights or other services being offered by Travelshop;

- withdraw its current advertising and in future ensure that full details are provided in its advertising of all conditions applicable to any offer being made by it;
- publish corrective advertising in each newspaper and publication in which the current advertising originally appeared; and
- institute a trade practices compliance/training program within the company.

Professor Fels said:

"Companies should be aware that by supplying or offering to supply goods and services to consumers on the condition that the buyer takes other goods or services from some other supplier, they may be placing themselves at risk of breaching the Act,"

"I would remind all businesses that they face penalties of up to $10 million, for companies, or $500,000 for individuals, should they be found to be involved in third line forcing activities. This matter also highlights the need for companies to be aware of their obligations and responsibilities to consumers to provide those consumers with accurate information to allow them to make an informed choice. It is essential that advertisements promoting an offer to consumers, particularly one involving significant price reductions, contain sufficient information to ensure consumers are fully informed as to the nature of any conditions that may be applicable to that offer."

―――― ಸುಡ ――――

Other Types of Anti-Competitive Conduct

[9.270] There are also various other types of anti-competitive conduct specified under Part IV. These include price fixing and mergers and acquisitions.

Price fixing (s 48)

[9.275] Section 48 of the *Competition and Consumer Act 2010* (Cth) prohibits a corporation from specifying a minimum retail price for its products. This prohibits the old price fixing activities of trade associations. See *Australian Federation of Travel Agents Ltd v Trade Practices Commission* (the AFTA case) [122] (see [11.375]) and the International Air Transport Association (IATA) cases [123] (see [12.710]).

---

122 *Australian Federation of Travel Agents Ltd v Trade Practices Commission* (1976) ATPR (Com) 15,553.

123 See the recent approval of IATA's Passenger Liability Agreements and also see *International Air Transport Association and Alitalia Linea Aera Italiana SPA* (1985) 7 ATPR 40-537.

Mergers and acquisitions (s 50)

[9.280] Section 50 of the *Competition and Consumer Act 2010* (Cth) prohibits the acquisition of shares or assets which would substantially lessen competition in a market. This raises the old problem in travel and tourism of how to define the market. Ansett was allowed to take over East West Airlines under this section. When Daikyo purchased the Four Seasons Hotel in Cairns in 1990 for $74m the Trade Practices Commission approved the transaction because the market was defined as the five star/four star/three star market of which Daikyo held 34%t rather than the five star/four star market of which Daikyo held 70%.[124]

Authorisations and Exemptions

[9.285] Under Part VII of the *Competition and Consumer Act 2010* (Cth) the ACCC may grant authorisations for conduct which would otherwise be in breach of the Act. In considering whether to grant authorisation the ACCC must be satisfied that the benefits to the public from the conduct outweigh any detriments.

Under s 51 various conduct is exempt from Part IV, including conduct authorised by legislation, industrial agreements about working conditions, restraint of trade clauses in employment contracts and partnerships, consumer boycotts and arrangements about patents and copyright arrangements.

ENFORCEMENT AND REMEDIES

[9.290] The *Competition and Consumer Act 2010* (Cth) provides a wide range of remedies and enforcement mechanisms.[125] These are much more innovative than those available at common law and are also subject to very few of the common law restrictions on use. The special statutory remedies apply to the consumer protection and competition law provisions of the legislation but the enforcement mechanisms and remedies vary from provision to provision.

Under the *Competition and Consumer Act 2010* (Cth) any person who aids, abets, counsels or procures the contravention of:

- Part IV may be ordered to pay the pecuniary penalties under s 76;
- Part V may be convicted and fined under s 79.

Under s 84 the conduct and knowledge of a director, servant or agent acting on behalf of a corporation or another person is deemed to be conduct and knowledge of the corporation or the other person for whom they act.

These provisions are wide enough to include many of the usual activities of travel agents in connection with the promotion, distribution and sale of travel suppliers' products.

The *Competition and Consumer Act 2010* (Cth), s 85 provides for a range of defences in the prosecution for an offence under Part V. These are discussed in Chapter 6 (see [6.165]).

---

124 See "Daikyo poses a luxury pose for TPC, Queensland", *Australian Financial Review* (7 August 1990). See also comments by W Pengilley, *The Law of Travel and Tourism* (Blackstone Press, 1990), p 948, n 63.

125 *Australian Consumer Law*, Chapter 5.

The *Australian Consumer Law* establishes a suite of national enforcement powers, penalties and remedies for use by State and Commonwealth consumer law enforcement agencies in administering the *Australian Consumer Law*.[126]

National enforcement powers include:

- court enforceable undertakings;
- substantiation notices; and
- public warnings.

National penalties may be imposed by a court in proceedings by enforcement agencies for non-criminal breaches of the ASCL proven to the civil (balance of probabilities standard). These penalties include:

- pecuniary penalties up to $1.1 million for a corporation and $220,000 for an individual;
- adverse publicity orders; and
- disqualification of managers.

National remedies available to enforcement agencies and private litigants to enforce their rights under the *Australian Consumer Law* include:

- injunctions;
- damages;
- compensation orders;
- orders for non-party consumers; and
- declarations relating to consumer contracts.

Simplified procedures are available through the complaints system and small claims tribunals discussed in Chapter 10. Further detail of these matters is beyond the scope of this book.

Baxter v British Airways Plc & Qantas Airways Ltd

[9.295] Baxter v British Airways Plc & Qantas Airways Ltd (1988) ATPR 40-877

Facts: British Airways and Qantas produce a joint brochure offering around-the-world tickets stating "You can fly almost anywhere" and listing 224 possible destinations on certain conditions. Baxter read the brochure and planned an itinerary with a friend which included Tel Aviv, one of the 224 possible stopovers offered in the brochure. Baxter's friend (who was an experienced traveller) instructed the travel agent, Jetset, to make the booking for them but it could not be made because the reservation computer refused to accept it. Further inquiry revealed that it was not possible to stop over at Tel Aviv without the purchase of an additional sector fare which was done under protest. As it happened, due to a terrorist incident Baxter decided not to visit Tel Aviv. Upon return Baxter and her friend brought an action against the defendants for compensation and for an injunction.

Decision: The Federal Court (Burchett J) found that the brochure was misleading. Although Tel Aviv was only one of 224 possible stopovers and only a small number of people would possibly be misled, that was sufficient for ss 52 and 53(c) of the *Trade Practices Act 1974* (Cth). Following the complaint the defendants had reprinted the brochure and taken steps to withdraw the original one, but original copies could still be obtained from travel agents some months later. The court accepted that to withdraw every single brochure would be a herculean task, and that the defendants had done all that was reasonable to replace the brochure and declined to grant an injunction. While accepting that damages for disappointment could be awarded under s 82 the court found that any

---

126 Attorney-General's Department, Commonwealth of Australia, *The Australian Consumer Law–A Guide to Provisions* (Barton, ACT, April 2010), p 40ff.

Baxter v British Airways Plc & Qantas Airways Ltd cont.

disappointment here would have been only during a brief period of anticipation and was thus negligible. As in the result there was no actual loss or damage suffered, no award of damages could be made. Accordingly the application was dismissed. Under the usual rules Baxter would have been ordered to pay the defendants' costs but here, as the breaches of the Act had been established, the order was that Baxter pay only one half of the defendants' costs.

───── ෩෬ ─────

PACKAGE HOLIDAYS

[9.300] This section considers the ultimate, mass-market product of the tourism and travel industry: the package holiday. A package holiday is a complex service product which is an experiential, intangible, perishable, consumable, composite, international export! These characteristics present special challenges for the legal system. [127]

Definition

[9.305] The law takes a simple view of what constitutes a package holiday. The European Community in Article 2 of the EC Directive on Package Tours [128] defined it thus:

> *Package [Holiday]* means the pre-arranged combination of not fewer than two of the following when sold or offered for sale at an inclusive price...:
>
> (a) transport
>
> (b) accommodation
>
> (c) other tourist services not ancillary to transport or accommodation...

Authors Nelson-Jones and Stewart define them as follows:

> *Package Holidays*...are holidays the elements of which are packaged together to form a whole which is sold at an inclusive price. The creator of the package is the *tour operator* who makes arrangements for transport companies, hotels etc to provide the travel, accommodation, meals and other items which together constitute a particular holiday. In some cases the tour operator, or companies under common ownership and control, will own the airline and hotels which feature in the package. But many substantial operators do not own any airplanes or hotels...and even operators who [do]...will often use some which they do not own. [129]

Damages for Disappointment

[9.310] What is the measure of the package holiday consumer's loss if expectations are not fulfilled?

The definitions above consider package holidays from the perspective of the producer. It is also useful to consider the same product from the point of view of the consumer because ultimately this is where the main problems arise in the regulation of package holidays. Just what is a tourist seeking in the purchase of a package holiday?

---

127 For further reading see TC Atherton, "Package holidays: tourists' trial buy or deal becomes operators' trial by ordeal", (1993) 1(3) *Current Commercial Law* 100-109; TC Atherton, "Package holidays: legal aspects" (1994) 15(3) *Tourism Management* 193-200; Atherton TC, "Tour operators' responsibility for package holidays: common law takes the EC Directive global" (1996) 3 *Travel Law Journal* 90-96; Dickerson, *Travel Law* (Law Journal Seminars Press, NY, 1993).

128 The EC Directive on Package Travel, Package Holidays and Package Tours (90/314/EC) ("the EC Directive").

129 J Nelson-Jones and P Stewart, *Guide to Package Holiday Law and Contracts* (3rd ed, Tolley Publishing, London, 1993); D Grant and S Masona, *Holiday Law* (4th ed, Sweet & Maxwell, London, 2007).

Middleton, a leading tourism marketing analyst, defines a package holiday in this way: "a series of individual products are included in it, from which customers, or tour operators acting as ... [assemblers] ... make their selection to produce the total experience ..." [130] and he warns:

> In practice, the ability to "engineer" intangible service products on paper and to *promise satisfactions* in brochures and in advertising, often exceeds a destination's or a producer's ability to deliver the satisfaction at the time of consumption. Because tourist products *are ideas at the time of purchase*, it is relatively easy to oversell such products... (emphasis added).

[131]

So tourists are seeking an experience, and will be satisfied or dissatisfied depending on whether or not their expectations are fulfilled. The common law has developed a special head of damages known as damages for disappointment to compensate for loss and damage in these circumstances. *Jarvis v Swan Tours* [132] and the other key cases in this development of the common law are discussed in Chapter 2, [2.215]ff. [133]

Who is Responsible?

[9.315] The package holiday product is synthetic: it involves a multitude of components and suppliers in different locations, making it difficult for tour operators to co-ordinate and control a composite product so that the desired holiday experience is delivered. This is compounded by the fact that each component is also usually marketed as a "stand-alone" product so that suppliers are independent of the tour operator. If something goes wrong it may also be difficult for consumers and any other innocent parties involved to identify who is legally liable. The complexity is illustrated in the diagram below.

---

130 VTC Middleton and J Clarke, *Marketing in Travel and Tourism* (3rd ed, Heinemann, Oxford, UK 2001).
131 VTC Middleton and J Clarke, *Marketing in Travel and Tourism* (3rd ed Heinemann, Oxford, UK 2001).
132 *Jarvis v Swan Tours* [1973] 1 All ER 71.
133 See also TC Atherton, "Package holidays: tourists' trial buy or deal becomes operators' trial by ordeal" (1993) 1(3) *Current Commercial Law* 100-109; TC Atherton, "Package holidays: legal aspects" (1994) 15(3) *Tourism Management* 193-200.

Distribution of Tourism and Travel Products

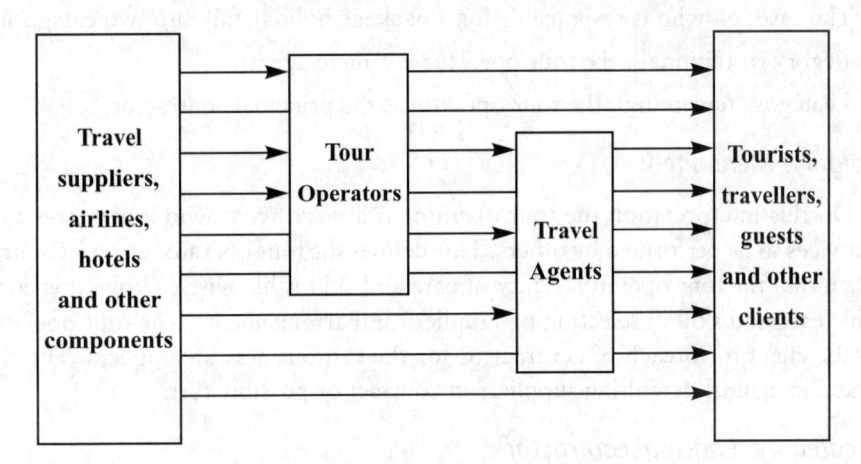

```
Travel
suppliers,          Tour                          Tourists,
airlines,        Operators                        travellers,
hotels                           Travel           guests
and other                        Agents           and other
components                                        clients
```

Note the roles of the travel agent and tour operator. They are the middlemen/women, that is, they are intermediaries. As discussed in Chapter 11, [11.220]ff, there are many intermediaries in the travel transaction, including tour wholesalers, tour operators, ground handlers, tour guides, consolidators and travel agents. All of them may fall within the legal definition of a "travel agent" (see [11.390]). Their names are misleading as they often play many roles and roles change during a transaction.

The tour operator has the key role. This is the party, regardless of name, who organises the package, that is, they select and arrange the components. The tour operator may also be a travel agent.

Agency

[9.320] As discussed in Chapter 11, [11.320], because the product is composite and intangible there is no stock or inventory for intermediaries to own or possess. Thus they all strive to structure their role as *agents* to minimise their legal responsibility. They try to ensure that the parties actually delivering the components (airlines, hotels or other travel suppliers) are the principals.

That leaves them with the limited responsibility of agents as discussed in Chapter 11, [11.165]. This can be summarised as:

- contract: not responsible to third parties (clients) under rivity of contract; and
- tort: not responsible to third parties (clients) for safety of the components provided by principals.

The position is more complicated than this, as discussed in Chapter 11. Travel agents have many roles and often act as advisers to clients, agents of clients and agents of principals. Moreover, often travel agents/tour operators are in fact principals.

Whom does the client rely upon? Clients deal mainly with the travel agent or tour operator. Clients rely on their skill and judgment. They are usually local and easier to sue. The client usually knows little about the airlines, hotels and other service providers. They are often foreign and difficult to sue.

Common law

[9.325] The cases on who is responsible for a package holiday fall into two categories:

- first category (traditional): the tour operator is a mere agent;
- second category (emerging): the tour operator is the principal contractor.

First category: Mere agent

[9.330] On this interpretation the tour operator is a *mere agent* who *undertakes to arrange* for the services to be performed by others. This defines the tour operator's services narrowly. It means then that the tour operator's duty of care and skill is likewise narrow: it is confined to reasonable care and skill in selection of suppliers and arrangements. The tour operator is not liable to the client for breach of contract or for the tortious acts of suppliers. The client will have an action against defaulting suppliers in contract or possibly tort.

Second category: Principal contractor

[9.335] On this interpretation the tour operator is the *principal contractor* who *undertakes to supply* the services whether or not they are performed by others. This defines the tour operator's services widely. It means that the tour operator's duty of care and skill is likewise wide: it involves a primary duty to ensure that the package of services (that is, the whole holiday) is provided with reasonable care and skill. The tour operator is liable to the client for breach of contract or tortious acts of suppliers. The client will have no action against defaulting suppliers in contract but may have one in tort.

The law is in transition from the first category to second category interpretation of the package holiday. The transition is being pushed by:

- consumer protection in developed countries; [134]
- the lack of effective remedies in developing countries (destinations);
- the *Wong Mee Wan case* (see [9.350]); [135] and
- the EC Directive on Package Holidays.

First category cases

[9.340] The traditional view that a tour operator is a mere agent in a package holiday is found in a series of cases from many leading common law countries: England, *Wall v Silver Wings Surface Arrangements Pty Ltd* (1981); [136] Canada, *Craven v Strand Holidays* (1981); [137] USA, *Rockard v Mexicoach* (1982); [138] and again in England in 1993, just before the EC Directive came into force, *Wilson v Best Travel Ltd*. [139] These cases are discussed in Chapter 11, [11.245]ff.

---

134 Compare the manufacturers and importers of goods who, under Part 3-5, Division 1 of the *Australian Consumer Law* are made strictly liable to the ultimate consumers for defects in their products.
135 Atherton, "Tour operators' responsibility for package holidays: common law takes the EC Directive global" (1996) 3 *Travel Law Journal* 90-96.
136 *Wall v Silver Wings Surface Arrangements Pty Ltd* (unreported, Hodgson J, 1981).
137 *Craven v Strand Holidays* (1981) 31 OR (2ED) 548.
138 *Rockard v Mexicoach* (1982) 689 FR 2d 1257.
139 *Wilson v Best Travel Ltd* [1993] 1 All ER 353.

Second category cases

[9.345] The new view that a tour operator is the principal contractor was established by the Privy Council in a 1995 decision on appeal from Hong Kong: *Wong Mee Wan v Kwan Kin Travel*.[140] There is also support for this view in several other cases: Australia, *Athens-Macdonald Travel Services v Kazis* (1970);[141] England, *Jarvis v Swan Tours* (1973);[142] and USA, *Elses v TWA* (1989).[143] These cases are also discussed in Chapter 11, [11.285]ff.

Wong Mee Wan v Kwan Kin Travel Services Ltd

[9.350] *Wong Mee Wan v Kwan Kin Travel Services Ltd* [1995] 4 All ER 745

Facts: HSY took a package tour to a lake in China organised and sold by KK, a tour operator/travel agent based in Hong Kong. The package included a tour guide and transportation. The group was delayed and missed the ferry which had been organised to take the group across the lake. The tour guide improvised and organised a speedboat to take the group across in three trips. On the third trip, due to the negligence of the driver, the speedboat crashed into a junk and HSY was drowned. Representatives of HSY sued the guide company, speedboat operator (both based in China) and the tour operator KK. Default judgment was given against the guide company and speedboat operator for HK $575,050. The plaintiff was unable to enforce the judgment in China and so pursued the Hong Kong-based tour operator KK. The plaintiff succeeded at trial but the decision was reversed by the Hong Kong Court of Appeal and the plaintiff appealed to the Privy Council.

Decision: The Privy Council (Lord Goff of Chieveley, Lord Jauncey of Tullichettle, Lord Slynn of Hadley, Lord Nolan and Lord Hoffman) held that under the contract between HSY and KK, KK undertook to provide the transport services as principal rather than merely to arrange for them to be provided by others. Thus the implied warranty in the contract was that those services, namely the lake crossing, would be supplied with reasonable care and skill whether or not KK chose to engage subcontractors to perform them.[144] In the course of its judgment the Privy Council formulated the distinction between this category of case and the first category of cases mentioned above where the travel agent is a mere agent of the travel supplier.

How is the distinction to be made between the first category and second category? Their lordships held that "in each case it has to be asked as a matter of construction into which category the contract falls", noting that "this may not always be easy". In the construction of the *Wong Mee Wan* contract it was accepted that the brochure contained the contractual terms between the plaintiff and first defendant. In construing the contract the Privy Council identified the following matters, each of which gave some indication that the first defendant tour operator was itself undertaking to supply and not merely to arrange for the services.[145]

- *Comprehensive package*

    The heading of the brochure "Kwan Kin Travel Tours – everything more comprehensively and thoughtfully worked out".

- *"We"*

    Throughout the itinerary included in the brochure the expression was always "we" who would do

---

140 *Wong Mee Wan v Kwan Kin Travel* [1995] 4 All ER 745.
141 *Athens-Macdonald Travel Services v Kazis* [1970] SASR 264.
142 *Jarvis v Swan Tours* [1973] 1 All ER 71.
143 *Elses v TWA*, 22 Aviation Cases 17,806 (NY Supp 1989).
144 *Wong Mee Wan v Kwan Kin Travel Services Ltd* [1995] 4 All ER 745.
145 *Wong Mee Wan v Kwan Kin Travel Services Ltd* [1995] 4 All ER 745 at 753-754. This case has since been followed in *Chan Shui Ying v HYFCO Travel Agency Limited* [2007] HKHC 1060/2005 and *Chea Kam Wing Victor v Kwan Kin Travel Services Ltd* [2007] 1 HKLRD 937.

Wong Mee Wan v Kwan Kin Travel Services Ltd cont.

- the things – board the bus, go for lunch, live in the hotel. This was considered not simply to refer to the tour group but to include the tour operator and to integrate it into each stage of the tour.
- *"Our"*

  Similarly the brochure provided that "our staff" would handle the customs formalities and the "escorts of our company" could request a member to leave the tour. There was nothing to indicate that the tour guide was other than an employee of the tour operator.
- *All-in price*

  The price was an all-in price including transportation, accommodation, meals and sightseeing.
- *Substituted transport*

  Transportation was as specified in the itinerary and the tour operator had the right to change the means of transport. The trial judge had found that this included the scheduled ferry trip across the lake and the substituted speedboat trip.

As a matter of construction the Privy Council found that:

> Taking the contract as a whole their Lordships consider that the first defendant here undertook to provide and not merely arrange for all the services included in the programme, even if some of the activities were to be carried out by others. The first defendant's obligation under the contract that the services would be provided with reasonable skill and care remains even if some of the services were to be rendered by others, and even if tortious liability may exist on the part of those others. It has not been suggested that Miss Ho Shui Yee [the traveller] was in contractual relations with the others. [146]

For a term to be implied into a contract, the Privy Council had previously laid down in *BP Refinery (Westernport) v Hastings Shire Council* [147] that generally, the term must be:

- reasonable and equitable;
- necessary to give business efficacy to the contract;
- so obvious that "it goes without saying";
- capable of clear expression; and
- not contradictory to any express term of the contract.

Through many decisions on similar contracts the courts have settled that special terms are implied into many classes of contracts at common law. Thus in package tour contracts it is well established in all the leading cases that at common law there is an implied term that the services will be supplied with reasonable skill and care. Indeed in many countries such a warranty is now implied by consumer protection statutes. [148] So long as the narrow view was accepted that tour operators merely arrange for services to be performed by others, this warranty remained similarly limited. By recognising the wider scope of the services provided by a tour operator in the second category the Privy Council in the *Wong Mee Wan case* opened the way for this warranty to become comprehensive.

The Privy Council in *Wong Mee Wan case* dismissed the objections raised by the Court of Appeal and in some of the previous cases against implying the comprehensive warranty. It was noted that the Court of Appeal had held that implying such a term would impose an "intolerable burden" on tour operators. It was also noted that Hodgson J in the *Silver Wings case* held that it would be "wholly

---

146 *Wong Mee Wan v Kwan Kin Travel Services Ltd* [1995] 4 All ER 745 at 754.
147 *BP Refinery (Westernport) v Hastings Shire Council* (1978) 52 ALJR 20.
148 For example, *Sale of Goods and Services Act 1982* (UK), s 13 and *Trade Practices Act 1974* (Cth), s 74.

Wong Mee Wan v Kwan Kin Travel Services Ltd cont.

unreasonable to saddle a tour operator" with such a burden.[149] The reasons given by the Privy Council for dismissing these objections and implying the comprehensive warranty were:[150]

- *Indemnity from subcontractors:* The tour operator has the opportunity to protect itself against claims made by travellers in respect of services performed by others "by negotiating suitable contractual terms with those who are to perform the services". Presumably this refers to requiring those who perform the services to indemnify the tour operator.
- *Insurance:* The tour operator may also "provide for insurance cover". Presumably this refers to the tour operator obtaining product liability or public liability cover. It should be noted that merely encouraging the traveller to take out travel insurance may not help the tour operator, given an insurer's usual rights of subrogation.
- *Exemption clause:* The tour operator "may include an appropriate exemption clause in his contract with the traveller." In all jurisdictions there are some difficulties with this approach, bearing in mind the principles of the ticket cases.[151] In some jurisdictions exemption may be unconscionable or contrary to public policy. It may even be prohibited where the warranty is implied by statute: see, for example, the *Australian Consumer Law*, ss 60, 61 and 64.[152]
- *Travellers' other rights and remedies limited:* "It also has to be borne in mind, in considering what is 'tolerable' or reasonable between the parties, that a traveller in the position of Miss Ho Shui Yee could have no influence on the terms negotiated by the tour operator with third parties, and if injured by their lack of care would, if having no right against the package tour operator, be obliged to pursue a claim in a foreign country. The difficulty involved in doing so does not need to be elaborated." In a package holiday contract in the second category the difficulties would be compounded by the absence of privity between the traveller and third parties, leaving the only available claim in tort.
- *EC Directive on Package Holidays 1990*: The Privy Council noted the provisions of the EC Directive which impose comprehensive primary liability on the tour organiser for the whole package holiday, including the components performed by others. The Privy Council acknowledged that "these terms do not of course apply to the present contract but they do throw some light on the contention that an unreasonable burden would be imposed if the contract were held to contain a term that reasonable skill and care were to be used". The Privy Council did not mention similar rules developed over 30 years under the US Charter Tour Operators Regulations and also the International Conventions on the Travel Contract (CCV)[153] which reinforce this point.[154]

―――― ❧☙ ――――

EC Directive on Package Holidays

[9.355] Package holidays usually involve interstate or international transactions which are subject to multiple regulatory systems with different and often conflicting requirements. Consider a package holiday through ten countries.

Pursuant to the *Australian Consumer Law*, s 67,

---

149 However the Privy Council did not address Philps J's view in the *Best Travel* case that "the implication of such a term was neither necessary, nor obvious nor desirable".
150 *Wong Mee Wan v Kwan Kin Travel Services Ltd* [1995] 4 All ER 745 at 754-755.
151 In *Kwan Kin Travel* itself, the trial judge refused a late application by the first defendant to amend to plead the exemption clause in the brochure which he noted "is couched in vague and unsatisfactory terms".
152 Refer to [9.185]ff for discussion these sections.
153 Brussells, 23 April 1970.
154 US Department of Transport, *Public Charter Tour Operators Regulation*, 14 CFR 380.

If:
(a) the proper law of a contract for the supply of goods or services to a consumer would be the law of any part of Australia but for a term of the contract that provides otherwise; or
(b) a contract for the supply of goods or services to a consumer contains a term that purports to substitute, or has the effect of substituting, the following provisions for all or any of the provisions of this Division:
  (i) the provisions of the law of a country other than Australia;
  (ii) the provisions of the law of a State or a Territory;
the provisions of this Division apply in relation to the supply under the contract despite that term.

In other words, Australia asserts jurisdiction whenever its law is the proper law of the contract regardless of any stipulation to the contrary in the contract. The EC Directive on Package Tours has gone much further and imposed an almost strict liability on the tour operator or travel agent involved at the EC end of the transaction. If, as is usual, the tour operator takes an indemnity from the Australian components, in many cases our industry will bear the ultimate liability imposed by these laws. In this way the EC Directive will be extended by private contractual arrangements to become the de facto world standard. It is interesting to note that a similar technique is employed under the *Australian Consumer Law* to deal with a foreign manufacturer of goods imported into Australia.[155]

The following provides a brief summary of the EC Directive and a checklist of issues to be considered in Australia.

Summary and checklist of Australian issues

[9.360] **Article 1: Object: packages sold or offered for sale in European Community**
Consider application outside Europe: conflict of laws and *Australian Consumer Law*, s 67.
Article 2: Definitions
"Package tour" see definition above, [9.305]
"Tour organiser": compare Tour Operator, Travel Agent
Article 3: Information to be provided
3.1 Descriptive material not to be misleading
- compare *Australian Consumer Law*, ss 18, 29

3.2 Brochure to provide adequate information and particulars are binding
- consider common law representations, terms or conditions
- compare general consumer protection law
- could this be covered by setting an information standard under *Australian Consumer Law*, s 134?

Article 4: Services to be provided
4.1 Essential information
- overlaps with Article 3.2 EC Directive

4.2 Essential information: Annex
- overlaps with Articles 3.2 and 4.1 EC Directive. Compare ticket case principles

4.3 Consumer's right to transfer

---

155 Manufacturer's liability under the *Australian Consumer Law*, s 7 (definition); s 56 (supply by description); s 61 (fitness for purpose); s 54 (acceptable quality); s 57 (supply by sample); Part 3-5 (Liability of manufacturers for goods with safety defects).

4.4 Restrictions on price variation
4.5 Restrictions on variation before departure
4.6 Consumer's rights on variation before departure
4.7 Variation after departure
- on Articles 4.4-4.7 consider fairness under *Australian Consumer Law*, ss 23, 24, 25, 62

Article 5: Liability

5.1 Tour organiser and/or retailer are deemed strictly liable for proper performance, with right to pursue suppliers (that is, common law's second category interpretation).
- consider consumer guarantees *Australian Consumer Law*, ss 60, 61, 62
- consider difficulty developing country suppliers have in meeting these standards

5.2 Tour organiser and/or retailer liable for damages unless fault of consumer or third party or force majeure
- similar to transport law common perils defences (see Chapter 12)
- also similar result to *Steiner v Magic Carpet Tours case* (see [13.55])
- Damages limited by international convention and, if not unreasonable, by contract
- compare *Australian Consumer Law*, ss 64, 139A

5.3 No exclusion of liability
- compare *Australian Consumer Law*, ss 64, 139A

5.4 Consumer to give prompt notification of defects

Article 6: Alternative Dispute Resolution

Article 7: Security for money received
- Compare Travel Compensation Fund (see [11.550]ff)

Article 8: Minimum standards

Article 9: Compliance

Exercise

Unpackaging holidays

[9.365] Select a package holiday brochure. Read it and analyse it, looking for answers to the following questions (all references are to sections of the *Australian Consumer Law* and principles discussed in this chapter).

1. Identify the key information about the holiday.
2. Categorise it into representations, terms, conditions on contract law principles from Chapter 4.
3. Is there any material in the brochure which potentially
    - is unconscionable (ss 20, 21)?
    - is misleading or deceptive (s 18)?
    - is false or misleading representation (ss 29, 34)?
    - requires full cash price to be stated (s 48)?
    - offers gifts or prizes (s 32)?
    - is bait advertising (s 35)?
    - requires payment in advance (s 36)?
4. Identify and compare terms which relate to consumer guarantees:

Unpackaging holidays cont.

- due care and skill (s 60);
- fit for the purpose (s 61(1));
- achieve the result (s 61(2));
- time for supply (s 62).

5. Are there any exclusion or limitation clauses?
   - Do these offend ss 64, 139A?
6. What is the role of the tour operator?
   - in substance (from the consumer's point of view)?
   - in form (using the checklist criteria from the *Wong Mee Wan case*):
     – first category interpretation: mere agent.
     – second category interpretation: principal contractor.
7. Does the EC Directive apply?
   - See checklist above.

CHAPTER 10

Dispute resolution

[10.05] METHODS 231
    [10.10]   Dispute Resolution Processes in Perspective 232
        [10.15]   Negotiation 232
            [10.30]   *Case Study: Fair Work Act 2009* 233
        [10.35]   Mediation 234
            [10.55]   *Case Study: Travel Agents as Mediators* 236
        [10.60]   Arbitration 236
            [10.75]   *Case Study: Travel Agent Commissioner* 238
[10.80] GOING TO COURT 238
    [10.80]   Jurisdiction of the Courts 238
        [10.85]   Defining jurisdiction 239
        [10.90]   Practical aspects of jurisdiction 240
    [10.95]   The Trial 240
        [10.100]   Some preliminary issues 240
        [10.105]   The pleadings 240
        [10.110]   Venue and method of trial 241
        [10.115]   Proceedings at trial 241
        [10.120]   Costs 242
[10.125] CONSUMER CLAIMS COURTS (DIY) 242
    [10.130]   Small Claims Jurisdiction 242
        [10.135]   Definition of small claim 243
        [10.140]   Parties 243
        [10.145]   Notice of claims 244
        [10.150]   Hearings 244
        [10.155]   Orders and appeals 245

METHODS

[10.05] The traditional legal method of resolving disputes has been through litigation in the courts. The parties present their case in an adversarial manner (that is, using opposing arguments) before the court and a decision is made by a third party called the judge, sometimes sitting with a jury. Once an action is initiated by one party (the plaintiff), the other party (the defendant(s)) is compulsorily caught on the litigation treadmill which only stops turning when the matter is resolved or withdrawn. The process is imposed on the parties. In other words, they have no control over the outcome or judgment of the court. The proceedings are public. See [10.75]ff for further discussion on public proceedings.

    The process is expensive, time consuming, fairly inflexible and results in disappointment for at least one of the parties because of the win/lose nature of litigation. Sometimes neither party is satisfied with the judgment. To address these apparent weaknesses in the existing system, a number of processes of alternative and additional non-litigious dispute resolution (ADR) have evolved to complement the traditional legal method of dispute resolution.

Figure 1: Comparing the different processes for settling disputes

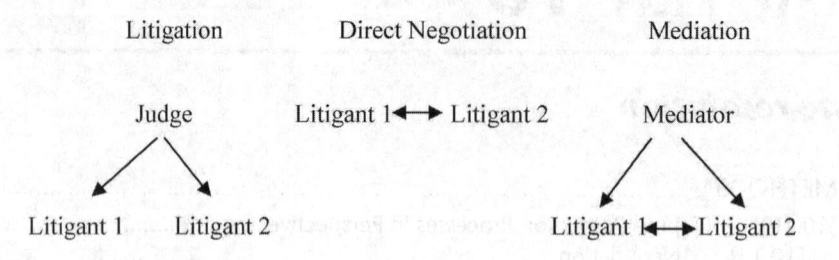

```
    Litigation          Direct Negotiation          Mediation

       Judge           Litigant 1 ←→ Litigant 2      Mediator
       ↙   ↘                                         ↙     ↘
Litigant 1  Litigant 2                    Litigant 1 ←→ Litigant 2
```

Dispute Resolution Processes in Perspective

[10.10] The ADR processes are many and varied. Their common theme is the empowering nature of the process which enables the parties themselves to determine the outcome or solution to the dispute rather than having the decision of a third party imposed upon them. The prospect of a win/win solution is a powerful incentive for parties to try ADR first. This section will concentrate on three of the better-known methods. They are:

- negotiation;
- mediation; and
- arbitration.

Negotiation

[10.15] In this process, the parties confer directly with each other without the intervention of a third party to reach an agreement which satisfies their mutual concerns or interests. To conduct a negotiation which is fair and balanced, each party should:

- be well informed on the topic;
- have allowed plenty of time for the discussions to take place; and
- have adequate resources at their disposal.

When one party has not properly sourced all the information or is labouring under some serious time constraint in reaching agreement, they are likely to get a deal which is less favourable than if they had done more homework or had taken more time to consider their options. Similarly, negotiations with a party whose available resources in terms of political, psychological or monetary power far outstrip the other party will probably result in an unfair agreement.

"Principled" negotiation

[10.20] Negotiation is often a game of tactics. Some negotiators adopt a reasonable and co-operative approach to negotiation and some use a more dominant and competitive style. Both may work. The underlying philosophy of "principled" negotiation [1] is that the negotiators should:

- separate the people from the problem;

---

1 R Fisher, WL Ury and B Patton, *Getting to Yes: Negotiating Agreements Without Giving in* (Houghton Mifflin, Boston, 1991).

- focus on interests not positions;
- invent options for mutual gain;
- insist on objective criteria. [2]

Parties should never enter into negotiations without assessing first what their best and worst alternatives to a negotiated agreement will be. [3]

Key features

[10.25] Negotiation is the most common ADR process. The process is voluntary and the parties have the greatest flexibility over a range of issues such as:

- venue;
- confidentiality;
- legal representation;
- content; and,
- solutions.

Case Study

[10.30] Fair Work Act 2009 (Cth)

In her second reading speech of the *Fair Work Bill 2008* (Cth), the Hon Julia Gillard [4] emphasised the importance of negotiations between employer and employee groups being conducted within a framework based on principles of fairness and flexibility in the terms and conditions of employment, including "*a comprehensive safety net of minimum wages and employment conditions that cannot be stripped away*". Later, she went on to say that with respect to the discussions between the parties:

> the bill sets out good faith bargaining requirements that a bargaining representative for a proposed enterprise agreement must meet, including: attending, and participating in, meetings at reasonable times; disclosing relevant information; responding to proposals; giving genuine consideration to the proposals of others and giving reasons for responses to those proposals; and refraining from capricious or unfair conduct that undermines freedom of association or collective bargaining.
>
> The bill specifies that the good faith bargaining requirements do not require a bargaining representative to make concessions during bargaining or to reach agreement on the terms that are to be included in the agreement. Parties are entitled to take a tough stance in negotiations. In the very unusual case where a negotiating party completely ignores good faith bargaining orders, the other party may apply to Fair Work Australia to intervene and to make a workplace determination. This will ensure there is no advantage to be gained by flouting the law.

The parameters of the negotiation between employer and employee groups are therefore quite restricted. This is in marked contrast with the more direct and less complicated negotiations which were previously encouraged under the *Workplace Relations Act 1996* (Cth). This legislation was

---

2   Fisher's four-point plan for "principled negotiation".
3   Referred to as BATNAs (best alternative to a negotiated agreement) and WATNAs (worst alternative to a negotiated agreement).
4   The then Deputy Prime Minister; Minister for Employment and Workplace Relations; Minister for Education; Minister for Social Inclusion.

Case Study cont.

"designed to empower employers and employees to make decisions about relationships at work, including over wages and conditions, based on their appreciation of their own interests".[5]

The tourism, travel and hospitality industry will be heavily influenced by this new federal legislation with its legislated National Employment Standards and modern award[6] system. It addresses the perceived power imbalance in the bargaining position of employers and employers and incorporates an award system which provides a safety net of minimum wages and conditions. For further discussion on the scope of the *Fair Work* legislation, see [8.120]ff.

─────── ෪ ───────

Mediation

[10.35] Mediation is assisted or facilitated negotiation. The parties meet face to face in the presence of a neutral third party, the mediator, who tries to help them isolate issues, identify common interests and generate options for settling the dispute. The role of the mediator is to control the process. In order to do this, he or she must:

- set certain ground rules of behaviour; and
- aim to create an environment in which the parties can communicate constructively towards finding a solution of the matters in dispute.

The content of the mediation is controlled by the disputants. The parties may discuss whatever matters they think fit in an informal atmosphere unhindered by the normal rules of evidence or other court procedures. The discussions are confidential and may not be used as the basis of evidence in later court proceedings. Entry into the process is generally voluntary[7] and if the parties fail to reach agreement, the mediator is not empowered to impose a decision upon them. When agreement is reached in mediation, the terms of agreement are usually reduced to writing although they may not be immediately binding.[8]

Because of the obvious benefits of mediating disputes rather than litigating them (time, money, control over process and possible outcomes and emotional cost, to name but a few) many contracts[9] now contain standard clauses referring the parties to mediation in the event of a dispute. In such cases, the parties will agree to mediate on certain terms, for example:

- who should be appointed mediator;
- scope and conduct of mediation;
- confidentiality and privilege;

---

5   The second reading speech of the then Minister for Industrial Relations, Mr Peter Reith introducing the *Workplace Relations Amendment (Transition to Forward with Fairness) Bill 2008*, 23 May 1996.
6   Hospitality Industry (General) Award 2010.
7   Exceptions include mandatory mediation. For example, the rules of the Federal Court and the Supreme Court of each State and Territory give the courts power to order parties to participate in mediation with or without their consent at any time. See *Federal Court of Australia Act 1976* (Cth), s 53A(1) and (1A); *Uniform Civil Procedure Rules 1999* (Qld), Division 3; *Uniform Civil Procedure Rules 2005* (NSW), Part 20; *Supreme Court Rules 2000* (Tas), Part 20; *Supreme Court (General Civil Procedure) Rules 1996* (Vic), Rule 50.07; *Supreme Court Act 1935* (SA), s 65; *Supreme Court Act 1935* (WA), s 69. See also *Family Law Act 1975* (Cth), s 63B, and *Family Law Rules 2004* (Cth), Rule 1.05.
8   Often parties who are unrepresented in mediation may want to have their lawyers review the terms of agreement before ratifying it.
9   For example, franchise agreements, building and construction contracts, commercial contracts, finance and lease agreements, joint ventures and so on.

- authority to settle;
- termination of mediation;
- enforcement of any settlement reached; and
- mediator's fee, amongst others. [10]

Conciliation

[10.40] The term "conciliation" is sometimes used in describing a process which looks much like mediation. Perhaps the main difference is that the neutral third party, the conciliator, is usually an expert with experience in the subject area of the dispute. Using her or his technical expertise to assist in identifying the issues, the conciliator may guide the parties to a resolution of the dispute actively canvassing settlement options. Just like mediation, the process is private and may be voluntary or a compulsory first step in litigation.

Role of the Ombudsman – investigator, conciliator or mediator?

[10.45] The Ombudsman [11] is a trusted intermediary whose role is to investigate complaints arising out of disputes between organisations (either government or industry based) and individuals and to make appropriate recommendations. More and more, however, the role is developing into one of dispute resolution, engaging the skills of conciliation and mediation. Certainly, the Ombudsman has more flexibility in dispute resolution than the traditional court adversarial processes allow. This view was endorsed by Burt CJ in *R v Dixon Ex parte Prince* [12] when he said:

> In the discharge of those functions and subject to the Rules of Parliament he is master of his own procedure.

Legislative interventions support the Ombudsman's role entrenching additional and alternative resolution mechanisms in disputes between, for example, employers and employees, [13] or travel insurers and consumers. [14] The introduction of the *Fair Work Act 2009* (Cth) established a Fair Work Ombudsman with wide ranging responsibilities including the promotion of harmonious and co-operative workplace relations and compliance by providing education, assistance and advice to employees, employers and organisations. [15]

Similarly, the travel insurance industry provides a free Ombudsman service [16] to consumers who may be complaining about a travel insurance claim, for example. The Ombudsman' case managers may gather all relevant information from the travel industry insurer and attempt

---

10   For example, the Institute of Arbitrators and Mediators suggest the inclusion of the following clause in business contracts: "Any dispute or difference whatsoever arising out of or in connection with this contract shall be submitted to mediation in accordance with, and subject to, The Institute of Arbitrators & Mediators Australia Mediation and Conciliation Rules." The mediation rules appear on the website at http://www.iama.org.au/pdf/MediationRules2007.pdf.
11   Meaning "agent" in Swedish.
12   *R v Dixon Ex parte Prince* (1979) WAR 11.
13   See generally Chapter 8.
14   See generally Chapters 7 and 11.
15   See *Fair Work Act 2009* (Cth), Part 5-2 and s 682.
16   It is called the Financial Ombudsman Service and is approved by the Australian Securities and Investments Commission.

resolution of the dispute between the travel insurer and the customer. If that process fails, the matter will be referred to an independent decision maker who must give reasons in writing for their decision.[17]

Advantages of mediation

[10.50] The main advantages of mediation are:
- informality of the process;
- private nature of the proceedings;
- the emphasis on the parties' needs and interests;
- generation of options for win/win solutions;
- prohibition on solutions imposed by the mediator;
- focus on maintaining the parties' future business relationship; and
- the parties' freedom to abandon the process if no agreement is reached.[18]

If there are numerous issues to resolve and/or many parties involved, mediation may not be the most appropriate forum for settlement of the dispute. Similarly, if emotions run high between the disputants, it may be impossible for the mediator to create a suitable environment in which the parties can communicate positively.

Case Study

[10.55] Travel Agents as Mediators

Travel agents may be the agents of either/or both of the consumer and travel supplier. See [11.220]ff for a discussion of the different roles of a travel agent. They are ideally placed to mediate disputes which arise between consumers and travel suppliers because they understand the needs and interests of both parties and both parties know and, presumably, have confidence in them.

They could draw on their knowledge of the transaction and technical expertise within the travel industry to suggest possible options for resolution of the dispute although, of course, they could not impose a solution of their own. Finally, travel agents who must deal with disgruntled travellers from time to time know only too well the importance of maintaining a good public relations image for the continuing health of their business relationship with consumers.[19]

Arbitration

[10.60] Arbitration was the first of the ADR processes to be formally recognised. It is the resolution of a civil or commercial dispute by an independent third party, called an arbitrator, instead of by a court or judge. Depending on the degree of formality of proceedings,

---

17   See the Financial Ombudsman Service homepage at http://www.fos.org.au/centric/home_page.jsp.
18   Unlike litigation, where they remain trapped on the treadmill until the dispute is resolved or the matter is withdrawn.
19   Query whether there is a conflict of interest in travel agents acting in this role.

arbitration may resemble a normal adversarial court hearing. The difference is that entry into the process is voluntary. The parties agree in writing on a recognised procedure for the settlement of disputes before they arise. [20]

One notable similarity between arbitration and litigation is that after the arbitrator has listened to submissions, he or she then makes a determination or award in the same way that a judge would hand down judgment. This award is final and binding on the parties pursuant to their arbitration agreement. This is a significant difference from the other forms of ADR examined here as they do not impose solutions on the parties. The arbitration hearing is often as costly, and as complicated and time consuming as ordinary litigation because of the complexity of some disputes.

Mediation/arbitration

[10.65] This chapter examines the operation of consumer claims' courts in [10.125]ff. These courts have jurisdiction in small claims and are generally presided over by referees whose function it is in the first instance to encourage the disputants to reach a negotiated settlement. If the parties cannot agree, arbitration takes place and a final and binding decision is imposed on them by the referee. The process moves from mediation to arbitration. Procedures are informal and technical rules of evidence do not apply. [21]

Key features

[10.70] Arbitration is the least flexible of the ADR processes and the parties have no control over the outcome. Nevertheless, some of the advantages of arbitration over litigation include:

- the choice of an arbitrator with the relevant technical skills and experience;
- the likelihood of a more commercial remedy;
- the determination of the dispute made without delay; and
- the private and confidential nature of proceedings.

Unlike a court hearing, which is a public service, the parties to arbitration must pay not only for their own legal representatives but also for the use of the venue, the arbitrator's time and the wages of any other support staff he or she may need, thus adding to the costs.

---

20 All States and Territories have adopted uniform Commercial Arbitration legislation which sets out recognised procedures for settling domestic disputes and allows parties some flexibility in the drafting of individual arbitration agreements. International disputes are governed by the *International Arbitration Act 1974* (Cth) which is based on the UNCITRAL *Model Law on International Commercial Arbitration*. There is much more scope under the domestic legislation for parties to apply to the courts for judicial supervision of an arbitration or for an arbitral award to be set aside than under the Model law. Noting this inconsistency in the existing system, the State and Territory Attorneys-General have agreed to introduce uniform Commercial Arbitration Acts based on the UNCITRAL Model Law. See, for example, *Commercial Arbitration Act 2010* (NSW).

21 Arbitration procedures apply under Part VIII of the *Family Law Act 1975* (Cth).

Case Study

[10.75] Travel Agency Commissioner

The Travel Agents' Handbook (IATA) [22] outlines the procedure for the conduct of review by the Travel Agency Commissioner [23] in disputes arising (for example) between applicants seeking approval as agents and the relevant accreditation body, the Agency Administrator. It specifies that:

> The Commissioner shall conduct each such review in an adversarial proceeding and decide, on the basis of all probative evidence presented during the proceeding, whether or not the Agent has failed to comply with or is in breach of the Agency Programme provisions alleged by the Agency Administrator....

In the past, decisions of the Travel Agency Commissioner were final and binding and constituted precedents for the resolution of similar future disputes. However, the situation has changed and now:

> Any party to a dispute settled in accordance with Resolution 820e shall have the right to submit the Travel Agency Commissioner's decision to *de novo* review by arbitration in accordance with this Section. [24]

This constitutes a limit on the Commissioner's jurisdiction to hear and decide cases and represents a paradigm shift in their authority. For some time, IATA has worked with the International Chamber of Commerce (ICC) to develop a special set of arbitration rules for resolving passenger sales agency disputes [25] so that:

> All disputes arising out of or in connection with a decision rendered by a Travel Agency Commissioner (a "Decision") shall be finally settled under the Rules of. Arbitration of the International Chamber of Commerce by one or more arbitrators appointed in accordance with said Rules and judgment upon the award may be entered in any Court having jurisdiction thereof. [26]

This process is more formal and more closely resembles a normal court hearing.

GOING TO COURT

Jurisdiction of the Courts

[10.80] There is a close link between where a court sits within its court hierarchy (either State or federal) and

(a) the types of matters with which it can deal; and

(b) the avenues of appeal which may lie from the court's decision to a higher court by an unhappy litigant.

Refer to [2.100]ff for a description of the various courts' powers in this respect. This section explains what the term "jurisdiction" means and identifies the factors which affect the courts' jurisdiction within the Australian court system.

---

22 Effective 1 June 2009 and available on the IATA website at http://www.iata.org.
23 Passenger Agency Conference Manual Resolution 820e, Reviews by the Travel Agency Commissioner, para 1.5 effective 1 June 2009.
24 Passenger Sales Agency Rules: Resolution 814, para 12.1.1.
25 Passenger Sales Agency Rules are found in Resolution 814 and 824.
26 Resolution 814, para 12.2.1.

Defining jurisdiction

[10.85] Jurisdiction is the extent of the power or authority of a court to hear and determine cases. There are a number of factors which influence a court's authority to decide matters and these include:

- the type of law involved in the case, for example, civil or criminal;
- the amount of money in dispute;
- the extent of penalty or fine prescribed for an offence;
- the method prescribed for hearing a criminal charge, for example, a summary hearing or jury trial;
- the place of residence of the parties;
- the geographical location of the subject of dispute;
- the nature of the matters, for example State or federal; and
- the avenues of appeal to and from the court.

Some of these categories overlap. For example, even if a court, such as the Magistrates' Court, has criminal jurisdiction it is still restricted to hearing simple offences or indictable offences of a minor nature because of the limits placed on the court's power to impose an appropriate sentence for the more serious crimes. Additionally, there are geographical limits placed on these courts so that only matters arising within their immediate geographical locality fall within their jurisdiction.

Similarly, intermediate courts such as District or County Courts have authority to hear civil matters but only if the amount in dispute is limited to a certain value.[27] This also applies to Magistrates' Courts exercising civil jurisdiction.[28] Again, there are geographical limits placed on these courts. For example, matters such as the defendant's residence within the geographical jurisdiction of the court or the fact that the dispute arose there are equally important factors.

Some (but not all) State courts have also been invested with federal jurisdiction. For example, State and Territory Supreme Courts have been invested with federal jurisdiction through cross-vesting legislation which is specifically designed to ensure that proceedings in State or federal courts do not fail for want of jurisdiction.[29]

27　For example, *District Court Act 1967* (Qld), s 68: more than $50,000 and less than$250,000; *District Court Act 1973* (NSW), s 4: $750,000; *Courts Legislation (Jurisdiction) Act 2006* (Vic), s 3: courts in Victoria to have unlimited civil jurisdiction; *District Court Act 1991* (SA), s 8 South Australia unlimited jurisdiction; *District Court of Western Australia Act 1969* (WA), s 6: $750,000 and unlimited jurisdiction in claims for damages for personal injuries.

28　This varies from jurisdiction to jurisdiction. For example, in Tasmania claims up to $50,000 and $5,000 in minor civil claims; in Western Australia claims up to $75,000; in South Australia claims involving personal injuries and property $80,000 and for other civil claims, $440,000. Small claims up to $4,000 are dealt with more informally; in Queensland claims up to $50,000 and small debts up to $7,500; in Victoria claims up to $100,000, in New South Wales claims up to $60,000 and unlimited for review of contracts. Small Claims Division $10,000; in Northern Territory $100,000 with claims less than $10,000 dealt with as small claims; in the Australian Capital Territory claims up to $50,000.

29　*Jurisdiction of Courts (Cross Vesting) Act 1987* (Cth); all States and Territories have introduced complementary legislation, for example, *Jurisdiction of Courts (Cross Vesting) Act 1987* (Qld). The validity of the legislation was challenged in the High Court case of *Re Wakim: ex parte Mcnally* (1999) 73 ALJR 839 which declared the legislation unconstitutional. Since then, however, the Commonwealth and States in the spirit of co-operative federalism made an agreement in 2001 on national uniform legislation effectively settling the matter.

Practical aspects of jurisdiction

[10.90] Jurisdiction is the link between court hierarchy and the doctrine of precedent (see [2.105]). This is because:

1. A party should commence their action at first instance in the court which has jurisdiction to resolve the dispute. To choose the wrong court to start civil proceedings may prove costly if the matter has to be transferred to a more appropriate court.
2. In terms of the doctrine of precedent it is important to know which other court decisions are binding on the court which is resolving the dispute presently before it.
3. In relation to the court system, it is necessary to know what avenues of appeal lie from the court in the event of an unfavourable decision.

The original and appellate division within the court hierarchy is one of the more important practical aspects of jurisdiction. A court presided over by a single judge (and perhaps a jury) exercises original jurisdiction when a dispute is first heard before it. If there is an appeal from that court to a higher court that higher court exercises appellate jurisdiction. Generally, more than one judge (usually three to five judges) will hear the appeal.

Some courts, like the Magistrates' Court, enjoy original but no appellate jurisdiction, while the intermediate courts such as the District and County Courts and the Supreme Courts exercise both original and some appellate jurisdiction. Other courts near the top of the hierarchy mostly exercise appellate jurisdiction, for example. the Courts of Appeal.

The Trial

[10.95] The trial process varies according to whether the matter is governed by the criminal or civil jurisdiction. The criminal trial procedure was outlined in [6.170]ff. This section will concentrate on the procedure in a civil trial.

Some preliminary issues

[10.100] There are a number of threshold questions which a potential litigant must answer before proceeding to trial. These include questions such as whether:

- the matter could be settled by some dispute resolution process apart from litigation;
- the court chosen to commence proceedings has appropriate jurisdiction;
- the action is still within time;[30] and
- all the parties who should be joined in the action have been properly identified.

Once these matters have been resolved, the plaintiff, as he or she is referred to, may commence proceedings by issuing a summons or writ and statement of claim against the other party or parties (the defendant).

The pleadings

[10.105] Once the initiating process has been served properly on the defendant, the case is largely conducted from that point until the day of trial by the exchange between the parties of a series of documents called pleadings. Their function is to pinpoint accurately the matters

---

30   This a reference to the fact that in general most claims, apart from personal injuries claims, become statute barred after six years. In the case of personal injuries, for those over the age of 18 years, most claims (with a few exceptions) are statute barred after three years. In the case of children, the three year period begins on the date of their eighteenth birthday.

actually in dispute between the parties and to define for the judge the issues on which both parties desire a judicial decision. The most important pleadings in all courts are the statement of claim and the defence.[31]

Venue and method of trial

[10.110] The venue for the trial may be influenced by such factors as:

- residence of witnesses;
- improbability of a fair trial; and
- the balance of convenience, generally.

In appropriate cases, the place of trial may be changed to accommodate the expense, delay or prejudice associated with holding the trial at the first venue.

Actions are sometimes tried before a judge and jury and sometimes before a judge sitting alone. The judge always determines questions of law. If there is a jury, then the jury rather than the judge determines questions of fact and, in a criminal trial, they determine whether the accused is guilty or not guilty. Subject to certain statutory restrictions,[32] either party is entitled to have an action tried with a jury,[33] and may indicate their desire to have the matter tried in this manner by endorsing the pleadings appropriately. The various State Juries Acts stipulate the number of jurors for a civil trial.[34]

It should be remembered that the standard of proof in a civil action is different from that in a criminal trial. The onus is on the plaintiff in civil proceedings to prove their claim on the "balance of probabilities", which is a lower standard of proof than that in criminal trials, where the prosecution bears the onus of proving the guilt of the accused "beyond reasonable doubt."

Proceedings at trial

[10.115] If the trial is with a jury, then the jury must be sworn in before the trial begins. After the jury is empanelled, the usual procedure is that the plaintiff's barrister makes an opening address summarising the issues and the case that he or she intends to make and outlining the evidence that will be called. Then, counsel for the plaintiff presents that evidence by calling witnesses who are examined in chief by the plaintiff's barrister and who may be subject to cross-examination by counsel for the defendant.

After the plaintiff's barrister has finished calling witnesses, it is the defendant's turn to begin her or his case. There will be another opening address, this time for the defendant, and then witnesses will be called in support of the defendant's version of events. At the close of the

---

31 M Aronson and J Hunter, *Litigation: Evidence and Procedure* (6th ed, Butterworths Sydney 1998), chapter 4 "Pleadings and Particulars".

32 See, for example, *Civil Liability Act 2002* (Qld), s 73 which states:
       A proceeding in a court based on a claim for personal injury damages must be decided by the court sitting without a jury.
    See also *Juries Act 1927* (SA), s 5 which bans jury trials in civil matters.

33 See, for example, *Defamation Act 2005* (NSW), s 21 which states: "Unless the court orders otherwise, a plaintiff or defendant in defamation proceedings may elect for the proceedings to be tried by jury."

34 The number of jurors varies from jurisdiction to jurisdiction. For example, *Juries Act 1957* (WA), s 19 – 6 persons; *Jury Act 1977* (NSW), s 20 and *Jury Act 1995* (Qld), s 32 – 4 persons; but see *Juries Act 2000* (Vic), s 22 "If a civil trial is to be tried by a jury, the jury is to comprise 6 jurors or, if the court makes an order in accordance with section 23, not more than 8 jurors."

evidence, the barrister for the defendant will sum up her or his case in a closing address. Finally, the plaintiff's barrister will do the same.

After counsel's addresses, if there is a jury, the judge will sum up for the jury, who will then retire to consider their verdict. After the verdict of the jury is announced, or if there is no jury, the judge will either deliver his or her judgment or reserve judgment until some later date.

Costs

[10.120] As a general proposition in litigation, "costs are an indemnity to the successful party and they, in general, include fees to counsel or solicitors, fees of court, necessary disbursements, and witnesses' expenses. The only limit to their amount is that they must be necessary and reasonable." [35]

Once judgment has been given, the question of costs may be argued. In most cases, costs follow the event, which means that they are awarded as a matter of course to the successful party. However, the judge has a discretion in this regard, particularly if the successful party has unduly prolonged proceedings or has failed to consider reasonable offers.

CONSUMER CLAIMS COURTS (DIY)

[10.125] Because of the high cost of litigation – legal expense, delay and emotional involvement – each of the States and Territories has introduced a procedure for the determination of small claims which moves more quickly and has costs efficiencies. [36] The special tribunals and other bodies which have been established [37] (referred to here as "consumer claims courts") provide a forum for consumers to bring their small claims against traders whom they believe have not performed work satisfactorily.

Small Claims Jurisdiction

[10.130] It has already been noted that in some States separate tribunals known as "small claims" courts, or "consumer claims" tribunals have been specifically established and in others special procedures have been devised within the existing court system. [38] These courts or tribunals are usually presided over by persons called referees, who may or may not be legally qualified [39] and who are sometimes magistrates. [40]

---

35   *R v Police Magistrate at Hughenden and Reid; Ex parte John Cumming* [1915] St R Qd 147 at 155 156 per Chubb J.

36   *Queensland Civil and Administrative Tribunal Act 2009* (Qld); *Victorian Civil and Administrative Tribunal Act 1998* (Vic); *Magistrates Court (Civil Proceedings) Act 2004* (WA); *ACT Civil and Administrative Tribunal Act 2008* (ACT); *Small Claims Act* (NT); *Consumer, Trader and Tenancy Tribunal Act 2001* (NSW); *Magistrates Court (Civil Division) Act 1992* (Tas); *Magistrates Court Act 1991* (SA); *Magistrates Court (Civil Division) Act 1992* (Tas).

37   For example, New South Wales, Victoria, Queensland and the Australian Capital Territory have established special tribunals. In Western Australia, Tasmania, South Australia, and the Northern Territory the small or minor claims jurisdiction is vested in the existing court system.

38   For example, New South Wales, Victoria, Queensland and the Australian Capital Territory have established special tribunals. In Western Australia, Tasmania, South Australia, and the Northern Territory the small or minor claims jurisdiction is vested in the existing court system.

39   For example, in the Northern Territory, Victoria, Western Australia, Tasmania and South Australia the referees must be legally qualified. In Queensland, the Australian Capital Territory and New South Wales, legal qualifications are not necessary, although if the claim appears complex or requires special expertise then the referees, adjudicators or decision makers may be assisted by an assessor or tribunal member with the necessary qualifications and experience.

Definition of small claim

[10.135] A small claim is generally defined as:

(1) a claim for:
- payment of money; or
- relief from payment of money;[41] or
- performance of work to rectify a defect in goods supplied or services provided; or
- return of goods; or
- a combination of any of the foregoing;

(2) a sum not exceeding the prescribed amount;[42]

(3) one that arises from a contract for the supply of goods or the provision of services; and

(4) one that is made between persons, who, in relation to those goods or services, are a consumer on the one hand and a trader on the other.

Some States have extended the jurisdiction of these consumer claims' courts to include the hearing of such matters as:

- applications under dividing fences legislation;[43]
- bond disputes in the case of residential tenancies;[44]
- claims for relief in neighbourhood disputes;[45]
- determination of certain building claims;[46] and
- compensation claims for property damage arising from motor vehicle accidents.[47]

Parties

[10.140] In those States with separate consumer claims courts[48], claims are generally made between persons called "consumers" and "traders." A consumer may be defined as either an individual[49] or may include an incorporated[50] person depending on the jurisdiction:

(a) who buys or hires goods other than–

---

40 In Western Australia, Tasmania, South Australia, and the Northern Territory magistrates preside over small claims.

41 In Victoria, the definition of "small claim" in s 2(1) of the *Small Claims Tribunals Act 1973* (Vic) excludes claims for relief from payment obligations.

42 The prescribed amount varies from jurisdiction to jurisdiction. For example, in Victoria there is no limit except that for the Magistrates Court itself, in Queensland it is $7500, in Tasmania it is $5,000, in South Australia it is $6,000. In the Australian Capital Territory, New South Wales, Northern Territory and Western Australia it is $10,000.

43 For example, disputes arising under the *Dividing Fences Act 1953* (Qld). See *Queensland Civil and Administrative Tribunal Act 2009* (Qld), s 12.

44 For example, disputes arising under the *Residential Tenancies and Rooming Accommodation Act 2008* (Qld).

45 For example, civil disputes arising out of trespass to land or nuisance and applications for common boundaries determinations. See *ACT Civil and Administrative Tribunal Act 2008* (ACT), s 15.

46 In New South Wales, the Consumer, Trader and Tenancy Tribunal is a specialist dispute resolution forum to hear such disputes.

47 For example, Western Australia deals with minor debt or damages up to $10,000. See *Magistrates Court (Civil Proceedings) Act 2004* (WA).

48 New South Wales, Queensland, Victoria and Australian Capital Territory.

49 *Queensland Civil and Administrative Tribunal Act 2009* (Qld), Schedule 3 Definition.

50 *Consumer Claims Act 1998* (NSW), s 3.

(i) for resale or letting on hire; or

(ii) in a trade or business carried on by the individual; or

(iii) as a member of a business partnership; or

(b) for whom services are supplied for fee or reward other than–

(i) in a trade or business carried on by the individual; or

(ii) as a member of a business partnership.... [51]

A trader, on the other hand, is:

a person who in trade or commerce–

(i) carries on a business of supplying goods or providing services; or

(ii) regularly holds himself, herself or itself out as ready to supply goods or to provide services of a similar nature... [52]

In all other States and Territories, any person may institute proceedings provided the matter is within the nature of a small claim as defined by the governing legislation of that jurisdiction.

Notice of claims

[10.145] Notice of claim is made by:

- completing the prescribed form;
- paying a lodgment fee; and
- filing the claim in the Small or Consumer Claims' registry or at the office of any clerk of a Magistrates' or Local Court.

The registrar or clerk, as the case may be, then gives notice of the claim and its particulars to the respondent (that is, the other party to the dispute), at the same time arranging a time and place for initial proceedings to take place. There is provision within the various Acts for claimants to withdraw their claims before they are determined with leave of the court. [53]

Hearings

[10.150] The primary function of the consumer claims courts is to achieve a negotiated settlement of the matters in dispute between the parties. [54] If this is not possible, then the court will make an order which is binding upon the parties and enforceable at law. In general, the proceedings are conducted in public [55] and the parties may be entitled to legal representation where, for example:

- all parties to the action agree; or

---

51   *Queensland Civil and Administrative Tribunal Act 2009* (Qld), Schedule 3 Definition.
52   *Queensland Civil and Administrative Tribunal Act 2009* (Qld), Schedule 3 Definition.
53   For example *Victorian Civil and Administrative Tribunal Act 1998* (Vic), s 74; *Queensland Civil and Administrative Tribunal Act 2009* (Qld), s 46.
54   For example, the court inquiry may be preceded by a preliminary conference in which the tribunal attempts by a process of conciliation to bring the parties to a settlement. See *ACT Civil and Administrative Tribunal Act 2008* (ACT), s 33; *Consumer, Trader and Tenancy Tribunal Act 2001* (NSW), s 55; *Small Claims Act* (NT), s 9.
55   *Queensland Civil and Administrative Tribunal Act 2009* (Qld), s 50; *Consumer, Trader and Tenancy Tribunal Act 2001* (NSW), s 33; *Victorian Civil and Administrative Tribunal Act 1998* (Vic), s 101; *Small Claims Act* (NT), s 18; *ACT Civil and Administrative Tribunal Act 2008* (ACT), s 38; *Magistrates Court (Civil Division) Act 1992* (Tas), s 31AA where hearings are public unless otherwise directed. However, see for an exception *Magistrates Court (Civil Proceedings) Act 2004* (WA), s 29.

- the court believes that the party would be unfairly disadvantaged if not legally represented.

These consumer claims courts are not bound by the rules of evidence so the hearings are more informal than normal court proceedings. Although they have control over their own procedures, however, the courts must:

- conform with the rules of natural justice; and
- act according to equity, good conscience and the substantial merits of the case.

The general rule is that no award of costs will be made in favour of one or other of the parties, in keeping with the policy that these are "low cost" proceedings, but exceptions exist. [56]

Orders and appeals

[10.155] In the exercise of its jurisdiction, a consumer claims court may make an order: [57]

- requiring the payment of money by a party to the proceeding;
- declaring that a person does not owe money to a person specified in the order;
- requiring a party (other than the claimant) to perform work to rectify a defect in goods or services to which the claim relates;
- requiring a party (other than the claimant) to replace any goods to which the small claim relates;
- dismissing the small claim.

These orders and settlements are final and binding. [58] In general, there is no right of appeal or review from the decisions of the court except in the case of:

(1) lack of jurisdiction; or

(2) denial of natural justice.

Denial of natural justice may occur if, for example:

- the referee or magistrate unreasonably refuses to grant an adjournment so that a party can properly prepare their case; or
- the party is not given sufficient notice in time for them to attend the hearing; or
- the respondent is not properly informed of the nature of the case they have to meet.

The overriding principle seems to be that proceedings must be conducted fairly and according to the substantial merits of the case. [59]

In summary, there are many good reasons to bring consumer claims to these courts, including:

---

56 For example, *Magistrates Court (Civil Division) Act 1992* (Tas), s 31AF – where the claim is frivolous or vexatious; or *Magistrates Court Act 1991* (SA), s 38(5) – where all parties have legal representation or the court is of the opinion that there were special circumstances justifying the award of costs.

57 For example, see *Magistrates Court (Civil Division) Act 1992* (Tas), Parts 3 and 5, Division 4; *Victorian Civil and Administrative Tribunals Act 1998* (Vic), Part 3; *Queensland Civil and Administrative Tribunal Act 2009* (Qld), Part 7; *Magistrates Court (Civil Proceedings) Act 2004* (WA), Part 4; *ACT Civil and Administrative Tribunal Act 2008* (ACT), Parts 4 and 6; *Consumer Claims Act 1998* (NSW), s 8; *Magistrates Court Act 1991* (SA), Part V, Division II.

58 For example, see *Queensland Civil and Administrative Tribunal Act 2009* (Qld), s 126. However, see also *Magistrates Court Act 1991* (SA), Part V, Division II, s 38(6), for examples of where a dissatisfied applicant may seek a review of the decision by a District Court judge.

59 For example, see *Queensland Civil and Administrative Tribunal Act 2009* (Qld), s 28; *Magistrates Court (Civil Proceedings) Act 2004* (WA), s 32; *ACT Civil and Administrative Tribunal Act 2008* (ACT) s 7.

(1) the minimal legal expense of personal as opposed to legal representation;
(2) the fact that costs will not be awarded against either party;
(3) the informality of procedures;
(4) the assurance of natural justice;
(5) the confidentiality of the hearing if deemed appropriate; and
(6) the finality of proceedings.

Exercise

The ball's in your court

You are a fanatical tennis fan and had planned to attend the second week of the upcoming Australian Open Tennis Tournament in Melbourne. Through your local travel agent you booked a package holiday with tour operator, *Grand Slam Tours Pty Ltd* with a registered office in your State. You paid an amount of $5,000, being the full cost of the package holiday covering travel, accommodation expenses and entry fees for each day of the final week of the tournament. You have taken out travel insurance with *Suretravel Pty Ltd* as recommended by your travel agent.

A week before the due date of your departure, you developed appendicitis and were hospitalised for three days. Your doctor prescribed complete rest for two weeks following the appendectomy.

Through your travel agent, you contact *Grand Slam Tours Pty Ltd* seeking a full refund of the $5,000. For its part, *Grand Slam Tours Pty Ltd* is relying on a clause in its tour brochure which states that "unless at least 14 days written notice of cancellation is received all deposit and other monies paid are forfeited for breach of contract" and is refusing to refund your money even though you have told your travel agent that you would like to re-book the holiday next year through *Grand Slam Tours Pty Ltd*. The travel agent suggests you should notify *Suretravel Pty Ltd* of your potential claim.

Suretravel Pty Ltd advises you in due course that it has assessed and rejected your claim. It is relying on the clause in the insurance contract which states in part "... The start date of this policy commences on the day of the holiday departure date." As your illness became apparent a week before the holiday start date, the travel insurer insists that you are not covered by its policy for the loss caused by this unexpected cancellation of your package holiday.

Consider your options.

1. (a) Obtain and complete the claim form the consumer affairs/fair trading department in your State.
   (b) Consider the likely outcomes of a small claim in your State against *Grand Slam Tours Pty Ltd*.
   (c) Consider the likely outcomes of a small claim in your State against *Suretravel Pty Ltd*.
2. (a) What alternative dispute resolution processes might work?
   (b) Reflect on the advantages and disadvantages of the different processes.
   (c) Which process might work best for you?

CHAPTER 11

Travel agency and distribution

[11.05]	AGENCY LAW		249
	[11.10]	Definition of Agency	249
		[11.15] Distinguish other relationships	250
	[11.50]	Creation of Agency	252
		[11.55] Agreement	252
		[11.60] Operation of law	253
		[11.65] Ratification	253
		[11.70] Estoppel	253
	[11.75]	Types of Agency	254
		[11.80] Special agent	254
		[11.85] General agent	254
		[11.90] Universal agent	254
	[11.95]	Rights and Duties of Agents	254
		[11.100] Duty to follow instructions	254
		[11.105] Duty to exercise due care and skill	255
		[11.110] Duty to act in person	255
		[11.115] Duty of loyalty	255
		[11.145] Right to remuneration	256
		[11.150] Right to indemnity and reimbursement	256
		[11.155] Right to a lien	256
	[11.160]	Liability of Agents	257
		[11.160] Liability to principal	257
		[11.165] Liability to third parties	257
		[11.190] Criminal liability of an agent	258
	[11.195]	Liability of Principal	258
		[11.200] Contract	258
		[11.205] Tort	258
		[11.210] Criminal liability	258
	[11.215]	Termination of Agency	259
[11.220]	TRAVEL AGENTS		259
	[11.220]	Travel Agents and Agency Law	259
		[11.225] Agent of the client	259
		[11.230] *Athens-Macdonald Travel Service Pty Ltd v Kazis*	260
		[11.235] *Kemp v Intasun Holidays Ltd*	260
		[11.240] *Re ILG Travel Ltd (in administration)*	261
		[11.245] Agent of the travel supplier	261
		[11.250] *Craven v Strand Holidays*	261
		[11.255] *Wall v Silver Wing Surface Arrangements Ltd (t/a Enterprise Holidays)*	262
		[11.260] *Wilson v Best Travel Ltd*	262
		[11.265] Broker	262
		[11.270] *Holt v Fynbout Pty Ltd NSW*	263
		[11.275] *Elsis v Transworld Airlines*	263
		[11.280] Principal/buyer for resale	264
		[11.285] *Odgers v McMiken*	264
		[11.290] *Anglo-Continental Holidays Ltd v Typaldos Lines (London) Ltd*	265

	[11.295]	*Thomas Cook Pty Ltd v Aviation and Tourism Services Pty Ltd*	265
	[11.300]	*Jarvis v Swan Tours Ltd*	265
	[11.305]	*Wong Mee Wan v Kwan Kin Travel Services Ltd*	266
[11.310]	Legal Analysis of the Travel Transaction		266
	[11.315]	Authority from suppliers	266
	[11.320]	Product information	266
	[11.325]	Advice and client instructions	267
	[11.330]	Reservations and documentation	267
	[11.335]	After sales service	267
[11.340]	Travel Agents and Child Sex Tourism		268

[11.345] SELF-REGULATION 268

[11.345]	Organisations		268
	[11.345]	International	268
	[11.370]	National	270
		[11.375] *Australian Federation of Travel Agents Ltd & Trade Practices Commission*	271
		[11.380] *AFTA Code of Ethics*	272

[11.385] TRAVEL AGENCY LICENSING 273

[11.385]	Uniform Scheme		273
[11.390]	Definitions and Exemptions		273
	[11.395]	Definition of carries on business as a travel agent	274
	[11.400]	Refinements and exemptions	275
[11.405]	Licensing Procedure		277
	[11.410]	Application	278
	[11.415]	Investigation	278
	[11.420]	Decision	278
		[11.425] *Mundro Pty Ltd v Commissioner for Consumer Affairs*	280
	[11.430]	Conditions	280
		[11.435] *Re Travel Compensation Fund, Dunn and Others*	281
	[11.445]	Appeal	281
		[11.450] *Frugtniet v Secretary to the Department of Justice*	282
[11.455]	Conduct of Business		282
	[11.460]	Name and notice	282
	[11.465]	Management and supervision	283
	[11.470]	Disqualified persons	284
		[11.475] *Roka v Collins (Court of Criminal Appeal (SA)*	284
	[11.480]	Accounting	285
[11.485]	Disciplinary Procedure		285
	[11.490]	Disciplinary action	285
		[11.500] *Australia and New Zealand Banking Group Ltd v Travel Agents Registration Board*	286
		[11.515] *Young v Travel Agents Registration Board*	287
		[11.525] *Re Number Two Janminga Pty Ltd and Travel Agents Licensing Authority*	288
	[11.535]	Unjust conduct and undertakings	289

[11.550] TRAVEL COMPENSATION FUND 290

[11.555]	Administration	291
[11.560]	Participation	292
	[11.565] Application	293
	[11.575] Investigation	294
	[11.580] Decision	294
	[11.585] Conditions	295
	[11.590] Appeal	296

	[11.595]	Re Gateway Management & Travel Compensation Fund	296
[11.600] CLAIMS			297
	[11.600]	Claims entitlement	297
	[11.605]	Claims procedure	299
		[11.610] Travel Compensation Fund v Digital Equipment Corporation	300
	[11.615]	Subrogation	300
		[11.620] Re Travel Compensation Fund, Dunn and Others	301
	[11.625]	Northern Territory Travel Industry Compensation Scheme	303
	[11.630]	Finance and Accounting	303
	[11.635]	Financial criteria	303
		[11.640] Travel World Service Pty Ltd v Rose Grisbrook Pty Ltd	304
	[11.645]	Trust moneys	305
		[11.650] Royal Brunei Airlines Sdn Bhd v Philip Tan Kok Ming	305
		[11.655] Stephens Travel Service (R&M Apptd) v Qantas Airways	307
	[11.660]	Practice of travel suppliers	308
[11.680] IMPACT OF THE WEB ON TRAVEL DISTRIBUTION			310
	[11.685]	Travel information and advice	310
	[11.690]	Travel advisories	311
	[11.695]	E-Commerce and Travel Portals	312
	[11.700]	Travel and E-commerce	312
	[11.705]	What's in a name?	313
		[11.710] ACCC v Trading Post and Google Inc	313
		[11.715] Mantra Group Pty Ltd v Tailly Pty Ltd	314

AGENCY LAW

[11.05] Every business and undertaking uses services provided by others, whether they are agents, employees, independent contractors or franchisees. Tourism, travel and hospitality are intangible, composite products often sold at a distance from the place they are delivered and consumed. As a result there is a heavy reliance upon others in the sale, distribution and delivery of these products.

Consider, for example, the many transactions involved in a typical package holiday:

- the client purchases a tour through a travel agent;
- the tour is organised by a tour operator;
- the transport, accommodation and other services in the tour are operated by others;
- the hotel is managed by an international operator;
- the restaurant is operated under an international franchise;
- the risks are underwritten by insurers;
- all these operators engage agents, employees and contractors.

Most of these transactions are governed by the law of agency.

Definition of Agency

[11.10] At common law an *agent* is a person who is authorised to represent or act on behalf of a second person, called a *principal*, to transact some business or affair between the principal and a *third person*.

The essential features of agency are service, representation and the power to affect the legal relationship between the principal and third parties. The extent of this power is determined by the scope of the actual, implied or apparent authority which the agent has. This authority is entrusted to the agent subject to a fiduciary duty [1] to exercise it in good faith and in the interests of the principal.

Distinguish other relationships

[11.15] While the transactions listed above all usually involve some elements of agency, they may also involve many other legal relationships. The party transacting the business may also be an employee, independent contractor, trustee, buyer for resale, creditor or franchisee. The mere fact that a party is called an agent (for example a "travel agent") does not mean they are acting as an agent in every transaction. Relationships may change from one transaction to another. To identify the elements of agency in a transaction it is useful to examine the distinguishing features from each of the other legal relationships.

Employee

[11.20] An employee works for an employer under a *contract of service* subject to a high degree of control by the employer over not only *what* is to be done but also *how* it is to be done. The distinction between an employee and an agent is not clear cut and the arrangements often overlap. To the extent that an employee is given authority to affect contractual relations between the employer and third persons, the employee may be regarded as an agent of the employer. For example, a resort manager may be an employee but will also have substantial authority to act as agent in dealings for the resort (see further Chapter 8).

Independent contractor

[11.25] An independent contractor works for an employer or principal under a *contract for services* which, like employment, defines *what* is to be done. However the contractor, unlike an employee, is usually subject to less control over *how* the work is to be done. Again the distinctions are not always clear cut. For example, a diving instructor is usually an employee, but the arrangement may be structured so that the instructor becomes an independent contractor. [2] Unlike an agent, an independent contractor generally has no authority to affect contractual relations between the employer and third persons. Again, exceptions are found where the work for which the contractor is engaged includes making such contracts. Thus, for example, a hotel management company may be engaged as agent or independent contractor of the hotel owner. [3] The choices are important because the distinctions have fundamental legal consequences. Independent contracting avoids many of the rights and duties of employment.

---

1   This is sometimes called a duty of loyalty.
2   See J Wilks and TC Atherton, "The lifestyle factor: Employment practices in the Queensland recreational diving industry" (1995) *Australian Journal of Hospitality Management* 2(1).
3   For a discussion of the different legal structures available see TC Atherton, *Negotiating International Hotel Management Agreements: The Last Resort* (Cahiers du Tourisme, Series C No 183, Janvier 1994, UniversitŽ de Droit, D'Economie et des Sciences, Centre des Hautes Etudes Touristiques, Aix-en-Provence, France), p 32.

Also, because there is less control, an employer or principal has less responsibility to third parties for the actions of an independent contractor.[4]

Trustee

[11.30] A trustee holds property for the use and benefit of another party called a beneficiary. Like an agent, a trustee owes fiduciary duties to act in good faith for the benefit of the beneficiary and is strictly accountable for moneys, including any secret profits made. However, unlike an agent, a trustee is legal owner of the trust property rather than a mere representative of the principal. That means that the dealings of a trustee with third parties bind the trust property rather than the beneficiary. If trust property is dealt with dishonestly the beneficiary may be able to trace and recover it and the trustee may be prosecuted for misappropriation. Trust arrangements are often made in conjunction with agency. For example, when travel agents receive moneys from clients on behalf of principals, those moneys are often trust property and should be deposited in a separate account (see [11.645]ff [5] Trusts are governed by the law of equity (see [2.60]) and a Trustee Act [6] in each State.

Buyer for resale

[11.35] Often an agent acts as agent for the buyer or seller of property or services. Sometimes an agent acts as agent for both the buyer and the seller, in which case the agent is a broker (see below, [11.265]). These relationships are to be distinguished from transactions where the party actually buys the property or services from the seller and on-sells them to the ultimate buyer. Though often called an agent, the buyer for resale is actually acting as principal. The buyer for resale is usually seeking to make as much profit as it can between its purchase price and its on-sale price, conduct which would usually be improper for an agent. An agent would usually be remunerated by commission. In the sale of travel, the travel agent may act in any of these ways provided the relationship is properly disclosed. Consolidators usually act as buyers for resale rather than common law agents.[7] ([11.610]). Tour operators are increasingly being regarded as buyers for resale, that is, principals (see [9.345] and the *Wong Mee Wan* casenote at [9.350]).

Creditor

[11.40] This is closely related to the buyer for resale relationship described above. The only obligation which a buyer for resale owes to the seller of the property or services is as creditor. The obligation of a buyer for resale to pay the seller for the property or services is independent of receipt of the moneys from the ultimate buyer. This means that the moneys received for the resale of the property or services belong to the buyer for resale beneficially and are not trust

---

[4] However they will remain responsible for "non-delegable" tasks. The High Court in *Burnie Port Authority v General Jones Pty Ltd* (1994) 179 CLR 520 has also now suggested that a land owner or occupier will remain responsible for dangerous substances or activities delegated to negligent independent contractors.

[5] While there is some industry resistance to making strict trust accounting compulsory for travel agents, it is highly desirable and is rewarded under the Travel Compensation Fund points system discussed later. It is interesting to contrast the position of real estate agents, who are required to have a formal trust account for client moneys.

[6] The Trustee Acts are: *Trustee Act 1925* (ACT); *Trustee Act 1925* (NSW); *Trustee Act* (NT); *Trustee Act 1936* (SA); *Trusts Act 1973* (Qld); *Trustee Act 1936* (SA); *Trustee Act 1898* (Tas); *Trustee Act 1958* (Vic); *Trustee Act 1962* (WA).

[7] See *Travel Compensation Fund v Digital Equipment Corp (Australia) Pty Ltd* (Sup Ct of NSW, Cole J, 18 February 1991, BC 9102336).

moneys. However it also means that the buyer for resale is obliged to pay the seller whether or not the buyer for resale is paid. In either case the seller's remedy is to sue on its own contract with the buyer for resale to recover the debt. See *Travel Compensation Fund v Digital Equipment Corporation (Australia) Pty Ltd*[8] casenote at [11.610]. These obligations may be varied by the terms of appointment of the travel agent (see [11.355], [11.680] and [11.685]).

Franchisee

[11.45] Franchises are more complex arrangements, often involving several of the other types of relationship. Under a typical franchise arrangement the franchisor owns the intellectual property (for example, a trademark, business name, operating system etc) and grants a right of use to the franchisees. A franchisee owns and operates the business (for example, the premises, plant, stock and labour) and pays fees to the franchisor. Fees usually comprise an initial franchise fee and continuing management fees calculated on turnover or profit. Franchises are used extensively in travel agency, hotel management and the fast food industry. They are now regulated by the general law and a mandatory Franchising Code of Conduct[9] and an international convention.[10]

Creation of Agency

[11.50] Agency can be created in any of the following ways:
- by agreement;
- by operation of law;
- by ratification; and
- by estoppel.

Agreement

[11.55] Agency is usually created by agreement between the principal and the agent and the agreement may be express or implied. However it need not be a contract, so no consideration is necessary to create a valid agency. An express agreement may be oral or in writing. Writing is often desirable to minimise misunderstandings and to simplify the resolution of disputes which do occur. Where arrangements are otherwise oral it is often a prudent practice to write to the other party confirming your understanding of what has been agreed. An agent also has the implied authority to do things in addition to those expressly authorised (but not inconsistent with them) which are necessary to give business efficacy to the agency. The mere appointment of a person to an office, for example a manager or director of a company, may give them implied authority to do the things usually required of a person in that office unless they are expressly restricted.[11] At common law there are no formalities for a valid agreement but these

---

8   *Travel Compensation Fund v Digital Equipment Corp (Australia) Pty Ltd* (Sup Ct of NSW, Cole J, 18 February 1991, BC 9102336).
9   The Franchising Code is prescribed under the *Competition and Consumer Act 2010* (Cth) and administered and enforced by the Australian Competition and Consumer Commission (ACCC).
10 UNIDROIT, *Draft convention on Franchising* (1996).
11 Contrast this with estoppel (discussed at [11.70]), where although they may be expressly restricted, a third party not knowing this may rely on the apparent authority of the office holder.

may be required under legislation for particular transactions. So a power of attorney must be signed and sealed, a real estate agency agreement must be in writing [12] and so must an insurance agency agreement [13] (see [7.110]).

Operation of law

[11.60] In certain special circumstances the law will deem an agency to exist even without agreement. These circumstances include cases where someone having custody of property (for example a carrier or bailee) is deemed to be authorised to take the steps necessary to save the property in an emergency). [14]

Ratification

[11.65] Agency by ratification occurs where the potential agent without authority purports to make a contract with a third party on behalf of the potential principal who subsequently acquiesces and adopts the contract. In effect the principal gives retrospective agreement to the agency. This may occur where in the first communication with a principal a travel agent presents a booking request on behalf of a client. Ratification may be express or implied by, for example, the principal commencing performance or taking benefits under the contract. Once ratified, the contract is binding on both the principal and the third party. If the principal does not ratify the contract the agent may be liable to the third party for breach of warranty of authority or personally on the contract if the principal was not disclosed (see [11.170]).

Estoppel

[11.70] Agency by estoppel is also known as apparent authority or ostensible authority to contrast it with the actual (express or implied) authority conferred in an agency created in the other ways discussed above. With agency by estoppel the potential principal, by words or conduct, gives the impression to a third party that it has given authority to the potential agent when in fact it has not. If the third party relies on the false impression, the principal is held bound by (that is, estopped from denying authority for) the actions of the agent. [15] Thus it is to some extent the converse of agency by ratification. It is also related to the implied authority of an office holder discussed above in [11.55], except that with estoppel there are express restrictions on the potential agent's authority unknown to the third party. [16] A travel agent who receives brochures and selling materials from a travel supplier has implied and apparent authority to make booking requests to the supplier on behalf of clients. However it is arguable that express authority is required to unilaterally make bookings binding on the supplier or to

---

12   See, for example, *Property Agents and Motor Dealers Act 2000* (Qld), Div 2, s 114.
13   See *Financial Services Reform Act 2001* (Cth) which replaced the former *Insurance (Agents and Brokers) Contracts Act 1984* (Cth).
14   The carrier cases concern cargo and ships' masters and railways: *Great Northern Railway v Swaffield* (1874) LR 9 Ex 132. There appears to be no reason in principle why it should not extend to luggage and even passengers.
15   In *Bolzan v Appolonio* (unreported, NSW Sup Ct, Giles J, 25 July 1988, BC 8801704) a tour leader was held to have apparent authority to obtain a refund of money for a tour operator from an Italian hotel supplier.
16   Because the restrictions are express the contrary authority cannot be implied but must be established by estoppel.

receive deposits or other moneys on behalf of suppliers.[17] Consider for example the limits on the authority of a travel agent without IATA accreditation.

Types of Agency

[11.75] The most important underlying question in any agency is the scope of the agent's authority. Some authors identify three types of agents based on the scope of their authority:

- special agent;
- general agent; and
- universal agent.

Special agent

[11.80] A special agent is authorised to deal with only one particular contract and has no apparent authority from the principal beyond that. In travel the closest analogy is when a travel agent is acting on behalf of a client to arrange a particular holiday.

General agent

[11.85] A general agent is authorised to deal with contracts for a certain type of trade or business and has the apparent authority usually involved in that trade or business. In travel, a general sales agent is the clearest example.[18] However, every travel agent has some general apparent authority to bind suppliers as principals, but the scope of that authority varies greatly depending on the circumstances. Compare for example a travel agent's relationship with a preferred supplier to that with an ordinary supplier. Compare also travel agents with and without IATA accreditation.

Universal agent

[11.90] A universal agent has the widest scope of authority and may do virtually anything the principal could do. It is usually created by power of attorney.

Rights and Duties of Agents

[11.95] Agents have various rights and duties at common law as well as fiduciary duties in equity (the specific fiduciary duties all flow from a general duty of loyalty). In many instances the principal's rights and duties are the converse of the agent's. These rights and duties may be varied by the usages and customs of the particular trade or business and by the expressed and implied terms of the agreement between the parties.

Duty to follow instructions

[11.100] An agent must act within authority and must observe lawful and reasonable instructions from the principal.

---

17   This has been confirmed for a real estate agent: *Egan v Ross* (1928) 29 SR (NSW) 328 at 388; *Peterson v Moloney* (1951) 84 CLR 91.
18   See RIR Abeyratne, "A New Look at the General Sales Agency Agreement in the Airline Industry" (1986) XI(1) *Air Law* 2-13.

Duty to exercise due care and skill

[11.105] An agent must exercise due care and skill in the exercise of the agency and the performance of duties. [19]

Duty to act in person

[11.110] At common law an agent must generally act in person and not delegate authority. However this is varied according to the usages and customs of the particular trade or business. Thus it is well established in the travel trade that the product is distributed through many layers of intermediaries, including general sales agents, consolidators, tour operators and retail travel agents. Accordingly, unless there were express instructions to the contrary, there could usually be no complaint if arrangements are made through other agents and intermediaries. However this may not relieve the travel agent from responsibility if something goes wrong. [20]

Duty of loyalty

[11.115] The remaining duties are all fiduciary duties which flow in equity [21] from the general duty of loyalty which an agent owes a principal. The scope of the duty depends on the terms of the agreement and the nature of the business, but usually the following specific duties apply.

Duty to act in the interests of the principal

[11.120] This duty means that an agent must not put its own interests above those of the principal and must avoid conflicts of interest. If a conflict of interest nevertheless arises, the agent must make full disclosure to the principal. This would generally preclude a travel agent from acting as general sales agent for competing carriers or competing hotels unless the principals agreed. It does not preclude a travel agent from acting as an ordinary retail agent for numerous competing carriers, hotels and other travel suppliers as this is the usual practice well known to all involved in the industry. However, preferred supplier and override commission arrangements may lead to potential conflicts which are best resolved by prior disclosure.

Duty to make full disclosure

[11.125] An agent must make full disclosure to the principal of all relevant facts relating to the transaction. Not only is this a separate duty in itself, it is also the best means an agent has of avoiding breach of any of the other duties. [22]

---

19 See for example *Elsis v Transworld Airlines* (1990) 167 AD 2d 285; 562 NYS 2d 433; 1990 NY App Div LEXIS 142422.
20 See for example *Odgers v McMiken* [1974] 8 SASR 119 at 126.
21 Fiduciary duties are also owed in many other relationships, including by trustees to beneficiaries, solicitors to clients and among partners: *Hospital Products Ltd v United States Surgical Corporation* (1984-1985) 156 CLR 41 at 68 per Gibbs CJ.
22 *Prebble v Reeves* [1910] VLR 88.

Duty to maintain confidentiality

[11.130] An agent must not disclose confidential information about the principal or the transaction.[23] If there is any doubt about whether particular information should be kept confidential prior permission of the principal should be sought.[24]

Duty not to make a secret profit

[11.135] As an agent is acting in the transaction on behalf of the principal, it follows that the agent's agreed remuneration and rewards must be disclosed and that all the profits belong to the principal. Potential breaches of duty where a travel agent acts as preferred agent or as broker are best avoided by prior disclosure.

Duty to keep accounts

[11.140] An agent must account to the principal for all money and property received on behalf of the principal. This involves keeping the principal's money and property separate from its own, keeping accurate accounts of all transactions and being prepared to produce them to the principal at any reasonable time. Upon request the agent must hand over to the principal the money, documents and papers relating to the transaction. Travel agents also have other more specific accounting obligations (see further [11.630]ff).

Right to remuneration

[11.145] At common law an agent is generally not entitled to remuneration unless that has been agreed. If remuneration is agreed but the amount is not, an agent is entitled to a reasonable remuneration. In the travel trade the agreed remuneration is frequently a percentage commission on the price of the travel sold by the agent. However, even if it has not been expressly agreed, the rates are usually fixed by the custom of the trade. Disagreements can arise when travel is cancelled by the principal or the client.[25]

Right to indemnity and reimbursement

[11.150] At common law an agent is entitled to be indemnified against losses and reimbursed for expenses incurred in reasonable performance of its duties, provided the agent has not breached any of its duties. However, by custom in the travel trade, a travel agent generally has no such right of indemnity and reimbursement from a supplier unless expressly agreed. The custom is changing between travel agents and clients with the growing practice of travel agents (by prior agreement) charging clients fees and expenses for advising and making travel arrangements on their behalf.

Right to a lien

[11.155] Under the right of lien an agent is entitled to retain possession of the principal's property and documents until paid the remuneration and expenses lawfully due. In travel it is

---

23 See, for example, *Guthrun Pty Ltd v Harvey World Travel Franchise Holdings Pty Ltd* (unreported, NSW Sup Ct, Hodgson J, 4 September 1989, BC 8901757) where a Harvey World travel agent's franchise was terminated for breach of confidentiality.

24 *Athens-Macdonald Travel Service Pty Ltd v Kazis* [1970] SASR 264. Although it is not entirely clear from the report it appears that A was acting as agent of the clients rather than as principal.

25 See, for example, *Holt v Fynbout Pty Ltd* (unreported, NSW Sup Ct, Cohen J, 28 May 1987, BC 8701344) where it was held that the agent had earned the commission.

usually the travel agent's responsibility to collect the deposit and balance of the price from the client on behalf of the principal and so this right would rarely arise in that situation. It can arise where the travel agent acts as agent of the client and there are outstanding fees or expenses and also where a travel agent has paid the supplier on behalf of the client. In those circumstances the travel agent would be entitled to retain the travel documents, such as tickets or vouchers, until paid by the client.[26] However, a travel agent must not retain a client's passport as this would be an offence under the *Australian Passports Act 2005* (Cth).[27]

Liability of Agents

Liability to principal

[11.160] The liability of an agent to the principal arises from breaches of the duties described above. The principal may claim or bring an action against the agent for:

- damages for breach of duty to follow instructions, use due care and skill or to act personally;
- an account and payment of any moneys received by the agent in breach of the (fiduciary) duty of loyalty; and
- in defence of any of the agent's claims for commission, indemnity or lien.

Liability to third parties

[11.165] The liability of an agent to third parties must be considered in contract, tort and for advice and representations.

Contract

[11.170] The general rule is that an agent who discloses the agency to a contracting third party is not personally liable on that contract. The agent is protected by privity of contract (see [4.395]). There are exceptions to this rule where:

- the agent agrees to be liable personally;
- the principal is non-existent;
- the agent personally signs a bill of exchange;
- trade, custom or usage would make the agent liable; or
- the agent exceeds actual authority.

If the agent does not disclose the existence of a principal and the contract is not ratified by the principal then the agent will be held personally liable on the contract with the third party.[28]

An agent may also be liable to a third party for breach of warranty of authority. The principle as stated by Wills J is:[29]

> I am of opinion that a person who induces another to contract with him as the agent of a third party by an unqualified assertion of his being authorized to act as such an agent, is answerable to the person who so contracts for any damages which he may sustain by reason of the assertion of authority being untrue.

---

26 The related right of an agent in the sale of goods to *stoppage in transitu* appears to have little application to an industry such as travel, which deals in services.
27 *Australian Passports Act 2005* (Cth), s 32; Penalty: Imprisonment for 10 years or 1,000 penalty units, or both.
28 See the argument abandoned by counsel in *Odgers v McMiken* [1974] 8 SASR 119 at 121.
29 *Collen v Wright* (1857) 120 ER 241.

Tort

[11.175] If an agent commits a tortious act (negligence or deceit) the victim can sue the agent and, if the agent was acting within actual or apparent authority, the victim can also sue the principal vicariously.[30]

Advice

[11.180] Although an agent may be acting for a principal in the sale of property or services to a third party, the agent may nevertheless provide advice to the third party. This often occurs where an agent, such as a travel agent, has or purports to have special skill or knowledge. In travel agency it is also possible for the travel agent to be acting as agent of the client for the purposes of giving this advice, whether for a fee or gratuitously. Recall that agency is created by agreement and consideration is not necessary. In all these circumstances the agent may be liable to the third party for negligent misstatement (see Chapter 5, [5.90]ff).

Consumer protection law

[11.185] An agent who makes a misrepresentation or provides misleading information to a third party will also be liable under the *Australian Consumer Law* (see Chapter 9, [9.90]ff).

Criminal liability of an agent

[11.190] An agent who commits a criminal offence such as theft or fraud will of course be personally liable under the general law (see Chapter 6).

An agent who takes secret commissions may also be prosecuted for a serious criminal offence under Commonwealth[31] and State legislation.[32]

Liability of Principal

[11.195] The liability of a principal is considered in contract, tort and under criminal law.

Contract

[11.200] A principal is liable to a third party on a contract entered on its behalf by an agent within actual or apparent authority. A principal who ratifies a contract entered by an agent without authority is also bound. Thus, apart from the exceptions outlined above ([11.170]), the only parties to the contract are the principal and the third party who each may sue and be sued upon it.

Tort

[11.205] A principal is vicariously liable to third parties for torts committed by an agent acting within the scope of its authority.

Criminal liability

[11.210] The criminal liability of a principal for the acts of an agent depends on the type of offence. If it is a strict liability offence, the principal may be liable for an agent's acts even

---

30   See *Deatons v Flew* (1949) 79 CLR 370 where an employer was held not vicariously liable for a barmaid who threw a glass of beer at an offensive customer because it was outside her authority.
31   *Criminal Code Amendment (Theft, Bribery and related Offences) Act 2000* (Cth).
32   See, for example, *Criminal Code 1899* (Qld), ss 442A – 442M.

though not aware of them. If the offence is not a strict liability offence, then the principal would need to be knowingly involved in the crime before he or she became liable.

Termination of Agency

[11.215] An agency may be terminated by:
- an act of the parties (that is, by mutual agreement or unilaterally by either principal or agent);
- death, unsoundness of mind, or bankruptcy of the principal or the agent;
- supervening illegality or impossibility of performance;
- expiration of the time for which the agent was engaged;
- destruction of the subject matter; and
- completion of the agency assignment.

TRAVEL AGENTS

Travel Agents and Agency Law

"A travel agent may perform any or all of the following functions: retailing, wholesaling or consolidating. Retailing is the direct sale of tickets to consumers on behalf of the airlines. A wholesaler organises and promotes a travel package (travel plus land content including accommodation), selling it to other agents. Consolidation is the practice whereby an agent performs a ticketing function for those agents who do not have particular airline credit facilities or do not have IATA accreditation, with the division of commission negotiated between the parties." [33]

[11.220] At common law there is no clear ruling on how a travel agent fits into the legal relationships described above. As discussed in [11.320], the travel product is intangible and there is no stock to own or deliver. This means that a variety of legal arrangements can be used to distribute it to the customers or clients. Agency is certainly the most common legal relationship but in practice a travel agent may be the agent of the client, an agent of the travel supplier, an agent of both (a broker) or an agent of neither but in fact a principal (buyer for resale). The different types of relationship are described in the following text and models and are illustrated by the case studies.

Agent of the client

[11.225] In this relationship the travel agent undertakes on behalf of the client to make arrangements to obtain travel services from travel suppliers. If the arrangements are defective the travel agent will be responsible to the client in agency law and, if the agency agreement is a contract, also in contract law. This relationship often arises as a corollary of the situation in [11.245] below so that the travel agent acts as agent for both parties and is, in effect, a broker (see [11.265] below). In other cases the travel services may be defined as merely making arrangements so that the travel agent supplies those services as principal, as in [11.280] below. [34]

---

33   Trade Practices Commission, *Determination on IATA Agency Accreditation* (1984), p 5.
34   *Odgers v McMiken* [1974] 8 SASR 119 at 122.

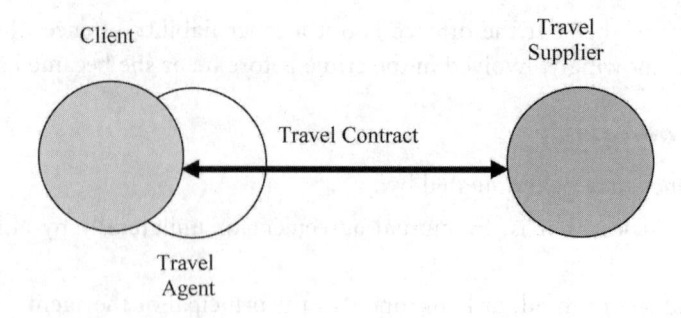

Athens-Macdonald Travel Service Pty Ltd v Kazis

[11.230] *Athens-Macdonald Travel Service Pty Ltd v Kazis* [1970] SASR 264

Facts: Travel agent AM contracted with clients to arrange for their three-month holiday in Cyprus. AM failed to make all the necessary arrangements and encouraged the clients to depart without disclosing that under the arrangements made the holiday would be shortened by 21 days. AM admitted liability for breach of contract.

Decision: The Supreme Court of South Australia (Zelling J) held that AM was liable for damages for disappointment for breach of contract and breach of duty to act in good faith and make full and frank disclosure to the clients. Although it is not entirely clear from the report, it appears that AM was acting as agent of the clients rather than as principal.

Kemp v Intasun Holidays Ltd

[11.235] *Kemp v Intasun Holidays Ltd* [1987] BTLC 353

Facts: Mrs K booked a package holiday for her family with tour operator IH through TC, a local travel agent. Before the booking arrangements were made Mrs K mentioned to an assistant at TC that her husband suffered from asthma and they arranged special insurance to cover this risk. However Mrs K did not mention the asthma problem in the special requirements section of the package holiday booking form. On arrival at the destination in Spain the hotel was overbooked and the K family had to spend 30 hours in the dirty and dusty staff quarters of another hotel, causing Mr K to suffer an asthma attack.

Decision: The English Court of Appeal (Kerr and Parker LJJ) held that IH was in breach of contract and K was entitled to damages for disappointment. However damages for the asthma attack were too remote and not in the reasonable contemplation of IH because TC was acting as agent for K and not as agent for IH at the time the information about his asthma condition was provided. [35]

---

[35] Contrast *Cameron v Qantas Airways Ltd* (1995) ATPR 51-417; (1995) 5 FCR 147 where the Federal Court (Beaumont J) held that information provided by passenger R J Aroney to her travel agent that she required a non-smoking seat because she had an asthma condition was received by the travel agent as agent for the carrier.

Re ILG Travel Ltd (in administration)

[11.240] *Re ILG Travel Ltd (in administration)* [1995] 2 BCLC 128

Tour operator ILG provided package tour holidays through a large number of travel agents in the UK. At the direction of the Civil Aviation Authority the standard form agency agreement between ILG and each travel agent and the booking conditions with clients provided that moneys ("pipeline moneys") paid by clients to travel agents for holidays were held on trust for the clients until confirmation and then on trust for ILG subject to the agent's entitlement to commission. These provisions were designed to ensure, amongst other things, that the travel agent was acting as agent (and trustee) for the client until confirmation so that the tour operator ILG would not be responsible to the client if the travel agent defaulted prior to confirmation.

───── ⦅⦆ ─────

Agent of the travel supplier

[11.245] In this relationship the travel agent undertakes on behalf of the travel supplier to make arrangements to supply travel services to the client. If the arrangements are defective the travel agent will be responsible to its principal, the travel supplier, in contract and agency law. However the travel agent will not be responsible to the client on the travel contract, which will be entered into between the client and the travel supplier. As this is so often the relationship in retail travel agency, travel suppliers are commonly called "principals".[36] These cases also fall into the first category of arrangement discussed in the *Wong Mee Wan case*[37] (see further casenote at [11.305]).

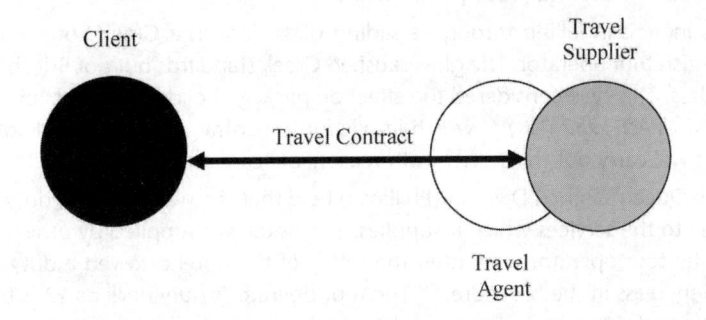

Craven v Strand Holidays

[11.250] *Craven v Strand Holidays* (1982) 142 DLR (3d) 31

Facts: A Canadian tour operator was not responsible to clients on its package tour who were injured when a South American bus company's bus overturned due to the negligence of the driver.

Held: The Ontario Canadian Court of Appeal (Howland CJO, Lacouriere and Weatherston JJA) held that the tour operator's contract with the client was only to arrange for the performance of the transport services, which was satisfied if it exercised due care in the selection of a competent bus line.

---

[36] However if the travel supplier is not disclosed then the travel agent will be liable as in relationship (c) as principal under the doctrine of undisclosed principal: *Odgers v McMiken* [1974] 8 SASR 119 at 121, 124.

[37] *Wong Mee Wan v Kwan Kin Travel Services Ltd* [1995] 4 All ER 745.

Craven v Strand Holidays cont.

The tour operator was not responsible for the actual performance of the transport services by the bus company. [38]

Wall v Silver Wing Surface Arrangements Ltd (t/a Enterprise Holidays)

[11.255] *Wall v Silver Wing Surface Arrangements Ltd (t/a Enterprise Holidays)* (unreported, 18 November 1981)

Facts: W was on a package holiday in Spain staying in a hotel which caught fire. W found the fire escape gate locked and was injured when exiting down a rope made from sheets. The tour operator had previously inspected the hotel and found the fire escape open. It had subsequently been locked by management to prevent burglars getting in.

Decision: The English High Court (Hodgson J) held it was well known that a tour operator neither owns nor operates the hotels or airlines used in a package holiday and is not responsible for the performance of those services. No term could be implied in W's contract with the tour operator that the hotel would be reasonably safe for use. W's only cause of action was against the hotelier who provided the services and not against the tour operator.

Wilson v Best Travel Ltd

[11.260] *Wilson v Best Travel Ltd* [1993] 1 All ER 353

Facts: W was injured in falling through a sliding glass door in a Greek hotel while on a holiday organised by a British tour operator. The glass satisfied Greek standards but not British standards which required safety glass. This case considered the effect on package holiday contracts of s 13 of the *Supply of Goods and Services Act 1982* (UK) [39] which implied into contracts for the supply of services a term "that the supplier will carry out the service with reasonable care and skill".

Decision: The Queen's Bench Division (Phillips J) held that the warranty and duty of care of a tour operator is limited to the services which it supplies. The hotel was supplied by others and it could not be implied that the tour operator warranted the safety of the hotel or owed a duty not to include a hotel without safety glass in the brochure. [40] The tour operator's duty under s 13 is to use reasonable care to exclude from the brochure accommodation whose standards are such that guests could not spend a holiday there in reasonable safety. The standards to be met are those of the destination unless the absence of a safety feature might lead a reasonable holidaymaker to decline to take the holiday there.

Broker

[11.265] A broker is an agent who acts on behalf of both the seller and buyer in a sale transaction. Common examples are stockbrokers and insurance brokers. Travel agents may also act in this way in a travel transaction. Despite the double responsibility of the broker and

---

38   A similar conclusion was reached in *Rookard v Mexicoach* 680 F 2d 1257 (1982).
39   Similar to the *Australian Consumer Law*, Subdivision B Guarantees relating to the supply of services.
40   Philps J agreed with the reasoning and conclusion of Hodgson J in the *Silver Wings* case.

the increased potential for conflict of interest, the broker usually remains just an agent and the travel contract is formed between the client and the travel supplier. The case studies concern transactions where the travel agent was clearly acting as agent for the travel supplier but was also held to be acting as agent of the client.

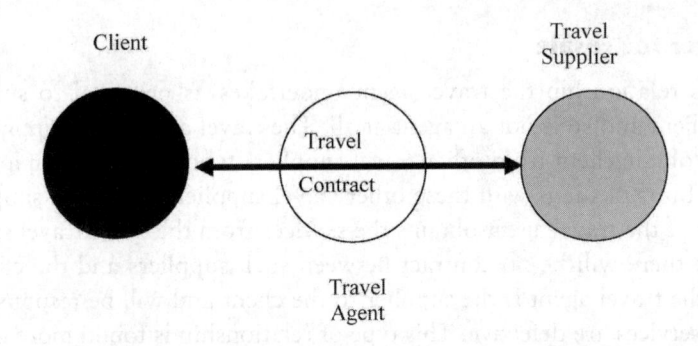

Holt v Fynbout Pty Ltd NSW

[11.270] *Holt v Fynbout Pty Ltd NSW* (Sup Crt, Cohen J, 28 May 1987, BC 8701344)

Facts: T, a travel agent, made bookings on behalf of clients with a cruise operator, F, for which it acted as general sales agent. Clients paid T the fares which T paid to F's trust account less commission. Without fault on the part of T or the clients the cruise did not proceed.

Decision: The Supreme Court of New South Wales (Cohen J) held that T was entitled to retain the commission because it had carried out the requirements of its agency contract with the client by accounting to the carrier for the fares less the commission which F agreed that T could retain as general sales agent. [41]

Elsis v Transworld Airlines

[11.275] *Elsis v Transworld Airlines* 167 AD 2d 285; 562 NYS 2d 433; 1990 NY App Div LEXIS 1424

Facts: Clients took a TWA package holiday of Egypt which included a seven-day cruise down the Nile River on the MS Pharoah. The brochure boasted of TWA's expertise, experience and quality assurance procedures which enabled clients to "sit back and relax, with the peace of mind which only TWA Getaway Egypt can offer". On the first morning of the cruise a fire broke out on the Pharoah and it burnt to the waterline in 30 minutes. The crew escaped in the only lifeboat and the passengers had to swim to shore without life jackets. The brochure disclaimed responsibility on the basis that TWA was a mere agent who made arrangements for the clients with the supplier principals, the operators of the Pharoah.

Held: The Supreme Court of New York Appellate Division (Kupferman JP, Ross, Carro, Asch and Ellerin JJ) held that although it was not responsible for the defaults of the Pharoah and its crew, TWA

---

41 It is respectfully submitted that his Honour's comment at p 16 – that in most cases the travel agent would be the agent of the client and not the carrier – is not correct.

Elsis v Transworld Airlines cont.

had a duty as agent of the clients to exercise good faith, reasonable diligence and skill in the inspection and selection of the cruise ship.

Principal/buyer for resale

[11.280] In this relationship the travel agent undertakes as principal to supply the travel services to the client and so is not an agent at all. The travel agent may supply its own travel services or may obtain them from other travel suppliers who act as its employees, agents or subcontractors. In its dealings with these other travel suppliers it may be simply a buyer for resale. However, if the travel agent obtains the services from the other travel suppliers, under this relationship there will be no contract between such suppliers and the client. Under the travel contract the travel agent is the supplier to the client and will be responsible directly to the client if the services are defective. This type of relationship is found more often where the travel agent is acting as a tour operator than as a retail travel agent. All of these cases fall into the second category of arrangement discussed in the *Wong Mee Wan case*[42] (see further casenote at [11.305]).

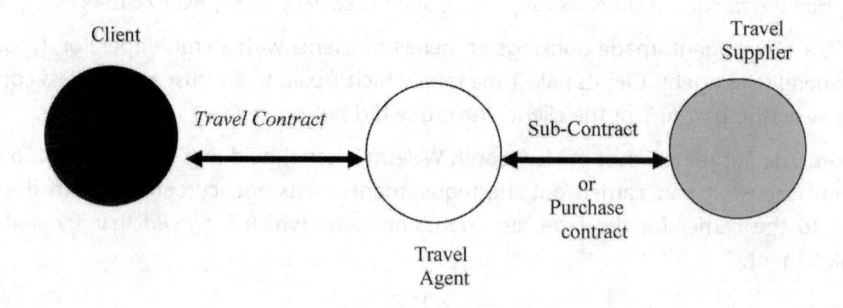

Odgers v McMiken

[11.285] *Odgers v McMiken* [1974] 8 SASR 119

Facts: Travel agent O undertook to supply a client with tickets and vouchers for return travel from Adelaide to London via Singapore by sea and air. O supplied vouchers issued by another undisclosed travel agent which were not honoured, leaving the client stranded in London.

Decision: The Supreme Court of South Australia (Bray CJ, Sangster and Jacobs JJ) held that O was liable as principal to the client for breach of contract.[43]

---

42   *Wong Mee Wan v Kwan Kin Travel Services Ltd* [1995] 4 All ER 745.
43   *Odgers v McMiken* [1974] 8 SASR 119 at 126.

Anglo-Continental Holidays Ltd v Typaldos Lines (London) Ltd

[11.290] *Anglo-Continental Holidays Ltd v Typaldos Lines (London) Ltd* [1967] 2 Lloyd's Rep 61

Facts: Travel agent AC obtained an allocation of ten berths on a take-or-pay basis from a cruise operator TL for a Mediterranean cruise on the ship "Atlantica". AC promoted the cruise and obtained bookings which were confirmed by TL. In fact TL had overbooked the cruise and one week prior to departure attempted to switch AC's bookings to an inferior ship, the "Angelika". AC's clients protested and AC cancelled the bookings.

Decision: The English Court of Appeal (Lord Denning MR, Davies and Russell LJJ) held AC that was entitled to rescind the bookings and recover damages from TL for breach of contract including loss of profits and damage to the goodwill of AC's travel agency. Although it is not entirely clear from the report, it appears that AC was acting as principal and suing TL as subcontractor. Contrast this with the usual way a travel agent arranges cruise bookings. [44]

Thomas Cook Pty Ltd v Aviation and Tourism Services Pty Ltd

[11.295] *Thomas Cook Pty Ltd v Aviation and Tourism Services Pty Ltd* (NSW Sup Crt, Yeldham J, 13 August 1985, BC 8500696)

Facts: Travel agent TC entered an agreement with ATS to promote a Concorde charter flight between Paris and Sydney. Acting as principal, TC paid a deposit of $75,000 and agreed to purchase 94 seats on the flight which it intended to on-sell to its clients. Department of Aviation approval for the flight was delayed, making it more difficult for the travel agent to on-sell the seats.

Held: The Supreme Court of New South Wales (Yeldham J) held that TC was entitled to rescind the contract and recover the deposit because of ATS's misrepresentation that the flight had been approved. Note how this differs from the usual arrangement between a travel agent and a carrier. [45]

Jarvis v Swan Tours Ltd

[11.300] *Jarvis v Swan Tours Ltd* [1972] 3 WLR 954

Facts: Mr J booked a 15-day holiday described in the tour operator's brochure as a "Swan's houseparty" at a Swiss hotel. The houseparty, skiing, yodelling and many other features of the holiday described in the brochure were not delivered as promised, much to the disappointment of J.

Decision: The English Court of Appeal (Lord Denning MR, Edmund Davies and Stephenson LJJ) held that J was entitled to recover damages for the disappointment caused by the tour operator's breach or warranty and misrepresentations. Note that the tour operator was held responsible as principal even though many of the services should have been provided by the hotel. [46]

---

44   Consider for example *Baltic Shipping Company "Mikhail Lermontov" v Dillon* (1993) 176 CLR 344.
45   See for example *Stephens Travel Service International Pty Ltd (Receivers and Managers Appointed) v Qantas Airways Ltd* (1988) 13 NSWLR 629.
46   See further discussion on damages for disappointment in *Vacations Pty Ltd v Young* [2010] NSWCA 137.

Wong Mee Wan v Kwan Kin Travel Services Ltd

[11.305] *Wong Mee Wan v Kwan Kin Travel Services Ltd* [1995] 4 All ER 745

Facts: HSY took a package tour to a lake in China organised and sold by KK, a tour operator/travel agent based in Hong Kong. The package included tour guide and transportation. The group was delayed and missed the ferry which had been organised to take the group across the lake. The tour guide improvised and organised a speedboat to take the group across in three trips. On the third trip, due to the negligence of the driver, the speedboat crashed into a junk and HSY was drowned.

Decision: The Privy Council (Lord Goff of Chieveley, Lord Jauncey of Tullichettle, Lord Slynn of Hadley, Lord Nolan and Lord Hoffman) held that under the contract between HSY and KK, KK undertook to provide the transport services as principal rather than merely to arrange for them to be provided by others. Thus the implied warranty in the contract was that those services, namely the lake crossing, would be supplied with reasonable care and skill whether or not KK chose to engage subcontractors to perform them. In the course of its judgment the Privy Council formulated the distinction between this category of case and the cases discussed in [11.245], above where the travel agent is mere agent of the travel supplier (see [9.345] for further discussion).

Aftermath: This reasoning was followed in another case involving the same tour operator which had arranged a package tour of an area in Taiwan on a bus which crashed because the driver was drunk causing injury to those on board.[47]

Legal Analysis of the Travel Transaction

[11.310] The previous section identified the variety of agency relationships which are possible in the travel transaction. It is now useful to analyse the wider legal responsibilities involved for a retail travel agent in a typical travel transaction.

Authority from suppliers

[11.315] A travel agent usually has arrangements to sell travel products on commission on behalf of many suppliers. These arrangements will often be informal in the case of hotels, resorts and tour operators, in accordance with the custom of the travel trade. In the case of transport suppliers the arrangements will usually be more formal and in the case of air carriers the agent will have authority to sell directly only under IATA's formal Passenger Sales Agency Agreement.[48] It is clear that these arrangements establish the terms of a contractual principal/agency relationship between the suppliers and the travel agent. As there are many competing suppliers the agent's (fiduciary) duty of loyalty to act in the interest of any one supplier is limited to acting fairly among suppliers.[49]

Product information

[11.320] Under the usual arrangements made to sell on commission, the travel products of suppliers are represented by brochures or other information displayed in the travel agency as invitations to treat. The actual products are intangible services and at the time of sale they are

---

47   *Chea Kam Wing Victor v Kwan Kin Travel Services* (Hong Kong Court of Appeal, No 82 of 2007).
48   IATA, Resolution 800b (IATA PSA Agreement).
49   This is complicated by any special arrangements with particular suppliers such as override commissions.

mere rights to participate in and enjoy the travel service product at some future time. This distinguishes the distribution arrangements in travel from the arrangements made by wholesalers and retailers of goods. There is no stock for a travel agent to possess or own or transfer and the travel product will usually be produced by the supplier only as it is provided to and consumed by the client. However travel agents have considerable responsibility. Clients rely upon the advice and information provided by travel agents. The rights of clients correspond with the obligations of travel suppliers to deliver. Production capacity is relatively fixed and travel products are perishable, so that if an airline seat or hotel room is not used on the scheduled day it is lost forever.[50]

Advice and client instructions

[11.325] Clients usually seek information and advice from travel agents on which travel products suit their needs. Travel agents investigate what travel products are available and advise and assist clients to choose the required mix of travel products. Clients instruct travel agents to make the reservations and arrangements necessary for the travel. Clients also expect travel agents to advise and assist with insurance, visas, health, customs and other formalities. In performing these functions the travel agent is acting as a professional adviser and agent of the client.

AFTA describes this role of a travel agent in this way:[51]

> Why use an AFTA Travel Agent? Today the travel industry is highly specialised and the average traveller is presented with numerous alternatives to choose from – the type of transport, the standard and location of accommodation, the dollar value of packaged holidays and the quality of service provided by staff. A good agent is something of a personal counsellor, a psychologist and an expert in the art and science of travel!

Unless the client has agreed to pay the travel agent a fee or an administrative charge for these professional services then they will be gratuitous and the agency will arise without a contract between client and travel agent. Nevertheless the travel agent will be liable to the client in tort and agency law for this work.

Reservations and documentation

[11.330] Travel agents are usually the intermediaries in the retail contracts which are ultimately entered into between clients and travel suppliers except in the principal/buyer for resale relationship described in [11.280]ff above. Travel agents transmit offers from clients to travel suppliers and communicate acceptances and confirmation back to clients. They arrange for clients to sign the suppliers' documentation, collect from clients the deposit and balance of the moneys and issue or obtain the tickets and vouchers required for the travel. Travel agents account to the travel suppliers for the price less their agreed commission. Although the moneys have come from the client upon confirmation they belong to the travel supplier, who contractually is the party liable for the travel agent's commission.

After sales service

[11.335] The travel agent is on standby during the travel to deal with any problems. When the client returns the travel agent should also debrief the client and endeavour to resolve any

---

50 See TC Atherton, "Package holidays: legal aspects" (1994) 15(3) *Tourism Management* 193-199.
51 Australian Federation of Travel Agents (AFTA) at http://www.afta.com.au.

dissatisfaction or claims which the client may have against the travel supplier. The role of a travel agent as mediator is discussed in Chapter 10.

Travel Agents and Child Sex Tourism

[11.340] Australia is at the forefront of international efforts to eradicate child sex tourism. The travel trade has an important responsibility to assist in this effort because the practice often involves travel from a developed country to a developing country where poverty and a weaker rule of law make children more vulnerable. The key initiative in this effort is the *Criminal Code Act 1995* (Cth) which makes such practices a serious criminal offence under Australian law even if they occur outside Australian territory.

Under Division 272 subdivision C of the Act a special legal responsibility is imposed upon travel agents. Under these provisions a travel agent who knowingly profits from or encourages child sex tourism may be prosecuted and the penalty upon conviction is imprisonment for up to 20 years and a fine of up to $500,000 for a corporation.

"Encourage" is defined extremely widely to include: [52]

(a) encourage, incite to, or urge, by any means whatever, (including by a written, electronic or other form of communication); or

(b) aid, facilitate, or contribute to, in any way whatever.

Examples given by the legislation are: [53]

(1) A person commits an offence if:

(a) the person engages in conduct; and

(b) the person does so with the intention of benefiting from an offence against this Division; and

(c) the conduct is reasonably capable of resulting in the person benefiting from such an offence.

In April 2010, the Australian Government introduced a new offence. It is now an offence to prepare for or plan to commit a child sex tourism offence, or to groom or procure a child for sexual activity overseas. These offences allow law enforcement to intervene before a child is abused. The offences carry penalties of up to 15 years imprisonment [54]

There have been several successful prosecutions of offenders under the legislation. AFTA has incorporated a specific item on the matter in its Code of Ethics (see [11.380] below).

SELF-REGULATION

Organisations

International

UFTAA

[11.345] The United Federation of Travel Agents Associations (UFTAA) [55] is the main international organisation concerned with travel agency. It was founded in Rome in 1966 and

---

52   *Criminal Code Act 1995* (Cth), Division 272.19(4).
53   *Criminal Code Act 1995* (Cth), Division 272.18.
54   *Criminal Code Act 1995* (Cth), Division 272.14 and Division 272.15.
55   United Federation of Travel Agents Associations (UFTAA at http://www.uftaa.org.

its membership comprises national travel agents associations as well as individual travel agencies and travel partners. UFTAA's objects are: [56]

- to encourage travel among people of all nations and to support freedom of travel throughout the World.
- to be an effective lobbying body, to oppose legislation directly harmful to tourism traffic and the free flow of travel for citizens of any country.
- to reduce bureaucratic obstacles to travel.
- to seek greater safety in aviation and land travel.
- to create a line of communication to all members and travel partners with periodic newsletters and information.
- to conduct international workshops and seminars on key topics of current interest to the Travel Industry.
- to promote and assist in the professional training of travel agents.
- to organise a members business Congress annually and provide a worldwide forum which will address mutual problems and matters affecting Tourism globally.

UFTAA deals with issues as they arise such as overbooking, uniform travel vouchers, travel insurance and ongoing needs (particularly training). It has negotiated and implemented arrangements with IATA for training and airline/travel agent relations as discussed below. It has also negotiated and implemented the IHA UFTAA Code of Practice on hotel/travel agency relations. [57] UFTAA also provides an international disputes resolution service for members.

WTAAA

[11.348] In 2005 a breakaway organisation called the World Travel Agents Association Alliance was formed. Its object was to take more dynamic approach to self regulation and deal more effectively with key providers on the challenges facing travel agency discussed in [11.680]. Some commentators call this process disintermediation. Australia is taking a leading role in the organisation with the initial headquarters in Sydney and the initial president being the former chair of AFTA. WTAAA now holds a majority of the 9 positions on the IATA Passenger Sales Agency Program Global Joint Council.

IATA

[11.350] The International Air Transport Association (IATA) [58] was founded in 1945 and is a private trade association of the world's air carriers (see [12.470]) IATA's goals include the regulation and standardisation of agency, booking, ticketing and payment procedures. As the major part of a travel agent's business is the sale of international air travel, IATA's regulations and requirements have a significant impact on travel agency.

---

56   Taken from the UFTAA website.
57   The most recent version is dated 1 September 1999. See http://www.uftaa.org/File/uftaa/doc-82_en.pdf.
58   International Air Transport Association (IATA) at http://www.iata.org.

Travel agent accreditation

[11.355] IATA maintains a strict training, approval, accreditation and retention scheme for travel agents. It publishes an annual *Travel Agent's Handbook* which sets out the relevant resolutions [59] and other provisions governing passenger sales agency. These requirements have some similarity to those required for licensing of travel agents under Australian law ([11.385]ff) and participation in the Australian Travel Compensation Fund [11.550]ff. Subject to the travel agent complying with the governing rules, accreditation gives an agent the following rights:

- to sell airline travel;
- to hold ticket stock and "Carrier Identification Plates"; and
- to hold money on behalf of airlines.

Travel agents without accreditation must deal through an accredited agent or "consolidator".

The IATA agency accreditation scheme was approved in Australia by the Trade Practices Commission. [60]

Billing and settlement plan

[11.360] Under the IATA Passenger Sales Agency Agreement moneys collected by travel agents on behalf of carriers are held on trust for the carrier (see [11.660]). [61] IATA operates a clearing bank (BSP) for the payment of airfares by travel agents on a 14-day basis. It also operates a clearing bank arrangement for monthly settlements among carriers.

Travel Agent Commissioner

[11.365] IATA also operates a sophisticated dispute resolution mechanism for travel agency/carrier disputes through the office of the Travel Agency Commissioner [62] (see [10.75]).

National

[11.370] The Australian Federation of Travel Agents (AFTA) [63] is the national representative body for travel agents. It was founded in 1957 to maintain a code of ethics for travel agents and its membership now comprises over 2,500 travel agency outlets along with over 500 travel partners. Tour operators are represented by the Australian Council of Tour Wholesalers (ACTW), a division of AFTA, and the Inbound Tour Operators of Australia (ITOA), a separate organisation founded in 1972. AFTA's mission is: [64]

> To be truly representative of the travel agents of Australia.
> To enhance the professionalism and profitability of its members through effective representation in industry and government affairs, education and training, and by identifying and satisfying the needs of the travelling public.
> To promote travel and domestic tourism.

AFTA's Code of Ethics provides a very important and effective self-regulatory mechanism for travel agency. In 1976 the Trade Practices Commission required various amendments to

---

59 For this region, particularly IATA Resolution 816 governs the Agency Program of Accreditation.
60 *Determination on IATA Agency Accreditation* (October 1984), p 5.
61 IATA Resolution 824(7).
62 IATA Resolution 820d.
63 Australian Federation of Travel Agents (AFTA) at http://www.afta.com.au.
64 Taken from AFTA's website.

ensure that the rules provide members with due process on disciplinary matters and are genuinely aimed at ethical conduct and standards.

Australian Federation of Travel Agents Ltd & Trade Practices Commission

[11.375] *Australian Federation of Travel Agents Ltd & Trade Practices Commission* (1976) ATPR (Com) 15,553

Facts: AFTA took disciplinary action against one of its members for discounting international air fares, an activity which at the time was a breach of its Code of Ethics. The member complained to the Trade Practices Commission, which reviewed the rules and Code and found various aspects which were anti-competitive in contravention of the *Trade Practices Act 1974* (Cth). AFTA redrafted the documents to overcome the objections and resubmitted them for clearance.

Decision: The Trade Practices Commission (Commissioner Dr Pengilley) granted clearance for the amended rules and Code of Ethics, noting that:

> There is, of course, no reason why the Trade Practices Act should discourage trade associations from fostering the common interests and ethical standards of members. It is only when these matters are used in an anti competitive manner, actual or potential, that questions of denial of clearance are raised. On the documentation and practices of the Federation considered in previous decisions, this anti-competitive use, actual or potential, was present. It presently is not.

Dr Pengilley observed that:

(i) Vague clauses which had the possibility of being utilised in an anti-competitive manner have now been either deleted or redrafted in reasonably precise language. These clauses no longer give rise to the likelihood that they will be interpreted in an anti-competitive manner.

(ii) Certain objectives which were clearly quite anti-competitive have now been deleted or appropriately amended so that they are no longer likely to have this effect.

(iii) The rights to members to a fair and impartial hearing have been assured as have the procedural processes associated with such hearing.

(iv) Requirements as to membership have been laid down with precision to prevent either arbitrary exclusion from membership or arbitrary expulsion from the Federation.

(v) The Federation's requirements as to standards are genuinely aimed at ethical conduct and not related to suppression or restriction of competition.

In 1982 clearance was granted to further amendments which tightened the requirements for financial security of members.[65]

The current Code of Ethics is in three parts: relations with the public; relations with carrier and other principals; and relations with fellow members. As can be seen from the extract provided below, the Code of Ethics incorporates many of the principles of law which regulate travel agents, including

---

65   *Re Australian Federation of Travel Agents Ltd* (1982) ATPR (Com) 50-047.

Australian Federation of Travel Agents Ltd & Trade Practices Commission cont.

consumer protection law (see Chapter 9) and agency law (see [11.95]ff). It provides a useful plain English summary of a travel agent's main obligations.

―――― ∞⌒∽ ――――

AFTA Code of Ethics

[11.380] AFTA encourages all members to embrace the Code of Ethics as shown below, in the interests of good business practice, however, it is acknowledged that this is not legally binding or enforceable by law. [66]

ACCURACY AFTA members will be factual and accurate when providing information in any form about their services and the services of any firm they represent. They will not use deceptive practices.

AFFILIATION - AFTA members will not falsely represent a person's affiliation with their firm.

COMPLIANCE AFTA members will abide by all Federal, State and local laws and regulations.

CONFIDENTIALITY AFTA members will treat every client transaction confidentially and not disclose any information without permission of the client, unless required by law.

CONFLICT OF INTEREST AFTA members will not allow any preferred relationship with a supplier to interfere with the interests of their clients.

CONSUMER PROTECTION AFTA members will use every effort to protect their clients against any fraud, misrepresentation or unethical practices which may arise in the travel industry.

COOPERATION AFTA members will cooperate with any inquiry conducted by AFTA o resolve any dispute involving consumers or another member.

DELIVERY AFTA members operating tours will provide all components as stated in their brochure or written confirmation, or provide alternative services of equal or greater value or provide appropriate compensation.

DISCLOSURE AFTA members will provide complete details about terms and conditions of any travel service, including cancellation and service fee obligations, before accepting payment for the booking.

NOTICE AFTA members operating tours will promptly advise the agent or client who reserved the space of any change in itinerary, services, features or price. If substantial changes are made that are written within the control of the operator, the client will be allowed to cancel without penalty.

QUALIFICATIONS & PROFESSIONALISM - AFTA Members must employ staff who have appropriate qualifications and are committed to continuing professional development, such as (but not limited to) the Australian Travel Professionals Program (ATPP). AFTA members must ensure that all staff offer truly professional advice by being fully informed on the various facets of Australian and International travel.

REFUNDS AFTA members will remit any undisputed funds under their control within the specified time limit. Reasons for delay in providing funds will be given to the claimant promptly.

RESPONSIVENESS - AFTA members will promptly respond to their client's complaints.

---

66   http://www.afta.com.au/MissionStatementCodeofEthics

AFTA Code of Ethics cont.

EXPLOITATION OF CHILDREN- AFTA members will not provide or assist in the provision of any travel service which, to their knowledge, is to be used for a purpose involving the sexual exploitation of children.

―――― ∽♡∾ ――――

TRAVEL AGENCY LICENSING

Uniform Scheme

[11.385] Australian travel agents are governed by the general law of agency as well as a special Australia-wide regulatory arrangement called the Co-operative Scheme for the Uniform Regulation of Travel Agents (the Scheme). The Scheme is designed to protect consumers by ensuring the competence, integrity, financial standing and business practices of travel agents and by compensating those consumers who nevertheless lose. There are two limbs to the Scheme:

1. **Licensing system** for travel agents under uniform State and Territory legislation.
2. **Travel Compensation** Fund ("TCF") under the industry-sponsored traveller insurance scheme.

The licensing system has been established by each State and Territory enacting legislation [67] (Travel Agents legislation) in substantially uniform terms. However there are numerous differences from State to State. The two limbs are linked and the TCF provisions are enforced by making participation in the TCF a condition of licensing [68] and vice versa. [69] They are also linked by the subrogation rights granted to the TCF trustees under the Travel Agents legislation as discussed below. The Northern Territory has provided an alternative private insurance scheme and at this stage NT travel agents do not participate in the TCF.

The Travel Compensation Fund is discussed in [11.550]ff. In this section of the chapter we will discuss the licensing system.

Definitions and Exemptions

[11.390] Under the Uniform Scheme any person who *carries on business as a travel agent* [70] (as that phrase is defined below) without the authority of a travel agent's licence commits an offence under the Act [71] which has serious criminal and civil consequences.

The possible penalties and other consequences for a person who breaches this provision are:

---

[67] Travel Agents Legislation comprises: *Agents Act 2003* (ACT); *Travel Agents Act 1986* (NSW); *Consumer Affairs and Fair Trading Act* (NT), Part XI; *Travel Agents Act 1988* (Qld); *Travel Agents Act 1986* (SA); *Travel Agents Act 1987* (Tas); *Travel Agents Act 1986* (Vic); *Travel Agents Act 1985* (WA).

[68] Travel Agents legislation: ACT: s 26; NSW: s 11(2)(a); NT: s 195(1)(b), s 221 (but see [11.120]); Qld: ss 20(1)(b), 37; SA: s 20; Tas: s 20(2); Vic: s 11(2); WA: s 13(2).

[69] See TCF Trust Deed Clause 1 for definition of "participant".

[70] It is also an offence to carry on business as a travel agent in partnership with an unlicensed person: Travel Agents legislation: ACT s 21; NSW: s 6(1)(b); NT: s 188(1)(b); Qld: s 12(1)(b); Tas: s 18(1)(b); Vic: s 6(1)(b); WA: s 7(2).

[71] Travel Agents legislation: ACT: s 21(2); NSW: s 6(1); NT: s 188; Qld: s 12; SA: s 7; Tas: s 18; Vic: s 6; WA: s 6(1).

- a fine;[72]
- imprisonment;[73]
- an injunction;[74]
- profits to be paid to the Crown and then into the TCF;[75]
- no fee or commission is recoverable;[76]
- the breach provides evidence that the person is not fit and proper to qualify for a licence.[77]

In addition, any other person who provides goods or services to an offender may themselves be convicted for an offence of aiding and abetting the unlicensed travel agent.[78] Further, they are deemed to be in partnership with the offender and so are jointly and severally liable with the offender under the TCF trustee's rights of subrogation[79] (discussed later) or at the suit of any third person who suffers loss.[80] These measures strongly discourage principals from dealing with unlicensed agents.

Definition of "carries on business as a travel agent"

[11.395] The Travel Agents legislation does not define a travel agent but rather includes all those who sell or arrange the sale of travel and then excludes employees and some of the principals. The result is to catch most agents as defined at common law and many other intermediaries in the other relationships described at the beginning of this chapter, such as independent contractors, buyers for resale and sometimes even principals (see [11.15]ff).

The Travel Agents legislation governs persons carrying on "business as a travel agent". This is defined in each Act with variations from State to State but generally according to one of two models.

In New South Wales, Tasmania, Victoria and Western Australia:

(1) ...a person carries on business as a travel agent if the person carries on a business of

   (a) selling tickets entitling another person to travel, or otherwise arranging for another person a right of passage, on a conveyance...;

   (b) selling to, or arranging or making available for, another person rights of passage...and hotel or other accommodation...;

---

72   Travel Agents legislation: Maximum penalty: ACT: s 21(2), 100 penalty units, imprisonment for 1 year or both; NSW: s 6(1), 500 penalty units ($50,000); NT: s 188, 500 penalty units ($50,000; body corporate 2,500 penalty units); Qld: s 12(1), 1,000 penalty units; SA: s 7, $50,000; Tas: s 18(2), 50 penalty units plus 5 penalty units daily; Vic: s 6(1), 500 penalty units or imprisonment for 12 months or both; WA: s 7, $25,000 or 9 months' imprisonment or both with minimum fine of $2,500 in the case of a second offence.

73   Travel Agents legislation: ACT: s 21(2), 1 year imprisonment; Vic: s 6(1), 12 months' imprisonment; WA: s 7, 5 months' imprisonment.

74   Travel Agents legislation: NT: s 189; Qld: s 13. There is a general power in other States and Territories.

75   Travel Agents legislation: ACT: s 94; NSW: s 38(3); NT: s 188(2), (3); Qld: s 12(3), (4); SA: s 7(2), (3); Tas: s 45(2), (10); Vic: s 35(2), (10); WA: s 32.

76   Travel Agents legislation: ACT: s 23; NSW: s 6(2); NT: s 188(4); Qld: s 12(5); SA: s 7(4); Tas: s 18(3); Vic: s 6(2); WA: s 31.

77   Travel Agents legislation: ACT: s 27; NSW: s 10; NT: s 193; Tas: s 21; Vic: s 10.

78   Travel Agents legislation: ACT: s 95; NSW: s 40(6); NT: *Criminal Code*, s 12; Qld: s 42(6); Tas: s 42(7), (8); Vic: s 37(6); WA: s 49(4), (5).

79   Travel Agents legislation: NSW: s 40(7); NT: s 222(4); Qld: s 42(7); Tas: s 42(6); Vic: s 37(7); WA: s 49(4).

80   Travel Agents legislation: Tas: s 44; Vic: s 38.

(c) purchasing for resale the right of passage on a conveyance...;

...holds out or advertises that the person is willing to carry on any activity referred to...[above].

...

(3) A person does not carry on business as a travel agent –
   (a) in respect of...(1)(a) if the person...is the proprietor [of the conveyance]...;
   (b) in respect of...(1)(b) if the person...is the proprietor [of the conveyance and place of accommodation]... [81]

A simplified model has been adopted in the Australian Capital Territory, Queensland, the Northern Territory and South Australia where:

(1) ...a person carries on business as a travel agent if the person, in the course of a business sells, or arranges for the sale of or advertises that he or she is willing to sell or arrange for the sale of –
   (a) rights to travel; or
   (b) rights to travel and accommodation.
(2) A person does not carry on business as a travel agent –...
   (b) by reason only of selling, or arranging for the sale of, rights to travel in a vehicle owned by him or her;
   (c) by reason only of selling, or arranging for the sale of, rights to accommodation at a place owned by him or her. [82]

Refinements and exemptions

[11.400] A number of points should be noted about these definitions:

- All intermediaries (that is, tour operators,[83] wholesalers, general sales agents and consolidators) would appear to fall within the definitions as well as the narrower industry concept of a retail travel agent.
- The key element in the concept is arranging for the sale of travel which in turn is defined in terms of transport. In contrast, the EC Directive on Package Holidays (discussed in [9.355]ff) takes a more comprehensive approach and regulates the organisation of any two of the three main components of tourism, namely transport, accommodation and other services.
- Principals are granted limited exclusions to permit transport and accommodation providers to sell their own products. A "proprietor" [84] or "owner" [85] is defined as the person who has lawful possession of the accommodation, vehicle or conveyance so as to include a lessee and exclude a lessor.
- Transport providers are included if they sell or arrange for the sale of any other travel or any accommodation even if in conjunction with their own transport.

---

81 Travel Agents legislation: NSW: s 4 which is similar to: Tas: s 5; Vic: s 4; WA: s 4.
82 Travel Agents legislation: Qld: s 9 which is similar to: AXT s 11; NT: s 186 and SA: s 4.
83 Tour operators usually arrange for most of the component services (for example the travel, accommodation and other activities) in a package tour to be provided by others.
84 Travel Agents legislation: NSW: s 4(4)(a); Tas: s 4(5); Vic: s 4(5).
85 Travel Agents legislation: NT: s 186(3); Qld: s 9(3); SA: s 4(3); WA: s 4(4).

- "Travel" and "rights of passage" have very wide meanings. "Vehicle" is defined to include any boat, aircraft or other means of transportation [86] and appears to be similar in meaning to the undefined "conveyance". These terms would appear to include self-operated hire cars, bare boat yachts, bicycles and perhaps even horses.

- Day trips and excursions which return to the point of departure in the same day are excluded from the definition in some States. [87]

- Accommodation providers are included if they sell or arrange for the sale of any travel. In some States this would appear to include a hotel arranging a hire car for a guest, which surely is an unintended consequence.

- Merely arranging for the sale of others' accommodation is not included. Thus a hotel, making forward accommodation bookings for guests at other establishments, would not be included. Nor would a business which dealt only in accommodation and not travel. [88]

- Accommodation is not defined but would clearly include hotels, motels, resorts, apartments, hostels, caravan parks and camp grounds. In the absence of a definition it may be difficult to classify mobile homes, sleeping compartments on trains, cruise ships, yachts and house boats. It would appear that these are both travel and accommodation and although the owner or proprietor would be excluded, any other person arranging for the sale may require a licence. However, although aircraft and coaches often travel overnight, the absence of proper sleeping facilities probably disqualifies them as accommodation.

- If a person is carrying on business as a travel agent by the definitions above, that business is deemed to include the making a "travel related arrangement" whether separately from or in conjunction with the other activities. A "travel related arrangement" is an arrangement that may commonly be made in connection with the other activities of a travel agent, such as an arrangement of accommodation, car hire or the provision of travellers' cheques. [89] This is designed to avoid previous problems [90] and ensure that the whole of a travel agent's business is licensed and accounted for under the scheme.

- "Carries on business" implies repetition, continuity and for profit rather than isolated, irregular and gratuitous activities of, for example, a school, club or social group. However, if such a group were to "hold out or advertise" willingness to carry out any of the activities then they would be regarded as carrying on business. Western Australia uses the phrase "carries on the activity" [91] which may be broader so as include not-for-profit operators.

---

86 Travel Agents legislation: NT: s 185; Qld: s 6; SA: s 3.
87 Travel Agents legislation: NSW: Reg 5; Qld: Order in Council 27/10/1988; Tas: reg 4; WA: reg 4.
88 Such a business would also appear to be outside the State legislation which requires real estate agents to be licensed because it would be dealing in mere contractual licences to occupy premises rather than proprietary rights of occupancy under letting or leasing arrangements tenancies, leases or other proprietary rights. See for example *Property Agents and Motor Dealers Act 2000* (Qld), s 128 (definition of "what a real estate agent's licence authorises").
89 TCF Trust Deed Clause 1.1 (definition of "travel-related arrangements"); Travel Agents legislation: for example NSW: reg 5.
90 See *Re Travel Compensation Fund, Dunn and Others* (unreported, Federal Court, Wilcox J, 2 December 1992) where an insolvent travel agency business was effectively split so that car hire arrangements for tours were made by a separate unlicensed entity sharing premises and overheads with the licensed travel agency. The apportionment of expenses was distorted so that the licensed travel agency appeared solvent and continued to trade until both entities collapsed.
91 Travel Agents legislation: WA: s 4.

- Merely advertising or holding out that a person is a travel agent or is willing to undertake any of the specified activities constitutes carrying on business as a travel agent. [92]
- Employees of a travel agent are excluded from the definition. [93] This would not exclude sub-agents and contractors who work under different arrangements as discussed above. They could be prosecuted for carrying on business without a licence and the travel agent could be prosecuted for aiding and abetting etc. This is illustrated in the *Janminga case* discussed below. [94]
- Certain government authorities are exempt from the licensing requirements of the Travel Agents legislation. [95] Such authorities include State tourism departments, rail authorities, tourism commissions and certain State banks. These authorities are all bound by the other provisions of the legislation.
- Any person carrying on business as a travel agent whose annual turnover (gross travel fares and accommodation sold, not just commission earned) does not exceed $50,000 is exempted from licensing provided they deal only in domestic travel. [96]

Licensing Procedure

[11.405] As there are two limbs to the uniform scheme, an application for a travel agent's licence must be made concurrently with an application to participate in the TCF.

Travel Agents Licence Application Process

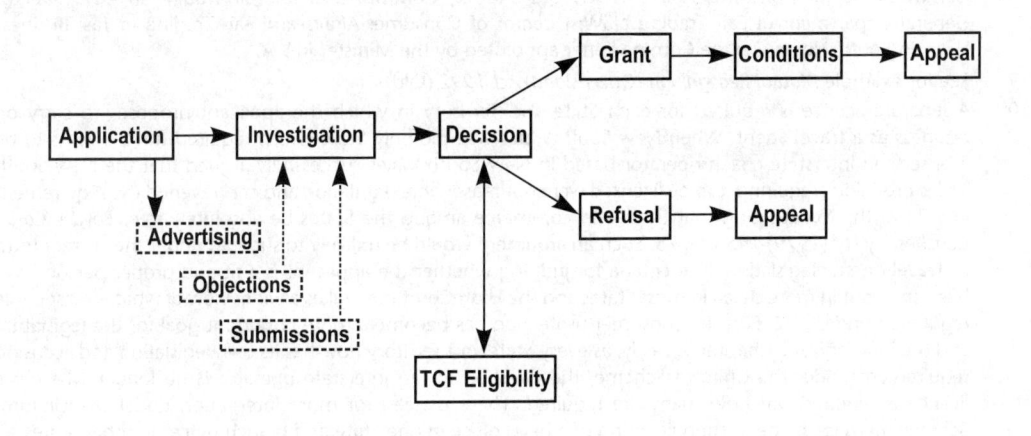

---

92 Travel Agents legislation: ACT: s 11; NSW: s 4(1); NT: s 186(1); Qld: s 9(1); Tas: s 4(1); Vic: s 4(1); WA: s 4(1)(e). In South Australia it is not included in the definition but it is made an offence under SA: s 7(1)(b).
93 Travel Agents legislation: ACT: s 13(d); NSW: s 4(2); NT: s 186(2)(a); Qld: s 9(2)(a); SA: s 4(2)(a); Tas: s 4(2); Vic: s 4(2); WA: s 4(2).
94 *Re Number Two Janminga Pty Ltd and Travel Agents Licensing Authority* (1991) 5 VAR 200 (Vic AAT).
95 Travel Agents legislation: ACT: s 6; NSW: ss 3(2), 5; NT: ss 3(2), 187(1); Qld: s 8; SA: s 5(2); Tas: s 3(2), (5); Vic: ss 3(2), 5; WA: ss 5, 6(1).
96 Travel Agents legislation: NSW: *Travel Agents Order 2005*, clause 4; Qld: *Travel Agents Regulations 1998* (Qld), s 6(1)(b).

[11.405] **277**

Application

[11.410] A travel agent's licence is obtained by making application [97] in the prescribed form to the licensing authority [98] in the State or Territory in which the applicant wishes to carry on business. Travel agents operating in more than one State require multiple licences. [99] Although the licensing process has been streamlined somewhat by the Mutual Recognition Acts, this remains an inefficient aspect of the system. [100] Fees are payable for the application, grant, annual renewal and for each branch office under a licence. These fees vary from State to State and through time. [101]

Investigation

[11.415] There are provisions in each State for inquiries to be made [102] into the application and for the Commissioner of Police to investigate and comment. [103] In some States the application is advertised in a newspaper, [104] objections may be lodged [105] and the applicant may have the opportunity to make submissions on the comments or objections. [106]

Decision

[11.420] To be eligible for the grant of a licence the applicant [107] must be: [108]

(a)   18 years or more of age;

---

97   Travel Agents legislation: ACT: ss 28, 29; NSW: s 8; NT: s 190; Qld: s 14; SA: s 8, Tas: s 19; Vic: s 8; WA: s 9.
98   Commissioner for Consumer Affairs in NT, Qld and SA; Commissioner for Fair Trading in ACT; Director General Department of Fair Trading NSW; Director of Consumer Affairs and Fair Trading in Tas; Business Licensing Authority in Vic; the Commissioner appointed by the Minister in WA.
99   See for example *Mutual Recognition (Queensland) Act 1992* (Qld).
100   A separate licence is required for each State and Territory in which the applicant proposes to carry on business as a travel agent. When New South Wales was the only State which required travel agents to be licensed, an interstate coach operator based in New South Wales successfully argued that the New South Wales provisions requiring it to be licensed were not reasonable regulation and contravened the requirement in s 92 of the Constitution that trade and commerce among the States be absolutely free: *Boyd v Carah Coaches Pty Ltd* (1979) 145 CLR 78. Such an argument would be unlikely to succeed under the current form of Travel Agents legislation. The criteria for judging whether the applicant is a fit and proper person have been spelt out in more detail in most States and the High Court now takes a wider view of what is reasonable regulation under s 92. Further, consumer protection has become a more important goal for the legislature and the judiciary. See Chapter 9. Lastly, as every State and Territory now has its own legislation and licensing requirement under the Uniform Scheme, the question for an interstate operator is no longer whether a licence is required but how many are required. There is need for more integration under the Uniform Scheme, perhaps by permitting licensing of a head office in one State and branch offices in other States.
101   For example in New South Wales the fees are: $105 application fee, $364 annual licence fee for each place of business: *Travel Agents Regulations 2006* (NSW), ss 6, Schedule 2.
102   Travel Agents legislation: ACT: s 12; NSW: s 9(1); NT: s 192; Qld: s 15(1); SA: s 8(2) (which merely states that the applicant is to provide information required to make a determination); Tas: s 20(1); Vic: s 9(2); WA: s 10(1), (2).
103   Travel Agents legislation: ACT: ss 29, 53 NSW: s 9(2); NT: s 191(1)(a); Qld: s 15(2); SA: s 37; Tas: s 20(2); Vic: s 9(3); WA: s 10(3).
104   Travel Agents legislation: ACT: s 28; NT: s 191(1)(b); Qld: s 14(3); WA: s 10(4).
105   Travel Agents legislation: ACT: s 30 by any person; NT: s 191(1)(b), (2), (3) by Commissioner of Police or any person; Qld: s 16 by any person; WA: s 11 by any person.
106   Travel Agents legislation: ACT: ss 31, 32; NSW: s 10(8); NT: ss 192, 193(9); Qld: ss 17, 18(5); Tas: s 21(8); WA: s 12(5).
107   And every partner in the case of a partnership and every controlling officer in the case of a body corporate.
108   Travel Agents legislation: ACT: ss 24, 26; NSW: s 10; NT: s 193; Qld: s 18; SA: s 9, Tas: s 21; Vic: s 10; WA: s 12.

(b) of good reputation and character;[109]

(c) likely to carry on the business honestly and fairly;

(d) otherwise a "fit and proper person" to be a licensee;

(e) have made suitable arrangements to fulfil the conditions of the licence;

(f) eligible to be, and admitted as, a participant in the TCF; and

(g) not disqualified from holding a licence or being involved in the business.[110]

There is no requirement that the *applicant* have any particular qualifications in travel agency.[111] However the licensee must ensure that each place of business is managed and supervised by a qualified person as discussed below in Conduct of Business. This is designed to encourage investment in travel agencies.

The key issue is whether the applicant is a "fit and proper person" to hold a travel agent's licence. Most States[112] provide guidelines to be considered in determining this. Specific matters which may be considered include whether the applicant and any person concerned in the management or supervision of the business have been charged with or convicted of an offence involving fraud or dishonesty or, under the Travel Agents legislation, have been refused a travel agent's licence or had any disciplinary action taken against them under the Travel Agents legislation.

The expression "fit and proper person" is used to define the personal standards required not only for travel agent licences but also for liquor licences, gaming licences and numerous other business licences. The High Court has consistently held that the purpose of the expression is "to give the licensing authority the widest scope for judgement and indeed rejection".[113] It has held that a travel agent licensing authority is "required to exercise its judgement as to the fitness of an applicant and that discretion is not limited to any defined criteria."[114] It has also held that:

> The question whether a person is fit and proper is one of value judgement. In that process the seriousness or otherwise of particular conduct is a matter for evaluation by the decision-maker. So too is the weight, if any, to be given to matters favouring the person whose fitness and propriety are under consideration.[115]

This issue has been considered in several cases, including *Re Number Two Janminga Pty Ltd and Travel Agents Licensing Authority*[116] (see casenote at [11.525]) and in the following case.

---

109 Not an express requirement in Queensland.

110 In any State or Territory.

111 Some other States also provide that the applicant must have the prescribed qualifications. However none have been prescribed, for example Travel Agents legislation: Qld: s 18(1)(c)(a).

112 Travel Agents legislation: NSW: s 10(3) – (5); NT: s 193(3) – (5); Tas: s 21(3) – (5); Vic: s 10(3) – (5); WA: s 12(3), (4) but not in other States and Territories. In *Boyd v Carah Coaches Pty Ltd* (1979) 145 CLR 78 the High Court majority (Barwick CJ, Gibbs, Stephen, and Mason JJ and Murphy JJ, Murphy J dissenting) held that the failure to set down guidelines in the former NSW provision gave the authority such a wide and unfettered discretion to refuse a licence that it could not be considered reasonable regulation for the purposes of s 92 of the Constitution.

113 Dixon CJ, McTiernan and Webb JJ in *Hughes & Vale v New South Wales (No 2)* (1955) 93 CLR 127 at 156, quoted with approval by Gibbs J in *Boyd v Carah Coaches Pty Ltd* (1979) 145 CLR 78 at 85.

114 Gibbs J in *Boyd v Carah Coaches Pty Ltd* (1979) 145 CLR 78 at 85.

115 Toohey and Gaudron JJ in *Australian Broadcasting Tribunal v Bond* (1990) 94 ALR 11 at 62.

116 *Re Number Two Janminga Pty Ltd and Travel Agents Licensing Authority* (1991) 5 VAR 200 (Vic AAT).

Mundro Pty Ltd v Commissioner for Consumer Affairs

[11.425] *Mundro Pty Ltd v Commissioner for Consumer Affairs* (1988) 4 SR (WA) 3181

Facts: In its application for a travel agent's licence M company proposed that S would be the qualified person employed in charge of the day-to-day conduct of the business. The Commissioner for Corporate Affairs objected to the application because of S's previous conviction for false pretences. The Licensing Authority upheld the objection and refused the application because it determined that S was not of good reputation or character or not a fit and proper person to hold a licence if he were to apply for it personally. S appealed.

Decision: The District Court of Western Australia (Clarke J) held that the scheme of the legislation is to demand good character of travel agents and their employees and the weighty reasons required to upset a Licensing Authority's determination on such matters were not shown here. S had been convicted of 55 counts of false pretences involving the passing of valueless cheques totalling $35,895 under assumed names over a considerable period of time. Goods worth $23,570 were recovered and S had pleaded guilty to the offences. Although a probation order rather than imprisonment was imposed, the Licensing Authority was entitled to consider the offender's actions and behaviour in the offences. Although the last offence was committed more than eight years ago S remained under a "very serious cloud of dishonesty" as a result of those actions.

See also *Caras International Tours v Travel Agents Licensing Authority* (unreported, Vic AAT, 16 May 1994).

———— ഓരു ————

Conditions

[11.430] Licences are issued subject to several conditions. These relate to the TCF; premises; and other conditions.

TCF

The licensee must be a participant in the TCF.[117] This is discussed below.

Premises

Each place of business must comply with the prescribed standards and requirements.[118] As with all businesses, the premises used for a travel agency must comply with all the relevant planning, building, health and safety laws.[119] In addition, New South Wales specifies the following standards:

- the premises must be easily identified as a travel agency;
- if shared with another activity, the travel agency section must be distinguishable from the other activity;
- the premises must be easily accessible during normal office hours;

---

117 Travel Agents legislation: ACT: s 91; NSW: s 11(2)(a); NT: s 195(1)(b), s 221; Qld: ss 20(1)(b), 37; SA: s 20; Tas: s 22(2); Vic: s 11(2); WA: s 13(2).
118 Travel Agents legislation: ACT: s 34; NSW: s 11(2)(b); NT: s 195(1); Qld: s 20(1)(a); SA: s 10(1); Tas: ss 19(d), (e), 26, 40; Vic: s 11(2); WA: s 13(2).
119 Travel Agents regulations: for example, Qld: reg 11.

- the premises must be adequately equipped for the conduct of business and security should be in place for the storage of ticket stock etc. [120]

The problems arising from splitting travel agency businesses and sharing premises were highlighted in the following case.

Re Travel Compensation Fund, Dunn and Others

[11.435] *Re Travel Compensation Fund, Dunn and Others* (1992) (unreported, Federal Court, Wilcox J, 2 December 1992)

Travel Abroad was a tour operator which specialised in European package holidays which it sold to the public directly as travel agent and indirectly through other travel agents. It was a licensed travel agent and member of the TCF. An associated company, Wheels Abroad, arranged and sold car hire in Europe. It was not a licensed travel agent or member of the TCF. When the companies collapsed in December 1988 a number of problems emerged resulting from the sharing of premises and overheads with this unlicensed associated company. It was found that $300,000 of Travel Abroad's overhead expenses had been wrongly allocated to Wheels Abroad, making it falsely appear that Travel Abroad was trading at a profit when the TCF renewed its participation in the scheme for the year of the collapse. Clients of Wheels Abroad had no claim against the TCF whereas clients of Travel Abroad successfully claimed $423,369 more from the TCF than it was able to recover from the liquidation of Travel Abroad. To avoid a repeat of these problems the definition of business as a travel agent has been widened to include travel-related arrangements such as car hire (whether conducted separately or in conjunction with the travel agency) and the TCF is authorised to take into account in determining eligibility the financial affairs and resources of any associated entities. [121] See also the later discussion of the subrogation issues in this case ([11.615]).

Other conditions

[11.440] In most States the Licensing Authority also has power to impose or revoke other conditions or restrictions upon the grant of a licence and at any time. [122]

Appeal

[11.445] A licensee dissatisfied with a refusal to grant a licence or with conditions imposed or varied on a licence has rights of appeal which vary from State to State. [123] The review and appeal procedures were tested to the limit in the following case.

---

120 NSW Department of Fair Trading, *Travel Agent Licensing Requirements* (2010) at http://www.fairtrading.nsw.gov.au/Businesses/Specific_industries_and_businesses/Travel_agent_licensing_requirements.html.

121 TCF Trust Deed, Clause 1.1 definition of "travel-related arrangements", Clause 1.3(b), (c); Travel Agents legislation: for example, NSW: reg 5.

122 Travel Agents legislation: NSW: s 11(1); NT: s 195(2), (3); Qld: s 20; SA: s 10(2), Tas: s 22(1); Vic: s 11(1); WA: s 13.

123 Travel Agents legislation: ACT: s 167 to the Civil and Administrative Tribunal; NSW: ss 22, 25 to the Administrative Decisions Tribunal by rehearing and from there on a question of law to the Supreme Court; NT: s 206 to the Local Court; Qld: s 26 to the Minister and from there to the District Court by rehearing; SA: s 11 against refusal to grant a licence, to the District Court by rehearing; Tas: s 34 to a magistrate (Administrative Appeals division); Vic: s 22 to the civil and Administrative Tribunal; WA: ss 23, 25 Administrative Tribunal.

Frugtniet v Secretary to the Department of Justice

[11.450] *Frugtniet v Secretary to the Department of Justice* (Victorian Court of Appeal, 24 April 1996, BC 9601695).

Facts: The Victorian Licensing Authority determined that F was not a fit and proper person to hold a travel agent's licence following an objection by the Director of Consumer Affairs. Her licence was cancelled and she was disqualified from holding a travel agent's licence or being involved in the direction, management or conduct of a travel agent's business for five years. Then began one of the most extensive appeal and review processes ever undertaken over a travel agent's licence.

Appeals: F appealed to the AAT, which allowed the appeal and set aside the decision and dismissed the objection. The secretary of the Department of Justice then appealed to the Full Court, which set aside the AAT decision and ordered a rehearing by the AAT. The AAT then affirmed the original determination and penalty save that the period of disqualification was reduced to two years. F then appealed against that decision to the Full Court, which unanimously dismissed the appeal. It upheld the original findings that F was not a fit and proper person due to several acts of dishonesty. These included: permitting her company to trade in breach of a condition of its licence by knowingly allowing her husband, himself a disqualified person, to be involved in the management of the business; falsely stating the ownership details of the company in an application to IATA for accreditation; forging certificates and falsely claiming qualifications in an application for renewal of the licence. [124]

Conduct of Business

[11.455] The conditions described must continue to be met throughout the conduct of the business. In addition, the Travel Agents legislation also sets out further requirements for the proper conduct of a travel agency business. Failure to conform with these requirements can lead to penalties, suspension or cancellation of the licence so that in effect they may operate as further conditions. The main requirements are listed below.

Name and notice

[11.460] Like any business, a travel agency must comply with the Business Names Act [125] of the relevant State. In addition, a licensed travel agent must:

- carry out the business as a travel agent under the name authorised in the travel agent's licence; [126]

- ensure that the authorised name appears in all advertisements, [127] letters, statements, invoices, cheques, receipts and other documents issued in the course of the business; [128]

---

124 *Frugtniet v Secretary to the Department of Justice* 1996 (unreported, Vic CA, 24 April 1996, BC 9601695).
125 The *Business Names Act 2002* (NSW); *Business Names Act 1996* (SA); *Business Names Act 1963* (ACT); *Business Names Act* (NT); *Business Names Act 1962* (Qld); *Business Names Act 1962* (Tas); *Business Names Act 1962* (Vic); *Business Names Act 1962* (WA).
126 Travel Agents legislation: ACT: s 171; NSW: s 12(2); NT: s 194(2); Qld: s 32(1); SA: s 34(1); Tas: s 24(2); Vic: s 12(2); WA: s 28.
127 Travel Agents legislation: ACT: s 15; NSW: s 34; NT: s 210; Qld: s 32(2)(a); SA: s 34(2)(a); Tas: s 38; Vic: s 31; WA: s 27.
128 Travel Agents legislation: NSW: s 35; NT: s 211; Qld: s 32(2)(b); SA: s 34(2)(b); Tas: s 39; Vic: s 32; WA: s 28.

- display in a conspicuous place at each place of business a notice showing the authorised name and prescribed particulars;[129]
- not transfer or lend the licence to another person or permit another person to carry on business under the name.[130] An exception is made following the death of a travel agent to permit administration of the estate.[131]

A travel agent who fails to comply with these requirements may be prosecuted and fined.

Management and supervision

[11.465] We have already noted that generally a licensee does not need to have any particular qualifications or experience in travel agency. However, in all States the licensee must ensure that each place of business is conducted under the day-to-day management and supervision of a person (whether or not the licensee) who does have prescribed qualifications and experience.[132] For this purpose, travel agency business is divided into two categories and the qualifications and experience required of the supervisor/manager vary with the complexity and responsibility of each category. For example in Queensland, the categories are:[133]

Category 1
The type of business for a category 1 licence is:
(a) selling or arranging for the sale of–
(i) a right to travel to or from a place outside Australia (*international travel*); or
(ii) a right to international travel and accommodation outside Australia; and
(b) the type of business that a licensee may carry on under a category 2 licence.

Category 2
The type of business for a category 2 licence is selling or arranging for the sale of–
(a) a right to travel between places in Australia (*domestic travel*); or
(b) a right to domestic travel and accommodation in Australia.

Each State has approved certain travel training courses. For a Category 1 licence, for example, the prescribed qualifications are:

(a) the successful completion of a unit of competency that–
(i) is titled SITTTSL013A (Construct normal international airfares); and
(ii) is provided by an organisation registered by a State registering authority [134] to–
(A) deliver training or conduct assessments; and
(B) issue nationally recognised qualifications under the Tourism Training Package
(THT02) in the Australian Quality Training Framework; or
(b) 1 year's full-time experience, during the 5 years before the application is made–
(i) selling or arranging for the sale of a right to travel to or from a place outside Australia; or

---

129 Travel Agents legislation: ACT: s 171; NSW: s 33; NT: s 209; Qld: s 31; SA: s 33; Tas: s 37; Vic: s 30; WA: s 26.
130 Travel Agents legislation: ACT: ss 97, 178; NSW: s 7; NT: s 196; Qld: s 21; Tas: s 23; Vic: s 7; WA: s 8.
131 Travel Agents legislation: NSW: ss 26, 27; NT: s 203; Qld: ss 29, 30; SA: s 14; Tas: ss 35, 36; Vic: ss 23, 24; WA: ss 33 – 35.
132 Travel Agents legislation: ACT: ss 69, 70; NSW: s 36; NT: s 213; Qld: s 34; SA: s 13; Tas: s 40; Vic: s 33; WA: s 29.
133 *Travel Agents Regulations 1998* (Qld), Schedule 1.
134 The organisation must be a registered training organisation within the meaning of the Vocational Education and Training legislation in each State.

(ii) in employment as the person in charge of the day-to-day conduct of a place of business of a licensed travel agent in a participating State, selling or arranging for the sale of a right to travel to or from a place outside Australia. [135]

For a Category 2 licence, the person in charge of the business does not need to have the prescribed qualifications. [136]

The curriculum for these courses must be designed to provide students with sufficient legal knowledge to ensure business compliance. These categories follow the principles of those specified by IATA for the accreditation of passenger sales agents (see [11.355]).

Disqualified persons

[11.470] The quality assurance derived by requiring a qualified person to manage and supervise each place of business is reinforced by prohibiting the employment in any capacity of a disqualified person without the approval of the Licensing Authority. [137] Disqualified persons are defined to include persons who in any State have been refused a licence or disqualified from holding a licence. The licensee bears the onus of proving in defence that reasonable enquiries were made and there was no reason for believing the person was disqualified. [138]

These provisions were applied in *Frugtniet v Secretary to the Department of Justice* [139] discussed above, [11.450]. In the following case study the agent was disqualified for, among other things, employing a disqualified person.

Roka v Collins (Court of Criminal Appeal (SA)

[11.475] *Roka v Collins (Court of Criminal Appeal (SA)*, Legoe J, 10 January 1994, BC 9400531)

Facts: C had carried on business as a travel agent for more than 12 years when he received notice from the TCF to provide an additional bank guarantee of $50,000 to meet the financial criteria. Unable to do so, C closed the business and surrendered his travel agent's licence. C was then convicted of a series of offences relating to the last years of the business. These included 21 counts of fraudulent conversion of clients' moneys totalling $82,000, for which a suspended sentence of three years' imprisonment was imposed under the criminal law. He was also convicted of failing to keep proper accounts under the Travel Agents legislation, for which he was fined $600. The Licensing Authority then lodged a complaint seeking disciplinary action based on these convictions.

Decision: The Court of Criminal Appeal of South Australia (Legoe J) held that C was not the type of person who should be involved in working in a travel agency in any capacity whatsoever. He had shown himself to be dishonest and unscrupulous with no sense of responsibility for his actions, had made no real attempt to comply with his obligations as a travel agent and had a lack of morality and ethics in fraudulently converting clients' money. He was disqualified from holding a licence or being

---

135   *Travel Agents Regulations 1998* (Qld), Schedule 3, s 1; *Travel Agents Regulations 2006* (NSW), s 12.
136   *Travel Agents Regulations 1998* (Qld), Schedule 3, s 2; *Travel Agents Order 2005* (NSW), clause 7.
137   Travel Agents legislation: ACT: s 27(1); NSW: s 37(1); NT: s 214(1); Qld: s 35(1); SA: ss 18B, 18C; Tas: s 41(1); Vic: s 34(1); WA: s 30(1).
138   Travel Agents legislation: ACT: s 27(2), (3); NSW: s 37(2); NT: s 214(2); Qld: s 35(2); Tas: s 41(3); Vic: s 34(2); WA: s 30(2).
139   *Frugtniet v Secretary to the Department of Justice* (unreported, Vic Court of Appeal, 24 April 1996, BC 9601695).

Roka v Collins (Court of Criminal Appeal (SA) cont.

employed or engaged in the business of a travel agent. C's appeal to the Supreme Court of South Australia seeking removal of the disqualification from employment was dismissed.[140]

───── ∞∞ ─────

Accounting

[11.480] A travel agent must keep the accounting records necessary to record and explain the transactions and financial position of the business, including sufficient information for the preparation and audit of the profit and loss account and balance sheet.[141] These requirements are discussed in more detail below, [11.630]ff.

Disciplinary Procedure

[11.485] The Licensing Authority monitors travel agency operations to ensure that the standards and other requirements of the scheme are being upheld. All States provide due process under the notice to show cause before disciplinary measures are imposed. New South Wales, the Northern Territory, Victoria and Western Australia also have an innovative procedure which gives an offender an opportunity to get its business in order before the more serious disciplinary measures are taken.

Disciplinary action

Objection and complaint

[11.490] The disciplinary process usually begins in response to a complaint or an objection to the continuance of the licence or the conduct of the licensee. An informal complaint or objection may be made at any time by any person, but some States also provide formal rights of complaint or objection to specified persons or authorities.[142]

Inspection and investigation

[11.495] The Licensing Authority has wide powers of inspection and investigation to ascertain whether the provisions of the Travel Agents legislation are being complied with. These powers are used to gather information to determine whether or not to issue a notice to show cause and, if issued, whether or not to take disciplinary measures.[143] They are usually delegated to an inspector, investigator or other officer[144] and include power to:[145]

- require production of records and translation into English if necessary;

---

140 *Roka v Collins* (unreported, SACCA, Legoe J 10 January 1994, 9400531).
141 Travel Agents legislation: ACT: ss 127 – 130; NSW: s 41; NT: s 212; Qld: s 33; SA: s 35; Tas: s 43; Vic: s 39; WA: s 41.
142 Travel Agents legislation: ACT: s 30 by any person; SA: s 17 the Commissioner or any other person; Vic: s 20(1) the Director; WA: s 21 by any person.
143 Travel Agents legislation: NSW: s 20(6), (7); NT: s 204(6), (7); Qld: s 24(6), (7); SA: s 37; Tas: s 36(6), (7).
144 Travel Agents legislation: ACT: s 42 Commissioner for Fair Trading; NSW: s 20(7) Commissioner of Police, s 44 public servant, s 18 *Fair Trading Act 1987* (NSW) investigator; NT: s 18 Commissioner or authorised officer; Qld: s 44 public servant, s 47 police officer; SA: s 27 public servant, s 37 police officer; Tas: s 48 a person authorised by director of Consumer Affairs and Fair Trading (Tas); Vic: s 20 director or Chief Commissioner of Police; WA: s 50 officer of Public Service Department.

- enter premises where the business is being carried on or the records are kept; [146]
- inspect and require explanations of records;
- take notes and copies or remove records for copying and return.

The travel agent and all employees must co-operate in this process and provide truthful explanations and answers to questions, or they commit a serious offence. [147] Some States relieve the obligation to answer questions or produce records which may be self-incriminatory. [148] There are also strict secrecy provisions governing information disclosed or obtained in the administration of the Travel Agents legislation to ensure that it is not revealed to competitors or otherwise misused. [149]

These provisions were tested in the following case.

Australia and New Zealand Banking Group Ltd v Travel Agents Registration Board

[11.500] *Australia and New Zealand Banking Group Ltd v Travel Agents Registration Board* (unreported, Sup Crt NSW, Lee J, 21 November 1985, BC 8500407)

Facts: ANZ Bank was licensed to carry on business as a travel agent at several of its banking branches. A rival travel agent complained to the Licensing Authority that ANZ had been carrying on business as a travel agent at a branch which was not licensed. The Licensing Authority sent two inspectors to the premises of one of the licensed branches with a letter requesting production of trust account records, which were duly produced. The inspectors asked questions about how bookings were made and what system was followed following bookings. They inspected client files, took client names, addresses and phone numbers and then interviewed several clients and asked them similar questions. Some clients complained to ANZ Bank. ANZ unsuccessfully sought injunctions to restrain the inspectors from making inquiries not connected with the trust account.

Decision: The Supreme Court of New South Wales (Lee J) held that the inspectors had power to ask these questions and make these inquiries under the general power to make inquiries to determine whether the Act was being contravened or complied with. It was not necessary that the specific questions asked should suggest specific breaches or other non-compliance so long as the questions asked were relevant to the carrying on of the business of a travel agent. No improper purpose could be imputed to the inspectors merely because the inspection was prompted by the complaint of a rival.

Grounds for disciplinary action

[11.505] The grounds for disciplinary action are: [150]

(a) improperly obtaining a licence;

(b) conviction for an offence

---

145 Travel Agents legislation: ACT: s 92; NSW: ss 43, 45; NT: ss 20 – 22; Qld: s 45; SA: s 36 powers are limited to requiring information to be provided; Tas: ss 48, 49; Vic: ss 41, 42A.
146 In Qld, a warrant may be required s 45A – C.
147 Travel Agents legislation: ACT: s 169; NSW: ss 44(4), 45; NT: s 23; Qld: s 45(3); SA: s 32; Tas: s 48(4), (5); Vic: s 42A.
148 Travel Agents legislation: NT: s 24; Qld: s 45(4).
149 Travel Agents legislation: NSW: s 54; Qld: s 46; WA: s 52.
150 Travel Agents legislation: ACT: s 65; NSW: s 20(1); NT: s 204(1); Qld: s 24(1); SA: s 16(1); Tas: s 32(1); Vic: s 20(1); WA: s 21(4).

(i) against the Travel Agents legislation,
(ii) against the consumer protection legislation, or
(iii) involving fraud or dishonesty punishable by three months' imprisonment;
(c) failure to comply with a licence condition or the Travel Agents legislation;
(d) insufficient financial resources to carry on business;[151]
(e) carrying on business dishonestly or unfairly;
(d) ceasing to carry on business for one month;
(e) refusal of a licence under corresponding Travel Agents legislation;
(f) disciplinary measures are imposed under corresponding Travel Agents legislation;
(g) ceasing to be eligible for the grant of a licence; and
(f) otherwise ceasing to be a fit and proper person.

Notice to show cause

[11.510] If the Licensing Authority believes there are reasonable grounds for disciplinary action it may serve upon the licensee[152] a notice to show cause why disciplinary measures should not be imposed. The notice must specify the grounds alleged. In some States the notice allows 14 days for the person served to make written submissions in defence[153] and the Licensing Authority then determines whether the grounds have been established.[154] In other States a hearing or inquiry is held[155] and the person served is given the opportunity to be heard before the determination is made.[156] The form and contents of the notice to show cause were considered in the following case.

Young v Travel Agents Registration Board

[11.515] *Young v Travel Agents Registration Board* (1987) 18 IR 173

Facts: The Licensing Authority served upon X and Y notice to show cause why disciplinary measures should not be imposed. The notice made allegations in general terms of a lack of care on their part as directors and officers of a failed corporate travel agent. X and Y challenged the validity of the notice because it did not give sufficient particulars of the ground alleged.

Decision: The New South Wales Supreme Court (Young J) held that the notice was invalid and could not be cured by amendment supplying the further particulars. The notice to show cause is an administrative law document, not a pleading. It must specify the ground alleged and must give sufficient particulars of that ground to enable the agents to know what is being alleged against them

---

151 This includes in some States winding up, official management, receivership, schemes of arrangement or insolvency of a corporation: Travel Agents legislation: WA: s 21(4)(f).
152 And upon all partners, an officer of a body corporate and the supervisor/manager if relevant.
153 Travel Agents legislation: NSW: s 20; NT: s 204; Qld: s 24; Tas: s 32.
154 Travel Agents legislation: NSW: s 21(1); NT: s 205(1); Qld: s 25(1); Tas: s 33(1).
155 Travel Agents legislation: ACT: s 167; SA: s 18 by the District Court; Vic: s 20; WA: s 21.
156 Travel Agents legislation: ACT: s 168; SA: s 18B(1); Vic: s 21(1); WA: s 22(1).

Young v Travel Agents Registration Board cont.

so that they can, by themselves, their solicitor or counsel, put evidentiary material and argument to the tribunal to counter what is alleged.

Disciplinary measures

[11.520] The Licensing Authority may suspend a licence for a limited period pending a determination of the disciplinary procedures.[157] Upon a determination that any of the grounds for disciplinary action is established the Licensing Authority has power to impose a wide range of disciplinary measures, including power to:[158]

(a)   reprimand the licensee;

(b)   require compliance with a stipulation;

(c)   suspend the licence for up to 12 months;

(d)   impose a condition or restriction on the licence;

(e)   impose a fine;[159]

(e)   disqualify the licensee or other person from holding or being engaged in the conduct of a travel agency, permanently or for a specified period; or

(f)   cancel the licence.

The appropriate penalty in disciplinary proceedings was discussed in *Roka v Collins*[160] in the case study above, [11.475]. It was also discussed in the following case.

Re Number Two Janminga Pty Ltd and Travel Agents Licensing Authority

[11.525]   *Re Number Two Janminga Pty Ltd and Travel Agents Licensing Authority* (1991) 5 VAR 200

Facts: A licensed travel agent, J, provided tickets on Philippine Airlines to a sub-agent, M, who carried on business as a travel agent without a licence. This continued for eight months and involved 24 transactions and 56 passengers. The Director of Consumer Affairs objected to J holding a licence on the grounds that J had failed to comply with the Travel Agents legislation (Victoria) and was not a fit and proper person to hold a licence. In disciplinary proceedings the Licensing Authority suspended J's licence for three months and J appealed to the Administrative Appeals Tribunal.

Decision: The Victorian Administrative Appeals Tribunal (Mr KR Howie, Member) held that J had clearly failed to comply with the Act by assisting an unlicensed person to carry on business as a travel agent. This was a serious offence striking at the very heart of the scheme and undermining the system.

---

157   Travel Agents legislation: NSW: s 20(8); NT: s 204(8); Qld: s 24(8); Tas: s 32(8); Vic: s 20(2) – (8).
158   Travel Agents legislation: ACT: s 167; NSW: s 21; NT: s 205; Qld: s 25; SA: s 18B; Tas: s 33; Vic: s 21; WA: s 22.
159   Only in some States: Travel Agents legislation: NT: s 207 50 penalty units for an individual and 250 penalty units for a body corporate only by Local Court on appeal; SA: s 18B(1)(b) $20,000; WA: s 22(1)(b) $1,000.
160   *Roka v Collins* (unreported, SA CCA, 10 January 1994, BC 9400531).

Re Number Two Janminga Pty Ltd and Travel Agents Licensing Authority cont.

However it did not in this case establish that J was not a fit and proper person to continue to hold a licence and so the appropriate penalty was not suspension or cancellation but rather a reprimand.

―――― ∞⌘ ――――

Appeal

[11.530] Determinations in disciplinary proceedings may be appealed under procedures which vary from State to State but which are similar to those provided for appeals against licence refusals of conditions.[161] The above appeal cases illustrate the approach.

Unjust conduct and undertakings

[11.535] Travel agents are subject to the general regulatory provisions on fair trading discussed in Chapter 9. These contain provisions for industry codes of conduct to be endorsed by the regulatory authority. No such code has yet been endorsed for travel agents. However AFTA has adopted a Code of Ethics which may in time evolve into a suitable fair trading code of conduct (see [11.380]).

Four States have enacted special provisions to regulate unjust conduct by travel agents.[162] Unjust conduct is defined as conduct which is:[163]

(a)   dishonest or unfair;

(b)   breach of contract;

(c)   breach of the Travel Agents legislation or the consumer protection legislation; or

(d)   failure to comply with a licence condition or restriction.

Such conduct would usually give rise to other rights and remedies, particularly conduct of the kind described in (b) to (d). However (a) is more vague and it is not clear how far "dishonest" may extend beyond the criminal law or "unfair" beyond the *Australian Consumer Law*. They may well extend to the customs and practices of the travel industry and the rules and standards set by the AFTA Code of Ethics. If so they would provide a useful enforcement mechanism.

The effect of the special provisions in the Travel Agents legislation is to give the Licensing Authority a graduated set of regulatory steps which bridge the gap between the carrot and the stick; that is, between the incentives of self-discipline and the sanctions of the disciplinary measures discussed above. If satisfied that a travel agent has repeatedly engaged in unjust conduct the following steps are available.

Undertaking

[11.540] The Licensing Authority (in Victoria, the director) may request the travel agent to execute a deed of undertaking[164] to cease the conduct and rectify the consequences of it. This undertaking is registered and prevents any other disciplinary action or measures being taken

---

161   Travel Agents legislation: ACT: ss 42, 167 to the Civil and Administrative Tribunal; NSW: ss 22, 25 to the Administrative Decisions Tribunal by rehearing and from there on a question of law to the Supreme Court; NT: s 206, 207 to the Local Court; Qld: s 26 to the Minister and from there to the District Court by rehearing; Tas: s 34 to a magistrate (Administrative Appeals division); Vic: s 22 to the Civil and Administrative Tribunal; WA: ss 23, 25 Administrative Tribunal.

162   Travel Agents legislation: NSW: ss 28 – 32; NT: ss 215 – 219; Vic: ss 25 – 29; WA: ss 36 – 40.

163   Travel Agents legislation: NSW: s 28; NT: s 215; Vic: s 25; WA: s 36.

164   Travel Agents legislation: NSW: ss 29, 30; NT: ss 216, 217; WA: ss 37, 38.

while it is observed. Failure to observe the undertaking may be penalised by a fine of up to $5,000 and it also provides grounds for obtaining a restraining order to observe the undertaking. [165]

Restraining order

[11.545] The tribunal or court (in Victoria, the business licensing authority) may order [166] the travel agent to cease the conduct and may impose conditions including action to rectify the consequences. Failure to obey the order may be penalised by a fine of up to $5,000 and it also provides grounds for the disciplinary action and measures described above. [167]

Despite the apparent usefulness of these provisions, they have been used only rarely. That probably explains why most of the later States to join the Uniform Scheme did not bother including them in their Travel Agents legislation. [168]

In one of the few cases relying on these provisions, a travel agent was selling frequent flyer award airline tickets notwithstanding that under the conditions of the awards they were not transferable. The Licensing Authority obtained an undertaking from the travel agent to cease the conduct. [169]

TRAVEL COMPENSATION FUND

[11.550] The TCF provides the second limb of the Co-operative Scheme for the Regulation of Travel Agents. The purposes of the TCF are: [170]

(a) to provide compensation to certain people who deal with travel agents; and

(b) to provide for the operation of the Fund; and

(c) to ensure that only persons who have sufficient financial resources to enable them to carry on business as a travel agent are participants of the Fund.

---

165 Travel Agents legislation: NSW: s 31(2); NT: s 218(2); Vic: s 28(3); WA: s 39(2).
166 Travel Agents legislation: NSW: s 31; NT: s 218; Vic: s 28; WA: s 39.
167 Travel Agents legislation: NSW: s 20(1)(c); Vic: s 20(1)(c); WA: s 21(4)(b).
168 Travel Agents Legislation comprises: ACT: *Agents Act 2003*; Qld: *Travel Agents Act 1988*; SA: *Travel Agents Act 1986*; Tas: *Travel Agents Act 1987*.
169 Register of Undertakings, Travel Agents Licensing Authority of Victoria. This is the only undertaking obtained in the first ten years in which the unjust conduct provisions were in force in Victoria.
170 Travel Compensation Fund Trust Deed amended to 4 December 2009, clause 3.

The TCF was established in 1986 and between the years 2001 - 2009, it has paid out more than $29 million in claims. There are over 4750 travel agencies (including branch offices) participating in the TCF.[171]

All States participate in the TCF scheme except the Northern Territory, which is discussed separately in [11.625].

Administration

[11.555] The TCF was established by a Deed of Trust (the TCF Trust Deed) on 12 December 1986 by agreement among the initial participating States in the Co-operative scheme.[172] All other States except the Northern Territory have since joined the compensation limb of the scheme. The TCF Trust Deed may be amended by a resolution of 75% of the Trustees and has been so amended many times.[173]

The Trustees comprise nominees (half of whom have knowledge of the travel industry) of the relevant Minister of each State together with one or two with knowledge of the interests of travel consumers nominated by the Ministers acting jointly.[174] The functions of the Trustees are undertaken by sub-committees,[175] the most important of which is the Management Committee which meets monthly and determines eligibility, approves claims and receives representations from travel agents on the Financial Criteria.[176]

The Travel Compensation Fund includes:[177]

- all contributions, fees and levies from applicants and contributors;
- the investments of the TCF and the income on those investments;
- all moneys recovered under the right of subrogation; and
- the illegal profits recovered by participating States from unlicensed travel agents.[178]

It is recognised that the TCF is not a bottomless pit. As discussed below, the right to compensation is quite narrow, with any wider claims being subject to the Trustees' discretion.[179] To offset some of the risk, the Trustees used to maintain a Catastrophe Back-up Insurance Policy. However, following the blowout in claims in 1993, the cost of this cover appears to have become unviable. The Trustees also have power to raise special levies where they consider the TCF is insufficient to meet existing or potential claims and this was used to meet the claims blowout in 1993.[180] Queensland's legislation provides that if the TCF is insufficient to meet all claims then the Trustees must apportion the amount available between the claimants.[181]

---

171 At 31 December, 2009: *Travel Compensation Fund Annual Report 2009*, pp 8-13.
172 New South Wales, Victoria, South Australia, and Western Australia.
173 TCF Trust Deed, Part 30.
174 TCF Trust Deed, Part 4.
175 TCF Trust Deed, Part 21.
176 *Travel Compensation Fund Annual Report 2009*, pp 22, 23.
177 TCF Trust Deed, Part 5.
178 Travel Agents legislation: ACT: s 92; NSW: s 38(3); NT: s 188(2), (3); Qld: s 12(3), (4); SA: s 7(2), (3); Tas: s 45(2), (10); Vic: s 35(2), (10); WA: s 32.
179 TCF Trust Deed, Part 15.
180 TCF Trust Deed, Clause 6.1(b).
181 Travel Agents legislation: Qld: s 41(2).

The Trustees must keep a register of the name and address of all participants and record all variations to names as approved and notified by the Licensing Authorities. [182] The accounts of the trust are audited [183] and an annual report is provided to each Minister. [184]

Participation

[11.560] As already noted, the TCF is linked to the first limb (the uniform licensing legislation) by making participation in the TCF a condition of licensing [185] and vice versa. If a licensee ceases to be a participant in the TCF its licence is usually suspended until the licensee again participates.

The TCF Deed defines a "participant" as a person whom the trustees determine is eligible to be a contributor of the TCF and who is licensed under the Travel Agents legislation. [186] Persons exempted from licensing may elect to become participants provided they pay the usual contributions. [187]

The number of participants in the Travel Compensation Fund at 31 December 2009 stood at 4,750, comprising 3,100 principal locations and 1,650 branch locations. [188] The numbers in each State are shown in the following chart.

Participants by State in the Travel Compensation Fund Approved at 31 December 2009

State	Head Office 2009	Branch Office 2009
ACT	25	39
NSW	1280	488
VIC	804	390
QLD	485	402
SA	166	125
WA	307	175
TAS	33	4
Total	3100	1650

Source: *Travel Compensation Fund Annual Report 2009* p 13.

As the procedure for becoming a contributor of the TCF has some similarity with the procedure for obtaining a travel agent's licence as depicted in the model above, it will be discussed under similar headings.

---

182 TCF Trust Deed, Part 14.
183 TCF Trust Deed, Part 24.
184 TCF Trust Deed, Part 25.
185 Travel Agents legislation: ACT: s 91; NSW: s 11(2); NT: ss 195(1)(b), 221; Qld: ss 20(1)(b), 37; SA: s 20; Tas: s 22(2); Vic: s 11(2); WA: s 13(2).
186 TCF Trust Deed, Clause 1 definition of "participant".
187 TCF Trust Deed, Part 10.
188 *Travel Compensation Fund Annual Report 2009*, p 13.

Application

Initial application

[11.565] Initial application must be made to the trustees in the prescribed form and accompanied by the prescribed fees and documents.[189] The fees payable[190] are $8,190 for a principal location and a further $5,470 for each branch location, made up as follows:

Travel Compensation Fund Fees

	Principal Location[191]	Branch Location
Administration Fee (non refundable)	760	470
Fund contribution (refundable)	7,430	50000
	$8,190	$5470

The documents which must accompany an initial application comprise:

- detailed monthly budgeted Profit and Loss Account;
- audited Balance Sheet (for companies, trusts and associations);
- verified Statement of Personal Assets and Liabilities (for sole traders, partners and individual trustees);
- Statement of Acquisition and Commencement Costs;
- auditor's letter confirming appointment; and
- vendor's letter advising proposed treatment of client deposits on changeover[192] and whether vendor will continue as a TCF member (for purchase of an existing agency).

The trustees may require an applicant to provide such additional information as they consider necessary to enable them to determine whether the applicant is eligible to be a contributor to the TCF.[193]

Renewal application

[11.570] A participant must also lodge a renewal application and annual review of the licensed travel agency[194] and pay annual renewal fees[195] within three months of the end of the agent's financial year. These fees are currently $390 for each principal location and $290 for each branch location.[196] The documents which must accompany the renewal application comprise:

- Annual Financial Review covering the performance of the agency measured against the Financial Criteria (see later) and signed by the agent and the auditor;

---

189 TCF Trust Deed, Claused 9.1-9.4.
190 TCF Trust Deed, Clause 6.1.
191 *Application for Participation in the Travel Compensation Fund*, TCF website at http://www.tcf.org.au/Agent_Participants.asp?Page=Fee_Schedule.
192 Once the agency changes hands and within one month of approval of the application by the trustees an Audit Certificate must be provided showing the amount of client liabilities transferred and the amount of cash deposited into the purchaser's bank account in satisfaction thereof.
193 TCF Trust Deed, Clause 12.
194 TCF Trust Deed, Clause 12A.
195 TCF Trust Deed, Clause 12B.
196 TCF website at http://www.tcf.org.au/Agent_Participants.asp?Page=Fee_Schedule.

- Audited Financial Statements;
- Detailed Profit and Loss Statement;
- Directors' Report and Directors' Statement (for companies, and by trustees for trusts);
- Verified Statement of Personal Assets and Liabilities (for sole traders, partners and individual trustees).

The trustees may also at any time require a participant to provide such additional information as they consider necessary to enable them to determine whether the participant remains eligible to be a contributor to the TCF. [197]

Investigation

[11.575] It can be seen that the application process requires the applicant to produce independently verified and audited information, thus reducing the need for the Trustees to make outside inquiries or investigations. This can be contrasted with the procedure for obtaining a travel agent's licence. The issues considered in a TCF application are also more objective than those considered in a travel agent's licensing application.

However, before they make a decision that an applicant is not eligible to become or remain a participant or to impose conditions, the Trustees must allow the applicant a reasonable opportunity to be heard. [198]

Decision

[11.580] A person is eligible to be a contributor to the TCF if the person has and is likely to continue to have *sufficient financial resources to enable the person to carry on business as a travel agent*. [199] However, in making that determination the trustees may take into account the following matters about any person concerned with the management of the business: [200]

- experience in the management of the financial affairs of a business; and
- involvement in the management of a failed travel agency; and
- involvement in the management of a travel agency in respect of which a claim has been made under this Deed; and
- has been a travel agent in respect of whom a claim has been made under this Deed; and
- has previously failed to meet a criterion in guidelines issued under clause 9.4; and
- has been involved in the management of another business; and
- has previously applied to be a participant.

It should be noted that the key issues for determining eligibility for a travel agent's licence – namely whether the applicant is a *fit and proper person* and the qualifications and experience in travel agency of the supervisor/manager – are not relevant to the TCF application.

The Trustees must publish guidelines on the criteria to be used to determine the issue of whether or not the applicant or a participant has sufficient financial resources. The financial criteria currently used are similar to those used to determine the eligibility of the travel agent

---

197 TCF Trust Deed, Clause 12A.
198 TCF Trust Deed, Clause 13.1.
199 TCF Trust Deed, Clause 9.1.
200 TCF Trust Deed, Clause 9.2.

to be accredited as a passenger sales agent under IATA's rules for the accreditation of passenger sales agents. They are discussed below in [11.635].

The Trustees may determine a reasonable date and time for compliance with any conditions.[201] If a participant fails to provide the required information[202] or pay any contribution, fee, levy or penalty[203] the Trustees may determine that the participant is not eligible to be a contributor.

If the applicant or participant has paid the required contributions and fees and the Trustees determine that they are eligible to be[204] or to remain[205] a contributor of the TCF, the Trustees certify this to the relevant Licensing Authority. That satisfies this condition of the travel agent's licence.[206]

If the Trustees determine that the applicant or participant is not eligible to become[207] or to remain[208] a contributor of the TCF, the Trustees must notify them and the relevant Licensing Authority of the determination and the matters taken into account in making it. Refusal of an initial application then disqualifies an applicant from obtaining a travel agent's licence. A person ceases to be a participant upon a determination that they are no longer eligible and they are then in default of this condition of their travel agent's licence.[209]

Conditions

[11.585] The Trustees may make their determination that a person is or remains eligible to be a contributor of the TCF subject to compliance with any one or more of the following conditions:[210]

(a) *Business operation*

The person may be required to:

(i) maintain a trust account for moneys received from clients;

(ii) increase the capital of the business; or

(iii) reduce the debt of the business.

(b) *Guarantee*

A guarantee of the person's business may be required. At 31 December 2009 the TCF was holding $1.697 million in recovered bank guarantees.[211]

(c) *Accounting*

Books and accounting records may be required to be maintained in a specified way.

---

201 TCF Trust Deed, Clause 9.7.
202 TCF Trust Deed, Clause 12A.
203 TCF Trust Deed, Clause 12B.2.
204 TCF Trust Deed, Clause 10.
205 TCF Trust Deed, Clause 12A.
206 Travel Agents legislation: ACT: s 91; NSW: s 11(2); NT: s 195(1)(b), s 221; Qld: ss 20(1)(b), 37; SA: s 20; Tas: s 22(2); Vic: s 11(2); WA: s 13(2).
207 TCF Trust Deed, Clause 10.2.
208 TCF Trust Deed, Clause 12B.4, 12B.5.
209 Travel Agents legislation: ACT: s 91; NSW: s 11(2); NT: s 195(1)(b), s 221; Qld: ss 20(1)(b), 37; SA: s 20; Tas: s 22(2); Vic: s 11(2); WA: s 13(2).
210 TCF Trust Deed, Clauses 9.6, 12A.2.
211 *Travel Compensation Fund Annual Report 2009*, p 26.

(d) *Auditor's report*

A report of a qualified auditor or accountant nominated by the Trustees may be required at the person's expense:

(i) stating that the accounting records give a true and fair view of the financial position of the business; or

(ii) providing the information required to permit the Trustees to determine the person's eligibility.

(e) *Floating charge*

A floating charge may be required over the assets and undertakings of the person's business in favour of the Trustees.

Appeal

[11.590] A person who was the applicant or participant has the following rights of appeal. After a determination that a person is no longer eligible to be a participant, the Trustees may, upon written application of the person who was the participant, reinstate the person as a contributor of the TCF.[212]

The TCF Trust Deed[213] also acknowledges that an applicant or a participant may also appeal under the Travel Agents legislation against a determination by the Trustees that they are not eligible or are no longer eligible or against conditions of eligibility.[214] Such an appeal was considered in the following case.

Re Gateway Management & Travel Compensation Fund

[11.595] *Re Gateway Management Pty Ltd and Travel Compensation Fund* (1993) 5 VAR 613

Facts: The Trustees had determined that travel agent G was no longer eligible to be a member of the TCF because it did not have sufficient financial resources to carry on business as a travel agent. Evidence had been given that, following the pilots' strike and recession, G had made losses of $85,000 in 1990, $30,000 in 1991 and $30,000 in 1992, that there was a shortfall in working capital of $110,000 and that G had not provided a bank guarantee of $70,000 required by the Trustees. Evidence was also given that overheads were relatively high at $24,000 per month on an annual turnover of $2.5m and there had been trust account transgressions. In all, G scored 3 out of the possible 20 points on the tests of financial criteria.

Decision: The Victorian Administrative Appeals Tribunal (Fagan J) held that "the absence of the required financial resources provides a reasonable motive for a licensee to resort to trust funds of its clients thereby exposing the Fund to loss in the event of the financial collapse of the licensee". There

---

212 TCF Trust Deed, Clause 12C.1.
213 TCF Trust Deed, Clause 13.2.
214 Travel Agents legislation: ACT: s 158 to the Civil and Administrative Tribunal; NSW: ss 22(3), 24, 25 to the Administrative Decisions Tribunal; NT: ss 206(3), 208 to the Local Court; Qld: s 26(7) to the Civil and Administrative Tribunal; SA: s 21 to the Disciplinary Division of the District Court; Tas: s 34(3) to a magistrate; Vic: s 46 to the civil and Administrative Tribunal; WA: ss 23(2), 24, 25 to the State Administrative Tribunal.

Re Gateway Management & Travel Compensation Fund cont.

were serious reservations about the accuracy of the accounts and projections for the company and the projections were "extremely optimistic". The decision of the Trustees was affirmed.

CLAIMS

Claims entitlement

[11.600] The Travel Agents legislation in some States purports to give claimants a much wider right to compensation than that actually delivered under the TCF Trust Deed.[215] New South Wales and Tasmania provide that regulations may be made prescribing "a scheme for compensating persons who suffer a pecuniary loss by reason of an act or omission by a person who carries on, or carried on, business as a travel agent".[216] Western Australia has a similar provision, except it does not confine the loss to pecuniary loss.[217] Queensland purports to provide claimants with an entitlement to recover compensation from the scheme for loss in consequence of:

(a) dishonesty or negligence of a person carrying on business as a travel agent;

(b) death, disappearance of insolvency; or

(c) failure to carry out contractual obligations properly;

of a person carrying on business as a travel agent, subject to the trust deed.[218]

All these provisions are misleading. The TCF Trust Deed actually provides for a very narrow right to compensation. It provides:

> 15.1 The Board must pay compensation out of the Fund in accordance with the terms of the Deed to a person who –
>
> (a) enters into travel arrangements or travel-related arrangements directly or indirectly with a participant; and
>
> (b) has suffered or may suffer direct pecuniary loss arising from a failure to account by the participant and the failure to account arises from an act or omission by the participant or an employee or agent of the participant; and
>
> (c) is not protected against the direct pecuniary loss by a policy of insurance.
>
> 15.1A The Board must not pay compensation under clause 15.1 in excess of $25,000 to any person in respect of any failure to account by a participant.

The end result is that a person has a right to compensation only so far as:

---

215 This problem does not arise in the Australian Capital Territory, Northern Territory, South Australia and Victoria which refer to the compensation scheme approved by the Travel Agents Board of Trustees or the relevant Minister: Travel Agents legislation: ACT: s 94; NT: ss 185; 220; SA: ss 3, 19; Vic ss 3, 46.

216 Travel Agents legislation: NSW: s 57(2)(a); Tas: s 55(2)(m).

217 *Travel Agents Act 1985* (WA), s 59(2)(h).

218 *Travel Agents Act 1988* (Qld), s 40.

1. the person [219] entrusted money [220] directly or indirectly to a participant for travel arrangements. [221] A non-resident is not covered for travel outside Australia; [222]
2. the participant [223] being a licensed travel agent and eligible TCF contributor [224] failed to account;
3. compensation is limited to pecuniary loss [225] not covered by insurance. [226]

So despite suggestions to the contrary in some States' Travel Agents legislation, a person cannot recover from the TCF for negligence, breach of contract, personal injuries or disappointment. A person cannot recover from the TCF for the default of a principal such as an airline or hotel. A client cannot recover if the travel agent was unlicensed subject to the discretion to pay, discussed below. Given the nature of the product and practices in the travel industry, consumers remain at considerable risk in all these circumstances. Compared with the position in Europe under the EC Directive, for example, these are serious deficiencies in the compensation limb of the Australian scheme.

However the TCF Trust Deed does give the Trustees a *discretion* to pay other claims. It provides:

15.2 The Board may pay compensation out of the Fund in accordance with the terms of the Deed to –

(a) a person referred to in clause 15.1 in relation to other loss arising from a failure to account as referred to in that clause; or

(b) a person who has suffered any loss arising from a failure to account in relation to any travel arrangement or travel-related arrangement and the failure to account arises from an act or omission by another person who is not a participant, or an employee or agent of that other person; or

(c) a person referred to in clause 15.1 in respect of any direct pecuniary loss suffered by that person which exceeds $25,000.

(d) a person other than a person referred to in clause 15.5 who suffers a loss in respect of travel arrangements or travel-related arrangements that are not within Australia.

The Trustees may develop and publish guidelines that apply to the payment of compensation arising under Clause 15.2. [227] The amount of compensation awarded by the Trustees is not to exceed the pecuniary loss suffered, except insofar as the payment is made by way of emergency compensation under Clause 18. [228]

Although the right to claim is confined to narrow grounds, the number of claims made and the value of claims paid under the scheme have been substantial, as shown in the following charts:

---

219 A client may also be a participant, ie a participant intermediary may claim for moneys entrusted to another participant intermediary.
220 Or valuable consideration.
221 Or "travel-related arrangements" which include accommodation, car hire and travellers' cheques: TCF Trust Deed, Clause 1.1 definitions.
222 Proviso to definition of "client": TCF Trust Deed, Clause 15.5.
223 Or an employee or agent of a participant TCF Trust Deed, Clause 15.1(b).
224 Definition of "participant": TCF Trust Deed, Clause 1.1.
225 TCF Trust Deed, Clause 151(b).
226 TCF Trust Deed, Clause 151(c).
227 TCF Trust Deed, Clause 15.3.
228 TCF Trust Deed, Clause 17.2.

Number and Value of Travellers' Claims on the Travel Compensation Fund

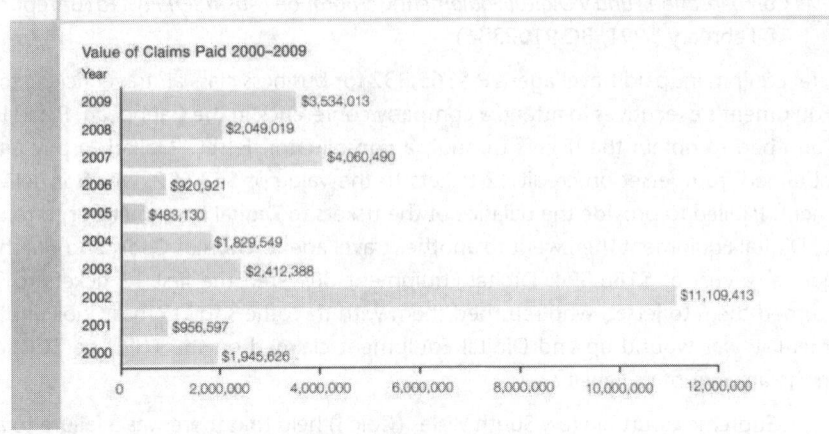

Value of Claims Paid 2000–2009

Year	Value
2009	$3,534,013
2008	$2,049,019
2007	$4,060,490
2006	$920,921
2005	$483,130
2004	$1,829,549
2003	$2,412,388
2002	$11,109,413
2001	$956,597
2000	$1,945,626

Source: Travel Compensation Fund Annual Report 2009, p 8.

Claims rose sharply in 2002 following the terrorist attacks on the World Trade Centre in September 2001 resulting in the collapse of several major participants. The TCF took urgent action to stem the tide and introduced more rigorous financial criteria to determine the eligibility of participants. Claims then settled back to more acceptable levels for the industry. Further "peaks" occurred in 2007 and 2009, the most recent one resulting from the collapse of 30 travel agencies.

Claims procedure

[11.605] Claims must be made in writing to the Trustees within 12 months after the failure to account arose, although the Trustees have a discretion to accept claims outside this time.[229] The Trustees are also authorised to disregard the formal claims procedure and pay such compensation under Part 15 as is necessary to meet emergency requirements in whole or in part where a participant fails to meet or is unable to meet its obligations.[230]

There is no time limit upon the Trustees to make a decision on a claim. The Trustees may decide to admit the claim in whole or in part or reject it and notice of the decision must be provided to the claimant within 14 days.[231]

A claimant has a right of appeal against the Trustee's decision under Clause 15.1 (but not under Clause 15.2). An Appeal Committee of three members appointed by the Minister of the relevant State rehears the matter and decides by majority.

In Queensland, a claimant dissatisfied with the decision of the Trustees on a claim may also appeal under the Travel Agents legislation.[232]

These matters were considered in the following case.

---

229 TCF Trust Deed, Part 16.
230 TCF Trust Deed, Part 18.
231 TCF Trust Deed, Part 16.8.
232 Travel Agents legislation: Qld: ss 26(7), 41 to the District Court.

Travel Compensation Fund v Digital Equipment Corporation

[11.610] *Travel Compensation Fund v Digital Equipment Corporation (Australia) Pty Ltd* (unreported Sup Crt NSW, Cole J, 18 February 1991, BC 9102336)

Facts: Digital Equipment paid travel agent P $165,332 for business class air travel tickets to enable 38 of Digital Equipment's executives to attend a company conference in the Caribbean. P had lost IATA accreditation and had to obtain the tickets through a consolidator, Jetset. P failed to pay Jetset any moneys but obtained from Jetset on credit 12 tickets to the value of $52,692, which it delivered to Digital Equipment. P failed to provide the balance of the tickets to Digital Equipment or to refund any of the moneys. Digital Equipment then went to another travel agent, Thomas Cook, and purchased all the tickets again at a cost of $186,894. Digital Equipment delivered the first 12 tickets to Thomas Cook, who returned them to Jetset, who returned them with the others to Thomas Cook and then to Digital Equipment. P was wound up and Digital Equipment claimed on the TCF. The TCF sought a declaration on the amount of its liability.

Decision: The Supreme Court of New South Wales (Cole J) held that there was a failure to account for the price paid for 26 tickets as conceded by the Trustees. Firstly, P dealt with Digital Equipment as a principal to deliver 38 tickets and was not required to account for the price at which it obtained the tickets or any profit even though Digital Equipment chose to return them and have them reissued. Secondly, there was no failure to account for the $52,692 because P had delivered 12 valid tickets for this and "the Trust Deed contemplates an accounting by an agent for monies received by the provision of tickets, travel vouchers and services as well as moneys". Accordingly the TCF was obligated to compensate Digital Equipment for the difference between the $165,323 paid to P and the $52,692 worth of tickets received.

Sequel: In an interesting sequel to this case, Digital Equipment then successfully sued Jetset and recovered the approximately $59,000 paid through Thomas Cook to Jetset for the unnecessary reissue of the 12 tickets. It was held that Digital Equipment was entitled to recover this sum from Jetset as moneys paid under a mistake of fact and for total failure of consideration.[233]

Subrogation

[11.615] It will be recalled from Chapter 7 ([7.60]) that subrogation is the right of an insurer who has paid a claim to step into the shoes of the claimant and exercise the claimant's rights to sue and recover from any other person legally liable to the claimant on the claim.

Where the TCF pays a claim arising from an act or omission of a travel agent the TCF trustees are subrogated to the rights of the claimant.[234] If the travel agent is a body corporate these rights are also enforceable against the directors unless the act or omission occurred without their knowledge or consent.[235] If the travel agent is not licensed then any person who

---

[233] *Digital Equipment Corporation (Australia) Pty Ltd v Jetset Tours (NSW) Pty Ltd* (unreported, SC NSW Windeyer J, 4 September 1995, BC 9505370).

[234] Travel Agents legislation: ACT: s 94; NSW: s 40(3), NT: s 222(1); Qld: s 42(3); SA: s 25(1); Tas: s 42(3); Vic: s 37(3); WA: s 49(1). Under Clause 15.7 of the TCF Trust Deed the Trustees may also make compensation payments in consideration or subject to assignments of the claimants rights and entitlement against a third person.

[235] Travel Agents legislation: ACT: s 94(4), (3), NSW: s 40(4), (5), NT: s 222(2), (3); Qld: s 42(4), (5); s 25(2), (3); Tas: s 42(4), (5); Vic: s 37(4), (5); WA: s 49(2), (3).

supplied the travel agent with goods or services in connection with the act or omission is deemed to have aided and abetted the act or omission [236] and is jointly and severally liable with the unlicensed travel agent. [237]

The leading case on the TCF's rights of subrogation is *Re Travel Compensation Fund, Dunn and Others* discussed previously in relation to travel agents splitting businesses and sharing premises (see [11.435]). It is considered further here on this issue.

Re Travel Compensation Fund, Dunn and Others

[11.620] *Re Travel Compensation Fund, Dunn and Others* (unreported, Federal Court, Wilcox J, 2 December 1992)

Facts: It will be recalled that Travel Abroad was the travel agent which put together European package tours and Wheels Abroad was the associated company which arranged car hire for the tours. These companies collapsed and the TCF paid out claims of $423,369 more than it was able to recover from the liquidation of Travel Abroad. The TCF claimed rights of subrogation against two groups of respondents.

1. Claim against directors (subrogation)

The companies grew from a turnover of $8 million in 1986/1987 to $20 million in 1987/1988. The companies were owned by the L brothers until their sale on 21 September 1988 to IPG for $200,000. IPG expected liabilities and contingencies to be $2 million. It appointed three new directors, D, B and S, who governed the companies until their collapse. They discovered liabilities substantially in excess of the $2 million. They resolved on 7 October 1988 that moneys received from all "new" bookings be paid into a new Travel Abroad client account from 12 October 1988. D interpreted "new" as excluding the balance of moneys received for bookings on which deposits had been received before 12 October 1988 and these continued to be paid into the general account. By 18 October IPG had injected $2 million working capital into the companies. They continued to discover further unpaid creditors. A list of assets and liabilities at 30 November 1988 prepared by staff showed assets of $860,000 and liabilities of $5,979,870 (including the $2 million injected by IPG) and a deficiency of $5,119,870. The manager informed the TCF on 15 December 1988. IPG was due to complete the purchase of the companies on 18 December but rescinded for breach of contract. The companies ceased trading and the directors resigned on 21 December 1988.

Decision on 1. The Federal Court (Wilcox J) held that the directors were liable as directors of the company whose "act or omission" caused the failure to account. The relevant act or omission was not the failure to account after the company ceased to trade and the directors resigned on 21 December 1988 but the failure to deposit each client's prepayments into a trust account as and when received. D was the chief executive and instructed the staff to establish the client account only after 12 October and then only for "new" bookings, and so could not establish the defence that it was without his knowledge or consent. P was a non-executive director who knew the company was insolvent and was continuing to trade and did nothing to ensure that client prepayments be kept in a separate trust account until 7 December 1988. So P was liable for the $11,100 in payments received up to 7 October. He was not liable under the Travel Agents legislation for moneys received after that as he was entitled to assume that D would carry out the decision of the board. However both directors were also fully

---

236   Travel Agents legislation: ACT: s 95, NSW: s 40(6), NT: s 222(4), *Criminal Codes* 12; Qld: s 42(6); Tas: s 42(7), (8); Vic: s 37(7); WA: 49(4), s 7 *Criminal Code*.

237   Travel Agents legislation: ACT: s 95, NSW: s 40(7), NT: s 222(4), Qld: s 42(7); Tas: s 42(6), 44; Vic: s 37(6); WA: s 49(4).

Re Travel Compensation Fund, Dunn and Others cont.

liable under the Corporations Law as directors of an insolvent company continuing to trade and there was no partial defence for P to that liability. His Honour Wilcox J summed the situation up neatly at paragraph 78 as follows:

> The purchase by IPG of Travel Abroad and Wheels Abroad was a transaction fraught with danger; not only to that company but, because it involved continued trading, to the creditors and clients of Travel Abroad.

Facts continued:

2. Claim against auditors (negligence)

Early in 1987 the TCF began requiring participants to submit audited financial accounts. The accounting firm P&M audited the company's 1987 accounts and the TCF relied upon these to renew Travel Abroad's participation. It was found that those accounts were negligently audited. Without the wrong allocation of $300,000 of Travel Abroad's overheads to Wheels Abroad, Travel Abroad's accounts would have shown a substantial loss and its participation would not have been renewed or would have been made conditional upon a substantial capital injection or security against claims. In 1988 P&M knew the companies were in serious financial difficulties. On 31 August 1988 they wrote to the directors advising that on an amalgamated basis Travel Abroad and Wheels Abroad were insolvent. They made several recommendations to the directors, including the operation of separate client accounts. They repeated this advice and recommendations to the new directors. The audited 1988 accounts due to be lodged with the TCF by 30 September 1988 were not lodged and P&M successfully applied for extensions on behalf of the company.

Decision on 2. The Federal Court (Wilcox J) held that the auditors were liable to the TCF for negligence in auditing the 1987 accounts. They knew that part of their task was to supply the information necessary for the TCF to consider Travel Abroad's continued participation in the fund. TCF was obviously a person so closely and directly affected by the audit that the auditors ought reasonably to have had it in mind in carrying out their duties. Thus they clearly owed a duty of care to the TCF. They breached that duty by simply accepting the allocation of overheads proposed by L. They should have either obtained amendments or refused to audit the accounts. If they had done so Travel Abroad would not have been allowed to continue to participate after 30 September 1987 without adequate security against claims and the TCF would not have incurred the losses. It was not necessary to decide whether P&M were liable to the TCF for negligence or misleading conduct in respect of the 1988 accounts. A cross claim by director P against the auditors failed because there was no evidence that IPG saw or relied upon the accounts.

Sequel: In an interesting sequel to this case, the TCF then claimed against the auditors' insurers.

In *Travel Compensation Fund v Travel Guide Pty Ltd (In Liquidation)*,[238] Lehane J upheld the TCF's rights of subrogation against the directors of the company on the basis that failure to establish a separate trust account for travel moneys received by a company in a parlous financial situation was a failure to account.

In *Travel Compensation Fund v Robert Tambree t/as R Tambree and Associates and Ors*,[239] the High Court unanimously upheld the right of the TCF to recover compensation from auditors and accountants who prepared misleading and deceptive financial information on which the TFC relied to renew a travel agent's participation in the scheme. In fact, the travel agent's business was failing and the travel agent herself was ineligible for a licence based on the TCF scheme's financial criteria. However, because of the misleading financial reports, these matters did not come to the attention of

---

238 *Travel Compensation Fund v Travel Guide Pty Ltd (In Liquidation)* (unreported, Federal Court, 13 February 1997).

239 *Travel Compensation Fund v Robert Tambree t/as R Tambree and Associates and Ors* (2005) 224 CLR 627.

Re Travel Compensation Fund, Dunn and Others cont.

the TCF for a further two months during which time the travel agent continued to trade illegally and unlicensed. The TCF paid out all claims including those made during the unlicensed trading period. In its decision, the High Court accepted the right if the TCF to protect itself against claims, including unlicensed trading claims and to recover the money from those liable for the deception.

The express right of subrogation of the TCF under the legislation should be contrasted with the uncertainties of relying upon an implied right at common law. [240]

―――― ෧ඏ ――――

Northern Territory Travel Industry Compensation Scheme

[11.625] The Northern Territory has provided an alternative private insurance scheme and at this stage Northern Territory travel agents do not participate in the TCF. The Northern Territory [241] also exempts participants in the alternative scheme from compliance with its Travel Agents legislation. [242] Exemption is granted on various conditions which in effect are similar to many of the provisions of the legislation except for participation in the TCF. As an alternative to participation in the TCF Northern Territory travel agents are required to participate in an approved insurance and/or compensation scheme. [243]

While the Northern Territory maintains the alternative scheme the TCF refuses to consider Northern Territory applications for participation in the TCF.

Finance and Accounting

[11.630] Finance and accounting involve travel agents in more litigation than any other aspect of the business except perhaps for consumer protection. The key problem is that moneys received from clients on behalf of principals are generally trust moneys but, unlike every other occupation and profession in a similar position, [244] the way is left open for imprudent travel agents to deal with these moneys as their own and use them to finance their travel agency or other interests. All too often travel agents who do this are unable to account and the client, principal or the TCF must bear the loss.

Financial criteria

[11.635] The whole thrust of the criteria for participation in the TCF is directed to this problem. To be eligible, a travel agent must have sufficient financial resources to be able to carry on the business with the minimum of financial risk of default. [245] The threshold for entry and continued participation in the compensation scheme is determined by financial criteria set

---

240 *Barclays Bank Ltd v TOSG Trust Fund Ltd* [1984] 2 WLR 49.
241 Pursuant to Travel Agents legislation: NT: ss 220 – 223.
242 Travel Agents legislation: NT: s 337.
243 Travel Agents legislation: NT: s 221.
244 For example insurance agents, real estate agents and solicitors.
245 TCF Trust Deed, Clause 9.1.

by the Trustees.[246] It may from time to time develop and publish guidelines [247] and if it is still not satisfied that a person is eligible to be a participant, it may require compliance with additional conditions.[248]

To ease the administration and expense of compliance these criteria are similar to those used by IATA for accreditation of passenger sales agents.

The financial criteria provide that a participant may be required to:[249]

(i) maintain a trust account or client account in respect of any money received in the course of that business; or

(ii) increase the capital of that business; or

(iii) reduce the debt of that business; or

(iv) provide in favour of the Board any security it requires in any form it determines; or

(v) pay any costs incurred in connection with providing or releasing that security.

In the case of persons seeking eligibility to be a participant, the Trustee Board may specify that:

- the business be guaranteed or insured;[250]
- the person maintain and operate books of account and other accounting records of the business;[251]
- a report be obtained at the expense of the person from a duly qualified auditor or accountant nominated by the Trustees–
    (i) stating that the accounting records of the business give a true and fair view of the financial position of the business; or
    (ii) providing any other information the Board requires to determine whether the person has sufficient financial resources to carry on the business;[252]
- the person provide full disclosure of the identity of any other person involved in the business.[253]

The practical application of the financial criteria and the financial injection mechanism are illustrated by the following case.

Travel World Service Pty Ltd v Rose Grisbrook Pty Ltd

[11.640] *Travel World Service Pty Ltd v Rose Grisbrook Pty Ltd* (Sup Crt Vic, Batt J, 22 September 1995, BC 9503975)

T Pty Ltd had carried on business as a travel agency for a decade until the national airline pilots' strike and recession of 1989. T Pty Ltd then got into financial difficulties and was unable to meet the financial criteria. In its financial analysis the TCF excluded from current assets loans made to related parties and other loans which the TCF doubted were recoverable. It required T Pty Ltd, among other things, to provide a capital injection or bank guarantee of $240,000. G agreed with the principals of T

---

246 TCF Trust Deed, Part 9.2.
247 TCF Trust Deed, Part 9.5.
248 TCF Trust Deed, Part 9.6.
249 TCF Trust Deed, Part 9.6 (b).
250 TCF Trust Deed, Part 9.6 (c).
251 TCF Trust Deed, Part 9.6 (d).
252 TCF Trust Deed, Part 9.6 (e).
253 TCF Trust Deed, Part 9.6 (f).

Travel World Service Pty Ltd v Rose Grisbrook Pty Ltd cont.

Pty Ltd to assist in the refinancing and restructuring of T Pty Ltd in exchange for financial control. In accordance with this agreement G and other investors paid substantial sums through G Pty Ltd to T Pty Ltd, its bankers and others in order to meet the TCF financial criteria. Then a dispute arose and G sought to recover $175,420 of the moneys. T Pty Ltd obtained a declaration that it was not indebted to G because technically the loan was made by G Pty Ltd.

———— ଛଠ ————

Trust moneys

[11.645] There are other remedies available to the client and principal when a travel agent fails to account for the moneys paid for travel. The moneys may be traced and recovered under the law of trusts. The travel agent and often others who have received the moneys or assisted in the breach of trust may be responsible for reimbursement. They may also have committed a serious criminal offence of misappropriation (see [6.95]).

At the outset it is necessary to distinguish those cases where the travel agent acts as principal (or buyer for resale) and undertakes to supply the service to the client whether or not the travel agent proposes to obtain the service from subcontractors or others. In those cases the travel agent is not acting as an agent at all but is liable as principal on its contract with the client [254] and on its contract with the service providers (subcontractors). [255] The relationship is debtor/creditor and it is not possible for the client or the service providers to trace the money (see above, [11.75]ff).

The more usual cases are where the travel agent acts as a mere intermediary, that is, as agent for the client [256] or service provider ("principal") [257] or both [258] (see above, [11.220]ff). In these cases the moneys (apart from commission) paid to the travel agent for the service do not belong to the travel agent and the law of trusts and tracing applies. These cases highlight the problems which arise in the absence of a strict insistence in the legislative scheme that these moneys be dealt with as trust moneys.

Civil liability of recipients and accessories

Royal Brunei Airlines Sdn Bhd v Philip Tan Kok Ming

[11.650] *Royal Brunei Airlines Sdn Bhd v Philip Tan Kok Ming* [1995] 2 AC 378

The leading common law case on the problem is the Privy Council decision as follows.

---

254   *Wong Mee Wan v Kwan Kin Travel Services Ltd* [1995] 4 All ER 745; *Jarvis v Swan Tours* [1972] 3 WLR 954.
255   *Anglo-Continental Holidays Ltd v Typaldos Lines (London) Ltd* [1967] 2 Lloyd's Rep 61; *Thomas Cook Pty Ltd v Aviation and Tourism Services Pty Ltd* (unreported, NSW Sup Ct, Yeldham J, 13 August 1985, BC 8500696).
256   *Re ILG Travel Ltd (in administration)* [1995] 2 BCLC 128; *Kemp v Intasun Holidays Ltd* [1987] BTLC 353; *Athens-Macdonald Travel Service Pty Ltd v Kazis* [1970] SASR 264. Although it is not entirely clear from the report, it appears that A was acting as agent of the clients rather than as principal.
257   *Wilson v Best Travel Ltd* [1993] 1 All ER 353; *Craven v Strand Holidays* (1982) 142 DLR (3d) 31, Canadian Court of Appeal; *Rookard v Mexicoach* 680 F 2d 1257 (1982); *Wall v Silver Wing Surface Arrangements Ltd (trading as Enterprise Holidays)* (unreported, Hodgson J, 18 November 1981).
258   *Elsis v Transworld Airlines* 167 AD 2d 285; 562 NYS 2d 433; 1990 NY App Div LEXIS 14242; *Holt v Fynbout Pty Ltd* (unreported, NSW Sup Ct, Cohen J, 28 May 1987, BC 8701344). It is respectfully submitted that his Honour's general comment at p 16 – that in most cases the travel agent would be the agent of the client and not the carrier – is not correct.

Royal Brunei Airlines Sdn Bhd v Philip Tan Kok Ming cont.

Facts: P was the principal shareholder and director of travel agent company BLT, which was a general sales agent for the Royal Brunei airline. The agreement incorporated the usual IATA provision that all moneys received by BLT on sales was the property of Royal Brunei and was to be held in trust for it until it was paid subject to BLT's rights to deduct commission. The moneys were not paid into a separate trust account but were paid into BLT's current account and under a standing arrangement with its bank the surplus was invested on fixed deposit from time to time. The money was to be paid to Royal Brunei within 30 days but from 1988 it fell into arrears. In 1992 Royal Brunei terminated the agreement and sought to recover B$335,160 outstanding moneys. There was no doubt that BLT was liable in debt and for breach of trust but it had used and lost the money in its other business activities. Royal Brunei sought to recover the money from P as an accessory to the breach of trust.

Decision: The Privy Council (Lord Goff of Chieveley, Lord Ackner, Lord Nicholls of Birkenhead, Lord Steyn and Sir John May) reviewed the authorities and (at 382) distinguished two circumstances in which third parties (non-trustees) may become liable to account in equity for trust property or its traceable proceeds:

1. **Recipient liability**, that is, where the third party knowingly (but not necessarily dishonestly)[259] receives trust property and is so held liable for restitution; and
2. **Accessory liability**, that is, where the third party knowingly (and dishonestly) assists a trustee to breach a trust and so is held liable as constructive trustee even though it did not itself receive any of the trust money.

This case fell into the second category because P did not take or keep the money for himself. It was lost in the business dealings of BLT. The Privy Council considered the authorities and concluded (at 392):

> Drawing the threads together, their Lordships' overall conclusion is that dishonesty is a necessary ingredient of accessory liability. It is also a sufficient ingredient. A liability in equity to make good resulting loss attaches to a person who dishonestly procures or assists in a breach of trust or fiduciary obligation. It is not necessary that, in addition, the trustee or fiduciary was acting dishonestly, although this will usually be so where the third party who is assisting him is acting dishonestly. "Knowingly" is better avoided as a defining ingredient of the principle...

Applying these principles to the facts their Lordships found B was liable, holding that (at 393):

> The money paid to BLT on the sale of tickets for the airline was held on trust for the airline. This trust, on its face, conferred no power on BLT to use the money in the conduct of its business. The trust gave no authority to BLT to relieve its cash flow problems by utilising for this purpose the rolling 30-day credit provided by the airline. Thus BLT committed a breach of trust by using the money instead of simply deducting its commission and holding the money intact until it paid the airline. The defendant accepted that he knowingly assisted in that breach of trust. In other words, he caused or permitted his company to apply the money in a way he knew was not authorised by the trust of which the company was trustee. Set out in

---

259 See *Stephens Travel Service International Pty Ltd (Receivers and Managers Appointed) v Qantas Airways Ltd* (1988) 13 NSWLR 629 below.

Royal Brunei Airlines Sdn Bhd v Philip Tan Kok Ming cont.

these bald terms, the defendant's conduct was dishonest. By the same token, and for good measure, BLT also acted dishonestly. The defendant was the company and his state of mind is to be imputed to the company.

The second category, accessory liability, was also involved in *Adamopoulos v Olympic Airways SA* [260] where Qantas and Olympic Airways successfully obtained Mareva injunctions to freeze the accounts of the travel agent company and its principal.

———— ଛଠଓ ————

The first category, recipient liability, is neatly illustrated by the following Australian case.

Stephens Travel Service (R&M Apptd) v Qantas Airways

[11.655] *Stephens Travel Service International Pty Ltd (Receivers and Managers Appointed) v Qantas Airways Ltd* (1988) 13 NSWLR 629

Facts: Qantas had a passenger sales agency agreement with travel agent ST in standard IATA terms which established an express trust similar to that in the Royal Brunei case, except that rather than monthly accounting it required fortnightly accounting through IATA's bank settlement plan. Here too, in breach of the agreement, ST paid the moneys into its general account, which in this case was a current account with ANZ Bank, usually in overdraft. ST acted as travel agent for the sales of tickets to its clients and as consolidator agent for sales to other travel agents who did not have IATA accreditation. Each fortnight it would draw a cheque on the current account and pay the sum due, which ranged from $500,000 to $800,000. ANZ refused to pay one cheque, closed the account and appointed receivers pursuant to a mortgage which gave it a floating charge over ST's assets. After the appointment of receivers operations continued and moneys were paid into a trust account in the joint names of the receivers and the administrators appointed under the former *Travel Agents Act 1973*. Qantas sought to recover all moneys received by the agent and the receiver which had not been accounted for.

Decision: The New South Wales Full Court (Kirby and Priestly JJA agreeing with Hope JA) held that ANZ was bound to account to Qantas for the moneys received. Under the passenger sales agency agreement, moneys received for the sale of Qantas tickets were to be held on trust for Qantas. That agreement had not been waived, varied or terminated. ANZ was aware of the terms of the agreement and that ST had no right to use the moneys in reduction of its overdraft and so was liable to account for all moneys received after it honoured the last cheque to Qantas through the bank settlement plan.

Thus it was a clear case of the recipient liability. The court noted that there was no suggestion of dishonesty on the part of ANZ as that is not a necessary ingredient of recipient liability. This is in contrast to the second category, accessory liability, in which, according the Privy Council's formulation in Royal Brunei, dishonesty is both a necessary and sufficient ingredient. Some further insight into the type of knowledge required in the first category is provided by these comments:

> Since it knew the terms of the agreement, it had notice of the trust obligations of Stephens under cl 10(b), whether or not it consciously appreciated the precise legal consequences. It must also have known that, in so far as Stephens received money belonging to Qantas and which it was required to pay to Qantas, Stephens had no right to use those moneys to reduce its overdraft [at 358].

---

260 *Adamopoulos v Olympic Airways SA* (1991) 25 NSWLR 75.

Stephens Travel Service (R&M Apptd) v Qantas Airways cont.

In these circumstances ANZ must be held to have had notice both of the existence of a trust in respect of moneys received for Qantas tickets not already paid for, and that the use of those moneys by Stephens to reduce its debt to ANZ would be a breach of trust [at 359].

On this formulation "knowledge" in the first category comes very close to constructive notice. It is not surprising that the banking industry is concerned about the loose arrangements which exist for trust moneys under the uniform scheme and is lobbying for compulsory use of formal trust accounts.

The main objection of travel agents is that given the number of principals and number of transactions it is not feasible to insist upon a formal trust account. The Privy Council in *Royal Brunei* noted the observation along these lines by the Court of Appeal in that case and, while stating that they expressed no view on it, did concede (at 393) that:

> It is possible that in certain circumstances these points might sustain an argument that, although there was a failure to pay, there was no breach of trust. They do not arise in this case because of the defendant's acceptance that there was a breach of trust.

Practice of travel suppliers

Carriers

[11.660] The situation as between travel agents and airlines is relatively clear as it is almost universally recognised that under the usual IATA arrangement the moneys are subject to an express trust in favour of the carrier.[261] Australian National Rail imposes a similar condition under its conditions of carriage. What is the position with other travel suppliers?

Tour operators

[11.665] Some tour operators have endeavoured to structure their arrangements with travel agents along IATA lines. In *Re ILG Travel Ltd (in administration)*[262] the operator ILG provided package tour holidays through a large number of travel agents in the United Kingdom. At the direction of the Civil Aviation Authority the standard form agency agreement between ILG and each travel agent and the booking conditions with clients provided that moneys ("pipeline moneys") paid by clients to travel agents for holidays were held on trust for the clients until confirmation and then on trust for ILG subject to the agent's entitlement to commission. These provisions were designed to ensure, amongst other things, that the travel agent was acting as agent (and trustee) for the client until confirmation so that the tour operator ILG would not be responsible to the client if the travel agent defaulted prior to confirmation. It was held that there was a charge in equity in favour of ILG over the pipeline moneys subject to the travel agent's rights to commission.

---

261 See, for example, the *Royal Brunei Airlines Sdn Bhd v Philip Tan Kok Ming* [1995] 2 AC 378 and the US cases cited with approval. Also see *Stephens Travel Service International Pty Ltd (Receivers and Managers Appointed) v Qantas Airways Ltd* (1988) 13 NSWLR 629.

262 *Re ILG Travel Ltd (in administration)* [1995] 2 BCLC 128.

Hotels

[11.670] Hoteliers have not attempted to address the problem in any organised manner. In the Code of Practice on Hotel/Travel Agency Relations drawn up by the International Hotels Association (IHA) and the United [263] Federation of Travel Agents (UFTAA) [264] the problem has been ignored. [265]

Criminal liability

[11.675] Last, but not least, there is the risk of criminal liability for the travel agent, recipient and accessory. The criminal law generally regards misappropriation as a serious offence (see [6.95]).

In *R v Hall* [266] the Court of Appeal allowed a travel agent's appeal against a conviction for theft. Travel agent R had paid deposits received for flights to America into his general account. His travel agency had not prospered and all the money was consumed so that he was unable to supply the tickets or make a refund. Under s 1 of the *Theft Act 1968* (UK) "theft" is defined as the dishonest appropriation of property belonging to another. Section 5(3) provides that:

> Where a person receives property from or on account of another, and is under an obligation to the other to retain and deal with that property or its proceeds in a particular way, the property or proceeds shall be regarded (as against him) as belonging to the other.

Although H had a contractual obligation to arrange the flights and buy the tickets that did not establish a special obligation on him within s 5(3). Their Lordships concluded (at 1012):

> It follows from this that, despite what on any view must be condemned as scandalous conduct by the appellant, in our judgement on this ground alone this appeal must be allowed and the convictions quashed.

However they also noted (at 1011-2) that each case turns on its facts and that:

> Cases could, we suppose, conceivably arise where by some special arrangement (preferably evidenced by documents), the client could impose on the travel agent an "obligation" falling within s 5(3).

It is submitted that, in the light of the trust obligations in the cases discussed above, the result may well have been different had the travel agent issued the tickets and failed to pay the airline. Under IATA's standard Passenger Sales Agency terms the travel agent would have an express special obligation as trustee to deal with the moneys for the benefit of the principal which would seem to satisfy the Court of Appeal's requirement in the dicta quoted above.

In the relevant provision of the Canadian Criminal Code the definition of theft relies upon there being a "direction" to deal with the property in a specified way. In *Lowden v The Queen*, [267] a case with similar facts to *R v HallR v Hall*, the Supreme Court of Canada upheld the conviction of a travel agent. While mere expectations of consumers were not directions, where those expectations are known to the travel agent they may constitute a direction. In 1994 a travel agent pleaded guilty on six counts of misapplying funds on similar facts to *Lowden v The Queen*. Lipton has noted that these cases were decided before the

---

263 Previously referred to as "Universal".
264 This replaces the former Convention of the same name which expired 14 June 1987.
265 Article 13, which covers Payment due to the Hotelier, deals with it simply in terms of contract and debt.
266 *R v Hall* [1972] 2 All ER 1009.
267 *Lowden v The Queen* (1982) 139 DLR 3d 257.

regulation 806/93 under the Canadian *Travel Industry Act* required travel agents to maintain a trust account for client funds and that it would now be easier for the prosecution because there was a direction.[268]

As far as the authors can find, there has not been a reported prosecution of a travel agent in Australia in similar circumstances. However it is submitted that a case could be made out.[269] These terms are very broad and would appear to capture the travel agent/client and the travel agent/principal relationship in most situations.

The cases show that failure to keep a trust account for client and principal's moneys is the root cause of most of the defaults, losses, claims for compensation and litigation. Moreover, the practice of using travel funds for other purposes is at best imprudent and at worst liable to result in criminal prosecution.

Mandatory trust accounting raises complex commercial and policy issues. Can the industry maintain pressure for both reduced commissions and strict accounting? How are travel agents to operate with the loss of valuable working capital? Would it be consistent with deregulation?

IMPACT OF THE WEB ON TRAVEL DISTRIBUTION

[11.680] Travel distribution increasingly takes place outside the traditional and well regulated travel agency system. There is now a heavy reliance upon online information, advice, bookings and transactions. This has raised numerous new regulatory issues and concerns and these have only begun to be addressed by regulators and the Industry. The following issues will be considered:

- Information and advice
- E-commerce and travel portals
- What's in a Name?

Travel information and advice

[11.685] Providing travel information and advice has traditionally been a key role of the travel agent. During the last 10-15 years many travel agents highlighted this expertise and developed fee structures for this service to diversify away from commissions which have been declining for the reasons discussed below. However the internet is also overtaking this role in many respects including:

- the internet now provides virtually unlimited information on travel products and destinations,
- advisory portals have evolved where real travellers share real experiences and appraisal of travel products.

Consider http://www.tripadvisor.com which provides the "world's most trusted travel advice" and information on over 400,000 destinations. It is impossible for a traditional travel agent to match this service. However this is not without its problems. Tripadvisor also invites visitors to "find hotels you can trust" based on publishing reviews and assessment provided by visitors

---

268 M Lipton, "The operation of a travel agent and the Criminal Code", [1996] 3 *Travel Law Journal* 103-104.
269 See, for example, *Criminal Code* (Cth), Divisions 134 and 135, Queensland *Criminal Code*, s 408C Fraud.

to the site. If these reviews or assessments are inaccurate, untrue or malicious then this is potentially defamatory of the subject accommodation provider.[270]

Travel advisories

[11.690] Most developed countries now provide official guidance to their citizens travelling to foreign countries mainly over the web. In Australia, it is the Department of Foreign Affairs and Trade (DFaT) which issues Travel Advisories for countries where there is some risk to Australian travellers.[271]

This has become increasingly stronger in tourism security. However, some tourism ministries in developing countries complain that the information is provided with "all care but no responsibility" for its content and that often the real situation on the ground is not nearly as serious as that portrayed in the travel bulletin. In this context, consider:

- the responsibility of travel agents, tour operators and carriers who operate in and out of these destinations to ensure safe passage of their customers;
- the responsibility of travellers for their own safety; and
- the impact on the destination if there is a real breach of tourism security.

For example, in 1995, Cambodia was ranked by a travel guide to be the World's most dangerous destination. Today, it is one of the World's most popular destinations attracting some two million visitors (and rising) per year. On the other hand, Bali used to be a favourite destination for Australian tourists abroad. However, since the Bali bombing incidents in 2002 and 2005 and the publicity surrounding the drug cases involving young Australians,[272] this destination has suffered economically from a decline in visitor numbers.

Considering the impact that travel advisories may have on a destination, particularly in the developing world, what responsibility should the issuing country be required to bear? Why is it the case that when similar incidents or risks occur in Western countries, for example, the terrorist attacks in New York, Madrid and London, they are so often ignored in travel advisories?

The Draft Annex on Tourism proposes a more specific treatment of tourism services under the *General Agreement on Trade in Services* (GATS). It was originally proposed in 1999 and then in 2000 a revised draft was tabled by a number of developing countries seeking to address certain anti-competitive practices in the tourism sector which they regarded as undermining sustainable tourism particularly in the developing world

Government officials from developing countries frequently complain that they are often concerned by the misleading informaiton contained in travel advisories which may portray their respective tourist destinations as a health, safety and security risk well beyond the reality on the ground.

In order to curb these anti-competitive practices, Article 4 of the Draft Annex sets out some strategies in subclause 4.1 for consumer protection which include adopting measures for their:

a) health and security;
b) economic interests;

---

270 300 hotels join potential defamation lawsuit against TripAdvisor http://hotelier.typepad.com/hotelier/2010/09/300-hotels-join-potential-defamation-lawsuit-against-tripadvisor.html.
271 See DFaT's website at http://www.smartraveller.gov.au.
272 Schappelle Corby was sentenced to 20 years imprisonment in 2005; Bali Nine: 7 members sentenced to life imprisonment and the 2 ringleaders put to death by firing squad in 2006.

c) information and education;

d) right to redress; and

e) representation.

Careful adherence to these principles by governments would ensure a more balanced approach to the information contained in travel advisories worldwide.

E-Commerce and Travel Portals

[11.695] The web allows providers (airlines, hotels and others) and clients to deal directly, bypassing the travel agent altogether, a process called "disintermediation". This has led to the development of complementary documentation and procedures to streamline travel including e-ticketing, self check-in and so on. It also allows providers (particularly airlines) to drive down commissions to uneconomic levels for travel agents.

The evolution of large travel portals often specialising in just one component, for example, accommodation, effectively bypasses the Travel Agent legislation and regulatory system. Similarly, the development of global travel portals which perform all the functions of Travel Agents are difficult for any one country to regulate (see exercise below [11:720]).

As a result, travel distribution increasingly:

- takes place outside the traditional and well regulated travel agency system;
- relies heavily reliance on online information and distribution; and
- introduces new regulatory issues and concerns which are just beginning to be addressed.

Travel and E-commerce

[11.700] UNCITRAL [273] first proposed a *Model law on Electronic Commerce* in 1996 [274] the object of which was to provide a regulatory framework that:

- facilitates the use of electronic transactions,
- promotes business and community confidence in the use of electronic transactions and
- enables business and the community to use electronic communications in their dealings with government.

This Model Law was adopted in Australia under the uniform Electronic Transactions Acts. [275] This was followed by the *UN Convention on the Use of Electronic Communications in International Contracts* (2005). [276] This Convention updates the Model Law and provides a more comprehensive regulatory framework for the distribution of travel and tourism including:

- Legal recognition of electronic communications in contract;(Art 8);
- Form not important and it satisfies requirement for writing; (Art 9);
- Time and place of despatch of electronic communications; (Art 10):

---

273 United Nations Commission on International Trade Law.
274 See UNCITRAL's website at http://www.uncitral.org/uncitral/en/uncitral_texts/electronic_commerce/1996Model.html.
275 See *Electronic Transactions Act 1999* (Cth) and State and Territory equivalents.
276 See UNCITRAL's website at http://www.uncitral.org/uncitral/en/uncitral_texts/electronic_commerce/2005Convention.html.

- When is it sent? When it leaves the information system of originator. It is received when it is capable of being retrieved at the electronic address of addressee.
- From where is it dispatched? It is despatched from the originator's physical place of business, to the addressee's physical place of business or residence (and see Art 6);
* Websites are generally "invitations to treat" (Art 11);
* Contract terms may be made available electronically (Art 12);
* Correction of errors (Art 14).

Australia and most developed countries are proposing to adopt the Convention

What's in a name?

[11.705] Search engine results are usually based on the relevance of material to the words searched. Complex algorithms are used in search engines and these are mirrored by complex strategies by web site builders to attract "hits" and improve their site's ranking including by using key words in meta-tags. Google and other search engines sell "sponsored links" so that searchers are directed to the sponsor's web site regardless of relevance or regardless of ranking. In this context, consider the relationship and interaction among:

* Place name
* Building name
* Business name
* Company name
* Brand
* Trademark
* Domain name
* Adwords
* Sponsored links

Travel providers use these names to describe and promote their products and travel customers often search these key words to find products which are relevant to their needs. Misuse of words can offend the consumer protection laws. The following case illustrates the point.

ACCC v Trading Post and Google Inc

[11.710] *Australian Competition and Consumer Commission (ACCC) v Trading Post and Google Inc* (2007) FCA 1419

Facts: ACCC alleged that the Trading Post contravened the *Trade Practices Act 1974* (Cth), s 52 (deceptive and misleading) and s 53(d) (false or misleading representation) when the business names "Kloster Ford" and "Charlestown Toyota" appeared in the title of Google sponsored links to the Trading Post website. Kloster Ford and Charlestown Toyota were Newcastle car dealerships who competed against Trading Post in automotive sales.

The ACCC also alleged that Google, by causing the two links to be published on its website and further by failing to adequately distinguish sponsored links from *organic* search results, had engaged in two separate counts of misleading and deceptive conduct in breach of *Trade Practices Act 1974* (Cth), s 52. The ACCC sought injunctions restraining Google from publishing search results that did not expressly distinguish advertisements from organic search results and orders that Trading Post and Google implement trade practices compliance programs.

ACCC v Trading Post and Google Inc cont.

Held: *Trading Post* (advertiser) settled and undertook not to use other business names as AdWords. The case continues against Google.

More recently, the European Court of Justice Advocate General has ruled that Google (France) has not committed a trademark infringement under EU law by allowing advertisers to select, in AdWords, keywords corresponding to trademarks. [277] The practice is widespread in travel and tourism.

Care must also be taken not to infringe intellectual property rights. This becomes difficult where the name of a building which is, in effect a place name, has been trademarked.

Mantra Group Pty Ltd v Tailly Pty Ltd

[11.715] *Mantra Group Pty Ltd v Tailly Pty Ltd* [2010] FCA 291 (26 March 2010)

Facts: Mantra is the exclusive on site letting agent and manger of a 261 apartment building called "Circle on Cavil" and has registered trademarks in Australia over that name. Tailly was an off site letting agent for a number of apartments in the building. To promote and advertise its properties Tailly registered several domain names incorporating the words, variations or misspellings of the words Circle on Cavil, used the name in its banner, text and title on its web sites and used the name in the meta tags on its web sites in order to achiever higher search engine rankings. Mantra brought proceedings against Tailly claiming infringement of its trademark and deceptive and misleading conduct.

Held: Reeves J upheld the claim and ordered Tailly to cease use of the name, to transfer the domain names to Mantra and an account of the profits from misuse. His Honour rejected Tailly's defences that the name was a geographical name and that the misuse had been in good faith.

Exercise

Things to consider: Travel agencies

The Issues:

- Is a travel web site a travel agent?
- Does it require a travel agent's licence?
- Does it require a real estate agent's licence?
- Where must it be licensed?

    From 2005, Travel Agents licensed in one State are exempted from licensing in other States if they have no physical presence there.

- Is the website an invitation to treat or is it an offer?

    Consider the ramifications of each.

- When and how does acceptance take place?

    Is it similar to faxes, telex or post?

- What terms and conditions apply?

    What is the significance (if any) of hypertext links/ticket cases/substitute documents?

---

277   *Google France & Google Inc. v Louis Vuitton Malletier*, Press Release No25/09, 22 September 2009.

Things to consider: Travel agencies cont.

- Which law applies?
  Choice of law?

---— ∞⋅∞ ——

CHAPTER 12

Passenger Transport

[12.10]	COMMON CARRIERS		318
[12.10]	Common Law		318
	[12.10]	History	318
	[12.15]	Definition	319
	[12.20]	Rights and duties of carriers at common law	320
	[12.55]	In transitu	324
	[12.60]	Special contracts: exclusion or limitation of liability	324
[12.65]	Legislation		325
	[12.65]	Australian Consumer Law: Statutory Guarantees	325
	[12.90]	Dillon v Baltic Shipping Co Mikhail Lermontov	327
	[12.100]	Other modifications by statute and conventions	328
[12.105]	CARRIAGE BY ROAD AND RAIL		329
[12.105]	Carrier Legislation		329
	[12.110]	Wallis v Downard-Pickford (North Queensland) Pty Ltd	329
	[12.115]	Implications for business travel	330
	[12.120]	Current Queensland position	330
	[12.125]	Carriers legislation in other States	331
[12.160]	Road Transport		333
	[12.160]	Regulation of Road Transport	333
	[12.185]	Liability in road transport	335
	[12.220]	International regulation of road transport: CVR Convention 1973	337
[12.230]	Rail Transport		338
	[12.235]	Regulation of rail transport	338
	[12.265]	Liability in rail transport	341
	[12.295]	International regulation of rail transport: COTIF Convention 1980	343
[12.300]	CARRIAGE BY SEA		343
	[12.305]	Oceanic Steam Navigation Co Ltd (the White Star Line) v Mellor (the Titanic)	344
[12.310]	History		344
	[12.310]	Freedom of the Sea	344
	[12.315]	Law of the Sea	345
[12.320]	Regulation of sea transport		345
[12.320]	Administration		345
[12.355]	Liability in Sea Transport		350
	[12.355]	Common carriers	350
	[12.360]	Seaworthiness	350
	[12.365]	History of liability limitation	351
[12.370]	Current Limitation of Liability		351
	[12.370]	Exclusion of liability for valuables	351
	[12.375]	Limitation of liability of seagoing ships: London Convention 1976	352
	[12.380]	Who may limit liability?	352
	[12.390]	Claims subject to limitation	353
	[12.395]	Limits of liability	354
	[12.410]	Breaking the limits	355
[12.415]	Unlimited Liability of Non-Seagoing Ships		356

[12.420]		Charter, hire and self-sail vessels	356
[12.425]		Other International Regulatory Systems	357
[12.425]		International passenger shipping liability: Athens Convention 1974	357
[12.430]		International inland navigation: CVN Convention 1976	358
[12.435]		History of cruise shipping	358
[12.440]		Policy to protect shipowners	359
	[12.445]	Case Study: Hijacking–Klinghoffer and the Achille Lauro	359
	[12.450]	Case Study: Accident on Board Ship–Oceanic Sun Line Special Shipping Company Inc v Fay	360
	[12.455]	Case Study: Ship Failures– The Titanic & The Mikhail Lermentov	360
	[12.460]	Case Study: Sexual Assault– Dianne Brimble and P&O	361
[12.470] CARRIAGE BY AIR			**362**
[12.470]		Regulation of Air Transport	362
[12.470]		Administration	362
[12.490]		Air Service Agreements (ASA)	366
	[12.495]	Case Study: Australia/SE Asia	367
[12.505]		World Trade Organization (WTO)	368
[12.520]		Outer Space	369
[12.525]		Space tourism	370
[12.535]		Liability in Air Transport	370
[12.535]		The Warsaw system	370
[12.550]		Australian law	372
[12.570]		Montreal and Warsaw system principles	374
	[12.655]	Newell v Canadian Pacific Airlines	386
	[12.660]	Goldman v Thai Airways International	387
	[12.665]	SS Pharmaceutical Co Ltd v Qantas Airways	388
[12.675]		Hijacking Conventions	389
[12.680]		Presumed Unlimited Liability	389
	[12.700]	Timney v British Airways PLC	390
[12.710]		IATA Passenger Liability Agreements 1997	391
[12.765]		Liability to Third parties	396

[12.05] Transport law governs the carriage of passengers and their luggage as well as the carriage of other peoples' goods, that is, freight and cargo. Most texts on transport law focus on freight and cargo. As this text is concerned with tourism, travel and hospitality, only those aspects concerning the carriage of passengers and their luggage will be discussed, although some of the principles are similar to those applying to freight and cargo.

COMMON CARRIERS

Common Law

History

[12.10] Carriers are one of the ancient common callings which attracted special rights and duties in order to improve the safety and efficiency of travel. Like innkeepers (see Chapter 13), carriers are the subject of some of the earliest recorded Roman law edicts and common law cases.[1]

The common law developed a strict set of rights and duties for common carriers which were applied to all means of transport. Advances in transport technology have always been

---

1 See the discussion of Roman law and common callings in Chapter 13.

fundamental to the growth of tourism. Consider the developments from transport by foot, horse, wagon, stage coach, train, car, taxi, bus and the like. What of the aeroplane and the prospects of space travel? These comments by pamphleteer J Cressel in 1681 catch the remarkable impact as the horse and wagon gave way to the stage coach: [2]

> These stage-coaches make gentlemen come to London upon every small occasion, which otherwise they would not do but upon urgent necessity, nay, the convenience of the passage makes their wives oft come up, who rather than come such long journeys on horseback would stay at home. Here when they come to town, they must presently be in the mode, get fine clothes, go to the plays and treats and by these means get such a habit of idleness, and love of pleasure.

However, the common law could not keep up with the developments. Although the strict rights and duties which evolved for common carriers still have some application today, they have been greatly modified by statutes and conventions [3] to suit contemporary conditions and the particular needs of each mode of transport. These will be discussed in subsequent parts of this chapter on carriage by land, sea and air respectively.

Definition

[12.15] At common law, a "common carrier" undertakes the business of providing transport services on standard terms to the general public. The law distinguishes a "private carrier" who selects passengers and strikes a special bargain or contract with each. The High Court has described the distinction in these terms: [4]

> It is in every case a question of fact whether the character of a common carrier has been assumed. In considering that question an important matter is whether the carrier holds himself out as ready without discrimination to carry...all persons who may choose to employ him...If instead of inviting all persons without discrimination to use his ships or vehicles, he reserves the right of choosing among them, independently of the suitability of...[them] for his means of transportation and without regard to the room or space he has available, then he is not a common carrier.

Historically, operators of coaches,[5] taxis,[6] railways,[7] ships,[8] ferries and aircraft who have conducted their business in this way have been found to be common carriers. Some authors

---

2   British Museum Document 816 mi2 (162) quoted in J Corke, *Tourism Law* (Elm Publications, UK, 1988), p 59.

3   For an interesting discussion of the conflict between international uniformity and the objectives of national courts which must interpret these conventions, see C Debattista, "Carriage conventions and their interpretation in English courts" (1997) *Journal of Business Law* 130-142.

4   *James v Commonwealth* (1939) 62 CLR 339 at 368 per Dixon J.

5   Coaches evolved from the earliest form of road vehicle, the wagon, which provided the basis of the early common law principles on common carriers. Improvements in shelter, comfort and schedule produced the "stage coach" (consider Australia's Cobb & Co) which was a classic common carrier: see, for example, *Clarke v West Ham Corp* (1909) 2 KB 858. So, too, are many modern coaches and buses: *Chitty on Contracts* (27th ed, The Common Law Library, Sweet & Maxwell, London, 1994), Vol II, [35-086].

6   Taxis are the contemporary equivalent of the "hackney" (derived from a French word meaning ambling horse) carriage which was a common carrier as discussed in *Lovett v Hobbs* (1680) 2 Shaw KB 187. See generally J Corke, *Tourism Law* (Elm Publications, UK, 1988), pp 59, 64, 65-66. The earliest Australian case the author could find was *Hancock v Cunnain* (1886) 12 VLR 9 where the Full Court of Victoria found that a taxi was negligent and so liable for the loss of a passenger's luggage whether or not the taxi was considered a common carrier.

7   Railways were found to be common carriers at common law even before they were declared to be by statute (for a time): *Great Northern Railway v LEP Transport* [1922] 2 KB 742.

have identified a sub-category of common carriers called public carriers who hold out a standing offer of carriage to the world at large to carry passengers in accordance with a published timetable and conditions.[9] On this interpretation anyone who presents themselves as ready, willing and able to travel may accept the offer, subject to vacancy.[10]

The common law itself has always permitted some flexibility by distinguishing between common carriers, who were subject to its strict rules of transport law, and private carriers, who were subject to the more lenient general law. However, as we shall see in later parts of this chapter, many carriers are now deemed by statute not to be common carriers but to be subject to statutory rights and duties especially designed for each mode of transport.

Rights and duties of carriers at common law

[12.20] The following discussion outlines the principal rights and duties of carriers at common law. It should be noted that these matters have been greatly modified by statute in several key ways. First, consumer protection legislation prohibits unconscionable, deceptive or misleading conduct and implies non-excludable guarantees into many contracts of carriage: see generally Chapter 9. Secondly, workplace health and safety legislation often applies to the equipment and premises used in transport: see generally Chapter 8. Thirdly, transport statutes and conventions make special provisions on many of these matters for particular modes of transport: see subsequent parts of this chapter on each of the main modes of transport.

Duty to accept passengers

[12.25] At common law, private carriers have no duty to accept passengers and, subject to the laws on discrimination,[11] are generally not subject to the restrictions on common carriers discussed in the next paragraph.[12] They are generally free to contract with whomever and on whatever terms they wish.

Common carriers, by definition, have a duty to carry anyone who is willing to pay and ready to travel on the carrier's usual route and they are not entitled to be selective about their passengers.[13] Wrongful refusal to carry is actionable in tort without proof of special damage.[14] However a common carrier may refuse if there is no space left or the person is intoxicated or otherwise unfit to travel.[15] While common law permitted common carriers some freedom of contract, if unreasonable charges or conditions are demanded this may constitute wrongful refusal to carry in tort[16] without proof of damage. This is a special duty imposed on common carriers outside the usual principles of contract and tort.[17]

---

8   *Bennett v Peninsular & Oriental Steamboat Co* (1848) 6 CB 775 and more recently confirmed in *Dillon v Baltic Shipping Co "Mikhail Lermontov"* (1990) ATPR 40-992 at 50-905 per Carruthers J.
9   J Corke, *Tourism Law* (Elm Publications, UK, 1989), p 59. Contrast DA Glass and C Cashmore, *Introduction to the Law of Carriage of Goods* (Sweet & Maxwell, London, 1989), [1.36].
10 *Carlill v Carbolic Smoke Ball Co* [1892] 2 QB 484 (see [4.55]).
11 See *Racial Discrimination Act 1975* (Cth); *Sex Discrimination Act 1984* (Cth) and similar laws at State level.
12 See, for example, *James v Commonwealth* (1939) 62 CLR 339 at 367-370 per Dixon J.
13 Unjustified refusal to carry is actionable in tort: *Bennett v Peninsular & Oriental Steamboat Co* (1848) 6 CB 775.
14 *James v Commonwealth* (1939) 62 CLR 339 at 367-368 per Dixon J.
15 *James v Commonwealth* (1939) 62 CLR 339 at 368.
16 *Garton v Bristol & Exeter Railway Co* (1861) 121 ER 656.
17 *Chitty on Contracts* (27th ed, The Common Law Library, Sweet & Maxwell, London, 1994), Vol II, [35-001].

Delay and deviation

[12.30] Carriers (private and common) have a duty to carry their passengers to their destinations by the usual route without unnecessary deviation and without unreasonable delay. [18] Breach may result in liability in contract and tort.

The common law permits carriers (common and private) some scope to contract out of this duty. However the courts will not permit a carrier (common and private) to contract out of responsibility for delay or deviation which is so extreme as to be considered outside the "four corners of the contract" [19] and common carriers are further restricted because they cannot demand unreasonable conditions.

Safety of passengers

[12.35] Carriers (private and common) do not insure the safety of their passengers and their liability is based on fault. They have a duty to take reasonable care for the safety of passengers which the House of Lords has described in these terms: [20]

> a carrier's obligation to his passengers, whether it be expressed in contract or in tort, is to provide a carriage that is as free from defects as the exercise of all reasonable care can make it.

Generally a plaintiff must prove that the defendant was at fault. This is often difficult for passengers (or their estates or dependants) in transport cases without detailed technical knowledge of the vehicle and the circumstances of the accident. However there are two legal principles which may make the plaintiff's task with proof easier in transport cases. One is the doctrine of res ipsa loquitur, which is an evidential principle that "the event speaks for itself" where negligence is the most probable cause of, for example, non-delivery of goods or some known particular of the accident itself. [21] The other is breach of statutory duty where failure to comply with a relevant statute or regulatory standard (of which there are many in transport) establishes prima facie proof of negligence. [22]

On the carrier's side, the usual defences of contributory negligence and voluntary assumption of risk discussed in Chapter 5 apply. [23] The common law also permits carriers (private and common) to contract out of their liability for the safety of passengers. [24]

18　*Hamlin v Great Northern Railway Co* (1856) 1 H&N 408; *Hobbs v London South West Railway* (1875) LR 10 QB 11.
19　See *Thomas Nationwide Transport (Melbourne) Pty Ltd v May & Baker (Australia) Pty Ltd* (1966) 115 CLR 353.
20　*Barkway v South Wales Transport Co Ltd* [1950] 1 All ER 392 at 403-404 per Lord Radcliffe.
21　Compare *Barkway v South Wales Transport Co Ltd* [1950] 1 All ER 392 (tyre blow-out was evidence of negligence) with *Hobbs v Petersham Transport Co Pty Ltd* (1971) 124 CLR 220 (broken axle was not evidence of negligence).
22　See, for example, the traffic law cases: *Mercer v Commissioner for Road Transport and Tramways (NSW)* (1937) 56 CLR 580; *Tucker v McCann* [1948] VLR 22; *Croston v Vaughan* [1938] 1 KB 540 at 551-552.
23　(27th ed, The Common Law Library, Sweet & Maxwell, London, 1994), Vol II, [35-074].
24　*Gregory v Commonwealth Railways Commissioner* (1941) 66 CLR 50.

Duty to accept luggage

[12.40] Private carriers are not obliged to accept passengers' luggage but may do so by special contract with additional charges and special conditions if they wish.[25] In contrast, although the point is not without doubt,[26] the better view is that common carriers have a duty to carry passengers' luggage without extra charge[27] but with the right to set reasonable limits and to charge extra for excess luggage.[28]

"Passengers' luggage" has a restricted meaning at common law and comprises packages of goods which are for the personal convenience of the passenger having regard for immediate necessities and the ultimate purpose of the journey.[29] In the old cases the emphasis was on immediate necessities and so it was held to exclude a bicycle (not a package),[30] a rocking horse purchased for a child at home (not for personal use)[31] and a typewriter[32] (articles required for a profession, trade or business). Customs have changed and modern travellers have less need for necessities as these are now more readily available along the way and at the destination. It is arguable that courts should now give more weight to the purpose of the journey and include these items for the adventure traveller, duty free or souvenir shopper and business traveller respectively.

It is doubtful whether the common law would permit common carriers to contract out of their duty to accept passengers' luggage.[33]

Responsibility for luggage

[12.45] If private carriers accept passengers' luggage without special conditions then they are strictly liable for it under principles similar to those for common carriers discussed in the next paragraph.

Common carriers are, in effect, insurers of their passengers' luggage. Even if the luggage is lost or damaged without their fault, common carriers are held strictly liable. Their only defence is where the loss or damage is caused by one of the classic defences (the perils of travel) which apply through much of transport law:

- **act of God**: this comprises natural forces which could not reasonably have been foreseen or guarded against, for example, earthquake, lightning or extraordinary weather;

- **act of the Queen's enemies**: this covers acts of the State's enemies or seizure by public (for example, customs);

- **inherent vice**: this is an inherent fault or defect in the luggage, for example faulty packing or labelling or perishable goods; or

---

25 *Macrow v Great Western Railway Co* (1871) LR QB 612.
26 Compare the conflicting views of *Chitty on Contracts* (27th ed, The Common Law Library, Sweet & Maxwell, London, 1994), Vol II, [35-086] and *Halsbury's Laws of Australia* (Butterworths, Sydney, 1992), Vol 3, Chapter 70 (A West), [70-195].
27 Confirmed in *Dillon v Baltic Shipping Co "Mikhail Lermontov"* (1990) ATPR 40-992 at 50-905 per Carruthers J.
28 *Macrow v Great Western Railway Co* (1871) LR QB 612 at 617-618 per Cockburn CJ.
29 *Macrow v Great Western Railway Co* (1871) LR QB 612 at 622 per Cockburn CJ.
30 *Britten v Great Western Railway* [1899] 1 QB 243. See comments of McCardie J in *Buckland v The King* [1933] 1 KB 329 at 340.
31 *Hudston v Midland Railway* [1869] LR 4 QB 366.
32 *Hastie v Great Eastern Railway* (1911) 46 LJ News.
33 Compare again the conflicting views of *Chitty on Contracts* (27th ed, The Common Law Library, Sweet & Maxwell, London, 1994), Vol II, [35-086] and *Halsbury's Laws of Australia* (Butterworths, Sydney, 1992), Vol 3, Chapter 70, [70-195].

- **the passenger's fault:** at common law there is no distinction between luggage which is stowed and hand luggage carried by the passenger, except that in the latter case it may be easier for the common carrier to establish the defence that the loss was caused by the passenger's fault. [34] However, items worn by the passenger or carried in a passenger's pocket, such as clothes, jewellery, watches and money, are not regarded as luggage and the common carrier is not responsible for them without fault. [35]

The position with excess luggage and items outside the definition of passengers' luggage above is more complicated. If the carrier knowingly takes them, with or without extra payment, then the carrier is strictly liable as if they were ordinary passengers' luggage. [36] Otherwise the carrier is not liable, even if negligent, because it never agreed to carry them. [37]

The common law permits carriers (private and common) to contract out of their responsibility for passengers' luggage.

Lien over luggage

[12.50] Although there is some doubt on the point, there is authority that private carriers have no right of lien over luggage or other goods carried unless it is stipulated in their contract of carriage. [38] Common carriers have a clear right of lien [39] over the goods (freight and cargo) carried which gives them the right to retain possession [40] until charges for their carriage are paid. In principle this right should extend to passengers' luggage because the right of lien balances the strict duty which the carrier bears as insurer and the law provides an innkeeper with a lien over a guest's luggage in similar circumstances. It follows from the discussion in [12.40] above that passengers' luggage is not carried free, but rather the passenger fare includes an unstated amount for the carriage of luggage. [41] As the lien is particular there may be doubt about the extent of charges covered. With the usual practice of requiring payment in advance this would rarely be an issue for luggage of the permitted quantity and type, and so it is not surprising that the authors could not find a case on the point.

However the issue often arises with excess luggage or items outside the definition of passengers' luggage above. The carrier is entitled to retain possession of the luggage until the charge has been paid. [42] In one case which found that an international airline was not entitled

---

34   *Chitty on Contracts* Chitty on Contracts (27th ed, The Common Law Library, Sweet & Maxwell, London, 1994), Vol II, [35-094].
35   *Smitton v Orient Steam Navigation Co* (1907) LT 848.
36   *Macrow v Great Western Railway Co* (1871) LR QB 612 at 619 per Cockburn CJ.
37   *Belfast & Ballymena Railway v Keys* (1861) 9 HLC 556.
38   *Electric Supply Stores v Gaywood* (1909) 100 LT 855. However some authors query this decision and argue that private carriers do have such a lien: See DA Glass and C Cashmore, *Introduction to the Law of Carriage of Goods* (Sweet & Maxwell, London, 1989), [1.110]. Such a lien would be justifiable on policy grounds where a private carrier accepts passengers' luggage and with it liability as insurer under the principles discussed in [12.45].
39   The lien is particular in the sense that it does not secure any other charges. In carriage of goods this means that only the freight on the particular goods is covered by the lien.
40   There is no power of sale.
41   *Cohen v South Eastern Railway* (1873) 2 Ex D 235 at 238.
42   *Rumsey v North Eastern Railway* (1863) 14 CB (NS) 641.

to certain excess baggage charges under the conditions of carriage, there was no challenge to the airline's asserted right to retain the passengers' luggage until the disputed charges had been paid. [43]

The common law also permitted carriers (common and private) to obtain a particular or general lien and a power of sale by special provisions in their carriage contracts.

In transitu

[12.55] The rights and duties of carriers apply beyond the vehicle and into the terminal facilities. [44] This is the concept of in transitu which is the carriers' equivalent of the innkeepers infra hospitium. In transitu or transit commences when the passenger's luggage is received for transport by the carrier or its employees a reasonable time before departure. [45] It concludes upon arrival and disembarkation at the destination allowing a reasonable time for the collection of luggage [46] after which the carrier holds the luggage as warehouseman. [47]

Special contracts: exclusion or limitation of liability

[12.60] At common law, carriers (private and common) had wide scope to contract out of their duties described above by incorporating into their contracts of carriage special terms which excluded or limited liability or otherwise reduced their obligations. The only restrictions upon this were that the common law generally did not permit common carriers to contract out of their duty to accept passengers (see [12.25]) and their duty to accept passengers' luggage (see [12.40]). However, even these duties were tenuous, as a general denial of these duties went a long way towards indicating that the carrier was a private carrier. [48]

The procedure for incorporating these special terms into contracts of carriage was established by the long line of cases (many of them involving carriers) known as the "ticket cases", which are discussed in Chapter 4. During the last century these procedures have been used so extensively that in practice they remove many of the basic duties from carriers, including responsibility for fault. It is only in recent times that the table has turned in favour of consumers and we have seen a growing aversion to exclusion and limitation of liability. Unfortunately, many in the transport industry have not realised their new and more vulnerable position under the wide-ranging statutory guarantees under the *Australian Consumer Law*. [49]

---

43 *Subramaniam a/l Paramasivam & Lain-lain lwn Malaysian Airline System Bhd* [1996] 3 MLJ 64.
44 *Timbrell v Waterhouse* (1885) LR (NSW) 77; *John v Bacon* (1870) LR CP 437.
45 *Soanes v London South Western Railway* (1919) 88 LJKB 524.
46 *Butcher v South Western Railway Co* (1855) 16 CB 13.
47 *Hodgkinson v London and North Western Railway Co* (1884) 14 QBD 228.
48 *Rosenthal v London County Council* (1924) 131 LT 563.
49 *Competition and Consumer Act 2010* (Cth), Schedule 2.

Legislation

Australian Consumer Law: Statutory Guarantees

[12.65] Building upon the statutory warranties implied under the *Trade Practices Act 1974* (Cth) (now repealed), the *Australian Consumer Law* applies statutory guarantees to the supply [50] of services to consumers in trade and commerce. The carriage of passengers and their luggage is a "service" within the meaning of the *Australian Consumer Law*. [51] However s 63 appears to exclude a business traveller's luggage and goods from the guarantees as discussed below [12.85]. [52]

The most important of these guarantees for passenger transport are as follows.

- **Due care and skill (s 60)**: Services must be rendered with due care and skill (similar to *Trade Practices Act 1974*, s 74(1). A similar *Trade Practices Act 1974* provision was held to apply to the luggage of a cruise ship passenger [53] by the Supreme Court in *Dillon v Baltic Shipping Co "Mikhail Lermontov"* [54] (see casenote at [12.90]) when the definition of services was quite narrow. Compare the duty of care in the tort of negligence (see [5.25]ff) which will also apply to the facts in many cases.

- **Fit for the purpose (s 61(1))**: Services (and any product resulting from the services) must be reasonably fit for any purpose disclosed by the consumer to the supplier unless it is shown that the consumer did not rely or that it was unreasonable for the consumer to rely on the skill and judgement of the supplier (similar to part of *Trade Practices Act 1974*, s 74(2).

    This guarantee ensures that services meet the *subjective* standards required by the consumer and made known to the supplier. It corresponds with the somewhat similar guarantee in relation to goods (s 55) which has widespread application in the tourism, travel and hospitality industry including in passenger transport where the vehicle is "supplied" where it reinforces the general requirement that it be roadworthy, seaworthy, airworthy and the like.

- **Time for supply (s 62)**: Services must be supplied within a reasonable time if the time of supply has not been otherwise fixed in a contract or agreed. (This is a new requirement.)

This has significant implications for tourism, travel and hospitality, particularly in relation to the intrinsic practices of overbooking and problems of delay (see Overbooking at [9.165]). Key issues include:

- standard contract provisions designed to avoid responsibility for delay may offend the unconscionable conduct and unfair contract terms provisions discussed above; and

- there will be a contest between express mention of times or dates to carry passengers (including convention obligations) and provisions seeking to relieve suppliers from responsibility and these may fall foul of the provisions restricting the right to limit or contract out of s 62 of the *Australian Consumer Law*.

---

50   The Sale of Goods legislation is limited to sales.
51   See *Australian Consumer Law*, ss 60 – 62.
52   However under s 63 the guarantees do not apply to the transportation and storage of goods for the purposes of a business, trade, profession or occupation carried on or engaged in by the person for whom the goods are transported or stored.
53   It would also now apply to the carriage of the passenger, following amendments to *Trade Practices Act 1974*, s 74 in 1986 which came into force shortly after the sinking of the ship. See now definition of "services" in *Australian Consumer Law*, s 4.
54   *Dillon v Baltic Shipping Co "Mikhail Lermontov"* (1990) ATPR 40-992.

These statutory guarantees apply independently of any contract and so they benefit all passengers even those who because of lack of capacity or package tour, agency, family, group or gift arrangements and the like do not have a direct contractual relationship with the supplier.

Exception: State or Territory Legislation

[12.70] Section 275 of the *Consumer Protection Law* provides if there is a failure to comply with one of the statutory guarantees that apply to the supply of services and a State or Territory law is the proper law of the contract then that State or Territory law prevails to limit or preclude liability. The equivalent *Trade Practices Act 1974* provision (s 74(2)A) was considered in *Insight Vacations Pty Ltd v Young* [2010] NSWCA 137 where the Court of Appeal held that this covers a law which in its own terms precludes or limits liability but does not cover a law which merely purports to permit a supplier to contract out of such liability. The former validates State and Territory legislation which has modified carrier liability as discussed in the following paragraphs. The latter would be invalid as the Commonwealth law prohibiting exclusion or limitation prevails over State and Territory law. This is illustrated in the cases discussed below.

Leisure travellers and their luggage and goods

[12.75] The statutory guarantees on the supply of services in the *Australian Consumer Law* clearly apply to the carriage of leisure passengers and their luggage and goods. Any term of a contract which purports to exclude, restrict or modify the guarantees is void: s 64. Limitation of liability under the guarantee provisions is not permitted under s 64A because leisure travel generally comprises "services of a kind ordinarily acquired for personal, domestic or household use or consumption". Any invalid attempt to do so would itself be deceptive and misleading conduct under s 18 and it may also be unconscionable conduct under s 20 as discussed in Chapter 9.

However, as discussed in Chapter 9, the *Australian Consumer Law*, s 139A permits a supplier of "recreational services" to exclude, restrict or modify in contract liability in respect of death or personal injury. This would include most adventure tourism activities. However this exclusion, restriction or modification is not permitted for a significant personal injury caused by the reckless conduct of the supplier. For more detailed discussion, see [9.200]. See generally Chapter 15 in respect of adventure travel which often includes a passenger transport component.

It is also still arguable that liability for a passenger's luggage is unlimited, subject to the Carriers Legislation discussed below.

Business travellers

[12.80] The *Australian Consumer Law* guarantee provisions [55] would apply to the carriage of business passengers but not their luggage or goods: s 63 (see below). Limitation of liability under the guarantee provisions may be permitted for business travellers if, for example, there is a designated business class and in any case provided the transport is not ordinarily used for personal, domestic or household purposes: s 64A. If permitted, liability may be limited under s 64A to the cost of providing the services again (effectively a refund of the fare) but only if

---

55   *Australian Consumer Law*, ss 60 – 62.

that is fair and reasonable having regard for the comparative strength of the relative bargaining positions, the availability of alternatives, and customs and experience. [56]

Business travellers' luggage and goods

[12.85] Under s 63 of the *Australian Consumer Law* (equivalent to 74(3) of the *Trade Practices Act 1974*) the guarantees do not apply to "the transportation and storage of goods for the purposes of a business, trade, profession or occupation carried on or engaged in by the person" for whom the goods are transported or stored.

This would appear to cover a business traveller's luggage and goods. The scope was considered in *Wallis v Downard-Pickford (North Queensland) Pty Ltd* [57] discussed below. Warranties would still be implied at common law but the carrier would be free to limit or exclude them subject to the ticket case principles and the consumer law restrictions discussed in Chapter 9 [9.175]ff.

The application of s 74 of the *Trade Practices Act 1974* (similar to ss 60 – 61 of the *Australian Consumer Law*) to passenger transport was considered in *Dillon v Baltic Shipping Co "Mikhail Lermontov"* (1993) 176 CLR 344.

Dillon v Baltic Shipping Co "Mikhail Lermontov"

[12.90] *Dillon v Baltic Shipping Co "Mikhail Lermontov"* (1993) 176 CLR 344

Facts: See [2.235].

Decision: The Supreme Court of New South Wales (Carruthers J) held that s 74 of the *Trade Practices Act 1974* (similar to the statutory guarantee under s 60 of the *Australian Consumer Law*) applied to the contract of carriage (though only the luggage part under s 74 as worded at that time) and so implied a warranty of due care and skill. His Honour held that:

(a) the passage ticket terms and conditions which purported to exclude, modify and limit this liability were not part of the contract on ticket case principles;

(b) even if they were part of the contract they were void under s 68 of the *Trade Practices Act 1974*; and

(c) the signed release agreement was unconscionable and unenforceable.

The subsequent appeal to the Full Court and then to the High Court upheld the decision on (a) and (c) and found it unnecessary to decide on (b).

Postscript 1: In this case the decision on (b) applied only to the luggage portion of the contract of carriage because at that stage s 74 had a restricted definition of "services", which did not include a contract for the carriage of passengers. Under amendments (made shortly after the sinking of the ship) s 74 of the *Trade Practices Act 1974* (and now ss 60 – 63 of the *Australian Consumer Law*) clearly would apply to the whole passenger carriage contract although there still appears to be some confusion on the matter. [58]

---

56   See TC Atherton, "Changes to TPA increase liability" (1992) 1(3) *Tourism and Travel Review* 7.
57   *Wallis v Downard-Pickford (North Queensland) Pty Ltd* (1994) 68 ALJR 395.
58   It appears the point could have been taken in a case which concerned an accident aboard the *Alexander Pushkin: Gill v Charter Travel Co* (unreported, Qld Sup Ct, De Jersey J, 16 February 1996, BC 9600812).

Dillon v Baltic Shipping Co "Mikhail Lermontov" cont.

Postscript 2: Also since the case, provision has been made for shipowners to limit liability under the *London Convention 1976* which came into force in 1991 under the *Limitation of Liability for Maritime Claims Act 1989* (Cth) (see [12.375] below). [59]

Exercise

The Rough Reef Trip

The Reef Warrior is a cruise ship which conducts daytrips to the Great Barrier Reef from the Port of Cairns. When returning from its last trip the weather blew up and the sea became very rough. The Captain warned passengers to remain seated and to hold on. However, the bar was kept open and the Captain maintained full speed ahead to try to keep to the schedule. Some passengers, particularly those drinking at the bar, ignored the Captain's warnings. The ship struck a freak wave and breached. Some passengers drinking at the bar fell overboard and three drowned. Several other passengers were injured. Luggage and goods damaged included watches, cameras, spare clothes, wetsuits and snorkelling gear belonging to tourists. It also included similar items plus scuba gear, submersible cameras and laptop computers belonging to a group of marine biologists who were on a research trip. Each passenger had been issued with a ticket which stated on the reverse side:

> Neither Reef Warrior nor its servants or agents accept any liability whatsoever for loss of life, personal injury and loss or damage to property howsoever caused.

You are requested to:

(a) Advise Reef Warrior on the likely claims and possible defences arising out of the incident.

(b) Considering your advice in (a), recommend management (including legal) procedures which Reef Warrior might use to avoid or minimise the risks of this type of incident.

Note that the Reef Warrior is a non-seagoing ship and so the *Limitation of Liability for Maritime Claims Act 1989* (Cth) and the *London Convention 1976* discussed in the subsequent part of this Chapter do not apply (see [12.375] below).

Other modifications by statute and conventions

[12.100] The general common law rules on carriers have also been modified in numerous ways by State and federal statutes and international conventions. These are discussed in the following parts on each of the major modes of transport. The general regulatory model for each mode of transport provides for:

- registration of the means of transport;
- setting standards for means of transport;
- licensing the operators;

---

59   See more generally K Lewins, "The Cruise Ship Industry – Liabilities for Passengers for Breach of s 52 and s 74 Trade Practices Act 1964 (Cth)" (2004) 18 MLAANZ Journal, pp 30-54.

- setting rules for operation;
- modifying liability.

This text will concentrate on the provisions which modify liability.

CARRIAGE BY ROAD AND RAIL

Carrier Legislation

[12.105] The common law on carriers (discussed above, [12.10]ff) has been extensively amended for carriage of luggage and other goods by land under special legislation in each State [60] ("Carriers legislation"). This legislation has its origins in the *Carriers Act 1830* (UK) and has some similarities to that used to protect innkeepers (see [13.130] ff). The object of the Carriers legislation was to provide carriers with a simple method of limiting their liability (risk management) for certain valuable goods so "they could protect themselves against huge losses from risks of which they could not be aware, and for which their charges are disproportionally low". [61] The interface between this legislation and the *Trade Practices Act 1974* (Cth) was considered in:

Wallis v Downard-Pickford (North Queensland) Pty Ltd

[12.110] *Wallis v Downard-Pickford (North Queensland) Pty Ltd* (1994) 179 CLR 388

Facts: A carrier was contracted by the Commissioner of Police to transport the household goods of a policeman who was being transferred from Ayr to Dalby. By its admitted negligence, the carrier caused $1,663 damages to the goods and sought to rely upon the Carriers legislation [62] which limited liability to $200.

Decision: The High Court (Deane, Dawson, Toohey, Gaudron, & McHugh JJ) held that the carrier was liable for full damages for breach of warranty under s 74 of the *Trade Practices Act 1974* (Cth): [63]

> It follows that the warranty created by s 74 carries with it full contractual liability for breach. Section 6(1) of the Queensland Act purports to limit that liability. The consequence is that there is a conflict between the two statutes, a conflict which amounts to a direct inconsistency in the sense that the Queensland Act detracts from the full operation of a right granted by the *Trade Practices Act*. The limitation is therefore, to that extent, invalid by reason of s 109 of the Constitution.

The High Court also found that various other sections of the Queensland Carriers legislation were invalid for similar reasons.

---

60 Carriers legislation comprises: ACT: *Common Carriers Act 1902* (NSW), *New South Wales Acts Application Act 1984* (ACT), Sch 2, Part 5; NSW: *Common Carriers Act 1902*; NT: *Carriers Act 1891* (SA), *Northern Territory Acceptance Act 1910* (Cth); Qld: (repealed by Act No 13 of 1993); SA: *Carriers Act 1891*; Tas: *Common Carriers Act 1874*; Vic: *Carriers and Innkeepers Act 1958*; WA: *Carriers Act 1920*.
61 *Penn Plastic Co Pty Ltd v Sadliers Transport Co (Vic) Pty Ltd* (1976) 136 CLR 28 per Stephen J.
62 *Carriage of Goods by Land (Carriers' Liability) Act 1967* (Qld).
63 *Wallis v Downard-Pickford (North Queensland) Pty Ltd* (1994) 179 CLR 388 at 396-397 per Toohey and Gaudron JJ.

Wallis v Downard-Pickford (North Queensland) Pty Ltd cont.

Postscript: s 275 of the *Australian Consumer Law* discussed above would now validate the State legislation.

Implications for business travel

[12.115] The case also analysed the meaning of the equivalent of s 63 which is of particular importance to the application of ss 60 to 64 on business travel luggage and goods as discussed above [12.85]. In this case the contract of carriage was entered between the Commissioner of Police and the carrier and the question also arose whether the exclusion under s 74(3) (now s 63 of the *Australian Consumer Law*) applied. Section 74(3) (similar to s 63: see [12.65]) provides that:

> (3) ...services does not include...a contract for...the transportation or storage of goods for the purposes of a business, trade, profession or occupation carried on or engaged in by the person for whom the goods are transported or stored...

All judges in the *Wallis* case held that this exception did not apply, but there were three different views on where to find the relevant purpose.

1. Deane and Dawson JJ held that the purpose of the actual transportation itself – that is, transportation of household goods – was the relevant purpose and the wider purpose of the contract was not relevant.
2. Toohey and Gaudron JJ held that the purpose of the contract was the relevant purpose but here it was for a public purpose, that is, the operation of the police force.
2. McHugh J held that the relevant purpose was the purpose of the consignor (Commissioner) not the consignee (policeman) and here the goods were not transported for any business, trade, occupation or profession of the Commissioner.

It appears that the court reads the exception very narrowly so as to give the widest operation to s 74 (now s 63). A similar distinction between private and commercial purpose is made in s 64A to determine whether or not limitation of liability under the whole contract (that is, not just for the transportation of goods) is permitted.[64] It will be interesting to see how this is interpreted for business travellers.

Current Queensland position

[12.120] Even before the *Wallis* case reached the High Court, the Queensland government responded and repealed its Carriers legislation in 1993.[65] However, this has had another important though unexpected consequence.[66] To understand the situation it is necessary to briefly consider the history. Queensland first departed from the model in the other States in 1967 when it replaced its 1866 Act with legislation which provided carriers with a limitation of liability for all goods, not just valuables. Further, the 1967 Act effectively abolished the

---

64 See TC Atherton, "Changes to TPA increase liability" (1992) 1(3) *Tourism and Travel Review* 7.
65 *Carriage of Goods by Land (Carriers' Liability) Repeal Act 1993* (Qld).
66 See C Turner, "The innkeepers' lien and liability for travellers' goods in Queensland" (1995) 16 *The Queensland Lawyer* 5-8.

common law rules on carriers' liability for goods [67] and introduced a code. However, when the 1967 Act was repealed in 1993 it is unlikely that the common law rules revived. [68] The result is that the common law rules on carriage of passengers apply in Queensland but those on carriage of their luggage and other goods do not.

The carriage of luggage and other goods in Queensland is now governed by the general law of contract, torts and bailment and the Australian Consumer Law provisions discussed above.

Carriers legislation in other States

[12.125] Under s 275 of the *Australian Consumer Law* discussed above the provisions of the Carriers legislation which limit or exclude a carrier's liability for luggage or goods will now prevail over the *Australian Consumer Law* guarantees (contrary to the *Wallis* case discussed above). The Carriers legislation follows the English model, but with variations from State to State.

Scope of legislation

[12.130] The Carriers legislation [69] applies only to carriage by land and generally only by common carriers. [70] It provides them with protection against claims for loss or damage to certain undeclared valuables. The legislation is particularly relevant for tourism and travel because it applies to valuables in parcels or packages, whether accompanying a passenger or as freight, and because of the nature of the items covered.

Valuables

[12.135] The list of goods and property covered by the Carriers legislation reflects a 19th century conception of "valuables" and generally comprises gold, silver, jewellery, precious stones, watches, clocks, trinkets, money, securities, stamps, maps, writings, title deeds, paintings, engravings, pictures, gold- and silver-plated items, glass, china, silks, furs and lace, with some variations from State to State. [71] No proper attempt has been made to update the list, which contains many anomalies. [72]

---

67   Section 5(1) of the *Carriage of Goods by Land (Carriers' Liability) Act 1967* (Qld).
68   This is a presumption of statutory interpretation under s 20(1)(a) and (2) of the *Acts Interpretation Act 1954* (Qld). The position is remarkably similar to that reached with innkeepers in Western Australia: see TC Atherton, "Innkeepers' Liability in WA: Tourist Accommodation operates under uncertain laws", *Western Australian Law Review* 1996 (26) 161-168 and with warehousemen' liens in Queensland: see (1974) Mod L Rev 240, 360, 480.
69   The legislation has been repealed in al but four States: NSW, Victoria, Tasmania and ACT and a recent report commissioned by the Victorian government reccmmends its aboltion. See *Carriers and Innkeepers Act Options Paper: Modernising Victoria's consumer Policy Framework* October 2008 (Consumer Affairs Victoria – Publisher).
70   Vic: *Carriers and Innkeepers Act 1958*; NSW: *Common Carriers Act 1902*; ACT: *Civil Law (Wrongs) Act 2002* (Part 11.2); TAS *Common Carriers Act 1874*.
71   Carriers legislation: ACT: Part 11.2; NSW: Sch 2; Tas: s 3; Vic: s 3.
72   For example, platinum is not covered because it had not been discovered when the legislation originated in the 1830s: DA Glass and C Cashmore, *Introduction to the Law of Carriage of Goods* (Sweet & Maxwell, London, 1989), [1.30].

Protection of carrier

[12.140] Under the Carriers legislation, the carrier is not liable for loss or damage to any item in the list worth over $20 unless, at the time of delivery of the parcel or package containing the item, the value and nature of the item is declared to the carrier and an increased charge is paid if required by the carrier for the extra risk. [73]

Notice and receipt

[12.145] The carrier must display a public notice in a conspicuous place at the premises where the items are received stating the rate of increased charges required as compensation for the risk of carrying the valuables safely. [74] The notice is binding on all persons whether or not they have actual knowledge of it. [75] No other public notice or declaration limits or affects the liability of a common carrier for valuables or other goods. [76] When the value has been declared and any increased charges have been paid or agreed to be paid, the carrier must (if required) give a signed receipt acknowledging that the item has been insured. [77] Failure to display the notice or give a required receipt deprives the carrier of the charges and of the protection of the legislation. [78] If a declared item is lost the passenger can recover the increased charges paid as well as the value of the item. [79] The passenger cannot recover more than the declared value but the carrier is not bound by it and may require strict proof of actual value. [80]

Fault of the carrier

[12.150] The legislation does not protect the carrier for loss or damage to valuables or any other goods if it was caused by the criminal or fraudulent acts of the carrier's employees and the employees are not protected, even for personal neglect or misconduct. [81]

In relation to goods other than valuables, the legislation varies among the States in its effect on the carriers' right to contract out of liability for negligence. The Australian Capital Territory, New South Wales and Tasmania provide that a carrier is liable for loss or damage caused by the neglect of the carrier or its employees unless a special contract or condition to the contrary is signed by the passenger and is just and reasonable. [82] Victoria does not require that it be signed or that it be just and reasonable. [83]

---

73 Carriers legislation: ACT: s 4; NSW: s 4; Tas: s 3; Vic: s 3.
74 Carriers legislation: ACT: Part 11.2; NSW: s 5(2); Tas: s 4; Vic: s 4.
75 Carriers legislation: ACT: Part 11.2; NSW: s 5(3); Tas: s 4(2); Vic: s 4.
76 Carriers legislation: ACT: Part 11.2; NSW: s 7(1); Tas: s 6; Vic: s 6.
77 Carriers legislation: ACT: Part 11.2; NSW: s 6(1); Tas: s 5; Vic: s 5.
78 Carriers legislation: ACT: Part 11.2; NSW: s 6(1); Tas: s 5; Vic: s 5.
79 Carriers legislation: ACT: no provision; NSW: no provision; Tas: s 9; Vic: s 9.
80 Carriers legislation: ACT: Part 11.2; NSW: s 11; Tas: s 11; Vic: s 11.
81 Carriers legislation: ACT: s 10; NSW: s 10; Tas: s 10; Vic: s 10.
82 Carriers legislation: ACT: s 9; NSW: s 9; Tas: s 14.
83 Carriers legislation: Vic: s 8.

In relation to valuables it is clear that the legislation in all the above States purports to protect the carrier even where the loss or damage is caused by the carrier's negligence. [84] The result is a grave injustice in many cases and Glass and Cashmore provide the following example: [85]

> Say for example a student takes his text books [which are "writings" in the list of valuables] in his brief case onto a scheduled bus and his briefcase is lost or destroyed by the gross negligence or the deliberate wrongdoings of the bus company's employees then, unless the student has taken the unlikely precaution of declaring the nature and contents of his briefcase to the bus conductor, the carrier would not be liable for any of the contents!

The *Wallis case* discussed above provided some relief when the *Trade Practices Act 1974* provisions were held to invalidate contrary State legislation. Section 275 of the *Australian Consumer Law* has reversed this and the possibility of grave injustice described above applies all over again. The result would seem to be accidental.

Road Transport

Regulation of Road Transport

Administration

International

[12.160] The International Road Transport Union (IRU), [86] Geneva, deals at an international level with various issues affecting this mode of transport, including border controls, [87] taxes and deregulation. The IRU has also established, with the International Hotels Association (IHA) (see [13.180]), standard form booking procedures, contracts and rules between coach operators and hoteliers for group accommodation.

National and State

[12.165] Although the Commonwealth government has no direct constitutional power over it, road transport is regulated at federal and State level. [88] Co-ordination and co-operation are procured through the Australian Transport Council (ATC). It is described in its website [89] as a "Ministerial forum for Commonwealth, State and Territory consultations and advice to governments on the co-ordination and integration of all transport and road policy issues at a national level". Through various agencies which deal with road issues, its initiatives include actions on national road infrastructure, road safety, design rules and vehicle emissions. The Commonwealth regulates interstate road transport [90] and each State also has its own road transport licensing and regulatory system.

---

84 *Hinton v Dibbin* (1842) 2 QB 646; 114 ER 253; *Great Western Railway Co v Rimell* (1856) 18 CB 575; 139 ER 1495.
85 DA Glass and C Cashmore, *Introduction to the Law of Carriage of Goods* (Sweet & Maxwell, London, 1989), [1.32].
86 See IRU website at http://www.iru.org.
87 Although Australia is an island state, this is an important issue here given our federal system and numerous State borders.
88 Uniformity of road transport law is sought by co-operative agreement between the Commonwealth and States and under the *National Road Transport Commission Act 1992* (Cth).
89 Australian Transport Council (ATC), http://www.atcouncil.gov.au.
90 *Interstate Road Transport Act 1985* (Cth).

Freedom of the highway

[12.170] Transport across land requires rights to travel over what would otherwise be public or private property.[91] The legal mechanism for this is the common law highway, described as:[92]

> A way over which there exists a public right of passage, that is to say a right for all Her Majesty's subjects at all seasons of the year freely at their will to pass and repass without let or hindrance.

At common law, highways included any means of travelling from one place to another, including roads, bridges, canals and rivers, all of which attracted similar rights and duties associated with transport. These days highways or roads are seen as distinct from waterways. In Australia, roads may be dedicated to public use at common law[93] or, more usually, under various statutes, but the result is the same. Detailed rules are prescribed under statutes and regulations for the use of roads. It is interesting to compare freedom of the road with the rights provided for the other modes of transport: freedom of the high seas (see [12.310]) and freedoms of the air (see [12.480]).

Public/private

[12.175] Traditionally, roads have been regarded as public infrastructure in Australia and it is only in more recent times that we have seen various moves towards privatisation to some extent through the growth of toll roads. Most vehicles are privately owned and operated, although many towns and cities own and operate their own scheduled bus services as part of the urban transport system.

Other regulation

[12.180] Special licences are required from State transport authorities to operate various types of road transport, including the following, which are particularly relevant for tourism and travel:

- taxis;
- limousines;
- off-road vehicles;
- hire vehicles;
- buses.

As a condition of licensing, the State transport authorities usually prescribe standards for the operator and vehicle and often regulate the conduct of the business.[94] The requirements vary from State to State and the detail is outside the scope of this text.

---

[91] Entering another's land without permission is trespass.
[92] *Ex parte Lewis* (1888) 21 QBD 321 per Willis J.
[93] *Attorney-General v Antrobus* (1905) 2 Ch 188 provides an interesting example of a public access way across private property to Stonehenge which was found not to be a road.
[94] See for example: NSW: *Passenger Transport Act 1990*; NT: *Commercial Passenger (Road) Transport Act*; Qld: *Transport Operations (Passenger Transport) Act 1994*; SA: *Passenger Transport Act 1994*; Tas: *Passenger Transport Act 1997*; Vic: *Transport Act 1983*; WA: *Public Transport Authority Act 2003*.

Liability in road transport

Common carriers

[12.185] Depending on the circumstances, each of these operators (apart from those who hire self-drive vehicles) can be a common carrier subject to the rights and duties applicable at common law (see [12.20]ff) and under the Carriers legislation (see [12.100]ff). However, many State transport authorities are deemed not to be common carriers.[95] Also, as discussed in the following paragraphs, they are also subject to the special principles developed at common law and by statute for carriage by road.

Roadworthiness

[12.190] In carriage by land, there was no absolute duty at common law that the vehicle be roadworthy.[96] The carrier's common law duty is only to supply a vehicle as safe as reasonable care can make it. However, vehicles must meet prescribed standards of roadworthiness under State transport legislation, as stated in the preceding paragraph, and failure to meet these standards may found an action for breach of statutory duty (see [5.175]). Similar results may follow where vehicles are found to be "factories" under OHS legislation (see [8.205]ff). The *Australian Consumer Law* applies guarantees that passenger transport services will be supplied with reasonable care and skill and will be fit for the purpose and without delay (see [12.65]ff) and also casts a duty on the vehicle supplier to ensure that vehicles supplied are fit for the purpose and of acceptable quality (see [9.175]).

Death or personal injury of passengers

[12.195] Where transport is provided by a motor vehicle such as a taxi, limousine, bus, motor cycle, hire car or the like special rules apply. Special legislation in each State[97] ("Motor Accident Insurance legislation") provides an accident insurance compensation scheme for passengers and others injured in motor vehicle accidents. The legislation requires the owner of the vehicle, as a condition of registration, to take out compulsory third party insurance to cover the liability of the owners and drivers of the vehicle for death or bodily injury to passengers or any third persons arising out of the use of a motor vehicle. Compensation under the scheme is available even if the vehicle is uninsured or unidentified and even if the owner or the driver is dead, bankrupt or cannot be found. The owner, and ultimately the insurer, is deemed to be liable for the driver even if the driver is unauthorised or unlicensed. In some States it is not even necessary to prove fault to establish liability in some circumstances.[98] Contracting out or limiting liability under the scheme is prohibited by the legislation.[99]

---

[95] See, for example, *Transport Administration Act 1988* (NSW), s 102. The State Transit Authority is not a common carrier.

[96] *John Carter v Hanson Haulage* [1965] 1 QB 495. Contrast carriage by sea at [12.360] below.

[97] Motor Accident Insurance legislation comprises: ACT: *Road Transport (Third Party Insurance) Act 2008*; NSW: *Motor Accidents Compensation Act 1999*; NT: *Motor Accidents (Compensation) Act*; Qld: *Motor Accident Insurance Act 1994*; SA: *Motor Vehicles Act 1959*, Part IV; Tas: *Motor Accidents (Liabilities and Compensation) Act 1973*; Vic: *Transport Accident Act 1986*; WA: *Motor Vehicle (Third Party Insurance) Act 1943*.

[98] Motor Accident Insurance legislation: NT: *Motor Accidents (Compensation) Act*; Tas: *Motor Accidents (Liabilities and Compensation) Act 1973*; Vic: *Transport Accident Act 1986*.

[99] See, for example, *Motor Vehicles Act 1959* (SA), s 133.

Delay

[12.200] At common law a road carrier has a duty in contract and tort to carry its passengers to their destinations by the usual route without unnecessary deviation and without unreasonable delay (see [12.30]).[100] At common law, carriers are permitted to contract out of such duty and it is common practice for Australian road carriers to attempt to do so in their conditions of carriage. Section 62 of the *Australian Consumer Law* now provides a statutory guarantee that services (including passenger transport) must be supplied within a reasonable time and contrary contractual provisions would generally be void and may be deceptive and misleading or false representations under the *Australian Consumer Law* (see [9.55]ff and in relation to carriage by air at [12.605]). Moreover, damages for delay are now likely to include damages for disappointment (see [2.215]ff).[101]

Loss or damage to luggage or other property

[12.205] The accident insurance compensation scheme described in the preceding paragraph is confined to death or bodily injury. Loss or damage to property is governed by the general law of bailment, contract and tort and, where the transport is provided by a common carrier, by the principles of common law, *Australian Consumer Law* and the Carriers legislation discussed in preceding sections. In South Australia the prohibition on contracting out of liability under the Motor Vehicles Accident Compensation legislation has been construed as extending to property damage as well.[102]

Road carrier's lien

[12.210] Subject to special enabling legislation, the common law principles on carriers' lien would apply to carriage by road (see [12.80]).

Hire cars and other self-drive vehicles

[12.215] In a contract for the hire of a vehicle there will be a duty of care and an implied term at common law that the vehicle will be supplied with due care and skill and will be reasonably fit for the purpose. Subject to the principles in the ticket cases, the common law permits exclusion or limitation of this liability.[103] However under the *Australian Consumer Law* statutory guarantees are applied under s 54 which, like ss 60 and 61 cannot be excluded (s 64) and can only be limited (s 64A) in the circumstances described in [12.65]ff above.

---

100 *Hamlin v Great Northern Railway Co* (1856) 1 H&N 408; *Hobbs v London South West Railway* (1875) LR 10 QB 11.

101 Established in *Jarvis v Swan Tours* [1972] 3 WLR 954 contrary to the earlier views in *Hamlin v Great Northern Railway Co* (1856) 1 H&N 408; *Hobbs v London South West Railway* (1875) LR 10 QB 11.

102 In *K&S Lake City Freighters Pty Ltd v Gordon & Gotch Ltd* (1985) 157 CLR 309 the High Court interpreted the South Australian provision as prohibiting contracting out of liability for property damage as well as personal injury.

103 *White v John Warwick and Co Ltd* [1953] 12 All ER 1021.

International regulation of road transport: CVR Convention 1973

[12.220] The International Institute for the Unification of Private Law (UNIDROIT) has sponsored the *Convention on the Contract for the International Carriage of Passengers and Luggage by Road* (CVR) [104] signed at Geneva on 1 March 1973 and the Protocol [105] signed on 5 July 1978. As Australia is an island state, this convention has no relevance to domestic or inbound travel and tourism but it is relevant to outbound. Under the convention the carrier is presumed liable up to specified limits for personal injury and luggage unless it can prove that all reasonable care and diligence was taken. Although the model is similar to aviation's Warsaw Convention (see [12.535]ff) the CVR has received little international support.

Exercise

The Turbulent Taxi Trip

Tim and Tracey have just arrived at the International Airport in your state. They are approached by a number of taxi drivers and eventually choose Mohammed because he indicates that he knows where "Central City Hotel" is located. He directs them to his vehicle.

They put their two suitcases in the boot of the car but Tracey decides she will carry the fine bone china Wedgwood teapot she bought duty free in Singapore on the way here. Tim has travelled this road between the hotel and the airport many times and he is familiar with the usual taxi fare (about AUD$35.00). Consequently, he does not bother to ask Mohammed how much the trip is likely to cost.

As it turns out, Mohammed has no idea where "Central City Hotel" is. (He just said so to get the booking.) In fact, he believes Tracey and Tim want to go to "Central City Plaza" which is in exactly the opposite direction across town from the Central City Hotel so that is where he takes them. Of course, once Tim realises the mistake he tries to direct Mohammed to the correct address. Mohammed's sense of direction is poor and his understanding of English is limited so the journey takes an additional 60 minutes when it should have taken only 20 minutes to reach the hotel if he taken the correct route in the first place. On the way, Mohammed's driving becomes more and more erratic and Tracey asks him to slow down on several occasions. At one set of traffic lights, he has to brake so hard that the teapot (which had been resting on Tracey's knee) flies off and hits the floor and breaks. At the same time, Tracey experiences a sharp pain in her neck which is later diagnosed by her doctor as a whiplash injury caused by the sudden stopping of the car.

Once outside the hotel, Tim is keen to get his luggage out of the boot. He asks for the fare and Mohammed says "AUD$100.00". Tim is furious and says he will pay nothing in view of the broken teapot, the unnecessary trip across town and the one hour delay in getting to the correct destination. With that, Mohammed gets back inside his taxi and drives away.

Discuss the issues. Compare and contrast the outcome of this dispute between Tim and Tracey and Mohammed:

- presently under the existing laws and regulations in your state; and

---

104 Cmnd 5622. "CVR" stands for "Convention relative au contrat de transport international des voyages et des bagages par route".
105 Cmnd 7481. The Protocol converts the limits set under the CVR to SDRs.

The Turbulent Taxi Trip cont.

- under the principles of Common Carriers legislation.

―――― ℘⋙ ――――

Rail Transport

[12.230] The link between rail and road is best reflected in the early name for this type of transport: railroad. In their heyday early last century, railroads introduced several key innovations to transport by road. First, the track or road of rails provided a smooth all-weather surface which was of great advantage compared with the unsealed highways of the time. Secondly, the rails provided a sure, self-steering guidance system for vehicles. Thirdly, the system supported the steam locomotive, which was the most efficient way of providing great pulling power at the time. Fourthly, the system incorporated multiple linked carriages, which provided large though flexible capacity. Finally, the common carrier manner of operation provided a very convenient and economical service which appealed to passengers. Although gradually displaced this century by the convenience of the motor car and the speed of the aeroplane, passenger rail transport is now enjoying something of a revival.

Regulation of rail transport

Administration

International

[12.235] There are several international organisations concerned with rail travel. The International Union of Railways (UIC),[106] Berne, was founded in 1922 and is concerned with harmonisation of railway operations. The Intergovernmental Organisation for International Carriage by Rail (OTIF),[107] Berne, acts as a depository of information on international railways and as a dispute resolution centre on the interpretation of international rail conventions. It also administers the COTIF Convention[108] and one of its principal objectives is to develop a uniform set of laws for passengers and freight in international through traffic by rail (see [12.295]).[109]

National and State

[12.240] Last century each Australian State established its own rail system to its own standards. Under the Australian Constitution the Commonwealth was granted general power over interstate rail transport[110] as well as power, subject to the consent of the State concerned, to construct, extend or acquire the railways of any State.[111] However it has been a slow and difficult process to overcome incompatible State gauges[112] and establish efficient interstate

---

106   International Union of Railways (UIC) See website at http://www.uic.org/spip.php?article528.
107   Previously the Central Office for International Railway Transport (COTIF).
108   *Convention concerning International Carriage by Rail* (COTIF) 9 May 1980.
109   See its website for more information at http://www.otif.org/en/about-otif/general-information.html.
110   Constitution, s 51(i) (trade and commerce power) and s 98 (extension to railways the property of any State).
111   Constitution, s 51(xxxiii), (xxxiv). These powers are additional to the Commonwealth's power over railways for defence purposes under s 51(xxxii).
112   See, for example, *Railway Standardization (New South Wales and Victoria) Agreement Act 1958* (Cth).

rail traffic. [113] In 1975 the Commonwealth [114] took over the railway systems in Tasmania [115] and South Australia [116] and has since then taken an increasing interest in developing the national railway system. [117] Co-operation and co-ordination are fostered through the Australian Transport Council (ATC) [118] (see [12.165]). Railways operations are governed by Commonwealth and State legislation [119] ("Railway Operation legislation").

Revival of rail travel and tourism in Australia

[12.245] Rail travel, like sea cruising, is enjoying a resurgence in popularity as a holiday experience. Each suffered a long period of decline as air travel emerged as a faster and more efficient means of long-distance passenger transport. Now they are being successfully repositioned to provide a more leisurely, comfortable and interesting trip than that provided by air.

Australia already has some outstanding rail journeys of this type. These include Australian Rail Track Corporation's transcontinental services [120] the Indian Pacific (Adelaide/Perth), the Ghan (Adelaide/Alice Springs) and the Overlander (Melbourne/Adelaide). They also include Queensland Rail's intrastate services the Queenslander (luxury Brisbane/Cairns) and the Spirit of the Tropics (backpacker Brisbane/Whitsunday/Cairns) and the ambitious Adelaide/Darwin link. [121] Future proposals include the high speed Sydney/Canberra connection. [122]

The Australian Rail Maps site [123] provides an excellent map of the major passenger rail routes in Australia, including links to detailed pages on the urban transit system in each major city.

The legal infrastructure also needs to be upgraded with uniform laws and regulations on responsibility for passengers and luggage, having regard for international standards and models such as the COTIF Convention discussed below ([12.295]).

Freedom of the railway

[12.250] Operator access to railways is much more restricted than it is to highways because railways are a later invention and need extensive rail and station infrastructure. Most railways have been established through special enabling legislation which grants the rights to acquire

---

113   See, for example, *Railways Agreement (Western Australia) Act 1961* (Cth).
114   The Australian National Railways Commission (AN) was established in 1978 by the amalgamation of the Commonwealth Railways, South Australian Railways and Tasmanian Government Railways. AN took over the operation of all Commonwealth and non-urban South Australian lines and the railways of Tasmania. In 1997/98 the Australian Government sold AN's interstate freight and interstate passenger services.
115   *Railways (Transfer to Commonwealth) Act 1974* (Tas) (since repealed).
116   *Railways (Transfer Agreement) Act 1975* (SA) (since repealed).
117   *Australian Land Transport Development Act 1988* (Cth).
118   Australian Transport Council (ATC) at http://www.atcouncil.gov.au.
119   Railway Operation legislation comprises: Cth: *Australian National Railways Commission Sale Act 1997*; NSW: *Transport Administration Act 1988*; Qld: *Transport Operations (Translink Transit Authority) Act 2008*; SA: *Passenger Transport Act 1994*; Tas: *Rail Company Act 2009*; Vic: *Transport Act 1983*; WA: *Railways(Access) Amendment Act 2000*.
120   ARTC, which is wholly owned by the Australian Government, manages over 10,000 kilometres of standard gauge track, primarily through direct ownership and long term leases of State owned track between Kalgoorlie in Western Australia and Acacia Ridge in southern Brisbane.
121   *AustralAsia Railway Corporation Act 1996* (SA) and *AustralAsia Railway Corporation Act* (NT).
122   Another initiative, the Great Southern Pacific Express between Cairns and Sydney ran from 1998 until 2003 when the service ended with losses of about $12m.
123   See the Australian Rail Map and Timetable Index, Railpage at http://www.railmaps.com.au.

and use land for the necessary facilities. Whether public or private, access to operators has traditionally been restricted to monopoly or near monopoly. It is only in recent times that the wisdom of this has been questioned and that a policy has been adopted to open up rail facilities to more competition.[124] Various methods are now being explored to provide multiple private operator access to rail infrastructure.[125]

Public/private

[12.255] In Australia, railways have traditionally been State owned and operated. Provision is now being made to privatise railways and this is expected to transform the industry (see [12.235]). Historically, the Australian National Rail Commission (ANR)[126] administered the rail system in the Australian Capital Territory and Northern Territory and took over the non-urban rail system in South Australia and Tasmania in 1975. Since 1997, railway operations have been administered by Australian Rail Track Corporation (ARTC)[127] which has established a *one stop shop* for rail operators seeking access to the interstate standard gauge rail network between Brisbane and Perth.

In November, 1996, the Australian Government introduced a number of rail reforms including:[128]

- the sale of the National Railways Commission (AN);
- the sale of the National Rail Corporation (NRC); and
- the establishment of the Australian Rail Track Corporation (ARTC).

The effect of these reforms has been to increase the overall involvement of the private sector and to lower the cost of transport to industry, amongst other things. ARTC operates the interstate and some non-metropolitan standard gauge lines in New South Wales,[129] Victoria,[130] Queensland,[131] Western Australia,[132] South Australia[133] and Tasmania.[134]

Other regulation

[12.260] Each rail authority operates under its own Rail Operation legislation as described above ([12.240]). Traditionally this legislation included power to make detailed by-laws

---

124 See *Competition Policy Reform Act 1995* (Cth) and the former *Competition and Consumer Act 2010* (Cth), Part IIIA.
125 These rights may take the form of leases, licences or easements. It is interesting to note that with similar intentions the *Railway Clauses Consolidation Act 1848* (UK) made provision for private carriers in England to lease time to run their own carriages on the public railway infrastructure but that this was never successful.
126 *Australian National Railways Commission Act 1983* (Cth).
127 *Australian National Railways Commission Sale Act 1997* (Cth).
128 *Australian National Railways Commission Sale Act 1997* (Cth).
129 Interstate and Hunter Valley lines and branch lines are leased to ARTC. The urban system is operated by RailCorp.
130 Interstate standard gauge lines are leased to ARTC. Broad gauge branch lines are owned by Victrack and the urban system is operated by Metro.
131 Queensland Rail owns and manages the system except for the interstate network between the NSW border and Acacia Ridge.
132 Interstate standard gauge line from Kalgoorlie to Adelaide is owned by ARTC. Rail lines in the southwest of the State are leased to WestNetRail, a private company. Pilbara lines are managed by mining companies.
133 Interstate standard gauge lines are owned by ARTC. The urban transport system is operated by TransAdelaide.
134 Rail is owned and operated by Tasmanian Railway Pty Ltd, TasRail, a Tasmanian Government-owned rail company established in December 2009.

regulating the conduct of their business and the rights and duties of carrier and passengers. In preparation for the entry of competitive private operators, some States have introducing legislation to promote the safe construction, operation and maintenance of railways by requiring accreditation of railway owners and operators and setting safety and competency standards. [135]

Liability in rail transport

Common carriers

[12.265] When railways evolved in the last century, they operated as common carriers because that type of service appealed most to the travelling public. Their legal status as common carriers was confirmed at common law [136] and rail transport generated much of the case law which developed and refined the rights and duties of common carriers. However, this has been altered by statute and the position of the various railways in Australia since 1997 is that the traditional rail networks have been reorganised and partially privatised. The Commonwealth and State railway authorities are declared not to be common carriers and their legislation contains various exclusions and limitations. [137] Public railway authorities are empowered under the Railway Operation legislation [138] to make regulations or by-laws governing the terms and conditions of carriage of passengers and their luggage and these powers are often used to further limit or exclude liability. [139] The validity of these limitations and exclusions is discussed below.

Railworthiness

[12.270] The position with railworthiness is similar to roadworthiness. Thus there was no absolute duty at common law that the track and rolling stock be railworthy. [140] The carrier's common law duty is only to supply track and rolling stock as safe as reasonable care can make it. However, with privatisation and competitor access to rail infrastructure, some States have introduced legislation requiring accreditation of railway owners and operators and setting safety and competency standards which cover railworthiness. [141] Failure to meet these standards may found an action for breach of statutory duty (see [5.175]). Similar results may follow where stations, track or rolling stock are found to be "factories" under OHS legislation (see [8.205]ff). Sections 60 and 61 of the *Australian Consumer Law* also imply guarantees into the contract of carriage that passenger transport services will be supplied with reasonable care and skill and will be fit for the purpose (see [12.65]ff). Sections 54 and 55 of the same Act impose a guarantee that the rolling stock supplied is fit for the purpose and of acceptable quality (see [9.175]).

---

135 See for example: *Rail Safety Act 2008* (NSW); *Rail Safety Act 2007* (SA); *Rail Safety Act 2006* (Vic).
136 *Great Northern Railway v LEP Transport* [1922] 2 KB 742.
137 See, for example, *Transport Administration Act 1988* (NSW), s 91.
138 See, for example, *Transport Administration Act 1988* (NSW), s 99.
139 For the scope of this power compare *Gregory v Commonwealth Railways Commissioner* (1941) 66 CLR 50 and *Australian National Railways Commission v Ranger Uranium Mines Pty Ltd* (1989) 97 FLR 134.
140 *Redhead v Midland Railway* (1869) LR 4 QB 379.
141 See, for example, *Rail Safety Act 2008* (NSW); *Rail Safety Act 2007* (SA); *Rail Safety Act 2006* (Vic).

Death or personal injury of passengers

[12.275] Generally at common law a rail carrier is liable only for death or injury of its passengers caused by its negligence (see [12.35]). However passenger claims are assisted by the evidentiary principles of res ipsa loquitur and breach of statutory duty (see [5.175]). Generally, neither the Rail Operations legislation nor the conditions of carriage purport to exclude or limit such liability for negligence.[142] If they did they might well be held void as contrary to the statutory guarantees of due care and skill and fitness for purpose under the *Australian Consumer Law* (like the Carriers legislation) (see [12.105]ff).

Delay

[12.280] Generally at common law a rail carrier (like a road carrier) has a duty in contract and tort to carry its passengers to their destinations by the usual route without unnecessary deviation and without unreasonable delay (see [12.30]).[143] At common law rail carriers are permitted to contract out of such duty and it is the standard practice of Australian rail carriers to attempt to do so in their conditions of carriage. In some States this practice is supported by power to make by-laws which are deemed to be part of the contract of carriage. The validity of these conditions is now doubtful. Section 62 of the *Australian Consumer Law* now provides a statutory guarantee that services (including passenger transport) must be supplied within a reasonable time and contrary contractual provisions would generally be void and may be deceptive and misleading or false representations under the *Australian Consumer Law* (see [9.55]ff and in relation to carriage by air at [12.605]). Moreover, damages for delay are now likely to include damages for disappointment (see [2.215]ff).[144]

Loss or damage to luggage or other property

[12.285] As discussed above, the Railway Operation legislation generally deems the Commonwealth and State rail authorities not to be common carriers. Thus these rail authorities successfully avoid the strict liability as insurer of passengers' luggage discussed previously (see [12.45]). With privatisation and the introduction of competitive private rail carriers it is unclear whether the enabling legislation will extend this privilege to private rail carriers. If not, their position some States[145] will be determined under the Carriers legislation discussed above (see [12.125]). It will be recalled that at common law they are also entitled to contract out of strict liability.

It has been standard practice for the Commonwealth and State rail authorities to attempt to exclude or limit liability for loss or damage to luggage and property even where they are negligent. This has been done in the conditions of carriage. The validity of these provisions is doubtful under the *Australian Consumer Law* where they offend the statutory guarantees of due care and skill and fitness for purpose under ss 60, 61 and 64 subject to the effect of s 245. See [12.105]ff.

---

142   Such limitations have been repealed in some Railway Operation legislation.
143   *Hamlin v Great Northern Railway Co* (1856) 1 H&N 408; *Hobbs v London South West Railway* (1875) LR 10 QB 11.
144   Established in *Jarvis v Swan Tours* [1972] 3 WLR 954 contrary to the earlier views in *Hamlin v Great Northern Railway Co* (1856) 1 H&N 408; *Hobbs v London South West Railway* (1875) LR 10 QB 11.
145   These are the Australian Capital Territory, New South Wales, Victoria and Tasmania where the Common Carrier legislation still exists.

Carrier's lien

[12.290] As the Railway Operation legislation deems the Commonwealth and other State rail authorities not to be common carriers, it is doubtful whether they would enjoy this lien unless it was obtained by special provision in the contract of carriage (see [12.270]).

International regulation of rail transport: COTIF Convention 1980

[12.295] The *Convention on International Railway Transport* (COTIF) [146] was signed at Berne on 9 May 1980 and came into force on 1 May 1985. Appendix A to COTIF contains the uniform rules regarding the carriage of passengers and their luggage (CIV). Again, as Australia is an island state, this convention has no relevance to domestic or inbound travel and tourism but it is important for outbound tourism and it applies through most of Europe.

Under the convention the railway carrier is presumed to be liable, but the amount of liability (expressed in Units of Account) is limited as follows: [147]

- passenger's death and personal injury: damages limited to 70,000 SDR;
- hand luggage: damages limited to 700 SDR per passenger;
- registered luggage: damages limited per kilo and per item. [148]

If the carrier can prove contributory negligence of the passenger, liability for luggage is avoided [149] but liability for death or personal injury is apportioned. [150] The carrier also escapes liability by proving that the accident was unavoidable and not connected with the operation of the railway. [151] However, if the damage has resulted from the wilful misconduct or gross negligence of the carrier, the limits on liability do not apply. [152]

Delay in delivery of registered luggage is covered by the CIV [153] but any other loss or damage for delay is not and is subject to the general law of the state in which it occurs.

Notice of a claim for personal injuries or death must generally be given within three months and proceedings must be commenced within three years. [154] Shorter time limits apply to other claims. [155]

Carriers [156] and passengers [157] are bound by the liabilities and limits provided under the CIV.

CARRIAGE BY SEA

[12.300] Until the arrival of the aeroplane, ships were the only means of transport between continents and, for isolated island countries like Australia, sea cruising was the only means of

---

146 Cmnd 8535.
147 *Convention on International Railway Transport*, Art 6(1): the unit of account is the Special Drawing Right (SDR) defined by the International Monetary Fund (IMF). This converts to approximately AUD$1.69 per SDR at rates of exchange as at June 2010.
148 34 SDR/kg or 500 SDR per item if actual value is established, otherwise 10 SDR/kg or 150 SDR per item.
149 *Convention on International Railway Transport*, Art 35(2).
150 *Convention on International Railway Transport*, Art 26(2).
151 *Convention on International Railway Transport*, Art 26(2).
152 *Convention on International Railway Transport*, Arts 30 – 31, 38 – 41.
153 0.40 SDR/kg or 7.0 SDR per item if actual value is established, otherwise 0.07 SDR/kg or 1.4 SDR per item.
154 *Convention on International Railway Transport*, Art 53.
155 *Convention on International Railway Transport*, Art 55.
156 *Convention on International Railway Transport*, Art 32.
157 *Convention on International Railway Transport*, Art 46.

international travel. Sea transport prevailed until the 1960s and then declined as rapidly as international aviation advanced. However, like rail travel, in recent years sea travel has enjoyed a revival by providing travellers with a more leisurely, comfortable and interesting trip than that provided by air. Consider how much has changed since this most famous case of shipping law.

Oceanic Steam Navigation Co Ltd (the White Star Line) v Mellor (the "Titanic")

[12.305] *Oceanic Steam Navigation Co Ltd (the White Star Line) v Mellor (the "Titanic")* (1914) 233 US 718 (US Supreme Court).

Facts: In the world's worst maritime disaster, the *Titanic*, on its maiden voyage from Southampton to New York, hit an iceberg and sank in the mid-Atlantic ocean. It was designed to be unsinkable and in accordance with shipping standards of the time there were lifeboats on board with capacity for only 1,000 people. In the result, 1,500 of the 2,200 passengers and crew on board drowned. The shipowner was negligent in failing to keep a proper lookout and of maintaining high speed in poor visibility. Under UK law (Merchant Shipping Acts) the shipowner's liability could be limited. Some claimants sought to avoid the UK limits by suing in the US. The owners sought to limit their liability under a similar US Limited Liability Act.

Decision: The US Supreme Court held that the shipowner was entitled to limit its liability under US law. Although the ship was registered in the UK and sank on the high seas, it was on a voyage to the US, some of the passengers were US residents and the claim was brought in the US. This was sufficient connection to apply US law.

Aftermath: As a result, the shipowners successfully limited their liability to US$91,805.54, the value of 14 salvaged lifeboats plus outstanding fares. Death claims alone were US$22 million.[158] The disaster forced a review of safety standards and eventually led to the formation of the International Maritime Organisation (IMO) ([12.320] below) and the adoption of the *International Convention for the Safety of Life at Sea* (SOLAS) ([12.345] below).

History

Freedom of the Sea

[12.310] Freedom of the seas is a fundamental principle of international maritime law. It can be traced back to the Romans. It was challenged in the sixteenth century by Portugal and Spain seeking to divide the Pacific Ocean between them to secure trade. In 1580, Queen Elizabeth rejected complaints by Spain and Portugal that Sir Francis Drake's voyages to the Pacific Ocean violated their claims of sovereignty over those waters.

As a result of England's stand, freedom of the sea has meant that any nation is entitled to use the sea and to navigate over it and through the air above it. However, freedom of the sea is not absolute, as there is a substantial body of international and national laws regulating activities at sea. This erosion of the principle began during the eighteenth century when the definition of territorial waters was extended to include a three-mile zone and has continued ever since.

---

158 M Davies, "Limitation of liability in international carriage of goods" (1992) 66 *Law Institute Journal* 984-988, 984.

The *Law of the Sea Convention 1982* now regulates most activities at sea as well as the conventions on liability discussed below ([12.375]ff). These regulations also include the extraterritorial operation of national laws under these conventions and in relation to registered ships discussed below ([12.335]). There are also rights of navigation over inland waters under principles similar to freedom of the highways discussed above ([12.170]).

Law of the Sea

[12.315] Historically, there were two conflicting approaches to the freedom of the seas:

1. *Closed* – that is, the seas should be subject to some level of ownership by nation States who could then make a claim or title to the body of water surrounding their coastal territories. Security was the main concern with nation States seeking to defend their coastlines from gunships firing and blockading ports and damaging coastal communities. Island States such as England supported this approach.[159]

2. *Open* – that is, the seas are not subject to ownership or title and are in fact resources available for all countries to use. The main concern here was that there should be equality for all and open seas for trade. The Dutch, in particular, supported this view.[160]

The second view prevailed until the mid twentieth century. Now the regulatory framework of the *Law of the Sea Convention* focuses on resources, sovereignty and environmental jurisdiction. It settled on a 12+12 nautical mile limit for territorial waters and contiguous zone and an exclusive economic zone (EEZ) of 200 nautical miles.

A State's continental shelf can extend as far as 350 nautical miles offshore. Really all that is effectively left of the freedom of the seas are the High seas – the area left over and beyond the legitimate claims of nation States.

Regulation of sea transport

Administration

International

[12.320] The International Maritime Organisation (IMO),[161] London, was founded by a 1948 Convention as the United Nations' specialised agency concerned with shipping. It is concerned with all international regulatory aspects of shipping, particularly safety, technology, navigation, trade, pollution and liability to passengers and it administers the main conventions on these matters. The United Nations, through its Division for Ocean Affairs and the Law of the Sea (DOALOS), administers the *United Nations Convention on the Law of the Sea* (LOS 1982), Montego Bay, 1982. This is the key international convention which "lays down a comprehensive regime of law and order in the world's oceans and seas; it is an umbrella convention which establishes rules governing all uses of the oceans and their resources. In so doing, it embodies in one instrument traditional rules for the uses of the oceans and at the same time introduces new legal concepts and regimes and addresses new concerns. The Convention provides the framework for further development of specific areas of the law of the

---

159 The idea was promoted by the Englishman John Selden.
160 This approach was promoted by Dutchman Grotius.
161 International Maritime Organisation (IMO) at http://www.imo.org.

sea".[162] The LOS Convention has been enacted into Australian law [163] and the effect on sovereignty and jurisdiction over seas and shipping is outlined in the Preamble as:

Australia as a coastal state has:

(a) sovereign rights in respect of the waters, the sea-bed and the subsoil that constitute the exclusive economic zone of Australia for the purposes of:

   (i) exploring the zone; and

   (ii) exploiting, conserving and managing the natural resources of the zone; and

(b) sovereign rights with regard to other activities for the economic exploitation and exploration of the exclusive economic zone of Australia, such as the production of energy from water, currents and winds; and

(c) jurisdiction in accordance with international law in relation to:

   (i) the establishment and use of artificial islands, installations and structures in the exclusive economic zone; and

   (ii) marine scientific research in the exclusive economic zone; and

   (iii) the protection and preservation of the marine environment in the exclusive economic zone; and

(d) other rights and duties in relation to the exclusive economic zone provided for in the United Nations Convention on the Law of the Sea;

...Australia as a coastal state has the right under international law to exercise control within a contiguous zone to:

(a) prevent infringements of customs, fiscal, immigration or sanitary laws within Australia or the territorial sea of Australia;

(b) to punish infringements of those laws.

The following diagram illustrates these zones, together with the division of responsibility between the Australian Commonwealth and States.

---

162 United Nations Division for Ocean Affairs and the Law of the Sea (DOALOS) at http://www.un.org/Depts/los/index.htm.

163 *Maritime Legislation Amendment Act 1994* (Cth) amending the *Seas and Submerged Lands Act 1973* (Cth).

Sovereignty over Waters

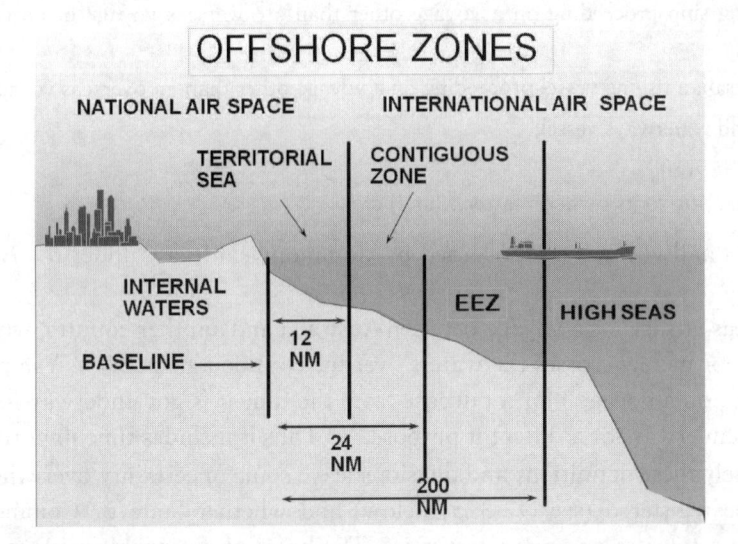

OFFSHORE ZONES

NATIONAL AIR SPACE | INTERNATIONAL AIR SPACE

TERRITORIAL SEA | CONTIGUOUS ZONE

INTERNAL WATERS | 12 NM | EEZ | HIGH SEAS

BASELINE

24 NM

200 NM

National and State

[12.325] The High Court has held that sovereignty over all these areas other than State Inland Waters in Australia vests in the Commonwealth rather than the States.[164] However, the actual division of jurisdiction and responsibility is quite complex. By agreement,[165] the States are permitted to exercise jurisdiction over the first three miles of the territorial sea[166] and the Commonwealth exercises jurisdiction from there out to the limit of the Exclusive Economic Zone and Continental Shelf.[167] Nevertheless both State and Commonwealth governments have some extra-territorial jurisdiction outside these boundaries over matters concerned with the peace, order and good government of their sovereign territory.[168]

The High Court has also held that the Commonwealth has wide powers to deal with navigation and shipping.[169] However by agreement[170] these powers have been divided not

---

164   *New South Wales v Commonwealth (The Seas and Submerged Lands Act Case)* (1975) 135 CLR 337.
165   The "Offshore Constitutional Settlement Agreement" between the Commonwealth and States enacted into legislation by the *Coastal Waters (State Powers) Act 1980* (Cth) and complementary legislation in each State and for the Northern Territory.
166   Queensland has a different power sharing arrangement with the Commonwealth in the Great Barrier Reef. See TA Atherton, "Revisiting Australia's Maritime Boundaries in the Great Barrier Reef: Implications for Regulation of Activities including Marine Passenger Transport" (July/August 2005) 143 *Maritime Studies Journal* 1-17.
167   To complement the powers and ensure the permanence of the arrangement the Commonwealth also granted title over the seabed of the territorial sea to the States under the *Coastal Waters (State Title) Act 1980* and similar legislation for the Northern Territory.
168   Compare *Pearce v Florenca* (1976) 135 CLR 507 and *Robinson v Western Australian Museum* (1977) 138 CLR 283.
169   *Australian Coastal Shipping v O'Reilly* (1962) 107 CLR 46 at 54 per Dixon CJ discussing s 51(i) (trade and commerce power) and s 98 (extension to shipping and railways) of the Constitution. Also, since *Tasmania v Commonwealth* (1988) 164 CLR 1 (*Tasmanian Dams case*) the Commonwealth also acquires jurisdiction through treaty making under s 51(xxix) (external affairs power).
170   Offshore Constitutional Settlement Agreement.

upon location [171] but upon the type of voyage. Thus under s 2 of the *Navigation Act 1912* (Cth) the States are permitted [172] to exercise jurisdiction over:

(a) a trading ship proceeding on a voyage other than an overseas voyage or an inter-State voyage;

(b) an Australian fishing vessel proceeding on a voyage other than an overseas voyage;

(c) an inland waterways vessel;

(d) a pleasure craft,

…[and] in relation to its owner, master…[and] crew.

All other ships and voyages are governed by Commonwealth law under the *Navigation Act 1912* (Cth).

An "overseas voyage" is a voyage between Australia and another country, whether the ship goes into port or merely crosses the waters over the continental shelf. [173] A ship is deemed to be "proceeding on a voyage" for a purpose from the time it is got underway for the purpose until it is got underway for a different purpose. [174] Thus it includes time in port.

Unfortunately these definitions and divisions leave some uncertainty over whether a ship is required to be registered (see [12.325] below) and whether State or Commonwealth law applies to many tourism and travel activities. The heart of the problem is the failure of the legislative draftsperson to recognise that tourism is a business. Does a fishing vessel include tourist and recreation activities such as fishing trips or game fishing? [175] In tourism, what is the distinction between a "trading ship" and a "pleasure craft"?

A "trading ship" is a ship that is used for any business or commercial activity including the carriage of passengers for hire or reward. [176] A "pleasure craft" is a ship that is used for recreational or sporting activities "whether or not let … for hire or reward or consideration of any kind". [177] It has been suggested that a trading ship takes individual passengers (rather like a common carrier) and a pleasure craft is let or hired as a vessel or to groups for recreational or sporting activities. [178] Registration is compulsory for a trading ship, not for a pleasure craft. If the voyage is overseas or interstate, Commonwealth law applies if it is a trading vessel, State law applies if it is a pleasure craft. These are important consequences which require a clearer distinction.

The Australian Transport Council is the body charged with responsibility for procuring co-operation and co-ordination on issues such as a Uniform Shipping Laws Code. [179] The other issues discussed above also warrant attention.

---

171 Except for collisions, which are governed by the law of the location.
172 Except where "expressly excluded by a provision of this Act".
173 *Navigation Act 1912* (Cth), s 6.
174 *Navigation Act 1912* (Cth), s 2(2).
175 These appear to catch, carry and process fish for trading purposes within the definition of a fishing vessel under s 6 of the *Navigation Act 1912* (Cth).
176 *Navigation Act 1912* (Cth), s 6.
177 *Shipping Registration Act 1981* (Cth), s 3(1); *Navigation Act 1912* (Cth), s 6.
178 M Davies and A Dickey, *Shipping Law* (3rd ed Law Book Co, Sydney, 2004), Chapter 3 Registration.
179 *Navigation Act 1912* (Cth), s 427.

Public/private

[12.330] In Australia, passenger ships have traditionally been privately or foreign owned and this issue is not as important as it is with other modes of transport. However, what is important in shipping law is the legal effect of a ship flying the flag of a particular nation.

Registration of ships

[12.335] For many purposes a ship, wherever it may be, is regarded as floating territory of the country in which it is registered. [180] This means that the flag state's national law, including criminal law, regulates most activities on board the ship wherever it may be. Ships owned by Australians and used for commercial purposes must be registered in Australia. [181] Certain vessels, including small ships (less than 24 metres in tonnage length), fishing vessels and pleasure craft, are exempt from registration (see discussion of definitions above). [182] However a pleasure craft – indeed any "vessel capable of navigating the high seas" – can be registered provided it is Australian owned. [183] This means that even small craft such as those used in sea kayaking are registrable. [184]

Other regulation

[12.340] The IMO no longer regulates the right to operate and the prices charged for passenger shipping. [185] Nor do the Commonwealth and States regulate such matters except in certain cases, where for example ferries are part of the urban transport system. However two other aspects of the regulatory system should be noted: Safety and Admiralty.

SOLAS Convention 1974

[12.345] The IMO has established international standards for seagoing ships. One of its most important conventions for travel and tourism is the *International Convention for the Safety of Life at Sea 1974* (SOLAS) and its Protocols, which evolved from the sinking of the *Titanic* (see [12.305]). New standards now require the upgrading of the world's cruise shipping fleet and the retirement of many famous passenger cruise ships. SOLAS has been enacted into Australian law by amendments [186] to the *Navigation Act 1912* (Cth). These standards are enforced in Australia by the Australian Marine Safety Authority (AMSA) [187] through a system of inspection and survey of all ships. [188] Although there is some degree of uniformity, [189] each State has its own system of regulating marine safety. [190]

---

180 For example, criminal law extends to Australian ships: *Crimes at Sea Act 2000* (Cth) and complementary State legislation under the Offshore Constitutional Settlement.
181 *Shipping Registration Act 1981* (Cth), s 12(1). The register is administered by the Australian Marine Safety Authority (AMSA): see below.
182 *Shipping Registration Act 1981* (Cth), s 13.
183 *Shipping Registration Act 1981* (Cth), s 14(a).
184 M Davies and A Dickey, *Shipping Law* (3rd ed Law Book Co, Sydney, 2004), Chapter 3 Registration.
185 The IMO's Liner Conferences are now concerned primarily with cargo.
186 *Transport Legislation Amendment Act 1995* (Cth).
187 *Australian Maritime Safety Authority Act 1990* (Cth); Australian Maritime Safety Authority at http://www.amsa.gov.au.
188 *Navigation Act 1912* (Cth), s 189.
189 *Navigation Act 1912* (Cth), s 427.
190 See, for example, the licensing and accreditation scheme used in Queensland: *Maritime Safety Queensland Act 2002* (Qld) and *Transport Operations (Marine Safety) Act 1994* (Qld).

Admiralty

[12.350] Shipping law is concerned with the law of the sea and the ships which ply it. Under the *Navigation Act 1912* (Cth) a "ship" is any vessel used in navigation by water, however propelled or moved.[191] Special rules and procedures have been developed under a branch of shipping law known as admiralty law.[192] These give rights to arrest and sue the ship itself as an alternative to suing those who own or who are responsible for the ship.[193] They also give rights of compensation to those who rescue or salvage a ship at sea.[194] In Australia these rules and procedures have been codified under the *Admiralty Act 1988* (Cth).

Liability in Sea Transport

Common carriers

[12.355] The liability of shipowners as common carriers can be traced back over 2,500 years to the earliest Roman edicts.[195] Although the focus of passenger shipping changed over the twentieth century from transport[196] to pleasure, ships often still fit the definition of common carriers.[197] The principles of common carriers' law discussed above ([12.20]ff) applies as modified by the common law for the special circumstances of carriage by water.[198] However, most shipowners have long had statutory protection from the unlimited and often strict liability of common carriers.

Seaworthiness

[12.360] At common law there is a an implied duty on a sea carrier to ensure that the ship is seaworthy. The duty is absolute; it is not simply a matter of taking reasonable care to ensure that the ship is seaworthy. This is to be contrasted with roadworthiness ([12.190]) and railworthiness ([12.270]) as discussed above. Seaworthiness embraces all those things required for the ship to cope with ordinary perils and safely complete the voyage. It includes the fitness

---

191 *Navigation Act 1912* (Cth), s 6. However there are different definitions in case law and in many other statutes. See M Davies and A Dickey, *Shipping Law* (3rd ed Law Book Co, Sydney, 2004), Chapter 3 Registration.
192 *Admiralty Act 1988* (Cth).
193 For an illustration where a ship was arrested and sued for salvage claim see *SG White v The Ship "Mediterranean"* (1966) Qd R 211.
194 In one amusing case, members of the Island Bohemian Club claimed salvage for saving the *Goring*, a small passenger cruise vessel they saw drifting down the Thames unmanned. The House of Lords held that there was no entitlement to salvage on a non-tidal river: *The "Goring"* [1988] 1 Lloyds Law Reports 397.
195 See T Atherton, "Innkeepers' liability for guests' property: contracting out is against the law" (1996) 24(6) *Australian Business Law Review* 448-462, 448.
196 See *Bennett v Peninsular & Oriental Steamboat Co* (1846) 6 CB 775 which held that a common carrier could be sued in tort for damages for unjustified refusal to carry.
197 The fact that the voyage may be for pleasure rather than transport, that it may be round trip rather than point to point and that the carrier may reserve the right to skip ports en route will not preclude a cruise ship from being a common carrier. See D E Eldridge, "Classifying cruise ships as common carriers under the Shipping Act, a jurisdictional struggle: American Association of Cruise Passengers v Carnival Cruise Lines" (1991) 15(2) *Tuland Maritime Law Journal* 397-410.
198 For an excellent analysis of the issues and principles in the US context see NGW Pieper and DW McCreadie, "Cruise ship passenger claims and defences" (1991) 21(2) *Journal of Maritime Law and Commerce* 151-197. See also TA Dickerson, "Laws leave passengers shipwrecked" (29 May 1995) *National Law Journal* 10-11.

of the hull, machinery, stores, equipment and crew. The concept is closely related to the implied term of fitness for purpose in contract law. The remedy for breach of the duty is damages.[199]

Further, the SOLAS and other conventions and standards described above prescribe in detail many of the minimum requirements for seaworthiness. Failure to meet these standards may found an action for breach of statutory duty (see [12.190] above). Similar results may follow where the ship is found to be a "factory" under OHS Legislation (see [8.210]. As with road and rail transport, ss 60 and 61 of the *Australian Consumer Law* applies a statutory guarantee that passenger transport services will be supplied with reasonable care and skill and will be fit for the purpose (see [12.65]ff above). Sections 54 and 55 of the same Act apply a guarantee that the ship supplied is fit for the purpose and of acceptable quality.[200]

History of liability limitation

[12.365] Liability for carriage of passengers by sea has been limited under English law for over 300 years.[201] The limits under this Imperial legislation[202] applied in Australia until they were repealed and replaced by the *Navigation Amendment Act 1979*[203] which also enacted the Brussels Convention 1957. This in turn was repealed by the *Limitation of Liability for Maritime Claims Act 1989* (Cth) which enacted the London Convention 1976[204] and introduced the current Australian system which has been operative since 1991.[205]

Current Limitation of Liability

Exclusion of liability for valuables

[12.370] The only part of the old system which remains current law in Australia is s 338 of the *Navigation Act 1912* (Cth) which excludes liability of certain shipowners for

any loss or damage happening without their actual fault or privity[206] where:

(a) any goods, merchandise or other things whatsoever…are lost or damaged by reason of fire on board the ship; or

(b) any [undeclared valuables]…are lost or damaged by reason of any robbery, embezzlement….

Exclusion (b) bears remarkable similarity to the undeclared valuables provisions of the Carriers Legislation discussed in [12.135]. However, in this case the valuables covered are

---

199 *Hong Kong Fir Shipping v Kawasaki Kaisen Kaisher Ltd* [1962] 2 QB 26.
200 It appears that this point could have been taken to defeat a limitation clause in a case which concerned an accident aboard the *Alexander Pushkin: Gill v Charter Travel Co* (unreported, Qld Sup Ct, De Jersey J, 16 February 1996, BC 9600812).
201 Maritime Ordinance of Louis XIV (1681).
202 *Merchant Shipping Act 1894* (UK).
203 The High Court held in *Kirmani v Captain Cook Cruises Pty Ltd* (1985) 159 CLR 351 that this effectively repealed the Imperial legislation limits for both State law and Commonwealth law.
204 *Convention on Limitation of Liability for Maritime Claims* (London, 1976).
205 The High Court held in *Victrawl Pty Ltd v Telstra Corporation Ltd* [1995] 131 ALR 465 that the Act was not retrospective and so the Brussells Convention 1957 governed incidents which occurred before 1991.
206 For a discussion of the meaning of actual fault and privity see MWD White, *Australian Maritime Law* (2nd ed, Federation Press, Sydney, 2000), [9.81].

more limited to "goods, being gold, silver, diamonds, watches, jewels or precious stones".[207] The exclusion from liability does not apply if a written declaration is provided stating both the nature and the value of the goods.[208]

Section 338 is stated to apply to all ships which are Australian owned, registered or operated, all ships engaged in the coasting trade[209] and all ships of prescribed countries.[210] However it would not apply to ships under State jurisdiction, namely those on voyages for the purposes listed in s 2 of the *Navigation Act 1912* (Cth) (as discussed above), because s 338 does not expressly exclude the operation of s 2.[211]

Limitation of liability of seagoing ships: London Convention 1976

[12.375] The *Limitation of Liability for Maritime Claims Act 1989* (Cth) enacted into Australian law the *Convention on the Limitation of Liability for Maritime Claims* (London Convention 1976) which was signed at London on 19 November 1976 and came into force in Australia on 1 June 1991. This provides the current system for the limitation of liability of seagoing ships in Australia and in many other countries. It has increased the limit on liability but made it much more difficult to break than under the old Brussels Convention 1957[212] which is still in force in some countries.

It should be noted that the limitation system under the Brussels Convention 1957 or the London Convention 1976 is relevant where there are many persons injured. The system enables the shipowner to apply to the court to set a maximum aggregate liability limit for all claims arising from the incident. This should be contrasted with other systems in force in many countries (but not Australia) which set a limit on the claim for each passenger. In the United Kingdom and many other countries both systems apply.[213]

The key issues arising under the London Convention are discussed as follows.

Who may limit liability?

Seagoing ships

[12.380] The London Convention 1976 applies only to "seagoing" ships.[214] A seagoing ship is one which actually goes to sea,[215] not one which could go to sea but does not.[216] "Sea" is not defined in the Act or Convention but it appears to mean the territorial sea and the high

---

207 *Navigation Act 1912* (Cth), s 338(b).
208 *Williams v African SS Co* (1856) 1 HLN 300.
209 *Navigation Act 1912* (Cth), s 10.
210 *Navigation Act 1912* (Cth), s 6(5).
211 See M Davies and A Dickey, *Shipping Law* (3rd ed Law Book Co, Sydney, 2004), Chapter 3 Registration.
212 *International Convention relating to Limitation of Liability of Owners of Sea-going Ships* (Brussells Convention 1957) signed at Brussells on 10 October 1957 and enacted by the *Navigation Amendment Act 1979* (Cth) (Limitation of Liability provisions in Part VIII) which in turn were repealed by the *Limitation of Liability for Maritime Claims Act 1989* (Cth).
213 See Athens Convention 1974 at [12.425] below.
214 London Convention 1976, Art 1.2.
215 *Union Steamship Co of New Zealand Ltd v Commonwealth* (1925) 36 CLR 130 at 145 per Isaac J.
216 *Salt Union Ltd v Wood* [1893] 1 QB 370; *Kirmani v Captain Cook Cruises Pty Ltd* (1985) 159 CLR 351 at 457 per Dawson J.

seas rather than the wider definition in other key legislation.[217] So ships which ply inland waters including lakes, rivers,[218] ports[219] and harbours such as Sydney Harbour[220] are non-seagoing and are now outside the protection of the Convention. While the Act[221] and the Convention[222] make provision for extension of the protection to cover non-seagoing ships, this has not been done. As non-seagoing ships had enjoyed this protection for almost 100 years this represents a very important change in the law for them.[223]

Not all seagoing ships are covered by the Convention. For the Convention to apply the ship must be registered in a nation which is a party to the Convention, or located in or crossing the territorial waters of such a nation, or on the high seas on a voyage between two such nations.

The Convention does not apply to air-cushion vehicles and "floating platforms constructed for the purpose of exploring or exploiting the natural resources of the seabed".[224] The latter appears wide enough to cover floating platforms of the type used at cruise ship mooring and dive sites on the Great Barrier Reef so as to exclude these from protection under the Convention.

Shipowners and others

[12.385] The Convention limits the liability of the "shipowner", which is defined to mean the owner, charterer, manager and operator.[225] The limits also cover actions against the ship itself[226] and, provided the shipowner is legally responsible for them, the shipowner's employees, agents and independent contractors.[227] This would provide some protection for travel agents and tour operators. The liability of insurers and salvors is also limited.[228]

Claims subject to limitation

[12.390] The London Convention 1976 governs cargo as well as passengers and the limits cover a wide range of matters.[229] For tourism, travel and hospitality the key claims limited are for:[230]

(a) ...loss of life or personal injury or loss or damage to property...occurring on board or in direct connection with the operation of the ship...and consequential loss resulting therefrom;

---

217 *Navigation Act 1912* (Cth), s 6 and *Admiralty Act 1988* (Cth), s 3 both define "sea" as including all waters within the ebb and flow of the tide.
218 A 142-ton screw steamer used exclusively to carry salt down the tidal river Mersey to Liverpool was held to be non-seagoing even though it was capable of going to sea: *Salt Union Ltd v Wood* [1893] 1 QB 370.
219 A ship which plied between Hobart and Port Esperence via the Derwent River and D'Entrecasteaux Channel was held to be seagoing only because it passed a lighthouse and was so deemed to be seagoing under special regulations: *Commonwealth v Huon Channel and Peninsular Steamship Co Ltd* (1917) 24 CLR 385.
220 *Kirmani v Captain Cook Cruises Pty Ltd* (1985) 159 CLR 351.
221 *Navigation Act 1912* (Cth), s 5.
222 London Convention 1976, Art 15.
223 Under s 504 of the *Merchant Shipping Act 1894* (IMP) and then under the Brussells Convention 1957.
224 London Convention 1976, Art 15.5.
225 London Convention 1976, Arts 1.1, 1.2.
226 London Convention 1976, Art 1.5.
227 London Convention 1976, Art 1.4.
228 London Convention 1976, Arts 1.1, 1.6 respectively.
229 Certain claims are excluded under London Convention 1976, Art 3 but these are not particularly relevant to tourism, travel and hospitality.
230 London Convention 1976, Art 2.

(b) ...loss resulting from delay in the carriage by sea of...passengers or their luggage;

(c) ...loss resulting from infringement of rights other than contractual rights, occurring in direct connection with the operation of the ship....

Damages for nervous shock (mental injury) would appear to be covered by the phrase "and consequential loss resulting therefrom" in (a). Damages for disappointment can be claimed in contract, tort and under consumer protection legislation. The phrase "other than contractual rights" in (c) may exclude such a claim in contract from limitation in appropriate cases.

Persons making a claim are required to prove liability in accordance with the general law discussed in [12.355], [12.360]. However if the shipowner is a common carrier then it is strictly liable for passengers' luggage (see [12.45]). Also under the general law shipowners are entitled to try to further limit or exclude liability by the conditions of carriage subject to the principles in the ticket cases (see [4.240]ff). This is in contrast with the position of persons claiming under the *Warsaw Convention* against an air carrier who bears strict liability and is prohibited from contracting out (see [12.535]ff).

However as discussed in [12.65] under ss 60 and 61 of the *Australian Consumer Law* there is a statutory guarantee that services (including passenger transport services) be supplied with due care and skill and be fit for the purpose and contracting out of these provisions is restricted.

Limits of liability

Loss of life and personal injury

[12.395] Article 7.1 was amended in 1996 [231] to provide that the limit for passenger claims is determined as follows:

> In respect of claims arising on any distinct occasion for loss of life or personal injury to passengers of a ship, the limit of liability of the shipowner thereof shall be an amount of 175,000 Units of Account multiplied by the number of passengers which the ship is authorized to carry according to the ship's certificate.

The Unit of Account is the Special Drawing Right (SDR) defined by the International Monetary Fund and its value varies from currency to currency and through time. [232] At the time of writing one SDR was worth approximately AUD$1.69 [233] so that the limit converted to:

$$175{,}000 \text{ Units of Account} = 175{,}000 \text{ SDR} = \text{AUD } \$295{,}750.$$

This is compared with the Australian limits for aviation of 350,000 SDR (international) and $500,000 (domestic) and per passenger (see [12.535]). However the shipping limit is calculated on the passenger carrying capacity of the ship and the aggregate is shared rateably among those suffering casualty, [234] whereas in aviation the limit is applied to each passenger. Shipping accidents also have a much higher survivor rate than aviation accidents.

---

231 LLMC Protocol 1996 entered into force 13 May 2004.
232 London Convention 1976, Art 8.
233 As at June 2010.
234 London Convention 1976, Art 9.

Ship liability under the London Convention

[12.400] Provision is made for the shipowner or insurer to guarantee or pay a sufficient sum into a fund to cover the total liability as limited under the Convention [235] so the ship, if arrested, can be released. [236] The claims are then determined by a court which distributes the moneys rateably among the claimants in accordance with the Convention and local law. [237]

Passengers' luggage and other property

[12.405] Article 6 limits liability for any claims other than for loss of life or personal injury arising out of a distinct occasion to 1,000,000 SDR for a ship not exceeding 2000 tons with additions per ton thereafter. [238] Where claims exceed the limit, the claimants share rateably. It will be recalled that valuables are excluded under s 338 of the *Navigation Act 1912* (Cth) ([12.370] above). It will also be recalled that if the shipowner is a common carrier it is strictly liable for passengers' luggage (see [12.45] above).

Breaking the limits

[12.410] Article 4 of the Convention provides a method of breaking the limits by proving conduct barring limitation. It provides:

> A person liable shall not be entitled to limit his liability if it is proved that the loss resulted from his personal act or omission, committed with the intent to cause such loss, or recklessly and with knowledge that such loss would probably result.

This is similar to Article 25 of the *Warsaw-Hague Convention for Aviation* (see [12.109]) in that it requires proof of either (a) intentional wrongdoing (unlikely and probably criminal) or (b) recklessness and with knowledge that the loss would probably result. As under Article 25 the alternative (b) is extremely difficult to establish especially if it must be proved subjectively and not objectively. [239] However it is even more difficult to break than Article 25 because Article 4 also requires proof that the loss was caused by the shipowner's *personal* act or omission.

The limits are effectively reduced by any counterclaim of the person entitled to limitation of liability. Article 5 provides:

> Where a person entitled to limitation of liability under the rules of this Convention has a claim against the claimant arising out of the same occurrence, their respective claims shall be set off against each other and the provisions of this Convention shall only apply to the balance, if any.

These counterclaims are not defined but would presumably include contributory negligence which, although it is a defence at common law, is apportionable under apportionment legislation (see Chapter 5, [5.155]).

---

235 London Convention 1976, Art 11.
236 London Convention 1976, Art 13.
237 London Convention 1976, Arts 12 – 14.
238 *LLMC Protocol 1996* (art 3) amends Article 6(b) of the London Convention 1976, so that the additions are: 400 Units of Account for each ton from 3002 to 30,000, 300 Units of Account for each ton from 30,001 to 70,000 tons and 200 Units of Account for each ton in excess of 70,000 tons.
239 See discussion of *SS Pharmaceuticals case* in [12.575] below.

Unlimited Liability of Non-Seagoing Ships

[12.415] In conjunction with the Brussels Convention 1957, the *Navigation Act 1912* (Cth) [240] deemed "sea going ships" to include ships used for purposes within s 2 of the *Navigation Act 1912* (Cth) over which States had jurisdiction as discussed above. In *Kirmani v Captain Cook Cruises Pty Ltd [No 1]* [241] the High Court held this was effective to limit the liability of a Sydney harbour cruiser to an injured passenger. However when the *Limitation of Liability for Maritime Claims Act 1989* (Cth) repealed the old regime it left non-seagoing ships unprotected. While there is provision in the London Convention 1976 for States' parties to limit the liability of non-seagoing ships [242] this has not been done at Commonwealth or State level. [243]

Only Western Australia purports to limit the liability of ships under the *Western Australian Marine Act 1982*. This legislation enacts the Brussels Convention 1957 into State legislation and is a carry-over from the old regime. To the extent that it purports to cover sea-going ships it is inconsistent with the Commonwealth legislation and is void under s 109 of the Constitution. [244] To the extent that it purports to limit the liability of non-seagoing ships it would be contrary to ss 60, 61 and 64 of the *Australian Consumer Law* but probably now validated by s 275 (see [12.65]). [245]

The result is that non-seagoing ships in Australia have no statutory limit upon liability. Any attempts by industry to limit or exclude liability contractually would be contrary to the statutory guarantees under ss 60 and 61 and void under s 64 of the *Australian Consumer Law* where it applies. [246] State legislation could establish limits which would prevail under s 275 of the *Australian Consumer Law*.

Non-seagoing ships would appear to include all inland water vessels and many tourist operators on Moreton Bay, Gold Coast Broadwater, Tweed River, Hawkesbury River, Botany Bay, Sydney Harbour, Murray River, Gippsland Lakes, Port Phillip Bay, Goolua, Swan River, Adelaide River, Alligator River, Yellow Water and the like.

Charter, hire and self-sail vessels

[12.420] The principles here are similar to those discussed for hire cars (see [12.215]). In a contract for the hire of a vessel there will be a duty of care and an implied term at common law that the vessel will be supplied with due care and skill and will be reasonably fit for the purpose. Subject to the principles in the ticket cases, the common law permits exclusion or limitation of this liability. [247] However statutory guarantees applied under ss 54 and 55 of the *Australian Consumer Law* are similar in effect and, like ss 60 and 61, cannot be excluded (s 64) and can only be limited (ss 64A) in the circumstances described in [12.65] above.

---

240 *Navigation Act 1912* (Cth), s 332 (since repealed).
241 *Kirmani v Captain Cook Cruises Pty Ltd [No 1]* (1985) 159 CLR 351.
242 London Convention 1976, Art 15(2).
243 *Limitation of Liability for Maritime Claims Act 1989* (Cth), s 5 makes way for State legislation giving effect to the London Convention.
244 See MWD White and Al Phillipides, *Shipping*, Vol 34.3 of *Laws of Australia* (Lawbook Co, Sydney), [116].
245 Compare the conclusion reached by MWD White and Al Phillipides, *Shipping*, Vol 34.3 of *Laws of Australia* (Lawbook Co, Sydney), [116]. See *Wallis v Downard-Pickford (North Queensland) Pty Ltd* (1994) 179 CLR 388.
246 See *Dillon v Baltic Shipping Co "Mikhail Lermontov"* (1990) ATPR 40-992.
247 *White v John Warwick and Co Ltd* [1953] 12 All ER 1021.

However shipping law will also apply so that the charterer may be liable to third parties as owner.[248] Interesting questions may arise as to whether others on the vessel are passengers or crew.[249]

Other International Regulatory Systems

International passenger shipping liability: Athens Convention 1974

[12.425] The *Convention Relating to the Carriage of Passengers and their Luggage by Sea 1974* (Athens Convention)[250] was signed at Athens on 13 December 1974 and came into force on 28 April 1987. Its Protocol was signed at London on 19 November 1976 and came into force on 19 April 1989.[251] It is not in force in Australia but is applied by many countries to seagoing ships and so is relevant to outbound tourism. Unlike the Brussels Convention 1957 and London Convention 1976 ([12.375] above), which set a maximum aggregate liability limit for all claims arising from an incident, the Athens Convention sets limits on the claim for each passenger. Where both conventions apply the overlap causes some difficulties.[252]

This convention applies to international carriage by certain ships. Carriage is international where under the carriage contract the places of departure and destination are in two different nations or in the same nation with an intermediate port of call in another nation.[253] For the convention to apply, one or more of the following must be a nation which is party to the Convention: the flag or place of registration of the ship, the place where the carriage contract was made or the place of departure or destination under the carriage contract.[254]

Under the convention the shipowner is presumed to be liable but the amount of liability[255] is limited as follows:[256]

- passenger's death and personal injury: damages limited to 46,666 SDR;
- cabin luggage: damages limited to 833 SDR per passenger;
- vehicles: 3333 SDR per vehicle;
- undeclared valuables: no liability;[257]
- other luggage: 1200 SDR per passenger.

---

248 *Navigation Act 1912* (Cth), s 258A. See also VM Bald, "Unlimitation of liability: vessel owners and the bareboat charter after *Baker v Raymond International Inc*" (1986) 7(4) *Cardozo Law Review* 1075-1102.
249 *Secretary of State for Trade v Booth (The "Boche")* [1984] 1 All ER 464.
250 *Convention Relating to the Carriage of Passengers and their Luggage by Sea 1974* (1975) 14 ILM 945.
251 A further Protocol dated 1 November 3002 which substantially increases the limits has not yet come into force. See also B Soyer, "Sundry Considerations on the Draft Protocol to the Athens Convention Relating to the Carriage of Passengers and their Luggage at Sea" (2002) 33(4) *Journal of Maritime Law and Commerce* 519-641.
252 See, for example, *The "Bowbelle"* [1990] 1 Lloyd's Reports 532. In this case the *Bowbelle* collided with the *Marchionesse*, a passenger cruise ship in the Thames causing loss of life, injury and property damage.
253 Athens Convention 1974, Art 1.9.
254 Athens Convention 1974, Art 2.
255 Athens Convention 1974, Art 9: the unit of account is the Special Drawing Right (SDR) defined by the International Monetary Fund (IMF). This converts to approximately AUD$1.69 per unit of account at exchange rates at June 2010.
256 Athens Convention 1974, Arts 7 – 10. The limits shown are for the Athens Convention 1974 and 1976 Protocol. Under the Convention alone the limits are expressed in francs. A 2002 Protocol (requires 10 States to accept it, not yet in force) substantially increases these limits. See for general discussion P Griggs and R Williams, *Limitation of Liability for Maritime Claims*, (2nd ed, Lloyds of London Press Ltd, London, 1991), p 98.
257 Athens Convention 1974, Art 5.

If the carrier can prove contributory negligence of the passenger, liability is apportioned according to the local law.[258] However, if the damage has resulted from the wilful misconduct or gross negligence of the carrier, the limits on liability do not apply.[259]

Notice of a claim for loss or damage to luggage must be given on disembarkation if apparent and within 15 days if not apparent, otherwise it is presumed undamaged.[260] Proceedings for death or injury or luggage must be commenced within two years.[261]

Carriers[262] and passengers are bound by the liabilities and limits provided under the Convention. However, higher limits can be expressly agreed in writing between carrier and passenger.[263]

International inland navigation: CVN Convention 1976

[12.430] As Australia is an island state this matter is relevant only to outbound travel and tourism. UNIDROIT has sponsored the *Convention on the Contract for the International Carriage of Passengers and Luggage by Inland Waterways* (CVN) signed at Geneva in 1976 and the Protocol signed in 1978. This proposes a presumed liability regime subject to limits (66,667 SDR). An alternative convention[264] proposes a maximum aggregate liability and a Limitation Fund similar to the Brussels Convention 1957 ([12.365] above). Neither of these conventions has yet received the support required to come into force. Renewed interest and revision is required for projects such as development of tourism through the various countries down the Mekong River.

History of cruise shipping

[12.435] We have already observed that early ship travel was more concerned with conveying cargo than with ferrying passengers. However, in 1867 Mark Twain was a passenger on the first cruise originating in America. He documented his adventures of the six month trip in the book, *Innocents Abroad*, and perhaps started a trend that continues to this day. By the beginning of the twentieth century, the concept of the "superliner" was a reality and Germany led the market in the development of these massive and ornate floating hotels.

At around the same time across the Atlantic, the American owned[265] White Star Line introduced the most luxurious passenger ships ever seen in the *Olympic* (complete with swimming pool and tennis court) and the ill-fated *Titanic*. The emphasis was on maximising passenger comfort by introducing elegant surroundings and lots of planned activities and minimising the extremes of ocean crossings by designing ships with reduced speed capacity and increased stability.

With the sinking of the *Titanic* in 1912 and the intervention of the two world wars, cruise shipping did not really see a revival unto the 1960s. The modern cruise ship industry created a "fun ship" image which was affordable and attracted many passengers who would have never

---

258   Athens Convention 1974, Art 8.
259   Athens Convention 1974, Art 13.
260   Athens Convention 1974, Art 15.
261   Athens Convention 1974, Art 16.
262   Athens Convention 1974, Art 18.
263   Athens Convention 1974, Art 10.
264   *Convention Relating to the Limitation of Liability of Owners of Inland Navigation Vessels* (CLN) (Geneva 1973) and its Protocol (Geneva 1978).
265   Financier JP Morgan.

had the opportunity to travel on the earlier much more exclusive "superliners". These fun ships provide a relaxed, informal environment with extensive on-board entertainment. This new breed of cruise ship places less emphasis on transporting people to a particular destination; but rather, seeks to focus on the voyage itself.[266]

Indeed, the English Court of Appeal endorsed this notion that ocean liners are no longer just another mode of transport when it acknowledged that:

> it is quite clear from the cases such as *Jarvis v Swan Tours* that, in contracting to provide a cruise, P&O were not merely undertaking a contract of carriage and the provision of accommodation and food on route, but were agreeing to provide an enjoyable and relaxing holiday of the kind so typically described in the brochure ....[267]

Policy to protect shipowners

[12.440] A review of the various Conventions and legislation governing the shipping industry discussed above clearly indicates that the limitations on liability for shipowners far outweigh the rights of their passengers to seek compensation when things go wrong. The policy behind such a generous approach to shipowners' obligations may well have been to provide incentive and encouragement to the shipbuilding industry.

As one observer[268] puts it:

> The unpleasant reality is that the cruise vessel's responsibilities and your rights as an injured passenger are governed not by modern, consumer oriented common and statutory law, but by 19th century legal principles, the purpose of which is to insulate the maritime industry from the legitimate claims of passengers... Although recent years have seen the expansion of travel consumers' rights and remedies in actions against airlines, domestic and international hotels, tour operators and travel agents (amongst others) there has been little, if any, change in the passengers' rights and remedies in actions against cruise lines.

The fact remains that cruise passengers appear to be at a distinct disadvantage in prosecuting their claims in cases of hijacking, shipboard accidents, sinking and the criminal acts of other passengers as the following case studies indicate.

Case Study: Hijacking–*Klinghoffer* and the *Achille Lauro*

[12.445] Facts: On 7 October 1985, off the coast of Egypt, four gunmen hijacked the Italian cruise ship, the *Achille Laur*, and demanded the release of Palestinian prisoners in Egypt, Italy, and elsewhere. When the demands were not met, they shot in the head Leon Klinghoffer, a 69-year-old wheelchair bound American tourist, and cast him into the sea near the Egyptian coast.[269] He and his wife, Marilyn, were celebrating their 36th wedding anniversary in the form of a pleasure cruise in the Middle East. Instead it became one of the formative events in the history of terror.

Aftermath: After his death, his daughters established the *Leon and Marilyn Klinghoffer Memorial Foundation*, whose mission it is to combat terrorism through educational, political and legal means. The foundation is funded by an undisclosed settlement paid by the Palestinian Liberation Organisation (PLO) to the Klinghoffers to settle a lawsuit seeking damages for the PLO's role in the hijacking

---

266 For a comprehensive discussion on this topic see *Brief History of the Passenger Ship Industry* at http://www.library.duke.edu/digitalcollections/adaccess/ship-history.html.
267 *P&O Steam Navigation Co & Ors v Youell & Ors* [1997] 2 Lloyd's Rep 136. This was a case assessing damages for disappointment.
268 Justice TA Dickerson, "The Cruise Passengers's Rights and Remedies" (2006) *The Travel & Tourism Law International Revue*.
269 See *Klinghoffer v PLO*, 739 F Supp 854 (SDNY 1990) and *Klinghoffer v PLO*, 937 F 2d 44, 50 (2d Cir 1991).

Case Study: Hijacking–Klinghoffer and the Achille Lauro cont.

It remains unclear if the Klinghoffer family received any compensation from the cruise ship company. The LLMC (London Convention 1976) would not have applied because substantial issues of law are determined by the flag the ship flies and in this case Italy is not a signatory to the LLMC Convention. It is, however, a signatory to the more generous *Convention on the Carriage of Passengers and their Luggage by Sea* (Athens Convention) although that particular convention only came into force on 19 April 1989.[270]

Case Study: Accident on Board Ship–*Oceanic Sun Line Special Shipping Company Inc v Fay*

[12.450] Facts: In June 1983 Dr Fay (Plaintiff) was a passenger on a Greek ship, the *MS Stella Oceanis*, during a cruise of the Aegean Sea in Greece.[271] He received serious injuries while taking part in trap shooting on board the ship. At that time the ship was sailing in Greek waters. Athens is a signatory to the *Carriage of Passengers and their Luggage by Sea* (Athens Convention) 1974 but this Convention only came into force on 19 April 1989.[272] Thus Greek law applied unless the Plaintiff could establish a sufficient nexus with the Australian jurisdiction so as to enforce his cause of action locally.

Held: The High Court was satisfied on the Plaintiff's evidence that Greece was the country in which the contract of carriage was to be performed but that New South Wales was the State in which the contract was made. This was based on a finding that the ticket was not given to the Plaintiff until the commencement of the cruise in Greece and therefore the foreign jurisdiction clause on the ticket (on which the defendant relied) was not a term of the contract. (Refer to the "ticket case" principles in [4.240].) The invocation of the local jurisdiction was not in the relevant sense oppressive, vexatious or in abuse of process. The Plaintiff was therefore entitled to have his case heard and determined by the Supreme Court of New South Wales.

Aftermath: The case was once again referred to the Supreme Court (NSW) for a decision on the substantive issues of negligence – all legal costs at the risk of the injured passenger – and many years after the incident.

Case Study: Ship Failures– "The Titanic" & The "Mikhail Lermentov"
[12.455] 1. The Titanic

This is one of the most famous and tragic tourism disasters and, though it happened 100 years ago, it still provides salutary lessons for tourism security, compliance and risk management today.[273]

Facts: The *Titanic* sank in 1912 and 1500 of the 2200 passengers and crew on board drowned. Death claims alone were US$22m

---

270 A further Protocol dated 1 November 2002 which substantially increases the limits has not yet come into force. See also M McCarthy, "Increase in liability for carriage by sea of passengers and their luggage", 5(5) *P&I International* 16.

271 See *Oceanic Sun Line Special Shipping Company Inc v Fay* (1988) HCA 32; (1988) 165 CLR 197 (30 June 1988).

272 A further Protocol dated 1 November 2002 which substantially increases the limits has not yet come into force. See also M McCarthy, "Increase in liability for carriage by sea of passengers and their luggage", 5(5) *P&I International* 16.

273 *Oceanic Steam Navigation Co Ltd (the White Star Line) v Mellor (the "Titanic")* (1914) 233 US 718 (US Supreme Court).

Case Study: Ship Failures– "The Titanic" & The "Mikhail Lermentov" cont.

Held: Liability of the White Star Line was limited to US$91,805, that is, the value of 14 salvaged lifeboats plus outstanding fares. For more discussion, refer to [12.305] above.

2. Mikhail Lermentov

This was another sinking ship case. For a more discussion of the facts, refer to [2.235], [12.90]. [274]

Facts: Mrs Dillon (recently widowed) paid $2205.00 for a 14 day Pacific cruise on board the *"Mikhail Lermentov"*. The ship struck a rock on the 10th day. Mrs Dillon was forced to abandon ship in the middle of the night and broke her leg in the process. She claimed damages for breach of contract including:

- restitution of balance of fare,
- loss of valuables,
- damages for personal injury,
- compensation for disappointment and distress.

Held: The High court awarded Mrs Dillon damages for her loss of items of personal property, damages for personal injuries (including emotional trauma) and damages for disappointment at the loss of enjoyment of the holiday and interest. Mrs Dillon had paid $2,205.00 for the cruise and she received about $50,000 in compensation including $5,000 damages for disappointment.

Aftermath: At the time of the sinking in 1986, Australia had not ratified the LLMC (London Convention 1976). The question remains whether Mrs Dillon would be better or worse off now that the Convention has come into force. Refer to [12.395]ff.

Case Study: Sexual Assault– *Dianne Brimble and P&O*

[12.460] Facts: On the first night of her cruise on the *Pacific Sky* in September 2002, Mrs Brimble had a few rum and cokes with her friends before heading to the ship's disco. She was last seen by staff leaving the club with a number of men she had met there. By 8.30am she was found partially dressed in a cabin shared by four male passengers, who were part of a group of eight men with whom she had been seen dancing until 4.20am. She died only 24 hours after boarding the ship.

An Inquest into Mrs Brimble's death began in 2006 and ended in 2007. Six years after male DNA was found under her fingernails, Mark Wilhelm was charged with her manslaughter and with supplying her with a prohibited drug. The case was finally brought to trial in September 2009. [275]

Held: In the first trial, the jury were unable to reach a verdict. At the second trial in April 2009, the defendant pleased guilty to the lesser charge of supplying drugs to Mrs Brimble and the prosecution dropped the manslaughter charge. No conviction was recorded against the defendant and no penalty applied because the trial judge decided:

> I am entitled to take into account not only the years of public humiliation of the offender but also the consequences of that on him and his mental health.

Aftermath: There are now stricter security measures onboard fun ship cruises including the introduction of sniffer dogs and closed circuit television throughout the ships on the P&O fleet.

Should the family of Mrs Brimble be compensated? Her former husband, Mark Brimble, who now looks after her children, and Mr David Mitchell who was her partner at the time of her death, reached

---

274   *Baltic Shipping Company v Dillon (The Mikhail Lermontov)* (1993) 176 CLR 344.
275   *R v Mark Wilhelm* [2010] NSWSC 378. Two other men were charged with the offences of perverting the course of justice or alternatively, the lesser charge of hindering the investigation.

Case Study: Sexual Assault– Dianne Brimble and P&O cont.

an out of court settlement with the chief executive of P&O in meetings held in Brisbane, Queensland in February 2007 for an undisclosed sum of money.

Exercise

Raising the Titanic

After reading this section on Carriage by Sea and perhaps watching one of the many excellent videos on the Titanic, consider how the Titanic case would be decided if the accident occurred today and the compensation claims were brought in Australia.

- Who might be made liable for the ship and what would be the average sum available per casualty?
- What limits of liability would apply? See worked example at [12.400].
- Could the limits be broken?
- Should liability for fault be unlimited as in international aviation (see [12.590] and following)?

CARRIAGE BY AIR

Regulation of Air Transport

Administration

International

[12.470] There are two main international organisations concerned with aviation. The International Civil Aviation Organisation (ICAO) [276] was founded [277] in 1947 as the United Nation's specialised agency concerned with aviation. It is an inter-governmental organisation concerned with all international regulatory aspects of aviation, particularly growth, technology, infrastructure efficiency and safety. [278] The International Air Transport Association (IATA) [279] was founded in 1945 and is a private trade association of the world's air carriers. Its goals are to promote safe, regular and economic air transport and to provide a means of collaboration among air carriers. [280] It also operates the interline clearing house and bank settlement plan.

ICAO was funded under the *Convention on International Civil Aviation*, Chicago, 1944 (Chicago Convention). The Chicago Convention confirmed that "every State has complete

---

276   International Civil Aviation Organisation (ICAO) at http://www.icao.int.
277   By Part II of the Chicago Convention 1944.
278   Chicago Convention 1944, Art 44.
279   International Air Transport Association (IATA) at http://www.iata.org.
280   See IATA's Mission Statement at http://www.iata.org/about/Pages/mission.aspx.

and exclusive sovereignty over the airspace above its territory"[281] and provided a framework for the development of international air transport in a safe and orderly manner under a system of multilateral and bilateral Air Service Agreements.

National and State

[12.475] Civil aviation became feasible only after the technological developments made in World War I to aviation occurred. When the Australian Constitution was drafted, civil aviation had not been conceived. Thus there was no express allocation of powers over aviation and the constitutional position has had to be determined through a series of High Court cases. It is interesting to trace the development of the Commonwealth's power over aviation under the Constitution.

Following the signing of the forerunner to the Chicago Convention,[282] the Commonwealth, by the *Air Navigation Act 1920* (Cth), enacted the Convention into domestic law and purported to regulate all aviation generally. This was challenged and the High Court, while upholding the Commonwealth's powers to ratify the Convention under the external affairs power[283] and acknowledging the power over interstate and international trade,[284] declined to recognise any Commonwealth power over intrastate aviation or aviation generally.[285]

The Commonwealth thereupon amended the *Air Navigation Act 1920* to restrict it to interstate and international trade and commerce. When this was challenged the High Court upheld its validity.[286] The Commonwealth also sought to change the Constitution by referendum to add "Air navigation and aircraft" to the s 51(vi) power on defence.[287] While 53.6% of voters overall supported it, there was a majority of voters only in Queensland and Victoria, and the referendum failed.

The Aviation Conference of Commonwealth and State Ministers (April 1937) was then convened with the object of achieving uniform air navigation rules throughout Australia. At the conference it was agreed that all States would enact uniform Air Navigation Acts as State law and that the Commonwealth's role in civil aviation would be restricted to licensing personnel and aircraft and registration of aircraft.

The Commonwealth then attempted, by second referendum in 1944, to add "air transport" to the Commonwealth's powers in Constitution. This time only 46% of voters supported it. The Commonwealth then attempted to nationalise the interstate air carriers.[288] This was challenged and the High Court held that the provisions of the Act purporting to give the Australian National Airlines Commission a monopoly over licensing interstate carriers offended s 92 (freedom of interstate trade and commerce) of the Constitution.[289]

Twenty years later the High Court had the opportunity to review its interpretation of the Constitutional position. It noted the tremendous development which had taken place in civil aviation and observed that it now considered that the Commonwealth had concurrent power

---

281 Chicago Convention 1944, Art 1.
282 The Paris Convention 1919.
283 Constitution, s 51(xxix).
284 Constitution, s 51(i).
285 *R v Burgess; Ex parte Henry* (1936) 55 CLR 608.
286 *R v Poole; Ex parte Henry* (1939) 61 CLR 634.
287 *Constitution Alteration (Aviation) Bill 1936* (Cth).
288 *Australian National Airlines Act 1945* (Cth).
289 *Australian National Airways Pty Ltd v Commonwealth* (1945) 71 CLR 29.

to regulate aviation matters now covered by State acts.[290] In response to the High Court's observations the Commonwealth amended its Air Navigation regulations to cover all air navigation: international, interstate and intrastate and to establish the Commonwealth licensing system for intrastate air transport. This was challenged and the High Court, by majority, upheld the validity of the amendments. The majority held that the Commonwealth now had power to regulate the air safety of intrastate aviation and no longer had to rely on authority ceded from the States.[291] In his judgment Barwick CJ observed:[292]

> The speeds at which aircraft move in the air, the narrow and narrowing margins of time in which consequences of error or malfunction may be avoided or reduced, the increasing density of air traffic, the interdependence of safety of one aircraft upon the performance of other aircraft, the hazards of weather and the variable performance of aircraft, leading to diversion and re-routing of aircraft in flight, the need for use of common facilities. ...all combine to demonstrate that all air operations irrespective of destination or of their particular nature must be subject to the same control if the air is to be safe.

Thus the Commonwealth now enjoys power over civil aviation and this is exercised through the *Air Navigation Act 1920* (Cth) (which enacts the Chicago Convention) and the *Civil Aviation (Carriers Liability) Act 1959* (Cth) which enacts the Warsaw Convention (see [12.550]).

Freedom of the air

[12.480] While there is general freedom of the air over the high seas, there is no such freedom over national territory.

At the level of the private landowner there was an ancient maxim which stated that the owner of the surface of land has title from the centre of the earth up to the sky. This concept of land title has had to be adjusted since the advent of flying, and at common law land title extends only as far up as the owner needs for reasonable use and enjoyment of the land.[293] The landowners' rights have been further diminished by Reg 20 of the *Air Navigation Act 1920* (Cth) which provides that no action in trespass or nuisance shall be brought for reasonable overflight. However, all overflying Australian and foreign aircraft operating in, from or over Australia are responsible under Commonwealth and State law for things falling to the ground and injuring people or damaging property.[294]

The Chicago Convention 1942 recognises that every nation has complete and exclusive sovereignty over the airspace above its territory[295] and requires that permission or authorisation be obtained before any civil aviation service can be operated over or into a nation's territory.[296] The types of permission and authorisation required have been categorised into a number of "freedoms of the air", as follows:

290　*Airlines of NSW P/L v NSW (No 1)* (1964) 113 CLR 1.
291　*Airlines of NSW Case (No 2)* (1965) 113 CLR 65.
292　*Airlines of NSW Case (No 2)* (1965) 113 CLR 65 at 92.
293　*Lord Bernstein of Leigh v Skyviews & General Ltd* [1978] QB 479.
294　See for example *Damage by Aircraft Act 1999* (Cth); *Damage by Aircraft Act 1952* (NSW).
295　Chicago Convention 1944, Art 1.
296　Chicago Convention 1944, Arts 6, 7.

Freedoms of the Air

First Freedom: the right for an airline of nation A to overfly nation B. [297]

Second Freedom: the right for an airline of nation A to make a technical stop at nation B. [298]

The first two freedoms are technical rights and were generally exchanged among nations under multilateral agreements annexed to the Chicago Convention.

Third Freedom: the right for an airline of nation A to transport passengers from nation A to nation B.

Fourth Freedom: the right for an airline of nation A to transport passengers from nation B to nation A.

Fifth Freedom: the right for an airline of nation A to transport passengers between nations B and C.

The 3rd, 4th and 5th freedoms are concerned with traffic rights and these have had to be negotiated and bartered between each pair of nations creating the labyrinth of Air Service Agreements (ASAs) in which international aviation operates.

Sixth Freedom: This is a combination of the 4th and 3rd freedoms creating a 6th freedom which is similar in effect to a 5th freedom.

ICAO characterizes all "freedoms" beyond the Fifth as "so-called" because only the first five "freedoms" have been officially recognized as such under the Chicago Convention and bilateral Air Service Agreements.

Seventh Freedom: 5th and 7th freedoms are distinguished as follows. 5th Freedom flight originates or terminates in the flag carrier Country A. 7th freedom: flight does not originate or terminate or pass through the flag carrier Country A.

7th freedoms are almost never granted.

Eighth Freedom = Cabotage: Pursuant to the *Convention on International Civil Aviation*, each State shall have the right to refuse permission for any foreign carrier to take on in its territory passengers, mail and cargo destined for another point in its territory. [299]

In other words, this is the domain of domestic aviation. Consider the impact on international aviation especially in places like Europe where there are so many different countries across one land mass. The EU has now negotiated as a bloc to redress this problem. Contrast this with the situation in a country like the United States of America which has fifty states but all are part of the one regulatory framework.

In 1996, Australia and New Zealand agreed to create a single market to allow each country's carriers to operate domestically in the other country and remove all barriers to international aviation between the two countries

Cabotage now restricts foreign carriers flying through Hong Kong to mainland China, and thus Hong Kong may cease to be the international gateway into China. However, since 1997, it has been emerging as a major hub in its own right.

---

297 Consequences where there is no First Freedom permission. Case Study 1: Korean Air Lines Flight 903, April 1978 Civilian airline shot down by Soviet fighters over Murmansk after it violated Soviet airspace and failed to respond to Soviet interceptors. Two passengers killed in the incident. 107 passengers and crew survived after plane was forced to make AN emergency landing on frozen lake. Case Study 2: Korean Air Lines Flight 007 September 1983. Civilian airline strayed into Soviet airspace and was shot down by Soviet interceptors. It killed all 269 passengers and crew on board.

298 Multilateral approval by 100 countries to International Air Transit Agreement under the Chicago Convention. Otherwise first and second freedoms freely granted between countries at peace.

299 Chicago Convention 1944, Art 7.

Australian domestic aviation policy

[12.485] Australian aviation policy has evolved from one extreme requiring public ownership and monopoly to the other favouring privatisation of carriers and airports and intense competition. This has been the trend around the world.

In domestic aviation Australia's first formal aviation policy was enshrined in the Two Airlines Agreement.[300] The objectives were to (a) develop the domestic civil aviation network and (b) achieve efficiency through a private/public duopoly. A delicate balance was sought between sufficient but not excessive competition. The duopolists were:

- Trans Australia Airlines (TAA): Commonwealth owned, later taken over by Qantas; and
- Australian National Airways (ANA): A private company which later became Ansett.

They shared mail and government business equally, shared or duplicated routes, timetables and tariffs and used the same type, size and capacity of aircraft.

The policy was enforced by prohibiting the import of any aircraft capable of competing with the two airlines on major trunk routes.[301] In 1965 IPEC Air sought to import aircraft to compete with the duopolists and challenged the legality of prohibition[302] under s 92 of the Constitution.[303] The High Court rejected the challenge, holding there had been no infringement of s 92 because importation precedes trade and commerce and is not part of it.

There the matter rested until 1990 when, in line with international trends, there was a complete change of policy in favour of competition. The Two Airlines Agreement was terminated[304] and new entrants were encouraged into the domestic aviation business. Unfortunately, on the eve of deregulation the Commonwealth had granted long-term leases over all the available airport terminal space to the duopolists. As a result (and for many other reasons) the new entrants Compass Mark I and II crashed financially. On the international front Ansett was permitted to compete with Qantas.[305]

The current policy also favours privatisation. TAA was taken over by Qantas in 1992 and Qantas was floated to the public in 1995.[306] In 1997 the main airports themselves were privatised. Despite privatisation there will always be a strong public element in the aviation industry, not the least because of the multitude of national interests in flag carriers.

Air Service Agreements (ASA)

[12.490] There was considerable controversy over the policy issues involved in treating air rights as property and restricting fifth freedom rights for the benefit of the national flag carrier. It is now becoming recognised that greater economic and social benefits can be obtained with a more open skies policy. These agreements are negotiated and administered by the

---

300 *Civil Aviation Agreement Act 1952* (Cth) (later the *Airlines Agreement Act 1981* (Cth)).
301 *Customs (Prohibited Imports) Regulations 1956* (Cth), reg 4A.
302 *R v Anderson; Ex parte IPEC Air P/L* (1965) 113 CLR 177.
303 Relying on *Australian National Airways Pty Ltd v Commonwealth* (1945) 71 CLR 29 discussed above.
304 *Airlines Agreement (Termination) Act 1990* (Cth).
305 Requiring a renegotiation of many ASAs to permit multiple designation.
306 Foreign ownership was capped to comply with provisions requiring ownership and control by nationals under bilateral ASAs.

Commonwealth government through its International Air Services Commission (IASC) which must now take these wider issues into account.[307]

In the Preamble to the Chicago Convention it says that air transport services are to be established on the basis of equality of opportunity. What happens in reality is that air rights are traded for the advantage of the state and usually the state's interests are advised and/or dictated by the nation's flag carrier. The fact is that only carriers substantially owned and controlled by nationals of the state are designated (or permitted) to fly the agreed routes.

The result is that third and fourth freedoms generally exchanged. In cases where there is unequal traffic between two nations, then the disadvantaged state will bargain for its air share of revenue or otherwise restrict or refuse the other nation third and fourth air freedoms. Fifth freedoms are mutually shared or refused. The following case study highlights these points.

Case Study: Australia/SE Asia

[12.495] Australia traditionally negotiated its ASA's following the "True origin and destination" (TOD) principle. This meant that it would only establish air services with a country if there was sufficient TOD traffic from end-to-end. In applying this principle, Australia negotiated ASA's with the UK, Europe, Japan, in exchange for third and fourth freedoms and sharing fifth freedom traffic

However, because Australia is at the end of a route it is at a commercial and geographical disadvantage. This has been used as an excuse to restrict and regulate this traffic to protect Qantas. This was the case with the South East Asian countries. Australian policy was that these were interim points on the main trunk routes so that whilst it would exchange third and fourth freedoms with these countries, it would limit its capacity on the TOD principle and refuse fifth freedoms to South East Asian carriers. It led to enormous cost in lost trade and tourism and contradicts Australia's otherwise general policy of promoting Australian/Asian interaction.

The South East Asian countries responded by creating the sixth freedom rights which effectively bypassed Australia's refusal to allow fifth freedom air traffic. The so-called "Asian tiger carriers" grew on this basis and now control strategic hubs like Singapore, Bangkok and Kuala Lumpur. The Gulf States (GCC) countries are now doing the same. For example, there is the Dubai/ Emirates' Air Services Agreement[308] and the more recent Abu Dhabi/Etihad.

Current regulatory framework for International Air Services

[12.500] Unlike most sectors of international trade where the presumption is that the market is open unless governments have imposed restrictions, in international aviation the market is closed unless governments act to open it up. It is regulated by a labyrinth of 3,500 Air Service Agreements. These include bilateral treaties plus protocols and secret Memorandums of Understanding (MoUs);

The restrictions imposed by Air Service Agreements (ASA's) include:

- which routes can be flown (that is, city to city);
- which carriers can fly and ownership requirements (that is, destination);
- type and capacity of aircraft;
- frequency and timetable of flights;

---

307 Under the *International Air Services Commission Act 1992* (Cth) the IASC allocates capacity in "the public interest" and must foster competition, consumer choice, trade and tourism, and competitive flag carrier.
308 *Dubai/ Emirates' Air Services Agreement* [2005] ATS 8.

- tariff;
- sharing of traffic and revenue (often secret);
- beyond rights if any (that is, fifth freedoms).

ASAs take years to negotiate and are always a compromise. Even when fully authorised by the ASA, new entrant carriers still need:

- National licensing;
- National approval of route, capacity and timetable;
- Air Operators Certificate (safety);
- Certificate of Carriers Liability Insurance (if required); and
- Capacity at relevant city airport.

World Trade Organization (WTO)

[12.505] Air rights are expressly excluded from the General Agreement on Trade in Services which covers only ancillary services including repair, maintenance, computer reservation systems (CRS) and distribution. Nor are Air rights are included in negotiations for accession to the WTO. They are also generally outside other multilateral and bilateral Free Trade Agreements.

This failure to liberalise air rights prevents the development of a true international aviation industry with enormous social and economic costs especially to tourism. It is little wonder then, that organisations such as ICAO, WTO and APEC [309] etc continue pressing to liberalise air rights.

Liberalisation: the first steps

[12.510] The first step towards liberalisation is the privatisation of national flag carriers. This has the effect of reducing the State's focus on the narrow issue of its carriers profitability rather than the much wider and greater social and economic benefits particularly through tourism. It also has the effect of encouraging new carriers to enter the market and compete.

Most countries have now privatised their national flag carrier but ASA restrictions on foreign ownership remain and also need to be renegotiated. For example, Australia's flag carrier, Qantas, privatised between 1992 and1996. Pursuant to the *Air Navigation Act 1920* (Cth) and the *Qantas Sale Act 1992* (Cth), foreign ownership is limited to not greater than 49% and requires incorporation, head office and board control in Australia

Many other countries have similar or even more restrictions which end up preventing the emergence of truly international carriers. Moves to remove these restrictions are hampered by the need to renegotiate ASAs which also require designated carriers to be substantially owned and controlled by nationals of the contracting states.

Airlines are trying "workarounds" by all manner of cross minority shareholdings, co-operation, affiliation and code sharing arrangements and these practices may raise issues of anti-competitive behaviour. For example, when an international airport is privatised, a public monopoly becomes a private monopoly because, unlike carriers, expansion or duplication of the airport capacity is a very difficult, slow and expensive process. The result is an increased risk of abuse. Sydney Airport was privatised in 2002 and the citizens of New South Wales are still awaiting the approval of a second airport site for their capital city.

---

309 Asia-Pacific Economic Co-operation.

Liberalisation: next steps

[12.515] The European Court of Justice has now ruled against the traditional clause in ASAs restricting rights to carriers owned or controlled by nationals. In 2004, the European Union (EU) merged all bilateral ASAs with the USA into a single ASA. This put EU carriers onto equal footing with US carriers and meant that EU carriers could merge without forfeiting their US route rights. Britain initially blocked the deal so as to protect the Heathrow hub unless the US agreed to allow majority foreign ownership of US based carriers.

In April 2007, the first ever EU /USA Aviation Treaty was signed and came into force in 30 March 2008. This treaty will enable the emergence of global carriers rather than just alliances and cross minority shareholdings. It has substantially liberalised "open skies" arrangements between the world's two major aviation markets and provides a template for negotiations in Asia which has so far been untouched by liberalisation.[310] The predicted benefits include improved safety, major cost cuts and additional jobs in the immediate future.[311]

Other countries are negotiating similar agreements with the EU and US. Already, Australia has entered the US/Australia open skies agreement in February 2008 and the EU/Australia treaty has been under negotiation since June 2008.

Outer Space

[12.520] Under the *Outer Space Treaty*:[312]

- the moon and other celestial bodies are the province of all humankind and are free for exploration and use by all States;[313]
- the moon and other celestial bodies are not subject to national appropriation or claims of sovereignty;[314]
- space activities and use shall be in accordance with international law;[315]
- there is a prohibition on militarisation;[316]
- astronauts are envoys of mankind;[317]
- there is international responsibility for national activities in outer space;[318] and
- the treaty encourages co-operation and mutual assistance in space activities.[319]

Australia ratified the *Outer Space Treaty* on 10 October 1967.

Under other treaties and conventions relating to Outer Space:

- states are to render all necessary assistance for the rescue and return of astronauts;[320]

---

310 For example, Qantas foreign ownership restrictions remain.
311 See EU website at http://www.eurunion.org/newsweb/HotTopics/OpenSkies.htm.
312 *Treaty on Principles Governing the Activities of States in the Exploration and Use of Outer Space, including the Moon and Other Celestial Bodies, 1967.*
313 *Outer Space Treaty* (1967) ATS No 24, Art I.
314 *Outer Space Treaty* (1967) ATS No 24, Art II.
315 *Outer Space Treaty* (1967) ATS No 24, Art III.
316 *Outer Space Treaty* (1967) ATS No 24, Art IV.
317 *Outer Space Treaty* (1967) ATS No 24, Art V.
318 *Outer Space Treaty* (1967) ATS No 24, Art VI.
319 *Outer Space Treaty* (1967) ATS No 24, Art IX.
320 The *Rescue Agreement Treaty* (1968) 672 UNTS 45 entered into force in Australia 18/2/1986.

- launching states have absolute liability for any damage death or injuries caused in space activities; [321]
- there is a compulsory registration system for objects launched into space; [322]
- there is a declaration that the moon and its resources are the common heritage of mankind. [323]

Space tourism

[12.525] Thus the technology and international legal framework are in place for space tourism. The USA, Australia, Russia etc, those with suitable launch sites are gearing up for it. The *Space Activities Act 1998* (Cth) facilitates it in the following ways:

- permit system for launch and retrieval;
- licensing system for operators;
- liability limited to insured amount not less than $750m;
- Commonwealth covers any further liability up to $3b.

The Russians are already in business charging the first space tourist, Dennis Tito, $20m for the trip. Others have followed. [324] Entrepreneurs like Richard Branson are gearing up to make it more commercial. [325] There are strong links here with Adventure Tourism (see Chapter 15).

Exercise

Negotiating ASAs

- Country B carrier would like to fly and take up/put down passengers along the way from Country A to country B and on to Country C and back.
- Country A carrier would like to fly and take up/put down passengers between Country B and Country C.
- Divide into groups of 3, comprising a negotiator for each of the 3 countries involved.
- Negotiate the required Air Service Agreements and associated rights and conditions required to authorise these new air services.

Try to achieve win/win outcomes.

Liability in Air Transport

The Warsaw system

Warsaw Convention 1929

[12.535] Air carriers' liability is generally determined by the principles of the *Convention for the unification of certain rules relating to international transportation by air* (Warsaw

---

321 The *Liability Convention* (1972) 961 UNTS 187 entered into force in Australia 20/1/1975.
322 *Registration Convention* 1975-1023 UNTS 15 entered into force in Australia 11/3/1986.
323 *Moon Treaty* (1979) ILM 1434. Few have ratified it. See http://www.greaterearth.org.
324 See Space Adventures: http://www.spaceadventures.com.
325 See Virgin Galacticat http://www.virgingalactic.com. See also D O'Nei, *General Public Space Travel and Tourism* (1998) at http://www.Spacefuture.com.

Convention 1929), which was signed at Warsaw in 1929 and came into force on 13 February 1933. It has been ratified by 152 countries [326] and in this respect is the world's most successful private law treaty.

The original objectives of the Warsaw Convention were to achieve international uniformity in air carriers' liability and documentation for air transportation. [327] It introduced a uniform system of strict but limited liability for passengers, baggage [328] and cargo. Uniformity was desirable to facilitate transactions across borders, languages and cultures and to avoid interminable conflicts of law problems. Liability was made strict to avoid the problems of proving fault and to compensate for the limits imposed on claims. It was argued that it was necessary to limit claims, otherwise a single disaster could bankrupt a carrier and insurance would be too expensive for carriers or for passengers if added to the price of each ticket. Advances in technology, safety and insurance have undermined the latter arguments and the Warsaw system has evolved through a series of increased limits to various attempts to remove the limits altogether. [329]

Key amendments: Hague Protocol 1955, Guadalajara Convention 1961, Montreal Protocols

[12.540] There was no mechanism in the Warsaw Convention to increase the limits to keep abreast of inflation and other factors. However, as inflation devalued the limits in real terms, the aviation industry spread to more and more diverse countries so that it became more difficult to achieve consensus among nations on revised limits. Sufficient consensus was reached for wide agreement under the Hague Protocol 1955 which doubled the limits under the Warsaw Convention and amended it to fix various other problems which had emerged. [330]

The *Guadalajara Supplementary Convention 1961* (Guadalajara Convention) further amended the Warsaw system to cover journeys performed by several carriers (interlining) and provides that passengers could sue either the contracting carrier or the actual carrier or both, but the total liability remained subject to the limits. [331]

There have been numerous other proposals and schemes to increase or avoid the limits on liability and many of these are found in various other agreements, conventions and protocols. Thus the "uniform" Warsaw Agreements now varies from country to country depending upon which of these have been adopted. It also varies from carrier to carrier as the Warsaw system leaves carriers free to voluntarily accept higher limits.

Major Developments: IATA Agreements and Montreal Convention

[12.545] In 1995 IATA sidestepped the delay in reforming the Warsaw system and brokered the *Intercarrier Agreement* which became effective in 1997. Under this carriers have agreed to

---

326 As at May 2009.
327 Warsaw Convention, Preamble, para 3.
328 The term "baggage" rather than "luggage" is used throughout the Warsaw Convention, CACLA, IATA Resolutions and air travel documentation, although the two terms appear to have identical meanings.
329 See E Giemulla, R Schmidt et al, *Warsaw Convention* (Kluwer Law International, The Hague), Introduction.
330 The US was the nation most dissatisfied with the low limits and it even refused to endorse the Hague Protocol because it considered the doubled limits too low. Instead, by threat of denunciation of the Warsaw system altogether, it forced Warsaw Convention international carriers to enter the Montreal Agreement 1966 which provided for special liability limits for carriers with a US stopover. These are per passenger US$75,000 inclusive or US$58,000 exclusive of legal fees.
331 Warsaw Convention, Art VI.

voluntarily waive the limits for fault based liability. The Intercarrier Agreement is a similar system to that of the Montreal Convention but operates independently of it and regardless of whether the relevant state has ratified it.

To restore uniformity and overcome objections to the limits, the Montreal Convention 1999 [332] which came into force in 2003 completely updates the Warsaw system and is replacing it. [333] As at July 2010, 97 Countries have ratified the Montreal Convention (including USA, all European and all OECD countries and Australia from January 2009).

Australian law

International aviation

[12.550] Australia, like most countries, has ratified the Warsaw Convention as amended by the Hague Protocol (Warsaw-Hague), the Guadalajara Convention and the Montreal Convention 1999. These are given the force of law by the *Civil Aviation (Carriers' Liability) Act 1959* (Cth). [334]

In 1995, Australia introduced radical amendments to the *Civil Aviation (Carriers' Liability) Act 1959* (Cth) for Australian international carriers. The *Transport Legislation Amendment Act 1995* (Cth) then increased the Warsaw system [335] limit per passenger to 260,000 SDR [336] and now requires carriers to hold insurance to cover compensation up to the limit for each passenger. [337]

Domestic aviation

[12.555] The *Civil Aviation (Carriers' Liability) Act 1959* (Cth) also applies similar provisions to the Warsaw system to interstate aviation and to the territories and corporations using the Commonwealth's constitutional powers. These provisions are also applied to other intrastate aviation by Civil Aviation (Carrier's Liability) Acts [338] in each State.

The *Transport Legislation Amendment Acts 1995* (Cth) also introduced radical amendments to domestic aviation and complementary amendments have been made to the relevant State Acts. The limit per passenger has been increased to $500,000 [339] and carriers are now required to hold insurance to cover compensation up to the limit for each passenger [340] similarly to Australian international aviation.

Comparison: international and domestic aviation

[12.560] The following table presents a comparison of the Montreal and Warsaw system articles, complementary sections of *Civil Aviation (Carriers' Liability) Act 1959* (Cth) relating to international aviation and corresponding sections of the *Civil Aviation (Carriers' Liability)*

---

332   *Convention for the unification of certain rules relating to international transportation by air* (Montreal, 28 May 1999).
333   It places limit of liability of SDR 100,000 plus unlimited liability in cases of fault. It also provides for ticketless travel.
334   *Civil Aviation (Carriers' Liability) Act 1959* (Cth), ss 8, 11.
335   Warsaw Convention, Art 22(1).
336   *Civil Aviation (Carriers' Liability) Act 1959* (Cth), ss 11A and 21A.
337   *Civil Aviation (Carriers' Liability) Act 1959* (Cth), Part IVA, ss 41A – 41L.
338   NSW 1967; Qld 1964; SA 1962; Tas 1963; Vic 1961; WA 1961.
339   *Civil Aviation (Carriers' Liability) Act 1959* (Cth), s 31(1).
340   *Civil Aviation (Carriers' Liability) Act 1959* (Cth), Part IVA, ss 41A – 41L.

Act 1959 (Cth) (and State legislation) relating to domestic aviation. Although the domestic provisions follow closely the Warsaw-Hague Convention discussed below, there are many differences and the more important of these are pointed out in the discussion.

Topic	International Montreal Convention	International Warsaw-Hague Convention Corresponding Articles	International Civil Aviation (Civil Liability) Act 1959, Part II, III Complementary Sections	Domestic Civil Aviation (Civil Liability) Act 1959, Part IV/State equivalent Corresponding Sections
Definitions	1	1	5, 20	26
Application	2	2	10 – 11, 17 – 18, 21 – 22, ss 24 – 25, 25B	25A, 27
Passenger ticket	3	3		40
Baggage check	3	4		40
Liability: bodily injury	17	17	12, 14, 15	28, 35, 37, 38
Liability: baggage	17	18		29
Liability: delay	19	19		
Defence: all reasonable endeavours	19	20		
Defence: contributory Negligence	20	21	16	39
Limits on liability	22	22	11A, 21A, 23, Part IVA	31, Part IVA
Prohibition on Contracting out	26	23, 32, 33		32
Exclusive remedy	29	24	12(2), 13	35(2), 36
No limit if intentional or reckless	22	25		
Servants, agents liability limited	30	25A (not in Warsaw)		33
Baggage complaints	31	26		30
Choice of forum	33	28	19	
Time limits	35	29		34
Successive Carriers	36	1		
Combined Transportation	38	31		
Extraordinary Circumstances	51	34		
Stowaways				42

Montreal and Warsaw system: world overview

[12.565] Despite its original objective of unification, the Warsaw system had become increasingly fragmented until the Montreal Convention 1999 which makes substantial progress towards establishing an updated and more uniform system. So far 99 countries have accepted the Montreal Convention.

Under the Warsaw system, there are variations from country to country depending on which conventions, protocols and agreements have been entered There are also variations from carrier to carrier as each is entitled to voluntarily offer higher limits under the IATA Intercarrier Agreement.

The instrument governing any flight is the one that has been accepted by both the Origin and Destination Country. The limits applying are the limits in that instrument subject to any higher limit under:

- national law;[341]
- IATA Intercarrier Agreement;[342] or
- carrier's voluntary offer of a higher limit.[343]

Montreal and Warsaw system principles

Definitions and documents

International carriage

[12.570] Under the Montreal and Warsaw system *international carriage* means any flight where the agreed place of departure and ultimate destination are:[344]

- in two different countries, or
- in the same country with a stopover in another country.

It should be noted that this includes domestic sectors of an international journey.

Passenger ticket

[12.575] Under the Montreal and Warsaw conventions the following information must be provided to the passenger prior to embarkation:[345]

- places of departure and destination;
- at least one stopping place in another country if places of departure and destination are in the same country;
- a reference to the fact that the Convention may apply to limit the carriers' liability for death, personal injury and loss or damage to baggage.

The Montreal Convention has done away with the need for a paper passenger ticket. The information required may be provided by "any other means" ie including electronic ticketing. Non compliance does not affect the existence or validity of the contract of carriage, the limitation of liability and other rules of the Convention still apply.

Under the Warsaw convention a ticket must be delivered to the passenger prior to embarkation containing the prescribed information. Under Article 22, if, with the carrier's consent, a passenger embarks without a ticket, or without reference to the Warsaw limit, the carrier is not entitled to the Warsaw limitation of liability.[346]

It is not necessary for any steps to be taken to bring notice of the Montreal/Warsaw/Warsaw-Hague limits to the passenger's attention nor that the passenger read or understand the notice for the limits to apply.[347] Although contemplated by the *Civil Aviation (Carriers'*

---

341 If the Montreal Convention has been ratified, then it overrides domestic law.
342 Limits similar to the Montreal Convention.
343 For example, Japanese carriers have abandoned liability limits.
344 Montreal and Warsaw Conventions, Art 1(2).
345 Montreal and Warsaw Conventions, Art 3.
346 *Civil Aviation (Carriers' Liability) Act 1959* (Cth), s 40: Regulations are similar.
347 Contrast the ticket cases and usual contractual principles.

Liability) Act 1959 (Cth), [348] there is no statutory requirement for a domestic passenger ticket or for notice or any other information to be supplied.

However, IATA prescribes the form and contents of air passenger tickets for domestic and international travel under its Resolutions. These include important provisions restricting the time for complaint about baggage or delay and purporting to diminish the carrier's responsibilities for meeting scheduled times (see [12.610]).

An international passenger ticket constitutes prima facie [349] (not conclusive) evidence of the entry into a contract of carriage and of its conditions [350] whereas the contractual status of a domestic ticket remains in doubt. The High Court decided in 1976 that for stamp duty purposes a domestic aviation ticket was not a contract. [351] Even key terms such as the price shown on the ticket have been held to be not conclusive. [352] While ticket case principles are not relevant to notice of the Warsaw Convention and statutory limits, they are important in determining whether the other terms and conditions contained in an airline passenger ticket form part of the contract of carriage so as to be binding on the passenger.

Baggage check

[12.580] The Montreal Convention [353] requires the carrier to provide a baggage identification tag for each piece of checked baggage. However non compliance does not affect the existence or validity of the contract of carriage and the limitation of lability and other rules of the Convention still apply.

The Warsaw Convention requires that a baggage check containing similar information to that prescribed for passenger tickets must also be delivered to passengers for checked baggage and the effects of compliance and non-compliance are also similar to passenger tickets. [354] Again, although contemplated by the *Civil Aviation (Carriers' Liability) Act 1959* (Cth), [355] there is no statutory requirement for a domestic baggage check or for notice or any other information to be supplied. However s 32(2) does permit a carrier to contract out of liability for damage resulting from the inherent defect, quality or vice of goods carried. These are the standard exceptions at common law and under the Warsaw convention. [356]

IATA also prescribes the form and contents of the baggage check [357] for domestic and international travel and the same issues arise as to whether or not these form part of the carriage contract and are binding on the passenger.

Provision is made under the Warsaw Convention for a passenger to declare a higher value of registered baggage and pay, if required, a supplementary charge to raise the limit on liability

---

348 *Civil Aviation (Carriers' Liability) Act 1959* (Cth), ss 31, 40, 41.
349 "Prima facie", that is, the onus is on the party alleging otherwise to prove it.
350 Warsaw Convention, Art 3(5).
351 In *MacRobertson Miller Airlines v Commissioner of Taxation (WA)* (1975) 133 CLR 125, Barwick CJ found the ticket was a mere receipt, Stephen J found the ticket was an offer and Jacobs J found the ticket was a voucher.
352 In *Sew Hoy & Sons Ltd v Stars Travel Ltd* (unreported, High Court of New Zealand, Dunedin, 5 September 1985, M186/84), upheld in appeal by Cook J, first-class passengers were required to pay an additional sum when it was found that the fare paid as endorsed on the ticket was less than the proper fare.
353 Article 3.
354 Warsaw Convention, Art 4. Similarly, cargo requires a waybill under Article 5, otherwise the carrier cannot rely on the limits under Articles 18 and 19.
355 *Civil Aviation (Carriers' Liability) Act 1959* (Cth), ss 31, 40, 41.
356 Warsaw Convention, Arts 17(2) and 18(2). The latter section is confined to cargo.
357 IATA Resolution.

to the higher value. However if the carrier can prove the passenger's actual interest in delivery of the baggage at the destination was less than the declared value then the carrier is not required to pay more than the actual value.[358] There are no equivalent provisions under the *Civil Aviation (Carriers' Liability) Act 1959* (Cth) for domestic aviation.

The term "checked baggage" used generally in the Warsaw Convention[359] and IATA conditions is equivalent to the term "registered baggage" used in the *Civil Aviation (Carriers' Liability) Act 1959* (Cth). It is to be contrasted with carry-on baggage and other property and valuables of which a passenger takes personal charge as discussed in [12.600] below.

Liability

[12.590] Article 17 of the Montreal and Warsaw Conventions provides that:

> The carrier is liable for damage sustained in case of death or bodily injury of a passenger upon condition only that the accident which caused the death or injury took place on board the aircraft or in the course of any of the operations of embarking or disembarking.

The *Civil Aviation (Carriers' Liability) Act 1959* (Cth) makes similar provision for domestic aviation.[360]

The following key points should be noted about the effect of these provisions:

- There is no need to show breach of contract or negligence or any other fault;
- There is need to show only that damage was sustained because of an accident in the course of international carriage;
- That creates an independent[361] and exclusive[362] cause of action in substitution for all other civil liability;[363]
- The liability is strict, although it is usually described as "presumed liability" under the Warsaw Convention because it (but not the *Civil Aviation (Carriers' Liability) Act 1959* (Cth) nor the Montreal Convention) provides a "best endeavours" defence.[364]

Several terms used in the provisions need some clarification:

- *Damages.* Damages may be recovered not only by injured passengers but also by other passengers and by employers, family and dependants.[365] However the total amount recoverable is subject to the limits. Damages are not reduced by amounts received from life insurance, superannuation, social security, inheritance of a dwelling and contents.[366] If medical or funeral expenses are paid under travel insurance only the insurer will be able to claim these expenses from the carrier under the right of subrogation. There is also authority

---

358 Warsaw Convention, Art 22(2).

359 "Checked baggage" is used in Warsaw Convention, Art 3, Warsaw Convention, Art 17(2)(3), "registered baggage" is used in Warsaw-Hague Convention, Art 22(2).

360 *Civil Aviation (Carriers' Liability) Act 1959* (Cth), s 28.

361 The US Supreme Court has held that Warsaw Convention, Art 17 creates a cause of action independent of national law: *Benjamins v BEA* 14 Avi 18,370 (1979).

362 The US Court of Appeals has held that the cause of action under Warsaw Convention, Art 17 is exclusive and the Supreme Court has denied certificates to appeal on the point: *Re Air Disaster at Lockerbie, Scotland 21 December 1988 v Pan Am*, 23 Avi 17,714 (1991); *Korean Airline Disaster case* 23 Avi 17, 505 (1991).

363 The Warsaw system is silent on the point but it has been so determined at common law (see references above); *Civil Aviation (Carriers' Liability) Act 1959* (Cth), ss 12(2), 13, 35(2), 36.

364 Warsaw Convention, Art 20: see [12.550] above.

365 *Civil Aviation (Carriers' Liability) Act 1959* (Cth), s 12, 14, 35, 37.

366 *Civil Aviation (Carriers' Liability) Act 1959* (Cth), s 15, 38.

that damages for disappointment are recoverable.[367] For a discussion of the principles applied in assessing damages for claims on the death of a passenger, see *McKenna v Avoir Pty Ltd*.[368]

- *Bodily injury.* The provision requires that the damages be sustained in the event of "bodily injury". There are conflicting decisions on whether this includes damages for nervous shock (mental injury).[369] This is an important issue in emergency landings, terrorist attacks and hijackings and for family or friends waiting at an airport for passengers on a missing flight. The Supreme Court of Israel has held that they are recoverable,[370] the United States Supreme Court has held that they are not[371] and in an Australian case, the Court of Appeal in New South Wales left the matter undecided.[372] If the nervous shock is associated with some physical injury then damages for nervous shock ought to be recoverable on the plain meaning of Article 17.[373] Many authors argue that they ought to be recoverable in any case.[374]

- *Accident.* The United States Supreme Court has held that the term includes most unexpected or unusual events external to the passenger.[375] It would not include any of the typical operational and accepted events of air carriage such as a "rough" landing, normal pressurisation or (after a warning to fasten seat belts), air turbulence.[376] An exceptionally rough landing, abnormal depressurisation causing deafness, or severe turbulence without warning would constitute accidents. However the dividing line is often difficult to draw.

---

367   *Newell v Canadian Pacific Airlines Ltd* 74 DLR 3d 574 (1976).
368   *McKenna v Avoir Pty Ltd* (1981) WAR 255.
369   E Giemulla, R Schmidt et al, *Warsaw Convention* (Kluwer Law International, The Hague), Ch III, p 6 argue that this is the only proper interpretation of the official French text; G Heilbronn, *Travel and Tourism Law* (Federation Press, Sydney, 1992), p 345.
370   *Air France v Teichner* (1988) ETL 187. Here the Supreme Court of Israel held that passengers on the Air France flight to Entebbe which was hijacked and detained could recover for mental injuries under Warsaw Convention, Art 17 even though they themselves were not physically injured.
371   *Floyd v Eastern Airlines* 23 Avi 17,367 (1992). All three engines failed, the aircraft plummeted several thousand feet and passengers were advised that the plane would ditch before the crew managed to restart one engine and land safely. No one suffered physical injury. The US Supreme Court ruled that damages for purely mental injury were not recoverable under Warsaw Convention, Art 17.
372   *American Airlines Inc v Georgeopoulos* (unreported, NSW CA, Clarke and Sheller JJA, Simos AKJA, 26 September 1996, 40762/93). The Magistrate decided that nervous shock and mental suffering were not within Warsaw Convention, Art 17. On appeal Ireland J determined that they were and on further appeal the Court of Appeal noted the conflicting decisions and referred the case back to the Magistrate for a more precise finding on the nature of the injuries suffered.
373   This would appear to be the way to reconcile *Air France v Teichner* 1988 ETL 187 and *Floyd v Eastern Airlines* 23 Avi 17,367 (1992). See also *Jack v Transworld Airlines Inc* 854 F Supp 654 (1994) which noted that *Floyd v Eastern Airlines* did not resolve this issue.
374   E Giemulla, R Schmidt et al, *Warsaw Convention* (Kluwer Law International, The Hague), Ch III, p 6 argue that this is the only proper interpretation of the official French text; G Heilbronn, *Travel and Tourism Law* (Federation Press, Sydney, 1992), p 345, n 54. argues that the issue will be clarified if and when the Guatemala City Protocol 1971 enters into force because it substitutes the wider term "personal injury" in Warsaw Convention, Art 17. These views were rejected by the NSW Court of Appeal in *American Airlines Inc v Georgeopoulis* discussed in fn 372 above.
375   *Air France v Saks* 18 Avi 18,538, 18,543.
376   E Giemulla, R Schmidt et al, *Warsaw Convention* (Kluwer Law International, The Hague), Ch III p 13.

Opinion is divided on whether hijacking [377] or terrorist acts [378] are accidents. [379]

In recent times, passengers have complained of Deep Vein Thrombosis (DVT), a potentially life threatening medical condition, allegedly arising out of long haul flights. However, these claims require proof that either there was an "accident" or that the airline had breached its duty of care to passengers. So far, the courts have rejected compensation claims from passengers who have developed DVT, finding that the illness was neither an "accident" under the Warsaw Convention, nor did it arise from poor seating arrangements but was rather a pre-existing medical condition of the claimant.

- *In the course of embarking and disembarking.* Accidents often occur while entering and leaving the aircraft, which is clearly within the provision. The definition also extends to accidents in the terminal where liability depends on the degree of carrier control. Thus an accident occurring in a queue while waiting for security or baggage checks is included [380] but one occurring on an escalator on the way to security and baggage checks was not. [381] The owners and operators of the air terminal and other facilities may also be liable.

Baggage

[12.595] Article 17(2) of the *Montreal Conventions* provides that

> The carrier shall be liable for damage sustained in the event of the destruction or loss of, or any damage to, any checked baggage, upon condition only that the event which caused the destruction, loss or damage took place on board the aircraft or during any period within which the checked baggage was in the charge of the carrier. In the case of unchecked baggage, including personal items, the carrier is liable if the damage resulted from its fault or that of its servants or agents.

Article 17(3) further provides that

> If the carrier admits the loss of the checked baggage, or if the checked baggage has not arrived at the expiration of twenty-one days after the date on which it ought to have arrived, the passenger is entitled to enforce against the carrier the rights which flow from the contract of carriage.

The Montreal Convention has a separate article covering liability for cargo (Article 18)

The Warsaw Convention Article 18 covers in similar terms to Montreal 17.2 both checked baggage and "any goods" the later designed primarily to cover cargo. This leaves the status of unchecked baggage unclear as discussed below.

The *Civil Aviation (Carriers' Liability) Act 1959* (Cth) makes similar provision for domestic aviation. [382]

---

377 Warsaw Convention, Art 17 accidents: *Husserl v Swiss Air Transport Co* 351 F Supp 702 SDNY (affirmed 185 F2d 1210) (Palestinian Liberation Organisation hijacking); *Karfunkel v Singapore Airlines and Air France* 14 Avi 17,674 (hijacking of the Air France jumbo jet to Entebbe).

378 Warsaw Convention, Art 17 accidents: *Day v Trans World Airlines Inc* 628 F2d 31 (second Circuit 1975) (terrorist attack on passengers in an international transit lounge in Athens) (certificate of appeal to US Supreme Court denied); *Hernandez v Air France* 14 Avi 17,421 (Japanese Red Army terrorists opened fire on passengers collecting baggage at Tel Aviv Airport) (held that accident occurred after disembarkation).

379 E Giemulla, R Schmidt et al, *Warsaw Convention* (Kluwer Law International, The Hague), Ch III, p 13 and G Heilbronn, *Travel and Tourism Law* (Federation Press, Sydney, 1992), p 345 doubt that hijacking is an accident. For an interesting review of the US cases see J Barrett, "Terrorism and the Airline Passenger" (1978) 129 *New Law Journal* 489-502.

380 *Day v TWA* 13 Avi 17,645 (1975).

381 *Felismina v TWA* 13 Avi 17,145 (1974).

382 *Civil Aviation (Carriers' Liability) Act 1959* (Cth), s 29(1).

The following key points should be noted about the effect of these provisions:

- There is no need to show bailment or breach of contract or negligence or any other fault (similar to liability for passengers);
- There is need to show only that damage was sustained because of the destruction, loss or injury to baggage caused by an occurrence during the transportation by air (contrast the wider term "occurrence" with "accident" for passengers);
- That creates an independent and exclusive cause of action in substitution for all other civil liability [383] (similar to liability for passengers) but subject to the comments below on carry-on baggage on international flights;
- The liability is usually described as "presumed liability" because both the Warsaw Convention [384] and *Civil Aviation (Carriers' Liability) Act 1959* (Cth) [385] provide a "best endeavours" defence (the Australian Act does not provide such a defence to passenger claims).

Several terms used in the provisions need some clarification:

- *Damage.* This includes damages for disappointment. See [12.655].
- *Checked baggage.* The carrier's presumed liability clearly covers checked baggage under the Montreal and Warsaw Convention and registered baggage, its equivalent under the *Civil Aviation (Carriers' Liability) Act 1959* (Cth).
- *Unchecked baggage.* Under the Montreal Convention the carrier is liable for unchecked baggage, including personal items, if the damage resulted from its fault or that of its servants or agents. [386]

Under the Warsaw Convention the extent to which carry-on baggage and other property and valuables ("carry-on baggage") is covered is not clear. [387] The phrase "or any goods", although designed primarily to cover cargo, would include carry-on baggage, but then it is excluded from presumed liability most of the time because it is not in the charge of the carrier under the definition of "transportation by air" discussed below. [388] Under the Warsaw Convention, liability for carry-on baggage on international flights will often have to be determined by general law as discussed below ([12.600]). This is unnecessarily complicated for the vast number of transactions involved and reform is overdue. [389]

The *Civil Aviation (Carriers' Liability) Act 1959* (Cth) takes a different approach by making no distinction between registered baggage and carry-on baggage, [390] but then reversing the onus of proof for carry-on baggage. It provides that the carrier is deemed to have proved that the damage resulting from the loss, destruction or injury to carry-on

---

383 Warsaw Convention, Art 17(2), *Civil Aviation (Carriers' Liability) Act 1959* (Cth), s 29(1).
384 Warsaw Convention, Art 20, no equivalent in Montreal Convention.
385 *Civil Aviation (Carriers' Liability) Act 1959* (Cth), s 29(1).
386 Warsaw Convention, Art 17(2).
387 *Baker v Landsell Protective Agency* 590 F Supp 165 US District Court SDNY.
388 Where the carrier has charge of carry-on baggage the carrier is presumed liable under Article 18: *Kabbani v International Total Services* US District Court, DC, Civil Action No 9-0391-LFO Order of 15 October 1992 (unpublished).
389 The Guatemala Protocol 1971, which has not yet come into force, simplifies the matter by amending Article 17 to include baggage (checked and carry on) and restricting Article 18 to cargo. This has some similarity to the *Civil Aviation (Carriers' Liability) Act 1959* (Cth) approach, discussed below.
390 *Civil Aviation (Carriers' Liability) Act 1959* (Cth), s 29(1).

baggage was caused by the contributory negligence of the passenger and that the carrier is liable only to the extent that the passenger proves that the passenger was not responsible.[391] The result is that the general law is not relevant to liability for carry-on baggage on domestic flights but the liability under the *Civil Aviation (Carriers' Liability) Act 1959* (Cth), which is independent and exclusive, is also very restricted. Whichever way liability is determined, claims for baggage are nevertheless subject to the limits discussed in [12.620] below.

- *Carriage by air.* The Warsaw Convention defines this phrase to mean the period while the baggage or goods are in the charge of the carrier whether on board the aircraft or during any period within which the checked baggage was in the charge of the carrier.[392] The *Civil Aviation (Carriers' Liability) Act 1959* (Cth) defines an equivalent phrase "carriage by air" in similar terms for registered baggage but for carry-on baggage, personal effects and other articles (carry-on baggage) defines it as the period while the passenger is on board the aircraft or is in the course of any of the operations of embarking or disembarking. The Warsaw Convention also includes transportation by land, sea or river if it is part of the contract for transportation by air.[393] The *Civil Aviation (Carriers' Liability) Act 1959* (Cth) provides that, for registered baggage, carriage by air does not extend beyond 12 hours after the baggage has been made available for collection.[394]

Carry-on baggage, international carriage and the general law

[12.600] As discussed above under the Warsaw Convention,[395] unless the carrier has taken charge of it, carry-on baggage is not covered by the carrier's presumed liability and so liability must be determined under the general law. It will be recalled from [12.45] that, if the air carrier is a common carrier, liability will nevertheless be strict at common law provided:

- the lost or damaged items fall within the definition of "passengers' luggage";
- they were not items being worn by the passenger or carried in the passenger's pocket such as clothes, jewellery, watches and money; and
- there are no contractual provisions to the contrary.

Otherwise, the passenger must prove that loss or damage was due to the fault of the carrier usually in contract, tort or bailment in order to recover. This task is assisted by the *Australian Consumer Law* which under ss 60 and 61 applies statutory guarantees that services (including passenger transport) be provided with all due care and skill and be fit for the purpose, achieve the result expected and provided in a reasonable time. Any carrier or IATA proposal to restrict or exclude this liability in the conditions of carriage would be void under s 64 (see [12.70] and [12.75]).

Delay

[12.605] Article 19 of the Montreal and Warsaw Conventions provides that "[t]he carrier is liable for damage occasioned by delay in the carriage by air of passengers, baggage or cargo". The *Civil Aviation (Carriers' Liability) Act 1959* (Cth) makes no such provision for domestic aviation and so it is governed by the conditions of carriage and the general law subject to s 62

---

391   *Civil Aviation (Carriers' Liability) Act 1959* (Cth), s 29(4).
392   Warsaw Convention, Art 17(2), *Civil Aviation (Carriers' Liability) Act 1959* (Cth), s 29(2)(b).
393   Warsaw Convention, Art 18(4).
394   Section 29(3) of *Civil Aviation (Carriers' Liability) Act 1959* (Cth).
395   Warsaw Convention, Art 18 applies only to checked baggage. *Montreal Convention*, Art 17(2).

of the *Australian Consumer Law* which applies a guarantee that services (including passenger transport) will be supplied within a reasonable time.

The following key points should be noted about the effect of Article 19:

- liability is established if it is proved that there was delay in the transportation by air;
- that creates an exclusive cause of action in substitution for all other civil liability; [396]
- the liability under the Montreal and Warsaw Convention on delay is usually described as "presumed liability" because the "best endeavours" defence applies; [397]
- the Montreal Convention sets specific limits for damages for delay whereas under the Warsaw Convention the general limits for passengers and baggage apply. [398]

Several terms used in the provision need some clarification:

- *Damage occasioned by.* Common law principles are used to define the scope of damages which are recoverable. These principles include remoteness of damage in contract [4.430] and foreseeability in tort [5.40]. Thus only losses arising as a natural consequence of a delay are compensable unless any special circumstances are communicated to the carrier or the carrier's agent. In practice passengers often do inform the carrier or the travel agent of such special circumstances and this can widen the scope of the carrier's liability significantly, subject to the comments below. For passengers on package holidays, damages for disappointment would generally be compensable.
- *Delay.* This term is not defined by the Montreal and Warsaw Conventions. Not just the lateness in arrival at the destination but also the scheduled duration of flight must be considered. A one-hour delay is more serious in a 30-minute flight than it is in a 30-hour flight. Passengers choose to travel by air because, although it is usually the most expensive, it is the fastest means of transport available. So passengers place considerable importance and reliance on flight schedules which indicate departure and arrival times. Few passengers appreciate how little responsibility a carrier accepts for this under the General Conditions of Carriage discussed below. If delay is so severe as to constitute non-performance then the general law applies and the passenger is entitled to rescind notwithstanding Article 26. [399]
- *In the carriage by air.* Although this appears to cover the period of operation as does a similar phrase in Article 18, that meaning is not relevant for Article 19. For delay, the only relevant time is the lateness of disembarkation and collection of baggage at the destination and so a later departure coupled with arrival on time due to a tailwind is not delay. [400]

General law on delay

[12.610] It will be recalled from [12.30] that carriers have a duty to carry their passengers to their destinations by the usual route without unnecessary deviation and without unreasonable delay. [401] Breach of this duty may result in liability in contract and tort. Routes and times shown in the flight schedule are at least representations which induce the contract or more

---

396   Warsaw Convention, Art 19, *Civil Aviation (Carriers' Liability) Act 1959* (Cth), s 29(1).
397   Warsaw Convention, Art 24.
398   Montreal and Warsaw Convention, Art 22.
399   *Cooke v Midland Railway* (1892) 9 TLR 147.
400   E Giemulla, R Schmidt et al, *Warsaw Convention* (Kluwer Law International, The Hague), Art 19, p 10.
401   *Hamlin v Great Northern Railway Co* (1856) 1 H&N 408; *Hobbs v London South West Railway* (1875) LR 10 QB 11.

likely terms of the contract especially as passengers choose air travel for speed and pay more for that quality. At common law carriers have considerable scope to contract out of these obligations.

However under the *Australian Consumer Law*, s 18 prohibits deceptive and misleading conduct, s 29 prohibits false representations about the standard, quality and performance characteristics of services and ss 60 and 61 imply guarantees that the carrier will use all due care and skill and that the services will be fit for the purpose. Further s 62 provides a statutory guarantee that services, including passenger transport will be provided within a reasonable time. These guarantees generally cannot be excluded and any provision purporting to do so is void. This greatly reduces the scope for carriers to diminish their responsibility by contract.

IATA ticket conditions on delay

[12.615] By using IATA's General Conditions of Contract, carriers purport to diminish the effect of Article 19 by Condition 9, which provides: [402]

> Carrier undertakes to use its best endeavours to carry the passengers and baggage with reasonable dispatch. Times shown in timetables or elsewhere are not guaranteed and form no part of this contract. Carrier may without notice substitute alternate carriers or aircraft, and may alter or omit stopping places shown on the ticket in case of necessity. Schedules are subject to change without notice. Carrier assumes no responsibility for making connections.

A number of issues are raised by this condition. First, under the ticket case principles, it may not form part of the contract of carriage so as to be binding on the passenger (see [4.165]ff). Secondly, for international carriage, this condition must come very close to offending Article 26 of the Warsaw Convention [403] which prohibits contractual provisions which purport to relieve the carrier from liability laid down under the Convention such as in Article 19. Thirdly, it seems clear that Condition 9 offends the provisions of the *Australian Consumer Law* referred to above. For international carriage, Article 26 of the Warsaw Convention would require that an action founded on the *Australian Consumer Law* could only be brought subject to the conditions and limitations of the Convention. The result is that the standard air carriage contract does not really mean what it says and international and domestic carriers have considerable legal responsibility for the damages caused by delay.

Limits on liability

[12.620] Under the Warsaw Convention, although liability is strict or presumed, the amount recoverable has traditionally been limited. The 1929 Convention contained no mechanism for automatic review of the limits and multilateral efforts have failed to reach general agreement on the issue ever since. The Hague Protocol doubled the original limits but even this was not sufficient for the United States, which instead made its own special arrangement with carriers. [404] Since then many other countries, [405] including Australia, have also made their own special arrangements for higher limits.

Multilateral efforts by governments have failed to restore uniformity. The intergovernmental multilateral negotiation process is so slow it becomes self-defeating. In the time required to reach consensus the new limits become inadequate.

---

402   IATA Resolution.
403   See also Warsaw Convention, Arts 47 and 49.
404   The Montreal Agreement with carriers raised the limit to US$75,000 per passenger for the US.
405   A limit of US$150,000 was set in most of Europe.

IATA, with the unanimous support of its carrier members, introduced a radical scheme to reform the limits and restore uniformity. Under the plan, which became effective on 14 February 1997, carriers which are party to the Agreement on Measures to Implement the IATA Intercarrier Agreement, accepted strict liability to 100,000 SDR per passenger and unlimited presumed liability. The IATA Passenger Liability Agreements are discussed in [12.710]ff.

This approach has been adopted in the *Montreal Convention 1999* which also provides for a general increase to 100,000 SDR. Critics may argue that this sum is already out of date.[406] Although still quite diverse, the limits on liability from the Australian perspective are summarised in the following table.

The *Montreal Convention* Article 24 introduced a mechanism to review the limits every five years and increase them in accordance with an index of inflation. The first increase took effect in January 2010 and the increased limits are reflected in the table below.

Current Limits on Air Carrier Liability/ Australia: Comparative table: International and Domestic

	Passengers	Baggage	
		Registered	Carry on
Warsaw Convention*	125,000 francs (about US$10K)	250 francs/kg	5,000 francs
Warsaw/Hague*	250,000 francs (about US$20K)	250 francs/kg	5,000 francs
Montreal No 1	8,300 SDR	17 SDR/kg	332 SDR
Montreal No 2	16,600 SDR	17 SDR/kg	332 SDR
Montreal No 3			
Montreal No 4			
Montreal Convention*	113,100 SDR (about US$174K)	1,131 SDR (about US$1.74K)	
[NB The convention which applies is the one which both the *origin and destination* countries have adopted]		*Delay 4,694 SDR (about US$6.640K)*	
IATA Intercarrier Agreement			
Strict liability	100,000 SDR		
Presumed liability	Unlimited		
Australia (CACLA)			
International	260,000 SDR	17 SDR/kg	332 SDR
Domestic	$500,000	$1600	$160

(1 SDR = approximately US $1.54 (at 25/09/10)

Servants and agents

[12.625] As servants or agents of the carrier are not party to the carrier's contract with the passenger they cannot be sued upon it or upon the grounds of liability provided by the Convention and *Civil Aviation (Carriers' Liability) Act 1959* (Cth) discussed above. Their liability to the passenger is determined by the law of tort.

However, they are protected by the limits on liability provided they prove that they were acting in the scope of their authority.[407] Under the Montreal and Warsaw Conventions but not the *Civil Aviation (Carriers' Liability) Act 1959* (Cth), servants and agents are not

---

406   Warsaw Convention, Art 21.
407   Warsaw Convention, Art 30, *Civil Aviation (Carriers' Liability) Act 1959* (Cth), s 33 and also at common law without these express provisions: *Reed v Wiser* 14 Avi 17, 848 US Court of Appeals.

protected by the limits if it is proved that the damage resulted from their own act or omission done with intent to cause damage or recklessly and with knowledge that damage would probably result.[408]

Interlining and successive carriers

[12.630] Where carriage is performed by several successive carriers or by carriers who are not party to a contract with the passenger, Article 36 of the Montreal and Warsaw Conventions and the *Guadalajara Convention 1961* determine who can be sued and ensure that no matter who is sued, the Warsaw rules apply and limit the aggregate amount recovered.

If the successive carriage is regarded by the parties as a single operation (successive carriage) then Article 36 of the Montreal or Warsaw Convention applies. Regardless of whether there is one contract or a series of contracts, it is deemed to be one undivided carriage and each sector is subject to the Warsaw Convention rules. However the only carriers liable to the passenger or the passenger's representative are:

- the actual carrier on the sector where the relevant accident, occurrence or delay occurred;
- in the case of passenger or passenger delay claims, the first carrier if it contracted to be responsible for the whole journey;[409] and
- in the case of baggage or baggage delay claims, the first carrier and last carrier.[410]

The Warsaw Convention rules and limits are further extended by the Guadalajara Convention, which applies wherever the person contracting as principal with the passenger or the passenger's agent (contracting carrier)[411] is different from the actual carrier who provides the carriage in whole or in part (actual carrier).[412] The Guadalajara Convention makes the contracting carrier liable and subject to the Warsaw Convention rules and limits as well as the actual carrier.

Under the Guadalajara Convention a travel agent or tour operator who contracts with the passenger for air travel as principal will be a contracting carrier and thus liable under the Warsaw Convention rules and limits. Usually the travel agent and tour operator are mere agents of the carrier and/or passenger in the first category situation discussed in [9.340]. The problem arises in the second category situation considered by the Privy Council in *Wong Mee Wan v Kwan Kin Travel Services Ltd*[413] as discussed in [9.350]ff.[414] This category is also potentially much wider in Europe, where the EC Directive on Package Holidays deems the travel agent or tour operator to be responsible as principal in package holidays. If the Warsaw Convention limits do not apply because of failure to provide documentation (see [12.535] above) or are broken because of carrier misconduct (see [12.650] below), the position of travel agents and tour operators in the second category is parlous. They are liable jointly and

---

408 *Montreal Convention 1999*, Art 43; Warsaw Convention, Art 25A.
409 Warsaw Convention, Art 36(2).
410 Warsaw Convention, Art 36(3). The first and last carrier can sue the actual carrier but all three carriers are jointly and severally liable to the passenger or the passenger's representative.
411 *Guadalajara Supplementary Convention 1961*, Art I(b).
412 *Guadalajara Supplementary Convention 1961*, Art I(c). It expressly excludes a successive carrier covered by Warsaw system, Arts 1(3), 36.
413 *Wong Mee Wan v Kwan Kin Travel Services Ltd* [1995] 4 All ER 745.
414 See also the author's discussion of this decision: TC Atherton, "Tour operator's responsibility for package holidays: common law takes the EC Directive model global" (1996) 3 *Travel Law Journal* 90-96.

severally for the acts and omissions of the actual carrier.[415] Other implications are discussed in the IATA Passenger Liability Agreements below ([12.710]ff).

Carrier defences

[12.635] The following defences to claims for passengers, baggage and delay are provided to the carrier under the Montreal and Warsaw Conventions and, where indicated, under the *Civil Aviation (Carriers' Liability) Act 1959* (Cth).

All reasonable measures

[12.640] Article 19 to the *Montreal Convention* removes this defence for all liability except delay. Article 19 provides, "the carrier shall not be liable for damage occasioned by delay if it proves that it and its servants and agents took all measures that could reasonably be required to avoid the damage or that it was impossible for it or them to take such measures". It is linked to the requirement in Article 17 that there be an "accident".

Under the Warsaw Convention this is a defence to all liability. Article 20 provides that the carrier is not liable if it proves that all reasonable measures were taken by it and its agents to avoid the damage or that it was impossible to take such measures. Because of this defence, many authors characterise a carrier's liability under the Warsaw Convention as presumed liability rather than strict liability. There is no equivalent defence for domestic aviation under *Civil Aviation (Carriers' Liability) Act 1959* (Cth).

This defence is akin to the principles of force majeure in contract and inevitable accident in tort. To satisfy Article 19, the range of avoidance measures required is all that were *reasonable* not merely those which were *desirable*. The precise scope of this defence remains uncertain but it would appear to arise in many hijack and terrorism cases.[416] There is also doubt over whether "agents" includes independent contractors.

The defence is waived in the United States under the Montreal Agreement and is limited or waived in several amendments of the Warsaw Convention which have not yet come into force. It is also waived generally for strict liability up to the limit under the IATA Intercarrier Agreement (see [12.715]).

Contributory negligence

[12.645] Under the *Montreal Convention* (Article 20), the *Warsaw Convention* (Article 19) and the *Civil Aviation (Carriers' Liability) Act 1959* (Cth),[417] if the carrier proves that the damage was caused by or contributed to by the injured person, the carrier may be wholly or partly exempted from liability in accordance with local law. At common law[418] and under the *Civil Aviation (Carriers' Liability) Act 1959* (Cth),[419] the procedure is to first determine the amount which would have been recoverable if there was no limit, and then to reduce it by the proportion of the passenger's fault. The limits are then applied to the reduced amount so that a negligent passenger may still recover up to the full limit. The negligence of a passenger does

---

415 Guadalajara Supplementary Convention 1961, Art III(1). They are not given protection similar to that provided to actual carriers for their acts or omissions under the proviso to Art III(2).
416 In *Bornier v Air Inter* RFDA 340 the defence failed because the passengers had not been subject to a security check.
417 Civil Aviation (Carriers' Liability) Act 1959 (Cth), s 39.
418 *The Khedive* (1880) 5 App Cas 876.
419 Civil Aviation (Carriers' Liability) Act 1959 (Cth), ss 16, 39.

not reduce the claim of any other party. A common example of contributory negligence is where a passenger fails to fasten the seatbelt as requested when warned of turbulence.

Breaking the limits

[12.650] The Warsaw-Hague Convention provides a method of breaking the limits by proving conduct barring limitation. Article 25 provides that:

> The limits of liability…do not apply if it is proved that the damage resulted from an act or omission of the carrier, his servants or agents, done with intent to cause damage or recklessly and with knowledge that damage would probably result…

The unamended Warsaw Convention has a similar provision based on the concept of "wilful misconduct". There is no equivalent under the *Civil Aviation (Carriers' Liability) Act 1959* (Cth) for domestic aviation. The Montreal Convention provides that the carrier will not be liable for damages in excess of the limit if it can prove that "such damage was not due to the negligence or other wrongful act or omission of the carrier or its servants or agents" [420] thus putting the carrier rather than the passenger to proof on the issues of negligence or other wrongful acts. This is a significant change to the Warsaw Convention and one which may well produce different outcomes from the court cases decided under Article 25 (see [12.655] below).

If Article 25 applies, the effect is to leave the carrier liable under Articles 17, 18 and 19 without the benefit of the limits. A similar provision has been introduced for seagoing ships under Article 4 of the *London Convention* (see [12.410]) and the following discussion also applies to it.

The principles outlined set out in Article 25 of the Warsaw-Hague Convention and the other conventions in the Warsaw Convention provide for two types of misconduct that will bar limitation:

(a) **Intentional:** Acts or omissions done with intent to cause damage would in most cases be trespass and/or criminal conduct, which is unlikely in commercial aviation.

(b) **Reckless and with knowledge of probable result:** While this is more likely than (a), it is difficult for the plaintiff to prove. The key question is whether a subjective or objective test is required for "knowledge"; that is, must it be proved that the carrier knew (subjective) or should have known (objective) of the probable result? The prevailing opinion is that the test should be subjective; however the objective test has been applied by French courts and in Australia's only case on the point. The following three cases are also instructive. [421]

Newell v Canadian Pacific Airlines

[12.655] *Newell v Canadian Pacific Airlines* 74 DLR 3d 574 (1976)

(objective test on reckless and intentional conduct under Art 25 Warsaw-Hague Convention)

Damages for disappointment recoverable for injury to pets carried as excess baggage

---

420 Warsaw Convention, Art 21(2)(a)
421 There is substantial US case law on Article 25 in hijackings and terrorism situations. However this is of limited use in Australia because in the US the Hague Protocol amendments of Art 25 do not apply (the older "wilful misconduct" concept is still in force) and carriers have waived the Art 20 defence under the Montreal Agreement.

Newell v Canadian Pacific Airlines cont.

Facts: The Newells were an elderly couple who had two pet dogs, Patachou and Bon Bon, which they regarded as part of the family. They wanted to take the dogs with them on holiday to Mexico City. Canadian Pacific would not permit the dogs to travel with the Newells in the first-class passenger compartment even though the Newells offered to buy all the other seats so it would not offend other passengers. After assurances from the carrier's staff that the dogs would be safe and comfortable, they were carried as "excess baggage". Unfortunately they were placed in the cargo compartment next to pharmaceuticals packed in dry ice which gave off poisonous carbon dioxide gas. On arrival in Mexico City Bon Bon was dead and Patachou was unconscious. The Newells were distraught and for the next 48 hours they took turns administering oxygen to Patachou. He revived but was too ill to fly back as baggage. The Newells bought four extra passenger seats for him to fly back to Toronto with them in the passenger compartment. The Newells sued for damages. The parties agreed that the carrier was liable under Article 18(1) of the Warsaw-Hague Convention. If Article 22(2) applied, damages would be limited to $560.

Decision: The County Court of Ontario, Canada (Borins J) found that the dogs had been carried at an extra charge of $56.56 as the Newells' "excess baggage" and that the combined "Passenger ticket and Baggage Check" satisfied the requirements of Art 4. The court further found that the carrier's cargo service department knew of the risk of placing animals and dry ice in the same compartment but failed to inform the carrier's ramp service department that the dry ice was in there. This was not merely a breach of the carrier's contract to carry them safely. It was held to be reckless with actual knowledge (that is, the subjective test) that damage would probably result within the meaning of Article 25. Thus the carrier could not rely on the limits under Article 22 and was liable for full compensatory damages. $608.27 of the special damages had been agreed. The court awarded a total of $1558.27, including two further sums which were awarded as compensatory damages under the principles in *Hadley v Baxendale*. $450 special damages was awarded for the cost of the four extra return seats for Patachou. $500 general damages was awarded for the Newells' "anguish, loss of enjoyment of life and sadness", applying the principles of *Jarvis v Swan Tours* on damages for disappointment.

Goldman v Thai Airways International

[12.660] *Goldman v Thai Airways International* (1983) TLR 7

Subjective test on reckless and intentional conduct under Art 25 of the Warsaw-Hague Convention

Facts: Goldman was on a Thai Airways flight from London to Bangkok when the plane encountered severe clear air turbulence (CAT) near Ankara. Goldman and 12 other passengers and crew struck the roof. Goldman was not wearing a seatbelt and he suffered serious spinal injuries. No warning or instruction to fasten seatbelts had been given to the passengers. However the incident occurred in one of two areas on the flight path where moderate CAT had been forecast in the weather chart provided to the flight Captain for the journey. Unlike a thunder storm, CAT is undetectable before it is encountered. CAT was described as "turbulent air, swirling and twisting about like a snake which may or may not foul a flight path". Under ICAO's definitions in moderate CAT passengers "feel strain against seatbelts; loose objects move about" whereas in severe CAT passengers "are forced violently against seatbelts; loose objects are tossed about". Thai Airways' flight operations manual contained instructions to pilots that the sign "fasten seat belts" should be lit while taxiing, takeoff, landing and "during all flying in turbulent air and when turbulence can be expected". Evidence from the experts was divided on the interpretation of this and whether good practice required warnings to belt up before entering a forecast moderate CAT area or only when some tell-tale signs of light turbulence were encountered.

Goldman v Thai Airways International cont.

Decision: The English Court of Appeal (Eversleigh, O'Connor and Purchas LJJ) held that the test to be applied under Article 25 of *Warsaw-Hague* when considering whether conduct was reckless and with knowledge that damage would probably result was subjective. That is, the plaintiff must prove not only that the conduct was reckless but also that the carrier or its agents knew that damage of the type suffered would probably result. Here, even if it were accepted that the flight Captain's conduct was reckless, it was not proven that he knew that damage would probably result. Further, it was not proven that he knew that damage of the type suffered would probably result. Accordingly, Article 25 did not apply and Goldman's damages of £41,852.42 were limited to £11,700.

SS Pharmaceutical Co Ltd v Qantas Airways

[12.665] *SS Pharmaceutical Co Ltd v Qantas Airways* (1988) 22 NSWLR 734; (1991) 1 LR 288

(Objective test on reckless and intentional conduct under Art 25 Warsaw-Hague Convention)

Gold francs under the Warsaw Convention are converted under the Civil Aviation (Carriers' Liability) Act 1959 (Cth), s 23 into AU$ at the market price of gold current at the date of judgment

Facts: One plaintiff sent to the other plaintiff five cartons of pharmaceutical products from Melbourne to Tokyo via Sydney as air cargo on the defendant carrier Qantas. Showers and occasional thunderstorms had been forecast for Sydney. During a change of planes in Sydney the cargo was stowed in the open during rain and was damaged. The cartons were clearly marked with umbrella symbols, an internationally recognised mark to warn carriers that they should be kept dry. The plaintiffs sought damages and the carrier did not deny liability but relied upon the limitation under Article 22. This test case was brought by Qantas' insurers to try and obtain an authoritative interpretation on the method of conversion of the limits expressed in francs into Australian dollars. The case took a surprising and, no doubt for Qantas, frustrating twist.

(Note that under Article 1 because the ultimate destination was foreign, even the domestic sector Melbourne to Sydney was regarded as international carriage subject to the Warsaw Convention. Thus the limits under Article 22(2) (baggage and goods) applied, subject to Article 25. There are no limits on liability for cargo under the *Civil Aviation (Carriers' Liability) Act 1959* (Cth).)

Decision at trial: The Federal Court (Rogers J) held that:

1. Article 25 applied so Qantas could not rely on the Art 22 limitation. Qantas had called no evidence and so the inference could be drawn that the conduct of its servants and agents was reckless and with knowledge of the likelihood of damage to specially vulnerable cargo in the weather conditions prevailing. Full damages of $144,193.83 were awarded, being $111,838 (the full value of the goods) and the balance interest.

2. Although unnecessary to decide in view of 1 (above) and hence obiter, the proper method of calculating the value of the franc under Article 22 is not SDR, nor the last official price of gold in Australia but the free market price of gold current at the date of judgment. Rogers J noted the uncertainty and that the SDR was the most logical and satisfactory, and called on the government for reform.

Decision on appeal: The Court of Appeal (Gleeson CJ and Handley J, Kirby J dissenting) upheld the finding on 1 and noted it was unnecessary to decide 2. In a strong dissenting judgment, Kirby J argued that the majority view constituted an objective test under Article 25 contrary to *Goldman v Thai Airways International* (1983) TLR 7 and prevailing world authorities and contrary to the object and spirit of the Warsaw Convention. Kirby J also called on the government for reform, stating (at 306-307):

> The average passenger and consignor using international air transport is almost certainly ignorant of the limitations on recovery which are imposed and the uncertainties and possible

SS Pharmaceutical Co Ltd v Qantas Airways cont.

injustices involved in the limitations provided by the Warsaw-Hague Convention. It would be preferable that these difficulties and injustices should be looked at in advance of, and not after, any major incident affecting large Australian interests.

The High Court refused leave to appeal.

Epilogue: The Commonwealth government amended the *Civil Aviation (Carriers' Liability) Act 1959* (Cth) in 1991 to increase the limits on liability and to ratify Montreal Protocols No 3 and No 4 which substitute the SDR for the franc in the limits on cargo. It did not ratify Montreal Protocols 1 and 2 which cover baggage. The government amended the *Civil Aviation (Carriers' Liability) Act 1959* (Cth) again in 1995 to substitute a limit of 260,000 SDR per passenger for the Warsaw Convention limit. The Montreal Protocols are still not in force. The limits on baggage remain in francs with all the uncertainties and potential injustices criticised in the decisions above.

―――― ෴ ――――

[12.670] On 1 September, 1983, Korean Air Lines Flight 007, a civilian aircraft, strayed into Soviet airspace over the sea of Japan without permission. Soviet jet interceptors shot it down killing all 269 passengers and crew. In the ensuing court cases, the courts held that the Warsaw limits did not apply because of the pilots' criminal negligence in deviating from the prescribed flight path.

Hijacking Conventions

[12.675] There are a number of conventions specifically relating to hijacking including:

- *Convention on Offences and Certain Other Acts Committed on Board Aircraft 1963;*
- *Convention for the Suppression of Unlawful Acts against the Safety of Civil Aviation 1971;*
- *Convention on the Prevention and Punishment of Crimes against Internationally Protected Persons, including Diplomatic Agents 1973;*
- *Convention against the Taking of Hostages 1979;*
- *International Convention for the Suppression of Terrorist Bombings 1997*

Presumed Unlimited Liability

[12.680] One of the major reforms of the Montreal Convention is Article 21(2) which provides in effect that in the case of death or personal injury of passengers, the carriers' liability shall not be limited by Article 17 unless the carrier proves that such damage was:

(a) not due to the negligence or other wrongful act of the carrier or its servants or agents, or

(b) was solely due to the negligence or wrongful act or omission of a third party

In effect this means presumed unlimited liability, similar to that accepted under the IATA Intercarrier Agreement.

Other Montreal Convention reforms

[12.685] To address the slowness of change to the limits of liability outlined in [12.620], Article 24 allows for the review of limits: every five years with limits to be increased by the CPI increase in the basket of SDR currencies. The first such review was implemented on 1 January 2010.

Article 28 provides that a carrier must make advance payments to claimants if the national law requires it. This is supplemented by ICAO which has developed a Code of Best Practice for airlines following an air crash. [422] The EU, Australia (2002) [423] and many other countries have developed national codes based on this code.

Finally, under Article 50, if the national law requires it, a carrier must provide proof of insurance sufficient to cover claims.

Procedure

Notice

[12.690] Notice of complaint of damage to baggage must be given:

- upon receipt of baggage, otherwise it is prima facie evidence that the baggage was received in good condition; [424]
- forthwith after discovery of damage and within seven days (three days for domestic) from the date of receipt. [425]

Notice of complaint of delay must be given within 21 days from the date baggage is available for collection. [426]

These notices must be in writing and must be given or despatched to the carrier within the time fixed. [427] Similar conditions are contained in IATA Conditions of Carriage. See [12.545].

Limitation period

[12.695] Plaintiffs must bring an action within two years after the date of intended or actual arrival at the destination or the date on which the transportation stopped. [428] Otherwise the claim is extinguished.

Timney v British Airways PLC

[12.700] *Timney v British Airways PLC* (1992) 56 SASR 287

(time limit cannot be extended)

Facts: A passenger suffered a broken thigh when she tripped on a metal plate in the floor in the corridor of the plane on a flight from Adelaide to London on 18 June 1985. She commenced an action by a summons issued on 2 May 1988.

Held: (Full Court King CJ, Bollen and Cox JJ) The time limit had expired and the claim was extinguished. The time limit under Article 29 was an integral part of the right to claim and was absolute. Although Article 28 provides that procedure is governed by the law of the forum, State laws

---

422 Civil Aviation Organization Circular 285, *Guidance on Assistance to Aircraft Accident Victims and their Families*.
423 For more information on the Family Assistance Code, see the website of the Department of Infrastructure, Transport, Regional and Local Government at http://www.infrastructure.gov.au/aviation/legislation/policy/family.aspx.
424 *Montreal Convention*, Art 31(1); Warsaw Convention, Art 26(1); *Civil Aviation (Carriers' Liability) Act 1959* (Cth), s 30(1).
425 *Montreal Convention*, Art 31(2); Warsaw Convention, Art 26(2); *Civil Aviation (Carriers' Liability) Act 1959* (Cth), s 30(2).
426 *Montreal Convention*, Art 31(2); Warsaw Convention, Art 26(2); *Civil Aviation (Carriers' Liability) Act 1959* (Cth), s 30(2).
427 *Montreal Convention*, Art 31(3); Warsaw Convention, Art 26(3); *Civil Aviation (Carriers' Liability) Act 1959* (Cth), s 30(2).
428 *Montreal Convention*, Art 35; Warsaw Convention, Art 29; *Civil Aviation (Carriers' Liability) Act 1959* (Cth), s 34.

Timney v British Airways PLC cont.

which allow extensions of time for infancy, incapacity and the like could not apply to alter the plain meaning of Article 28. To the extent that they purported to do so, they would be contrary to the Convention and the *Civil Aviation (Carriers' Liability) Act 1959* (Cth) and void under s 109 of the Constitution.

Forum shopping

[12.705] Plaintiffs are given the opportunity to exploit the fragmentation in the Warsaw Convention by choosing the forum with the fewest obstacles and the largest potential damages for their claim. This is facilitated by Article 28, which permits a plaintiff to choose the courts of any of the following jurisdictions in which to bring an action:

- carrier's domicile;
- carrier's principal place of business;
- carrier's place of business through which the contract was made;
- the destination.

The *Montreal Convention* Article 33 and the IATA Intercarrier Agreements introduced a fifth option, much fairer and more convenient for the passengers and their dependents:

- domicile or permanent residence of the passenger.

IATA Passenger Liability Agreements 1997

[12.710] As mentioned in [12.615] above, IATA bypassed the inertia of inter-governmental multilateral negotiations and introduced a radical scheme to reform several key problems of the Warsaw system.[429] In 1995 IATA obtained unanimous approval from its member carriers for the Intercarrier Agreement on Passenger Liability (IIA). The agreement acknowledged that although the "Warsaw Convention system is of great benefit to international air transportation" the "Convention's limits of liability, which have not been amended since 1955, are now grossly inadequate in most countries".[430] Under the IIA the carriers agreed:

1. To undertake action to waive the limitation of liability on recoverable compensatory damages in Article 22 paragraph 1 of the Warsaw Convention as to claims for death, wounding or other bodily injury of a passenger within the meaning of Article 17 of the Convention so that recoverable compensatory damages may be determined and awarded by reference to the law of the domicile of the passenger.

2. To reserve all available defences pursuant to the provisions of the Convention; nevertheless any carrier may waive any defence, including any defence up to a specified monetary amount of recoverable compensatory damages, as circumstances may warrant.

---

[429] The following discussion of the issues has also been published in the *Journal of Air Law and Commerce*: TC Atherton, "Unlimited liability for air passengers: The position of carriers, passengers, travel agents and tour operators under the IATA Passenger Liability Agreement Scheme" (1997) (Dec) 63 *Journal of Air Law and Commerce*.

[430] Agreement on Measures to Implement the IATA Intercarrier Agreement IIA, Preamble.

Following approval of the EU and United States [431] regulatory authorities, the Agreement on Measures to Implement the IATA Intercarrier Agreement (MIA) was declared effective on 14 February 1997. Under the MIA, signatory carriers [432] agree to incorporate into their conditions of carriage and tariffs the following provisions:

I [Mandatory]

1. [The carrier] shall not invoke the limitation of liability in Article 22(1) of the Convention as to any claim for recoverable compensatory damages arising under Article 17 of the Convention.

2. [The carrier] shall not avail itself of any defence under Article 20(1) of the Convention with respect to that portion of such claim which does not exceed 100,000 SDR....[II. 2. provides the option of setting different limits for different routes subject to government approval]

3. Except as otherwise provided in paragraphs 1 and 2 hereof, [the carrier] reserves all defences available under the Convention to any such claim...

II. [Optional]

1. [The carrier] agrees that subject to applicable law, recoverable compensatory damages for such claims may be determined by reference to the law of the domicile or permanent residence of the passenger.

Summary of reforms

[12.715] The IATA Passenger Agreements reformed the Warsaw system in the following key ways:

- uniform strict liability of 100,000 SDR per passenger. This involves waiver of the Article 22 per passenger limits [433] and the Article 20 best endeavours defence [434] up to this limit;

- unlimited presumed liability above 100,000 SDR. This involves waiver of the Article 22 per passenger limits; [435]

- optional law of domicile or permanent residence of passenger. This involves adding a fifth jurisdiction to the plaintiff's choices under Article 28; [436]

- optional variation of 100,000 limit according to route, subject to government approval. [437]

- the measures designed to achieve these reforms are discussed in the following paragraphs.

---

431 For an analysis of the issues in the US DOT approval see AJ Harakas, "The status of the Warsaw Convention limits on liability – the International Air Transport Association and Air Transport Association of America file Applications with the US DOT for approval of the Intercarrier Agreement and Implementing Agreement of Passenger Liability" (1996) (Oct) *The Aviation Quarterly*, Part 2, 115-123.

432 As of 1 June 2000, 122 international carriers, representing more than 90% of the world's air transport industry had signed the IATA Inter-carrier Agreement. For an updated list see IATA website at http://www.iata.org.

433 Agreement on Measures to Implement the IATA Intercarrier Agreement IIA, clause I.1; *Montreal Convention*, Art 21.

434 Agreement on Measures to Implement the IATA Intercarrier Agreement IIA, clause I.2.

435 Agreement on Measures to Implement the IATA Intercarrier Agreement IIA, clause I.1. *Montreal Convention*, Art 21(2).

436 Agreement on Measures to Implement the IATA Intercarrier Agreement IIA, clause II.1. *Montreal Convention*, Art 33.

437 Agreement on Measures to Implement the IATA Intercarrier Agreement IIA, clause II.2. *Montreal Convention*, Art 24, 25.

Only Article 17 claims covered

[12.720] The IATA Passenger Agreements apply only to claims for damages for injury to passengers under Article 17. They do not cover claims for loss or damage to baggage under Article 18 [438] or for delay under Article 19, which remain subject to the usual convention provisions. However it will be a rare case where the amount at stake will justify litigation on the Article 20 best endeavours defence [439] up to the limit or to try to break the limit for carrier's misconduct under Article 25. [440] These will continue to be important practical issues for cargo which is also outside the IATA scheme.

Waiver of Article 20 best endeavours defence

[12.725] The scope of the defence has always been uncertain and controversial [441] (see [12.630]). Its removal for damages up to 100,000 SDR introduces a truly strict liability regime with presumed liability now operating above that limit. [442]

Waiver of Article 22 limits

[12.730] The most radical part of the IATA scheme is the removal of the Article 22 and other limits on liability under Article 17. This has marked the coming of age of the aviation industry in terms of technical and commercial responsibility. It has put pressure on long-standing limited liability regimes in place for international road, rail and sea transport. [443]

Article 25 now irrelevant

[12.735] One the main objectives of the IATA scheme is to avoid the increasing cost, delay and frustration of litigation trying to establish misconduct [444] of the carrier in order to break the Article 22 limits ([12.650] above). With removal of the Article 22 limits on Article 17 damages such litigation will in future be confined to cargo cases.

5th jurisdiction added to Montreal Convention Article 28

[12.740] Proponents of the IATA scheme described the addition of the fifth jurisdiction in these terms: [445]

> This provision is key to assuring that passengers and their families receive compensatory damages commensurate with their reasonable expectations. The law of the passenger's domicile is the law around which he or she made plans before the accident, the law where (in the event of death), the estate will be probated and where the passenger's survivors will most likely continue to live. [446]

Aviation has spread so widely it has long been impossible to reach consensus on a universal limit or absolute measure of damages for death or personal injury. By adding the fifth jurisdiction, the IATA scheme taps into a formula which in most cases will be fairer and more convenient. Unfortunately, as discussed below, there must be some doubts about its legality.

---

438   *Montreal Convention*, Art 17(2).
439   Not available under the *Montreal Convention*.
440   There is presumed unlimited liability for negligence or other wrongful acts under *Montreal Convention*, Art 21(2).
441   Under the Montreal Agreement 1966 carriers in the US were required to waive this.
442   *Montreal Convention*, Art 21(2).
443   *Montreal Convention*, Art 21(2).
444   "Wilful misconduct" under *Warsaw*, "recklessly with intention" under *Warsaw-Hague*, Art 20.
445   *Montreal Convention*, Art 33.
446   American Transport Association application to US Department of Transport approval of the scheme.

Legal basis of the scheme

[12.745] Authority for the scheme comes from the Warsaw system, Article 22(1), which provides that by special contract the carrier and passenger may agree upon a higher limit of liability.[447] This will usually be done through the passenger ticket, which under Article 1(2) is prima facie (but not conclusive) evidence of the terms of the contract[448]. As discussed in [12.710], the ordinary principles of contract law (ticket cases) will determine whether or not the MIA terms have been effectively included in the contract. It will take some time before knowledge of the terms is so widespread that notice is presumed and even longer before they become part of the custom of the trade. Many passengers are still not aware of the limits under the Warsaw system. However, as the MIA terms are generally more favourable to the passenger than the Warsaw system terms,[449] a passenger is unlikely to challenge them on this basis.

Could a carrier or its insurers avoid the MIA terms because they have not been effectively incorporated into the contract on ticket case principles, for example because the passenger has inadequate notice, language skills, age or capacity? Passengers are unlikely to make admissions against their own interest on this to assist the carrier. Estoppel would appear to require the passenger to have similar knowledge of the terms to that required to incorporate them into the contract.

Do the IIA and MIA provide a sufficient legal basis for the special terms even if they are not incorporated into the contract between carrier and passenger? This issue is especially important between 14 February 1997, when the MIA was declared effective, and the date when each carrier:

(a) introduces the documents and systems to incorporate the terms into their conditions of carriage and tariffs; and

(b) organises insurance cover for the increased liability.

The IIA is in wider and more general terms than the MIA and it does not specify the 100,000 SDR threshold which marks the transition between strict and presumed liability under the MIA. Nevertheless the IIA does clearly establish the general agreement to waive the limit on liability and the further details and method agreed are clearly enough established through the MIA. However these are agreements among carriers for the benefit of passengers who are not themselves parties to the agreements. Traditionally, privity of contract would prevent passengers from suing directly on the agreements to enforce the rights in England.[450] This is to be contrasted with the long-standing position in the United States[451] and more recently in Australia[452] where passengers may well be able to enforce the rights even though they are not parties to the agreement.[453]

Is the so-called fifth jurisdiction provision legal? IIA clause 1 and MIA optional clause II.1 purport to allow the law of the domicile of the passenger to determine recoverable

---

[447] *Montreal Convention*, Art 25.
[448] *Montreal Convention*, Art 3(1).
[449] Apart from the *Montreal Convention 1999*.
[450] *Beswick v Beswick* (1968) AC 58.
[451] *Lawrence v Fox* 20 NY 268 (1859).
[452] *Trident Insurance v McNeice Bros* (1988) 165 CLR 107.
[453] Consider also statutory provisions such as s 55 of the *Property Law Act 1974* (Qld) which grant third party beneficiaries similar rights of enforcement.

compensatory damages. While this is likely to be fairer and more convenient for the plaintiff passenger, it is not one of the four jurisdictions from which the plaintiff must choose under Article 28.[454] This appears to directly offend *Warsaw Convention 1929*, Article 32 [455] which provides that:

> Any clause contained in the contract and all special agreements entered into before the damage occurred by which the parties purport to infringe the rules laid down by this convention, whether by deciding the law to be applied, or by altering the rules as to jurisdiction, shall be null and void.

Thus again it appears that a carrier or its insurers could avoid this clause in the MIA even if appears to be agreed and included it in their conditions of carriage.

Implications for travel agents and tour operators

[12.750] In [12.630] above the potential liability of a travel agent or tour operator under the Guadalajara Convention was discussed. It was noted that a travel agent or tour operator who contracts as principal with the passenger for air travel will be a contracting carrier under Article I and thus personally liable jointly and severally with the actual carrier to the passenger by virtue of Article II under the Warsaw system rules and limits. It was also noted that under Article III the acts and omissions of an actual carrier are deemed to be those of a travel agent or tour operator who is a contracting carrier.

When these principles are applied to the Passenger Liability Agreements some very important issues arise for travel agents and tour operators. It would appear that they too become liable to the passenger for the actual carrier's waiver of limits and defences under the Warsaw system. Article III(1) which makes the contracting carrier liable for the acts or omissions of the actual carrier is in similar terms to Article III(2) which provides for the converse. However Article III(2) goes on to also provide:

> Any special agreement under which the contracting carrier assumes obligations not imposed by the Warsaw Convention or any waiver of rights conferred by that Convention ... shall not affect the actual carrier unless agreed to by him.

There is no such proviso to the contracting carrier's liability for the actual carrier's acts or missions under Article III(1). On a plain meaning interpretation of the provision it would appear that the contracting carrier is liable on the terms set by the actual carrier.

This conclusion is reinforced if, as is usual, the travel agent's or tour operator's brochure or contract with the passenger states: "The carriage of passengers and baggage by the carrier is performed subject to the conditions of carriage endorsed on the relevant travel tickets and documents issued by the carrier." Such a provision, which is designed to ensure the carrier's limitation conditions apply to protect the travel agent and tour operator, would have the unwelcome effect of expressly binding them to the carrier's waiver of Warsaw system limits and defences under the IATA scheme. Could the travel agent or tour operator alter this term and try and avoid responsibility for an actual carrier's waiver of defences or limits? This would be difficult to enforce because Article IX prohibits contracting out.

Under Article VII the passenger or the passenger's representatives may sue the travel agent or tour operator with or without the actual carrier. While any rights to indemnity against the party at fault are preserved by Article X, this may be of little comfort if the actual carrier or its

---

454 *Montreal Convention*, Art 33.
455 Reinforced by *Warsaw Convention*, Art 24.

insurer is unable or unwilling to pay. At the least, travel agents and tour operators should insist that the actual carrier is insured and that the policy is extended to cover the contracting carrier. However the innocent travel agent and tour operator are still likely to be left with unreimbursed legal costs and some risk of bearing unlimited liability.

Thus the position of a travel agent or tour operator acting as a principal remains unsatisfactory under the scheme as presently structured.

Arbitration

[12.755] Another element of the IATA scheme provides for claims to be settled generally by arbitration rather than by the normal courts. The *Warsaw Convention*, Article 32 [456] expressly permits arbitration clauses for goods but is silent on the point for passengers and baggage and the strong implication is that it is not permitted for them. Further analysis must await the release of further details on the arbitration scheme.

Montreal encapsulates the IATA scheme reforms

[12.760] As mentioned, the Montreal Convention reflects the IATA reforms and they are now promulgated as international law between contracting states. However the IATA reforms are still quite relevant wherever the origin or destination or both countries have not ratified the Montreal Convention.

Liability to Third parties

[12.765] Aircraft accidents often cause death, injury and damage to property on the ground. [457] The *Rome Convention 1952* attempted to provide a standard approach to liability on this by imposing strict liability. However, it has unreasonably low limits and has not been updated (rather like Warsaw system). [458] Australia and most developed countries have renounced it and introduced alternative legislation. [459]

The disastrous events that took place on September 11, 2001, highlighted weaknesses in carrier third party liability including:

(a) the enormous death, injury and damage to property; and

(b) the impossibility for carriers to obtain insurance.

These observations forced more international action and resulted in ICAO now sponsoring two new conventions to modernise this area of carriers' liability. These conventions were finalised at the diplomatic conference in April 2009 and are called:

- *Unlawful Interferences Convention 2009,*
- *General Risks Convention 2009.*

Unlawful Interferences Convention 2009

[12.770] The *Unlawful Interferences Convention 2009* includes terrorism activities and imposes on carriers:

- strict liability;

---

456 *Montreal Convention* Art 34.
457 For example, the Lockerbie disaster in Scotland in December 1988 when 11 people on the ground were killed; September 11, 2001 terrorist attack which killed almost 3000 people in the World Trade Centre.
458 Only 49 signatories at May 2009.
459 *Damage By Aircraft Act 1999* (Cth) and State equivalents.

- capped to limits based on the weight of the aircraft (SDR 0.75m to SDR 700m);
- liability of all defendants is channelled through the carrier for convenience;
- funded by a levy on all passengers and cargo.

General Risks Convention 2009

[12.775] The *General Risks Convention 2009* applies principles similar to the *Montreal Convention 1999*. That is:

- strict liability to a threshold (limits as in [12.765] above based on weight of aircraft)
- unlimited liability unless the carrier proves it is not negligent or the damage is solely due to the negligence of another party.

Exercise

A Frightful Flight

- A and B took a Garuda Airlines flight Sydney to Bali via Darwin.
- Late departure because flight from Bali was 2 hours late (as usual).
- Transit in Darwin did not coincide with the flight of A and B's daughter, D, so they missed meeting at the airport to celebrate D's 18th birthday. A, B and D's Travel Agent had carefully selected and recommended this route for that purpose as it was so important to them.
- Severe air turbulence between Darwin and Bali and A damaged her laptop and B, whose seatbelt was unfastened, broke his left arm when the plane was thrown around violently. "Fasten seat belt" sign was not working since Sydney and B, listening to his iPod, did not hear the pilot's warning.
- C sitting next to A and B was on her way to the Maldives.
- Weather foul in Bali and pilot was advised by air traffic control to circle until it cleared. Pilot was keen to save fuel, meet deadlines and secure his bonus so he decided to try and land straight away. Plane overshot the runway and A and C were killed, B broke his right arm. Destroyed several houses in the local village and several villagers were killed and injured.
- Assume:
    - Indonesia has ratified the Warsaw Convention and the Rome Convention.
    - The Maldives have ratified the Montreal Convention.
    - Garuda has not implemented the IATA Intercarrier Agreement.
    - Its booking conditions are in the form circulated.

Advise A, B and C and their dependents.
Advise the local villagers.
Advise the Travel Agent.
Advise Garuda Airlines.

CHAPTER 13

Traveller Accommodation

[13.10]	COMMON INNKEEPERS		400
[13.10]	Common Law		400
[13.10]	History		400
	[13.15]	*The Innkeepers case*	400
[13.20]	Current position		401
[13.25]	Definitions		402
[13.50]	Rights and duties of innkeepers at common law		406
	[13.65]	*Garzilli (Connie Francis) v Howard Johnson's Motor Lodges Inc*	408
	[13.90]	*Irving v Heferen*	414
[13.95]	Infra hospitium		415
[13.100]	Special contracts: exclusion or limitation of liability		415
	[13.105]	*Olley v Marlborough Court*	416
	[13.110]	*Williams v Linnitt*	417
[13.120]	LEGISLATION		419
[13.120]	International		419
[13.125]	Australian Consumer Law guarantees and prohibition on exclusion or limitation		420
[13.130]	Innkeepers legislation		420
[13.155]	Holiday rental		424
[13.180]	ADMINISTRATION AND REGULATION OF TRAVELLER ACCOMMODATION		427
[13.180]	International		427
[13.180]	IHA		427
[13.185]	IYHA		428
[13.190]	National		428

[13.05] This chapter discusses the special rights and duties of accommodation providers under the ancient innkeepers' doctrine and the modifications made to these rules by legislation in most States. The structure and headings in this chapter are similar to those used in the previous chapter to highlight the interesting parallels between the laws governing traveller accommodation and the laws governing passenger transport.

COMMON INNKEEPERS

Common Law

History

[13.10] The common law on innkeepers, like that on carriers, is derived from ancient Roman law which prescribed special rights and duties for those providing travellers with essential services, particularly shipowners, innkeepers and stable keepers.[1] In those ancient times travel was dangerous and carriers and innkeepers were notorious for exploiting and robbing their customers, who were particularly vulnerable given the conditions of the time.[2] Proof of fault was difficult especially if they secretly connived with any of the numerous pirates, robbers and highwaymen[3] who preyed upon travellers. The practical solution devised at Roman law was to impose strict duties and responsibilities upon carriers and innkeepers.[4] The same Roman rules, survived by custom throughout the Dark Ages, emerged in medieval common law in one of the earliest recorded court cases.[5] This case was heard in 1368 – coincidentally (perhaps), the same year in which Chaucer began to write *The Canterbury Tales*, one of which (The Nonne Preestes Tale) concerns an unfortunate traveller who is robbed and murdered by an innkeeper.[6]

The Innkeepers case

[13.15] *The Innkeepers case* (1368) YB 42 Edw III 11 No 13

...The said Thomas...complains...that...according to the law and custom of the king's realm innkeepers, who keep common inns for the accommodation of men travelling through the districts where the inns are situated and staying in them, are bound to look after the goods of those who are staying in the said inns, day and night, without impairment or loss, so that...loss may not in any way befall such guests.

... [C]ertain malefactors...broke at night with force and arms, that is to say, with swords etc, into a room in which Thomas, on a journey to London..., was accommodated within such an inn...at Huntingdon, and took and carried away the said Thomas's goods and chattels namely, one belt, a seal with a silver chain, one sword with buckler, linen and woollen cloths and one dagger to the

---

1   *Justinian's Institutes* published in 533 AD codified the edicts on *Nautae, Caupone and Stabularii* which were developed by the Praetors (Roman magistrates) from 500 BC. The edict Receptum provided that a shipowner, innkeeper or stablekeeper, who takes charge of property belonging to a traveller, is answerable for such property strictly unless he can prove the loss was caused by the traveller's own negligence or inevitable accident.

2   Travellers' problems with innkeepers feature prominently in literature. For example, the Bible records the humble beginnings of Jesus Christ, born in the stable of a common inn; Chaucer describes the innkeeper who accompanied him, in *Canterbury Tales*; and consider also the confessions of the Master of the House in *Les Miserables*.

3   See Alfred Noyes (1880-1958), *The Highwayman*, which describes one such sinister character.

4   See DS Bogen, "Ignoring History: the liability of ships' masters, innkeepers and stablekeepers under Roman Law" (1992) (July) 36 *American Journal of Legal History* 326-320 for an excellent discussion of Roman law on this subject.

5   For more recent applications of this doctrine see *Turner v Queensland Motels Pty Ltd* [1968] Qd R 189 at 197 per Hart J; *Burns v Royal Hotel (St Andrews) Ltd* (1957) Scots Law Times 53 at 56 per Lord Guthrie. However, some authors deny the connection.

6   WW Skeat (ed), *The poems of Geofrey Chaucer* (Oxford University Press, London, 1912), p 545, [4174]-[4252].

The Innkeepers case cont.

value of four pounds, as well as nine pounds of the king's money..., in contravention of the king's peace, whereby he says that he is wronged and has suffered loss to the value of fifteen pounds... And [the innkeeper's stableman, says that he]...provided Thomas and his servants with a room with adequate locks...and that at that time they expressed themselves content with the said room, and he says that the said inn was adequately barred etc, so that Thomas lost no goods or chattels by his negligence, as he complains.

And after the arguments and answers of the parties had been read and examined, it is awarded that Thomas is to recover thirteen pounds from [the innkeeper] for the aforesaid chattels as well as forty shillings for the damages awarded to him on the aforesaid account... [7]

Medieval travelling conditions had changed little from Roman times and the common law took the same practical approach to making travel safer:

- remove the incentive to rob by making carriers and innkeepers strictly liable for traveller's property;
- also make them responsible (fault based) for travellers' personal safety;
- impose a duty to provide travellers with transport and accommodation so they cannot leave a traveller stranded and vulnerable;
- in return provide innkeepers and carriers with a lien over travellers' property to secure the costs of services provided.

Current position

[13.20] Although travelling conditions today have changed dramatically the same rules, with statutory modifications and variations from place to place, are still in force in most common law and civil law countries. At common law these special rules for the "common callings" of carriers and innkeepers are independent of the laws of contract, tort and bailment which may also apply.[8] In Civil law countries the rules derived directly from the Roman law edict.[9] In other legal systems, such as in Bedouin customary law, similar principles apply.[10]

In transport, international conventions have achieved considerable uniformity (see Chapter 12). Efforts by UNIDROIT since the 1930s to achieve international uniformity on innkeepers' laws have so far been unsuccessful (see [13.120]). National reform and uniformity have also proved to be elusive.[11]

Considering the developments which have taken place in transport, accommodation and hospitality since the adoption of these rules and the impact now of communications, banking and insurance.

---

7   The extracts are taken from another report of the case in MS Arnold (ed), Selden Society, *Select Cases of trespass from the King's courts 1307-1399* (London, 1985). There is considerable inconsistency between the two reports although the Selden Society (Vol 1, p lxvi note 507) claims they are the same case.

8   In other words, the rules are derived indirectly from Roman law through the "custom of the realm". See Hart J in *Turner v Queensland Motels Pty Ltd* [1968] Qd R 189 at 197.

9   See Lord Guthrie in *Burns v Royal Hotel (St Andrews) Limited* (1957) Scotts Law Times 53 at 56.

10 Bedouin law was the product of harsh conditions in the desert where survival was difficult. The whole system was based on honour, honesty, trust and respect. In hospitality the "tent" was protected to a line in front where the camels lay and a stranger (even if a criminal) could seek refuge (and hospitality) with a family for up to 3 days before being turned out into the desert again. Source: Dr S Al Sudairy: *Justice Among the Bedouins* (Thesis).

11 TC Atherton, "Innkeepers' liability for guests' property: contracting out is against the law" (1996) 24(6) *Australian Business Law Review* 448-462, 462.

- Are travellers still vulnerable?
- Is the strict liability rule still appropriate?
- What other ways are there now of dealing with the risks?

To put this into perspective, in 2007, the World Bank sponsored a private sector tourism industry forum in Laos, a developing country, and one recommendation was the introduction of Tourism Police in that country because:

- In recent years there has been an increase in the number of thefts committed against tourists especially in guesthouses and hotels. The stealing of money and valuables left in hotel rooms has become a real problem in certain tourist places.
- Often the offence is committed with the knowledge of when the client will check out – the tourist who needs to continue his trip (by boat, flight or bus) is helpless and has no time or means to call the police.
- Often the tourist receives little support from the guesthouse or hotel where the theft occurred. The security Laos was able to offer a tourist in the past was one of the country's positive points and travellers felt particularly welcome.
- This feeling of security is being threatened by a few criminals and these crimes affect not just the tourists but the country's tourism industry and Laos' image as a whole.

Definitions

[13.25] The special rights and duties under the common law innkeepers' doctrine apply only between innkeepers and guests. These and other associated terms have technical meanings at common law. These meanings have evolved through the dramatic changes in customs and technology over the last 1,000 years.

"Inn"

[13.30] An inn is an establishment which provides accommodation, food and beverage to the travelling public. Accommodation must be available [12] though it may not necessarily be required by every customer. [13] At common law liquor is neither necessary nor sufficient to make an establishment an inn. [14] Food, though originally essential, may no longer be necessary. The Supreme Court of Victoria (O'Brien J) held in *Oakford Executive Apartments v Van der Top* [15] that an establishment of self-contained executive apartments was an inn even though there was limited food service. It is arguable that with self-catering apartments let to travellers or with the proliferation of independent restaurants and fast food outlets, food service should no longer be necessary to qualify an establishment as an inn. [16]

Traveller accommodation has evolved from the ancient concepts of the inn which were revived in the Renaissance period (14th and 15th centuries) and developed through the coffee house (from 1650) and the hotel (from the 1790s) then quickly in this century to include the

---

12   *Doe d Pitt v Laming* (1814) 4 Camp 73 NP: Held that coffee house was not an inn; *Miller v Federal Coffee Palace* (1889) 15 VLR 30: Held that Coffee Palace with accommodation was an inn.
13   *Williams v Linnitt* [1951] 1 KB 565: Held that innkeeper was liable for stolen car of a local farmer who went to inn for "temporary refreshment".
14   *Webster v Orlitz* [1917] VLR 107: Held that an inn could continue the other parts of its business on Sunday despite a prohibition on liquor trading.
15   *Oakford Executive Apartments v Van der Top* (Unreported, Vic Sup Ct, O'Brien J, 23 January 1992).
16   In *Gemmell v Goldsworthy* [1942] SASR 55 an innkeeper who had food service facilities was held liable for damages for failure to supply food. Would unavailability of food facilities be a reasonable defence?

motel (from 1926) and now serviced apartments and resorts.[17] The common law concept has adapted this and an "inn" today would include most hotels, motels,[18] backpacker hostels, serviced apartments (as discussed above), resorts and other establishments which provide accommodation for the travelling public. Where accommodation is restricted to owners (for example in timeshare resorts) or members of a club (such as YHA hostels) then the establishment would not generally be an inn as it does not provide accommodation to the travelling public. However, to the extent that these establishments provide their accommodation to the travelling public, without such restrictions (as many now do), they would qualify as inns for the transactions.

"Innkeeper"

[13.35] The innkeeper is the proprietor or person carrying on the innkeeping business, that is generally the person who is in possession of the premises. Thus where the establishment is leased to the operator the innkeeper would be the lessee rather than the lessor/owner. This is not affected by the fact that individual rooms will be occupied by guests because guests usually have a mere licence to occupy rather than legal possession (see discussion in [13.45] below on lodgers).

Where the establishment is run by one of the hotel operator chains, such as Hilton, Sheraton or Hyatt, who are usually mere agents of the owner, it is considered that the owner as principal would be the real innkeeper at law (see [11.165]ff). Similarly if a company runs the inn and employs a person as manager the company rather than its employee is the innkeeper even if the manager holds the liquor licence.[19] Where the hotel operator is a subcontractor the position is less clear, but in any event the operator invariably takes an express indemnity from the owner for any liability which it may incur from this position so the owner would still be ultimately liable.

Less clear still is the question of who is the innkeeper in the more recent operating structure for apartment buildings (and now strata title hotels) where units are individually owned but collectively let under management rights or some similar arrangement. As mentioned above these establishments have been held to be an inn where they provide accommodation to the travelling public: *Oakford Apartments case* ([13.40] below). In that case the operator, Oakford Apartments, was taken to be the innkeeper but the nature of the operating structure is not apparent from the report. Again, the uncertainty over responsibility can be resolved by appropriate indemnities as between the managing agent and the owners.[20]

"Guest"

[13.40] The innkeepers' doctrine applies only where the customer is a "guest" rather than a "lodger". Historically a "guest" was a traveller who arrived at an inn and demanded food or accommodation. In contrast, a "lodger" was a person who stayed as a friend or tenant of the

---

17   Early dates are from DE Lundberg, *The Hotel and Restaurant Business* (3rd ed, CBI Publishing Boston, 1979), pp 24-25.
18   *Turner v Queensland Motels Pty Ltd* [1968] Qd R 189; *Irving v Heferen* [1995] 1 Qd R 255.
19   *Dixon v Birch* (1873) LR 8 Exch 135.
20   See also the definition of "innkeeper" in *Traveller Accommodation Providers (Liability) Act 2001* (Qld), s 8(4)(a): "an accommodation provider, and only an accommodation provider, is an innkeeper".

landlord on a special contract.[21] This relatively clear distinction was blurred for a while in Australia as the courts adapted the innkeepers' doctrine to the age of telecommunications and intermediaries. In these authors' view it is now relatively clear that a traveller will be a "guest" within the meaning of the innkeepers' doctrine even if accommodation is booked in advance, through a travel agent or as part of a package holiday ([11.220]ff discusses the different possible relationships). It is instructive to examine how the innkeepers' doctrine has evolved in this way in Australia.

The confusion began in 1947 with the Full Court of New South Wales case of *Ex parte Coulson; Re Jones*[22] where Davidson J (at 184) stated in dicta that:

> From the earliest times a "guest" of an inn was a person who, without prior or special contract, arrived at the premises and demanded food and sleeping accommodation, and was received on reasonable terms. A "lodger" on the contrary, was one who arrived at the inn and was received on the terms of his contract.

This formulation was applied too literally by the majority of the Full Court of Victoria in 1953 in *Daniel v Hotel Pacific*.[23] Daniel and 12 other customers of a seaside resort hotel at Lorne sought to recover from the hotel as innkeeper for the loss of their money and other valuables deposited in the hotel safe which was robbed during their Christmas holiday stay. The majority applied Davidson J's test literally and held that the plaintiffs were not "guests" because they had made prior bookings for their accommodation for a fixed period by telephone or post and so arrived and were received on their "special contract". Thus innkeepers' strict liability did not apply. The hotel was not negligent and was therefore not liable.

In a strong dissent Sholl J commented (at 463):

> The use in modern times of the telephone, telegraph and the post is so universal, and accommodation at hotels is often so much in demand, that it would seem mere anachronistic eccentricity for the law to impose on a hotelkeeper a greater duty towards a small class of mere casual arrivals, who come without any notice at all, and are fortunate enough to obtain accommodation, than to the many who have the common sense and the courtesy to send a prior communication; or to impose towards a person who refuses to state the duration of his stay a greater duty than towards one who is prepared to book for a definite time.

His Honour (at 467) formulated the following test which, in the light of the subsequent decisions, must be regarded as the better view of the law:

> The test to be adopted to distinguish when a person is or has become a "lodger" or "boarder", and not a "guest", for the purpose of this branch of the law, should, I think, be…whether there has been initially or subsequently – ie before, on, or at some time after the visitor's reception – and either expressly or by implication, an arrangement
>
> (a) which contemplates or involves an intended "permanence" of stay, ie a stay for a long time, whether defined, or left indefinite as to duration…; especially

---

21   At common law a guest may stay on and become a boarder or lodger. Usually a guest or boarder or lodger will have a mere licence to occupy the room rather than a tenancy. For example, the *Residential Tenancies Act 1994* (Qld) prescribes rights and remedies for residential tenancies in addition to all other rights and remedies. A residential tenancy is a right of occupancy for residential purposes and premises can include part of a hotel or motel: s 26. However it does not apply to a right of occupancy for holiday purposes (generally less than six weeks): s 21. This would exclude most "guests" for innkeepers' liability purposes and does not apply to a boarder or a lodger: s 22. In practice the provision causes problems for the industry when live-in managers are dismissed but cannot be evicted immediately as required so a new manager can take over and continue the operation.

22   *Ex parte Coulson; Re Jones* (1947) 48 SR (NSW) 178.

23   *Daniel v Hotel Pacific* [1953] VLR 447.

(b) if accompanied by the absence of any other permanent home…

(c) or which in some other way makes the visitor a member of the innkeeper's household in a character differing from that of an ordinary hotel guest…

In 1968 the Full Court of Queensland in *Turner v Queensland Motels Pty Ltd* [24] dealt with a couple travelling from Adelaide who had made through a business associate a prior booking at a motel in Brisbane for ten days with the possibility of an extension. The booking was made by telephone and was confirmed by letter. The court cited passages with approval from *Daniel v Hotel Pacific* but distinguished it on its particular facts. They held that despite the prior booking through an agent they were "guests", so that the innkeeper was strictly liable for the theft of money from their room. Hart J (with whom Hanger J agreed) defined "special contract" in these terms (at 200):

> It seems to me that what…[was] meant by a special contract was, at the very least, some contract whereby a person is received on terms other than those on which the owner of an inn holds out that he will receive all travellers, who are willing to pay a price adequate to the sort of accommodation provided and who come in a situation in which they are fit to be received.

In 1973 in *Theeman v Forte Properties Pty Ltd* [25] the Full Court of New South Wales was faced with a case on identical material facts to *Daniel v Hotel Pacific*. The court unanimously upheld the finding that the Theemans were guests for the purposes of innkeepers' liability. Hope JA (with whom Moffat AP and Reynolds JA agreed) acknowledged (at 429) that it was a question of fact but expressly disagreed with the comments by the majority in *Daniel v Hotel Pacific* that a prior booking for a fixed period precluded a person from being a guest. His Honour agreed with Sholl J's interpretation of the authorities and with Hart J's definition in *Turner v Queensland Motels* of what is meant by a "special contract".

The issue returned to the Victorian Supreme Court in 1992 in *Oakford Executive Apartments v Van der Top*. [26] In that case two apartment-style rooms were robbed. The occupiers were visitors from overseas. One room had been booked in advance by a son for ten nights. The other had been booked in advance by an employer for an indefinite period while the employee sought permanent accommodation. One occupant from each room signed the pro forma "Reservation Agreement". O'Bryan J discussed *Daniel v Hotel Pacific*, noting the strong dissenting judgment of Sholl J, and quoted with approval the passages from his judgment referred to above. He also agreed with Hart J's definition of a special contract and upheld the finding that the occupants of both rooms were "guests" for the purposes of innkeepers' liability.

Thus it is now clear that prior booking by any means of communication through a travel agent for a fixed or indefinite period will not preclude a traveller from being regarded as a "guest". Nor, it is submitted, should the position be any different if the accommodation is arranged by a tour operator as part of a "package". A holidaymaker on a package tour is an itinerant traveller and cannot sensibly be regarded as a "lodger" or "boarder".

"Lodger"

[13.45] As mentioned above, a "lodger" is a person who stays as a friend or tenant of the landlord on a special contract. The distinction from a guest is usually clear. Thus in *Alldis v*

---

24   *Turner v Queensland Motels Pty Ltd* [1968] Qd R 189.
25   *Theeman v Forte Properties Pty Ltd* [1973] 1 NSWLR 418.
26   *Oakford Executive Apartments v Van der Top* (unreported, Vic Sup Ct, O'Brien J, 23 January 1992).

Huxley,[27] where a horse trainer made a special arrangement for board and lodging of himself, his staff and horses at a lump sum per week and stayed for some months, the members of the group were held to be lodgers and the relationship was landlord and tenant, not innkeeper and guest. Similarly in *Hanson v Barwise*[28] a husband and wife who moved from one part of Mackay to another to board at the George Hotel, bringing with them their own linen and household articles and paying rent monthly in arrears, were held to be mere lodgers (boarders), not travellers (guests).

At common law a guest may stay on and become a lodger (for example, a boarder or tenant as in the examples above) and from that point the innkeepers' doctrine will cease to apply to them. Like a guest, a boarder usually has a mere licence to occupy the room rather than a tenancy.

The advent of serviced apartment accommodation for travellers has blurred some of the traditional distinctions and practices. Because a guest usually has a mere licence to occupy a room and is not a tenant, traveller accommodation is sold mainly by travel agents rather than real estate agents: see Chapter 11. However with the sale of short-term occupancy of self-contained apartments to travellers there is an overlap of responsibility and both types of agent are often involved. If sold by a travel agent the occupant would usually be a mere licensee and the innkeepers' doctrine would usually apply. If sold by a real estate agent the apartment may be let on a tenancy for the short term or from week to week so that the occupant has possession and is a lodger as discussed above. In that case the innkeepers' doctrine does not apply and the arrangement may be subject to the residential tenancy laws.[29]

The residential tenancy laws provide occupants with special additional rights and remedies, including termination and eviction procedures, which would be cumbersome and unworkable for operators of traveller accommodation. The impact of these laws on travel and tourism varies from State to State. For example in Queensland[30] a residential tenancy is a right of occupancy for residential purposes and premises can include part of a hotel or motel.[31] However it does not apply to a right of occupancy for holiday purposes (generally less than six weeks),[32] which would exclude most "guests" for innkeepers' liability purposes, and it does not apply to a boarder or a lodger.[33] In practice the provisions have caused problems for the industry when live-in managers are dismissed but cannot be evicted immediately as required so a new manager can take over and continue the operation.

Rights and duties of innkeepers at common law

[13.50] The principal rights and duties of innkeepers at common law are outlined in the following discussion. It should be noted that, as with carriers, the common law rights and duties of innkeepers have been greatly modified by statute in several key ways. First, consumer protection legislation prohibits unconscionable, deceptive or misleading conduct and implies

---

27 *Alldis v Huxley* (1891) 8 WN (NSW) 23.
28 *Hanson v Barwise* [1930] QSR 285.
29 This was discussed in *Oakford Executive Apartments v Van der Top* (unreported, Vic Sup Ct, O'Brien J, 23 January 1992), p 9.
30 *Residential Tenancies Act 1994* (Qld). Also see *Residential Tenancies Act 1987* (NSW); *Residential Tenancies Act 1995* (SA); *Residential Tenancies Act 1997* (Vic); *Residential Tenancies Act 1997* (Tas); *Residential Tenancies Act 1987* (WA); *Residential Tenancies Act 1997* (ACT); *Residential Tenancies Act* (NT).
31 *Residential Tenancies Act 1994* (Qld), 26.
32 *Residential Tenancies Act 1994* (Qld), 21.
33 *Residential Tenancies Act 1994* (Qld), 22.

non-excludable warranties and conditions into many accommodation contracts (see generally, Chapter 9). Secondly, occupational, health and safety legislation often applies to the premises and equipment of the inn (see generally, Chapter 8). Thirdly, special Innkeepers legislation in most States limits the strict liability of the innkeeper and in some States grants a power of sale (see [13.130]ff on Innkeepers legislation).

Duty to receive and entertain guests

[13.55] Innkeepers have a common law duty to receive and entertain all travellers as guests and must not be selective or discriminatory.[34] Common carriers have a corresponding duty (see [12.20]). The innkeepers' duty to entertain involves supplying guests with accommodation, food and beverage at reasonable prices. Innkeepers are permitted to refuse on reasonable grounds, for example if the establishment is already fully occupied or booked out or if the traveller has a contagious disease or is otherwise in an unfit state to be entertained. For example in *Steiner v Magic Carpet Tours Pty Ltd*[35] the innkeeper was entitled to refuse to accommodate a guest in a drunken state even if there was a prior booking. Wrongful refusal is actionable in tort without proof of damage.[36] This duty has been confirmed in Australia in *Lambert v Monaghan*,[37] *Gemmell v Goldsworthy*[38] and by Lee J in a leading Queensland case of *Irving v Heferen*.[39]

No such duty is owed to a lodger.

Duty to take reasonable care for guest's safety

[13.60] Like carriers (see [12.35]), innkeepers do not insure the safety of their guests and their liability is based on fault. Innkeepers have a duty to take reasonable care for the safety of guests and this includes a warranty that the premises of the inn are as safe for the personal use of guests as reasonable care and skill can make them.[40] This duty has also been confirmed by the Australian courts in dicta in many cases such as *Nott v Maclurcan*[41] and *Irving v Heferen*.[42]

However the authors could not find an Australian case directly in point. Perhaps this is because the scope of liability as innkeeper appears to be little different from liability under the general law of tort, particularly negligence and occupier's liability. In Western Australia occupiers' liability for premises is prescribed by legislation[43] while liability for activities at the premises is preserved at common law according to the general law of negligence.[44] In States without such legislation, occupiers' liability has now been completely overtaken by the general law of negligence with the relationship between the parties establishing no more than the

---

34 Halsbury's Laws of England (4th ed, Butterworths, London, 1991), Vol 24, [1113].
35 Steiner v Magic Carpet Tours Pty Ltd (1984) ATPR40-490.
36 In Gemmell v Goldsworthy [1942] SASR 55 an innkeeper was held liable for damages for failure to supply food.
37 Lambert v Monaghan (1917) 19 WAR 99 at 101.
38 Gemmell v Goldsworthy [1942] SASR 55.
39 Irving v Heferen [1995] I Qd R 255 at 262.
40 Compare the duties of a travel agent or tour operator who selects (agent) or supplies (principal) accommodation for a guest (see [9.310] ff, [11.220] ff).
41 Nott v Maclurcan (1903) 20 WN (NSW) 135.
42 Irving v Heferen [1995] Qd R 255 at 261.
43 Occupiers Liability Act 1985 (WA).
44 Ogwo v Taylor [1988] AC 431; Revill v Newbery [1996] 2 WLR 239.

existence of an ordinary duty of care.[45] Arguably this is also happening to innkeepers' liability for the personal safety of guests; that is, that the innkeeper/guest relationship does no more than establish the ordinary duty of care.[46] See generally, Chapter 5. However in *Northern Sandblasting v Harris*[47] the High Court held a landlord liable to a tenant under a strict, non-delegable duty and the principle would appear to extend to traveller accommodation subject to the effect of the civil liability legislation[48] (for further discussion see [5.100]).

Where there is a contractual relationship between hotel and guest the reasonable care and fitness term would also be implied, probably under the general law (see Chapter 4). The *Trade Practices Act 1974* (Cth), s 74 used to imply a similar warranty into contracts for the supply of services to a consumer. Now, even without a contractual relationship ss 60 and 61 of the Australian Consumer Law provide a statutory guarantee in the supply of services such as those supplied by an innkeeper[49] (see [9.185]ff).

Garzilli (Connie Francis) v Howard Johnson's Motor Lodges Inc

[13.65] *Garzilli (Connie Francis) v Howard Johnson's Motor Lodges Inc* (1976) 419 F Supp 1219; NY 1976

Facts: The famous singer Connie Francis was sexually assaulted in her motel room. The assailant entered the room through a sliding patio door. Although the door appeared to be locked it was quite easily opened from the outside. There was evidence that the motel had been broken into four times previously through the patio doors and that safer locks had been ordered but had not yet been received and installed.

Decision: The New York District Court (Platt J) upheld the finding that the motel was responsible in negligence. Connie Francis was awarded almost US$2.5m for pain, suffering, mental anguish, humiliation and loss of earnings.

Postscript. This represents an interesting illustration of the relationship between legal responsibility and technology in risk management. The case sent a warning to US hoteliers to review their room security systems. The practice of using the same locks is flawed as guests could copy the key and use it to break in later. Even master keys were available for sale in the streets in front of hotels in some cities in the USA. The solution was relatively inexpensive. Computer card locks overcome these problems and they have been widely adopted in US traveller accommodation. In fact some travel agents in the USA now refuse to book hotels without this system for fear that they will also be held liable for negligent advice to clients. These principles apply to the Australian accommodation sector. Is it

---

45 *Australian Safeway Stores Pty Ltd v Zaluzna* (1987) 69 ALR 615 where the High Court approved this formulation by Dean J in *Hackshaw v Shaw* (1985) 155 CLR 614 at 662-663.
46 Compare *Chordas v Bryant* (Wellington) Pty Ltd (1988) FCR 91 and *Wormald v Robertson* (1992) Aust Torts Reports 81-180 where one patron was injured by another with a beer jug and the operator was found negligent in failing to act on complaints of unruly behaviour.
47 *Northern Sandblasting v Harris* (1997) 146 ALR 572.
48 Pursuant to that legislation, a person sued for breach of a non delegable duty will have their liability determined as if they were vicariously liable for the negligence of the person in connection with the performance of the work or task.
49 See T C Atherton, "Changes to TPA increase liability" (Nov 1992) 1(3) *Tourism and Travel Review* 7.

Garzilli (Connie Francis) v Howard Johnson's Motor Lodges Inc cont.

negligent not to adopt best practice in security? Do travel agents have a duty to warn or advise clients on this?

Duty to receive, stable and feed a guest's horse and receive a carriage

[13.70] It has always been an important part of innkeepers' duties to look after guests' means of transport. The common law has followed the development from the horse and buggy to the motor car and the transition is neatly marked in *Gresham v Lyon*: [50]

> It is clear on authority that today the keeper of a "common inn" is under obligation to provide accommodation not only for the guest himself, but for his motor car, as he was in the olden days obliged to provide accommodation for the traveller's gig and horse...

This has been confirmed in dicta in Australia. [51]

Arguably, innkeepers would now be justified in refusing to provide stabling and feed for a guest's horse, but it could make for an interesting test case in the appropriate circumstances. More practically, the question now arises whether innkeepers have a common law duty to provide adequate car parking space and porte-cochere and other facilities for motor coaches. Even here, planning laws now prescribe the minimum car parking space required and the innkeeper's self-interest dictates the facilities provided for motor coaches. It is not clear whether the usual carport facilities provided for each room by motels are the result of innkeepers' duty, planning laws or self-interest.

Motor vehicles, except in jurisdictions where they have been excluded by statute, also form a substantial part of guests' property for which innkeepers are strictly liable and over which they enjoy a lien under the rights and duties discussed below.

No such duty is owed to a lodger.

Duty to safeguard a guest's property

[13.75] At common law, innkeepers are in effect insurers of their guests' property. Common carriers have a corresponding duty (see [12.45]). Even if guests' property is lost or damaged (subject to comments below on damage) without their fault, innkeepers are held strictly liable. Their only defence is where the loss or damage is caused by one of the classic defences (the perils of travel) which also apply to common carriers:

- **act of God:** This comprises natural forces which could not reasonably have been foreseen or guarded against, for example earthquake, lightning, extraordinary weather; [52]
- **act of the Queen's enemies:** This covers acts of the state's enemies or seizure by public (for example customs) authorities; [53]

---

50   *Gresham v Lyon* [1954] 2 All ER 786 at 788 per McNair J.
51   Lee J in *Irving v Heferen* [1995] 1 Qd R 255 at 262: "In addition to the obligation to receive a traveller, an innkeeper is bound to receive, stable and feed a traveller's horse, receive his carriage (now his car), if facilities are available": *Williams v Linnitt* [1951] 1 KB 565.
52   In *Burns v Royal Hotel (St Andrews) Ltd* (1957) Scots Law Times 53 the innkeeper argued in defence that the fire was damnum fatale. Lord Guthrie (at 55) acknowledged that the defendant bore a heavy onus in proving Act of God but accepted that it could be shown indirectly by absence of fault as well as by proof of an independent cause. Further evidence was sought on the point.
53   The authors could find no modern cases on this point.

- **inherent vice:** This is an inherent fault or defect in the property, such as faulty packing or labelling or perishable goods; or
- **the guest's fault:** There are various aspects of this defence which warrant discussion as below. [54]

There is some doubt whether strict liability applies for mere damage as opposed to loss of a guest's property. Some English cases support strict liability; [55] others suggest proof of negligence is required. [56] In 1954, the Law Reform Committee (England) [57] reviewed the cases and concluded that there was no reason and no clear decision requiring a distinction, but acknowledged that there was some doubt about the matter. [58] The Australian cases all support strict liability and the authors support this view but could not find a case directly in point. [59]

It is difficult for an innkeeper to prove the defence that the loss or damage was the result of the guest's fault. [60] For example in *Shacklock v Ethorpe* [61] the guest placed her jewels in a jewel case, which she locked, but did not deposit the case in the security safe or lock her guest room. This was held not to be negligence on the part of the guest. There is also doubt about whether negligence of the guest is an absolute defence or whether the apportionment legislation would apply (see [15.150]). [62]

Innkeepers are generally responsible for all the property which a guest brings to the inn while it is infra hospitum; that is, within the precincts of the inn (see [13.95]). Property is not limited to goods or luggage, as it is with common carriers (see [12.40]). Thus it includes trade stock [63] and vehicles, whether or not they are owned by the guest or someone else. [64] However, as with common carriers, innkeepers are not responsible where the guest retains

---

54 Failure to heed a notice warning guests to deposit valuables with reception was held in one case to be sufficient evidence of negligence: *Jones v Jackson Ltd* (1873) 29 LT 399 but this decision should be confined to its facts: see *Carpenter v Haymarket Hotel Limited* [1930] TLR 11 discussed later. For a more usual example see *Shacklock v Ethorpe* (1939) 3 All ER 372 where the guest placed her jewels in a jewel case which she locked. She did not deposit them in the security safe or lock her guest room. This was held not to be negligence on the part of the guest. See also *Levy v Curran* (1909) 9 SR (NSW) 725 and compare the comments of Lord Esher MR in *Huntley v Bedford Hotel* with the comments of Hart J in *Turner v Queensland Motels*. These matters are reconciled in the discussion on Rules of the House in [13.80].

55 *Morgan v Ravey* (1861) 158 ER 109.

56 *Winkworth v Ravey* [1931] 1 KB (1861) 652; *Williams v Owen* [1956] ER 1.

57 Second Report (*Innkeepers' liability for property of travellers, guests and residents*), (1954) Cmnd 9161.

58 In England, the matter was then settled by the *Hotel Proprietors Act 1956* which does not distinguish between loss and mere damage.

59 Dicta in *O'Dea v O'Hara, South Australian Advertiser* 17 May 1895. The other cases concern the special case of fire where there is an independent strict liability for damage: *Nott v Maclurcan* (1903) 20 WN NSW 135 and *Kellett v Cowan* [1906] Qd St R 116.

60 The authors could find no modern cases on this point.

61 *Shacklock v Ethorpe* (1939) 3 All ER 372.

62 See Hart J in *Turner v Queensland Motels Pty Ltd* [1968] Qd R 189 at 201. Also note that the *Law Reform (Tortfeasors Contribution, Contributory Negligence, and Division of Chattels) Act 1952* (Qld) defines "fault" for which liability may be apportioned in terms of liability in tort. However innkeepers' liability is not founded in tort. Thus the Act may not apply leaving any negligence of the guest as an absolute defence to the innkeepers' liability. For a discussion of these issues see NE Palmer, *Bailment* (2nd ed, Law Book Co, Sydney, 1991), Ch 24. However note that some references to State innkeepers' laws are out of date.

63 In *Robin v Gray* [1895] 2 QB 501 the guest was a commercial traveller selling sewing machines owned by the company which employed the guest and the court upheld the innkeeper's lien.

64 In *Park v Berkley* (1930) 25 Tas LR 67 the guest brought a car to the inn on the last day of his stay and the innkeeper's lien was upheld against it even though it was on hire purchase.

exclusive possession of the property.[65] With common carriers this is achieved by limiting the definition of luggage (see [12.40]) but with innkeepers it is usually provided as a defence of the innkeeper. It covers similar situations, such as items worn or carried in a guest's pocket. Beyond that it is very difficult to prove that a guest has assumed exclusive responsibility for the property so as to relieve the innkeeper of responsibility.[66]

Innkeepers, unlike carriers, cannot limit or exclude liability for guests' property by contract or otherwise. It is a strict liability imposed under the common law innkeepers' doctrine and is independent of the law of contract, tort or bailment. Any attempt to limit or exclude it is void at common law (see [13.100]ff).[67]

The common law duty imposing strict and unlimited liability on an innkeeper for guests' property is extremely harsh. In many cases where the innkeeper is without fault, the result will be widely regarded as unjust.[68] It is difficult to find an equivalent liability cast upon any other commercial activity under contemporary law. A carrier may limit or exclude such liability at common law. Even an insurer limits its liability and is able to require an insured to take precautions and to describe the insured property and declare its value before accepting the risk (see Chapter 7). An innkeeper cannot and is left vulnerable to fraudulent claims by guests.[69]

For over a century, the harshness of these common law rules has been mitigated in most countries by Innkeepers legislation ([13.120]ff), which leaves an innkeeper liable for fault but limits the amount of strict liability. South Australia repealed its Innkeepers' legislation in 1985 and to date remains the only Australian State with unlimited strict liability for guests' property under the common law rules.[70] Some attempts have been made to exclude or limit this liability by notices setting out Conditions of Bailment. These are ineffective for several reasons, particularly because contracting out is prohibited at common law as discussed above.[71] The only solution is to reintroduce legislative limits.[72] In Western Australia, innkeepers' liability for guests' property applies incidentally on licensed premises only.[73]

No such duty applies to a lodger. The duties of an accommodation provider to a lodger's property is determined by the general law of contract, tort and bailment.

The prohibition on limiting or excluding liability for guests' property is to be contrasted with the innkeepers' rights to set and enforce reasonable Rules of the House.

---

[65] It is very difficult to prove that a guest has assumed exclusive responsibility for his property so as to relieve the innkeeper of responsibility. See dicta of Swift J in *Carpenter v Haymarket Hotel Ltd* [1930] TLR 11 at 12 discussed below.

[66] See dicta of Swift J in *Carpenter v Haymarket Hotel Ltd* [1930] TLR 11 at 12 discussed in [13.80].

[67] For a detailed discussion of this issue see TC Atherton, "Innkeepers' liability for guests' property: contracting out is against the law" (1996) 24(6) *Australian Business Law Review* 448-462.

[68] See the comments of Hart J in *Turner v Queensland Motels* mentioned below.

[69] Protecting innkeepers from fraudulent claims by guests was one of the reasons for the original Innkeepers Laws. See for example the recital to the *Innkeepers Liability Act 1863* (ENG).

[70] See TC Atherton, "Tourist accommodation operators beware: the Inns and outs of innkeepers' strict liability for guests' goods" (1996) 16(5) *Proctor* 4.

[71] These notices may also constitute a breach of s 29(m) of the Australian Consumer Law which prohibits false representations about the existence, exclusion or effect of any warranty, right or remedy.

[72] See TC Atherton, "Innkeepers' liability for guests' property: contracting out is against the law" (1996) 24(6) *Australian Business Law Review* 448-462.

[73] The *Liquor Control Act 1988* (WA) primarily regulates licensed premises and other matters related to liquor licensing.

Right to set Rules of the House

[13.80] Innkeepers have always had the right to set reasonable Rules of the House for guests at the inn. [74] Notice of them must be brought to the attention of guests, who are then bound to follow them. If they do not follow house rules, and thereby suffer loss, then that may establish negligence on the part of the guest which, as discussed in [13.75] above, is the innkeeper's most effective defence.

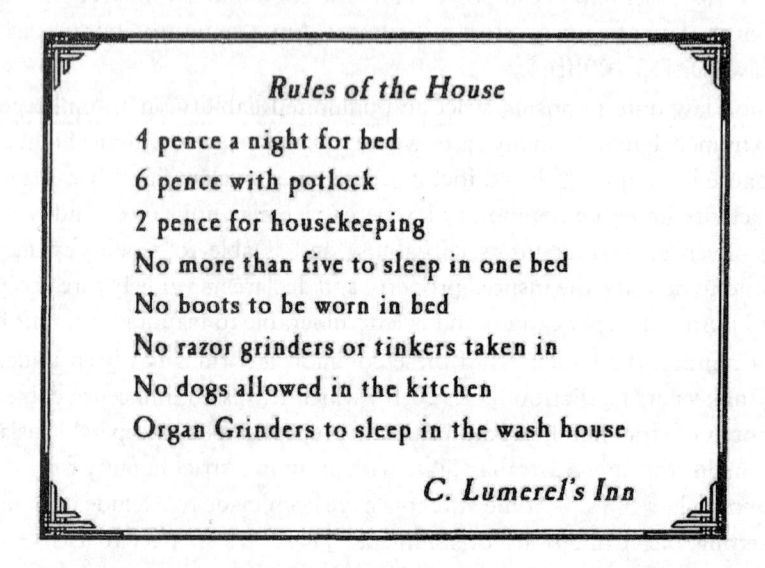

> **Rules of the House**
>
> 4 pence a night for bed
> 6 pence with potlock
> 2 pence for housekeeping
> No more than five to sleep in one bed
> No boots to be worn in bed
> No razor grinders or tinkers taken in
> No dogs allowed in the kitchen
> Organ Grinders to sleep in the wash house
>
> *C. Lumerel's Inn*

(A sign for a local inn of the Tudor period (1458-1603).) [75]

It is important to distinguish house rules from attempts to limit or exclude innkeepers' liability by contract, which are declared void as contrary to public policy (see [13.100]ff). House rules do not operate contractually, but failure to comply is evidence of negligence on the part of the guest which if proved, is effective to relieve the innkeeper from liability. US authors JR Goodwin and JM Rovelstad frame the distinction in this way: [76]

> An innkeeper is free to develop and place into use reasonable rules to be followed by guests in the inn. Once a guest has notice of such rules, he must obey them. If he fails to do so, and if loss results, then the guest is negligent because of the failure to observe the rules and recovery is barred. However an innkeeper cannot use such rules to avoid duties imposed by the law, such as the duty to receive, the duty to be careful and the duty to be responsible for the loss of the goods of a guest caused by the negligence of the innkeeper.
>
> A common rule found in all inns is that valuables must be deposited at the front desk if the innkeeper is to be responsible for them. If a guest has notice of such a rule, failure to abide by it would relieve the innkeeper of liability for the loss. Such rules apply to excessive amounts of cash or jewellery when not being carried by the guest. They would not apply to clothes and other items that a guest constantly uses, such as a wrist watch.

---

74 The right of an innkeeper to set reasonable Rules of the Inn has long been recognised in the common law. See for example the 1566 Queen's Bench case *Saunders v Spencer* (1566) 73 ER 591.
75 DE Lundberg, *The Hotel and Restaurant Business* (3rd ed, CBI Publishing Boston, 1979), p 16, Figures 1-2.
76 J R Goodwin and J M Rovelstad *Travel and Lodging Law: Principles, Statutes and Cases* (Grid Publishing, Ohio, 1980), p 306. See also TA Dickerson, *Travel Law* (Law Journal Seminars Press, NY, 1993), [4.04(3)].

This distinction rationalises some otherwise apparently conflicting decisions and judicial comments. For example in *Jones v Jackson* [77] failure to heed a warning notice (house rule) and lodge money with reception was found to be negligent. In *Carpenter v Haymarket Hotel Limited* [78] failure to deposit a ring was found to be not negligent because the notice (house rule) was not reasonable and to the extent that the notice purported to exclude liability contractually it was void. It also reconciles the comments of Hart J in *Turner v Queensland Motels* [79] with the comments of Lord Esher MR in *Huntley v Bedford Hotel*. [80] Innkeepers have the right to specify safety precautions required of guests in respect of their property in any Notice of Bailment but not to use the Notice to limit and exclude liability contractually which is void.

The distinction indicates a better approach to risk management. It would be prudent for innkeepers to establish formal house rules to reinforce the system for the security of guests' property. Not only will this reduce the chance of property being lost, it will also reduce the innkeeper's liability for losses which do occur. If the guest has not followed the house rules it will be easier for the innkeeper to establish that the guest has been negligent, which is the innkeeper's only practical means of defence. Ideally the accommodation industry organisations (see [13.180]ff below) should set the framework for these house rules in an industry code of practice which allows sufficient scope for adaptation to the special circumstances of each property.

There appears to be no reason why any accommodation provider should not have the right to set house rules.

Right to a lien over property

[13.85] Innkeepers have the right to a lien over property brought to the inn by guests. The rationale for the lien is to compensate innkeepers for their strict duties, as discussed above, to receive and entertain guests and to safeguard their property. [81] The lien applies regardless of who else owns or has an interest in the property. Thus in *Robins v Gray* [82] the guest was a commercial traveller selling sewing machines owned by the company which employed the guest and the court upheld the innkeeper's lien. In *Park v Berkley* [83] the guest brought a car to the inn on the last day of his stay and the innkeeper's lien was upheld against the car even

---

77 *Jones v Jackson* (1873) 29 LT 399.
78 *Carpenter v Haymarket Hotel Limited* [1930] 47 TLR 11. In this case Swift J said: "[counsel for the hotel] admitted that he would not expect a lady to trot down from her bedroom to the office in order that she might deposit the ring which she took off her finger with the clerk at the office rather than put it in her suit-case." Nor could it be construed as an election by the guest to undertake the custody of her property herself. Thus the notice could not relieve the innkeeper from liability. See also *Wright v Embassy Hotel* (1934) 39 SJ 12.
79 *Turner v Queensland Motels* [1968] Qd R 189 at 201 per Hart J: "it seems to me that there is no reason whatsoever why people should leave such large sums [£268] in cash in their rooms at night in a motel. By doing so they expose moteliers to the risk of having to recompense them if the money is stolen. Personally I think that if this is not negligence, it is at least getting very close to it."
80 *Huntley v Bedford Hotel* (1892) 56 JP 23. In this case Lady Huntley kept £1,300 worth of jewellery in a locked jewellery box in a locked trunk in her dressing room. Lord Esher MR observed that it was unreasonable to expect her to comply with a notice in the guest room which read: "articles of value, if not kept under lock, should be deposited with the manager, who will give a responsible receipt for the same".
81 *Gordon v Silber* (1890) 25 QBD 491; *Robins & Co v Gray* [1895] 2 QB 501 at 504 per Lord Esher; *Hanson v Barwise* [1930] St R Qd 285 at 290 per EA Douglas J; *Irving v Heferen* [1995] I Qd R 255 at 263 per Lee J.
82 *Robins v Gray* [1895] 2 QB 501.
83 *Park v Berkley* (1930) 25 Tas LR 67.

though it was on hire purchase. Thus, to the surprise of many in the car hire industry, it is arguable that the innkeeper's lien would apply to a hire car unless excluded by statute.

The lien gives the innkeeper the right to retain possession of the property until the guest's account at the inn is paid. It is only a right to retain possession; there is no power of sale except where it has been granted expressly by statute. The lien traditionally covered accommodation, food and beverage charges. It does not cover other debts such as a loan given by the innkeeper to the guest. Thus in *Robins v Gray* above the innkeeper's lien covered the accommodation charges of £10 but not the loan of £3 made by the innkeeper to the guest. Logically, however, it should now extend to telephone, business centre and similar charges. This was confirmed in a Queensland case which also provides an interesting insight into the rights and duties of innkeepers.

Irving v Heferen

[13.90] *Irving v Heferen* [1995] 1 Qd R 255

Facts: Irving was convicted of possessing and supplying marijuana found among his belongings in his motel room by the manager, who alerted the police. Irving had paid for the room in advance but ran up a phone bill to massage parlours, 0055 numbers etc (52 calls totalling $72.40). The manager was concerned that Irving would leave without paying. Early in the morning, after phoning and knocking with no answer, he entered the room with the master key and found Irving asleep. The manager woke him and demanded payment but Irving said "Too bad" and went back to sleep. He then searched Irving's belongings and took possession of his boots, a syringe, scales and a carry bag of belongings. The manager later opened the bag and found a wallet with $40. He took the money and put a receipt for part payment of the phone bill back in the wallet. He also found the marijuana and reported it to the police. He then locked it all up in the motel safe. Irving was tried and convicted. He appealed against his conviction, arguing that, in the circumstances outlined above, the evidence against him was unlawfully obtained and should have been excluded at his criminal trial. Irving argued that the manager had invaded his privacy and illegally taken and gone through his belongings.

Decision: The Queensland Court of Appeal (Macrossan CJ, Pincus JA and Lee J) unanimously dismissed the appeal. Lee J at 261-267 made a detailed analysis of the innkeepers' doctrine and the current rights and duties of innkeepers at common law. Pincus JA agreed with his conclusions on the lien and the other rights and duties of the innkeeper in this case. Macrossan CJ decided the appeal on different grounds.

Lee J held as follows. The motel was an inn and Irving a guest so that the innkeepers' doctrine applied. The innkeeper's lien covered the telephone charges and all services provided by the inn. When a guest refuses to pay, the innkeeper is entitled to detain the guest's goods and this includes the right to take them into possession peaceably as was done in this case. The innkeeper is also entitled to enter the guest's room. However here, when finding Irving asleep, the innkeeper should have left and waited for his departure. What he did was an "unwarranted invasion of his privacy in the circumstances". Lee J said (at 265):

> The demand for immediate payment, and the seizure of goods of [Irving] who was still in bed asleep at 6.15 am, even if strictly lawful, were most unwise. Such conduct would be warranted only in exceptional circumstances.

(Emphasis added.)

The manager's further actions were unlawful. The innkeeper is only entitled to passively retain possession.

Irving v Heferen cont.

The searching of [the guest's] belongings and the removal of the $40 from the wallet were acts contrary to the rights which a common law lien may have conferred upon [the innkeeper] and were unlawful [that is, not authorised in civil law].

It may also have been stealing subject to s 22 of the *Criminal Code* defence of an honest claim of right.

So, even though the lien existed, the evidence was obtained illegally as the result of the unlawful search of guest's bag. However, as the illegality arose only because of the manager's mistake and was not in deliberate and reckless disregard of the law, it was proper to exercise discretion to admit the evidence.

There is no right of lien over the property of a lodger.

―――― ಸಂಃ ――――

Infra hospitium

[13.95] The special rights and duties of innkeepers apply only while the guests or, where relevant, their property are infra hospitium, that is, within the precincts of the inn. This corresponds with the concept of in transitu or transit in transport law which defines the scope of the carriers' rights and duties (see [12.55]). Infra hospitium includes the buildings of the inn and the precincts so intimately related to those buildings as to be treated as forming part of them: *Williams v Linnitt*[84] (see [13.110]). In that case the majority found that the open car park was infra hospitium and so the innkeeper was strictly responsible for the stolen car, while Denning LJ agreed with the principles but found the innkeeper was not strictly liable because the car park was outside the precincts of the inn.[85]

With more and more business, recreational and entertainment facilities being supplied with the core accommodation, these car park cases provide some guidance on whether these facilities are infra hospitium and so subject to the strict innkeepers' rights and duties. It is considered that a hotel restaurant, shop or business centre would usually be infra hospitium. However they may not be so if there is sufficient separation from the accommodation in physical terms (that is, distance and structure) or legal terms (that is, independent operation or lease) or functional terms (that is, unrelated to accommodation). Where the accommodation is provided as part of a resort including swimming pool, tennis courts, golf course, gymnasium and recreational shopping the limits may be more difficult to define.

Special contracts: exclusion or limitation of liability

[13.100] Under the innkeepers' doctrine a distinction is made between a guest and a lodger and the doctrine applies only to guests. The rights and duties between an accommodation provider and a lodger are determined by the general law of contract, tort and bailment rather than under the innkeepers' doctrine. It is only with the duty to take reasonable care for the personal safety of guests that the duty is identical whether the customer is a guest or lodger (see [13.60] above). There is some correspondence with the distinction made in transport law between common carriers and private carriers, who carry under a special contract and are not subject to the special rights and liabilities of common carriers (see [12.15]). As mentioned above in [13.45], a "lodger" is a person who stays as a friend or tenant of the landlord on a special contract.

---

84   *Williams v Linnitt* [1951] 1 KB 565 at 580.
85   See also *Nott v Maclurcan* (1903) 20 WN (NSW) 135 where a car park was held to be infra hospitium even though it was not contiguous with the hotel.

However it is not open to an innkeeper to avoid the special rights and duties under the innkeepers' doctrine by simply declaring so in a special contract.

The most important duty which innkeepers might wish to avoid is the duty to safeguard guests' property (see [13.75] above). Innkeepers, unlike carriers, cannot limit or exclude liability for guests' property by contract or otherwise. It is a strict liability imposed under the common law innkeepers' doctrine and is independent of the law of contract, tort or bailment. Any attempt to limit or exclude it is void at common law: *Williams v Linnitt* (discussed below). This is a fundamental obstacle and is in addition to any difficulties the innkeeper may face in trying to incorporate an exclusion or limitation clause into the guest contract under the ticket case principles: *Olley v Marlborough Court* (discussed below). Note the different issue in each case: the establishment in *Williams v Linnitt* was a common inn, in *Olley v Marlborough Court* it was not.

Olley v Marlborough Court

[13.105] *Olley v Marlborough Court* [1949] 1 KB 532

Facts: Mr and Mrs Olley left the key to their self-locking room on the keyboard at reception of a residential hotel. Due to the negligence of the hotel staff their key was removed by persons unknown and furs and other property belonging to Mrs Olley were taken from their room. The hotel had a notice in the form of section 3 of the *Innkeepers Liability Act 1863* in reception and in the room behind the door there was another notice in the following form:

> The proprietors will not hold themselves responsible for articles lost or stolen, unless handed to the manageress for safe custody. Valuables should be deposited for safe custody in a sealed package and a receipt obtained.

The trial judge found that Marlborough Court was not a common inn but a boarding house catering for residential lodgers. Mrs Olley, like many others, had lived there for months at a time and she knew the place quite well.[86] She was found to be a lodger, not a guest. Thus neither the strict liability of innkeepers at common law nor the provisions of the *Innkeepers Liability Act 1863* applied. In any case the hotel's employees were found to have been negligent in failing to safeguard the key and so the *Innkeepers Liability Act 1863* would not have helped the hotelier.

Decision: On appeal to the English Court of Appeal (Bucknill, Singleton and Denning LJJ) the question was whether the notice in the room could protect the hotelier. The court found unanimously that the contract had been made before Mrs Olley got to the room and the notice could not form part of it. A majority (Singleton and Denning LJJ) held that even if it did form part of the contract its terms were inadequate to exempt the hotel from liability for the negligence of its employees. In the course of his judgment Denning LJ presented the following classic formulation of the ticket case principles:

> People who rely upon a contract to exempt themselves from their common law liability must prove that contract strictly. Not only must the terms of the contract be clearly proved but also the intention to create legal relations – the intention to be legally bound – must also clearly be proved. The best way of proving it is by way of a written document signed by the party to be bound. Another way is by handing him before or at the time of the contract a written notice specifying its terms and making it clear to him that the contract is on those terms. A prominent public notice which is plain for him to see when he makes the contract or an express oral stipulation would, no doubt, have the same effect. But nothing short of one of these three ways will suffice. It has been held that mere notices put on receipts for money do not make a contract [reference deleted]. So, also in my opinion, notices put up in bedrooms do not of themselves make a contract. As a rule, a guest does not see them until after he has

---

86   Singleton LJ at 544. This raises a question of whether it could have been argued that Mrs Olley had knowledge of the terms from her prior dealings as in *Balmain New Ferry Co Ltd v Robertson* (1906) 4 CLR 379.

Olley v Marlborough Court cont.

been accepted as a guest. The hotel company no doubt hope that the guest will be bound by them, but the hope is vain unless they clearly show that he agreed to be bound by them, which is rarely the case.

Williams v Linnitt

[13.110] *Williams v Linnitt* [1951] 1 KB 565

Facts: A farmer who lived a mile from the local inn used to drive there several evenings a week to drink beer with his friends. On the night in question he left his car in the car park in front of the inn but when he returned on closing time it had been stolen. The car park had a sign bearing the name of the inn and a notice saying:

> Car Park. Patrons only. Vehicles are admitted to this parking place on condition that the proprietor shall not be liable for loss or damage to (a) any vehicle; (b) anything in, or on or about any vehicle, however such loss or damage may be caused.

The farmer sued for the full value of the vehicle because under the *Innkeepers Liability Act 1863* (UK) there was no statutory exclusion or limit on an innkeeper's liability for motor vehicles.[87]

Decision: The English Court of Appeal by majority (Lord Tucker and Asquith LJ, Denning LJ dissenting) held the innkeeper liable. Denning LJ dissented on the grounds that the car park was not infra hospitium (see [13.95]).[88] However the court held unanimously that the farmer was the guest of the inn and innkeepers could not contract out of their liability for guest's property.

Lord Tucker noted (at 575) that

> the judge found that the plaintiff had not seen or, at any rate, read the notice, and that in any event, if the carpark was part of the inn, such a notice would not relieve the innkeeper of his common law liability. The defendant, on appeal, did not seek to rely on this notice as contractually relieving him from liability, and conceded that, if the carpark was within the "hospitium", he could not contract out of his liability...

Asquith LJ agreed (at 580):

> Goods placed within these limits by the traveller are "infra hospitium" and, except by notice under the Innkeepers' Acts and to the extent that such a notice operates, the innkeeper cannot limit his absolute liability for them. He cannot by a special agreement contract out of his strict liability.

Denning LJ dissented on the finding that the car park was "infra hospitium" but agreed with the principles on liability. He outlined the history and policy of the rule (at 584-585):

> In the seventeenth and eighteenth centuries an innkeeper could not lawfully contract out of his liability for goods which were brought by the guest within the precincts of the inn. There was a very good reason for this rule. It was because the innkeeper was obliged to accept the goods, and the law would not allow him to derogate from his obligation by attaching

---

[87] Before statutory intervention, the common law treated motor vehicles no differently from any other property of the guest.

[88] If the goods are not infra hospitium (the scope of which may vary according to the nature of the goods) then they are not protected by innkeepers' strict liability and in some jurisdictions exclusion or limitation clauses may be effective. See for example *Gresham v Lyon* [1954] 2 All ER 786.

Williams v Linnitt cont.

conditions to his acceptance. If he refused to accept the goods except at the owner's risk, he was in effect refusing to honour the obligation which the law imposed upon him; and that he was not allowed to do. [89]

He pointed out that while the courts subsequently allowed common carriers to contract out of a similar duty, this privilege was regretted and was never extended to innkeepers:

> The law as to common innkeepers was, however, never altered by the judges. No retrograde step was taken there. Innkeepers have never been allowed to contract out of the liability imposed on them by the custom of the realm. It is true that this involved them in hardships and Parliament passed the *Innkeepers Liability Act, 1863*, to protect them in some respects; but the very passing of that Act implicitly affirms the rule that at common law they cannot make a special contract out. So the law still is that, in respect of goods brought within the precincts of the inn, the innkeeper cannot contract out of the liability which the common law imposes upon him. No one disputed this before us, [90] but the matter is of such importance that I think that we should declare it specifically. [91]

Williams v Linnitt has been cited with approval in Queensland [92] and confirmed in the *Oakford Executive Apartments case*. It has also been followed in Scotland [93] and a similar principle applies in the United States. [94]

Bailment

[13.115] The special rules imposing strict liability on innkeepers and carriers for guests' property were developed long before the general principles of fault-based liability and also before a related branch of the law known as bailment. In 1704, Holt CJ [95] laid down in *Coggs v Barnard* the modern principles of the liability of bailees based on negligence. [96] However, the strict liability of the innkeepers and common carriers [97] was too firmly entrenched and was retained as an anomalous exception [98] distinguished on the grounds of public policy:

> And this is a politick establishment, contrived by the policy of the law, for the safety of all persons, the necessity of whose affairs oblige them to trust these sorts of persons, that they may

---

89   It should be noted that the principles of liability outlined by Denning LJ in this case stand in stark contrast to his comments on this point in the earlier case of *Olley v Marlborough Court* [1949] 1 KB 532 at 549-550 where he suggested in obiter dictum that there may be some scope for contracting out of innkeepers' liability.

90   Indeed Gardiner KC for the plaintiff argued that "There has not in 400 years been a case in which it has been held that an innkeeper can contract out of his common-law liability": *Williams v Linnitt* [1951] 1 KB 565 at 568.

91   *Williams v Linnitt* [1951] 1 KB 565 at 585.

92   *Irving v Heferen* [1995] 1 Qd R 255 Qld CA per Lee J.

93   *Burns v Royal Hotel (St Andrews) Ltd* (1957) Scots Law Times 53.

94   JEH Sherry, *The Laws of Innkeepers* (3rd ed, Cornell University Press, Ithaca, NY, 1993), p 485.

95   *Coggs v Barnard* (1704) 2 Ld Raym 909.

96   Again the common law borrowed from Roman law and used the Roman rules of negligence: Holdsworth, *A History of English Law*, Vol viii, p 458. However, like innkeepers' liability, bailment is not a tort or contract but is a separate form of action in itself.

97   The strict liability of common carriers was not settled till well after that of innkeepers. TFP Plucknett, *A Concise History of the Common Law* (5th ed, Butterworth, London, 1956), p 482 identifies the first reference to it in *Doctor and Student*, II c 38.

98   Holdsworth, *A History of English Law*, Vol viii, p 458.

be safe in their ways of dealing; for else these carriers [99] [and innkeepers] might have an opportunity of undoing all persons that had any dealings with them, by combining with thieves etc, and yet doing it in such a clandestine manner, as would not be possible to be discovered. And that is the reason the law is founded upon in that point. [100]

The law of bailment affects many aspects of the tourism, travel and hospitality industry. It determines the liability of accommodation providers for the property of lodgers and the liability of private carriers for passengers' luggage and goods. It also determines the rights and duties of anyone having possession or custody of another's goods and thus is very important in car and equipment hire and hospitality cloakroom and custody services. [101]

In *Hobbs v Petersham Transport* [102] Windeyer J defined bailment in these terms:

> A bailment comes into existence upon a delivery of goods by one person, the bailor, into the possession of another person, the bailee, upon a promise, express or implied, that they will be redelivered to the bailor or dealt with in a stipulated way.

In the present context the main duty of a bailee is the duty to take care of the goods. It is now settled law that the standard of care required of a bailee is the ordinary standard of reasonable care found in the general law of negligence. [103] However in determining what is reasonable care the court will consider all the circumstances, including what charge if any the bailee has made for providing the custody service. [104] Thus a lower standard may be reasonable where the bailment is gratuitous or for nominal consideration compared with cases where substantial charges are made for providing safe custody of the goods.

As in the general law, the onus usually rests upon the plaintiff to prove that the bailee is at fault. However bailment represents a very important application of the evidentiary principle of res ipsa loquitur; that is, the incident speaks for itself (see [5.180]). In bailment, if the goods are lost or damaged, the evidential onus shifts on to the bailee to prove that it was not at fault. [105]

At common law, a bailee is entitled to exclude or limit its liability by special contract. [106] This is of course subject to the ticket case principles (see [4.240]ff) and ss 60 and 61 of the Australian Consumer Law discussed below.

LEGISLATION

International

[13.120] The common law innkeepers' doctrine as amended by legislation to limit strict liability applies throughout most of the common law. Interestingly, in civil law countries the

---

99 "And this is the case of the common carrier, common hoymaster, master of a ship etc, which case of a master of a ship was first adjudged 26 Car 2, in the case of *Mors v Slew*, Raym 220 1 Vent 190, 238." Holt CJ at 112.
100 *Coggs v Barnard* (1704) 2 Ld Raym at 918.
101 The classic example of bailment is that of the valet parking service which many accommodation providers offer.
102 *Hobbs v Petersham Transport* (1971) 124 CLR 220 at 238.
103 *Houghland v RR Low (Luxury Coaches) Ltd* [1962] 1 QB 696 at 698 per Ormerod LJ. The requirement of gross negligence in gratuitous bailment under the original *Coggs v Barnard* formulation is no longer good law.
104 *Pitt Son & Badgery v Proulefco SA* (1984) 153 CLR 644 at 647 per Gibbs J, Wilson, Brennan, Deane and Dawson JJ concurring.
105 *Houghland v RR Low (Luxury Coaches) Ltd* [1962] 1 QB 696; *Pitt Son & Badgery v Proulefco SA* (1984) 153 CLR 644.
106 *TNT (Melbourne) Pty Ltd v May & Baker (Aust) Pty Ltd* (1966) 115 CLR 353.

principles of the Roman edict also prevail, with limits on strict liability introduced around the same time last century as they were introduced into common law countries. Despite the broad similarity of principles there remains formidable diversity, which is incompatible with fairness, transparency and efficiency for travellers, intermediaries, accommodation providers and insurers. A strong case can also be made for uniformity at an international level.

To this end UNIDROIT has proposed a *Draft Convention on the Hotelkeepers Contract* and the matter has been debated internationally since the 1930s. Europe has had a uniform approach to innkeepers' laws since 1967 but little progress has been made on wider uniformity. The International Hotel Association (IHA) initially supported but eventually opposed the Convention (see [13.180]). It is interesting to compare the progress made in reaching international consensus on the liability of the transport components of tourism (see Chapter 12). The *General Agreement on Trade in Services* (GATS) made at Marrakesh 15 April 1994 now requires more concerted action to achieve transparency in these laws.

Australian Consumer Law guarantees and prohibition on exclusion or limitation

[13.125] The provision of accommodation or bailment are "services" within the meaning of s 2 of the *Australian Consumer Law*. Sections 50 and 61 impose a statutory guarantee in the supply of services that they will be provided with due care and skill and will be reasonably fit for the purpose for which they are supplied. Under s 64 these guarantees cannot be excluded and there is little scope to limit this liability in tourism, travel and hospitality under s 64A. Section 139A permits exclusion or modification in supply of "recreational services" provided it is limited to liability for death or personal injury. This covers most tourism services, see [9.200]. Section 275 facilitates tort law reform measures in the respective civil liability legislation of the States and Territories which limit liability for personal injuries in certain circumstances: see Chapter 5 [5.185]. These matters are also discussed in detail in Chapter 12 ([12.65]ff) in relation to transport services and the principles outlined apply equally to accommodation and bailment services.

Innkeepers legislation

[13.130] The common law on innkeepers discussed earlier in the first part of this chapter has been amended under special legislation in most States [107] ("Innkeepers legislation"). [108] This legislation has its origins in the *Innkeepers Liability Act 1863* (UK) and has some similarities to that used to protect carriers (see [12.105]ff). The effect of the Innkeepers legislation is to provide innkeepers with a simple method of limiting their strict liability (risk management) for guests' goods and in some States to grant a power of sale to supplement the innkeepers' lien. Unlike the Carriers legislation, as the effect of the Innkeepers legislation is not to exclude or limit fault-based liability, it does not generally offend the *Australian Consumer Law*. The Innkeepers legislation varies from State to State.

---

107 South Australia has repealed its legislation.
108 Innkeepers legislation comprises: ACT: *Civil Wrongs Act 2002* (Chapter 11), NSW: *Innkeepers Act 1968*; NT: *Accommodation Providers Act*; Tas: *Civil Liability Act 2002* (Part 10A); Vic: *Carriers and Innkeepers Liability Act 1958*; WA: *Liquor Control Act 1988*; Qld: *Traveller Accommodation Providers (Liability) Act 2001*.

South Australia

[13.135] South Australia had Innkeepers legislation until it reviewed its Liquor Licensing Legislation in 1985 when it was (apparently accidentally) repealed and not replaced.[109] The result was that the unamended common law innkeepers' doctrine applies in that State. Most seriously for the accommodation industry, innkeepers in that State have a duty of strict and unlimited liability for guests' property.

Many operators have still not caught up with the change in the law and still display the old statutory limitation notice.[110] Not only is this legally ineffective, it may also constitute a breach of s 29(m) of the *Australian Consumer Law*, which prohibits false representations about the existence, exclusion or effect of any condition, warranty, guarantee, right or remedy. The only solution is to reintroduce legislative limits.[111]

It is interesting to note that Tasmania and Queensland for a time followed South Australia's lead and repealed their relevant Innkeepers legislation in 1990 and 1992 respectively. However, following an outcry from the industry, Queensland re-introduced its regulation of innkeepers' liability in 2001, and Tasmania followed in 2002.

Western Australia

[13.140] Western Australia is somewhere in between the common law position of South Australia and the limited strict liability in the other States. This curious position comes about because in 1970 Western Australia repealed its old Innkeepers legislation[112] and also abolished the special duties and liability of an innkeeper at common law.[113] Then in 1988 Western Australia purported to revert to the general model of the common law innkeepers' doctrine, modified to limit strict liability.[114] However on conventional statutory interpretation the effect appears to be that the common law duties and liability were not effectively revived and applies to the property of guests on licensed premises only.[115] This leaves innkeepers in Western Australia enjoying the rights under the common law innkeepers' doctrine but with some uncertainty as to whether the duties apply and if not as to the interpretation of the statutory limitation provisions. This position is entirely unsatisfactory and warrants urgent reform.[116]

Other States

[13.145] The Innkeepers legislation follows the English model but with variations from State to State. The following discussion will include Western Australia but this is subject to the general comments made above on the curious position there. A detailed Comparative Table of Innkeepers' Legislation (including England for comparison) is provided in the Appendix to this chapter at [13.200]. A summary of the effect of these provisions is provided below.

---

109   *Liquor Licensing Act 1985* (SA) repealed and did not replace ss 120 – 121 of the *Licensing Act 1967-1975* (SA).
110   *Licensing Act 1967-1975* (SA), s 120.
111   See TC Atherton, "Innkeepers' liability for guests property: contracting out is against the law" (1996) 24(6) *Australian Business Law Review* 448-462.
112   *Liquor Act 1970* (WA) repealed *Innkeepers Act 1920* (WA).
113   *Liquor Act 1970* (WA), s 173.
114   *Liquor Control Act 1988* (WA), s 107 reintroduced statutory limitation and s 176 repealed the *Liquor Act 1970* (WA), s 173.
115   See *Carriers and Innkeepers Act Options Paper* October 2008, a paper prepared by Consumer Affairs Victoria.
116   See TC Atherton, *Innkeepers' liability in WA: Tourist Accommodation operates under uncertain laws* (1996) 26(1) *The University of Western Australia Law Review* 160-168.

- **Definitions:** The Innkeepers legislation generally adopts the common law or similar definitions of "inn" [117] and "innkeeper". [118] Most States also adopt the common law definition of "guest" but require in addition that sleeping accommodation be engaged. [119] This undoes that part of the common law in *Williams v Linnitt* [120] (see [13.110]) which held that a farmer calling into an inn for a drink on his way home was a guest.

- **Exclude vehicles:** In most States horses, carriages and motor vehicles and their contents are excluded from strict liability [121] and in some States also from the innkeepers' lien. [122] This follows the English legislature [123] and amends the common law in *Williams v Linnitt* [124] (see [13.110]) which held the innkeeper strictly liable for the farmer's car.

- **Loss and damage the same:** Most States declare that liability for loss or damage to property is to be treated in the same way. [125] Despite some conflicting decisions, it was concluded in [13.75] that this is also the better view of the position at common law.

- **No limit unless notice:** The limits to liability do not apply unless the innkeeper displays a notice in the prescribed form in the reception area [126] and in some States also in the guest room. [127] As previously discussed these notices are statutory and not contractual and so their effectiveness does not depend on the guest actually seeing, reading or understanding them. The form of notice under the New South Wales legislation is set out below.

---

117 Innkeepers legislation: ACT: *Civil Wrongs Act 2002* (Chapter 11) "traveller accommodation", NSW: *Innkeepers Act 1968*, s 3(1) "common inn" plus hoteliers' licensed premises: *Liquor Act 1982* (NSW), s 100; NT: *Accommodation Providers Act* "accommodation establishment"; Tas: *Civil Liability Act 2002* (Part 10A "tourist accommodation premises"); Vic: *Carriers and Innkeepers Liability Act 1958*, s 26(1) plus any hotel or motel; WA: *Liquor Control Act 1988*, s 105, plus any hotel or motel licensed premises providing sleeping accommodation; Qld: *Traveller Accommodation Providers (Liability) Act 2001*: "traveller accommodation".

118 Innkeepers legislation see for example NSW: *Innkeepers Act 1968*, s 3; Vic: *Carriers and Innkeepers Liability Act 1958*, ss 26(1), 27(1) proprietor of the inn; WA: *Liquor Control Act 1988*, s 105 licensee.

119 Innkeepers legislation see for example NSW: *Innkeepers Act 1968*, s 4; Vic: *Carriers and Innkeepers Liability Act 1958*, s 27(2); WA: *Liquor Control Act 1988*, s 105 and provided they are not employees or family of the licensee.

120 *Williams v Linnitt* [1951] 1 KB 565.

121 Innkeepers legislation: see for example NSW: *Innkeepers Act 1968*, s 6(a); Vic: *Carriers and Innkeepers Liability Act 1958*, s 29(a).

122 Innkeepers legislation: see for example NSW: *Innkeepers Act 1968*, s 8; Vic: *Carriers and Innkeepers Liability Act 1958*, s 31.

123 *Hotel Proprietors Act 1956* (UK), s 2(2).

124 *Williams v Linnitt* [1951] 1 KB 565.

125 Innkeepers legislation: see for example NSW: *Innkeepers Act 1968*, s 5; Vic: *Carriers and Innkeepers Liability Act 1958*, s 28; WA: *Liquor Control Act 1988*, s 107 but in effect common law.

126 Innkeepers legislation: see for example NSW: *Innkeepers Act 1968*, s 7(2); Vic: *Carriers and Innkeepers Liability Act 1958*, s 30(4); WA: *Liquor Control Act 1988*, s 107(c).

127 Innkeepers legislation: see for example NSW: *Innkeepers Act 1968*, s 7(2); Vic: *Carriers and Innkeepers Liability Act 1958*, s 30(4).

INNKEEPERS ACT 1968 – SCHEDULE 1

(Sec 7)

NOTICE

LOSS OF OR DAMAGE TO GUESTS' PROPERTY

UNDER the *Innkeepers Act 1968*, an innkeeper may in certain circumstances be liable to make good any loss of or damage to a guest's property even though it was not due to any fault of the innkeeper or any servant in the innkeeper's employ.

This liability however:

(a) extends only to the property of guests who have engaged sleeping accommodation at the inn;

(b) is limited to one hundred dollars to any one guest except in the case of property which has been deposited, or offered for deposit, for safe custody;

(c) does not cover motor-vehicles or other vehicles of any kind or any property left in them, or horses or other live animals.

This notice does not constitute an admission either that the Act applies to these premises or that liability thereunder attaches in any particular case.

- **No limit if in safe custody:** The limits to liability do not apply if the goods have been lodged for safe custody,[128] or in some States if safe custody facilities are not offered.[129] In Victoria, a special limit of $2,000 applies to goods lodged in safe custody, or if safe custody facilities are not provided, the innkeeper or its servants were not at fault.[130] In Queensland, there is a special limit of $50,000 unless the guest discloses a larger sum to the accommodation provider in writing and a fee is paid.[131]

- **Limit on liability if without fault:** Except where:

    (a) the goods have been lodged for safe custody; or

    (b) the loss or damage is caused by the fault of the innkeeper or its servants or agents,[132]

    the liability of the innkeeper is limited to the sum in the following table.[133]

---

[128] Innkeepers legislation: see for example NSW: *Innkeepers Act 1968*, s 7(3)(a); Vic: *Carriers and Innkeepers Liability Act 1958*, s 30(1)(a)(i); WA: *Liquor Control Act 1988*, s 107(b).

[129] Innkeepers legislation: see for example NSW: *Innkeepers Act 1968*, s 7(3)(b); Vic: *Carriers and Innkeepers Liability Act 1958*, s 30(1)(a)(ii).

[130] Innkeepers legislation: Vic: *Carriers and Innkeepers Liability Act 1958*, s 30(1)(a), 30(5).

[131] Qld: *Traveller Accommodation Providers (Liability) Act 2001* s 14(4).

[132] Innkeepers legislation: see for example NSW: *Innkeepers Act 1968*, s 6; Vic: *Carriers and Innkeepers Liability Act 1958*, s 30(5); WA: *Liquor Control Act 1988*, s 107(b).

[133] Innkeepers legislation: ACT: s 4; NSW: *Innkeepers Act 1968*, s 7(1); NT: *Accommodation Providers Act* s 6(1); Tas: *Civil Liability Act 2002*, s 158A(3); Vic: *Carriers and Innkeepers Liability Act 1958*, s 30(1)(b); WA: *Liquor Control Act 1988*, s 107.

Innkeepers' Limits on Strict Liability

ACT	NSW	NT	Tas	Vic	WA	Qld
$40	$100	$200	no liability	$100, $2,000 if safe custody	$200	$250 $50,000 if in safe custody subject to conditions

- **Power of sale:** The Northern Territory grants an innkeeper a statutory power of sale of guests' property to supplement the innkeepers' lien. [134]
- **Guest register:** In some States an innkeeper is required to keep a guest register.

Need for uniform Traveller Accommodation Act

[13.150] These authors have advocated reform of the common law and statutory provisions governing innkeepers for the following reasons since 1995: [135]

> Australia's hotels, motels and guest houses now host 62 million visitor nights per year. [136] However the law governing this enormous number of transactions is a confusing mix of medieval common law principles of doubtful contemporary relevance and obscure statutory provisions which create idiosyncratic technical variations from state to state. It is not surprising that few accommodation operators or guests really understand what their rights and obligations are...The law must catch up with the remarkable development of the tourism industry. There is an urgent need for a uniform Tourist Accommodation Act to provide a clear, fair and simple legal framework for these transactions.

Finally, the Australian Standing Committee on Tourism (ASCOT) established an Inter-Governmental Standing Committee in National Innkeepers Legislation and in 2003 it commissioned the authors to undertake the Review of International Law on Innkeepers Liability and to make recommendations for reform and uniformity. Unfortunately little progress has been made since.

Holiday rental

[13.155] This Chapter has traced the origins and development of the law regulating accommodation providers from ancient Rome to the current times. It is instructive to consider the regulation of what used to be an informal and obscure form of traveller accommodation which has recently undergone rapid expansion to where it now forms a substantial portion of the traveller accommodation capacity at many destinations. [137]

Holiday rental may be defined as the short term rental of houses and apartments for holiday purposes. In comparison with commercial accommodation holiday rental has these features:

- Premises usually no different from dwellings occupied by long term residents except usually located in areas of high appeal to visitors and fully furnished and equipped;

---

134 *Accommodation Providers Act*: NT: *Accommodation Providers Act* ss 10, 11.
135 TC Atherton, "Innkeepers' liability for guests' property: contracting out is against the law" (1996) 24(6) *Australian Business Law Review* 448-462, 448.
136 Tourism Forecasting Council, *Forecast 1995*, 2(1), p 9: 1995-1996 Domestic 41.29 million; *Forecast 1996*, 2(2), p 6: 1996 International 20.8 million.
137 According to a survey by BIS Shrapnel, currently some 8.5% of Australian households own a holiday home (500,000). More than half of these offer them for holiday rental when not required by the owner household. Similar trends have emerged throughout the developed world.

- Unlike a resort, hotel or motel usually self catering and serviced only weekly rather than daily;
- Houses: usually have no on site management, unlike bed and breakfast accommodation; and
- Apartments: may be only one but usually many in each building, may have on site management.

Recall from Chapter 1 that "Tourism" means the activities of persons travelling to and staying in countries outside their country of ["place of" for domestic tourism] *residence for not more than one consecutive year* for leisure, "business and other purposes." [138]

"Residence" is your home, where you live, where you store your personal property (see Wikipedia). It is clear that a person may have more than one residence (eg second homes). If a person moves between the two each year are they a tourist in one (or both?)

"Domicile" = residence + the intention to make it your permanent home (common law and s 10 of the *Domicile Act 1982* (Cth) and equivalent in States and Territories). Legally you can only have one domicile at any one time. But is this practically correct in 2010. This has important legal and policy implications including:

- Nationality
- Immigration
- Choice of law
- Taxation

When a second home (house or apartment) is rented out when the owner is not occupying it, this raises many other legal and policy issues, most of which are unresolved. This section briefly considers two of these:

- Planning approvals
- Licensing

The sector has developed because of a combination of lifestyle changes, changes in consumer preferences and because the internet has allowed suppliers to market and distribute their properties cost effectively directly to consumers over the internet. Specialist holiday rental portals have developed to facilitate these transactions. [139]

The growth of this sector into a major form of tourist accommodation has generally occurred without any special approvals, licensing or other regulatory arrangements. Many of the regulatory arrangements developed for commercial accommodation do not apply. Consider the following issues.

Distribution: few restrictions on owners.

[13.160] Owners renting their property directly to occupiers do not require a licence. Renting short term for holiday purposes is not a residential tenancy. [140] So there is generally no restriction on rights and duties owner can impose.

---

138   Draft Annex World Trade Organisation.
139   For a discussion of these factors and the legal implications see T C Atherton, "The Legality of Letting Holiday Homes International Travel Law Journal" [2006] 4 *Issue* 207-211.
140   See *Residential Tenancies Act* (Qld) s 21 (if less than 6 weeks unless contrary proved), (NSW) s 6 (if less than 2 months).

Licensing intermediaries

[13.165] Generally, negotiating rents, letting places of residence, collecting rents etc as an agent for others requires a real estate agent's licence.[141] A licence is also available for management rights, which are special rights and a licence for a resident manager to let units in a building.[142]

Under the legislation, "letting" includes every form of leasing or letting of places of residence. Arguably holiday rental is only a contractual occupancy, not an interest in land as under a lease or tenancy because:

- owner/manager reserves the right to supervise, enter, inspect, service, clean, maintain and to evict summarily for breach, and
- Residential Tenancy Acts expressly exclude short term holiday rental.

The result would be that travel agents could handle holiday rentals. In practice real estate agents assert exclusive rights over the business and in New South Wales this is supported because the definition of "letting" which includes mere licences. In any event, through holiday rental, real estate agents and resident letting agents are substantial participants in the tourism industry and perform many of the functions of travel agents.

Distribution via the web

[13.170] Concurrently with and in many respects driving the development of holiday rental, specialist travel portals have emerged which deal only in accommodation. Because they deal in only one component (ie accommodation) they can avoid travel agents licensing and regulation (see Chapter 11). Further, if structured so that the web site merely facilitates communication (for instance, as a conduit), they may also avoid real estate agents licensing and regulation. Portals like Stayz.com have undergone exponential growth. There are numerous copies and variations nationally and internationally.

Regulatory issues

[13.175] Holiday rental is opposed by residents at some destinations for various reasons including:

- Inflates property values and rents making housing unaffordable for locals
- Takes residential property out of the permanent rental market
- The argument that it causes an intrusion of strangers into their community and results in anti social behaviour and additional noise, traffic and garbage.

They argue that it is "illegal" because it is a commercial activity which is not permitted in residential areas under the relevant planning laws.[143] Some industry associations and lobby groups argue that as holiday rental is unregulated it enjoys unfair advantages over hotels, motels and other forms of commercial traveller accommodation.

Holiday rental owners argue they have invested in good faith and in compliance with relevant laws and are merely exercising their fundamental rights as property owners.

---

141   See *Property Agents and Motor Dealers Act 2000*, (Qld) s 128, s 160, *Property, Stock and Business Agents Act 2002* (NSW) s 3, s 8).

142   See *Property Agents and Motor Dealers Act 2000* (Qld) Ch 2 s 111 – 127, *Property, Stock and Business Agents Act 2002* (NSW) s 3, s 23.

143   The issue came to the fore at Byron Bay. See Atherton TC, *Storm over Holiday Letting*, Australian Property Investor (June 2006).

This matter is generally determined under the relevant local planning laws. Local government is also responsible for maintaining residential amenity and, together with the police, regulating anti social behaviour.

The main problem has occurred where there is no resident innkeeper or caretaker to control anti social behaviour. Often the police are unavailable or slow to respond to neighbour complaints of antisocial behaviour because of other more pressing priorities. Holiday rental owners groups have been formed at Byron Bay and on the Gold Coast to self regulate and organise a private security firm service to provide a call out service to respond to neighbour complaints. If implemented in conjunction with strict booking conditions by owners prohibiting antisocial behaviour and reinforced by local council regulations this system would go a long way towards solving the problems.

If left simply to planning laws the problems are likely to continue. Local planning laws usually permit the residential use of houses and apartments without restriction on the length of stay.[144] In some areas it has been found that short term occupancy is not permitted.[145] In many areas the laws are uncertain and untested. The situation varies from one local government area to another and from time to time. If at any time during operation and owner can show that the activity was permitted under the local laws then in place then they will continue to enjoy the right to continue under existing use rights even if the local laws are subsequently changed.

Both Queensland and New South Wales are developing standard template planning laws and this matter needs to be resolved and regulated more effectively and fairly for all stakeholders.

ADMINISTRATION AND REGULATION OF TRAVELLER ACCOMMODATION

International

IHA

[13.180] The International Hotel Association (IHA)[146] was founded in 1956 as a trade association for the hotel and restaurant industry. It is concerned with:[147]

> questions of interest to the international hotel and restaurant industry, including in particular, governmental policy affecting hotels and restaurants, restrictions affecting international tourism, the legal framework governing relations between hotels and their clients, travel agencies and other intermediaries and international labour conditions.

Its main legal initiatives have been:

- **International Hotel Regulations,** Kathmandu 1981 which provides a code of international trade practices on the contract between hoteliers and their guests;

---

144 For example, Gold Coast City Council where the matter is currently the subject of much debate.
145 In New South Wales apartments: See the Court of Appeal leading case *North Sydney MC v Sydney Serviced Apartments P/L* (1990) 71 LGRA 432 and many subsequent cases in other NSW local government areas. In Queensland houses on the Sunshine Coast: See *Sunshine Coast Regional Council; v Ebis Enterprises Pty Ltd* [2010] QPEC 52 currently on appeal.
146 International Hotel Association (IHA) at http://www.ih-ra.com.
147 Article 2(a)-(d) of the IHA Constitution and Statutes.

- **Code of Practice on hotel/travel agency relations IHA/UFTAA,** 1987 (see [11.345]) [148] which similarly provides a code of international trade practices on transactions between hoteliers and travel agents;
- **Standard Voucher IHA/UFTAA,** 1982 for hotel reservations by travel agents;
- **Standard form booking procedures, contracts and rules between coach operators and hoteliers for group accommodation,** IRU/IHA, (see [12.160]);
- **Environmental Action Pack for Hotels,** IHA/UNDP, 1996.

IHA effectively blocked the adoption of the International Convention on the Hotel Contract promoted by UNIDROIT ([13.20] above) because many of its membership were concerned about some of the more radical consumer protection measures proposed. However, attitudes are changing and under the GATS there is increasing pressure for reconsideration of this matter.

Other matters which warrant further consideration include a code of conduct on overbooking procedures (see [9.165]) and a unified hotel approach to the issue of travel agency trust accounting ([11.630]).

IYHA

[13.185] The International Youth Hostel Federation (IYHF) [149] is an international non-governmental, non-profit-making organisation recognised by UNESCO. It was originally created to help young people experience the countryside and cities of the world but its appeal has broadened to a wider age group and it has developed into a major international tourism accommodation organisation. The Hostelling International (HI), or Youth Hostelling International (YHI) name and logo with the blue triangle, hut and tree are the brand name and symbol of youth hostels across the world. Hostels provide over 31 million overnight stays a year through 4,000 hostels in 90 countries.

The IYHF publishes annual Hostelling International Guides in two volumes across the Americas, Europe Africa, Asia and the Pacific. An International Booking Network (IBN) has been introduced to enhance customer service. More importantly from a legal point of view is the Assured Standards scheme designed to provide a grading service for hostels. It began voluntarily but now all member countries are required to have in place regular inspection programmes.

National

[13.190] The Australian Hotels Association (AHA) is the national equivalent of the IHA. It is the main trade association of Australian hoteliers and is a powerful lobby group, particularly on liquor licensing issues. At a national level there is also the more recently reorganised Hotel Motel and Accommodation Association (HMAA) which is the trade association of (mainly) moteliers. Each of these organisations has State branches or counterparts. The Australian Youth Hostels Association (AYHA) is the national counterpart of the IYHF.

---

148   This replaces the 1979 IHA-UFTAA International Hotel Convention.
149   The International Youth Hostel Federation (IYHF) at http://www.iyhf.org. The information in this section was obtained from this site.

Exercise

Murphy's Accommodation Law

Mr and Mrs Murphy stayed at the Faulty Hotel for seven days in January. The hotel accommodation was booked for them by their travel agent as part of a motoring holiday around Australia. During their last night at the hotel thieves got into their room using a copied key obtained from a former guest. They stole the following property:

- $5,000 in cash taken from Mr Murphy's wallet which he had left on the bedside table;
- $20,000 worth of Mrs Murphy's jewellery which she had stored in the in-room coin-operated safe. The thieves guessed the digital combination: 1, 2, 3, 4. A notice on the side of the safe reads "Neither Safeworld nor the Hotel accept any responsibility for loss or damage however caused to property stored in this safe."
- $1,500 laptop computer which had been deposited for safe custody with reception.

This was the last straw for the Murphys. They had already had a run of bad luck. Mrs Murphy had injured her back when she slipped over in the porcelain bath. During the week they had also lost:

- $10,000 Rolex watch which Mr Murphy left on the cabana chair beside the swimming pool while he went in for a dip;
- $2,500 digital camera which was stolen from the Murphys' hire car while it was left unlocked in the hotel's open carpark.

On checking out, the Murphys demanded that the hotel provide compensation for their losses. The manager pointed to an old statutory notice on the wall behind reception and said that under Australian law the hotel's liability was limited to a nominal sum. She said that in any case the hotel could accept no responsibility at all because all the losses were the Murphys' own fault.

The Murphys became angry and refused to pay their hotel account totalling $2,500 which they had run up for food, beverage, telephone, business centre and day trips booked through the hotel tour desk. The manager then instructed the car park attendant to seize the Murphys' hire car as security for the outstanding charges. The Murphys protested and said they had to return the car that morning to the hire car company as they were flying back home to America in the afternoon.

Advise the manager on the hotel's legal rights and duties based on the law of your State.

Appendix

[13.200]

CURRENT LAW	England	ACT	NSW	NT	Qld	SA	Tas	Vic	WA
Current Act	Hotel Proprietors Act 1956	Civil Law (Wrongs) Act 2002 (Chapter 11)	Innkeepers Act 1968	Accom. Providers Act 2002	Traveller Accommodation Providers (Liability) Act 2001	common law	Civil Liability Act 2002 (Part 10A)	Carriers and Innkeepers Liability Act 1958 Liquor	Liquor Control Act 1988
"inn" defined	s 1(3), like common law	s 145 "traveller accom."	s 3(1) common law plus any hotelier's licenced premises	s 3(1) "accom. establishment"	s 6 "traveller accom.";	common law	s 49A(1) "tourist accom. premises"	s 26(1): like common law plus any hotel or motel	s 105: licensed premises providing sleeping accom. Other inns uncertain
"innkeeper" defined	common law	s 146 "accom. provider"	s 3: common law	s 3(1)(c) "accom. provider"	s 7 "accom. provider"	common law	s 49A(1) "accom. provider"	ss 26(1), 27(1): proprietor of the inn	s 107: licensee of premises providing sleeping accom. Other innkeepers uncertain
"guest" defined	s 2(1)(a): common law if sleeping accom. is engaged	s 148	s 4: common law if sleeping accom. is engaged	s 4 Not explicit	s 9	common law	s 49A(1)	s 27(2): common law if engaged sleeping accom.	s 105: person if sleeping accom. is engaged and not licensee's employee or family. Other guests uncertain
Vehicles and contents and horses excluded	s 2(2): from strict liability and lien	s 149	ss 6(a), 8: from strict liability and lien	s 7	S 10	common law	no provision	ss 29(a), 31: from strict liability and lien	no provision
Loss and damage the same	s 1(3)	s 144 pt 11,1	s 5	s 5	s 8(2)	common law	s 49A(3)	s 28	s 107: uncertain
No limit unless notice in reception	s 2(3)	s 154 or other system of notification	s 7(2): and in guest room	s 6(2)		common law	s 49A(3)(c)	s 30(4): and in guest room	s 107(c)

Traveller Accommodation CHAPTER 13

CURRENT LAW	England	ACT	NSW	NT	Qld	SA	Tas	Vic	WA
No limit if in safe custody	s 2(3)(b)	s 152(1)(b) unlimited	s 7(3)(a)	s 6(3)(b) unlimited	$50,000 unless disclosed in writing and fee paid	common law	s 49A(3)(b) unlimited	s 30(i)(a)(i), s 30(5): limit $2,000	s 107(b)
No limit if safe custody not provided	s 2(3)(c)	s 153(5) safe custody facilities not necessarily provided	s 7(3)(b)	s 6(3)(e) refusal to receive safety deposit	s 14(7)) safe custody facilities not necessarily provided	common law	no provision	s 30(1)(a)(ii)	no provision
No limit if fault	s 2(3)(a)	s 152(1)(a)	s 6	s 6(3)(a)	s 13(1)(a)	common law	s 49A(3)(a)	s 30(5)	s 107(b)
Innkeepers' lien		No provision	s 8 except for vehicles and live animals	s 9 except for vehicles	s 8(3)	common law	No provision	s 31 except for vehicles and live animals	No provision
Power of Sale		No provision	No provision	ss 19, 11	No provision	common law	no provision	no provision	No provision

[13.200] **431**

CHAPTER 14

Food and Beverage

[14.05] INTRODUCTION 434
    [14.10]   History 434
[14.15] ORGANISATIONS 435
    [14.15]   International 435
    [14.20]   National 437
[14.25] FOOD LEGISLATION 437
    [14.25]   Co-operative Scheme 437
        [14.30]   FSANZ 437
        [14.35]   The Council 438
        [14.40]   The Code 439
        [14.45]   Food legislation 439
    [14.50]   Definitions 440
    [14.55]   Sale and Preparation 440
    [14.60]   Labelling 441
    [14.65]   Trade measurement 442
    [14.70]   Hygiene and Premises 443
    [14.75]   Administration and Enforcement 443
[14.80] GENERAL LAW 444
    [14.80]   Contract Law 444
    [14.85]   Contract Terms and Statutory Guarantees 444
    [14.90]   Tortious Liability 444
    [14.95]   False Representations 445
    [14.100]   Product Liability 445
       [14.105]   Class Actions for Product Liability 445
    [14.110]   Workplace Health and Safety 446
    [14.115]   Criminal Liability 446
              [14.120]   *Garibaldi mettwurst case* 446
[14.130] LIQUOR LICENSING 448
    [14.130]   The Rum Rebellion 448
    [14.135]   Legislative history 449
    [14.140]   Liquor licensing legislation 449
    [14.145]   Objects of liquor licensing 450
    [14.150]   Government revenue from liquor 450
    [14.155]   Definitions and Exemptions 452
    [14.160]   Nature of a liquor licence 452
              [14.165]   *Dalgety Wine Estates Pty Ltd v Rizzon* 453
    [14.170]   Types of licence 454
    [14.175]   Licensing Procedure 455
    [14.185]   Application 456
    [14.190]   Investigation 456
    [14.195]   Decision 456
    [14.200]   Conditions 457
    [14.205]   Review 458
    [14.210]   Conduct of Business 458
       [14.215]   General responsibilities 458

[14.220]	Disciplinary Procedure		459
[14.225]	Inspection and investigation		460
[14.230]	Grounds for disciplinary action		460
[14.235]	Disciplinary measures		460
[14.240]	Appeal		460
[14.245]	Alcohol Servers' Statutory Liability		460
[14.250]	The Meaning of intoxication		461
[14.255]	Harm minimisation campaigns		461
[14.260]	Alcohol Servers' Common Law Liability		462
[14.265]	Dram Shop liability		462
	[14.270]	*Menow v Hosenberger*	463
[14.275]	Australian Context		463
[14.280]	Responsibility for Intoxicated Guests		464
[14.285]	Conduct of patrons on the premises		464
	[14.285]	*Chordas v Bryant*	464
	[14.290]	*Wormald v Robertson*	465
[14.300]	Conduct of staff on the premises		465
	[14.300]	*Exchange Hotel Ltd v Murphy*	465
[14.305]	Conduct of patrons off the premises		466
	[14.310]	*Johns v Cosgrove & ors*	466
	[14.315]	*Cole v South Tweed Heads Rugby League Football Club*	467
[14.320]	Fallout from the case		468
[14.325]	Civil Liability legislation		468

INTRODUCTION

[14.05] The development of food and beverage law has followed the advancement in scientific analysis of the quality of food and the development of consumer protection laws generally. The important milestones in food and beverage law are:

- Contract law remedies (Chapter 4);
- Statutory guarantees (Chapter 9, [9.175]ff);
- *Donoghue v Stevenson* tortious liability to consumers (Chapter 5, [5.25]ff);
- Consumer protection laws (Chapter 9, [9.15]);
- Product liability laws [Chapter 9, [9.205];
- OHS legislation (Chapter 8, [8.160]ff);
- Criminal liability (Chapter 6);
- Food legislation; and
- Liquor licensing.

In this list the only topics which have not been discussed in previous chapters are food legislation and liquor licensing and this chapter will concentrate on those topics.

History

[14.10] The earliest food and beverage legislation in England was the *Assize of Bread and Ale 1266*,[1] which regulated the quantity rather than the quality of what was supplied. Such was the technology of the day that that was about the only characteristic of these products which was capable of objective measure. For the rest, the buyer relied upon the subjective measures

---

1   *Assisa Panis et Cerevisaiae* (1266) 51 Henry 3 Stat 1.

of look, feel, touch, smell and taste and, as discussed in Chapter 9, [9.10], it was very much buyer beware. In practice it is often woe betide even the most cautious buyer because the bacteria which causes food poisoning are everywhere and cannot always be seen, smelled or tasted.[2]

Some of the commonly used additives in the 19th century were poisonous. For example, to whiten bread, bakers sometimes added alum and chalk to the flour, while mashed potatoes, plaster of Paris (calcium sulphate), pipe clay and even sawdust could be added to increase the weight of their loaves. Rye flour or dried powdered beans could be used to replace wheat flour and the sour taste of stale flour could be disguised with ammonium carbonate. Brewers too, often added mixtures of bitter substances, some containing poisons like strychnine, to "improve" the taste of the beer and save on the cost of hops.

The use of these substances in manufactured foods and drinks was so common that town dwellers developed such a taste for adulterated foods and drinks that white bread and bitter beer were in great demand.

Even in the 21st century, there are examples of such food adulteration practices. In 2008, Chinese authorities discovered that food manufacturers were adding the chemical, melamine, to baby milk products to enrich its protein content. The chemical has been blamed for causing kidney failure in infants with the death of at least four children in China. More than 53,000 other infants and small children fell ill after drinking the toxic milk.

> The act of debasing a food or drug with the object of passing it off as genuine, or the substitution of an inferior article for a superior one to the detriment of the purchaser, whether done in fraud or negligence, appears to be as old as trade. These practices, in an organised society, naturally lead to official suppressive action (by the twin needs to protect the purchaser and the honest trader) and in various forms such action has existed in England certainly since the thirteenth century.[3]

The earliest legislation dealt with false weights and measures, as mentioned above, and then later dealt with adulteration of food substances and finally false advertising. Current legislation:

- outlaws harmful products;
- prohibits false advertising; and
- requires disclosure of certain information on packaging.

ORGANISATIONS

International

[14.15] International food trade and foreign travel are increasing and bringing with them important social and economic benefits. To avoid the adverse human health and economic consequences of foodborne injury, illness and food spoilage, effective hygiene control is vital.

---

2 Bacteria are found not only in animal (including human) intestines and faeces or human sores, wounds and orifices but also in air, water and in most types of food and beverage itself. They become a problem if there is poor food handling or hygiene because, given the right temperature, pH balance, moisture and air, one bacterium can become 16 million bacteria in just eight hours: Tweed Shire Council, *Bacterial Growth Fact Sheets*, pp 31-32.

3 Bell & O'Keefe's *Sale of Food and Drugs* (14th ed, Butterworths, 1968).

Growers, manufacturers and processors, food handlers and even tour operators [4] have a responsibility to ensure that the food offered to consumers is safe and suitable for consumption.

The key UN organisations concerned with food safety and standards are the Food and Agriculture Organisation of the United Nations (FAO) [5] and the World Health Organisation (WHO). [6] In 1962 they established the FAO/WHO Codex Alimentarius Commission to set international food standards. The Commission has produced a *Model Food Law* which has been influential in the improvement of national food standards in many countries, including Australia. [7] WHO has described the continuing challenges in food safety in these terms: [8]

> Despite advances in modern technology and attempts to provide safe food, foodborne diseases remain a major public health problem both in developed and developing countries. Every year WHO receives reports of hundreds of thousands of cases of foodborne diseases from all over the world. Reports from many industrialized countries indicate that, like in the developing countries, most foodborne diseases are caused by microbiologically-contaminated food. Statistical data also show that in many countries, the incidence of these diseases has dramatically increased over the past several years. WHO has an active programme in food safety with the objective to reduce morbidity and mortality related to foodborne diseases.

Similarly, the World Trade Organisation's [9] *General Agreement on Tariffs and Trade* (CATT) Article 20 permits member States to act on trade in food and to adopt or enforce necessary measures to protect human, animal or plant life or health provided they do not discriminate or use this as disguised protectionism. [10] It confirms that international trade in food should be conducted on the principle that

- all consumers are entitled to safe, sound and wholesome food and
- to protection from unfair trade practices.

There are numerous relevant international industry organisations, including (most importantly for tourism, travel and hospitality) the International Hotels and Restaurant Association (IHA) (see [13.180]ff).

---

4   First Choice Holidays, a UK based tour operator paid out almost £300,000 in compensation in 2009 to a Mr Julian Hurley who suffered long term health problems from a debilitating bout of food poisoning caused by eating contaminated food in the restaurant of the hotel where he and his wife were staying on their honeymoon as part of their package holiday in Venezuela. As a result First Choice Holidays cancelled all future package holidays in that country.

5   Food and Agriculture Organisation of the United Nations (FAO) at http://www.fao.org.

6   World Health Organisation (WHO) at http://www.who.org.

7   Other useful FAO/WHO publications have included: *Guidelines for Developing or Strengthening the National Food Safety Programme, A Guide on Safe Food for Travellers, Hygiene in Food-service and Mass Catering*.

8   From World Health Organisation (WHO) at http://www.who.org.

9   http://www.wto.org.

10   See also specific agreements on food safety and product standards including the Phyto Sanitary Agreement (SPS Agreement).

National

[14.20] Australia has a Uniform Scheme for the regulation of the sale of food and this is administered at national level by Food Standards Australia New Zealand (until recently referred to as Australia New Zealand Food Authority [11]) and at State level, by State Health Departments and by Local Government officers. These matters are discussed in more detail in [14.25]ff.

There are many national and State trade associations for the food and beverage industry, the most important for tourism, travel and hospitality being the Restaurant and Caterers Association (R&CA), which focuses on food and beverage, and the Australian Hotels Association (AHA) (see [13.190]), which focuses on accommodation and beverage. Each of these has State affiliated bodies.

FOOD LEGISLATION

Co-operative Scheme

[14.25] Australia has a Co-operative Scheme for the Regulation of the Sale of Food. The Scheme includes the following components:

(1) Food Standards Australia New Zealand (FSANZ);

(2) Australia New Zealand Food Standards Council (the Council);

(3) Australian New Zealand Food Standards Code (the Code); and

(4) State food authorities and the substantially uniform State and Territory legislation (Food legislation).

The object of the regulatory framework is to provide for matters relating to the handling and selling of food, securing the safety and suitability of food and fixing standards for food, and for other purposes.

FSANZ

[14.30] FSANZ is a bi-national food authority established by the *Food Standards Australia New Zealand Act 1991* (Cth).[12] It comprises a chairperson, State and Territory representatives, two New Zealand representatives, a consumer representative and two relevant experts.[13] The functions of the FSANZ are to:[14]

- develop, vary and review food standards;
- make recommendations to the Council about food standards;
- oversee food surveillance;
- carry out research and surveys;
- develop food safety education;
- co-ordinate food recalls;

---

11 Established pursuant to the *Food Standards Australia New Zealand Act 1991* (Cth).
12 New Zealand was included in the Scheme by the *National Food Authority Amendment Act 1995* (Cth). See also *Bilateral Treaty – Agreement with New Zealand Establishing a System for the Development of Joint Food Standards*, 5 December 1995 (Treaties Library).
13 *Food Standards Australia New Zealand Act 1991* (Cth), s 40.
14 *Food Standards Australia New Zealand Act 1991* (Cth), s 7.

- develop policies on importing food; and
- develop codes of practice for industry on food standards.

Food standards may relate to the composition, production, packaging, storing or handling of food; information about food including labelling, promotion and advertising; interpretation of other standards; and other matters relating to food as prescribed. [15]

In setting food standards the objectives, in descending order of priority, are: [16]

- protection of public health and safety;
- provision of adequate information relating to food to enable consumers to make informed choices and prevent fraud and deception;
- promotion of fair trading in food;
- promotion of trade and commerce in the food industry;
- promotion of consistency between domestic and international food standards where these are at variance.

FSANZ may develop, vary or review food standards at its own initiative [17] or on the application of any person. [18] It is currently reviewing all the standards in the Code. In the process it is required to publish a draft standard for public comment, hold an inquiry and make a recommendation on the matter to the Council. [19] For an interesting analysis of the role of FSANZ in rejecting an application to vary the standard set for alcoholic content of imported Scotch whisky see *National Food Authority v Scotch Whisky Association*. [20]

The Council

[14.35] The Council was established under the National Food Standards Council Agreement (1991) between the Commonwealth and the States and Territories. The Council comprises one Minister from each of the Commonwealth, States and Territories and a representative of New Zealand. [21] Its role is to oversee the implementation and operation of the uniform food standards.

When the Council receives a draft standard recommended by FSANZ the Council may adopt it, amend it, reject it or return it to FSANZ for reconsideration. When the Council adopts a draft standard it is published in the Commonwealth Gazette specifying the date it is to come into effect. [22] The standard then automatically becomes part of the Code. [23]

---

15 *Food Standards Australia New Zealand Act 1991* (Cth), 9.
16 *Food Standards Australia New Zealand Act 1991* (Cth), s 10.
17 *Food Standards Australia New Zealand Act 1991* (Cth), Part 3 Standards Div 2.
18 *Food Standards Australia New Zealand Act 1991* (Cth), Part 3 Standards Div 1. If it rejects an application FSANZ must give its reasons and the decision to reject is reviewable by the Commonwealth Administrative Appeals Tribunal.
19 *Food Standards Australia New Zealand Act 1991* (Cth), ss 14 – 19.
20 *National Food Authority v Scotch Whisky Association* (1995) 129 ALR 357; (1995) 21 AAR 260; (1995) 38 ALD 1. See also *Distilled Spirits Industry Council of Australia Inc v National Food Authority* (1994) No V94/85 AAT No 9685. (Commonwealth Administrative Appeals Tribunal).
21 New Zealand was included by the *National Food Authority Amendment Act 1995* (Cth).
22 *Food Standards Australia New Zealand Act 1991* (Cth), ss 20, 28, 32.
23 Section 3 definition of "Food Standards Code" in *Food Standards Australia New Zealand Act 1991* (Cth).

The Code

[14.40] The Code contains the national standards established on food sale and preparation, labelling, packaging and hygiene. It is continually being developed, varied and reviewed under the process outlined above. Compliance with the Food Standards Code is required as part of the food law of each State and Territory under the Food legislation discussed below. [24]

The Code presently sets General Standards in Chapter 1 on the following matters:

- 1.2 Labelling and other information requirements;
- 1.3 Substances added to food;
- 1.4 Contaminants and residues;
- 1.5 Food requiring pre-market clearance;
- 1.6 Microbiological and processing requirements

It also sets out Food Product Standards in Chapter 2 on the following specific matters:

- 2.1 Cereals;
- 2.2 Meat, eggs and fish;
- 2.3 Fruits and vegetables;
- 2.4 Edible oils;
- 2.5 Dairy products;
- 2.6 Non-alcoholic beverages;
- 2.7 Alcoholic Beverages;
- 2.8 Sugars and honey;
- 2.9 Special purpose foods;
- 2.10 Standards for other foods.

Chapter 3 refers to Food Safety Standards that apply in Australia only and Chapter 4 addresses Primary Production Standards. [25]

Food legislation

[14.45] Under the scheme, a Model Food Act was developed influenced by the FAO/WHO Model Food Law. Following the *Food Regulation Agreement 2000* [26] between the Commonwealth, States and Territories, each of the States and Territories has now introduced substantially uniform Food legislation [27] providing national consistency on food regulation. This legislation adopts the standards set in the Australia New Zealand Food Standards Code. The following discussion focuses on the general principles in the Code and the Food legislation.

---

24 For example: Food legislation: *Food Act 2001* (ACT), s 27; *Food Act 2003* (NSW), s 21; *Food Act 2004* (NT), s 20; *Food Act 2006* (Qld), s 39; *Food Act 2001* (SA), s 21; *Food Act 1984* (Vic), s 16; *Food Act 2003* (Tas), s 21; *Food Act 2008* (WA), s 22.

25 For further information about the Food Standards Code, see Food Standards Australia New Zealand at http://www.foodstandards.gov.au/foodstandards/foodstandardscode/#_one.

26 It has subsequently been amended in 2002 and July 2008.

27 Food legislation comprises: (ACT); (NSW); (NT); (Qld); (SA); (Vic); (Tas); (WA).

Definitions

[14.50] "Food" is defined widely to include: [28]

(a) any substance or thing of a kind used, capable of being used, or represented as being for use, for human consumption (whether it is live, raw, prepared or partly prepared); and

(b) any substance or thing of a kind used, capable of being used, or represented as being for use, as an ingredient or additive in a substance or thing referred to in paragraph (a); and

(c) any substance used in preparing a substance or thing referred to in paragraph (a); and

(d) chewing gum or an ingredient or additive in chewing gum, or any substance used in preparing chewing gum; and

(e) any substance or thing declared to be a food under a declaration in force under section 6.

[It does not matter whether the substance, thing or chewing gum is in a condition fit for human consumption.]

(2) However, *food* does not include a therapeutic good within the meaning of the *Therapeutic Goods Act 1989*.

(3) To avoid doubt, *food* may include live animals and plants....

Thus food means food and beverages, including alcoholic beverages but excluding therapeutic drugs.

Sale and Preparation

[14.55] The Code, Chapter 3, sets out the food safety and hygiene issues for Australia and the Food legislation requires compliance with the Code. For the purposes of the Food Safety Standards, food is not suitable if it:

(a) is damaged, deteriorated or perished to an extent that affects its reasonable intended use; or

(b) contains any damaged, deteriorated or perished substance that affects its reasonable intended use; or

(c) is the product of a diseased animal or an animal that has died otherwise than by slaughter, and has not been declared by or under another Act to be safe for human consumption; or

(d) contains a biological or chemical agent, or other matter or substance, that is foreign to the nature of the food. [29]

However, food is not "unsuitable" if it is permitted by the Food Standards Code [30] nor is it "unsafe" even though a particular consumer may have an allergic reaction to it. [31] Similarly, the authors argue that even if an injurious substance in food causes harm, such as a chicken or fish bone, the food is not necessarily unsafe thus giving rise to a cause of action. The common test used to be whether the substance is natural or foreign to the food. That test is probably now giving way to a more equitable test that when a person suffers injury from consuming a food product, the manufacturer, seller, or distributor of the food product is liable to the extent that the injury-causing object or substance in the food product would not be reasonably expected by an ordinary consumer

---

28 *Food Standards Australia New Zealand Act 1991* (Cth), s 5. Definitions under Food legislation are similar.
29 Food Standards Code, Chapter 3.11, Clause 2(4).
30 See, for example, *Food Act 2003* (NSW), s 9(2)(d).
31 See for example *Food Act 2003* (NSW), s 8(2).

Consequently, an upset stomach is not necessarily a cause of action. The injured person must show that the discomfort was caused by something that the law considers to be a defect such as:

- a foreign object like a toothpick found in a hamburger;[32] or
- damaged or deteriorated food like "toxic" asparagus sauce.[33]

The Food Legislation requires all persons selling or advertising food for sale to comply with the Food Standards Code.[34] "Selling" includes advertising or offering for sale, bartering, sale for resale and supplying in conjunction with accommodation, service or entertainment.[35] Furthermore, regardless of the fact that the food is safe, a food business must not sell food that is not of the nature or substance demanded by the purchaser.[36]

This corresponds with the Consumer Protection legislation on guarantees in relation to the supply of products discussed below.

Labelling

[14.60] Labelling is the primary means of communication between the producer and seller of food on the one hand, and the purchaser and consumer on the other. It is most important to consumers who suffer from a wide range of allergies and for whom failure to declare the inclusion of a particular ingredient could lead to life threatening situations.[37]

The Code, Chapter 1.2.4 sets out the detailed requirements for the labelling of ingredients on food packaging. The Food legislation also prohibits false description of food including:

(a) the food is represented as being of a particular nature or substance for which there is a prescribed standard under the Food Standards Code and the food does not comply with that prescribed standard,

(b) the food is represented as being of a particular nature or substance and it contains, or is mixed or diluted with, any substance in a quantity or proportion that significantly diminishes its food value or nutritive properties as compared with food of the represented nature or substance, ...[38]

Examples abound of such false advertising in the hospitality industry including selling:

- cheap wine in bottles labelled with expensive brands;
- understrength milk or spirit;
- inexpensive fish as expensive fish, for example, Nile perch as barramundi, Blue eye cod as jewfish etc;

---

32 See *Carman v Smithfield Tavern FNQ Pty Limited t/as Palmer Kate's Saloon* [2000] ACTSC 11 (11 February 2000).
33 Mr William Hodgins, 81, died on 13 January 2007 after treating his wife Audrey to a meal at an upmarket Sydney Restaurant where he ordered the fish of the day with an asparagus sauce. Tests on the sauce carried out found there was a presence of bacillus cereus at 9.8 million per 10 million parts. Levels of 1.0 million parts per 10 million is toxic.
34 Food legislation: (ACT), s 27; (NSW), s 21; (NT) s 20; (Qld), s 39; (SA), s 21; (Vic), s 16; (Tas), s 21; (WA), s 22.
35 Food Standards Code, Chapter 3.11, Clause 1.
36 For example, see *Food Act 2003* (NSW), s 19.
37 For example, additives such as sulphur dioxide which is widely permitted in food, tartrazine, peanuts, royal jelly (bee saliva) and pollen are well known for their ability to affect susceptible consumers.
38 See *Food Act 2003* (NSW), s 22.

- cheap cuts of meat as expensive cuts, for example, rib steak sold as sirloin, [39] large boiling fowls as turkeys, hoggett as lamb and so on.

The test is generally what the ordinary person understands by the label or advertisement and this is a question for the courts after the hearing of evidence. There is no need to prove that the consumer was actually misled or deceived. [40] This corresponds with the Consumer Protection legislation provisions on fair trading discussed below.

Trade measurement

[14.65] An issue closely related to false packing or labelling is incorrect measurement. Regulations on this can be traced back as far as the *Assize of Bread and Ale 1266* mentioned at the beginning of this chapter. Although the Commonwealth has constitutional responsibility for weights and measures it has not enacted trade measurement legislation. This responsibility remains with State and Territory governments which have enacted special Trade Measurement legislation [41] that regulates the use of measuring instruments in trade. "Measurement" means determination of physical quantity by means such as number, volume or weight. Measuring instruments must be certified and marked in accordance with the legislation. There are also detailed requirements for packaging and the sale of prepacked articles and inspectors have similar powers to health officers: see below, [14.75].

Serious offences are created for unjust measurement, which means:

- using an correct or unjust measuring instrument; or
- using a measuring instrument in a manner which is unjust; or
- an act or omission which causes or is likely to cause an instrument to give incorrect measurement or information provided it was done intentionally or with reckless indifference.

Conviction for an offence results in a substantial fine, [42] any transaction based on the instrument is voidable and there is civil liability to compensate for any loss caused by the offence. Employers are liable for employees and directors and managers are liable for company offences as under the Food legislation.

On 13 April 2007, the Council of Australian Governments formally agreed that the Commonwealth should assume responsibility for trade measurement. The transition period

---

39   see *Tonzo Pty Ltd v Amore* (unreported NSW DC, Dunford J, 11 Dec 1987).

40   On 23 November 2006, the Australian Competition and Consumer Commission (ACCC) launched the *Food and beverage industry – Food descriptors guideline to the Trade Practices Act* (the *Guideline*) to guide businesses on the standards of advertising and labelling expected of the food industry. The Guideline is designed to supplement existing food standards, such as those developed by Food Standards Australia New Zealand. *Case Study:* Uncle Tobys Roll Ups. The packaging claims included representations that the roll-ups were "Made with 65% real fruit"; representations on the ingredients panel that the fruit content of the product was equivalent to a specified percentage of fresh fruit; and television advertisements with images of an apple being flattened into a roll-up and an associated description. The ACCC expressed concern that the representations were likely to mislead or deceive consumers.

41   Trade Measurement legislation comprises: ACT: *Trade Measurement Act 1991, Trade Measurement Administration Act 1991*; NSW: *Trade Measurement Act 1989; Trade Measurement Administration Act 1989; Trade Measurement (Repeal) Act 2009*, Qld: *Trade Measurement Act 1990, Trade Measurement Administration Act 1990, Trade Measurement Legislation Repeal Act 2009*; SA: *Trade Measurement Act 1993, Trade Measurement Administration Act 1993*; Tas: *Trade Measurement Act 1999, Trade Measurement (Tasmania) Administration Act 1999*; Vic: *Trade Measurement Act 1995, Trade Measurement Administration Act 1995*; WA: *Trade Measurement Act 2006, Trade Measurement Administration Act 2006*; NT: *Trade Measurement Act, Trade Measurement Administration Act; Trade Measurement Legislation Repeal Act.*

42   $20,000, for example, in Queensland (s 8).

for the transfer of responsibility from the States and Territories to the Commonwealth was three years. From 1 July 2010, the National Measurement Institute (NMI) will take responsibility for trade measurement nationwide. This will make NMI responsible for the full spectrum of measurement, from the peak primary standards of measurement to measurements made at the domestic trade level. [43]

Hygiene and Premises

[14.70] Under the Food Standards Code, Chapter 3.2.3 adopted in the Food legislation, the premises, appliances and other equipment used in the storage, preparation and sale of food must be licensed and must meet prescribed standards. Standards must also be met in the processes used. However, until recently no particular training or skills have been required of those controlling or engaged in the processes although the functions of the various food authorities under the Food legislation require them

> to undertake or facilitate the education and training of persons to enable them to meet the requirements of the Food Standards Code and food safety schemes. [44]

Legislative initiatives in some States [45] require certain food businesses [46] in the hospitality and retail food service sector to have at least one trained food safety supervisor wherever a business is serving food that is:

- ready to eat
- potentially hazardous, and
- not sold and served in its package. [47]

All of these measures address concerns previously raised by the authors regarding the necessity for mandatory training and skills standards given the responsibility and the consequences for malpractice.

Administration and Enforcement

[14.75] The Food legislation is administered by the relevant Health Authority and enforcement is usually delegated to local government and their health inspectors. Health inspectors have wide powers to inspect premises and take samples for analysis. Where a health inspector considers that premises or appliances are unclean or insanitary he or she may give notice requiring rectification. If the defects are not rectified within the time fixed further orders may be made that the premises be closed and the activities be stopped.

Breach of the Food legislation and Food Standards Code is a criminal offence. The health inspector's report and analyst's certificates are admissible into evidence. The onus of proof that the food was fit for human consumption or use is on the defendant. It is a defence to show that the food was purchased in reliance upon a written warranty of its fitness for consumption and that there were no grounds to believe or suspect that it did not conform to the warranty.

43　See National Measurement Institute website at http://www.measurement.gov.au/Pages/Home.aspx.
44　For example, *Food Act 2003* (NSW), s 108(e).
45　For example, the New South Wales *Food Amendment (Food Safety supervisors) Act 2009* inserting Part 8, Division 3 Requirements relating to food safety supervisors.
46　Including restaurants, cafes, takeaway shops, caterers, bakeries, pubs, clubs, hotels and supermarket hot food sales.
47　See NSW Food Authority site at http://www.foodauthority.nsw.gov.au/industry/industry-sector-requirements/retail-outlets-and-restaurants/food-safety-supervisor-initiative/#New-legislation.

The usual penalty for an offence is a fine. Employers are also liable for the offences of employees and the directors and managers of companies are also liable for company offences.[48] The rights of appeal vary from State to State.

GENERAL LAW

Contract Law

[14.80] In contract law the remedies for misrepresentation are limited. A person suffering food poisoning would usually have a right of action for damages for breach of contract against the party who sold the food to them and damages for disappointment may be recoverable in many cases. However privity of contract prevents action by the consumer in contract against others who may be at fault, such as manufacturers or wholesalers. These matters are discussed in more detail in Chapter 4.

Contract Terms and Statutory Guarantees

[14.85] In every contract for the sale or supply of food there are implied terms that it will conform to the description, will be fit for the purpose and will be of merchantable quality. As discussed in Chapter 9, this was the case under the Sale of Goods Legislation (and arguably at common law) and these warranties and conditions were strengthened by the *Trade Practices Act 1974* (Cth) whether food was regarded as a good (ss 70, 71) or a service (s 74) in which case there was a warranty that it would be supplied with due care and skill and that it and any ingredients within it, would be fit for the purpose. In food service the fitness for purpose term means fit for human consumption and this makes the seller or supplier who contracts with the consumer strictly liable, even where the real fault lies with a party further up the chain of supply. That party may be protected from direct suit from the consumer by privity of contract. However if the seller or supplier is held liable it may itself sue the supplier to it in contract. Provisions for limitation of liability would not apply to food supplied to a consumer.

Now these matters are further strengthened by the *Australian Consumer Law* which imposes similar obligations on the supplier of food as statutory guarantees independent of contract and regardless of whether food is considered as a good or a service. So the supplier is now liable directly to the consumer whether or not there is a contract between them. Sections 54 – 56 cover the supply of goods and ss 60 – 63 cover the supply of a service. These matters are discussed in more detail in Chapter 9.

Tortious Liability

[14.90] The classic tort case of *Donoghue v Stevenson* (see casenote [5.35]) illustrates how the consumer may recover damages for negligence against the manufacturer or other party at fault even if there is no contract between them and the consumer. Breach of the Food Legislation and Food Standards Code may also found an action for damages for breach of statutory duty. These matters are discussed in more detail in Chapter 5.

---

48   For example, see *Food Act 2003* (NSW), s 133(2)(e).

False Representations

[14.95] False labelling and misrepresentation in relation to food will also offend the deceptive and misleading conduct and false representation provisions of the Consumer Protection legislation which is now contained in the *Australian Consumer Law*. They are not restricted by privity of contract and the misconduct need not be intentional. They will found civil liability for damages and a wide range of other remedies. False representations will also risk quasi-criminal prosecution and substantial pecuniary penalties greatly in excess of those applying under the Food legislation. These matters are discussed in more detail in Chapter 9.

Product Liability

[14.100] The manufacturer or importer of food may also be directly liable to the consumer if the product liability provisions of the *Australian Consumer Law* [49] apply. "Manufacture" is defined widely [50] to include food grown, extracted, produced, processed or assembled. Liability is based on either a contractual approach by reference to express or implied terms or on a tortious approach for defects in the standard of safety that consumers are entitled to expect. Either way, the action is not restricted by privity of contract and there is a range of remedies available besides damages. Provisions for limitation of liability would not apply to food supplied to a consumer. These matters are discussed in more detail in Chapter 9, [9.175]ff.

Class Actions for Product Liability

[14.105] The combination of the introduction of Part IVA of the *Federal Court of Australia Act 1976* (Cth) and a statutory code on defective goods under the *Australian Consumer Law* [51] imposing a product liability regime (in some cases creating strict liability) upon manufacturers, suppliers and importers of defective goods has led to an upsurge in representative proceedings (otherwise known as "class actions"). The class action procedure provides a convenient way for a large number of people affected by anti-competitive conduct, such as a food poisoning episode, to seek compensation. A major advantage of such a class action is that legal costs are shared.

The essential elements for commencement of a class action are that:

- there must appear to be seven or more persons with a claim against the same person;
- the claims must arise out of related circumstances;
- the claims must give rise to a substantial common issue of law or fact. [52]

Subject to fulfilment of these elements there is no limit to the subject matter of class actions.

There have been a number of claims on behalf of consumers for loss caused by contaminated products, including oysters, [53] peanut butter [54] and pork rolls. [55]

---

49   This is Division 3 – 5: Liaility of Manufacturers for goods with safety defects.
50   *Australian Consumer Law*, s 7.
51   *Australian Consumer Law*, Division 3 – 5.
52   *Federal Court of Australia Act 1976* (Cth), s 33C.
53   Wallis Lake Oyster case: *Graham Barclay Oysters Pty Ltd v Ryan* (2002) 211 CLR 540.
54   In 1996, 550 people filed a class action suit against Kraft Foods Ltd, Melbourne, Australia after they became ill from eating contaminated peanut butter. This resulted in the first ever settlement of a Federal Court class action under the product liability provisions of the *Trade Practices Act 1974* (Cth).

Workplace Health and Safety

[14.110] Restaurants and other food processing premises would usually be factories under OHS legislation. This generally imposes a duty upon employers and those in management and control of factories and processes to ensure that employees and others present at the premises are not injured. Because food is often consumed at the factory (for example, in a restaurant) these provisions may also apply to protect consumers. Breach of the duty is measured against standards and the Food Standards Code would provide strong evidence of the required standard. As in the Food legislation, breach results in criminal prosecution but the penalties under the OHS legislation are much more severe than under the Food legislation. Also, as in the Food legislation and Food Standards Code, breach does not give rise to direct civil liability but it may do so indirectly for breach of statutory duty. These matters are discussed in more detail in Chapter 8, [8.160]ff.

Criminal Liability

[14.115] Finally, in extreme cases, where the conduct in relation to the food is malicious, grossly negligent or reckless, those responsible may be criminally liable at common law as well as under statute. Where the person who eats the unwholesome food dies, those responsible may be indicted for manslaughter.[56] This occurred in the Garibaldi mettwurst case.

Garibaldi mettwurst case

[14.120] In the summer of 1994-1995 there was an outbreak of food-related diseases in South Australia involving 150 cases of illness, the hospitalisation of 23 children, some of whom suffered serious and permanent disabilities, and the death of a four-year-old child. The coronial inquest found that the child had died from disease caused by eating Garibaldi mettwurst contaminated with E coli.[57]

Criminal prosecution under the *Food Act* was not possible because the six-month time limit was exceeded by the time investigations were complete. Manslaughter charges were laid under the criminal law against the Garibaldi company, two directors and the financial controller. These charges were eventually dropped, but it did raise the prospect of personal criminal liability for defective or dangerous food products. The Directors pleaded guilty to the charge of creating risk of harm and were fined $10,000 each

Civil claims for damages were made against the company and many of these were settled by its insurers. The Garibaldi company subsequently ceased business and went into liquidation.[58] Since that time, some twenty of the children who survived the food poisoning have undergone kidney transplants and require ongoing medical care the State Government which had initially offered to

---

55   In 2003, more than 200 people fell sick after eating pork rolls from the Thanh Phu restaurant. Many of those who were poisoned by the pork rolls joined a class action to sue for damages and over $1m was paid out to victims as compensation. See article in *Sydney Morning Herald* 13 August 2003 at http://www.smh.com.au/articles/2003/08/13/1060588445827.html?from=storyrhs
56   MW and RJ Gerkens, *Food Law in Australia* (Looseleaf Service, LBC, Sydney), [4.6].
57   Coronial Inquest report (28 September 1995).
58   Information obtained from T Weekes, "Private remedies for public poisonings" (1996) (Nov/Dec) 3(2) *Foodmonitor* 44-45.

Garibaldi mettwurst case cont.

fund. A District Court action was brought against the State Government in 2008 to pay for these life saving operations. [59]

Exercise

Fawlty Food

Watch an episode of *Fawlty Towers* titled "Basil the Rat" (Episode 3). Pause at the times indicated and discuss the issues listed.

Minutes	
0	Sybil and Basil enter hotel
1	Carnegie (Health Inspector) checks kitchen
2	
3	Carnegie gives list of defects
4	Carnegie threatens Food Hygiene Notice
	Chef and Basil argue

Pause and discuss:
- Hygiene and premises
- Enforcement: inspection, notice
- Effect of failure to comply

5	Manuel and Basil the rat
6	
7	Manuel and Basil meet two ladies, rat frightens guests, Manuel and Polly
8	Sybil and Basil rat in kitchen
9	Sybil and Basil and Manuel
10	Polly and Manuel
11	Polly and Sybil, and Basil, and Chef in kitchen
12	Manuel and Polly and Chef, Manuel and rat, Polly and guest, Polly and Manuel
13	Major and Basil

Pause and discuss:
- Innkeepers' doctrine (see [13.10]ff)
- Fawlty Towers is an "inn", Major and two old ladies are "lodgers", Honeymooners (yet to arrive) are "guests"
- Compare guests' and lodgers' rights and liabilities re property

14	Major with gun
15	Basil looks for Manuel, Basil and Polly
16	Basil and Manuel, Basil and Chef
17	Basil and rat poison and veal, Carnegie arrives
18	Major shoots, TV explodes, Carnegie says Basil is responsible under Health and Safety Act

Pause and discuss:
- OHS liability (see [8.160] and following)
- Hotelier's liability for guests injuring another guest (see [14.200]) and compare *Chordas v Bryant* and *Wormald v Robertson*)

---

59 Report in the *Adelaide Advertiser*, 3 June 2008 entitled "Garibaldi survivors' 13-year fight".

Fawlty Food cont.

	19	Polly and Manuel, ratatouille, meat gets mixed
	20	Basil and Major, Basil and cat
	21	Veal substitute
	22	Inspector gives clearance, wants veal lunch
	23	Basil and Chef and Polly, cat is OK
	24	Basil slaps Manuel, Basil sees cat choke, takes back veal

Pause and discuss:
- Food legislation liability for contaminated food
- Criminal negligence: *Garibaldi case* (see [14.120], [6.55]ff)

	25	Chef cooks another veal
	26	Honeymoon couple, cat OK, Basil takes it back
	27	Basil, Manuel, honeymoon couple, rat
	28	Honeymoon couple want veal
		Honeymoon couple leave

Pause and discuss
- Honeymooners "guests" (see [13.40] and following)
- Assume first day of week's honeymoon
- Duty to mitigate, damages for disappointment (see [2.405]ff)

	29	Rat goes into restaurant
	30	Rat in biscuit tin for Carnegie, Basil faints

LIQUOR LICENSING

The Rum Rebellion

[14.130] Liquor licensing triggered one of the most notorious events in Australian history: a coup d'ètat. It began in 1793 when, to prevent the "secret and clandestine sale of spirits", Lieutenant-Governor Grose issued an order that thenceforth spirits could be sold only by licensees, which meant the official store or officers of the New South Wales Corps.[60] By 1798 a formal cartel agreement had been entered into between the officers of the New South Wales Corps and the principal inhabitants of the colony.[61] Rum, imported or distilled, became the currency of the colony, to the enormous profit of the cartel and the poverty and often ruin of many of the citizenry.

In 1807 Governor Bligh (already famous as the victim/hero of the 1789 mutiny on the *Bounty*) sought to regulate the importation, distillation and sale of alcohol and to prohibit its use as a barter currency.[62] The result was a bitter dispute with the cartel and particularly its main protagonist, Captain John Macarthur, who just two years earlier had received his land grant to found the Australian wool industry. On 26 January 1808 the New South Wales Corps marked the 20th anniversary of Australia Day by staging a rebellion in which they marched on

---

60 J Legrand, *Chronicle of Australia* (Ringwood, Victoria, 1993), p 93.
61 J Legrand, *Chronicle of Australia* (Ringwood, Victoria, 1993), p 107.
62 J Legrand, *Chronicle of Australia* (Ringwood, Victoria, 1993), p 136.

Government House, arrested and jailed Governor Bligh [63] and usurped authority over the colony for almost a year until the arrival of the new Governor Paterson. [64]

Legislative history

[14.135] It should be noted that liquor licensing is a creature of statute as at common law there were no restrictions on the sale of intoxicating liquors. [65] Under the early English statutes local justices were given jurisdiction to grant licences to fit and proper persons for the keeping of inns, alehouses and victualling houses. In Australia, regulation continued from the Rum Rebellion through ordinances and proclamations.

In 1828 the English *Alehouses Act* [66] consolidated various statutes and introduced comprehensive regulation of the retailing of liquor. It set out the duties of licensees, such as not to: adulterate liquor; use illegal measures; permit premises to be used by drunk or disorderly persons; and to keep premises closed on holy days except to receive travellers. [67] This statute was received into the law of Australia. The English *Licensing (Consolidation) Act 1910* introduced the universal system of licences for the retail trade in liquor and this system was copied in most Australian States. [68]

Liquor licensing legislation

[14.140] Each State and Territory still has its own Liquor Licensing legislation. [69] Most Australian liquor licensing legislation now reflects the English "on licence" and "off licence" structure and numerous other innovations have been introduced. Although there is some broad similarity, there is such diversity among the States that a full comparative analysis is beyond the scope of this text. Instead, this section discusses the general principles of liquor licensing in Australia. For detailed requirements readers should refer to the particulars of the relevant State legislation and scheme.

It is interesting to compare the scheme for liquor licensing with that for travel agency discussed in Chapter 11 [11.385]ff). To facilitate comparison, a similar structure is used in this section.

---

63   J Legrand, *Chronicle of Australia* (Ringwood, Victoria, 1993), p 40.
64   J Legrand, *Chronicle of Australia* (Ringwood, Victoria, 1993), p 143.
65   *R v Fawkner* (1669) 2 Keb 506; *Resolution of the Judges* (1624) Hut 99.
66   Alehouses Act 6 Geo IV No 4.
67   J Corke, *Tourism Law* (Elm Publications, England, 1988), pp 189-190.
68   See, for example, *Liquor Act 1912* (NSW) since repealed and replaced by *Liquor Act 2007* (NSW). The *Liquor Act 1912* (Qld) has since been repealed and replaced by *Liquor Act 1992* (Qld).
69   Liquor Licensing legislation comprises: ACT: *Liquor Act 1975*; NSW: *Liquor Act 2007*; NT: *Liquor Act*; Qld: *Liquor Act 1992*; SA: *Liquor Licensing Act 1997*: Tas: *Liquor Licensing Act 1990*; Vic: *Liquor Control Reform Act 1998*; WA: *Liquor Control Act 1988*.

Objects of liquor licensing

[14.145] John Rockefeller once said:

> When Prohibition was introduced, I hoped that it would be widely supported by public opinion and the day would soon come when the evil effects of alcohol would be recognized.
>
> I have slowly and reluctantly come to believe that this has not been the result. Instead, drinking has generally increased; the speakeasy has replaced the saloon; a vast army of lawbreakers has appeared; many of our best citizens have openly ignored Prohibition; respect for the law has been greatly lessened; and crime has increased to a level never seen before. [70]

The objects of modern Liquor Licensing legislation as set out in the *Liquor Act 2007* (NSW), section 3 are:

(a) to regulate and control the sale, supply and consumption of liquor in a way that is consistent with the expectations, needs and aspirations of the community, [71]

(b) to facilitate the balanced development, in the public interest, of the liquor industry, through a flexible and practical regulatory system with minimal formality and technicality,

(c) to contribute to the responsible development of related industries such as the live music, entertainment, tourism and hospitality industries. [72]

(2) In order to secure the objects of this Act, each person who exercises functions under this Act (including a licensee) is required to have due regard to the following:

(a) the need to minimise harm associated with misuse and abuse of liquor (including harm arising from violence and other anti-social behaviour), [73]

(b) the need to encourage responsible attitudes and practices towards the promotion, sale, supply, service and consumption of liquor, [74]

(c) the need to ensure that the sale, supply and consumption of liquor contributes to, and does not detract from, the amenity of community life.

One further and important objective which this section does not directly address is the need to obtain revenue for the state to enable the attainment of the objects of the legislation and for other purposes of government (see [14.150] below). [75]

Regulating liquor is a challenge for every government, given the generally negative social impacts, the generally positive economic impacts, the enormous returns to the state from licence fees, the monopolising effect of licensing and the power of the liquor lobby. The dilemma is highlighted by the longstanding contradiction between those laws which promoted public bars designed for drive-in drinkers and those which now impose the most severe penalties on drive-out drinkers.

Government revenue from liquor

[14.150] The State and federal governments are substantial stakeholders in the liquor trade. The Commonwealth government takes its share by levying customs duty on all liquor

---

70 See Brief History of BC Wine & Liquor Laws at http://www.winelaw.ca/cms/index.php?option=com_content&task=view&id=4&Itemid=26.
71 Compare with Liquor Licensing legislation: Qld: *Liquor Act 1992*, s 3(d)(ii).
72 Compare with Liquor Licensing legislation: Qld: *Liquor Act 1992*, s 3(a); SA: *Liquor Licensing Act 1997*, s 3(b).
73 Compare with Liquor Licensing legislation: Qld: *Liquor Act 1992*, s 3(d)(i); SA: *Liquor Licensing Act 1997*, s 3(a).
74 Compare with Liquor Licensing legislation: SA: *Liquor Licensing Act 1997*, s 3(a).
75 Liquor Licensing legislation: Qld: *Liquor Act 1992*, s 3(e).

imported and excise duty on all liquor produced in Australia. The State governments take their shares through liquor licence fees based on a percentage of liquor purchasers made by licensees.

Under s 90 of the Constitution the Commonwealth government has the exclusive power to impose customs and excise duties. When States first sought to impose liquor licence fees based on a percentage of purchasers it was challenged in a series of cases claiming it was unconstitutional. In 1904 the High Court interpreted excise narrowly and upheld the validity of a State licence fee for carrying on business as a brewer (business franchise fee) in *Peterswald v Bartley*.[76] Two cases in 1960 confirmed the validity of retail liquor licences structured in this way. In *Dennis Hotels Pty Ltd v Victoria*[77] the High Court split, holding by a bare majority that a licence fee of 6% of liquor purchasers by a licensed victualler was not an excise but that a temporary licence fee which imposed an additional £1 per day was an excise and therefore unconstitutional. The matter was thought to be clarified in *Whitehouse v Queensland*[78] where the High Court clearly upheld the validity of a liquor licence fee based on a percentage of the value of liquor purchased in a past period. This formed the constitutional basis of the State taxes on liquor, tobacco and petrol until 1997.

Currently the Commonwealth imposes excise duty on beer, spirits, liqueurs and certain other ready to drink products[79] (but not wine which is subject to wine equalisation tax [WET][80]) and this raised an estimated $3.1 billion in the 2008-2009 financial year.

The States used to impose a liquor licence fee based on a percentage of the value of liquor purchases but in *Ha v New South Wales; Hammond & Associates v New South Wales*[81] the High Court by majority[82] upheld constitutional challenges by retailers and wholesalers to the validity of tobacco taxes and in so doing rejected the narrow interpretation of excise fees upon which State taxes on liquor, tobacco and petrol were based. The majority rejected the argument that the licence fees could be justified on goods such as tobacco and liquor for regulatory reasons and said:

> The maintenance of constitutional principle evokes a declaration that the Dennis Hotels formula cannot support what is, on any realistic view of form and of "substantial result", a revenue raising inland tax on goods. The States and Territories have far overreached their entitlement to exact what might properly be regarded as fees for carrying on businesses. The imposts which the Act purports to levy are manifestly duties of excise on the tobacco [or liquor] sold during the relevant period. The challenged provisions of the Act are beyond power [under s 90 of the Constitution].

In response, the Commonwealth almost immediately enacted legislation[83] under which it now imposes the taxes on liquor, tobacco and petrol to raise and reimburse the States for the revenue lost.

---

76   *Peterswald v Bartley* (1904) 1 CLR 497.
77   *Dennis Hotels Pty Ltd v Victoria* (1960) 104 CLR 529.
78   *Whitehouse v Queensland* (1960) 104 CLR 609.
79   Otherwise referred to as "alcopops". The rate of excise duty for ready-to-drink alcoholic beverages increased by 69.4% to the same rate for full-strength spirits on and from 27 April 2008 and is expected to raise a further $2bn from 2008-2012.
80   WET is a value-based tax applied to wine consumed in Australia. It is paid on the value of the goods at the last wholesale sale. The WET rate for 2009-2010 is 29%.
81   *Ha v New South Wales; Hammond & Associates v New South Wales* (1997) 189 CLR 465.
82   Brennan CJ, McHugh, Gummow and Kirby JJ; Dawson, Toohey and Gaudron JJ dissenting.
83   *Franchise Fee Windfall Tax (Imposition) Act 1997* (Cth) and *Franchise Fee Windfall Tax (Collection) Act 1997* (Cth).

It is not clear whether s 90 is confined to goods or could be construed as also covering duties of excise on services. If so then the States' taxes on gaming (see Chapter 15) may also be open to challenge on these grounds.

Definitions and Exemptions

[14.155] Under the Liquor Licensing legislation, it is an offence punishable by a fine for any person to sell liquor without a licence or permit or to supply liquor other than from licensed premises. These key terms need to be defined. [84]

- "**liquor**" is generally defined as a beverage which at 20 $^1/_4$ Celsius contains more than 1.15% ethanol by volume. [85] It includes any substance prescribed by regulations to be liquor.
- "**to sell**" includes to barter or exchange, offer or attempt to sell, carry or expose for sale.
- "**to supply**" includes similar activities to sale but for direct or indirect pecuniary benefit or advantage.
- "**premises**" include land, buildings or structures on land and any vehicle, train, vessel or other means of transport.

These provisions provide control over the sale and distribution of liquor. There are also restrictions on the consumption of liquor in designated public places. These are designed to confine the commercial consumption of liquor to licensed premises and the non-commercial consumption to private premises or permitted public places.

Nature of a liquor licence

[14.160] It is important to appreciate the economic effects of licensing. Licensing creates a barrier to entry so that an existing licence becomes a thing of value. The effect is illustrated by comparing travel agency and liquor licensing. In travel agency licences are freely available provided the applicant satisfies the personal and financial conditions of approval. There is no restriction on numbers and viability is left to market forces. Thus travel agency is very competitive and travel agency licences, while essential, are of nominal value.

In liquor licensing there is a deliberate policy of restricting the number of licences for social and other reasons. In practical terms licensees often gain a franchise area which can be extremely lucrative. Then the liquor licence is not only essential for operations but is also an important part of the capital assets of the business. However, as the monopoly is a creature of statute, the liquor licensee is extremely vulnerable to changes in law and policy, especially the National Competition Policy implemented by Competition Policy Reform legislation (see Chapter 9, [9.240]ff). Thus obtaining and protecting a liquor licence are among the primary business objectives of every hospitality operator.

It has not been fully settled whether a liquor licence is a mere personal right or privilege or whether it is property. In the United States liquor licences are now generally regarded as property rights which are granted the protection of due process under the 14th Amendment of

---

84   See for example Liquor Licensing legislation: NSW: *Liquor Act 2007*, s 4; Qld: *Liquor Act 1992*, s 4; SA: *Liquor Licensing Act 1997*, s 4, Vic: *Liquor Control Reform Act 1998*, s 3.

85   Compare *Liquor Act 1992* (Qld), s 4B which specifies 0.5% and includes a spiritous or fermented fluid of an intoxicating nature intended for human consumption.

the US Constitution.[86] In Australia the prevailing view is that a liquor licence is a mere personal right or privilege rather than a property right: it merely authorises a specified person to do specified acts in a specified place which would otherwise be illegal.[87] Nevertheless, for the reasons discussed above liquor licences can have a substantial capital value.

Important consequences follow from this, especially where the original licensee mortgages or leases the licensed premises. As the licence itself is not property the lessor or mortgagee must be careful to make contractual arrangements with the licensee for protection, extension and transfer of the licence on termination or default. The courts will enforce such contractual arrangements provided they are not inconsistent with the Liquor Licensing legislation. However the effectiveness of contractual arrangements is limited in bankruptcy or in any dealing where privity of contract breaks the link with the licensee. Further protection can be obtained by attaching the liquor licence to the property in the premises in various legal ways which can have the effect of elevating the status of the licence to that of the property. Several principles of property law assist this including:

- a licence which is coupled with an interest in property and is necessary for its enjoyment is enforceable as a proprietary interest;
- if the licence is held as trustee then equitable remedies are available to prevent dealings with it in breach of trust;
- provisions in a lease or mortgage which touch and concern the land are also proprietary and so run with the land and bind successors in title;
- a restrictive covenant over land is enforceable as a proprietary interest in most States.[88]

However there is a wider public interest in a liquor licence and so there always remains some risk, as illustrated by the following case.

Dalgety Wine Estates Pty Ltd v Rizzon

[14.165] *Dalgety Wine Estates Pty Ltd v Rizzon* (1979) 141 CLR 552

Facts: A sublease contained an implied covenant that the sublessee would not transfer the liquor licence away from the premises. In breach of the covenant the sublessee made application to the Licensing Court for transfer of the liquor licence. The sublessor's application for an injunction to restrain the application was refused by the Full Court of South Australia and the High Court granted special leave to appeal.

Decision: The High Court by majority (Stephen, Mason and Murphy JJ, Barwick and Gibbs J dissenting) refused to grant an injunction on the ground that the decision on the transfer was one for the Licensing Court which under the licensing legislation was bound to consider the wider public interest as well as the private interests. The court noted that in *Slatter v Railway Commissioner of New South Wales*[89] an injunction had been granted in similar circumstances. Stephen J described the licence in these terms at 568:

> Because the rights in question relate to licensed premises and to dealings in a liquor licence, a species of monopoly property regulated by the licensing legislation, the appellant can scarcely complain that the court established under that legislation is to adjudicate upon

---

86 D Van Loenen, "Liquor Licensing", 10(3) *International Journal of Hospitality Management* 261-265.
87 T Ryan, *Liquor Licensing Issues,* paper given to the Pubs, Resorts and Package Holidays conference, Sydney, 27 March 1993, pp 15-16.
88 Except Queensland: *Norton v Kilduff* [1974] Qd R 47; *Ryan v Brain* (1994) 1 Qd R 681.
89 *Slatter v Railway Commissioner of New South Wales* (1931) 45 CLR 68.

Dalgety Wine Estates Pty Ltd v Rizzon cont.

them.

⸺ ⧢ ⸺

Types of licence

[14.170] Under the Liquor Licensing legislation the authority to sell liquor has been bundled in many combinations of terms and conditions which creates a wide variety of liquor licences. The names of these licences and the terms and conditions which go with them vary from State to State. Nevertheless, following the English model, most States now distinguish between two broad categories of liquor licence based upon where the liquor sold may be consumed: [90]

- **On licences** confer the right to sell liquor for consumption only *on* the licensed premises;
- **Off licences** confer the right to sell liquor for consumption *off* the premises, that is, take-away.

The general terms and conditions of four types of licence will be considered: hotel, restaurant, night club and club licences.

- **Hotel licence.** A hotel licence generally gives the licensee widest authority to sell liquor, including the right to sell for consumption both on and off the premises. [91] In most States the number of these licences is restricted and the licence is the most valuable available. The hotel licence was originally intended for the inn style of accommodation, food and beverage establishment. However the limited number and valuable monopoly on liquor saw the accommodation service, and in many cases, even the food service deteriorated at many hotels which concentrated on the more lucrative liquor business. This has caused many teething problems over the last few decades as tourism has developed and demanded a better standard of accommodation, food and beverage facilities. First, motel developers had to battle for an appropriate form of licence. Then when international standard hotel facilities were developed many had great difficulty in obtaining a hotel licence. More recently, resort developers have also had difficulty in obtaining an appropriate form of licence. Fortunately liquor laws have now been reviewed in most States to provide the licences required by these different types of operation.

- **Restaurant licence.** A restaurant licence generally authorises the licensee to sell liquor for consumption only on the premises. [92] Originally, restaurants could sell liquor only for consumption with meals but this has been relaxed in many States so that restaurants now often provide bar service for diners and non-diners. In reaction to the expense, formalities and facilities required for the licence to sell liquor, many restaurants now choose to be unlicensed so that diners bring their own liquor (BYO) and only consumption, not sale, of liquor takes place on the premises.

---

90 See for example *Liquor Act 2007* (NSW), Part 3, Divisions 1 – 7.
91 Liquor Licensing legislation: (ACT): s 45 general licence; (NSW): s 15 hotel licence; (NT): s 24 on and off licence; (Qld): Part 4 Div 2 commercial hotel licence; (SA): s 32 hotel licence; (Tas): s 7 general licence; (Vic): s 8 general licence; (WA): s 41 hotel licence.
92 Liquor Licensing legislation: (ACT): s 46 on licence; (NSW): s 24 on premises licence (restaurant); (NT): s 24 on and off licence; (Qld): s 67A commercial other licence with meals; (SA): s 34 restaurant licence; (Tas): ss 8, 11 special licence; (Vic): s 9A restaurant and cafe licence; s 15 BYO permit,; (WA): s 50 restaurant licence.

- **Night club licence.** A night club licence generally authorises the licensee to sell liquor for consumption only on the premises in conjunction with the provision of entertainment.[93] Originally night clubs were an offshoot of restaurants and were required to provide meals but this requirement has now been relaxed in most States.
- **Club licences.** A club licence generally authorises the licensee to sell liquor to members of the club and their guests.[94] The club must generally be a not-for-profit association formed to pursue some bona fide sporting or social objective. Originally club licences were restricted to consumption on premises but most States have extended this to permit limited sales to members for off-premises consumption. These establishments have undergone tremendous growth with the additional revenue provided by gaming machines (see Chapter 15).

Licensing Procedure

[14.175] The procedure for obtaining a liquor licence varies from State to State and according to the type of licence involved. Some of the steps are also required for transfer of an existing licence. The main steps are similar to those required for a travel agency licence and the following diagram (which is similar to travel agency, [11.405]) illustrates the application process.

Liquor licencing procedure: application process
[14.180]

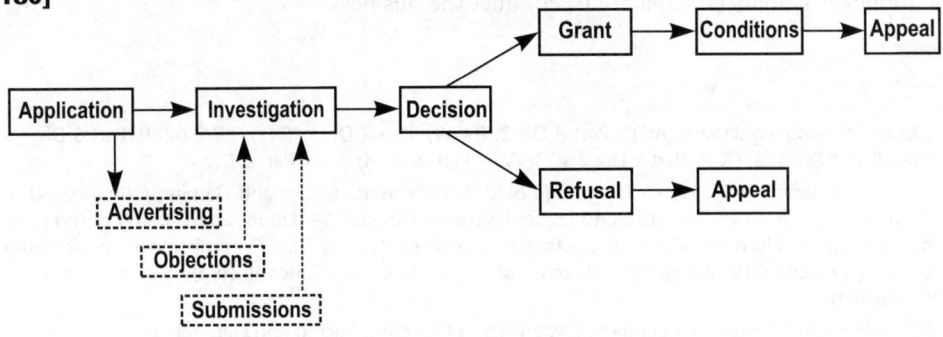

```
                                              ┌─Grant──→ Conditions ──→ Appeal
                                              │
Application → Investigation → Decision ───────┤
     │            ↑  ↑                        │
     ↓            :  :                        └─Refusal ──→ Appeal
  Advertising     :  :
                  :  :
              Objections
                     :
                Submissions
```

---

[93] Liquor Licensing legislation: (ACT): s 49 special licence; (NSW): s 16 general bar licence; (NT): s 24 on and off licence; (Qld): s 67AA commercial other licence with entertainment; (SA): s 35 entertainment venue licence; (Tas): s 8 on licence; (Vic): s 9 on premises licence; s 11A late night licence; (WA): s 42 nightclub licence.

[94] Liquor Licensing legislation: (ACT): s 48 club licence; (NSW): s 19 and see *Registered Clubs Act 1976*; (NT): s 24 on and off licence; (Qld): s 76 community club licence; (SA): s 36 club licence; (Tas): s 10 club licence; (Vic): s 10 club licence; (WA): s 48 club or club restricted licence.

Application

[14.185] A liquor licence is obtained by making application [95] in the prescribed form to the licensing authority [96] in the State or Territory in which the premises are located. The nature of the licensing authority varies from State to State. For example, applications in Queensland are decided administratively by the Chief Executive of the relevant Department. [97] All States also make provision for transfer [98] of licences and some States make special provision for removal, [99] variation, [100] surrender [101] and, where required, renewal [102] of liquor licences. The procedures for these other dealings vary but generally follow the steps for an application so far as they are relevant. The fees payable for applications and these other dealings vary from State to State.

Investigation

[14.190] The formality of the investigation process also varies from State to State. In some States it is quite general [103] whereas in others there are specific requirements for notification of the Commissioner of Police [104] and the local authority, [105] advertisement [106] and public objections. [107]

Decision

[14.195] The matters to be considered in deciding an application include:

- whether the applicant or transferee is a fit and proper person; [108]
- the applicant's financial capacity to conduct the business; [109]

---

95 Liquor Licensing legislation: (ACT): Part 4 Div 2; (NSW): Part 4 Div 1; (NT): s 26; (Qld): Part 5 Div 1 s 105; (SA): Part 4 Div 1, 3; (Tas): Part 2 Div 2 s 23; (Vic): Part 2 Div 4; (WA): Part 3 Div 7.

96 Licensing Authority: ACT: Liquor Licensing Board; NSW: Casino. Liquor and Gaming Authority; NT: Liquor Commission; Qld: Chief Executive and Liquor Licensing Tribunal; SA: Liquor and Gaming Commissioner (if not contested), Licensing Court of South Australia (if contested); Tas: Commissioner for Licensing; Vic: Director of Liquor Licensing; WA: Director of Liquor Licensing (uncontested), Liquor Licensing Court (contested).

97 Liquor Licensing Division, Queensland Department of Tourism, Racing and Fair Trading.

98 Liquor Licensing legislation: (ACT): Part 4 Div 4.5; (NSW): Part 4 Div 3 s 60; (NT): ss 40 – 41; (Qld): Part 5 Div 1 s 113; (SA): Part 4 Div 5; (Tas): Part 2 Div 2 ss 27 – 29; (Vic): Part 3 Div 5 s 69; (WA): Part 3 Div 9.

99 Liquor Licensing legislation: (NSW) Part 4 Div 3 s 59; (SA): Part 4 Div 4; (WA): Part 3 Div 8.

100 Liquor Licensing legislation: (NT) ss 32A, 33; (Qld): Part 5 Div 1 s 111; (SA): Part 4 Div 9; (Vic): Part 2 Div 5 s 30.

101 Liquor Licensing legislation: (ACT): Part 4 Div 4.6; (NT) s 39; (Qld): Part 5 Div 3; (SA): Part 4 Div 6; (Tas): Part 2 Div 1 s 30; (Vic): Part 2 Div 9; (WA): Part 3 Div 12.

102 Liquor Licensing legislation: (ACT): Part 4 Div 4.3; (Vic): Part 2 Div 8.

103 Liquor Licensing legislation: (NSW): s 42; (NT): s 28.

104 Liquor Licensing legislation: (Qld): ss 117, 117A; (SA): ss 28A, 75A; (Vic): ss 39; (WA): s 68.

105 Liquor Licensing legislation: (Qld): ss 117, 117A; (SA): s 76; (Vic): s 40; (WA): s 68.

106 Liquor Licensing legislation: (NT): s 27; (Qld): s 118; (SA): s 52; (Tas): s 23; (Vic): s 35; (WA): s 67.

107 Liquor Licensing legislation: (NSW): ss 44; (NT): ss 29, 46F; (Qld): ss 118A, 119; (SA): ss 77 – 79; (Vic): s 38; (WA): ss 73 – 74.

108 Liquor Licensing legislation: (ACT): ss 52, 64; (NSW): s 68; (NT): s 31, regulations; (Qld): s 107(1); (SA): ss 56, 63; (Tas): s 22; (Vic): s 46; (WA): s 37.

109 Liquor Licensing legislation: (NT): s 31, regulations; (SA): s 55.

- the applicant's understanding of the obligations of a licensee; [110]
- the applicant's training and experience; [111]
- whether the premises meet the prescribed standards; [112]
- proof of title; [113]
- whether the application meets the needs of the public; [114] and
- whether the application affects the amenity of the neighbourhood. [115]

The applicant must be an adult and if a corporation must usually appoint a nominee who meets the personal criteria for an applicant. The "fit and proper person" criterion is used to define the personal standards required for many business licences in the tourism, travel and hospitality industry, including liquor licences, gaming licences and travel agency licences (see [11.420]ff). The purpose of the expression is "to give the licensing authority the widest scope for judgment and indeed rejection". [116] In the transfer of a licence this is the main matter for consideration.

The applicant must generally prove that the licence is necessary to provide for the reasonable "needs of the public" in terms of liquor and related services in the locality of the premises, having regard for matters including existing licensed premises. In many States existing licensees use this ground to endeavour to keep out competitors.

Conditions

[14.200] Liquor licences are issued subject to the general terms and conditions which apply to licences of the type. The licensing authority may also apply such further reasonable and relevant special conditions for the particular licence. It may also vary or revoke the special conditions of the licence, as happens regularly with the hours of trade permitted for some licences. [117]

---

110   Liquor Licensing legislation: (ACT): s 52; (NT): s 31, regulations; (Qld): s 107(1); (SA): s 55; (Tas): s 22; (Vic): regulations.
111   Liquor Licensing legislation: (NSW) s 68; (SA): s 55; (Tas): s 221 Vic: regulations.
112   Liquor Licensing legislation: (ACT): s 52; (NSW): Part 5; (NT): s 31, regulations; Qld: regulations; (SA): s 57; Vic: regulations; (WA): s 66.
113   Liquor Licensing legislation: (NT): s 31, regulations; (SA): s 59; (WA): s 72.
114   Liquor Licensing legislation: (NSW): s 44; (Qld): s 116; (SA): s 58; (Vic): ss 44 – 47; (WA): s 37.
115   Liquor Licensing legislation: (NSW): s 48; (Qld): s 119; (SA): s 57; (Vic): ss 44 – 47; (WA): s 37.
116   Dixon CJ, McTiernan and Webb JJ in *Hughes & Vale v New South Wales (No 2)* (1955) 93 CLR 127 at 156, quoted with approval by Gibbs J in *Boyd v Carah Coaches Pty Ltd* (1979) 145 CLR 78 at 85. This has been the approach in liquor licensing cases from the outset of the uniform liquor licensing system: *R v Hyde Justices* [1912] 1 KB 645.
117   Liquor Licensing legislation: (NT): s 59; (Qld): Part 5 Div 1 s 111; (SA): Part 4 Div 9; (Tas): ss 37 – 38; (Vic): Part 2 Div 3.

Review

[14.205] Any person aggrieved by a decision of the licensing authority has rights of appeal which vary from State to State.[118] This includes not only the applicant who might be dissatisfied with refusal to grant a licence or with conditions imposed or varied on a licence but also, in most States, an objector or competitor.

Conduct of Business

[14.210] The licensee must conduct the business in accordance with the terms and conditions of the particular licence and also in accordance with the following requirements which apply generally to all licences (although there are variations from State to State).

General responsibilities

[14.215]

- **Management and supervision:** [119] The licensee is generally required to maintain control of the licensed premises and the management and supervision of the business.
- **Name and notice:** [120] The business must be conducted in the name of the licensee or nominee and the name must be displayed on the premises.
- **Maintenance of premises:** [121] The premises must generally be maintained with the facilities and to the standards required by the licensing authority and other relevant authorities.
- **Alterations require approval:** [122] Alterations of the premises require prior approval of the licensing authority and other relevant authorities.
- **Prohibition on profit sharing:** [123] A licensee is generally not permitted to share profits with unlicensed persons. Care must be taken not to breach this requirement where dealings such as franchises or leases are involved.
- **Register of guests:** [124] Where accommodation is provided as part of the licensee's business some States require the licensee to maintain a register of guests. Clubs are also required to maintain a register of members and usually also a register of their guests.
- **Record of liquor purchases:** [125] To facilitate the calculation of licence fees licensees are required to maintain a record of all liquor purchases. See discussion on licence fees below.

---

118   Appeals Court: ACT: Civil and Administrative Tribunal; NSW: Administrative Decisions Tribunal; Qld: Civil and Administrative Tribunal; SA: from Commissioner to Licensing Court to the Supreme Court; Tas: Licensing Board; Vic: Director of Liquor Licensing; WA from Director of Liquor Licensing to the Liquor Licensing Court to the Supreme Court.
119   Liquor Licensing legislation: (ACT) s 33; (NSW): s 91; (NT) s 110; (Qld): ss 143 – 144; (SA): ss 71, 97: (Tas) Part 2 Div 5; (Vic): Part 7; (WA) Part 4 Div 3 s 99.
120   Liquor Licensing legislation: (ACT): s 33; (NSW): s 91; (NT) ss 107, 108; (Qld): ss 143 – 144; (SA): ss 97, 109: (Tas): ss 53 – 55; (Vic): Part 7.
121   Liquor Licensing legislation: (ACT): s 33; (Qld): s 154; (Tas): Part 2 Div 5; (WA): Part 4 Div 2.
122   Liquor Licensing legislation: (ACT): Part 6: Part 10; (Qld): s 154; (SA): Part 4 Divs 7 – 8A; (SA) s 101; (Tas): s 47; (Vic): Part 2 Div 4.
123   Liquor Licensing legislation: (SA): Part 6 Div 2; (WA): Part 4 Div 4.
124   Liquor Licensing legislation: (SA) ss 100 – 101; (Vic): s 108; (WA): Part 4 Div 5.
125   Liquor Licensing legislation: (NT): ss 111 – 113; (SA): s 38.

- **Disorderly or intoxicated persons:** [126] Some States have made specific provisions on responsibility of licensees with disorderly or intoxicated guests. This matter is discussed in more detail in [14.245].
- **Amenity:** [127] Licensees are generally required to ensure their operations are conducted so as to minimise the noise and other interference with the surrounding community.
- **Minors:** [128] All States have detailed provisions prohibiting the supply of liquor to minors or the consumption of liquor by minors on licensed premises. Responsibility is cast on the licensee, employees and the individuals themselves.
- **Licence fees:** [129] Licensees are required to keep proper records and until 1997 were required to pay a State licence fee, which ranged from 11% to 13% of the value of liquor purchases. [130] Following the High Court's decision in *Ha v New South Wales; Hammond & Associates v New South Wales* [131] these provisions are invalid under s 90 of the Constitution. The Commonwealth now imposes similar taxes on liquor purchases and reimburses the States for the revenue lost. See the discussion in [14.140] above.
- **Definition of Intoxicated Persons:** [132] Several States have now defined drunkenness in their Liquor Licensing legislation. A good example is Queensland's definition of "unduly intoxicated" which reads:

    a state of being in which a person's mental and physical faculties are impaired because of consumption of liquor so as to diminish the person's ability to think and act in a way in which an ordinary prudent person in full possession of his or her faculties, and using reasonable care, would act under the circumstances.

Disciplinary Procedure

[14.220] The licensing authority monitors the operations of licensees to ensure that the standards and other requirements of the Liquor Licensing legislation are being upheld. Under the legislation there are wide grounds for disciplinary action and a range of disciplinary measures which may be imposed. Unfortunately the procedures vary so much from State to State that it is not possible to discuss them fully in general terms. The reader should refer to the Liquor Licensing legislation of the relevant State [133] and to the general discussion of criminal procedure in Chapter 6, [6.170]ff. Notwithstanding this, the following general points can be made.

---

126 Liquor Licensing legislation: (ACT) s 138; (NSW): s 77; (NT): ss 102, 105; (Qld): s 156; (SA): Part 6 Div 8; (Tas): s 62; (WA): Part 4 Div 6.
127 Liquor Licensing legislation: (NSW): s 3; (Qld): s 164; (SA): Part 6 Div 6; (WA): Part 4 Div 7 s 117.
128 Liquor Licensing legislation: (ACT): s 152; (NSW): Part 7 Div 2; (NT): s 106, ss 106A – 106E, ss 116A – 118; (Qld): s 145B, s 155, s 155AA; (SA): Part 7; (Tas): ss 60 – 61; (Vic) Part 8 Div 2: (WA): Part 4 Div 9.
129 Liquor Licensing legislation: (ACT): s 179; (NSW): s 47; (NT): s 31; (Qld): Part 9; (Vic): s 49; (WA): Part 5.
130 *Ha v New South Wales; Hammond & Associates v New South Wales* (1997) 189 CLR 465.
131 Lower fees apply to low-alcohol beer and wine.
132 Liquor Licensing legislation: (NSW): s 5; (Qld): s 44; (SA): ss 124, 131A; (Vic): s 3AB; (WA): s 3A.
133 Liquor Licensing legislation: (ACT): Part 2; (NSW): Part 5; (NT): s 19; (Qld): Parts 7, 10; (SA): Parts 8 – 11; (Tas): Part 2 Div 4 – 5, 7; (Vic): Parts 6 – 7; (WA): Part 6.

Inspection and investigation

[14.225] The licensing authority and its officers in conjunction with the police have wide powers of inspection and investigation [134] to ensure that the licensee is complying with the terms of its licence and with the requirements of the Liquor Licensing legislation.

Grounds for disciplinary action

[14.230] Disciplinary action generally may be taken where the licensee has breached the terms of its licence or the provisions of the Liquor Licensing legislation, particularly the responsibilities in the conduct of business discussed above in [14.210]ff. Many States also prescribe a list of specific offences for which disciplinary action may be taken. [135]

Disciplinary measures

[14.235] The disciplinary measures which may be imposed include: [136]

- a fine; [137]
- suspension and cancellation of the licence; [138]
- seizure and forfeit of liquor; [139] and
- recovery of illegal profits. [140]

Appeal

[14.240] The rights of appeal mentioned in [14.205] also generally apply against the findings in disciplinary actions and against the disciplinary measures imposed. [141]

Alcohol Servers' Statutory Liability

[14.245] The Liquor Licensing legislation imposes a statutory duty [142] on licensees and their employees to prevent excessive consumption of alcohol on licensed premises. For example:

> (1) A *licensee* must not permit:
>
> (a) intoxication, or
>
> (b) *any* indecent, violent or quarrelsome conduct,
> on the licensed premises.

---

134   Liquor Licensing legislation: (NSW): Part 9 s 138; (Qld): Part 7; (SA): Part 9 Div 1; (Tas): Part 2 Div 7; (Vic): Part 7; (WA): Part 6.
135   Liquor Licensing legislation: (ACT): Part 10; (NSW): Part 10; (NT): s 124; (Qld): Part 10; (SA): Part 8; (Tas): Part 2 Div 6; (Vic): Part 8; (WA): Part 6.
136   Liquor Licensing legislation: (NSW): Part 9; (NT): s 124; (WA): ss 95 – 96.
137   Liquor Licensing legislation: (SA): s 132; (Vic): Part 8.
138   Liquor Licensing legislation: (NT): s 48A, Part 7 Div 3; (Tas): Part 2 Div 4; (Vic): s 96.
139   Liquor Licensing legislation: (NT): 101AN; (SA): s 123; (Tas): ss 95 – 97.
140   Liquor Licensing legislation: (SA): s 133.
141   Appeals Court: ACT: Civil and Administrative Tribunal; NSW: Administrative Decisions Tribunal; Qld: Civil and Administrative Tribunal; SA: from Commissioner to Licensing Court to the Supreme Court; Tas: Licensing Board; Vic: Director of Liquor Licensing; WA from Director of Liquor Licensing to the Liquor Licensing Court to the Supreme Court.
142   Liquor Licensing legislation (ACT) s 138; (NSW): ss 73, 77, 99; (NT): ss 102, 105; (Qld): s 156; (SA): Part 6 Div 8; (Tas): s 62; (WA): Part 4 Div 6.

(2) A licensee or an employee or agent of a licensee must not, on the licensed premises, sell or supply liquor to an intoxicated person. [143]

Heavy fines for breach of the provisions apply.[144] Queensland, for example, imposes maximum fines of $3,000 on the bar attendant, $18,750 on the supervisor/manager on duty at the time and $18,750 on the licensee. The licensee also risks losing its liquor licence after two offences in two years.

These provisions may have the effect of extending the civil liability of the licensee and employees for damages for negligence. See discussion in [14.275]ff.

The Meaning of "intoxication"

[14.250] It has been observed already in [14.210] that several States have defined intoxication for the purposes of their Liquor Licensing legislation. To augment this definition, the Liquor Licensing Division of the Department of Employment, Economic Development and Innovation in Queensland which governs the administration of its Liquor Licensing legislation [145] in that State has published on its website a "Intoxication - the signs" to assist licensees and staff to recognise when a person is intoxicated including:

- mood changes
- slurring or mistakes in speech
- raised speaking voice
- clumsiness, fumbling with change
- loss of balance or co-ordination, swaying or staggering
- confusion, lack of ability to hear or respond
- bumping into, or knocking over furniture
- falling down
- dozing while sitting at a bar or table
- crude behaviour
- spilling drinks, or the inability to find one's mouth with glass
- inappropriate sexual advances
- aggression or belligerence
- inability to light a cigarette. [146]

Harm minimisation campaigns

[14.255] The (NSW) *Liquor Act 2007*, section 52 states in part:

(1) Conditions relating to harm minimisation The Authority may impose conditions on a licence prohibiting or restricting activities (such as promotions or discounting) that could encourage misuse or abuse of liquor (such as binge drinking or excessive consumption)...

---

143   *Liquor Act 2007* (NSW), s 73.
144   In *Director v Phoenician Club (1997)* (unreported) a prosecution before the NSW Licensing Court, the Magistrate fined "The Phoenician Club" pursuant to breaches of the *Registered Clubs Act 1976* (NSW) $100,000 for its irresponsible and inadequate supervision of premises which resulted in the tragic death of Anna Wood (15 yrs) who took the drug ecstasy at a dance party organised by the Club in October 1995.
145   *Liquor Act 1992* (Qld).
146   See Office of Liquor and Gaming Regulation website at http://www.olgr.qld.gov.au/consumers/responsible_drinking/intoxication/index.shtml.

Complementing this regulatory measure, a number of harm minimisation campaigns have been launched in response to community concerns regarding problems associated with alcohol abuse amongst young people in particular and with drink driving and the like. These promotional campaigns have been used to:

- raise awareness of the rules in the industry and among its customers;[147]
- target peak festival celebration periods like Schoolies Week, Easter, Christmas, New Year and University Orientation Weeks; and.
- focus on responsible serving of alcohol to patrons.

Postscript: It is also important to consider these issues under the OHS legislation (see Chapter 8). This imposes duties on persons in charge of workplaces to safeguard employees and other persons at workplaces. In some States it may be arguable that this legislation also applies in the circumstances discussed above.[148]

Alcohol Servers' Common Law Liability

[14.260] At Common Law, generally, the seller of intoxicating liquors is not liable for injuries resulting from intoxication of a customer where such injuries are inflicted on a third party through the action of the customer while intoxicated or are sustained by the customer personally. Courts have held the view that the *consumption* of the liquor rather than its *sale* was the proximate cause of any damage resulting from the intoxication of the one who consumed it.[149]

"Dram Shop" liability

[14.265] To overcome some of the perceived injustices inherent in the Common Law[150], the State of New York (US) in 1873 passed an Act entitled *An Act to Suppress Intemperance, Pauperism and Crime* which effectively prohibited the sale of liquor without a licence. It provided that:

> Every husband, wife, child ... or other person who shall be injured in person, or property, or means of support, by any intoxicated person ... shall have a right of action in his or her name, against any person or persons who shall, by selling or giving away intoxicated liquors, [have] caused the intoxication in whole or in part...[151]

The philosophy behind the legislation was that by imposing civil liability upon the seller, he or she would be more careful in the manner of sales and would demonstrate a greater consideration for the consumer and their dependants. One writer has observed that:

---

147 For example, Queensland introduced a concerted "No more it's the law" promotional campaign to increase awareness of the rules in the industry and among its customers in 1996 which was later followed in other States. Other campaigns include "If you drink and drive, you're a bloody idiot!" (2003); Thinking Drinking (2009). The latest round of such advertisements highlight parents' attitudes to alcohol consumption in front of their children and its effect on them.
148 See, for example, s 28(2) of the *Workplace Health and Safety Act 1995* (Qld).
149 Sherry JEH, *The Laws of Innkeepers* (3rd ed, Cornell University Press), p 695.
150 "Dram" means a small drink of alcoholic liquor. "Shop" means any retail outlet.
151 Sherry JEH, *The Laws of Innkeepers* (3rd ed, Cornell University Press), p 710.

Dram shop liability laws are a potentially powerful tool for changing the environment in which alcohol is sold because they hold alcohol servers responsible for harm that intoxicated or underage patrons cause to other people (or, in some cases, to themselves). [152]

The following case illustrates this approach.

Menow v Hosenberger

[14.270] *Menow v Hosenberger* 7 DLR (3d) 494

Facts: The plaintiff had a tendency to drink to excess and act recklessly. The hotelier had instructed its employees not to serve the plaintiff unless he was accompanied by a responsible person. One night after becoming intoxicated and annoying other guests the plaintiff was evicted. While hitch-hiking home he was struck by a car and injured. He sued the driver of the car and the hotelier.

Decision: The Canadian High Court held the hotelier, driver and the plaintiff himself equally liable. The hotelier's duty of care to the guest extended beyond the premises. Haines J held that the hotelier had breached the equivalent of s 156(1) of the Queensland *Liquor Act 1992* and that established liability in tort for breach of statutory duty:

> I find as a fact that the [hotelier] sold the plaintiff beer up to and past the point of visible or apparent intoxication. In so doing it contravened [provisions equivalent to s 156(1)] which were enacted not only to protect society generally...but to provide some safeguard for persons who might become irresponsible and place themselves in a position of personal danger.

Australian Context

[14.275] No similar "dram shop" legislation exists in Australia. However public concern over the increasing number of drink driving related road fatalities has led to the harm minimisation campaigns mentioned in [14.255], as well as to other measures such as:

- lowering culpable blood alcohol levels in most States; and
- compulsory roadside breath testing; and
- heavy criminal sanctions against licensees and employees serving alcohol to intoxicated persons. [153]

However, there is no statutory *civil* liability for alcohol servers. That matter has been left for the Courts to determine. In *Chordas v Bryant* [154] the Court decided that the ACT Liquor Licensing equivalent provision on responsible alcohol servers' liability did not establish a breach of statutory duty. However, the Full Court in *Wormald v Robertson* [155] did not endorse this and while leaving the matter undecided it observed that *Chordas v Bryant* was distinguishable.

The duty of care may extend to guests after they leave the licensed premises and even to persons injured by intoxicated guests after they leave the premises as the cases below illustrate.

---

152 Sherry JEH, *The Laws of Innkeepers* (3rd ed, Cornell University Press), p 711.
153 For example, see *Liquor Control Reform Act 1998* (Vic), s 108; maximum penalty exceeds $13,000 and on the spot fines exceed $1,300.
154 *Chordas v Bryant* [1988] 92 FLR 413.
155 *Wormald v Robertson* (1992) Aust Torts Reports 81-180.

Responsibility for Intoxicated Guests

[14.280] A licensee owes a duty of care for the safety of its guests, whether based on the fact that it is the occupier of the premises or that it is engaged in the activity of providing hospitality. If the duty is breached then the licensee will be liable for damages in the tort of negligence (see Chapter 5, [5.25]ff).[156] The common law imposes a stringent standard of responsibility for intoxicated guests. For example, in *Hogan v Rusty Rees Pty Ltd*[157] there was a space at the top of a staircase in a country hotel with a barrier at the bottom to block entry and a sign warning that the stairs were out of order. Nevertheless, the hotelier was held liable for damages in negligence to an intoxicated guest who climbed through the barrier, climbed the stairs and fell through the space.

It is clear that much depends on where the alcohol related incident took place. Did it occur:

(1)   on the premises; or

(2)   off the premises?

In the past, alcohol server liability related only to the first possibility – *on the premises* – and typically included analysis of the:

- conduct of patrons; and
- conduct of staff

The following cases show how this responsibility even includes a duty to protect guests from the criminal actions of intoxicated guests.

Conduct of patrons "on the premises"

Chordas v Bryant

[14.285] *Chordas v Bryant* [1988] 92 FLR 413

Facts: C was struck over the head with a beer jug by another patron, K, who was "well affected" by alcohol. There was evidence that C had provoked K and it was not proved that K's intoxication was a cause of the incident. C sued the hotelier for damages for negligence.

Decision: The Federal Court (Davies, Kelly and Neaves JJ) dismissed C's appeal and confirmed the trial judge's finding that the hotelier was not responsible. The court confirmed that a hotelier owes a general duty to take reasonable care to avoid foreseeable risks to patrons. However a hotel is not liable for the acts of its guests unless it knew or ought to have known of facts requiring intervention in order to protect other guests. The court relied heavily on the fact that the hotelier had a duty under the licensing legislation to accept all customers and that limited its ability to exercise control (compare innkeepers). Even if it were established that the hotel knew or ought to have known that K was intoxicated it was held not foreseeable that C would provoke him and that broke any causal link. Note that the court rejected the alternative view that C's provocation constituted contributory negligence.

---

156   This is augmented by the duties imposed under the OHS legislation (see [8.175]ff).

157   *Hogan v Rusty Rees Pty Ltd* (Queensland Supreme Court Writ No 174/85 upheld on appeal No 82 of 1988, decided 19 June 1989).

Chordas v Bryant cont.

It was also found that s 79 of the *Liquor Ordinance* (ACT) did not confer any private right of action for breach of statutory duty.

— ∽⃝∾ —

Wormald v Robertson

[14.290] *Wormald v Robertson* (1992) Aust Torts Reports 81-180

Facts: The facts were similar to those in *Chordas v Bryant* apart from these features. There was evidence that the assailant, R, had been misbehaving for half an hour before the incident. R had been jumping on tables, breaking glass and molesting other guests. Two complaints had been made to the licensee about R's behaviour but the licensee had done nothing. Finally the plaintiff, W, intervened and said "Enough is enough Robbo, you have been carrying on all night". R then struck W with a beer jug as in *Chordas v Bryant*. The trial judge applied *Chordas v Bryant* and found the hotelier not responsible.

Decision: The Full Court of Queensland (Macrossan CJ, Davies JA and Ambrose J) allowed the appeal and held the hotelier negligent. *Chordas v Bryant* was distinguished because here causation was clearly established. The hotelier knew or ought to have known of the risk which R posed and should have taken action, with the assistance of the police if necessary, to evict him. W's actions did not break the causal link. They were reasonable and it was reasonable that any one of a number of guests would have intervened if R's behaviour were allowed to continue. The defences of contributory negligence or volenti non fit injuria had not been made out. It was not necessary to decide whether there had been a breach of duty based on s 78 of the Queensland *Liquor Act 1912*. *(This earlier Act was the relevant law at the time of this case.)*

— ∽⃝∾ —

[14.295] In *Bowron v Lucock* [158] the plaintiff, Bowron, broke his arm when he slipped on the greasy residue left on the floor of the Jannali Inn in Sydney by another patron, Lucock, who used pork chops as shoes to satisfy a dress code requiring all patrons to wear foot attire inside the premises of the hotel. The judge found that the Jannali Inn had breached its duty of care by failing to clean the area that Lucock had made into a greasy mess after taping the meat to his feet, and therefore did not prevent the risk of injury to patrons. The Court awarded the plaintiff $460,000. However, the judge held that Lucock owed no duty of care to the plaintiff. [159]

Conduct of staff *"on the premises"*

Exchange Hotel Ltd v Murphy

[14.300] *Exchange Hotel Ltd v Murphy* (1947) SASR 112

Facts: The plaintiff who had been drinking at the hotel was injured when he was ejected from the licensed premises after he became angry and disorderly when told the hotel was closing. The barman escorted the plaintiff to the doorway, pushed him in the back and slammed the door. The barman failed to notice that the plaintiff had clung to the door frame with one hand, and as the door slammed shut, it had chopped off the top of one of his fingers.

---

158   *Bowron v Lucock* (unreported, District Court of NSW, 2002).
159   See also *Preston v Star City Limited (No 3)* [2005] NSWSC 1223 (unreported). In that case, Hoeben J permitted a claim in negligence to proceed to trial because the plaintiff claimed Star City knew of the plaintiff's problem drinking and actively encouraged and exploited it.

Exchange Hotel Ltd v Murphy cont.

Held: Although the barman had used reasonable force, he was negligent in failing to notice that the plaintiff's hand was not clear of the door jamb. The barman was acting in the scope of his employment and therefore the hotel was vicariously liable in damages for assault.[160]

Conduct of patrons "*off the premises*"

[14.305] The previous cases examined a licensee's duty of care to prevent reasonably foreseeable risk or danger to customers and/or intoxicated persons on their premises. The next cases examine the extent to which a licensee has a duty of care to his or her customers for damage suffered outside the premises. Compare the intent expressed by the Court's decision with that of the "Dram Shop" (Civil Damages) Acts in the United States and Canada referred to in [14.265] and [14.270].

Johns v Cosgrove & ors

[14.310] *Johns v Cosgrove & ors* (1997) QSC 229

Facts: The plaintiff, Johns, was a regular heavy drinker at the licensee's Chevron Hotel on the Gold Coast! Some of the hotel staff were aware of Johns' usual route home, across a busy road, to catch a bus and that he often left the hotel in a drunken state. On the night of 24 April, 1990, the plaintiff was waiting for the bus at the side of the highway when he lost his grip of a bus stop sign and staggered into the path of an oncoming car. He suffered serious head and leg injuries. His blood alcohol level measured shortly afterwards was 0.332.

During the course of his judgment, Derrington J said:

> It is not negligence merely to serve a person with liquor to the point of intoxication; but it is so *if because of the circumstance it is reasonably foreseeable that to do so would cause danger to the intoxicated party*, such as, for example where the intoxication is so gross as to cause incapacity for reasonable self-preservation when it is or should be known that he or she may move into dangerous circumstances, and where no action is taken to avert this. This is not to impose an excessive burden on publicans if it is fully understood.

[emphasis added]

Held: In the result, the judge awarded damages in favour of the plaintiff although he held him 45% liable. The judge held the driver of the car that struck the plaintiff 30% liable and the Hotelier 25% liable. In other words, the Chevron Hotel was found to have breached its duty of care to Johns by serving him liquor till he was clearly drunk. It then failed to ensure that his homeward journey was a safe one.

In a stunning sequel to this case, subsequent evidence came to light on appeal suggesting that the initial judgment may have been obtained by fraud.[161] A retrial was ordered.

---

160   Compare the result in this case with that in *Deatons Pty Ltd v Flew* (1949) 79 CLR 370 where the barmaid "glassed" an unruly patron while trying to evict him from the premises. On that occasion, the Court held that it was not within the scope of the barmaid's duty to discipline patrons and therefore the hotel was not liable for her actions.

161   *Cosgrove & Anor v Johns* [1998] QCA 110. It was alleged, amongst other things, that Johns promised to pay one key witness $20,000 to give false evidence and to procure others to do likewise.

Johns v Cosgrove & ors cont.

The principles set down in this case (and not challenged on appeal) sent a shudder through the hospitality industry, especially those responsible for the service of alcohol. In fact, it changed industry practice towards intoxicated patrons as the next case demonstrates.

Cole v South Tweed Heads Rugby League Football Club

[14.315] *Cole v South Tweed Heads Rugby League Football Club Ltd and Anor* (2004) 217 CLR 469

Facts: The appellant Cole was seriously injured when she was run down by a car in the early evening of 26 June 1994, while drunk. Shortly before, she had left the premises of the Respondent football club where she had been drinking for most of the day. At about 3 pm she had been refused further alcohol by the club staff and at 6.15 pm had been asked to leave the premises by the club manager, who offered to provide transport to her home, which she refused.

Cole claimed that the club owed her a duty of care to monitor and moderate her drinking during the day and should not have allowed her to leave the club without proper assistance.

Held: Per Gleeson J.[162]

(i) Except in extreme cases the *law makes intoxicated people legally responsible for their actions*, and they should not, as a general rule, be able to avoid responsibility for the risks that accompany a personal choice to consume alcohol;

(ii) It is *impractical to impose on a supplier of alcohol a general duty* to protect consumers against risks of injury attributable to alcohol consumption. The supplier has only a limited capacity to monitor the level of risk to which a consumer maybe exposed. That risk may be affected by circumstances that the supplier usually is in no position to assess;

(iii) Even if the club did owe Cole a duty of care, on the evidence it had not failed to take reasonable care: it had last supplied Cole with alcohol at 12.30 pm and refused her further alcohol at 3 pm, and had offered her safe transport home.

Per Gummow and Hayne JJ:[163]

(iv) It was unnecessary to decide whether the club owed Cole duties of care to monitor and moderate her drinking and to prevent her from coming to harm on leaving the club, since any breach of the first duty was not a cause of her injuries, and the second duty was discharged by the club's offer of safe transport home;

Per Callinan J:[164]

(v) *Except for extraordinary cases, the law should not recognise a duty of care to protect persons from harm caused by intoxication following a deliberate and voluntary decision on their part to drink to excess. The voluntary act of drinking until intoxicated should be regarded as a deliberate act taken by a person exercising autonomy for which that person should carry personal responsibility in the law;*

---

162 *Cole v South Tweed Heads Rugby League Football Club Ltd and Anor* (2004) 217 CLR 469 at [1]-[26].
163 *Cole v South Tweed Heads Rugby League Football Club Ltd and Anor* (2004) 217 CLR 469 at [48]-[83].
164 *Cole v South Tweed Heads Rugby League Football Club Ltd and Anor* (2004) 217 CLR 469 at [112] - [133].

Cole v South Tweed Heads Rugby League Football Club cont.

(vi) Even assuming a relevant duty of care, the club would have fully discharged it by doing what it did, offering Cole transport home.

(McHugh and Kirby JJ dissenting.)

Fallout from the case

[14.320] Some commentators have suggested that this was a lost opportunity for the High Court to embrace community concerns and attitudes about who should bear the social and economic costs associated with the irresponsible consumption of alcohol.[165] These authors suggest that if the appeal in *Cole v South Tweed Heads Rugby League Football Club Ltd and Anor* had succeeded, alcohol service providers would have faced similar liability at common law to that imposed by the Canadian and US "Dram Shop" legislation. See [14.265] above. As one commentator observed:

> Attributing some responsibility for alcohol-related injury to those who both benefit from and are in a position to control alcohol abuse, would promote safety, deter irresponsible self-interested conduct, and set meaningful standards of acceptable behaviour. The result could be a much needed cultural and social shift towards more responsible alcohol practices.
[166]

Civil Liability legislation

[14.325] Perhaps *Johns v Cosgrove & ors*[167] will remain the high water mark for determining an alcohol servers' duty and standard of care to an intoxicated patron once they have left the premises. The Civil Liability legislation[168] (State and Territory) now directly addresses issues of foreseeability, breach of duty, voluntary assumption of risk, contributory negligence and in some jurisdictions, the legislation addresses the duty and standard of care which will apply in cases of intoxication in future.

For example, the *Civil Liability Act 2003* (Qld), section 46 states:

(1)

 (a) it is not relevant to consider the possibility that a person may be intoxicated or that a person who is intoxicated may be exposed to increased risk;

 (b) a person is not owed a duty of care merely because the person is intoxicated;

 (c) the fact that a person is or may be intoxicated does not of itself increase or otherwise affect the standard of care owed to the person.

---

165 G Orr & G Dale, "Impaired judgements? Alcohol server liability and "personal responsibility" after Cole v South Tweed Heads Rugby League Football Club Ltd" (2005) 13 TLJ 103.

166 P Watson, ""You're not drunk if you can lie on the floor without holding on" – Alcohol Server Liability, Duty, Responsibility and the Law of Torts" [2004] JCUL Rev 6; (2004) 11 *James Cook University Law Review* 108.

167 *Johns v Cosgrove & ors* (1997) QSC 229.

168 *Civil Liability Act 2002* (NSW), ss 47 – 50; *Civil Liability Act 2003* (Qld), ss 46 – 49; *Recreational Services (Limitation of Liability) Act 2002* (SA); *Wrongs Act 1958* (Vic), ss 14F – 14H; *Civil Liability Act 2002* (WA), ss 5L, 5AE; *Civil Liability Act 2002* (Tas), ss 4A – 5; *Civil Law (Wrongs) Act 2002* (ACT), ss 95-86; *Consumer Affairs and Fair Trading Amendment Act* (NT).

(2) Subsection (1) does not affect a liability arising out of conduct happening on licensed premises. [169]

Where a person who suffers harm is intoxicated, there is a presumption of minimum 25% contributory negligence. [170]

Exercise

A Night on the Town

Albert has spent the evening at Barry's restaurant and bar "The Watering Hole". He is a regular Friday night customer and as usual for this time of the evening, he is feeling a little tipsy. As he was attempting to get up from his chair to leave, he tripped and fell heavily onto Donald, the diner at the next table. Donald was not amused and muttered something to the effect that he felt like making a citizen's arrest. With that, Albert saw red and picked up a fork menacing it in Donald's face. When Albert calmed down a bit, he staggered over to the bar and ordered another whisky.

When Donald complained to Barry about Albert's behaviour, Barry came over to Albert and demanded that he finish his drink immediately and leave the premises or he would call the police. Albert agreed to go but asked Barry to pay for his taxi fare home. Barry declined. Donald, who was still angry with Albert, said "Enough is enough" and with that frogmarched Albert out of the restaurant. At the front door, Donald pushed Albert into the footpath where he slipped and fell injuring his head.

Shortly afterwards, Albert was seen getting into his motor vehicle in the restaurant car park. As he drove out into the street, he didn't stop to give way to passing cars and collided with an oncoming vehicle, injuring himself and the three occupants of the other vehicle.

Discuss whether Albert has a cause of action against

(a) Barry; and

(b) Donald.

Who should the occupants of the vehicle involved in the collision with Albert's vehicle sue?

---

169 For example, Civil Liability legislation in New South Wales (*Civil Liability Act 2002* (NSW), s 49) is similar except it does not contain a paragraph similar to the subs 46(2) and adds that if a person who suffers harm is intoxicated then no award of damages is to be made unless it is proved that the person would have suffered the harm whether or not they were intoxicated (*Civil Liability Act 2002* (NSW), s 50(2)); Victoria has no equivalent but (*Wrongs Act 1958* (Vic), s 14G provides that intoxication is a factor that must be considered when determining whether the plaintiff has established there has been a breach of duty of care owned by the defendant; South Australia has no equivalent.

170 For example see Civil Liability legislation: *Civil Liability Act 2002* (NSW), s 50; *Civil Liability Act 2003* (Qld), s 47.

CHAPTER 15

Activities and attractions

[15.10]	THEME PARKS, SPORTING AND OTHER EVENTS		473
	[15.15]	Rights and Duties of Proprietors	474
	[15.20]	No duty to accept licensees	474
		[15.25] *Cole v PC 443A*	475
	[15.30]	Rights of Licensees	475
		[15.35] *Cowell v Rosehill Racecourse*	477
	[15.40]	Consumer protection	478
	[15.43]	Ticket scalping	478
		[15.45] *Australian Rugby Union v The Hospitality Group Pty Ltd*	478
	[15.55]	Rights of a Proprietor over a Spectacle	481
		[15.60] *Victoria Park Racing & Recreation Grounds v Taylor*	481
	[15.65]	Duty to Safeguard Licensees and their Property	482
	[15.70]	Torts and contract	482
		[15.75] *Hall v Brooklands Auto Racing Club*	483
		[15.80] *Australian Racing Drivers Club v Metcalf*	483
	[15.85]	Consumer and Civil Law legislation	484
	[15.90]	Workplace health and safety	484
	[15.95]	Criminal liability	484
	[15.100]	Crowd control	485
	[15.105]	Unauthorised advertising	486
	[15.110]	Major Events	486
	[15.115]	Case Study: street car racing	486
[15.120]	GAMING LAW		487
	[15.120]	Definitions	487
	[15.125]	History	488
		[15.130] *Firebrasse v Brett*	489
	[15.135]	Australian law	491
	[15.140]	Gambling policy	492
	[15.145]	Casinos	494
	[15.155]	Casino policy formulation	495
		[15.160] *Registrar of Titles v Keddell*	498
	[15.165]	Casino development and capacity	499
	[15.175]	Control of casinos	501
	[15.180]	Responsibility of Casino Operators to their customers	503
		[15.185] *Preston v Star City Pty Ltd*	503
		[15.190] *Foroughi v Star City Pty Ltd*	504
		[15.195] *Kakavas v Crown Ltd and John Williams*	504
	[15.200]	Signs of problem gambler	505
	[15.205]	Gaming machines	505
		[15.215] *Mendonca and Santiago v South Sydney Junior Rugby League Club Ltd*	508
[15.225]	WORLD HERITAGE		510
	[15.225]	History and Objectives	510
	[15.230]	Australia's properties inscribed on the World Heritage List	511
	[15.235]	World Heritage Convention	512

[15.240]	World Heritage Committee	513
[15.245]	Cultural heritage	513
[15.250]	Natural heritage	515
[15.255]	State party obligations	515
[15.260]	Presenting World Heritage Sites	516
[15.265]	Australian Developments	517
[15.270]	Australian cases on World Heritage	517
[15.275]	Recurrent themes	519
[15.280]	Towards a co-operative approach	520
[15.285]	Sustainable Tourism	520
[15.290]	World Heritage Sustainable Tourism Programme	520
[15.295]	Sustainable tourism at World Heritage Sites	521
[15.320]	Native title	525
[15.325]	Implementation	528
[15.330]	Management models	528
[15.335]	Management strategies	529
[15.340]	Laws and regulations	529
[15.345]	Tourism operators' accreditation	529

[15.355] ADVENTURE TOURISM 531

[15.360]	Compare Innkeepers/Carriers' Duties	531
[15.365]	Contract	532
[15.370]	Torts	533
[15.375]	Hotels' Responsibility for Beach Safety	533
[15.380]	*Case Study 1*	534
[15.385]	*Case Study 2*	534
[15.390]	*Case Study 3: Bondi Beach (1997)*	535
[15.395]	*Case Study 4: Sahara Tours (1999)*	535
[15.400]	Consumer Protection	536
[15.405]	Unfair practices	536
[15.410]	Statutory guarantees	536
[15.415]	Exclusion or modification	536
[15.420]	Reforms	537
[15.425]	Reform–consumer protection	537
[15.435]	Australian Consumer Law and Tort law reform	538
[15.445]	Civil Liability Legislation	539
[15.450]	Cases on obvious risk	539
[15.455]	Tourism and recreation	540
[15.460]	Cases on dangerous recreational activity	540
[15.460]	*Lormine v Zenereb*	540
[15.465]	Public authorities	541
[15.470]	Other liabilities	541
[15.475]	Occupational health and safety legislation	541
[15.480]	Breach of statutory duty	541
[15.485]	Criminal liability	541
[15.490]	*R v Geoffrey Ian Jack Nairn*	542
[15.495]	Risk Management	542
[15.500]	Concepts in risk management	542
[15.505]	Risk management process	543
[15.510]	Difficulties in tourism	543
[15.515]	Limiting and shifting responsibility	543
[15.520]	Exclusion/limitation clauses	543
[15.525]	Insurance	544
[15.530]	Regulatory Compliance	544

[15.05] Most definitions of tourism identify three key components: first, travel; secondly, accommodation; and thirdly, activities and attractions. For example:

> Tourism denotes the temporary, short term movement of people to destinations outside the places where they normally live and work and their *activities* during their stay at these destinations.[1]

or

> Tourism' means the *activities* of persons travelling to and staying in countries outside their country of residence for not more than one consecutive year for leisure, business and other purposes.[2]

Travel has been discussed in Chapter 12 and Accommodation in Chapter 13. The third component, activities and attractions, is the subject of this chapter. Activities and attractions are often the main motivations for travel and are also often the centre of hospitality operations. It should be noted that food and beverage, the subject of Chapter 14, could be regarded as ancillary to transport or accommodation or as independent activities and attractions in their own right. Because of this dichotomy they have been discussed in their own chapter in this text.

Activities and attractions are so diverse that it would be impossible to review the law on every one of them. Instead, the approach taken in this chapter is to consider first the general rights and duties between the parties and to then consider the regulatory issues in several representative case studies which involve key activities and attractions, namely:

- theme parks, sporting and other events;
- gaming law;
- World Heritage and ecotourism; and
- adventure tourism.

THEME PARKS, SPORTING AND OTHER EVENTS

[15.10] This section will examine the key issues for theme parks, sporting and other major events arising under the general law and by statute. Various Australian States have already passed special enabling legislation to facilitate street car racing, the Olympics, World Youth day and so on.[3] More recently, however, competition is growing among the States to be the "event capital of Australia" leading to the introduction of generic enabling legislation for major events.[4]

As the then Victorian Sports Minister, James Merlino, described it:

> The *Major Sporting Events Act* [2009 Vic] is the most comprehensive major sporting event-related legislation anywhere in the world and will further enhance our unparalleled reputation as the destination for major sporting events.[5]

Similarly, the NSW Tourism Minister Ms Jodi McKay said:

---

1   A.J Burkadt & S Medlik, *Tourism: Past, Present and Future* (London, Heinemann, 1974).
2   Draft Annex on Tourism under the General Agreement on Trade in Services (GATS), World Trade Organization (30 September 1999).
3   For example, *Gold Coast Motor Racing Events Act 1990* (Qld); *Australian Grand Prix Act 1994* (Vic); *Homebush Motor Racing (Sydney 400) 2008* (NSW).
4   *Major Events Act 2009* (NSW); *Major Sporting Events Act 2009* (Vic); *Major Sports Facilities Act 2001* (Qld).
5   Second reading speech, Victorian Parliament, 26 February 2009.

These types of events involve enormous amounts of planning, coordination and logistical support from government agencies, including transport and traffic management, health, police and emergency services, crowd management and use of venues. The events, in turn, bring increased international and domestic tourism to New South Wales, economic benefits, jobs and an enhanced international profile. Special legislation has often been enacted to facilitate the conduct of particular major events in New South Wales. Over time, a standard set of provisions has been developed for major events legislation.

Although the types of events have varied widely, many of the legislative provisions necessary to support the events have been essentially the same. To increase certainty for event organisers and to further encourage the economic investment produced by the staging of events in New South Wales, the Government is introducing the *Major Events Bill 2009*. The bill collects together the provisions that have been regularly used in such special legislation and allows specified provisions to be applied to an event that is declared in regulations to be a major event for the purposes of the legislation. [6]

To facilitate major events, this special enabling legislation has been required to modify the rights and duties of the promoters and proprietors of activities and attractions under the general law as discussed in the following sections.

Rights and Duties of Proprietors

[15.15] The following discussion outlines the general rights and duties of proprietors of activities and attractions, who, unlike carriers and innkeepers, have no special rights and duties at common law. They are subject to the general common law as well as the consumer protection legislation (see Chapter 9) and OHS legislation (see Chapter 8, [8.180]ff). There is also often special legislation for the regulation of each type of activity and attraction. The owners or operators of activities and attractions are variously called owners, operators, promoters or proprietors. The term "proprietor" will be used in this chapter as this term encompasses both owner and operator. Visitors to activities and attractions are variously called customers, patrons, entrants, fans or spectators and the like. The terms "licensee" (general) will be used in this chapter as appropriate to describe the visitor. "Licensee" captures the essence of the relationship. More specific subsets of this term such as "spectator" will be used where appropriate.

No duty to accept licensees

[15.20] Unlike carriers and innkeepers, the proprietors of activities and attractions have no common law duty to accept customers, patrons, entrants, fans or spectators and the like. Possession of the premises carries with it the general right to exclude others or to permit them to enter on such terms as the proprietor sees fit. [7] Generally the discrimination laws provide the only restriction on the right of exclusion.

This general right of exclusion applies also to tour operators, tour guides and others seeking to conduct commercial activities at the proprietor's premises. Consider the following case.

---

6   Second reading speech, NSW Parliament, 20 October 2009.
7   See PZ Binder, "Arbitrary exclusions of "undesirable" racetrack and casino patrons: the courts' illusory perception of common law public/private distinctions" (1983) 32 *Buffalo Law Review* 699-730; M Schechter, "Uston v Resorts International Hotel: an unwarranted intrusion on the common law right of exclusion" (1984) 20 *California Western Law Review* 511-531. The case concerned the right of a casino to exclude card counters.

Cole v PC 443A

[15.25] *Cole v PC 443A* [1936] 3 All ER 107

Facts: Cole had, for some time, conducted a business as a tour guide to Westminster Abbey under a permit issued by the Dean of the Abbey. Although there was no suggestion of misconduct, in 1932 the Dean refused to renew his permit. In 1935 Cole, wearing a badge "Cole's Sightseeing Tours", was present at a divine service in the Abbey. On the Dean's orders a policeman was called and, after requesting him to leave, ejected him without unnecessary force. Cole sued the policeman for assault.

Held: The King's Bench Division (Lord Hewart LCJ, du Parq and Goddard JJ) dismissed the action. The court noted that Cole's living depended upon admission to the Abbey and noted that he had previously brought similar unsuccessful actions for eviction from Westminster Hall and the Houses of Parliament. In this case Cole argued that he had a general right to be present as a parishioner of the church. Lord Goddard LCJ dismissed this argument in the following terms:

> That, in my opinion, is really humbug. It is an afterthought designed to cover what the man was really doing ... He never said, and nobody would have believed him if he had said: "My real object in being there was to worship." In these circumstances, and especially when one remembers that with engaging frankness on the application for this case it was stated that what was being interfered with was Mr Cole's livelihood – not his immortal soul but his livelihood – it seems to me that the excursions into constitutional and ecclesiastical law and history, which we have had, however edifying and however ably done, are absolutely irrelevant.

Rights of Licensees

[15.30] The rights of a customers, patrons, entrants, fans or spectators and the like at activities and attractions are limited to those rights granted by the proprietor. The usual rights granted are permission to enter the premises and enjoy the activity or attraction. Without this permission licensees become trespassers and could be evicted at any time with reasonable force if necessary. As long as the permission is current it provides a defence to trespass.

In law the permission to enter the premises and enjoy the activity or attraction is a licence, whether it is called a licence or a permit, a ticket, a pass, an invitation or the like. Diners at a restaurant, drinkers at a bar or guests at a hotel have similar licence rights. Greeson P in *Baikie v Fullerton-Smith*[8] provides a useful description of the nature of licences:

> there are all sorts of licences but basically each is an authority which prevents the individual to whom it is granted from being a trespasser on someone else's property. Every licence is a limited permission both as to how long it will endure and as to what it allows to be done on the premises...It is a purely personal and temporary permission – a permissive occupation.

Whether there is a right to transfer (assign) the licence depends on the circumstances and proprietors often expressly prohibit transfer in the terms of the permission so as to invalidate transactions by ticket "scalpers", particularly for popular events or entertainment. However, the trade continues despite this risk as it is often difficult or impractical for the proprietor to detect the breach or enforce the penalty. For more discussion see [15.43].

---

8   *Baikie v Fullerton-Smith* [1961] NZLR 901 at 906.

The other rights of a licensee depend upon whether or not there is a contract: [9]

- **Gratuitous licence:** If the licence is gratuitous, i.e. free, then the proprietor (licensor) may cancel (revoke) it at any time and the former licensee becomes a trespasser and must leave the premises. In fact a request to leave is the most usual way of cancelling such a licence. The former licensee will have no right or remedy for the cancellation.

- **Contractual licence:** If the licence is contractual, that is if there is an entry or participation fee, then the proprietor's right to cancel it is subject to the contract. The proprietor may still revoke the licence at any time (for example, by requesting the licensee to leave) and the former licensee becomes a trespasser and must leave in the same way as under a gratuitous licence. However in cancelling the licence the proprietor may be breaching the contract which gives the licensee the right to bring an action for damages. Where the fee has been paid by someone else, as often happens in a group or family situation, then the licensee's rights on the contract may be more limited by the privity of contract rule unless the licensee can show they had an agency or trust arrangement with the person paying. [10] Otherwise the person who paid could sue for breach of contract. [11]

So the result is that under a licence, whether gratuitous or contractual, the proprietor can cancel permission at any time and the licensee then becomes a trespasser and must leave the premises. The proprietor is in possession of the premises and cancellation is an exercise of the proprietor's general right of exclusion as discussed in [15.15]. This rule highlights the contrast between licences and lease or tenancy arrangements. If the customer, patron, entrant, fan or spectator and the like has a lease or tenancy then that includes an interest in the land (usually possessory) which restricts the proprietor's right of exclusion. Under a lease or tenancy the proprietor must follow the more complicated procedures required to terminate their interest in the land.

If the proprietor cancels a licence in breach of contract then in most tourism, travel and hospitality (and in sporting and entertainment) situations the damages recoverable will include damages for disappointment. [12] These are the circumstances expressly contemplated in *Jarvis v Swan Tours* [13] and *Baltic Shipping Company v Dillon (the "Mikhail Lermontov")* [14] (see Chapter 2, [2.215]ff). Before the development of this remedy, damages were limited to the

---

9   There is also a third category, namely a licence coupled with an interest in the land. In this case the operator's rights of cancellation are restricted because the licence is protected along with the interest in the land. It was so held in *Hurst v Picture Theatres Ltd* [1915] 1 KB 1 although it is difficult to identify what was the interest in land and this case was not followed in the leading Australian decision, *Cowell's case*, discussed in [15.35].

10 In Queensland the guest as a third party beneficiary would have a direct claim against the operator under s 55 of the *Property Law Act 1974* (Qld). It is also arguable that there is a general right to do this at common law in the circumstances covered by *Trident Insurance v McNiece Bros* (1988) 165 CLR 107.

11 In *Jackson v Horizon Holidays* [1975] WLR 1468 Lord Denning even awarded damages to the contracting father for the disappointment of his family members; however this was overruled by the House of Lords in *Woodar Investments v Wimpey* [1980] 1 All ER 571.

12 For a discussion of the principles involved see TC Atherton, "Package Holidays: legal aspects" (1994) 15(3) *Tourism Management* 193-199.

13 *Jarvis v Swan Tours* [1972] WLR 954 per Denning LJ: "in a proper case damages can be recovered for mental distress in contract. One such case is a contract for a holiday, or any other contract to provide entertainment or enjoyment".

14 *Shipping Company v Dillon (the "Mikhail Lermontov")* (1993) 176 CLR 344, approving the proposition by Bingham LJ in *Watts v Morrow* (1991) 1 WLR 1421 at 1445: "Where the very object of a contract is to provide pleasure, relaxation, peace of mind or freedom from molestation, damages will be awarded if the fruit of the contract is not provided or if the contrary result is procured instead."

price of the ticket and there was a concerted effort to obtain injunctions and other equitable relief in cases where proprietors cancelled the licence of the customer, patron, entrant, fan or spectator and the like in breach of contract.[15] However these authors believe the better view in Australia is that the licence remains a mere personal interest and the only remedy of the licensee under general law is damages for breach of contract.[16] This is illustrated in the leading Australian case discussed below.[17]

Cowell v Rosehill Racecourse

[15.35] *Cowell v Rosehill Racecourse* (1937) 56 CLR 605

Facts: Cowell claimed £5,000 damages for assault after being forcibly removed from a racecourse part way through the meeting. He had paid 4 shillings to attend a race meeting and had refused to leave when requested.

Held: The High Court (Latham CJ, Starke, Dixon, McTiernann JJ, Evatt J dissenting) held that the contractual licence did not confer any proprietary interest in the land but was only a contractual right which could be cancelled at common law. Upon cancellation Cowell had a reasonable time to leave and then he became a trespasser. For cancellation in breach of contract, Cowell's only remedy was damages for breach of contract.

Dixon J described the nature of the licence and rights under it in this way:[18]

> A licence ... is revocable at law. It operates as a bare permission to do what would otherwise be an invasion of the licensor's rights. If the permission is terminated, further continuance of the acts it authorised becomes unlawful. A licensee does not become a trespasser until he has received notice that the licence is countermanded and until a reasonable time has elapsed in which he may withdraw from the land and remove whatever property he has brought in pursuance of the licence. But if he then refuses to leave he cannot complain of his forcible removal.

Latham CJ made these observations:

> I cannot regard the transaction of buying a ticket for an entertainment as creating anything more than a contractual right in the buyer against the seller – a right to have the contract performed. For the breach of such a right there is a remedy in damages, but the remedies applicable to proprietary rights are not legally (or equitably) appropriate in such a case. There is strictly no grant of interest. What is granted is something quite different, namely, contractual rights and obligations.[19]
>
> If his licence was effectively revoked, though wrongfully, he was a trespasser, and the removal of him from the racecourse without the use of undue force did not constitute an assault. It is clear that equity would never have decreed the specific performance of a contract

---

15   Stein and Stone, *Torrens Title* (Butterworths, Sydney, 1991), p 290 argue that the courts strained the principles of property law to try and find a better remedy when damages were inadequate. See also Bradbrook, MacCallum and Moore, *Australian Real Property Law* (4th ed, Lawbook Co, Sydney, 2008), chapter 1.

16   *Wood v Leadbitter* 153 Eng Rep 351 (1845); *Naylor v Canterbury Park Racecourse* (1935) 35 SR (NSW) 281; *Ashburn Anstalt v Arnold* [1989] 1 Ch 1. However in *Forbes v NSW Trotting Club* (1975) 25 ALR 1 the High Court did express some reservations about *Cowell's* case.

17   There is authority to support equitable relief in principle if there is a constructive trust: *Ashburn Anstalt v Arnold* [1989] 1 Ch 1 at 25-26; an irrevocable licence (express or implied): *Mayfield Holdings Ltd v Moana Reef Ltd* [1973] 1 NZLR 309 at 314-315; *Winter Gardens Theatre (London) Ltd v Millennium Productions Ltd* [1946] 1 All ER 678 at 685 (reversed on other grounds [1948] AC 173); or estoppels, NP Gravall, *Land Law: Texts and Materials* (1995, Butterworths, London), pp 511-512.

18   *Cowell v Rosehill Racecourse* (1937) 56 CLR 605 at 630-631.

19   *Cowell v Rosehill Racecourse* (1937) 56 CLR 605 at 617.

Cowell v Rosehill Racecourse cont.

to provide an entertainment. Equity would never have granted an unconditional injunction restraining the proprietor of a place of entertainment from excluding from the place a person who had bought a ticket of admission. [20]

Consumer protection

[15.40] If the termination of the licence (gratuitous or contractual) is unconscionable or deceptive and misleading then the *Australian Consumer Law* protections may provider wider remedies than available at common law (see [9.55]ff). The remedies available in appropriate circumstances, would include injunction and specific performance for wrongful cancellation of a licence (see [9.290]ff).

Exercise

Gold Coast V8 Car Racing Event

The event organiser sells 4 day ticket to a spectator from Sydney, Adelaide or Melbourne. On the first day the crowd controller excludes spectator and cancels the 4 day ticket. The spectator has incurred incurs expenses for airfare, accommodation and the ticket to the event.

Discuss issues including:

– Licensee's rights
– Consumer Protection
– Remedies?

Ticket scalping

[15.43] Do licensees have a right to assign their licence to another person? Usually a licence granted or sold is personal and not assignable and this is usually set out in the terms and conditions of the licence. This issue has most often arisen in relation to the widespread practice of "ticket scalping" where intermediaries (resellers) with no intention of attending themselves buy up scarce tickets to popular events with the intention of on selling them at a profit to genuine customers, patrons, entrants, fans or spectators and the like. The practice disrupts the orderly distribution of tickets, causes considerable loss of revenue for promoters and forces end users to pay exorbitant prices. There have been a number of cases where the legal issues have been examined.

Australian Rugby Union v The Hospitality Group Pty Ltd

[15.45] *Australian Rugby Union v The Hospitality Group Pty Ltd* (2000) 173 ALR 702

Facts: The Hospitality Group (THG) purported to sell hospitality packages including tickets for the international rugby tests including the Bledisloe Cup. The ticket conditions prohibited resale for commercial purposes without the Australian Rugby Union's (ARU) written consent.

---

20   *Cowell v Rosehill Racecourse* (1937) 56 CLR 605 at 619.

Australian Rugby Union v The Hospitality Group Pty Ltd cont.

Held: The condition prohibiting the resale was entirely reasonable and enforceable. The ARU was entitled to prevent scalping to capture all available profit from the event and also had a legitimate interest to protect in selling tickets at a reasonable price to promote the sport.

Postscript: This approach is now mirrored in the more recent legislative interventions as discussed below.

[15.48] The Office of Fair Trading (OFT) promotes the Entertainment Industry Code of Fair Conduct on this subject but it does not cover online or offsite scalping and thus leaves it as a problem for promoters as these next cases illustrate.

eBay International AG v Creative Festival Entertainment Pty Limited (2006) 170 FCR 450

Facts: The promoters of "The Big Day Out" music festival sought to restrain scalping over eBay. Ebay brought an action against the promoters for threatening and cancelling tickets resold over eBay.

During the ticket sales, the promoters had changed condition 6 from:

"if resold, ticket *may* be cancelled or holder *may* be refused entry" to:
"*will* be cancelled and holder *will* be refused entry".

Held: The promoter engaged in deceptive and misleading conduct contra to s 52 of the *Trade Practices Act 1974* (Cth) (now s 18 of the *Australian Consumer Law*) because:

- the change was ineffective on ticket sales already made;
- the changed term was not part of the new ticket conditions on the ticket case principles;
- the change was without proper notice in accordance with ticket case principles;
- of the difficulty in enforcing such a condition against an assignee or donee of a ticket because there was no privity unless purchased as an agent.

After the case, eBay issued a statement

> I think the ruling illustrates the need for promoters to improve primary distribution in order to get tickets into the hands of genuine fans rather than trying to shut the gate after the horse has bolted. [21]

[15.50] In 2009 The Big Day Out Sydney sold out almost instantly. The promoters were forced to do a second show to keep fans happy. In 2010 the promoters further strengthened their ticketing conditions by specifying:

> DUE TO OUR CONTINUING BATTLE AGAINST TICKET SCALPERS AND PROFITEERING, THE BIG DAY OUT REQUIRES YOU TO READ AND AGREE TO THE FOLLOWING CONDITIONS BEFORE YOU PURCHASE TICKETS TO THE SHOW CONDITIONS OF SALE AND ADMISSION
>
> ...
>
> 2. This ticket may not, without the prior consent of the promoter, be resold or offered for resale at a premium over the face value of the ticket (including via on-line auction sites) or used for advertising, promoting or other commercial purposes (including competitions and trade promotions) or to enhance the demand for other goods or services either by the original purchaser from the Promoter or any subsequent ticket holder.

---

21 Examples of ticket scalping continue to abound. For example, at the 2009 AFL Grand Final, tickets were sold by promoters at $120 per ticket but the scalping price rose to $1900 a ticket!

If a ticket is sold or used in breach of this condition, the Promoter reserves the right to cancel the ticket without a refund. This ticket is only valid when purchased from official agents. Tickets bought from other sources may be refused entry.

3. The Promoter reserves the right to enforce published ticket purchase limits and cancel any tickets obtained above said limits by any one customer....

10. The Promoter reserves the right to refuse a ticketholder admission to the event or to evict that person from the event in any of the following circumstances: ...

... b) if the ticket has been sold or used in breach of condition 2;

So the ticketing conditions and contractual position is made clear. The problem is this is very difficult to enforce given the large numbers of transactions, minimal paperwork, impracticality of screening, requiring ID, investigating transactions and attempting to refuse entry when large numbers of licensees are queued and requiring entry without delay

Ticket scalping legislation

[15.52] Several States have sought to deter ticket scalping by making it a criminal offence at certain events. This legislation includes:

- *Major Sports Facilities Act 2001* (Qld) [22] which prohibits unauthorised resale or purchase of tickets;
- *Major Sports Events Act 2009* (Vic) [23] which is similar to the Queensland legislation but contains more extensive measures for enforcement; and
- *Major Events Act 2009* (NSW) [24] which prohibits unauthorised sale of tickets at the venues of major events.

The Commonwealth Consumer Affairs Advisory Council is, at time of writing, conducting a national review into ticket scalping and its impact on consumers. The Review is examining current practices related to ticket on selling and considering possible marketplace responses, including both regulatory and non-regulatory options, and their cost and effectiveness. The Issues Paper is available at http://www.treasury.gov.au which will also provide other reports as they are produced.

Exercise

Ticket scalping AFL Grand Final

Consider the following facts, identify the legal issues and propose possible solutions (legal and practical) to the problem.

- Tickets sold by promoter at $120 each
- Scalping price up to $1900 each, sold by online auction
- Country fans must pre book flights and accommodation in January with no guarantee of a ticket to the game

---

[22] *Major Sports Facilities Act 2001* (Qld), Part 4A – Resale or purchase of tickets.
[23] *Major Sports Events Act 2009* (Vic), Part 9 – Sports Event Ticketing.
[24] *Major Events Act 2009* (NSW), s 41(b).

Ticket scalping AFL Grand Final cont.

- Clubs receive allocations of 1000 tickets and some clubs scalp.

―――― ⁂ ――――

Rights of a Proprietor over a Spectacle

[15.55] Under copyright law the owner of the copyright in an original work has the exclusive right to perform and broadcast it.[25] However, at common law there is no property in a mere spectacle, that is, it is only where it has been transformed into printed words, sound or image that copyright law applies. Thus in *Bernstein of Leigh (Baron) v Skyviews & General Ltd*[26] Baron Bernstein failed in an action to recover photographs from an aerial photographer who had overflown his estates and taken photographs of them for sale. Baron Bernstein had no property in the spectacle and no legal right to privacy. In fact the photographer had copyright in the photographs of Baron Bernstein's estates. This creates serious problems for the proprietors and promoters of activities and attractions, particularly major events, and it often has to be overcome by special enabling legislation.[27] Consider the following case.

Victoria Park Racing & Recreation Grounds v Taylor

[15.60] *Victoria Park Racing & Recreation Grounds v Taylor* (1937) 58 CLR 479

Facts: T erected a platform on land adjoining a racecourse and broadcast by radio descriptions and the results of the races conducted by the proprietor of the racecourse, VPR. As a result attendances at the racecourse, entrances and other revenue fell. VPR sought a permanent injunction to restrain T from making the broadcasts.

Held: The High Court (Latham CJ, Dixon and McTiernan JJ, Rich and Evatt JJ dissenting) held that T had not infringed any property right of the VPR and so was not entitled to an injunction. Latham CJ said:[28]

> I am unable to see that any right of the plaintiff has been violated or any wrong has been done to him. Any person is entitled to look over the plaintiff's fences and to see what goes on in the plaintiff's land. If the plaintiff desires to prevent this, the plaintiff can erect a higher fence...At sports grounds and other places of entertainment it is the lawful, natural and common practice to put up fences and other structures to prevent people who are not prepared to pay for admission from getting the benefit of the entertainment. In my opinion, the law cannot by injunction in effect erect fences which the plaintiff is not prepared to provide. The defendant does no wrong in looking at what takes place on the plaintiff's land. Further, he does no wrong to the plaintiff by describing to other persons, to as wide an audience as he can obtain, what takes place on the plaintiff's ground. The court was not referred to any principle of law which prevents any man from describing anything which he sees anywhere if he does not make defamatory statements, infringe the law as to offensive language, etc, break a contract, or wrongfully reveal confidential information. The defendant

---

25   *Copyright Act 1968* (Cth), s 31(3).
26   *Bernstein of Leigh (Baron) v Skyviews & General Ltd* [1978] QB 479.
27   For example, see *Gold Coast Motor Racing Events Act 1990* (Qld); *Australian Grands Prix Act 1994* (Vic); *Homebush Motor Racing (Sydney 400) Act 2008* (NSW), Part 5 s 35ff.
28   *Victoria Park Racing & Recreation Grounds v Taylor* (1937) 58 CLR 479 at 494.

Victoria Park Racing & Recreation Grounds v Taylor cont.

did not infringe the law in any of these respects.

Major events: To facilitate major events and assist the promoter/organiser to capture all the commercial benefits the special enabling legislation creates intellectual property in the event and vest it in the promoters. Such legislation includes:

- *Gold Coast Motor Racing Events Act 1990* (Qld)
- *Australian Grand Prix Act 1994* (Vic)
- *Homebush Motor Racing (Sydney 400) Act 2008* (NSW), Part 5 ss 35ff
- *Major Sporting Events Act 2009* (Vic), Part 3 Div 3ff Authorised Broadcasting

Duty to Safeguard Licensees and their Property

[15.65] Unlike the public callings of carriers and innkeepers discussed in Chapters 12 and 13 respectively, at common law there are no special duties upon proprietors of theme parks, sporting and other events to safeguard licensees and their property.

In relation to licensee's property, if the proprietor takes custody (eg, in a cloak room), then the principles of bailment apply. Under the law of bailment the proprietor is liable for negligence but the doctrine of res ipsa loquitor reverses the onus of proof (ie, the proprietor must prove that although the property has not been returned this was not as a result of the proprietor's negligence).

In relation to the licensee personally, the general principle is that proprietors of activities and attractions owe a duty to ensure that reasonable care and skill are taken for the safety of licensees and others affected by their operations. This duty of care is imposed in a variety of ways in activities and attractions and most of these have been discussed in detail in previous chapters, as indicated below:

- Contract law (Chapter 4)
- Torts (Chapter 5)
- Product liability and statutory guarantees under the *Australian Consumer Law* (Chapter 9)
- OHS legislation (Chapter 8, [8.180]ff)
- Criminal law gross negligence (Chapter 6, [6.55]ff), and
- Specific legislation for particular activities and attractions (see case studies below).

Torts and contract

[15.70] The general duty of care imposed on the proprietor of premises under the tort of negligence applies independently of contract and covers licensees whether they are contractual or gratuitous licensees and even if they are trespassers [29] on the premises. [30] So too does the general duty of care in tort imposed on the proprietors of dangerous activities or dangerous

---

29   For example, if the guest has not paid the required fee for entry or participation.
30   In *Australian Safeways Stores Pty Ltd v Zaluzna* (1987) 162 CLR 479 the High Court abandoned the old model of occupiers' liability based on the status of the guest and assimilated it into the general law of negligence.

materials.[31] However, existence of the duty and the extent of the duty descend along with the lowering in status of the person on the property and ascend with the risk and danger of the activity on ordinary principles of negligence.

In contract, provided there is no inconsistent express provision, the courts imply a term that the premises and activities will be supplied with due care and skill. This is augmented by similar statutory guarantees discussed in [15.85]ff.

All those involved with activities and attractions need to be mindful of the potential risks and possible responsibilities.[32]

Hall v Brooklands Auto Racing Club

[15.75] *Hall v Brooklands Auto Racing Club* (1933) 1 KB 205

Facts: A racing car crashed through a safety fence, killing two and injuring other spectators. The race track had been operating for 23 years without an accident like it.

Decision: The English Court of Appeal (Scrutton, Greer and Slesser LJJ) held that the racetrack proprietor was not liable. Under an implied term of the contract the duty of the proprietor was to see that the racetrack was as free from danger as reasonable skill and care could make it. However motor racing involves risks which no reasonable diligence could avoid and there was also an implied term that the plaintiff knew of the risk and agreed to accept it. Scrutton LJ said:[33]

> A spectator at Lords or the Oval runs the risk of being hit by a cricket ball…[those] at football or hockey or polo matches run similar risks…those who pay for admission or seats in stands at a flying meeting run a risk of the performing aeroplanes falling on their heads…What is reasonable care would depend on the perils which might reasonably be expected to occur, and the extent to which the ordinary spectator might be expected to take the risk of such perils…No-one expects the persons receiving payment to erect such structures or nets that no spectator can be hit by a ball kicked or hit violently from the field of play towards the spectators. The field is safe to stand on and the spectators take the risk of the game.

Comment: Note this case proceeded in contract but the principles are very similar to those which would apply in tort. In *Wilks v Cheltenham Cycle Club*[34] a motor cycle scramble rider who crashed against a fence, injuring W and his daughter, was held not liable on similar principles.

Australian Racing Drivers Club v Metcalf

[15.80] *Australian Racing Drivers Club v Metcalf* (1961) 106 CLR 177

Facts: This case involved the Bathurst 1000. During the race a car crashed through the fence on Con Rod Straight injuring M, a 16-year-old spectator who had paid a fee of 6/- to enter and watch the race. Cars had twice before crashed through the other side but never this side.

Decision: The High Court (Dixon CJ, McTiernan, Kitto, Taylor and Owen JJ) upheld the finding that the proprietor was liable for breach of contractual duty. There was an implied condition of the admission contract that the premises would be as reasonably safe for enabling him to watch the races

---

31   In *Burnie Port Authority v General Jones Pty Ltd* (1994) 179 CLR 520 the High Court abandoned the old *Rylands v Fletcher* model of strict liability and also assimilated it into the general law of negligence.
32   For example, recent tragedies such as the collapse of the overhanging cliffs at Margaret River, the Port Arthur massacre and the Thredbo disaster illustrate the point.
33   *Hall v Brooklands Auto Racing Club* (1933) 1 KB 205 at 209.
34   *Wilks v Cheltenham Cycle Club* (1971) WLR 608. Denning LJ (at 670-671) set out the responsibilities of participants in such activities.

Australian Racing Drivers Club v Metcalf cont.

as reasonable care and skill could make them. The common experience of mankind was that racing cars travelling at very high speed may frequently get out of control and measures should be taken (that is, an effective safety fence) to prevent them from injuring spectators. The defence did not argue that under the contract M had voluntarily assumed the risk as M was a child attending his first race meeting.

Comment: This case was argued in contract. Note the shift from the previous racing cases towards a stricter liability. This is especially important for proprietors with the non-excludable warranties and conditions which now apply, as discussed in the next part. Today the facts would also support a claim under the *Australian Consumer Law*.

Consumer and Civil Law legislation

[15.85] The *Australian Consumer Law* imposes a statutory guarantee that services will be supplied with all due care and skill. As discussed in Chapter 9. These provisions usually prevail over the exclusion and limitation clauses often found in the signs, tickets and documentation at theme parks, sporting and other events.

The *Civil Liability* legislation discussed in Chapters 5 and 9 now limits liability for dangerous recreational activities as well as addressing issues of foreseeability, breach of duty, voluntary assumption of risk, contributory negligence amongst others.

Workplace health and safety

[15.90] OHS legislation generally imposes a duty of care on proprietors of activities and attractions in two ways. First, the premises are usually held to be a "factory" for the purposes of the legislation so that the proprietor's duty of care for employees and other visitors to the "factory" usually encompasses customers, patrons, entrants, fans and spectators and the like. Secondly, equipment used in some activities may also fall within the definition of "amusement device" and so be subject to further standards and duties. As discussed in Chapter 8, [8.210], the breach of these duties may result in criminal prosecution. Civil liability arises only indirectly where breach of a standard or duty founds an action for damages for breach of statutory duty.

Criminal liability

[15.95] In extreme cases of gross negligence or recklessness the proprietor of activities and attractions may be prosecuted for similar offences. Again these offences usually arise from breach of duty of persons in charge of dangerous things [35] or of persons doing dangerous acts. [36]

The point is illustrated in the findings of the Coronial inquest into the death of a volunteer track marshal at the Australian Grand Prix Formula One car race in March 2001. The volunteer marshal was killed when he was struck by one of the wheels of a disintegrating racing car following a high speed crash. The wheel found its way through a "gap" in the

---

35 See, for example, Queensland *Criminal Code*, s 289: duty of persons in charge of dangerous things.
36 See, for example, Queensland *Criminal Code*, s 288: duty of persons doing dangerous acts.

barrier fence used for photography and for access. Coincidentally, the tether system designed to keep wheels on crashing cars also failed (all 4 flew off). The venue, Albert Park, had been converted for racing and there was evidence that it provided inadequate fencing and distance from spectators. The Coroner found that the accident was "avoidable".[37] In the aftermath to this enquiry, the organisers doubled the fence height.

The Tort Law Reform Legislation (see [5.185]) probably saved the event. See also the "balloon-kissing" case *R v Sanby*[38] (see [6.60]).

Crowd control

[15.100] Crowd control is part of the proprietor's general duty of care in contract and tort to take reasonable measures to ensure the safety of customers, patrons, entrants, fans or spectators and the like. A proprietor has authority to enforce conditions of contract and entry even if it is necessary to physically restrain: *Balmain Ferry Co v Robertson* (1906) CLR 379, see [4.235].

It is strengthened by Events legislation including:

- *Gold Coast Motor Racing Events Act 1990* (Qld);
- *Australian Grands Prix Act 1994* (Vic);
- *Major Sporting Events Act 2009* (Vic), Part 4 Crowd management;
- *Major Events Act 2009* (NSW), Div 5 Safety and crowd management at major events.

Case Study: Crown Control at the Big Day Out

A spectator was crushed in a mosh pit during a performance by a rock band at the Big Day Out festival in Sydney 2001[39]. She was revived and rushed to hospital, but died five days later. The frontman for the band claimed "We begged, we screamed, we sent letters, we tried to take precautions, because … we know we cause this big emotional blister on a crowd".

The Senior Deputy State Coroner issued a statement saying responsibility was on the Big Day Out's promoters as there was overwhelming evidence that crowd density was dangerous when the band went on stage. The band was also criticised in the report for making "alarming and inflammatory" comments and failing to take the situation more seriously.

Wrongful death claims were filed by the spectator's parents against the promoters, security personal and the band. The New South Wales court found the band was not liable and dismissed them from the claim.

Later, the insurer also sued the band claiming that the band's frontman incited the spectators to rush the stage.

The promoters of the Big Day Out have included specific provisions on this risk in their conditions of ticket sale and admission 2010 which state.

10. The Promoter reserves the right to refuse a ticketholder admission to the event or to evict that person from the event in any of the following circumstances:

  e) if the ticketholder is affected by the consumption of alcohol or drugs.

  f) if the ticketholder participates in dangerous activities including aggressive dancing, moshing, stage diving, crowd surfing and climbing

---

37 *Coroner's Case* No 621/01.
38 *R v Sanby* (Unreported, NT CCA, No CA8 of 1992).
39 Source: ABC and Wikipedia

Case Study: Crown Control at the Big Day Out cont.

13. The Promoter and the owner and or lessee of the Venue shall not be held liable for any loss, injury or damages sustained entering or within the Venue whether caused by the negligence of the Promoter or that owner or lessee or otherwise.

Unauthorised advertising

[15.105] A proprietor may enforce intellectual property rights over the use of the name and logo amongst other things relating to the event. This is also strengthened by events legislation. What about other advertising and marketing? In *Lord Bernstein v Skyviews*[40] the proprietor had no action in trespass against overflight. The Events legislation now restricts this. See, for example:

- *Major Sports facilities Act 2001* (Qld), Part 4B Advertising;
- *Major Sporting Events Act 2009* (Vic), Part 7 Advertising and part 8 Aerial Advertising;
- *Major Events Act 2009* (NSW), Div 4 Commercial and airspace controls.

Major Events

[15.110] The common features of major events are:

- Public/Private partnership;
- Special enabling legislation to deal with issues, for example, like ownership of the spectacle;
- Special administering organisation; and
- Winners and losers not just among the participants but in the broader community.

Major events require extensive regulation and how the regulators determine what is in the public interest? See the discussion on cost benefit analysis in [15.150]ff below. Using these principles, the challenge for the regulator of major events to:

- maximise the benefits;
- minimise the costs;
- capture sufficient benefits from the winners to compensate the losers;
- incorporate mechanisms for compensation.

Case Study: street car racing

[15.115] Street car racing requires special enabling legislation such as:

- *Gold Coast Motor Racing Events Act 1990* (Qld);
- *Australian Grands Prix Act 1994* (Vic);
- *Homebush Motor Racing (Sydney 400) Act 2009* (NSW);

to overcome all the problems discussed previously.

More recently, this legislation is evolving into a general regulatory framework for major events. See, for example:

- *Major Sports Facilities Act 2001* (Qld);

---

40   Lord Bernstein v Skyviews [1977] 1 QB 479.

Case Study: street car racing cont.

- *Major Sporting Events Act 2009* (Vic);
- *Major Events Act 2009* (NSW).

The most common complaints of "locals" to these events are the costs of: noise; crowding; and traffic; restrictions on access for which they argue they are not properly compensated.

Take as an example, the Australian Grand Prix and try to identify:

- "winners" who do not contribute to the cost of staging the event;
- "losers" who are not compensated by the event;
- the mechanisms for compensation.

Suggest improvements.

GAMING LAW

"All ye, who owe your wealth's advance

To games of skill and gambling chance,

Though weighted down with treasure;

Yea, iron nerved gambler, risking all

Take heed lest deaths and Fire recall

Your gold, at grim Fate's pleasure.

Seneca [41]

Definitions

[15.120] *'Wagering contracts'* – Hawkins J in *Carlill and Carbolic Smoke Ball Co* [42] said (emphasis added):

> A wagering contract is one by which two persons professing to hold opposite views touching the issue of a future uncertain event, mutually agree that, dependent upon the determination of that event, one shall win from the other, and that other shall pay or hand over to him, a sum of money or other stake; *neither of the contracting parties having any other interest* in that

---

41   Cited in WC Firebaugh, *The Inns of Greece and Rome* (Benjamin Blom, New York, 1928), p 151.
42   Carlill v Carbolic Smoke Ball Co [1892] 2 QB 484; [1893] 1 QB 256 at 490 (QB) affirmed.

contract other than the sum or stake he will so win or lose, there being no other real consideration for the making of such contract by either of the parties.

The italicised text distinguishes insurance from wagering contracts. Traditionally, in insurance contracts the insured generally had an insurable interest, that is some enforceable right or interest whether contractual or proprietary in the subject matter of the policy. However, that has changed since the introduction of the *Insurance Contracts Act 1984* (Cth) which requires only a 'pecuniary or financial loss'[43] (see also [7.20]). Under current State legislation, wagering may be defined as:

(a) betting conducted by means of a totalisator; or

(b) betting conducted on a fixed odds basis; or

(c) other betting prescribed under a regulation.[44]

Gaming contracts–A gaming contract is like a wagering contract except that the event is determined by a game of chance[45] and there may be more than two persons who win or lose. Games of chance may involve skill or luck and include horse racing, dice, card games, bingo, machine games and the like.[46] Some authors do not distinguish between wagering and gaming.[47]

In this discussion the term 'gambling' will be used to include both gaming and wagering.

History

[15.125] Gambling has been a popular activity throughout history. At the inns of ancient Greece and Rome the essential food and accommodation service was usually augmented by liquor, gambling and prostitution.[48] These activities have always posed some of the greatest challenges for regulators. The problems have changed little through time and it is instructive to trace the historical development of law and policy on gambling.

As with liquor, there were generally no restrictions on gambling at common law. The courts, though often reluctant,[49] generally enforced wagering contracts. However most

---

43 See, for example, *Macaura v Northern Assurance Co Ltd* [1925] AC 619 where the major shareholder and creditor of a company could not recover under a policy he had effected over timber which lay on his land but was owned by the company. See also *Insurance Contracts Act 1984* (Cth), ss 16 – 18.

44 See *Wagering Act 1998* (Qld), Schedule 2. Compare with the definition in the *Gaming and Wagering Commission Act 1987* (WA), s 3 which states:
> wagering includes the staking or hazarding of money or other value –
> (a) on some question to be decided;
> (b) in support of an assertion or on the issue of a forecast; or
> (c) on the outcome of an uncertain happening, or in the event of a doubtful issue, and the collection or payment of winnings on a wager

45 *Ellesmere v Wallace* [1929] 2 Ch 1 at 55.

46 See, for example, *Unlawful Gambling Act 1998* (NSW); *Lottery & Gaming Act 1936* (SA); *Wagering Act 1998* (Qld); *Liquor Control Reform Act 1998* (Vic); *Gaming and Wagering Commission Act 1987* (WA); *Gaming Control Act 1993* (Tas); *Gambling Regulation Act 2003* (ACT); *Gaming Control Act* (NT).

47 See for example *Halsbury's Laws of Australia* (Butterworths, Sydney), Vol 6 Contracts at [110-7070].

48 See generally WC Firebaugh, *The Inns of Greece and Rome* (Benjamin Blom, New York, 1928).

49 In a case brought to enforce a wager on a cock fight Lord Ellenborough said: "It is impossible to be engaged in ludicrous inquiries of this sort, consistently with the dignity which is essential to the public welfare that a court of justice should always preserve": *Squires v Whisken* (1811) 3 Camp 140 at 141.

gaming was made unlawful under a series of statutes from 1388 [50] which regulated particular games, premises, gamblers and proprietors. [51] Illegal games included not only cards, dice and table games but also sports such as bowls, skittles, quoits, and tennis. The first general policy against excessive gambling emerged in 1664 by *statute 16 Car II c 7* which aimed to discourage it by introducing a penalty for cheating and making certain gambling debts and securities unenforceable. The title and preamble provided:

An Act against deceitful, disorderly and excessive gambling.

Whereas all lawful games and exercises should not be otherwise used, than as innocent and moderate recreations, and not as constant trades or callings to gain a living, or make unlawful advantage thereby; and whereas by the immoderate use of them, many mischiefs and inconveniences do arise, and are daily found, to the maintaining and encouraging of sundry idle, loose and disorderly persons in their dishonest, lewd, and dissolute course of life, and to the circumventing, deceiving, cousening and debauching of many of the younger sort, both of the nobility and gentry, and others to the loss of their precious time, and the utter ruin of their estates and fortunes, and withdrawing them from noble and laudable employment and exercises.

Section 2 introduced a penalty for cheating at gaming and wagering of treble the amount won, payable half to the crown and the other half to the loser, by action brought within six months and otherwise to any informer action brought within the next 12 months. Section 3 provided that any gambling losses on credit (that is, not paid at the time in cash) in excess of £100 and all associated conveyances, pledges, mortgages and securities were unenforceable. There were weaknesses in the legislation. It protected only the very wealthy, for whom the loss of £100 in 1664 was not ruinous. [52] It did not prevent gentlemen from paying and securing their gambling debts out of a sense of honour. [53] It provided no protection for losses in cash. The following case illustrates the last problem.

Firebrasse v Brett

[15.130] *Firebrasse v Brett* (1687) 1 Vern 489; (1688) 2 Vern 71

Facts: Sir Bazil Firebrasse had dinner at his home with Brett and Sir William Russell. After dinner, which included considerable wine, he played dice with his guests and lost £900 to Brett. Brett himself had started with a stake of about £10. 'Inflamed with wine,' Sir Bazil fetched a bag of guineas containing a further £1,500. Brett won that as well. Sir Bazil and his servants seized the £1,500 from Brett as he was leaving. Sir Bazil brought an information against Brett for using false dice but this was acquitted. Brett brought an action in trespass against Sir Bazil for forcibly taking back from him the bag of guineas. Sir Bazil defended this action again alleging fraud and sought to be relieved from the debt.

Decision: The Lord Chancellor found no grounds for declaring gaming and wagering itself unlawful. However he 'declared he thought it a very exorbitant sum to be lost at play in one sitting,

---

50 *Statute 12 Rich II c 6 (1388)* encouraged servants and labourers to spend their Sundays and holidays playing sport rather than games of chance.

51 For an excellent description of early English statutes and cases see RA Moodie, "Gaming and wagering contracts" (1975) (Aug) 8(1) *Victoria University of Wellington Law Review* 22-47, 22.

52 In *1710 Statute 9 Anne c 14* "An act for better preventing excessive and deceitful gaming" reduced this to £10.

53 This was the usual and often ruinous practice. See Blackstone, *Commentaries*, Book IV p 172 where he notes that this left gentlemen in a no-win situation in that they were bound to pay losses out of honour but were liable to be sued by less gentlemanly losers for triple any winnings. This problem was partly overcome in the *Statute 8 Anne c 14 (1710)* discussed below.

Firebrasse v Brett cont.

between persons of their rank, and that he would discourage, as much as in him lay, such extravagant gaming'.[54] Ultimately the case was settled (by gentlemen's agreement?) with Sir Bazil keeping the £1,500, Brett keeping the £900 and the action for trespass and the allegations of fraud being withdrawn.

Comment: If Sir Bazil had proven cheating then Brett would have been liable to pay triple the sum, half to Sir Bazil and half to the state under s 2 of the statute of 1664. Perhaps Brett took the hint from the Lord Chancellor's critical comments and this encouraged the settlement. Section 3 of the statute of 1664 did not apply because the £1,500 loss had been paid initially in cash and was thus not a gambling loss on credit.

The problems were addressed again in 1710 by *statute 9 Anne c 14*, 'An act for better preventing excessive and deceitful gaming'. Section 1 removed the £100 limit which applied under the 1644 statute and provided that all conveyances, pledges, mortgages and securities to pay or secure gambling debts or losses or where the consideration was gambling winnings were utterly void and of no effect. Section 2 greatly extended the 1644 statute triple penalty concept. It provided that all gambling losses of £10 or more, whether or not there was cheating involved, could be sued for and recovered by the loser within three months and if not any informer could then sue the winner for triple the amount, with half to go to the informer and half to the poor of the parish. It is interesting to compare the 'Robin Hood' policy in this transfer from the winners to the poor with the policy underlying Australia's community benefit levy on gaming revenue (see [15.170] below).

These *Imperial Acts of 1664* and 1710 were received into the Australian colonies under the general principles on reception of English laws at 1828 and are still in force today to the extent that they have not been repealed or amended by the Australian States. O'Connor J in *Quan Yick v Hinds*[55] said:

> It cannot, I think, be doubted that the English laws prohibiting lotteries came into force in New South Wales on the passing of 9 Geo IV c 83. They are, like the laws against gaming and wagering, of general application, and intended to safeguard the moral well-being of the community, and there would appear to be no reason why they should not have been in force from the very beginning of the settlement.

These statutes were amended by *5 & 6 Will 4 c 41 (1835)* which provided that the notes, bills and securities referred to in the statutes of 1664 and 1710 were deemed to be made for illegal consideration and were enforceable by innocent third parties against the party with whom they dealt, who could then recover from the party who originally took the security.

The problems continued in England until gambling reached scandalous proportions publicised by *Smith v Bond*[56] in 1843. In this case parish officers sought to stamp out gambling by bringing a common informer's action under the 1710 Act for all gaming losses in the parish. They won a verdict of £3,508 and this prompted the House of Commons to appoint a Select Committee on Gaming to examine the issues.[57] The Committee found that although statutes prohibited certain games and rendered keepers of gaming houses liable for severe penalties, gaming and gaming houses nevertheless proliferated around the country with little police control.

The *Gaming Act 1845*[58] sought to deal with these problems more comprehensively. It repealed the statute of 1664 and so much of the statute of 1710 as was not amended by the statute of 1835. It also repealed statutes which made games of skill and sports such as bowls, skittles, quoits, and tennis illegal. However it outlawed wagering, gaming and common gaming houses and provided for:

---

54 *Firebrasse v Brett* (1688) 2 Vern 71.
55 *Quan Yick v Hinds* (1905) 2 CLR 345 at 378.
56 *Smith v Bond* (1843) 11 M&W 549.
57 *Journals of the House of Commons* (1844) Vol 99 24 at 31.
58 *Gaming Act 1845* (IMP) 8 & 9 Vic c 109.

Firebrasse v Brett cont.

- search warrants for premises suspected of being used for the purpose;
- offences for keepers, employees, gamblers and others found on the premises; and
- forfeiture of all money and securities found on the premises.

In addition, s 18 declared

> That all contracts or agreements, whether by parole or in writing, by way of gaming or wagering, shall be null and void; and that no suit shall be brought or maintained in any court of law or equity for recovering any sum of money or valuable thing alleged to be won upon any wager, or which shall have been deposited in the hands of any person to abide the event on which any wager shall have been made... .

Australian law

[15.135] The 1845 Imperial legislation was expressly adopted in New South Wales in 1850 and in most of the other Australian colonies [59] and forms the basis of legislation on gaming and wagering in Australia. The Australian law was also based on similar policy as stated by Rich J of the High Court in *Defina v Kenny*: [60]

> Formerly at common law wagers were not illegal and actions were brought and maintained to recover money won upon them. But [under the 1850 legislation] betting contracts were made null and void and money won under them was not recoverable. The legality of wagering contracts was not affected, but the law was no longer available for their enforcement and the parties to them were left to pay wagers or not as their sense of honour might dictate...

However in most States the law on gaming and wagering is now a fragmented mix of these old statutes and numerous subsequent enactments dealing with various aspects of these activities. [61] In each State, legislation ('Gaming Contract legislation') provides that gaming and wagering contracts are void and that money alleged to be won is not recoverable. [62] Exceptions are made for specific lotteries, pools, bingo, TAB [63] and bookmakers at licensed racecourses. Exceptions are also made for casinos and gaming machines which are discussed in more detail later.

Usually where these exceptions apply, the gambling must be conducted strictly in accordance with the permitted exception, otherwise it is illegal. Then, even if the legislation

---

59 *The Gaming Act 1850* (NSW); *The Gaming Act 1850* (Qld).
60 *Defina v Kenny* [1946] 72 CLR 164 at 171 per Rich J.
61 For example in Queensland the main criminal provisions historically have been:
- *Gaming Act 1850*, which adopted the Imperial *Gaming Act 1845* and established offences by gaming house proprietors and patrons;
- *Vagrants Gaming and Other Offences Act 1931*, which established offences including: s 19 Unlawful games, s 20 Cheating at games, s 21 Places of access to games, s 21A Seizure of fruit machines, s 22 Betting on (liquor) licensed premises (now see the *Gaming Machines Act 1991* (Qld)); *Criminal Code* Part IV Acts Injurious to the Public including offences against morality (Chapter XXII), Prostitution (Chapter XXIIA) including, s 232 Operating a House for Unlawful Games.

62 Gaming contract legislation: *Gambling Regulation Act 2003* (ACT): *Unlawful Gambling Act 1998* (NSW): *Gaming Control Act* (NT): *Wagering Act 1998* (Qld); *Lottery & Gaming Act 1936* (SA): *Gaming Control Act 1993* (Tas); *Liquor Control Reform Act 1998* (Vic); *Gaming and Wagering Commission Act 1987* (WA).
Gaming contract legislation: ACT: ss 13, 13A; NSW: s 16; NT: s 135; Qld: s 248; SA: s 50, 50A; Tas: s 114; Vic: ss 15, 16; WA: s 4.

63 See, for example, definition of "wagering" in the *Wagering Act 1998* (Qld), Schedule 2.

does not itself so declare, a gaming and wagering contract entered pursuant to the illegal gambling may be held unenforceable at common law. Even an indirect connection with illegal gambling is enough to render a contract unenforceable, for example the action for hire charges on a roulette wheel failed in *JM Allen (Merchandise) Ltd v Cloke* [64] and an action to recover a gambling debt even where there was a fresh promise to pay and fresh consideration failed in *Hill v Wnm Hill (Park Lane)*.[65] *Mendonca & Santiago v South Sydney Junior Rugby League Club Ltd*[66] (see case study at [15.215]) provides an interesting illustration of these principles in relation to unauthorised gambling on poker machines.

Gambling policy

[15.140] The policy issues involved in gambling are complex and vary according to country, culture and religion. In many countries gambling, like alcohol, drugs, prostitution and similar activities,[67] has been regarded traditionally as so undesirable as to warrant severe restriction or prohibition. In some cultures gambling is contrary to fundamental moral and religious principles[68] whereas in others it is regarded as a more secular social problem.[69]

Gambling is denounced in many religions, including Islam, Buddhism and Christianity. Consider the long tension between Christianity and gambling, highlighted perhaps at the crucifixion of Christ when the Roman soldiers threw dice for his possessions. That tension has continued. Consider these opposing views:

> Traditionally Protestant opposition [to gambling] has been based on moral and social grounds. Gambling was seen as immoral in itself though some situations make it more so. Gambling encouraged greed and materialism, debased rewards for genuine work and replaced faith in God with dependence on 'chance'.[70]
>
> Gambling can be split into two parts – the playing of games without betting is not immoral, the addition of betting to those games does not in itself alter the moral situation. The playing of games may interfere with the welfare of the player or dependents, but so could flying a plane – this does not make flying a plane immoral.
>
> If the immoral stance does not lie in the game or betting then it must lie in the involvement of money – but given the roles we now allow for money, how could this be? Risking money is an essential part of the free enterprise system, and interfering with it substantially would be an interference with liberty – many small businesses lose money on ventures, but it is not immoral.[71]

Simple prohibition has rarely been a successful policy. As with alcohol, drugs, prostitution and similar activities, prohibition discourages but does not eliminate gambling: it merely drives the activity underground and into the hands of criminals and often beyond the reach of the regulators. Ironically prohibition may in fact increase the associated social problems. It also

---

64   *JM Allen (Merchandise) Ltd v Cloke* [1963] 2 QB 340.
65   *Hill v Wnm Hill (Park Lane)* [1949] AC 530.
66   *Mendonca & Santiago v South Sydney Junior Rugby League Club Ltd* (Unreported, NSW Sup Ct, Sully J, 16 December 1993, BC 9302359).
67   These activities are among the most difficult to regulate successfully. See Scott, *Law and Leisure Services Management* (1988), particularly Chapter 6.
68   For example, it is contrary to religion for Muslims to gamble.
69   For example, China.
70   SA Reid, "The church's campaign against casinos and poker machines in Victoria", in Cardwell et al (eds), *Gambling in Australia* (Croomhelm, Sydney, 1985).
71   R and L Sylvan, "The ethics of gambling", in Cardwell al (eds), *Gambling in Australia* (Croomhelm, Sydney, 1985).

keeps the activity out of reach of the revenue collectors. Governments around the world [72] have recognised this and have gradually relaxed prohibitions on milder forms of gambling such as lotteries, racecourse bookmaking, [73] bingo, poker machines and the like. With the growth of tourism, prohibitions on gambling have created strong push and pull effects. Many gamblers, denied the opportunity to pursue the activity at home, have sought out destinations where it is available. Some destinations seeking more visitors at any cost have added gambling as an attraction.

Australia has experienced this internationally and domestically:

- **Internationally: Asian high rollers**–'High rollers' are gamblers who can be relied upon to bet substantial sums of money in casinos. They are courted by casino operators and provided with special facilities and services. They have spawned a subgroup of intermediaries known as 'junket tour operators' who collect and deliver groups of high rollers to selected casinos on a commission basis. Many of the Australian casinos are depending on attracting particularly lucrative Asian high rollers [74] who are unable to gamble at home because of religious or legal restrictions. High rollers used to comprise some 40% of the market for Burswood casino in Perth and most of the market for the Christmas Island casino but this is changing with the opening of several new casinos in Macau, a small country bordering China. This has become a real threat to the Asian high roller market in Australia with other Asian countries also reviewing the success of these operations. [75]

- **Domestically: New South Wales poker machines**–Australia has also experienced the push/pull effects domestically with gaming machines, particularly with cross-border trade from Queensland, Victoria and South Australia into New South Wales clubs, which were the first to offer poker machine gambling from 1960. It is instructive to consider the current demise of many of these border clubs now that these other States have changed policy to provide gaming machines in clubs and hotels in their own States. [76] Our casinos are being similarly affected by Asian countries now relaxing their prohibitions on casino gambling.

Some countries overreacted and legalised many forms of gambling without putting in place the proper controls. For example, England in the *Betting and Lotteries Act 1963* legalised most types of gaming in the United Kingdom but lost control of the industry so that there was a proliferation of casinos and infiltration by organised crime and protection rackets. The

---

72 For example, the *Betting and Lotteries Act 1963* (UK) legalised most types of gaming in England. See S Fitzgerald, "The Gaming Act 1968 in 1990", in WR Eadington and JR Cornelius, *Gambling and Public Policy: International Perspectives* (Institute for the Study of Gambling and Commercial Gaming, College of Business Administration, University of Nevada, Reno, 1991), pp 395-407.

73 The introduction of off-course totalisator betting in 1960 marked the turning point in policy: see A Neilson, "Government regulation of casino gambling in Australia: the political and bureaucratic components and some of the myths" in WR Eadington and JR Cornelius, *Gambling and Public Policy: International Perspectives* (Institute for the Study of Gambling and Commercial Gaming, College of Business Administration, University of Nevada, Reno, 1991), pp 363-396 and 361.

74 For example, Crown Casino in Melbourne offers the services of its own private jet and golf course to lure high rollers there.

75 This author was adviser to the Government of Cambodia on its international tender for a casino licence aimed at this market.

76 See R McKercher and O Vaughan, *Adjusting to changes in State government tourism policy: the reaction of NSW border clubs to the introduction of legalised gaming in Victoria*, paper delivered at the Australian tourism and hospitality research conference, Sydney (6-9 July 1997).

Gaming Act 1968 was passed to reduce the number of casinos and establish strict controls over gaming and wagering. [77] Legalisation subject to strict controls has emerged as the most successful regulatory policy.

Many challenges lie ahead in the regulation of gambling. International efforts are required to reflect the newer forms of gambling, such as floating casinos, in-flight gambling and internet gambling, which are not confined by country, cultural or religious boundaries. As they are transnational they are very difficult for any one state to control.

Two types of gambling which particularly affect the tourism industry sector will be considered in further detail: casinos and gaming machines.

Casinos

[15.145] Casinos are the modern form of that old establishment which for so long has been outlawed: the common gaming house. Thus legalisation of casinos is arguably the ultimate act in changing traditional policy on gambling.

In the United States, the State of Nevada led the way in 1931 with legalised casino gambling centred on the city of Las Vegas. While the US monopoly ensured its economic success, the State lost control and the industry was infiltrated by organised crime. It was not until 1976 that this monopoly was broken by the State of New Jersey legalising casino gambling in Atlantic City. While New Jersey based its laws on the Nevada model, it introduced variations to try to avoid some of the problems experienced in Las Vegas. These variations included confining licences to resort-hotel complexes operated by large and reputable organisations and using licences to stimulate urban redevelopment. [78] Many other countries experimented with legalisation of casinos in the 1960s and 1970s and the results have often been disastrous. [79]

For example Lea [80] argues that the costs of casinos can exceed the benefits in developing world countries, based on the experience in the South African states of Botswana, Lesotho and Swaziland where casino development sparked a tourist boom at the expense of enormous local social costs. Similarly when a casino was opened in pre-communist Cambodia, Chandler [81] describes the results in these terms:

> His [King Sihanouk's] decision to open a casino in Phnom Penh to raise revenue had disastrous results. In the last six months of 1969, thousands of Cambodians lost millions of dollars at its tables; several prominent people, and dozens of impoverished ones, committed suicide after sustaining losses; and hundreds of families went bankrupt. [82]

Australia has drawn from these experiences in developing its law and policy on casinos. Given this background it is useful to examine more closely the policy issues involved and the refinements to the regulatory approach which have been made in Australasia to maximise the

---

77 See Fitzgerald, in WR Eadington and JR Cornelius, *Gambling and Public Policy: International Perspectives* (Institute for the Study of Gambling and Commercial Gaming, College of Business Administration, University of Nevada, Reno, 1991), pp 395-407.

78 For a comparison of the two systems see AJ Hicks, "No longer the only game in town: a comparison of the Nevada and New Jersey regulatory systems of gaming control" (1981) 12 *Southwestern University Law Review* 583-626.

79 TC Atherton, *Developing a policy on the regulation of international casino gambling*, Presentation to the Council of Ministers of the Royal Government of Cambodia, Phnom Penh, July 1994.

80 J Lea, *Tourism and development in the third world* (Routledge, London, 1998), p 5.

81 DP Chandler, *A history of Cambodia* (2nd ed, Westview Press, Colorado, 1993), pp 203-204.

82 When Cambodia reintroduced a casino in 1994 this author endeavoured to establish the Australian model of international tender and strict regulatory controls but with mixed success.

benefits and minimise the costs to the destination. It is arguable that Australia has developed and tested a new regulatory model which will produce more reliable net benefits and so may be of use in other countries.

Costs and benefits of casino gambling

[15.150] The costs and benefits of casino gambling have been studied extensively by others and may be summarised as follows:

Costs	Benefits
• increased crime and immorality; • money laundering; • costs to the gambler; • costs to the gambler's family and dependants.	• employment; • government revenue; • foreign exchange; • infrastructure; • regional development; • added tourist attraction.

Two points should be noted from these costs and benefits:
- the costs are mainly social and the benefits mainly economic; and
- the costs generally fall upon different parties from those who benefit.

These dimensions add to the complexity of the debate on casino gambling policy. From the narrowest point of view, that of the developer and operator, the financial analysis for a casino usually shows lucrative returns. From society's point of view the cost benefit analysis usually shows less tangible but nonetheless dramatic potential social costs or 'externalities'. To assess the costs and benefits accurately it is also necessary to carefully define the boundary of the society whose interests are to be considered.

Casino policy formulation

[15.155] Regulating casino gambling provides an interesting application of the philosophies of law and economics which underlie government policy formulation.[83] Under these philosophies there are two main criteria for determining whether a regulatory policy is 'efficient' or whether it could be improved:[84]

- **Paretto.** Under the Paretto criterion a policy change is justifiable if it will make someone better off and no one worse off. This provides little guidance on casino policy and because few, if any, regulatory measures would satisfy this criterion it has generally been rejected as too restrictive.
- **Kaldor Hicks.** Under the Kaldor Hicks criterion a policy change is justifiable if it will make at least one person so much better off that they could theoretically compensate all those who will be made worse off and still be better off. This is more useful for casino policy because of the opportunity it provides for trade-off between winners and losers. This is in fact the underlying philosophy of all cost benefit analysis and environmental impact assessment.

---

83   See TC Atherton, "Casinos as instruments for tourism development in Australia and Asia", in J-C Eude (ed), (French), *Casinos et Tourisme* (Cahier Espaces, Paris, 1994), pp 85-96.

84   See generally TC Atherton, *Regulation of tourism destination planning, development and management* (MSc thesis (Tourism Management), Surrey University, 1991).

Veljanovski [85] and others criticise the Kaldor Hicks criterion for several reasons, including:

- it violates the Paretto condition that no one be made worse off; and
- if those made worse off go uncompensated it results in an unjustified redistribution of welfare.

The development of casino policy in Australia has provided, perhaps unwittingly, a classic illustration of these philosophies and the scope for a more creative approach to regulation. The potential for trade-off is highlighted by reconsidering the costs and benefits of casino gambling in terms of who wins and who loses:

Those who benefit (the winners)	Those harmed (the losers)
• casino owners, operators, financiers, employees, suppliers; • government (federal, State and local); • compatible industries.	• gamblers; • family and friends of gamblers; • competing industries; • when the gambler becomes dishonest then the impact widens to employers, customers, victims of fraud, robbery etc.

If those who benefit could theoretically compensate those who are harmed, then the casino could be justified on the Kaldor Hicks criterion. In the usual casino regulatory system the government collects a gaming tax (from those who benefit) which it redistributes to the wider society (including those who are harmed) through general public expenditure. Gaming tax provides substantial government revenue in Australia, as shown in the following table: [86]

Aggregate Gambling Taxation Revenue Australia 2005-2006 [87]

ACT	NSW	NT	Qld	SA	Tas	Vic	WA	Total
$55m	$1,522m	$55m	$835m	$408m	$75m	$1,460m	$283m	$4,693m

Much of this revenue comes from casino gambling. However this raises Veljanovski's second criticism. If the gaming tax is used for general public expenditure it does not provide compensation to those who bear the social costs.

Community benefit levy. In answer to this Australia has introduced a special community benefit levy in addition to normal gaming tax. It comprises a special levy of 1-2.5%t of gaming revenue [88] amounting to $32.64m in 2007 [89] which is dedicated to providing social benefits to the community. In addition, the casino industry makes additional community contributions including support of charities, community groups, sporting events and special events amounting to a further $8.8m. [90] In overall terms, then, it can be argued that the social benefits offset the social costs. However because in Australia these community benefit funds are distributed to broader charitable purposes rather than targeted at the specific social costs

---

85   CG Veljanovski, "The new law and economics: a research review" in Ogus and Veljanovski (eds), *Readings in the Economics of Law and Regulation* (Clarendon Press, Oxford, 1984), pp 12-24.
86   There may be some doubts about the constitutional validity of these State taxes. See [14.150].
87   Source: Australasian Gaming Council Fact Sheet 06/08.
88   See, for example, *Control Act 1992* (NSW); *Casino Act 1997* (SA); *Casino Control Act 1982* (Qld); *Casino Control Act 1991* (Vic).
89   *Australian Casino Industry Economic Report Financial Year 2007*, p 20.
90   *Australian Casino Industry Economic Report Financial Year 2007*, p 20.

of those who are harmed (that is, the problem gamblers and their families) it does not answer Veljanovski's criticism. What it does very effectively, however, is to improve the net result of the cost benefit analysis and encourage political support for the casino policy.[91]

Casinos for tourists. An even more effective policy has been to target the casinos at the tourist market. In this way much of the harm done to the gambler and the gambler's home community are removed from the equation because the cost benefit analysis focuses only on the destination community. The effect on the analysis is illustrated in the following diagrams.

Figure 1: Casino for Locals: Boundary of Society Includes Losers

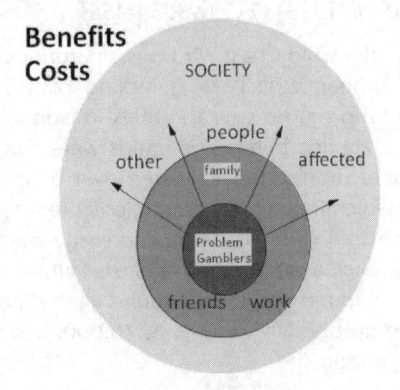

Figure 2: Casino for Tourists: Boundary of Society Excludes Losers

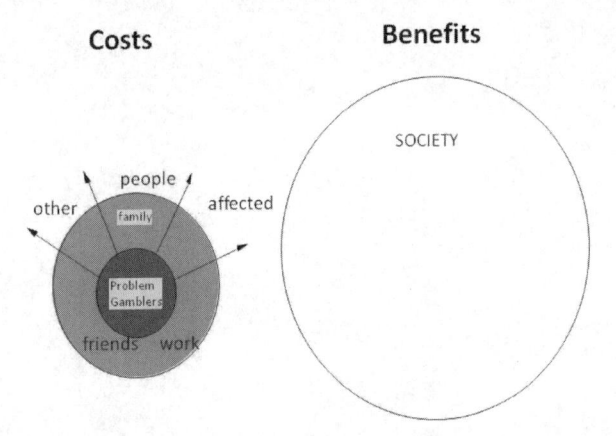

In Australia this is partly achieved by requiring casinos to be developed in tourist destinations and in conjunction with major hotels and convention facilities. Thus it can be argued that many of the gamblers are temporary visitors who take their problems away with

---

91   See Jupiter Casino (Gold Coast Qld): Mission Statement:
    The Queensland Government established the Jupiter's Casino Community Benefit Fund (JCCBF) in 1987 to provide funding to community groups in Queensland. The JCCBF receives money from taxes on casinos. It distributes these funds to community projects on a quarterly basis. The JCCBF is just one way the Government returns taxes from gambling activities. In redistributing gambling taxes through its grants program, the JCCBF plays an important role in ensuring, on balance, the whole State benefits from gambling in Queensland.

them when they leave; that is, it shifts the costs away from the destination, which is left to enjoy only the benefits. If locals were prohibited from gambling the solution could be enforced, but at the expense of civil liberty. [92] However, the experience with Australian casinos has been that the majority of the patrons are locals. [93] Problem gamblers range from those who lose their pension on the poker machines to those who gamble with other people's money in the high rollers' room.

Registrar of Titles v Keddell

[15.160] *Registrar of Titles v Keddell* (1993) Q Conv R 54-455

Facts: Palmer was a solicitor on the Gold Coast who was a notorious gambler at the races and at the high roller room of the casino. To finance his huge gambling losses Palmer abused his position as a solicitor and forged transfers and mortgages over the titles to land and other property which clients entrusted to him for safekeeping. He fled before the frauds were discovered and many of his clients were left with forged transfers and mortgages registered over their land titles. This is one of those cases. It concerned a mortgage which Palmer had fraudulently registered on Keddell's title. In earlier proceedings Keddell had obtained an order that the mortgage be released upon payment of the $535,000 plus interest owing and a judgment against Palmer's company for that amount. Unfortunately Palmer could not be found and even if found all the moneys had been gambled away. More unfortunately the land had dropped in value to $275,000. Keddell sought compensation from the State under the land title legislation.

Decision: The court awarded compensation of only $300,000, being the market value of the land plus expenses. The reasoning was that the mortgagee would sell up the land for default and Keddell would have the opportunity to buy back the property at market price. Thus the client, Keddell, was put to the risk and inconvenience of the legal proceedings and the buy back. The State bore the rest of the

---

[92] This was the approach favoured in Cambodia in 1994 where the author assisted in the drafting of a law which required casino gamblers to produce a foreign passport and thus targeted foreigners and also those Cambodians who had lived abroad where there were casinos and who presumably were more resistant to the social problems of excess gambling. Other destinations such as Russia require that all gambling takes place using US dollars thus restricting local involvement and still others place the casinos in remote destinations so far away from local communities that locals cannot access them easily.

[93] At Jupiter's Casino on the Gold Coast approximately 45% of the customers are tourists. The proportion of tourists is much lower at casinos in lesser destinations such as Breakwater casino at Townsville. McMillan (reported in N Chenoworth, "Casino Boom you can bet on it", *The Bulletin* (26 May 1992), pp 54-55) estimates that Australia-wide casino clientele in 1992 was 75-85% local.

Registrar of Titles v Keddell cont.

cost of Palmer's fraud. This is just one of many such cases arising out of the frauds which Palmer perpetrated to support his gambling problem.

―――― ഇറ ――――

Casino development and capacity

[15.165] There have been three distinct phases in the development of casinos in Australia as detailed in the table below. [94]

Original Development and Capacity: Australian Casinos [95]

Year opened	Location	Casino name	Casino operator	Hotel rooms	Convention capacity	Gaming machines number*	Gaming tables number*	Annual patronage casino*
1997	Sydney	Star City	Showboat	489	2500	1500	200	5m
1995						500	150	
1997	Melbourne	Crown	Crown	1120	3000	2500	350	12m
1994						1300	200	
1996	Cairns	Reef		128	600	564	47	1.3m
1995	Brisbane	Treasury	Conrad	137	150	1224	102	3.3m
1993	Christmas Island	Christmas Island		156		80	26	
1994	Canberra	Canberra	Casinos	0		0	49	700,000
1992			Australia	294		37		
1986	Townsville	Hypiters	Sheraton	196	700	218	34	600,000
1985	Perth	Burswood	Victoria Holdings	417	3600	1120	111	2.8m
1985	Adelaide	SkyCity	ASER	369	3500	870	89	2.9m
1985	Gold Coast	Jupiters	Conrad	609	2300	1095	101	4.8m
1982	Launceston	Country Club	Federal	104	620	188	25 Club	600,000
1981	Alice Springs	Lasseter's	IOOF	75	0	196	21	400,000
1979	Darwin	SkyCity	MGM Grand	147	650	386	28	300,000
1973	Hobart	Wrest Point	Federal	278	1600	272	29	1.1m
Total				4519	19,220	10,213	1212	35.8m

First phase. This began with the development of the Wrest Point Casino in Hobart (1973) followed by casinos in Darwin (1979), Alice Springs (1981) and Launceston (1982). These were all relatively small casinos located in relatively remote places and they demonstrated the potential for casino gambling to draw patrons. They also demonstrated that with strict regulation and control, organised crime could be kept out of the industry.

---

[94] For an interesting analysis of early casino developments see D A Mossenson, "The Australian casino model" in WR Eadington and JR Cornelius, *Gambling and Public Policy: International Perspectives* (Institute for the Study of Gambling and Commercial Gaming, College of Business Administration, University of Nevada, Reno, 1991), pp 303-362.

[95] **Source:** Compiled by author from various sources including columns marked * from C Forbes, "Scant figures hide dark side of chance", *The Australian*, Tuesday 28 January 1997 p 4.

Second Phase. Between 1985 and 1986 four new casinos were established in the Gold Coast, Adelaide, Perth and Townsville. These projects were located in major population or tourist centres, were on a much larger scale, and three of the four projects were owned by publicly listed entities.

Third Phase. There was a lull until 1992, when the current surge of development commenced. In this phase the number of casinos in Australia has doubled and the capacity has nearly trebled as the Brisbane, Melbourne and Sydney casinos are very large even by world standards. Since the forecasts in the preceding table, Australia now has a casino industry with about 1,265 gaming tables, 12,234 gaming machines and an expected annual patronage of 47.9 million visitors.[96] The gaming facilities are complemented by around 4,000 hotel rooms and convention facilities catering for almost 600.00 people [97] reinforcing the efforts to attract tourists with the policy implications discussed in [15.155].

Casino licensing, tax and investment

[15.170] The Australian approach to casinos is fundamentally different from that taken in Britain and the United States, where the number of casinos is determined largely by market demand and competition. The result in the US has been that Las Vegas and Atlantic City each have many casinos (Las Vegas has over 190 casinos) within their region.

In contrast each Australian State has divided its casino market up into exclusive franchise areas each with a single licence which has usually been offered to the highest and best bidder by international tender. This approach has numerous advantages over the US and British models, including:

Easier to administer and control. Having only one casino licence in each region minimises the difficulties of administration and control discussed in the next part. The task of surveillance, revenue collection and administration is made much easier especially where the licensee is a major public corporation with extensive corporate and financial responsibilities to ensure compliance.

Monopoly. Granting the licensee a substantial period of exclusivity over a region creates a monopoly, and the opportunity for super profits gives the licence great value. The Australian model effectively appropriates much of this profit and value for public use. First, the gaming tax and community benefit levy can be set at relatively high levels and this is discussed below. Secondly, in the international tender process one important criterion for selection is the size of the premium or 'up-front fee' bid for the licence. This more sophisticated approach has been developed in the third phase in Australia. These fees have been $20m for Canberra, $135m for Brisbane, $55m for Cairns, $250m for Melbourne and an astonishing $365m for Sydney. This is not only a reflection of the projected profitability of these casinos but it is also a very efficient means of transferring the capitalised value of these super profits from the licensee to the State. Exclusivity has also provided security for the substantial investment being made into the casino industry which spent a total estimated at $4.8 billion on the original development of casino projects. The casino industry has spent a further $290.8m on expansion and refurbishment of facilities to 2007.[98]

Technology transfer. International tender is arguably the most effective means of tapping the best talent available in the world for the design, construction, financing, operation, marketing and entrepreneurial skills required for a major casino project. The winning bidder is usually a

---

96 *Australian Casino Industry Economic Report Financial Year 2007*, pp 14 and 21.
97 *Australian Casino Industry Economic Report Financial Year 2007*, pp 6-7.
98 *Australian Casino Industry Economic Report Financial Year 2007*, p 13.

consortium including a construction company, international hotel operator, international casino operator and institutional investors. Their relative capability is tested against the criteria established by the government in a very competitive bidding and selection process.

Public float. Tenderers have usually been encouraged to include a public float of shares in the casino so as to provide all willing Australians with the opportunity to share in the risks and rewards of ownership and operation. Public listing also adds another layer of surveillance and control over the integrity of the licensee.

Transparent selection process. International tender and selection against published criteria limits the scope for infiltration of organised crime and corruption in the licensing process. Even though international tender is arguably the most efficient and transparent method of finding the best casino developer, the selections have still been controversial [99] and there continues to be public scrutiny and inquiry into the credentials of the bidders and the fairness of the process. [100]

Taxation and Community Benefit. As mentioned above, the artificial monopoly created by exclusive licensing provides the opportunity to collect higher gaming taxes. Surprisingly, there has not been any obvious competition among the States over casino tax rates except in the premium player market. The approach which appears to have been taken in each case has been to charge as much as the market will bear. The range is from 8% (Alice Springs, Darwin and Christmas Island) to 20% (Gold Coast, Brisbane, Melbourne) and 22.5% (Sydney), but this is a reflection of the relative profitability of the locations. The community benefit levy of 1-2.5% of gaming revenue has become firmly established in casino policy. With Australia's 13 casinos making total gaming revenue of $3.68 billion, [101] gaming tax ($402.6m) [102] and community benefit levy ($32.64m) [103] do provide a substantial annual income to State governments and community organisations.

Australia developed its casino model by observing and building upon the United States experience in Las Vegas and Atlantic City. The Australian model has now been followed in some other States of the US. It remains to be seen whether the model can be successfully applied in developing countries where the absence of a strong rule of law makes it more difficult to control casinos.

Control of casinos

[15.175] The key to the success of the Australian casino model has been the rigorous control system established by special Casino Control legislation in each State and Territory. [104] The key elements of the control system are as follows.

---

99 Some authors argue the problem is that the selection is political: see A Neilson in WR Eadington and JR Cornelius, *Gambling and Public Policy: International Perspectives* (Institute for the Study of Gambling and Commercial Gaming, College of Business Administration, University of Nevada, Reno, 1991), pp 363-396.

100 See *Darling Casino Ltd v New South Wales Casino Control Authority* (unreported, High Court of Australia, 3 April 1997), where Brennan CJ, Dawson, Toohey, Gaudron and Gummow JJ unanimously dismissed a challenge by a rival bidder for the Sydney casino licence.

101 *Australian Casino Industry Economic Report Financial Year 2007*, p 8.

102 *Australian Casino Industry Economic Report Financial Year 2007*, p 14.

103 *Australian Casino Industry Economic Report Financial Year 2007*, p 20.

104 Casino Control legislation comprises: ACT *Casino Control Act 2006*; NSW: *Casino Control Act 1992*: NT: *Gaming Control Act*: Qld: *Casino Control Act 1982*; SA: *Casino Control Act 1997*; Tas: *Gaming Control Act 1993*: Vic: *Casino Control Act 1991*; WA: *Casino Control Act 1984*.

Administration. Each State has established a casino authority [105] with the responsibility and wide powers to administer the casino control system. [106]

Licensing. As discussed in [15.140], gaming is generally declared to be illegal under legislation in each State. The Casino Control legislation excepts licensed casinos from this general prohibition and declares gaming in licensed casinos to be lawful. [107] Licences have usually been granted to the selected tenderer following the most rigorous of inquiries to ensure that the premises and the licensee, and all persons associated or connected with the ownership, administration or operation of the casino are fit and proper for the purpose. The matters considered particularly include links with organised crime. As the principal casinos have now been licensed these issues are somewhat academic as far as initial licensing is concerned. However any adverse change in these matters may provide grounds for suspension or cancellation of a licence. As the casino licence is fundamental to the operation and a thing of great value this provides a very powerful method of control. The employees of casinos must also be licensed. [108] For an interesting analysis of the principles involved in licensing casino employees see *R v Specker; Ex parte Alvaro*. [109]

Fees, taxes and levies. In addition to the gaming taxes and community benefit levies discussed in [15.155], casinos are also required to pay substantial periodic fees to cover the cost of the administration of the casino control system. [110]

Operation and control. Control is exercised over the facilities, including the premises, maintenance, gaming equipment and chips, and over the hours of operation, permitted games, rules of games and the conduct of games. In accordance with the lessons from history, gaming and wagering on credit are generally not permitted. However, as casino bets are usually cash transactions, they are particularly difficult to manage and control. A key object of the Casino Control legislation is to minimise the problems experienced in other countries. [111] McMillen described the Australian approach in the following terms: [112]

> The Wrest Point model of control, which set the pattern for later casinos in Tasmania and Northern Territory, was a synthesised hybrid system, incorporating the best surveillance procedures and internal control practices from Europe and Nevada into an Anglo-Australian regulatory structure. More comprehensive internal auditing controls were pioneered in the Wrest Point casino, tightening government control over money laundering and skimming, two major problems in casino regulation.

---

105   ACT: Gambling and Racing Commission; NSW: Casino Liquor and Gaming Control Authority; NT: Licensing Commission; Qld: Casino Control Division of the Treasury Department; SA: Independent Gambling Authority; Tas: Tasmanian Gaming Commission; Vic: Victorian Casino and Gaming Authority; WA: Gaming and Wagering Commission.

106   Casino Control legislation: ACT: Part 2; NSW: Part 3; NT: Section 13ff; Qld: Part 2; SA: Part 6; Tas: Part 7; Vic: Part 10; WA: Part 2.

107   Casino Control legislation: ACT: Part 5; NSW: Part 2; NT: s 26ff; Qld: Part 3; SA: Part 4; Tas: Part 3; Vic: Part 2; WA: Part 4.

108   Casino Control legislation: ACT: Part 4; NSW: Part 4; NT: s 46H; Qld: Part 4; SA: Part 4; Tas: Part 4; Vic: Part 4; WA: Part 5.

109   *R v Specker; Ex parte Alvaro* (1986) 44 SASR 60.

110   Casino Control legislation: Christmas Island: Part 5; Part 10; NSW: Part 8; NT: s 26; Qld: Part 5; Tas: Part 9; Vic: Part 8; WA: Part 3.

111   See for example: RW Maxwell, "Casino Development in Atlantic City: Abuses and Remedies" (1985) 10 *Vermont Law Review* 384-415; TR O'Brien and MJ Flaherty, "Regulation of the Atlantic city gambling industry and attempts to control its infiltration by organised crime" (1985) 16 *Rutgers Law Journal* 721-758.

112   J McMillen, *When the chips are down: a comparison of Australian casino developments*, at pp 19-20 of *Faces of Gambling, Proceedings of the Second National Conference of the National Association of Gambling Studies* (Department of Psychology, University of Sydney Australia, 1986).

The basic principle of the control systems is that there are people watching people watching people. The New South Wales Inquiry into Casinos described the Tasmanian system as follows: [113]

> All equipment is subject to the closest scrutiny by the government inspectors and staff. It is most impressive and includes checks of tables before opening of games. Further tests may be made at any time. All equipment is checked for interference prior to issue and on its return. At least one set of cards are checked for marks by magnifying glass daily...The chip control is treated with the security accorded to banknotes. Physical stock is taken regularly and all floats are recorded and examined by inspectors. The audit system is most detailed and documented at all points. A Government inspector is always present at any money count and countersigns the documents. The entire count is recorded on videotape and sixteen cameras generally form part of casino security.

The Commonwealth *Financial Transaction Reports Act 1988* now provides an additional layer of regulation on many of these matters.

Casino agreements. Complex financing, ownership and management structures have been required for the scale and mix of businesses in the casino projects. The Casino Control legislation provides for the scrutiny and approval of these arrangements to prevent the indirect infiltration of organised crime and to ensure that the other standards and objectives of the system are met. [114]

Casino project legislation. The scale and complexity of the casino projects has usually required special enabling legislation for each project.

Responsibility of Casino Operators to their customers

[15.180] There are strong parallels between alcohol servers' liability and responsible gambling practice. For example, casino operators are regulated by the same restrictions on

- smoking/no smoking areas;
- serving of alcohol to already intoxicated customers.

In addition, patrons are now suing casino operators alleging that they are responsible for the customer's gambling losses if the customer:

- continues gambling once intoxicated; [115]
- breaches a 'self exclusion' contract and returns to the casino to gamble. [116]

The following cases illustrate these two arguments.

Preston v Star City Pty Ltd

[15.185] *Preston v Star City Pty Ltd* (1999) NSWSC 1273

Facts: The Plaintiff alleged negligence and breach of statutory duty relating to losses of approximately $3 million suffered by him in gambling at the Sydney Star City Casino. He alleged (amongst other things) that that the defendant casino offered him inducements to gamble. These included the provision of a cheque cashing facility, the supply of complimentary products, services and

---

113 EA Lusher QC, *Report on the Inquiry into the Legalisation of Gambling Casinos in New South Wales* (1977), [600]-[601].
114 Casino Control legislation: ACT: Part 8; NSW: Part 3 Div 2; NT: ss 46J – N; Qld: Part 8; Tas: Part 9; Vic: Part 3; WA: Part 3; SA: Part 5.
115 *Preston v Star City* (1999) NSWSC 1273.
116 *Kakavas v Crown Ltd* (2007) VSC 526 (December 13); *Foroughi v Star City Casino* (2007) 163 FCR 131.

Preston v Star City Pty Ltd cont.

privileges, such as liquor, free of charge and the defendant informing the plaintiff 'that if he remained a "high roller" patron it would make available various business contracts related to its procurement needs or promotions'.

In addition, the Plaintiff claimed for breach of statutory duty by the defendant casino in allowing him to gamble whilst intoxicated, which was alleged to constitute a breach of section 163 of the *Casino Control Act 1992* (NSW) which prohibits intoxicated persons from gambling at the casino.

Held: Wood CJ (on appeal) acknowledged that a duty of care may exist in these circumstances but might not 'go so far as preventing the offer of a limited or reasonable range of inducements and complimentary services…'.[117] However, he stated that a duty of care may exist to prevent 'the provision of significant credit facilities or excessive encouragement through incentives, of a person who has specifically asked to be barred or to go beyond a limit that he has asked the casino to set'.[118]

This case did not involve any allegation that the defendant had engaged in active inducement or deliberate conduct designed to take advantage of the plaintiff's personal failings but the next two cases do rely on these specific allegations.

Foroughi v Star City Pty Ltd

[15.190]   *Foroughi v Star City Pty Ltd* (2007) 163 FCR 131

Facts: The Plaintiff was a problem gambler who sought permanent exclusion from Star City Casino in 2004. Despite being aware that he was a compulsive gambler, Star City Casino staff admitted the Plaintiff 65 times even inviting him to the High Roller room. He claimed $600,000 from the Defendant casino operator which he alleged he had lost since his self exclusion because he had an expectation that he would no longer be allowed to gamble at the establishment.

Held: The application for damages was dismissed. Jacobson J said:

> Any loss suffered by [the Plaintiff] was caused not by Star City Casino but by the Plaintiff's deliberate and voluntary conduct in entering the casino and gambling in breach of his written undertakings [119]… In the ordinary case, a gambler who enters a casino in breach of a voluntary exclusion order and suffers losses will have no redress in the form of a damages claim against the casino … That is not to say that the casino does not have some obligation to try to detect such persons and remove them. However the questions of what measures the casino should have in place are a matter for the Casino Control Authority.

This idea that a self exclusion clause will forever prevent a problem gambler from successfully claiming against the casino operator has been tested again in the following case with the judge leaving the question open.

Kakavas v Crown Ltd and John Williams

[15.195]   *Kakavas v Crown Ltd and John Williams* [2007] VSC 526

Facts: The Plaintiff was a problem gambler who self excluded from the Crown Casino in 1995. He sued the Defendant casino for $30m because he claimed that the casino 'devised a scheme' to induce him to recommence gambling in 2004 including providing him with a false name 'Harry Ray'. Some of

---

117   *Preston v Star City* (1999) NSWSC 1273 at 190.
118   *Preston v Star City* (1999) NSWSC 1273 at 133.
119   *Preston v Star City* (1999) NSWSC 1273 at 150.

Kakavas v Crown Ltd and John Williams cont.

those inducements alleged to have been made by Crown Casino included the use of a jet on about 30 occasions to fly him to Melbourne, gifts of thousands of dollars on many occasions including when he boarded the plane or arrived at the casino hotel, and, on several occasions, being extended lines of credit by the casino of up to $1.5 m. [120]

The Plaintiff also alleged that the Defendant did not advise him that any of his winnings would be forfeited to the State. He further alleged that if the Defendant had done so, the result would have been to deprive the inducements of any effect Pursuant to section 78B of *Casino Control Act 1991* (Vic), the winnings of a person who is subject to an exclusion order are forfeited to the State.

Held: Harper J found (in part), that those parts of the amended statement of claim that pleaded separate causes of action in negligence, misleading and deceptive conduct and restitution should be struck but that the cause of action labelled by the plaintiff as 'unconscionable conduct' was not so clearly untenable that it could not possibly succeed. The plaintiff was given leave to re-plead his claim in accordance with this judgment.

The door is now slightly open on the question of whether there is any duty of care owed to problem gamblers to prevent them from suffering gambling loss.

Signs of problem gambler

[15.200] Various authorities have identified a number of telltale signs of a problem gambler including:

- a strong, uncontrollable urge to gamble;
- failure at repeated attempts to reduce or stop gambling;
- spending more money and/or time on gambling activities than originally intended;
- continuing to gamble to recoup losses;
- gambling whenever money is available;
- lying to family members, friends or employers to conceal involvement with gambling;
- placing gambling as a priority, above other previously important relationships and activities;
- committing illegal acts such as forgery, fraud or theft to finance gambling activities.

Gaming machines

Gaming machine policy

[15.205] The policy issues involved with gaming machines are similar to those discussed for casinos above. In fact at present casinos provide 12,234 gaming machines.[121] However, unlike table games, gaming machines have also been licensed for two other types of establishment: hotels and clubs. This has greatly extended the impact of this type of gambling facility and raises some interesting policy issues.

- The 'losers' argument favours the casinos. As discussed above, casinos have been established in conjunction with substantial tourist facilities and so may argue that the

---

120 ABC Radio National Transcript, *Background Briefing: The law and gambling* (29 April 2007).
121 *Australian Casino Industry Economic Report Financial Year 2007*, p 14.

harmful impacts associated with the losers fall outside the local community. In contrast the losers at hotels and clubs are much more likely to be from the local community.

- The 'winners' argument favours the hotels and clubs. Casinos are owned and operated by large corporations, often publicly listed with substantial foreign ownership, so that little of the profits stay in the local community. In contrast, hotels are smaller enterprises and often locally owned, and clubs are by definition operated for the benefit of locals so that the profits are more likely to be reinvested in the local community.

However there are also competing policy arguments between hotels and clubs. There has long been great rivalry between hotels and clubs over liquor, food and entertainment, and gaming machines now provide another dimension to this contest. The arguments include:

- Hotels argue that they have established their premises and facilities on commercial lines and suffer unfair competition from supposedly not-for-profit clubs, which in reality are large commercial enterprises enjoying unfair income tax and other concessions.
- Clubs argue that they reinvest all surplus from gaming machines and other operations into the local community in the form of cultural, sporting, recreational and entertainment facilities and are more careful of the welfare of their customers whom they must represent and account to as an association.

The political solution to these arguments has been to permit casinos, hotels and clubs to all provide gaming machines in most States.[122] This has led to a proliferation of this type of gambling, which can be addictive and is particularly harmful to problem gamblers in its clientele who are often from already disadvantaged socio-economic groups. There is a trend developing in Australia for patrons to sue the owners of gambling establishments holding them responsible for their own addictive gambling habits and losses. See the discussion in [15.180]ff above. There are close parallels with the cases on a liquor licensee's responsibility for intoxicated customers, discussed in Chapter 14, [14.280]ff.

Gaming machine law

[15.210] New South Wales pioneered the approval of gaming machines in licensed clubs in 1960. As discussed in [15.140], this generated substantial cross-border trade from Queensland, South Australia and Victoria (until recently, as these States eventually moved to also permit gaming machines). Now each State and Territory has established a system for the licensing and use of gaming machines under special Gaming Machine legislation.[123] The policy of the Gaming Machine legislation was analysed by Scully J in *Mendonca & Santiago v South Sydney Junior Rugby League Club Ltd 1993* (see case study in [15.215]). The key elements of the control system are as follows.

Definitions–Gaming machines include the traditional slot machines, poker machines and fruit machines ('one-armed bandits') as well as many of the newer devices developed using information technology which can turn a simple game of chance into a virtual reality

---

122   Only in the Australian Capital Territory is the casino not permitted to provide gaming machines, see *Casino Control Act 2005* (ACT), s 107.
123   Gaming Machine legislation comprises: ACT: *Gaming Machine Act 2004*; NSW: *Gaming Machines Act 2001*; NT: *Gaming Machine Act*; Qld: *Gaming Machine Act 1991*; SA: *Gaming Machines Act 1992*; Tas: *Gaming Control Act 1993, Racing and Gaming Act 1952*; Vic: *Gambling Regulation Act 2003*; WA: *Gaming and Wagering Commission Act 1987*.

experience. In the struggle to keep up with technology, 'gaming machine' is usually defined widely as any device with the following key features:[124]

- it may be used for the purpose of playing a game of mixed chance and skill;
- it may be operated by inserting, using or electronically transferring money, tokens or credit; and
- as a result of making a bet on the device, winnings may become payable.

Administration–Each State has established a Gaming Machine authority[125] with the responsibility and wide powers to administer the Gaming Machine legislation.[126]

Licences–In all States and Territories except the Australian Capital Territory, casino licences generally include approval to operate a number of gaming machines, as discussed previously. However hotels and clubs provide the greatest number and the greatest geographical spread of gaming machines. In most States the qualifications for a gaming machine licence are similar to those for a hotel liquor licence or a club licence (see Chapter 14, [14.175]), except the inquiries and checks are more rigorous to prevent the infiltration of organised crime.[127] Qualifying hotels and clubs are issued with a renewable, non-transferable site licence for the approved number and type of gaming machines. Manufacturers, suppliers, service contractors, repairers and machine managers are also usually required to be licensed or approved.[128]

Supervision and control–As with casinos, control is exercised over the premises, number and location of the gaming machines and over the hours of operation, permitted games, rules of games and the conduct of games.[129] However the primary control is exercised over the machines themselves to ensure that they operate correctly and deliver the required percentage win to gamblers and record gaming revenue for the purposes of gaming tax. In some States gaming machines are owned and supplied by the Gaming authority whereas in others the machines are manufactured and supplied by approved private providers.

Accounting, taxes, levies and fees–The Gaming Machine legislation provides for gaming tax, community benefit levies, administration fees and rental on machines supplied by the Gaming authority.[130] The rates and mix of charges vary from State to State.

Inspection and enforcement–The Gaming Machine authority has wide powers to give directions to licensees about the conduct of gaming and administration of the premises and to

---

124 Gaming Machine legislation: ACT: Part 1 and Dictionary; NSW: Part 1; NT: s 3; Qld: Part 1 and Schedule 2; SA: *Gaming Machines Act 1992*Part 1; Tas: Part 1; Vic: Chapter 3 Part 1; WA: Part 1.
125 Gaming Machine authority: ACT: Gambling and Racing Commission; NSW: Casino, Liquor and Gaming Control Authority; NT: Northern Territory Licensing Commission; Qld: Queensland Gaming Commission; SA: Liquor and Gambling Commission; Tas: Tasmanian Gaming Commission; Vic: Victorian Commission for Gambling Regulation; WA: Gaming and Wagering Commission of Western Australia.
126 Gaming Machine legislation: ACT: Parts 2, 3; NSW: Part 5; NT: s 17; Qld: Part 2; SA: *Gaming Machines Act 1992*Part 2; Tas: Parts 7, 8; Vic: Chapter 3, Part 4; WA: Part 2.
127 Gaming Machine legislation: ACT: Parts 4 and 5; NSW: Part 5; NT: ss 28 – 34; Qld: Parts 3, 4; SA: *Gaming Machines Act 1992*Parts 3, 4, 4A; Tas: Parts 3, 4, 4A – C; Vic: Chapter 3, Part 4A; WA: Part 5.
128 Gaming Machine legislation: ACT: Part 6; NSW: Part 4; NT: ss 116 – 120; Qld: Part 4; SA: *Gaming Machines Act 1992*Parts 4, 4A; Tas: Part 4, 4A – C; Vic: Chapter 3, Part 5; WA: Part 5 Div 5.
129 Gaming Machine legislation: ACT: Part 6; NSW: Part 5; NT: ss 98 – 115; Qld: Parts 5, 6, 7; SA: *Gaming Machines Act 1992*Parts 4A, 5; Tas: Parts 4, 5, 6; Vic: Chapter 3, Parts 4, 4A; WA: Part 4.
130 Gaming Machine legislation: ACT: Parts 11, 12; NSW: Part 7; NT: ss 143 – 157; Qld: Parts 8, 9; SA: *Gaming Machines Act 1992*Part 8; Tas: Part 9; Vic: Chapter 3, Part 7; WA: Part 5.

make inspections and inquiries to ensure compliance and if necessary to bring proceedings for offences and to review and terminate licences.[131]

Mendonca and Santiago v South Sydney Junior Rugby League Club Ltd

[15.215] *Mendonca and Santiago v South Sydney Junior Rugby League Club Ltd* (unreported, Sup Ct NSW, Sully J, 16 December 1993, No 14099 of 1989)

Facts: M and S went to the Club to play the poker machines. The Club was registered under the *Registered Clubs Act 1976* (NSW) which permitted the operation of poker machines subject to stringent requirements, including conditions which defined and restricted the persons authorised to play to various classes of members and registered customers. M's father was a member but neither M nor S were members or registered customers. M and S were playing a machine in turns when it hit the jackpot of $97,328.33. The Club refused to pay because they were not members or registered customers and they sued to recover the win.

Decision: The Supreme Court of New South Wales (Scully J) held that the contract was unenforceable at common law. The Club argued that there was no contract. Sully J found that S was playing the machine at the time of the win and there was a contract between S and the Club. He said:[132]

> The acceptance by the operator of a poker machine of the money which a player of the machine must insert into the machine in order to have a chance of winning a prize from the operator of the machine, seems to me to satisfy the classic description of a wagering contract, as to which description see *Carlill v Carbolic Smokeball Co* [1892] 2 QB 484 per Hawkins at 490...[133]

The Club argued that if there was a contract it was subject to the condition set out on a notice exhibited over the machines and at the change room. The notice set out five rules of the Club, which included a rule that jackpots would be paid out only to members or registered customers. Scully J found that S did not have sufficient command of English to read or understand the rules and, applying the ticket case principles from *Balmain New Ferry Co Ltd v Robertson* [1906] 4 CLR 379 at 386 per Griffith CJ held:[134]

> I am not satisfied on the probabilities that the defendant has proved that it did what was reasonably sufficient to give to...[S] clear notice of the rules...In other words, I am not satisfied that the defendant has established on the probabilities that the wagering contract between it and...[S] had incorporated into it by notice the exclusionary rule...

The Club successfully argued that the contract was unenforceable for illegality. Scully J found that S and M had breached s 45 of the Act which made it an offence punishable by a fine of up to $200 for a person not a member or registered customer to use any facilities (including poker machines) of a club. However the Act did not expressly prohibit the making of a wagering contract in breach of s 45 and Scully J held that such a prohibition could not be implied into the statute. Scully J held that the wagering contract was unenforceable at common law based on the principle that the court will not enforce a contract at the suit of a party who has entered into it with the object of committing an illegal act. Scully J provided the following reasons for reaching this conclusion:

---

131 Gaming Machine legislation: ACT: Part 13; NSW: Parts 6 and 7; NT: ss 45 – 51, 165; Qld: Part 10; SA: *Gaming Machines Act 1992*Part 7; Tas: Part 8; Vic: Chapter 3, Parts 8, 9; WA: Part 3.

132 *Mendonca and Santiago v South Sydney Junior Rugby League Club Ltd* (unreported, Sup Ct NSW, Sully J, 16 December 1993, No 14099 of 1989) at 6.

133 See [15.120] above.

134 *Mendonca and Santiago v South Sydney Junior Rugby League Club Ltd* (unreported, Sup Ct NSW, Sully J, 16 December 1993, No 14099 of 1989) at 14.

Mendonca and Santiago v South Sydney Junior Rugby League Club Ltd cont.

- The history of the regulation of gaming.

    For more than 140 years the statute law of New South Wales has consistently proscribed unregulated gaming and wagering. A consistent feature of that statutory proscription has been to deny expressly the enforcement in the courts of New South Wales of gaming and wagering contracts. The prototype legislation is... [the *Gaming Act 1850* (NSW) (see [15.140]). This statutory provision has been consistently re-enacted whenever the statute law of gaming and wagering has been revised and updated – see the *Gaming and Betting Act 1912* s 16 above, n 48, and Rich J in *Defina v Kenny* at [15.135]]. [135]

- Exceptions were made only subject to strict regulation.

    That sequence of legislation has always recognised and expressly permitted certain stated exceptions to the otherwise general rule. As social conditions, standards and expectations have changed, so has the number of permitted exceptions expanded, but always upon the basis that the public law of New South Wales regards gaming and wagering as, at least, potential social mischiefs, to be permitted, if at all, only subject to strict legislative regulation. [136]

- The *Registered Clubs Act 1976* (NSW) is such an exception.

    The Registered Clubs Act is in that settled tradition of the public law of New South Wales. The Act accepts that people want to gamble on poker machines, but seeks to provide for that expectation in a way that stops far, and deliberately far, short of permitting simple unrestricted access to poker machines. That the Act seeks, as it plainly does, to manipulate the public regulation of poker machines in order to raise revenue for the State Government, does not detract, in my opinion, from the public policy, evident throughout the history of gaming and wagering legislation in New South Wales, of legalising gaming and wagering only on strict conditions. [137]

- The policy of the Act.

    So far as the Act now in question is concerned, the intended operation of that public policy is, in my opinion, clear. Certain premises will be licensed as registered Clubs. They will be permitted to have certain categories only of members. Persons who are such members are authorised by law, – not, it is to be noted, by the Clubs autonomously, – to enter upon such premises and there to enjoy all available lawful amenities, including in particular, access to poker machines. A person who is not so authorised...but who nevertheless uses those amenities, commits a punishable misdemeanour. [138]

- Contrary to public policy to enforce the contract.

    To permit such a person to profit from such a misdemeanour would be, in my opinion, to strike a serious blow against the integrity of the public policy previously discussed. That is especially so in the present case where the disproportion between the unauthorised gain and the prescribed penalty is so gross.

    It would be, in my opinion, wrong for the Courts to lend any aid to such a subversion of the intended public policy of the legislature as expressed generally in the current gaming

---

135 *Mendonca and Santiago v South Sydney Junior Rugby League Club Ltd* (unreported, Sup Ct NSW, Sully J, 16 December 1993, No 14099 of 1989) at 29.

136 *Mendonca and Santiago v South Sydney Junior Rugby League Club Ltd* (unreported, Sup Ct NSW, Sully J, 16 December 1993, No 14099 of 1989) at 29.

137 *Mendonca and Santiago v South Sydney Junior Rugby League Club Ltd* (unreported, Sup Ct NSW, Sully J, 16 December 1993, No 14099 of 1989) at 29.

138 *Mendonca and Santiago v South Sydney Junior Rugby League Club Ltd* (unreported, Sup Ct NSW, Sully J, 16 December 1993, No 14099 of 1989) at 30. Scully J noted at 26 that S knew the Club was not a place of unregulated public resort and that it was open only to categories of members.

Mendonca and Santiago v South Sydney Junior Rugby League Club Ltd cont.

and wagering legislation, and more particularly in the Act now in question. [139]

Exercise

Russian Roulette

Perry Klapper is a real estate agent with a compulsive gambling habit losing on average $5000.00 each time he visits Twinkle Town Casino. His family is so worried about his gambling debts (a whopping $100,000 since January this year) that they have convinced him to enter a self exclusion contract with the Casino which he has done. Unfortunately Perry cannot help himself and is now visiting the Casino in disguise so as to avoid being photographically identified on the Casino's banned list.

The Casino, in turn, recognises a potential 'High Roller' when it sees one and is offering all kinds of inducements to Perry in disguise such as free tickets to upcoming concerts, limousine transport, free food, drinks and even accommodation at the Casino. Some of the Casino staff even suspect that it is Perry in disguise but don't want to 'rock the boat'.

Discuss, what liability, if any, the Casino may face when it realises its mistake. Alternatively, could Perry bring an action for the recovery of his gambling losses blaming the casino for failing in its duty of care to prevent him from suffering further losses?

WORLD HERITAGE

'The Convention's focus on both cultural and natural heritage makes it a unique legal instrument. This is expressed in the World Heritage emblem, which is round, like the world, but at the same time it is a symbol of protection. The central square is a form created by man and the circle represents nature, the two being intimately linked.' (UNESCO, 1978) [140]

History and Objectives

[15.225] UNESCO's publication *The World Heritage* provides a succinct description of the historical context and objectives of the World Heritage Convention:

---

139   *Mendonca and Santiago v South Sydney Junior Rugby League Club Ltd* (unreported, Sup Ct NSW, Sully J, 16 December 1993, No 14099 of 1989) at 30. Scully J said at 27 that to refuse enforcement of the wagering contract would "give a distinct and painful sting to [s 45]" whereas the s 45 penalty of $200 was "the merest drop in the financial ocean".
140   UNESCO World Heritage Centre: http://www.whc.unesco.org/en/list.

The ancient Greeks referred to the Seven Wonders of the World. Today, practically all of these have disappeared, leaving no trace.[141] However there remain in the world today many more than those Seven Wonders: irreplaceable testimonies of past civilisations and natural landscapes of great beauty and significance, their preservation concerns us all.

That is the objective of the 'Convention Concerning the Protection of the World Cultural and Natural Heritage' [the World Heritage Convention, 1972]. This international Convention to which there are [186] States Parties [142] was adopted by the General Conference on UNESCO in 1972. Its primary mission is to define the worldwide natural and cultural heritage and to draw up a List of sites and monuments considered to be of such universal value that their protection is the responsibility of all humanity. The aim of the Convention is therefore to promote co-operation among all nations and peoples in order to contribute effectively to this protection.

The Convention is thus profoundly original in its conception. It embodies some important new ideas linking together the conservation of nature and of culture which until recently had rarely been seen in conjunction with each other. For a long time nature and culture were perceived as opposing elements in that man was supposed to conquer a hostile nature, while culture symbolised spiritual values. However nature and culture are of course complementary: the cultural identity of different peoples has been forged in the environment in which they live and frequently, the most beautiful man-made works owe part of their beauty to their natural surroundings. Moreover some of the most spectacular natural sites bear the imprint of centuries of human activity. Sadly, in our modern world, cultural monuments and natural sites appear to be equally threatened by degradation.

At 1 July 2010 there were 890 sites listed, comprising 689 cultural sites, 176 natural sites and 25 mixed cultural and natural sites. These sites are located in 148 different countries.

Australia's properties inscribed on the World Heritage List

[15.230] Australia is fortunate to have 18 World Heritage Sites; 3 cultural, 11 natural and 4 mixed sites. These are set out in the table below, together with their date of listing and category of site. They are also illustrated geographically on the following map.

Australian World Heritage Sites [143]

Date of listing	Category of Site	Site name
	Cultural	
2004		Royal Exhibition Building and Cultural Gardens
2007		Sydney Opera House
2010		Australian Convict Sites
	Mixed (cultural and natural)	
1981		Kakadu National Park Uluru-Kata Tjuta
1981		Willandra Lakes Region
1982		Tasmanian Wilderness

---

141 Professor Ralph Slayter, former Australian ambassador to UNESCO (1978-81) and head of our delegation to the World Heritage Committee and chairman from 1981 to 1983, believes that the Convention represents "a contemporary example of the ancient Seven Wonders of the World" – "the difference being that when the Seven Wonders list was drawn up the 'world' was Mediterranean and natural heritage was not even considered. There being no mechanism to preserve the ancient wonders, only the Pyramids of Egypt have survived more or less intact": B Cohen, "Our Great Natural Wonders", *The Weekend Australian Review*, 12-13 December 1992, p 3.

142 As at September 2010.

143 For a more detailed description of Australia's World Heritage sites, see http://www.whc.unesco.org/en/list.

Date of listing	Category of Site	Site name
1987		Uluru-Kata Tjuta National Park
	Natural	
1981		Great Barrier Reef
1982		Lord Howe Island Group
1986		Central Eastern Rainforest Reserves (Australia)
1988		Wet Tropics of Queensland
1991		Shark Bay
1992		Fraser Island
1994		Australian Fossil Mammals Sites
1997		Heard and McDonald Islands
1997		Macquarie Island
2000		Greater Blue Mountains Area
2003		Purnululu National Park

Map of Australian World Heritage Sites

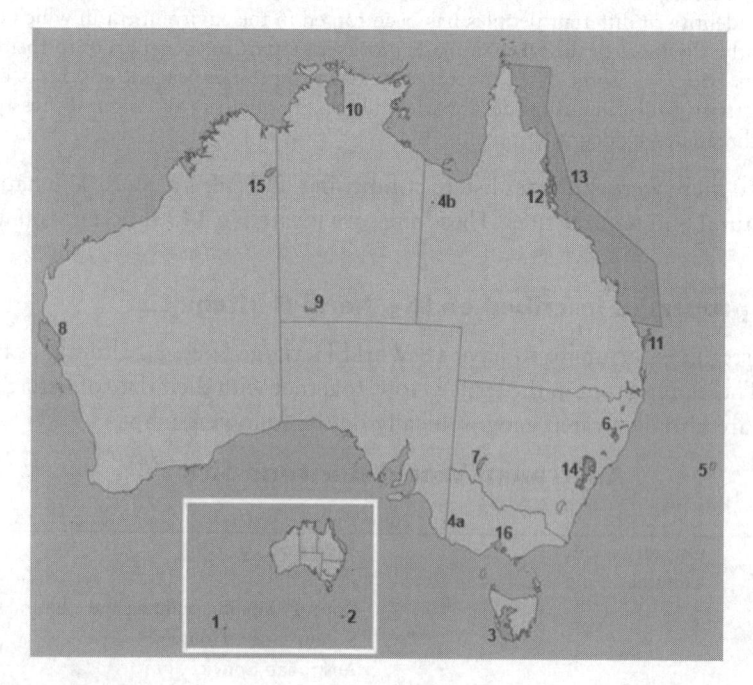

Source: World Heritage Sites in Australianhttp://www.thesalmons.org/lynn/wh-australia.html. The Australian Convict Sites (11) are situated variously in New South Wales, Norfolk Island, Tasmania and Western Australia.

World Heritage Convention

[15.235] The *Convention Concerning the Protection of the World Cultural and Natural Heritage 1972* UNESCO ('World Heritage Convention') is designed to respond to actual and threatened damage to world cultural and natural heritage, on the basis that 'deterioration or disappearance of any item of the cultural or natural heritage constitutes a harmful impoverishment of the heritage of all nations of the world' (Preamble, 2nd recital).

The main aims of the Convention are to:

- identify;

- protect; and
- present

world cultural and natural heritage. [144]

The strategies used to protect sites include:

- Listing of heritage sites (World Heritage List); [145]
- Listing of heritage sites in danger (List of World Heritage in Danger); [146]
- Assistance to states in maintenance and restoration of sites (World Heritage Fund). [147]

World Heritage Committee

[15.240] The World Heritage Convention is administered by the World Heritage Centre [148] at UNESCO's offices in Paris. Twenty-one state parties are elected for six-year terms (one-third of the seats are elected at each General Assembly). The Committee approves applications to the World Heritage List and develops policy and guidelines called the Operational Guidelines for the Implementation of the World Heritage Convention.

In order to qualify for the World Heritage List, a nominated property must meet specific selection criteria of outstanding universal value from either a natural or cultural point of view. The Operational Guidelines define selection criteria from (i)-(x) for assessing such nominations. [149] Paragraphs (i) to (vi) relate to cultural heritage and paragraphs (vii) to (x) relate to natural heritage. The specific criteria for cultural and natural heritage are detailed in the following [15.245] and [15.250] respectively.

Even with the additional particulars laid down in the Operational Guidelines the criteria are unavoidably imprecise and selection involves subjective judgment by the Committee as the ultimate decision-making body. In this selection the Committee is advised by the International Council of Monuments and Sites (ICOMOS) on cultural sites and by the International Union for the Conservation of Nature (IUCN) on natural sites. The listing process involves identification and nomination by the country of location, evaluation including investigation and report by ICOMOS or IUCN and then decision by the Committee.

Australia's World Heritage is administered by the World Heritage Unit [150] of the Department of Environment Water, Heritage and the Arts, and the relevant State Departments of Environment. Each site also has its own local management authority and arrangements for this vary from site to site as discussed below.

Cultural heritage

[15.245] Cultural heritage is the work of humans and to qualify for World Heritage listing a site must include:

monuments: architectural works, works of monumental sculpture and painting, elements or structures of an archaeological nature...groups of buildings...which, because of their

---

144   Article 4.
145   Article 11(1), (2) and (3).
146   Article 11(4). As at July 2010 there were 31 sites in danger.
147   Article 15.
148   UNESCO World Heritage Centre: http://www.whc.unesco.org/en/list.
149   Operational Guidelines, [77]ff. See http://www.whc.unesco.org/archive/opguide08-en.pdf.
150   Australian World Heritage at http://www.environment.gov.au/about/publications/annual-report/08-09/cross-cutting.html.

architecture, their homogeneity or their place in the landscape, are *of outstanding universal value* from the point of view of history, art or science.

(Article 1)

There are presently 704 cultural World Heritage Sites, 3 of which are in Australia (7 including mixed sites). See table in [15.230]. In order to establish that a cultural property is of 'outstanding universal value', it must fit within at least one of the following six selection criteria, That is:

i. Represent a masterpiece of human creative genius;

ii. Exhibit an important interchange of human values, over a span of time or within a cultural area of the world, on developments in architecture or technology, monumental arts, town planning or landscape design;

iii. Bear a unique or at least exceptional testimony to a cultural tradition or to a civilization which is living or which has disappeared;

iv. Be an outstanding example of a type of building, architectural or technical ensemble or landscape which illustrates (a) significant stage(s) in human history;

v. Be an outstanding example of a traditional human settlement, land-use or sea-use which is representative of a culture (or cultures) or human interaction with the environment, especially when it has become vulnerable under the impact of irreversible change;

vi. Be directly or tangibly associated with events or living traditions, with ideas, or with beliefs, with artistic and literary works of outstanding universal significance (preferably used in conjunction with other criteria.

The cultural criteria have caused some difficulties for Australia, which, until recently, did not have a site listed solely on its cultural merit. The problems stem mainly from the original Eurocentric concept of cultural heritage. Aboriginal cultural heritage had sufficient antiquity but did not have sufficient monuments and structures to fit the concept. Australia's later European settlement had produced the monuments and structures but at less than 200 years old, it did not have sufficient antiquity.

Australian Aboriginal cultural heritage is now accommodated by a sub-category of sites called 'Cultural Landscapes'[151] which include diverse examples of the interaction between humans and the natural environment. The Uluru-Kata Tjuta site, originally listed only as a natural site, was successfully renominated as a cultural landscape in 1994, becoming the world's second site to be listed in that category.[152] This recognises the vital and continuing relationship between the Aboriginals and the natural environment at the site. This category also now accommodates many sites in the highly developed countries of Europe which have relatively few pristine natural sites.

Despite their lack of antiquity Australia's monuments and buildings have now also been considered for listing under the revised cultural heritage criteria. The Sydney Opera House provides an interesting example of this development. When first nominated, the World Heritage Committee indicated unofficially their view that it would not satisfy the criteria and

---

151 Cultural landscapes represent the "combined works of nature and of man" designated in Article 1 of the Convention.

152 See SM Titchen, "The Uluru-Kata Tjuta cultural landscape" (Mar 1996) 10 *The World Heritage Newsletter* 8-11.

it was withdrawn by the Australian government so as to avoid embarrassment. It was later renominated and is now listed under the revised criteria.

Originally proponents of ecotourism focused exclusively on natural attractions and denied the significance of the cultural dimension. Gradually the concept has matured so that most definitions now recognise the cultural component and in some acclaimed ecotourism experiences the cultural component is clearly dominant. As discussed above, the World Heritage Convention has pioneered this broader view and embraced the inextricable link between humans and nature and the heritage value of both. This is important for Australia, as the majority of our sites, although listed for natural values, also have an important cultural dimension and indeed four are also listed for their cultural values. See mixed cultural and natural sites at [15.230].

Natural heritage

[15.250] Natural heritage comprises the works of nature and to qualify for World Heritage listing a site must include:

> natural features consisting of physical and biological formations or groups of such formations, which are of outstanding universal value from the aesthetic or scientific point of view; geological and physiographical formations and precisely delineated areas which constitute the habitat of threatened species of animals and plants of outstanding universal value...natural sites or precisely delineated natural areas of *outstanding universal value*.... (Article 2)

There are presently 180 natural World Heritage Sites in the world, 11 of which are in Australia (15 including mixed sites). See Table in [15.230].

In order to establish that a property is of 'outstanding universal value', for the purposes of natural heritage, it must fit within at least one of the following four selection criteria, That is to:

vii. Contain superlative natural phenomena or areas of exceptional natural beauty and aesthetic importance;

viii. Be outstanding examples representing major stages of earth's history, including the record of life, significant on-going geological processes in the development of landforms, or significant geomorphic or physiographic features;

ix. Be outstanding examples representing significant on-going ecological and biological processes in the evolution and development of terrestrial, fresh water, coastal and marine ecosystems and communities of plants and animals;

x. Contain the most important and significant natural habitats for in-situ conservation of biological diversity, including those containing threatened species of outstanding universal value from the point of view of science or conservation.

State party obligations

[15.255] Each State party, so far as possible and with its consent, is encouraged to identify and nominate potential sites situated on its territory for inclusion on the World Heritage List.[153] As previously indicated, these sites must be of 'outstanding universal value' in

---

153   Article 11(1), Article 3.

accordance with criteria established by World Heritage Committee.[154] If selected, the site is placed on the World Heritage List which is updated at least every two years.[155]

> Each State party recognizes that the duty of ensuring the identification, protection, conservation, presentation and transmission to future generations of the cultural and natural heritage ...belongs primarily to that State. (Article 4)

However, not all sites of 'outstanding universal value' are nominated by a State Party and this simply reflects the fact that a particular State Party may not wish to lose some of its sovereign power over the site. This dilution of sovereign power is an inevitable result of the World Heritage listing process which involves international monitoring and reporting of management strategies.[156] For example, once listed, a site becomes subject to 'international protection'.

> While fully respecting the sovereignty of States on whose territory the cultural and natural heritage...is situated...[that] heritage constitutes a world heritage for whose protection it is the duty of the international community as a whole to cooperate. (Article 6)

For example, once a State Party has listed a site, the World Heritage Committee may then later reclassify it as a threatened site on its List of World Heritage Sites in Danger without State Party consent.[157] There are presently 31 such World Heritage Sits in Danger. The kinds of threats which could trigger such listing may be either ascertained or potential and are quite extensive in nature.[158] Once the process has begun, it will set in motion programs for corrective measures and monitoring.

Other specific measures which a State Party is required to undertake once a site on its territory is listed for World Heritage include:

- establishment of policies and services for the protection, conservation and presentation of cultural and natural heritage;
- development of study and research methods to counteract dangers that threaten cultural or natural heritage;
- development of appropriate legal, scientific, administrative and financial measures for conservation; and
- establishment or development of national or regional centres for training in the protection, conservation and presentation of the cultural and natural heritage.[159]

Presenting World Heritage Sites

[15.260] Within the context of the tourism industry sector, the concept of 'presentation' referred to in Article 4 of the *World Heritage Convention* has special significance. From the tourist's perspective, a good cultural or natural heritage experience is one which exhibits the following attributes:

---

154 Article 11(2).
155 Article 11(3).
156 See TA Atherton and TC Atherton, "The Power and the Glory: a discussion paper on National Sovereignty and the World Heritage Convention" (1995) 69 *Australian Law Journal* 631-649.
157 Article 11(4).
158 See Article 11(4) "...such as the threat of disappearance caused by accelerated deterioration, large- scale public or private projects or rapid urban or tourist development projects; destruction caused by changes in the use or ownership of the land; major alterations due to unknown causes; abandonment for any reason whatsoever; the outbreak or the threat of an armed conflict; calamities and cataclysms; serious fires, earthquakes, landslides; volcanic eruptions; changes in water level, floods and tidal waves."
159 Article 5.

- something that is unique;
- a well presented site, facility or experience;
- easy and safe access;
- clean and tidy;
- an appropriate scale of visitor services;
- polite, friendly, knowledgeable staff;
- accurate, attractively presented information; and
- the opportunity to participate in some way.

These are the standards tourists expect and demand when visiting World Heritage Sites. Most World Heritage Sites are open to the public subject to restricted access to parts of the site in some cases or restricted numbers of visitors in others. Very few are limited to a particular group of people only.[160] This reflects the obligation that World Heritage Listing process imposes upon a State Party. That is the recognition that World Heritage belongs to all of humankind and that listing should not be used as a tool to 'lock up and throw away the key' to a particular property in an overzealous desire to protect and conserve it.

Australian Developments

[15.265] Australia, an early signatory[161] to the World Heritage Convention, has enacted domestic legislation at both State and Commonwealth level to reflect the principles of World Heritage.[162] Since the Commonwealth has been given no specific power over the environment in the Australian Constitution,[163] State and local authorities share this jurisdiction with the federal government.[164]

The tensions existing between State and federal politics on issues of conservation and development in World Heritage areas and the adversarial approach taken by both parties to the resolution of these issues have resulted in the development of uniquely Australian World Heritage case law.

Australian cases on World Heritage

[15.270] There have been a number of disputes involving not only all the usual issues of conservation versus development[165] but also the added tension between State and federal government over the way the world Heritage Convention augments the federal government's external affairs power over the States under the Australian constitution.[166]

---

160 For example, Mount Athos World Heritage Site in Greece. The "Holy Mountain", is forbidden to women and children.
161 22 August 1974.
162 The earlier *World Heritage Properties Conservation Act 1983* (Cth) has now been replaced by the *Environmental Protection and Biodiversity Conservation Act 1999* (Cth) (EPBCA). See also *Environmental Planning and Assessment Act 1979* (NSW).
163 *Commonwealth of Australia Constitution Act 1900* (IMP).
164 G Bates, *Environmental Law in Australia* (5th ed, Butterworths, 2002), at [3.1].
165 See TC Atherton and TA Atherton, "Mediating disputes over tourism in sensitive areas: Part I Advantages of alternative dispute resolution techniques" (1994) 5(1) *Australian Dispute Resolution Journal* 1-21.
166 See TA Atherton and TC Atherton, "Mediating disputes over tourism in sensitive areas: Part II Adapting and applying alternative dispute resolution techniques" (1994) 5(2) *Australian Dispute Resolution Journal* 135-155.

The series of cases involving World Heritage Values include the following:

Tamanian Dam case

Commonwealth v Tasmania (1983) 158 CLR 1 ('Tasmanian Dam Case').

Facts: In 1982, the Commonwealth (with initial Tasmanian support), nominated three parks in South West Tasmania for World Heritage Listing. In that same year, Tasmania commenced work towards construction of a dam within the designated World Heritage Area which would have flooded the Gordon-below-Franklin river wilderness area in south west Tasmania. In 1983, the Commonwealth enacted the *World Heritage Properties Conservation Act 1983* [167] and effectively blocked the Tasmanian government from constructing its hydro-electric scheme.

Held: The High Court (by majority of 4 to 3) upheld the constitutional validity of the Commonwealth legislation. It recognised that State sovereignty and jurisdiction are conditional upon the Commonwealth's trade, foreign affairs and other external powers [168] to give effect in Australia to international conventions on the environment.

The later *Tasmanian Forests Case* [169] confirmed this approach.

In other words, the obligations imposed on the federal government by the World Heritage Convention cannot be wholly delegated to any State or Territory. There must be an ongoing system of checks and balances to protect World Heritage values at listed sites in the Australian States and Territories from potential risks such as oil drilling on the Great Barrier Reef, [170] flooding of lakes for hydro-electric purposes or logging of ancient forests.

Queensland v Commonwealth

Queensland v Commonwealth (1988) 62 ALJR 143

Facts: Queensland sought an injunction to prevent the nomination of the Wet Tropics in North Queensland for World Heritage listing. It argued an Environmental Impact Assessment (EIA) under the *Environmental Protection (Impact of Proposals) Act 1974* should have been required in view of the likely adverse social and economic impacts on the local community.

Held: The High Court found this argument quite ironic in view of Queensland's delay and risk to World Heritage values and declined to order an injunction.

---

167 Since repealed and replaced by the *Environmental Protection and Biodiversity Conservation Act 1999* (Cth).
168 Constitution, s 51(xxxix).
169 *Richardson v Forestry Commission* (1988) 164 CLR 261.
170 A former Queensland State government once proposed this and is partly responsible for the enactment of the *Great Barrier Reef Marine Park Act 1975* (Cth).

Queensland v Commonwealth cont.

Postscript: In 1988, the federal government amended the *Environmental Protection (Impact of Proposals) Act 1974* to exclude World Heritage nomination from actions requiring environmental impact assessments.

Friends of Hinchinbrook Society Inc v The Minister

Friends of Hinchinbrook Society Inc v The Minister for the Environment and Ors [1997] 55 FCA (Feb '97); [1997] 789 FCA (Aug '97) [171]

Facts: On 9 July, 1996, the Minister for the Environment gave his consent (pursuant to sections 9 and 10 of the *World Heritage Properties Conservation Act 1983* (Cth) for certain activities to be carried out in the World Heritage area of a proposed tourist resort development site including removal of fallen mangroves and dredging of an access channel for the marina. The Plaintiffs challenged the grant of the consent and argued (amongst other things) that these activities were not consistent with the protection, conservation and presentation of the World Heritage values of the area.

Held: Sackville J upheld the validity of the consents issued by the Minister pursuant to sections 9 and 10 of the Act. In reaching this conclusion, His Honour noted that it would be difficult for the Minister to have regard to the conservation and protection of Heritage Listed sites, as required by the Act, if he did not consider 'the prospect of serious or irreversible harm to the property in circumstances where scientific opinion is uncertain or in conflict.'

Recurrent themes

[15.275] It is clear from the discussion in [15.270] that listing sites has often been controversial. In most cases consumptive activities such as mining, logging or hydro damming, listings have had to be discontinued. Also in most cases tourism has been advanced as the method of replacing lost industries and generating long-term sustainable economic benefits from the sites. Suter [172] has observed that:

> Australia has a unique relationship with the UNESCO World Heritage Convention: in no other nation has the convention created as much controversy as it has in Australia. Insofar as calculation is possible, Australia has probably had more litigation and political challenges to the Convention than all the other [145 as at January 1997] parties to the Convention combined.

In summary, the tensions existing between competing (un)sustainable activities and conflicting World Heritage Values are highlighted in the listing of a number of Australian World Heritage Sites. For example:

- Great Barrier Reef: listed to prevent oil drilling;
- Kakadu National Park: extended to prevent uranium mining;
- Tasmanian Wilderness: listed to prevent damming, logging;
- Fraser Island: first prevented sand mining, then logging;
- Central Eastern Australian Rainforest: listed to prevent logging.

---

171 There were a series of seven cases and appeals during 1996-98 relating to this matter. See, for example, [1997] 55 FCA (Feb '97); [1997] 789 FCA (Aug '97).
172 KD Suter, "The UNESCO World Heritage Convention" (1992) 8 EPLJ 4.

Towards a co-operative approach

[15.280] Over time, the Commonwealth, State and local authorities have shown a greater willingness to co-operate in harmonising the regulatory framework for environmental protection in the Australian context. For example:

- *Offshore Constitutional Agreement (OCS)* 1979;
- *Intergovernmental Agreement on the Environment (IGAE)* 1992;
- *Australian Local Government Association (ALGA) Accord with the Commonwealth Government* 1995;
- *Council of Australian Governments (COAG)* 1997 review of Commonwealth's role in environmental matters.

These initiatives will hopefully prevent a return to the litigious approach to protection of World Heritage values adopted by all sides in the 1980s and 1990s.

Sustainable Tourism

[15.285] World Heritage sites are by definition usually outstanding international tourist attractions – they are the present Wonders of the World. The listing procedure and the management obligations under the World Heritage Convention indirectly provide an objective international system of quality assurance for visitors to these attractions. Despite the incredible diversity of sites, international visitors can usually be assured that they are worthy of the visit and that the unique values of the site will be protected and presented. Listed sites comprise the bulk of the world's most outstanding cultural and natural attractions and collectively they provide the motivating force for a substantial proportion of international tourism. There is no similar international system of quality assurance yet available for attractions outside World Heritage.

In other words, a World Heritage Site:

- adds a new element to the tourism product of a destination;
- provides a Unique Selling Proposition (USP) for specific tourism markets; [173]
- attracts tourism which in turn can help to raise funds for protecting and conserving cultural or natural heritage;
- creates and sustains awareness and understanding of the past amongst local communities and tourists, leading to a desire to protect and conserve.

World Heritage Sustainable Tourism Programme

[15.290] In 1994, the authors defined 'ecotourism' in the following way:

> Ecotourism is sustainable tourism focused on natural (and associated cultural) attractions which is both educational for visitors as well as beneficial for destination communities

[174]

The elements identified in that definition appear now to be embedded in the UNESCO World Heritage Sustainable Tourism Programme 2001 ('the Programme') which encourages

---

[173] These include cultural tourists, nature adventure tourists and so on.

[174] The authors attempted to encapsulate the criteria for ecotourism in the definition they developed for the Queensland Ecotourism Strategy 1995.

sustainable tourism actions at World Heritage sites, to preserve them for future generations to appreciate. The Programme uses tourism to contribute to:

- environmental protection,
- limit negative socio economic impacts, and
- benefit local people economically and socially.

It is composed of seven activities: [175]

- Building the capacity of World Heritage site management to deal with tourism
- Training local community members in tourism related activities to participate in the industry and receive tourism's benefits.
- Aiding communities around the sites to market their products.
- Raising public awareness of World Heritage and building pride with local communities and visitors through conservation education.
- Using tourism generated funds to supplement site conservation and protection costs.
- Spreading the lessons learned to other sites and protected areas.
- Building increased awareness of World Heritage and its activities and policies for tourism industry officials and their clients.

Sustainable tourism at World Heritage Sites

[15.295] It is also instructive to consider how well ecotourism fits with the provisions of the World Heritage Convention.[176] Tourism is the only major industry consistent with World Heritage values pursuant to the World Heritage Convention because it satisfies the requirements of:

1   Sustainability: Article 5;
2   Cultural and Natural attractions: Articles 1 and 2;
3   Education: Article 27;
4. Benefits locals (indigenous and others): Article 5(a).

Sustainability

[15.300] Sustainable tourism is the conceptual solution to the long-standing conflict between conservation and development.[177] In essence it recognises that human activities such as tourism have a range of impacts on the environment and that the quality of life of current and future generations depends upon ensuring that those impacts do not exceed the capacity of the environment to withstand them.[178] The sustainability concept is the most important feature of ecotourism, and promotes environmentally friendly tourism.[179]

---

175   Source: http://www.whc.unesco.org/en/sustainabletourism.
176   See also the author's evidence to the House of Representatives, Standing Committee on Environment, Recreation and the Arts, Reference World Heritage Areas, *Hansard*, 15 November 1995, pp 191-202.
177   See TC Atherton, *Sustainable Tourism Development*, Invited keynote paper delivered at the roundtable on Sustainable Tourism at the 10th General Assembly of the World Tourism Organisation (WTO) (Bali, Indonesia, 7 October 1993).
178   See TC Atherton, *Tourism: The Regulation of Destination Planning, Development and Management* (MSc thesis, University of Surrey, 1991), p 178.
179   However what is appropriate tourism in national parks and other protected areas is often controversial. See for example *Australian Conservation Foundation v South Australia* (1990) 53 SASR 349.

It is also the central focus of the World Heritage Convention, which requires each State to 'ensure that effective and active measures are taken for the protection, *conservation, presentation* and rehabilitation (if necessary) of the natural and cultural heritage situated on its territory' (emphasis added).[180]

The italicised words show that the Convention imposes dual obligations on party States: on the one hand to present these wonders of the world for the appreciation of those who are attracted to them and, on the other, to protect and preserve their outstanding features and values for posterity.

The reconciliation of these potentially contradictory objectives presents a major challenge for managers of World Heritage sites and the tourism industry. UNESCO, UNEP and WTO have jointly developed guidelines on the issues involved.[181] Commonwealth and State legislation now usually requires sustainability as a condition of approval of industry development and operation. Sustainability is also the focus of the management plans prepared or being prepared for Australia's World Heritage sites.

Attractions and activities at World Heritage Sites

[15.305] Tourism is one of the few potentially sustainable economic activities in World Heritage Sites.[182] The importance of tourism relative to other industries is shown in Figure 1.

---

180   Article 5.

181   UNESCO/UNEP/WTO, *Guidelines for management of tourism in natural World Heritage Sites* (UNESCO/UNEP/WTO Paris, 1994). The authors of this text conducted an international survey of natural World Heritage sites and assisted in drafting the guidelines and writing the report.

182   In 1993 the authors undertook research with UNEP, UNESCO and the WTO on a study of the issues involved with tourism in natural World Heritage sites. The UNESCO/UNEP/WTO project aimed to develop and improve management guidelines for tourism in World Heritage areas. International surveys of tourism in world natural and mixed heritage sites were conducted in 1992 and 1993 (called "the 1993 World Heritage Tourism Survey") and while the diversity of sites means the findings are only indicative, they still do provide some useful insight into world trends and issues involved in tourism in natural World Heritage areas.

Figure 1: Economic Activities in Natural World Heritage Sites

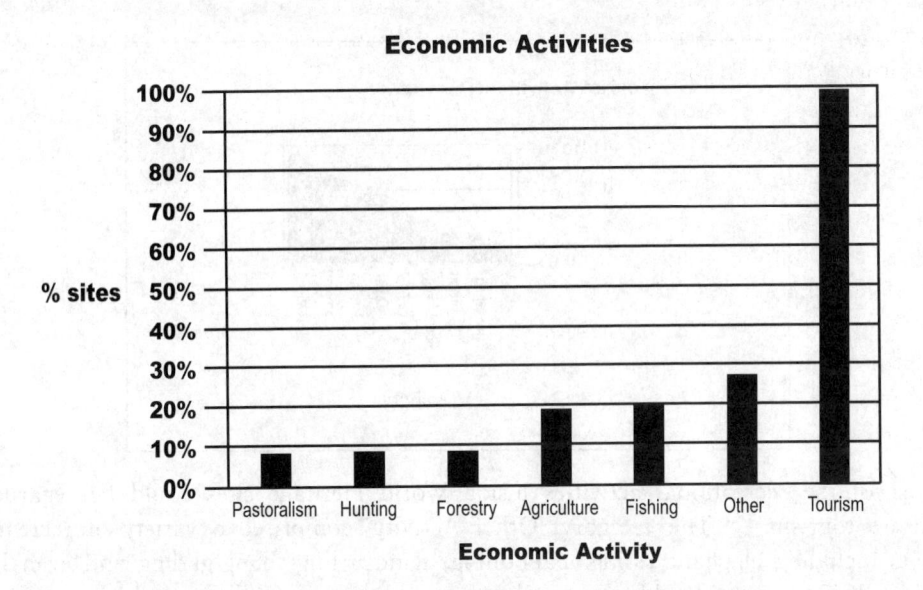

Economic Activities

(Bar chart showing % sites by Economic Activity: Pastoralism ~8%, Hunting ~9%, Forestry ~9%, Agriculture ~20%, Fishing ~21%, Other ~28%, Tourism 100%)

Tourist activities in World Heritage can be divided into the passive observation and enjoyment of the attractions ('attractions') and the more active engagement in recreational activities ('activities'). The main attractions in natural World Heritage sites are shown in Figure 2 below.

Figure 2: Attractions in Natural World Heritage Sites

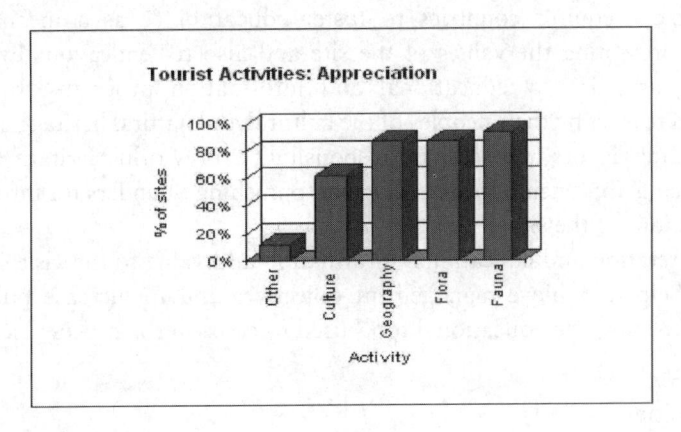

Tourist Activities: Appreciation

(Bar chart showing % of sites by Activity: Other, Culture, Geography, Flora, Fauna)

The main tourist activities in natural World Heritage sites are shown in Figure 3 below.

Figure 3: Recreational Activities in Natural World Heritage Sites

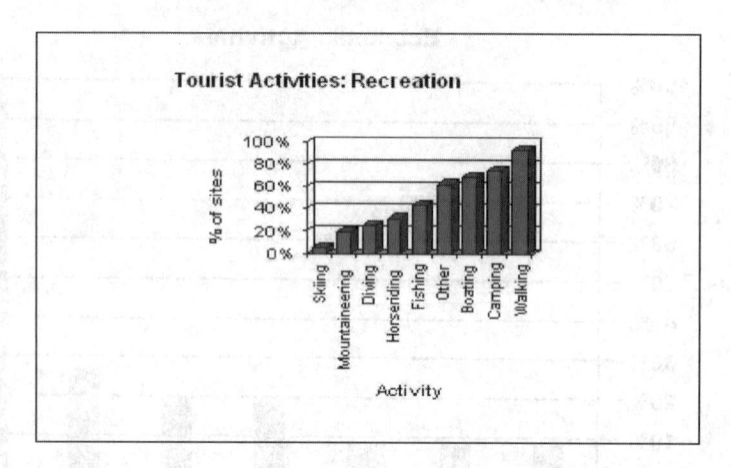

Tourist Activities: Recreation

(Bar chart showing % of sites for activities: Skiing, Mountaineering, Diving, Horseriding, Fishing, Other, Boating, Camping, Walking — increasing from near 0% to near 100%)

Most of the recreational activities inside World Heritage sites could be regarded as adventure tourism.[183] The category 'Other Activity' comprised a variety of recreational pursuits including elephant riding, ballooning, windsurfing, hang-gliding and even bungy jumping. There is considerable overlap between tourist attractions and tourist activities in World Heritage sites. The activities often afford the transport, vantage, or other opportunity to experience the sight, feel, sound and smell of the attractions.

Education

[15.310] A key feature of sustainable tourism is the requirement that it be informative and educational about the sites visited. This is also one of the objectives of the World Heritage Convention, which requires countries to foster education[184] as a means of protecting, conserving and presenting the values of the site and also to 'endeavour by all appropriate means and in particular by educational and information programs, to strengthen the appreciation and respect by their peoples of the cultural and natural heritage'.[185] It is far more effective to educate visitors and so share responsibility for World Heritage than it is to rely simply on a policing approach of prosecuting and punishing offenders for infringements of the rules and regulations of the site.[186]

Visitor interpretation and educational information add value to the visitor experience and they may also help to achieve management objectives and to increase public support for management decisions. The educational tools used to assist in the process include:

- guides, rangers, trackers;
- local communities;
- printed materials;
- audio tapes;

---

183 See T C Atherton, *Licensed to thrill: regulating adventure tourism in World Heritage areas* (12 pages, paper presented at the Australian Tourism Research Conference, Griffith University 10-11 February 1994).
184 Article 5(e) – Fostering education.
185 Article 27.
186 See TC Atherton, "Visitor management in World Heritage sites" (1994) *Environment & Development* 3 (newsletter of the World Travel & Tourism Environment Research Centre, Oxford).

- self-guided trails;
- visitor centres;
- art;
- websites.

Local involvement

[15.315] Most proponents of sustainable tourism emphasise the importance of involving the local community in the management and presentation of the attractions for a number of reasons:

- to ensure the quality and authenticity of the presentation and interpretation;
- on the ethical grounds that economic benefits from the use of the site should accrue to the community most responsible for it; and
- on the pragmatic ground that providing benefits to the local community makes them stakeholders in *continued conservation* [187] rather than *consumptive uses* [188] of the resources of the site.

The World Heritage Convention promotes a similar approach by requiring each country to 'adopt a general policy to give cultural and natural heritage a function in the life of the community and to integrate the protection of that heritage into comprehensive planning programs'. [189]

The local community includes indigenous as well as non-indigenous people. Unfortunately in the early days of listing sites in Australia insufficient attention was given to the impact of listing of sites on local communities, who were often thereby deprived of livelihoods in mining, logging, farming, grazing and hydro damming. Where this has happened in other countries which do not have Australia's strong rule of law, the consequences have been disastrous, not only for the local communities but also for the poaching, plundering and pilfering of the site itself.

As sustainable tourism is the only potentially sustainable economic use of World Heritage sites a concerted effort should now be made to promote and involve the local community in this endeavour.

Native title

[15.320] The World Heritage Committee has acknowledged that there are significant cultural values in most of Australia's World Heritage sites and four are listed for their cultural values as

---

187 **Nepal Case Study 1:** Sagamartha National Park. There were an estimated 3,500 Sherpas residing in the park in 1997 mainly in the south and distributed among 63 settlements. The traditional economy is subsistence agro-pastoralism, supplemented by barter trading with Tibet and the middle hills of Nepal. The local economy has become dependent upon tourism, with activities such as provision of guides, porters, lodges and trekking services providing employment.

188 **Nepal: Case Study 2:** Royal Chitwan National Park: Considerable antagonism has long existed between the park and local people over loss of life (three to five people are killed each year by rhinoceros and tiger), loss of livestock (domestic cattle may constitute up to 30% of tiger kills in settled areas peripheral to the park), damage to crops (estimated to range from 10% to 100%) and restrictions concerning the use of the park's resources (hunting, fishing, grazing, and collection of timber, fuel wood and other forest products for food and medicine are prohibited within the park). There has also been a rapid increase in the number of foreigners visiting Chitwan which has led to locally inflated prices for basic foods and household products. Few local people are employed in the park.

189 Article 5(a).

well as their natural values: Kakadu National Park, Willandra Lakes Region, Tasmanian Wilderness and Uluru/Kata-Tjuta. Title to two of these sites, Kakadu and Uluru/Kata-Tjuta, was transferred to the traditional Aboriginal owners under the *Land Rights Act* (NT) subject to a lease-back to the government for national park purposes. The following discussion focuses on World Heritage, but these principles apply to all national parks. For the reasons discussed below, native title is likely to be recognised over most of Australia's World Heritage sites and many national parks.

In 1992 native title was recognised at common law by the High Court of Australia in *Mabo v Queensland [No 2]*[190] (*Mabo*), a case involving the Murray Islands off Queensland. The majority (Mason CJ, Brennan, McHugh, Deane, Gaudron, Toohey JJ, Dawson J dissenting) held that:[191]

> In the result, six members of the court (Dawson J dissenting) are in agreement that the common law of this country recognizes a form of native title which, in the cases where it has not been extinguished, reflects the entitlement of the indigenous inhabitants, in accordance with laws and customs, to their traditional lands and that, subject to the effect of some particular Crown leases, the land entitlement of the Murray Islanders in accordance with their laws or customs is preserved, as native title, under the law of Queensland.

Under the *Mabo* principles, the nature and incidents of native title are ascertained by reference to traditional laws and customs which may change through time.[192] Native title will usually include the rights and interests involved in traditional hunting, gathering and fishing[193] together with the right to observe and maintain spiritual customs and values.

Following *Mabo*, the *Native Title Act 1993* (Cth) was passed with corresponding State legislation to provide a framework for processing native title claims, to grant native title claimants the 'right to negotiate' for approval of future activities affecting land claimed and to validate land dealings from 1975 which may have been contrary to the *Racial Discrimination Act 1975* (Cth). The right to negotiate makes native title claimants legal stakeholders in the land as soon as their application is accepted by the registrar.

In applying the *Mabo* principles to mainland Australia it was generally thought at the time that common law native title was extinguished over most of Australia by the grant of pastoral leases. However in 1996 the High Court majority in *Wik Peoples v Queensland*[194] (*Wik*) (Toohey, Gaudron, Gummow and Kirby JJ; Brennan CJ, McHugh and Dawson JJ dissenting) rejected this limitation and held that native title can coexist with pastoral leases and merely 'yields' to the extent of inconsistency. The further implication from this is that when pastoral leases terminate, native title may revive.

Subsequent court cases have sought to further define and refine the scope of the native title legislation including that:

- certain types of pastoral leases can extinguish native title;[195]

- any native title in relation to the territorial sea is subject to the common law public rights of fishing and navigation and the public international law right of innocent passage;[196]

---

190 *Mabo v Queensland [No 2]* (1992) 175 CLR 1.
191 *Mabo v Queensland [No 2]* (1992) 175 CLR 1 at 15.
192 *Mabo v Queensland [No 2]* (1992) 175 CLR 1, see particularly Brennan J at 51-52.
193 Section 223 of the *Native Title Act 1993* (Cth).
194 *Wik Peoples v Queensland* (1996) 187 CLR 1.
195 *Wik Peoples v Queensland* (1996) 187 CLR 1.
196 *Commonwealth of Australia v Yarmirr* (2001) 208 CLR 1.

- any exclusive right to fish in tidal waters is extinguished and that there are no native title rights to or interest in any mineral or petroleum. However, the *Native Titles Act 1993* (Cth) does protect hunting, gathering and fishing rights in relation to land or waters where the indigenous peoples concerned have a connection with the land or waters by tradition. [197]

The lasting legacy of *Mabo* and *Wik* is that common law native title probably continues to exist over most Australian World Heritage sites. While the native title claims over the sites are being processed (which may take many years) the claimants are legal stakeholders and their approval, involvement and compensation will usually be required for future activities affecting the land. [198] There is likely to be a high success rate in the determination of native title claims over World Heritage sites and in many cases the result will be that legal ownership is transferred to the traditional owners with a leaseback to the State for national park purposes on the Uluru-Kata Tjuta and Kakadu models.

Native title will have substantial impacts on tourism. Aboriginal culture is already a significant part of the attraction and interest of many sites and this is likely to be reinforced and extended. Aboriginal peoples themselves are going to be large stakeholders in the tourism industry, with extensive potential involvement as traditional owners, landlords, joint venturers, investors, managers, interpreters, employers and employees. The extent to which native title assists Aboriginal peoples to achieve self-determination and social and economic development (self-empowerment) depends upon refinement of the native title concept and the legal methods for claiming and using traditional lands. [199] At the outset it will be important to resolve the potential conflicts between traditional rights to hunt, gather and fish and the fundamental conservation objectives of World Heritage.

Native title will also have a substantial impact on visitors to sites and others involved in the tourism and travel industry. Aboriginal spiritual customs and values will need to be reflected and observed in the interpretation and activities at the site. Formal education and accreditation systems will be required for guides and tour operators. On the one hand this will add significant cultural interest for visitors, but on the other, where there is a clash of cultures or values, it will also require restrictions and regulations. [200] The most successful operators will be those who respect traditional values and customs and work with Aboriginal peoples to present the natural and cultural values of the sites in an interesting and informative way in accordance with Article 5 of the World Convention Heritage discussed in [15.295]ff. [201] For more discussion on Native Title, see [2.65].

---

197   *Western Australia v Ward* (2002) 213 CLR 1.
198   *Native Title Act 1993* (Cth), s 21.
199   See TC Atherton, *Indigenous development requires a redefinition of native title* (presentation to National Conference of Land Law, Bond University, July 1997).
200   For example, the visitors' desire to climb Uluru conflicts with indigenous spiritual beliefs.
201   TC Atherton, *Strategy for Aboriginal and Torres Strait Islander Tourism* (submission to ATSIC, May 1995).

Implementation

[15.325] At the heart of management objectives in World Heritage Sites, there are three driving principles. They are, first, to protect the heritage values (resource) above all else. Secondly, they seek to generate as much income from the site as possible so as to continue its conservation activities. Finally, they attempt to facilitate so much public access as the site can accommodate sustainably.[202]

With these objectives in mind, this section will explore the various models used to manage sites along with some of the strategies adopted to implement the objectives.

Management models

[15.330] There are three types of management arrangements for Australia's World Heritage sites:

1. *Management by State government agencies*
   - Willandra Lakes Region (New South Wales)
   - Gondwana Rainforests of Australia (Queensland/New South Wales)
   - Lord Howe Island (New South Wales)
   - Shark Bay (Western Australia)
   - Fraser Island (Queensland)
   - Australian Fossil Mammal Sites (Riversleigh/Naracoorte) (Queensland/South Australia)
   - Tasmanian Wilderness (Tasmania)
   - Macquarie Island
   - Greater Blue Mountains Area (New South Wales)
   - Purnululu National Park (Western Australia in a joint management plan with Purnululu Aboriginal Corporation)
   - Royal Exhibition Building and Carlton Gardens (Victoria)
   - Sydney Opera House (New South Wales)

2. *Management under joint State/Commonwealth arrangements with day-to-day management by State government agencies*
   - Great Barrier Reef (Queensland/Commonwealth)
   - Wet Tropics of Queensland (Queensland/Commonwealth)
   - The Heard and McDonald Islands Group (Australian Territory with day-to-day management being the responsibility of the Australian Antarctic Division)

3. *Owned by Aboriginal community and leased to the Director of National Parks and Wildlife who manages it from day to day as a national park*
   - Uluru-Kata Tjuta National Park
   - Kakadu National Park (Stage 1) (Stage 1 and 3 Northern Territory)

---

202 There is evidence that fewer than 20% of World Heritage sites allow access across the whole site. Some 8% of sites restrict overall visitor numbers (based on a 2000 survey by PLB of 50 WHS managers).

The key instrument is the management plan prepared or being prepared for each Australian World Heritage site. These management plans address Australia's obligations under the World Heritage Convention and deal with the issues discussed in the below. [203]

Management strategies

[15.335] The most common tools used in regulation and management are: [204]

- zoning;
- restricting access to guided tours only;
- using fixed interpretation and self-guided trails;
- traffic management.

Zoning is required if there is some measure of cultural or environmental sensitivity within and just outside the site. In emerging destinations, where there is no existing development outside the site, zoning works particularly well because there is an opportunity to create an orderly commercial 'buffer' around the site where investment can be directed more easily. The situation is more problematic in established destinations because of the need to accommodate existing uses and the close proximity of residential housing in some cases.

Laws and regulations

[15.340] Management models and strategies also require an effective regulatory framework. In Australia, at State and Territory level, there are many environmentally protective laws and regulations covering a range of specific topics which impact on World Heritage sites including:

- Environment Protection and Biodiversity;
- National Parks and Wildlife Conservation;
- Indigenous peoples heritage; and
- flora and fauna.

At the Commonwealth level, the *Environment Protection and Biodiversity Conservation Act 1999* (Cth) performs a similar task. This one piece of legislation addresses the obligations Australia has made to the international community under the following environmentally protective conventions:

- 1971-*Ramsar Convention 1971*
- 1972-*World Heritage Convention 1972*
- 1973-*Convention on International Trade in Endangered Species 1973*
- 1974-*Environment Protection (Impact of Proposals) Act 1974*
- 1976-*Convention on Conservation of Nature in the South Pacific 1976*
- 1979-*Convention on the Conservation of Migratory Species of Wild Animals 1979*
- 1992-*Convention on Biological Diversity 1992*.

Tourism operators' accreditation

[15.345] At the industry level, it is important to ensure that tourism operators who are granted concessions to operate their businesses inside or adjacent to World Heritage areas are

---

203 For more information, see Australian Government, *Department of Environment, Water, Heritage, and the Arts, Management of Australia's World Heritage Listed Places* at http://www.environment.gov.au/heritage/about/world/managing.html.

204 This information is based on a 2000 survey by a UK consulting company, PLB, of 50 WHS managers.

meeting the industry standards. One bad report can bring a whole tourism sector into disrepute (for example, reef diving, bungy jumping) and may even reflect adversely on the broader tourism community. Thus the need for quality assurance measures, particularly in the case of ecotourism and adventure tourism operators. Quality assurance may take a number of forms including:

- Industry codes of conduct;[205]
- Accreditation (for example, Eco Certification Program);[206]
- Consumer protection legislation;[207]
- health and safety checks (OHS legislation);[208]
- common law damages for disappointment.[209]

Exercise

Gambling with World Heritage

[15.350]

Choose your favourite Australian World Heritage Site.

- Assume you are an adviser to the Aboriginal Land Council which owns or has claimed native title over the site.
- The concessionaire of the main Visitor Information Centre for the site has requested approval from the Aboriginal Land Council to install five gaming machines.
- Assume the local and State government authorities have no objections to the proposal.
- The Aboriginal Land Council has asked you to prepare a report on the proposal outlining the advantages, disadvantages and other matters which should be considered and recommending whether it should be refused, approved or approved on conditions.

In your report consider the economic and social impacts of gambling, the impact on traditional customs and values and the impact on the World Heritage values of the site.

Postscript. Ironically this exercise from the 1998 first edition was unexpectedly put into practice in 2000 when the authors were engaged by the Asian Development Bank to prepare the first tourism management plan for the Preah Vihear cultural site in Cambodia on the border with Thailand. At the time there were proposals to establish a casino at the site which had just been cleared of mines from civil war. The casino would have catered mainly for cross border visitors from Thailand which also has strong cultural links to the site and the ancient Khmer culture. The authors' report recommended Word Heritage listing and the site was listed as a cultural site in 2008. Listing was delayed by a dispute with Thailand over the territory which was originally awarded to Cambodia by the International Court of Justice in 1962.[210] Shortly after listing hostilities broke out between Cambodia and Thailand over the site and it was closed to tourists. If a settlement could be reached the site could be expanded to

---

205 For example, Charter Fishing Code of Conduct; Code of Conduct for Inbound Tour Operators.
206 It has been developed to address the need to identify genuine nature and ecotourism operators. It is also now being exported to the rest of the world as the International ECO Certification Program. See Ecotourism Australia at http://www.ecotourism.org.au/eco_certification.asp.
207 See Chapter 9 for further discussion.
208 See Chapter 8 for further discussion.
209 When the expectation exceeds the experience.
210 *Cambodia v Thailand ICJ* 1962/16.

Activities and attractions CHAPTER 15

Gambling with World Heritage cont.

include the spectacular surrounding natural landscape which was included in the original application to list as a mixed site.

ADVENTURE TOURISM

[15.355] Definition. 'Tourism' has already been defined in Chapter 1. An 'adventure' is *'an unusual, exciting, and daring experience...'* or *'excitement arising from or associated with danger or risk'* [211] or, in other words, the taking of a *risk*. Therefore:

adventure tourism = tourism + risk

The key issue for tourism operators carrying on business in this area is their potential and actual legal liability because:

responsibility + risk = liability

Adventure tourism operators face a particularly onerous range of liabilities because of the nature of the activity. They need to understand all possible causes of action in order for better compliance, risk management and possible defences. On the other hand, tourists (plaintiffs) need to explore all possible causes of action.

Approach

This section will analyse the topic from first principles because it brings together and applies material from previous chapters and it raises new issues and challenges because of the risky nature of the activity. The principles will be illustrated mainly with beach and watersport activities although the principles and approach are similar for most adventure tourism activities because they all usually involve [212]

- Multiple operators, distributors
- + public authority or other entity responsible for the venue eg, beach, mountain, river, national park.

Compare Innkeepers/Carriers' Duties

[15.360] Chapter 13 reviewed Innkeepers' liability including their duty to take *reasonable care for the safety of their guests* and that they are *strictly liable for their guests' property, subject to limitation of liability under State legislation*. Innkeepers have responded to these challenges with various risk management strategies including the setting of appropriate 'Rules of the House'. [213] They must be brought to the notice of guests who are then bound by them. House rules do not operate contractually and any attempts by contract to limit or exclude the Innkeepers' liability will be declared void. However, failure to observe House rules is evidence of the guest's (contributory) negligence which is the innkeeper's best defence. For further discussion see [13.80].

---

211 *Oxford English Dictionary* online.
212 The material in this section is based upon the author's presentation to the Beach Safety & the Law Summit (8-9 November 2007, Surfers Paradise Marriott (QUT, QLS, SLSA)), Year of the Lifesaver.
213 Similarly, common carriers could make rules of the vehicle.

The Innkeepers' doctrine applies only 'infra hospitium'[214] that is, within the precincts of the hotel although the case law has extended this to include a hotel car park.[215] Beyond that, it is uncertain, especially with resort style facilities including swimming pool areas, golf courses, tennis courts, gymnasiums and the like. Does the precinct also extend to the beach, lake or river adjacent to the resort? To answer these questions, it is necessary to determine who *has care, control and management over the area.*

Just like innkeepers, care, control and management are some of the recurring themes for tourism operators involved in activities and attractions. For example, who has:

- legal ownership and responsibility for the beach and adjacent waters?
- management and operation of the activity?
- ownership and supervision of the equipment?
- Who it the tour operator/promoter?

Once the answers to these questions are made clear, then liability is more easily established.

Contract

[15.365] At common law, there is an implied term that goods and services will be supplied with all due care and skill and be reasonably fit for the purpose.[216] The liability can be limited or excluded subject to the ticket case principles, and it applies to goods and services supplied by the hotel. Services providers are also liable in contract for misrepresentation about the safety of the activity, for example.

However these principles may not be applicable where:

- there is no contract between the guest and hotel, passenger and carrier, tourist and operator such as in the case of group, package, or incentive travel;
- often, the ticket case principles render attempted exclusion or limitation ineffective;[217]
- some licensees may lack capacity (for example, minors);
- attempts to rely on agency or privity of contract do not succeed;[218]
- they are overridden by the *Australian Consumer Law* (see later).

However, the principles may apply specifically in relation to advice given by the concierge, or by the tour desk in arranging activities or by the sports convenor in supplying equipment or instruction. For further discussion, see [9.315]ff.

---

214 For common carriers, this is the time during which the passenger is in transit.
215 *Williams v Linnitt* [1951] 1 KB 565.
216 *White v John Warwick* [1953] 1 WLR 1285.
217 See *Olley v Marlborough Court* [1949] 1 KB 532; *eBay International AG v Creative Festival Entertainment Pty Limited* (2006) 170 FCR 450.
218 *EC Directive on Package Holidays 1990* and associated indemnities from component providers; *Wong Mee Wan v Kwan Kin Travel* (1995) 4 All ER 745.

Torts

[15.370] The innkeepers'/carriers' duty to take reasonable care for the safety of guests/passengers has probably been overtaken by the general law of negligence although infra hospitium and in transitu are helpful in defining the scope of the duty of care and breach of *Rules of the House/Vehicle* provide prima facie evidence of guest/passenger negligence. The same is true for occupiers' liability. [219]

At common law, landlords, in some circumstances, have even been held to have a 'non-delegable' personal liability to ensure that rental premises are safe for their tenants. [220] The principle may extend to persons who have control of premises such as in the case of hotel and guest relationships although they are not usually landlord and tenant. However, since the introduction of the Civil Liability legislation, a person sued for breach of a non delegable duty will have their liability determined as if they were vicariously liable for the negligence of the person in connection with the performance of the work or task. [221]

In Australia, private title on beachfront land generally ends at the high water mark so Australian hotels and resorts generally do not have sufficient care, responsibility and management to attract liability in tort for accidents occurring on public beaches (subject to exacerbating circumstances discussed in [15.375] below). In fact, most of the Australian cases on beach safety are against the relevant public authorities having the care, control and management of the beach. Hotels and resorts have a duty to their guests which does not extend much beyond the premises (the infra hospitium principle). Similarly, the extent of a carrier's duty in transporting passengers to the beach probably does not extend beyond the trip (in transitu principle) but may include the activity if the vehicle waits to return the passenger to the hotel, especially if the carrier has some involvement in the care, control and management of activity.

Hotels' Responsibility for Beach Safety

[15.375] There are a number of special circumstances in which a hotel may be responsible for beach safety in tort. This happens:

- if the hotel has title to the beach or nearby waters under licence or seabed lease from the public authority;
- if the hotel is the only facility in a remote location and the beach is promoted as an attraction for the hotel; [222]
- if the hotel conducts an activity on the beach for guests such as organised swimming, surfing, diving, sailing, parasailing and the like;
- if the hotel rents or provides the equipment used in the activity;
- if the hotel arranges for the activities or equipment hire by others through the hotel tour desk (tour operator responsibility); or

---

219 Australian Safeway Stores v Zaluzna (1987) 162 CLR 479.
220 Northern Sandblasting Pty Ltd v Harris (1997) 188 CLR 313.
221 For example, see Civil Liability Act 2002 (NSW), s 50.
222 Enright v Coolum Resort [2002] QSC 394; Tashis v Lahaina Investment Corp 480 F2d 1019 (9th Circuit 1979). Brochure stated "The Royal Lahaina Beach resort stretches along a 3 mile secluded white sand beach on the West side of the island of Maui. The sea is safe and exhilarating for swimming". Held: that Hotel has a duty to warn guests of dangerous surf conditions. Arguably it should also provide lifeguards.

- if the hotel concierge provides negligent advice.

The following case studies highlight and canvass some of the issues raised here.

Case Study 1

[15.380] *Wyong Shire Council v Shirt* (1980) CLR 217

Facts: Wyong Shire Council controlled and managed a lake. They dredged a channel into a jetty and erected four 'Deep Water' signs along one side. A passing skier misinterpreted them to mean deep water on the other side, fell off and suffered quadriplegic paralysis. Wyong Shire Council conceded it owed a general duty but argued that as the risk of misinterpretation was minimal it had not breached the standard of care required.

Decision: The High Court (Stephen, Mason, Murphy, Aickin JJ; Wilson J dissenting) held that Wyong Shire Council breached its duty. The risk of misunderstanding and injury was foreseeable even though extremely unlikely. This was because the measures required to avoid the risk were relatively simple and inexpensive while the gravity of harm which could be caused if they were not taken was severe.

Comment: Note that there was no contract, so this case was argued in tort. This case illustrates the risk management approach which the law takes in these situations. The concept can be reduced to the following formula:

$$\text{Liability} = \text{Probability of harm} \times \text{Gravity of harm} - \text{Cost of avoidance}$$

Postscript: This is exactly the same methodology as that used in risk management (see later).

Case Study 2

[15.385] *Enright v Coolum Resort, Maroochy Council & Hyatt* [2002] QSC 394

Facts: The deceased, Enright, was a 46 year old Harvard lawyer. He caught an overnight flight from the Philippines to Brisbane arriving at 5.00 am to attend a conference at the Coolum Beach Resort. He transferred to Coolum in a chauffeured car which diverted along Yaroomba Beach so he could see the surf. The driver advised him that the surf was dangerous and he should swim at Coolum Beach where there were more people and it was safer, or he should swim in the resort pool. Enright attended the conference all day and when it concluded at 4.30pm, he headed for the beach with a colleague.

The resort patrolled an area of the beach in front of the resort and operated a beach shuttle and Beach Club till 4.30pm. The brochure and signs at the Resort advised of this. There was a warning sign at the Beach Club to swim between the flags and when the lifeguard was on duty. Enright and his friend took the wrong turn, got lost, caught a bus and eventually arrived at a Yaroomba Beach, late in the afternoon. There were no warning signs on that track from the road to the beach.

The beach was deserted, there were high winds, rough and dangerous sea conditions. Enright was experienced with water sports, beach and surfing conditions from Long Beach USA. He surfed for some time until he became tired and his friend suggested that they return to the resort. Enright wanted one more wave. No wave came, so he turned ashore and saw that the current had taken them a long way off shore. Both surfers were exhausted, but the friend managed with difficulty to save himself. Enright drowned and his wife brought this action.

Held: Moynihan J decided there had been no breach of duty of care. Against the driver's advice, Enright had decided to surf. He had made no attempt to obtain further information. Being an

Case Study 2 cont.

experienced surfer himself, the hotel had no duty to warn of obvious risks. Consequently, the Council, Hotel Operator (Hyatt) and Hotel owner were not liable. For further discussion of this case, see [5.60].

Case Study 3: Bondi Beach (1997)

[15.390] *Swain v Waverley Municipal Council* [2005] 220 CLR 517

Facts: In 1997, the Plaintiff was swimming between the flags off Bondi Beach at 4.30pm some 15-20 metres from the beach. He dived in waist deep water, struck a submerged sandbar and suffered quadriplegia. The beach was under the care, control and management of the Defendant Council which employed three lifesavers. At first instance, the Supreme Court found the Defendant negligent and awarded $3.75m, after deducting 25% for contributory negligence. The Defendant appealed and the case eventually went all the way to the High Court.

Held: The High Court (by majority 3:2) upheld the trial judgment confirming that here was sufficient evidence for the jury to find that the Council had been negligent. Even though the beach usually had moving channels and sandbars and diving was risky, there may have been reasonably practical alternatives, for example, continually moving the flags or closing the beach.

Postscript: The Supreme Court decision and subsequent litigation prompted the intervening tort law reform legislation.

Case Study 4: Sahara Tours (1999)

[15.395] *Preti v Conservation Land Corp; Sahara Tours; Parks & NT Wildlife Commission* [2007] 20 NTLR 97

Facts: The deceased, a 38 year old Swiss tourist, took a 5 day guided adventure tour through the Northern Territory with Sahara Tours. The deceased was unable to read or understand much English. At one location, there was a rope swing over a deep muddy brown waterhole. The deceased did not see the warning sign at the Information Centre and if he did he could not have understood it. The guide instructed how to use the rope (no clear warnings of rocks as at several waterholes on previous days) but there was no evidence that the deceased would have heard or understood it. Another tourist collided with him while waiting his turn and knocked him into shallow water where he struck his head and was killed. The defendant *Parks & NT Wildlife Commission* (PWC) had a formal Risk Management Strategy but it was not rigorously implemented until after the accident. It had identified the risks and removed the rope several times over the years but the rangers were aware that others kept reinstalling it and they let it happen. The deceased's dependants sued the defendants for damages for negligence

Held: Southward J: the rope swing was dangerous and the consequences as here could be catastrophic. More effective action was required on behalf of Sahara Tours and PWC to ameliorate the risk. The guide should have clearly warned of the danger and PWC should have erected warning signs and ensured the rope was removed. However, the obviousness of the risk and the expectation that persons should take reasonable care for their own safety are relevant so the judge found the deceased 50% contributory negligence which was later reduced to 20% by the Court of Appeals.

Case Study 4: Sahara Tours (1999) cont.

Postscript: *Conservation Land Corp* (the owner) was not liable as PWC had the care, control and management of the waterhole under the relevant *National Parks and Wildlife* legislation. The Tour Operator contract conditions (exclusions and limitations) were not considered

---- ℘℃ ----

Consumer Protection

[15.400] The *Australian Consumer Law* creates responsibilities for adventure tourism activities through Unfair Practices provisions (Part 3-1) and statutory guarantees as discussed in detail in Chapter 9. They incorporate special provisions to limit liability in the case of certain 'Recreational Services' along with other significant Tort law reforms which are discussed further below.

Unfair practices

[15.405] Under the *Australian Consumer Law* (and State Fair Trading Act equivalents), failure to provide accurate information on the risks involved in the use of the beach or associated equipment or activities may be a breach of either:

- Section 18 Misleading and deceptive conduct

    This founds an action in damages and other remedies; or

- Section 29 False representation that

    (a)   Goods or (b) services are of a particular standard, quality or grade...

    (g)   Goods or services have performance characteristics, uses or benefits they do not have.

    This founds an action in damages and other remedies and /or prosecution. [223]

Statutory guarantees

[15.410] In relation to the supply of services, the *Australian Consumer Law*, s 60 states:

> If a person supplies, in trade or commerce, services to a consumer, there is a guarantee that the services will be rendered with due care and skill ... and

Section 61 states in part that:

> ...there is a guarantee that the services...will be reasonably fit for [the] purpose ...

Section 54 of the *Australian Consumer Law* has similar *guarantees* implied into contracts for the supply of goods.

These guarantees are imposed independently of the law of contract and so the old contract defences of privity, agency and the like are not applicable. [224]

This is discussed in more detail in Chapter 9.

Exclusion or modification

[15.415] Under s 64 of the *Australian Consumer Law*, statutory guarantees imposed on the supply of goods (s 54) and services (ss 60, 61) cannot be excluded, restricted or modified

---

223   Consider *Tashis v Lahaina Investment Corp* 480 F2d 1019 (9th Circuit, 1979) where the brochure stated that "the sea is safe and exhilarating for swimming".

224   Unlike the *Trade Practices Act 1974* (Cth) which used to imply these as conditions and warranties in the contract.

(unlike a common law warranty) but it permits limitation of liability in certain cases]. Section 64A of the *Australian Consumer Law* generally confirms that ss 54, 60 and 61 cannot be limited if they relate to goods or services 'of a kind ordinarily acquired for personal, domestic or household use or consumption'. Most tourism services fall into this category including adventure tourism. Liability may also not be limited if the consumer establishes that it would not be fair or reasonable for the supplier to rely on the limitation having regard for relative strength of bargaining position, standard contract terms etc circumstances which are commonly found in adventure tourism

Before 2002, it was very difficult for tourism operators to manage risk using limitation or exclusion clauses. and the effect of similar *Trade Practices Act 1974* (Cth) provisions was particularly onerous for adventure and recreational activities as discussed below. This was criticized by this author and others. [225]

Reforms

[15.420] The insurance industry reached a 'crisis point' in liability insurance in 2001/2. This was partly driven by the September 11, 2001 terrorist attacks on the World Trade Centre which caused worldwide difficulties in re-insurance and an increase in costs and the reduction in the value of/and returns of insurers from global assets and investments. Problems in the Australian insurance industry were compounded by the fact that a series of high profile adventure tourism type cases (as described earlier) were working their way through the legal system.

Councils, national parks and other public authorities were concerned at the increasing responsibility, liability and payouts in personal injury and death cases and that public liability insurance was becoming unobtainable or 'unaffordable'. For all these reasons, the insurance industry began lobbying the State and federal governments hard for 'reform'. The Ipp Report [226] reviewed the civil law and recommended a series of 'reforms' which were largely adopted by State and federal governments.

Reform–consumer protection

[15.425] Up until 2002 the law as described so far was the high point in onerous liability for adventure tourism operators and other defendants in civil claims for personal injuries and death. In 2002, a series of 'reforms' was introduced to implement the Ipp Report and in the process substantially reduced:

(a)   the circumstances in which damages can be recovered for negligence; and

(b)   the types and quantum of damage that can be recovered.

Exclusion and modification

[15.430] In 2002, the *Trade Practices Act 1974* (Cth) was amended [227] to permit, in supply of 'recreational services', limitation of liability for death or personal injury. This has been carried into in the *Australian Consumer Law*, s 139. Section 139A(2) defines 'recreational services' as services that consist of participation in

---

225   TC Atherton, *Regulating adventure tour operators* (1994) Proceedings of the World Adventure Travel & Ecotourism Conference (Hobart November 1994).

226   *Review of the Law of Negligence Report* (August 2002) at http://www.revofneg.treasury.gov.au/content/Report/PDF/LawNegFull.pdf.

227   Section 68B relating to the implied warranty in supply of services under s 74.

(a) a sporting activity or similar leisure-time pursuit, or
(b) any other activity that:
  (i) involves a significant degree of physical exertion or physical risk, and
  (ii) is undertaken for the purposes of recreation, enjoyment or leisure.

This definition is sufficient to cover most adventure tourism activities. It may include integral accommodation, for example, the Milford Sound trail huts or it may include integral transport, for example, horse riding, white water rafting, jet skiing, sea kayaking, parachuting and so on.[228] The component parts of tourism are of course, recreation (activities and attractions) transport and accommodation

The *Australian Consumer Law* introduces an exception[229] (not in the former *Trade Practices Act 1974*) so that s 139 does not apply if significant personal injury is caused by supplier's 'reckless conduct' which means:

- Supplier is or should be aware of significant risk, and
- Engages in the conduct despite the risk and without adequate justification

Under this exception the operators in the balloon kissing, whitewater rafting in flood, reckless diving cases would quite rightly not be protected. However the scope and application to other adventure tourism cases is uncertain and yet to be clarified by case law.

This illustrates how the law is continuing to evolve to deal with the difficult issues arising in the regulation of adventure tourism.

Australian Consumer Law and Tort law reform

[15.435] The civil liability legislation (State and Territory)[230] as discussed in Chapter 5 and below now limits liability for dangerous recreational activities which particularly affects adventure tourism operators as well as addressing issues of foreseeability, breach of duty, voluntary assumption of risk, and contributory negligence, amongst others. To ensure the validity of these laws the federal *Australian Consumer Law* which would normally prevail over State legislation deems in s 275 that if the State is the proper law of the contract, then its laws will apply to limit or preclude liability for failure to comply with a guarantee in the supply of services.

Conclusion on Australian Consumer Law

[15.440] Under the *Australian Consumer Law* it is now possible by contract to limit liability for tourism and other recreational services in respect of death or personal injury subject to the restrictions and exceptions discussed above. However it is important to remember that this is still also subject to the difficulties in contract law discussed above [15.365] including:

- limitation clauses may be inapplicable when there is no contract between the tourist and the service provider;
- often the 'ticket case' principles render attempted exclusion or limitation ineffective;

---

228 However it does not seem to include a bus journey as part of a package holiday. See *Insight Vacations Pty Ltd v Young* [2010] NSWCA 137.
229 *Australian Consumer Law*, s 139A(4).
230 *Civil Liability Act 2002* (NSW); *Civil Liability Act 2003* (Qld); *Recreational Services (Limitation of Liability) Act 2002* (SA); *Wrongs and Other Acts (Public Liability Insurance Reform) Act 2002* (Vic); *Civil Liability Act 2002* (WA); *Civil Liability Act 2002* (Tas); *Civil Law (Wrongs) Act 2002* (ACT); *Consumer Affairs and Fair Trading Amendment Act* (NT).

- some tourists may lack capacity, for example, minors or,
- the term may be found unconscionable or unfair under the *Australian Consumer Law*.

Liability and quantum for death or personal injury is generally now also subject to State and Territory *Civil Liability* legislation which is discussed in more detail in the next section.

Civil Liability Legislation

[15.445] As previously indicated, each State and Territory enacted far reaching tort law reform under Civil Liability legislation [231] as discussed in Chapter 5. This chapter will focus on the application of the legislation to tourism, travel and hospitality and particularly adventure tourism. The following analysis is based on the *Civil Liability Act 2003* (Qld) with reference to other States' legislation highlighting similarities and differences.

The *Civil Liability Act 2003* (Qld) states (in part):

- 'No liability for materialization of an *inherent risk* ie, risks that *could not be avoided by reasonable care and skill*' (s 16); [232]
- '*No duty to warn of obvious risk* ie, risk that would have been obvious to a reasonable person' (s 15); [233]
- Chapter 3 reduces the quantum of damages which can be awarded for personal injury; [234]
- Reforms civil liability law generally,

This reinforces the tortious defence of voluntary assumption of risk – volenti non fit injuria. In general terms, there is nothing unreasonable or unusual in requiring an individual to accept responsibility for their actions in the face of an 'obvious risk'. However, in the tourism industry, by definition, a tourist is a newcomer to the area and probably has little knowledge of conditions and risks which are obvious to locals. The following examples illustrate this problem.

Cases on 'obvious risk'

[15.450] In *Doubleday v Kelly* [235] a seven year old rollerblading on a trampoline was not an obvious risk as she was an inexperienced child but in *Great Lakes SC v Dederer* [236] a fourteen and a half year old diving from a 9m high bridge into a murky river was an obvious risk even for someone of that age. It seems that the peculiar knowledge and experience of the plaintiff is relevant in determining what an 'obvious risk' is. In other words, it is a *subjective test*.

If culpability does turn on the peculiar knowledge and experience of the plaintiff, then tourists visiting an area for the first time must surely be more vulnerable than locals to 'obvious risks'. As one commentator put it:

---

231   *Civil Liability Act 2002* (NSW); *Civil Liability Act 2003* (WA); *Civil Liability Act 2002* (Tas); *Civil Liability Act 2003* (Qld); *Wrongs Act 1958* (Vic); *Law Reform (Contributory Negligence and Apportionment of Liability) Act 1991* (SA); *Civil Law (Wrongs) Act 2002* (ACT); *Proportionate Liability Act* (NT).

232   Similar to *Civil Liability Act 2002* (NSW), s 5I; *Law Reform (Contributory Negligence and Apportionment of Liability) Act 1991* (SA), s 39; *Wrongs Act 1958* (Vic), s 55.

233   Similar to *Law Reform (Contributory Negligence and Apportionment of Liability) Act 1991* (SA), s 38; but see *Civil Liability Act 2002* (NSW), s 5G: Injured person presumed to be aware of obvious risks; *Wrongs Act 1958* (Vic), s 56: Plaintiff to prove unawareness of obvious risk which enforce the tortious defence of voluntary assumption of risk – volenti non fit injuria.

234   Similar to *Civil Liability Act 2002* (NSW), Part 2; *Law Reform (Contributory Negligence and Apportionment of Liability) Act 1991* (SA), Part 8 "prescribed maximum", *Wrongs Act 1958* (Vic), Part VB.

235   *Doubleday v Kelly* [2005] NSWCA 151.

236   *Great Lakes SC v Dederer* [2006] NSWCA 101.

[for] a plaintiff foreign tourist, travelling under supervision of a defendant tour company or guide, who, through unfamiliarity, does not know of, or fully appreciate some of the local dangers, particularly in non-urban regions (for example, injury from dingoes, irukandji crocodiles, cyclones or large tides

[these would not be obvious risks]. [237]

Tourism and recreation

[15.455] 'Recreational activity' is defined in the Civil Liability legislation in similar terms to that used for 'recreational services' in the *Australian Consumer Law*. [238]

A *dangerous* recreational activity is one where there is a significant degree of risk of physical harm. *The Civil Liability Act 2003* (Qld), section 19 states: [239]

(1) A person is not liable in negligence for harm suffered by another person as a result of the materialisation of an obvious risk of a dangerous recreational activity engaged in by the person suffering harm.

(2) This section applies whether or not the person suffering harm was aware of the risk. [240]

Again, what is an obvious risk to a local may not be so apparent to a tourist unfamiliar with local conditions.

Cases on 'dangerous recreational activity'

Lormine v Zenereb

[15.460] *Lormine v Zenereb* [2006] NSWCA 200

Facts: The Plaintiff was standing at the invitation of the crew on the front deck of a dolphin tour vessel when he was washed overboard and injured when a rogue wave struck. The tour brochure promoted the activity as one to be undertaken 'in calm ocean waters ... (and one which would) ... suit people of all ages'.

Held: The Court of Appeal decided that it was not a 'dangerous recreational activity'. The test is *objective* and is one of fact and degree in each case.

This leaves foreign tourists in a difficult situation as the following observation highlights:

Adventure travel, under a package travel contract which enables a tourist to travel to remote parts of the globe, may be dangerous because of the risks of assault or other injury which may

---

237   R.J. Douglas SC G.R. Mullins & S.R. Grant, *Annotated Civil Liability Act 2003 (Qld)* (2nd edition Australia Lexis Nexis 2007) at [13.6].

238   *Australian Consumer Law*, s 139A; *Civil Liability Act 2002* (NSW), s 5M–No duty of care for recreational activity where risk warning, See also *Recreational Services (Limitation of Liability) Act 2002* (Qld).

239   See also *Civil Liability Act 2003* (Qld), ss 17, 18.

240   Similar to *Civil Liability* provisions in NSW: *Civil Liability Act 2002* (NSW), s 5J – N. There is no equivalent provision in Victoria. South Australia takes a different approach to the other States based on establishing and complying with a code of practice: *Recreational Services (Limitation of Liability) Act 2002* (SA).

Lormine v Zenereb cont.

be common there as opposed to conventional travel in Europe. [241]

Public authorities

[15.465] Under the *Civil Liability Act 2003* (Qld) [242] public and other authorities, for example, national parks, beach authorities as well as lifesavers enjoy restricted liability. [243] Does this mean that the pendulum has now swung too far the other way in favour of protecting public authorities when in fact they do have clearly defined care, control and management roles and responsibilities?

Other liabilities

[15.470] The tourism industry may be subject to other liabilities in respect of beach activities including occupational health and safety, breach of statutory duty and criminal liability.

Occupational health and safety legislation

[15.475] Occupational Health and Safety (OHS) legislation at federal level and in all States and Territories [244] causes particular problems for tourism. Unlike most other products, tourism is consumed at the factory/workplace as it is produced. Provisions designed to protect employees at the workplace may also cover tourists. For example, was the voluntary track marshal killed in the Australian Grand Prix coronial case a tourist or employee? [245]

OHS laws also produce some specific regulatory codes now for activities, such as *Diving – Marine Safety Code of Conduct* (Qld).

Breach of statutory duty

[15.480] Breach of statutory duty is the common law dimension of statutory obligations. It requires a legislative intent to create strict civil liability at common law. Generally, the plaintiff need not prove foreseeability. For further discussion see [5.175].

Criminal liability

[15.485] In order to attract criminal liability in negligence, a person must be proved to have been grossly negligent or reckless beyond a reasonable doubt. This is indeed a heavy onus of

---

241 RJ Douglas, SC Douglas, GR Mullins & SR Grant, *Annotated Civil Liability Act 2003 (Qld)* (2nd edition Australia Lexis Nexis 2007) at [18.2].

242 *Civil Liability Act 2003* (Qld), Chapter 2, Part 3, ss 34ff "Liability of public authorities", and "volunteers" at s 38.

243 Similar to *Civil Liability Act 2002* (NSW), Parts 5 and 9; and in *Wrongs Act 1958* (Vic), Part 9 and 12 which is similar. See also *Law Reform (Contributory Negligence and Apportionment of Liability) Act 1991* (SA), s 42 "road authority" and s 74 "good Samaritan".

244 *Australian Workplace Safety Standards Act 2005* (Cth); *Occupational Health and Safety (Commonwealth Employees) Act 1991* (Cth); *Occupational Health and Safety (Maritime Industry) Act 1993* (Cth); *Work Safety Act 2008* (ACT): *Occupational Health and Safety Act 2000* (NSW): *Workplace Health and Safety Act 2009* (NT): *Workplace Health and Safety Act 1995* (Qld): *Occupational Health, Safety and Welfare Act 1986* (SA): *Workplace Health and Safety Ac 1995* (Tas): *Occupational Health and Safety Act 2004* (Vic): *Occupational Safety and Health Act 1984* (WA).

245 See Victorian Coroner's Case No 621/01.

proof. Those at greatest risk of prosecution when things go wrong and tourists get injured or worse, killed, are those persons who are doing dangerous acts or who are in charge of dangerous things. These prosecutions arise more commonly in adventure tourism where there have been a number of cases involving dangerous activities and equipment such as diving accidents [246] and 'balloon-kissing' [247] events.

R v Geoffrey Ian 'Jack' Nairn

[15.490] *R v Geoffrey Ian 'Jack' Nairn* (unreported, Supreme Court, Cairns 1999)

Facts: A case which illustrates the point is that of Tom and Eileen Lonergan who disappeared while diving on the Great Barrier Reef from the *Outer Edge* in January 1998. Due to an inaccurate headcount, the boat returned to Port Douglas without them. The skipper did not notice that their hire equipment was still missing and that they had possibly not returned from the trip until two days later. The boat returned to the Reef but the Lonergans could not be found and were presumed to have died from exposure, drowning or sharks or a combination of these events.

Held: The Coroner committed the skipper to trial for manslaughter requiring proof of criminal negligence. At trial, the jury acquitted him. The skipper was also prosecuted and fined under the *Workplace Health and Safety Act 1995* (Qld) because it was argued that the dive site was a 'factory' and prescribed standards applied.

Risk Management

[15.495] For any organisation, the rational approach to handling risks is to manage them. The world's first risk management standard is the Australian Standard [248] which has been adopted or adapted in many countries. Its central philosophy is that it may prevent a crisis or disaster from developing or at least reduce the harmful impacts and speed up the recovery. The Standard describes a methodological process designed to assist organizations manage risks

Concepts in risk management

[15.500] *Risk* is 'the chance of something happening that will have an impact on objectives. Risk is measured in terms of the consequences of an event and their likelihood.'

Crisis is 'any situation that has the potential to affect long-term confidence in an organisation [or community] or a product, or which may interfere with its ability to operate normally.'

Disaster is 'a catastrophic event that severely disrupts the fabric of a community and requires the intervention of the various levels of government to return the community to normality.'

Recovery is the process of restoring the conditions or circumstances (as far as practicable) which prevailed before the disaster occurred.

---

246 The skipper of the boat which abandoned the Lonergans at sea was unsuccessfully prosecuted.
247 *R v Sanby* Court of Appeal NT 1993. For more discussion, see [6.11] Unsuccessfully prosecuted for gross negligence but found guilty on a lesser charge.. There was a canyoning case in Switzerland which also successfully prosecuted the operators of a tour company who led a group of young people including Australians to their death.
248 AS/NZ 4360 1999-2004.

Risk management process

[15.505] The key steps to risk management are to identify, analyse, evaluate and to treat risks. This methodology is the same as that which the courts use in determining liability in negligence. That is:

$$\text{Liability} = \text{Probability of harm} \times \text{Gravity of harm} - \text{Cost of avoidance}$$

Lawyers have a key role in risk management throughout the process and especially in treating risks by limiting and shifting responsibility.

Difficulties in tourism

[15.510] It is difficult to apply the methodology practically and effectively to tourism. The main obstacles have been: [249]

- **Single entity model:** The Standard and most other methodologies on risk management are designed for a single organisation or entity. Impacts on others are categorised as externalities. Shared roles and responsibilities are usually ignored.
- **Tourism complexity:** Any tourism destination is an amalgam of multiple private and public entities and stakeholders with separate interests, roles and responsibilities. Achieving a coordinated and planned response is no easy task.
- **Security complexity:** The complexity is compounded by the sheer complexity and additional number of entities involved in security.
- **Sensitivity and vulnerability:** More than any other industry or human endeavour, tourism is extremely sensitive and vulnerable to risks.

Limiting and shifting responsibility

[15.515] There are a number of legal principles and mechanisms which help to limit or shift liability in the tourism, travel and hospitality industry. These include:
- force majeure, act of God or act of the State's enemies;
- agency;
- notice: voluntary assumption of risk;
- contributory negligence;
- disclaimer: exclusion and limitation of liability;
- indemnity;
- insurance; and
- regulatory compliance

Exclusion/limitation clauses

[15.520] This is the traditional risk management method used by most operators, many of whom do not appreciate the legal complexities and pitfalls involved. However the prospects and problems in excluding and limiting and excluding liability in common law, contract, tort

---

249   TC Atherton, *Tourism Security* (workshop paper presented at the World Security Forum Conference Malaysia 27-18 June 2006).

and under the *Australian Consumer Law* and Civil Liability legislation are discussed above. Under the Occupation Health and Safety legislation, it is not possible to exclude liability.

Insurance

[15.525] Insurance (if available and affordable) is an important part of any risk management strategy and in many cases is the last resort for many operators. However they must ensure compliance with the industry regulations and standards in order to satisfy the requirements of most insurance policies.

For their part, tourists should take out travel insurance to cover some of the risks. Many operators require tourists to take out travel insurance which is a prudent strategy. However it will not protect the operator if there is a substantial claim because of the principle of subrogation. Subrogation gives the insurer the right to:

- commence proceedings against third parties in the name of the insured;
- recover the amount of the insured's losses from third parties even though the insured has been indemnified for such loss by the insurer.

It must be remembered that pursuant to the subrogation principle, the insurer is entitled to exercise only rights which the insured already enjoys. For example, if there is a contract between the insured and a third party containing an effective exclusion or limitation clause then both the insured and the insurer are bound by that clause. For further discussion, see [7.60].

Regulatory Compliance

[15.530] One of the most important aspects of any risk management strategy is a proactive regulatory compliance program. Identifying and analysing the relevant laws and regulations for the tourism travel and hospitality industry is the central theme of this book. As discussed in Chapter 1, Australia introduced the world's first regulatory compliance standard.[250] The authors hope that this book will be of some assistance in this task.

Exercise

Risk Management Strategy

Gold Coast Surfing Tours Pty Ltd (GCST) operates day trip surfing excursions for tourists including basic instruction and then body or board surfing wherever the waves are best on the day. GCST sells directly to the public through its website and indirectly through package tour operators, travel agents and hotel tour desks. It provides a hotel pick-up-and-return service.

Outline the key points you would recommend to be included in a risk management strategy for GCST. How might other stakeholders manage their risk from the operation and activity including Tour Operator, Travel agent, Hotel, Gold Coast Council (responsible for beach)?

---

250   AS 3806 1998-2006.

INDEX

A

Acceptance — *see also*
Contract,
[4.80]-[4.115]

Accommodation
administration,
[13.180]-[13.200]
holiday rental,
[13.155]-[13.175]
innkeepers — *see*
Innkeepers
international travellers,
[13.180]-[13.185]
legislation, [13.120]-[13.175]
national travellers, [13.190]
regulation, [13.180]-[13.200]
travellers, [13.180]-[13.190]

Accounts
travel agents, — *see* **Travel agent**

Accreditation, travel agents,
[11.355]

Act — *see* **Statutes**

Activities — *see also*
Attractions; Sporting events
Australian Consumer Law,
[15.85]
Civil Liability legislation, [15.85]
consumer protection, [15.40]
contract, [15.70]-[15.80]
criminal liability, [15.95]
crowd control, [15.100]
duty to safeguard licensees and their property,
[15.65]-[15.80]
licensee's rights,
[15.30]-[15.35]
licensees, no duty to accept,
[15.20]-[15.25]
major events, [15.110]-[15.115]
proprietors, rights and duties,
[15.15]-[15.10]
rights and duties of proprietors,
[15.15]-[15.50]
spectacle, rights of a proprietor over, [15.55]-[15.60],
[15.110]
street car racing, [15.115]
ticket scalping, [15.43]-[15.45]
torts and contract,
[15.70]-[15.80]
unauthorised advertising,
[15.105]
workplace health and safety,
[15.90]

Administrative Appeals Tribunal, [2.180]

Admiralty law, [12.350]

Adventure tourism — *see also*
Sustainable tourism
— *see also* **Tourism**
Australian Consumer Law,
[15.400]-[15.440]
beach safety and hotels' responsibility,
[15.375]-[15.395]
breach of statutory duty,
[15.480]
cases on obvious risk, [15.450]
Civil Liability legislation,
[15.445]-[15.465]
consumer protection,
[15.400]-[15.435]
consumer protection reform,
[15.420]-[15.425]
contract, [15.365]
criminal liability,
[15.485]-[15.490]
definition, [15.355]
difficulties, [15.510]
exclusion / limitation clauses,
[15.520]
hotels' responsibility for beach safety, [15.375]-[15.395]
innkeepers / carriers' duties compared, [15.360]
insurance, [15.525]
liabilities, [15.470]-[15.490]
public authorities, [15.465]
reform - consumer protection,
[15.420]-[15.425]
regulatory compliance,
[15.530]
responsibility, limiting and shifting, [15.515]
risk management,
[15.495]-[15.530]
risk, obvious, [15.450]
safety legislation, [15.475]
statutory duty, breach of,
[15.480]
statutory guarantees, [15.410]
torts, [15.370]
unfair practices, [15.405]

Advice, provision by agent,
[11.180], [11.325]

Agency
agreement, [11.55]
buyer for resale, distinguished,
[11.35]
creation, [11.50]-[11.70]
creditor, distinguished, [11.40]
definition, [11.10]
employee, distinguished,
[11.20]
estoppel, [11.70]
franchisee, distinguished,
[11.45]
independent contractor, distinguished, [11.25]
liability of agents,
[11.160]-[11.190]
liability of principal,
[11.195]-[11.210]
mere, [9.330]
operation of law, [11.60]
package holiday, liability for,
[9.320]-[9.355]
ratification, [11.65]
rights of agents, [11.95],
[11.145]-[11.155]
termination, [11.215]
travel — *see* **Travel agent**
trustee, distinguished, [11.30]
types, [11.75]-[11.90]

Agent
advice, provision of, [11.180]
anti-competitive offences,
[9.250]
consumer protection law,
[11.185]-[11.190]
contract, liability for, [11.170]
criminal liability, [11.190]
definition, [11.10]
duties, [11.95]-[11.140]
accounts, duty to keep,
[11.140]
act in person, duty to,
[11.110]
confidentiality, of, [11.130]
disclosure, of, [11.125]
due care and skill, to exercise, [11.105]
instructions, to follow,
[11.100]
interests of the principal, to act in, [11.120]
loyalty, of, [11.115]
secret profit, not to make,
[11.135]
general, [11.85]

545

Agent — cont
  indemnity and reimbursement,
      right to, [11.150]
  insurance, [7.110]
  liability, [11.160]-[11.190]
  lien, right of, [11.155]
  misrepresentation by, [11.185]
  principal, liability to, [11.160]
  remuneration, right to, [11.145]
  rights, [11.145]-[11.155]
  secret commission, [6.110]
  special, [11.80]
  third parties, liability to,
      [11.165]-[11.185]
  tortious act, [11.175]
  universal, [11.90]

Air transport
  administration,
      [12.470]-[12.485]
  Air Service Agreements (ASA),
      [12.490]-[12.500]
  arbitration, [12.755]
  Australian law,
      [12.550]-[12.565]
  freedom of the air, [12.480]
  Guadalajara Convention 1961,
      [12.540]
  hijacking conventions, [12.675]
  IATA Passenger Liability
      Agreements 1997,
      [12.710]-[12.760]
  international, [12.470]
  international and domestic,
      comparison of, [12.560]
  liability in, [12.535]-[12.775]
  liability to third parties,
      [12.765]-[12.775]
  Montreal and Warsaw system
      principles,
      [12.570]-[12.670]
  Montreal Convention 1999,
      [12.565]
  national and State, [12.475]
  outer space, [12.520]-[12.530]
  presumed unlimited liability,
      [12.680]-[12.705]
  regulation, [12.470]-[12.515]
  space tourism,
      [12.520]-[12.530]
  third party liability,
      [12.765]-[12.775]
  uniform system,
      [12.570]-[12.670]
  Warsaw Convention 1929,
      [12.535]-[12.540]
  Warsaw system,
      [12.535]-[12.545]
  World Trade Organization
      (WTO),
      [12.505]-[12.515]

Anti-competitive practices
  arrangements, [9.250]
  authorisations and exemptions,
      [9.285]
  cartel conduct, [9.245]
  contracts and arrangements,
      [9.250]
  enforcement and remedies,
      [9.290]-[9.295]
  exclusive dealing,
      [9.260]-[9.265]
  exemptions, [9.285]
  market power, misuse of,
      [9.255]
  mergers and acquisitions,
      [9.280]
  price fixing, [9.275]
  remedies, [9.290]-[9.295]

Appeal
  court, definition, [2.100]
  jurisdiction, and, [10.90]
  Privy Council, [2.185]
  Arbitration
  case study, [10.75]
  definition, [10.60]
  features, [10.70]
  mediation, after, [10.65]
  what constitutes, [10.60]

Arrest
  citizen, [6.190]
  criminal investigation, [6.175]
  private property, entry on,
      [6.180]
  warrant, [6.185]

Assault, [6.80]

Athens Convention 1974,
  [12.425]

Attractions — see also **Sporting
  events**
  Australian Consumer Law,
      [15.85]
  Civil Liability legislation, [15.85]
  consumer protection, [15.40]
  contract, [15.70]-[15.80]
  criminal liability, [15.95]
  crowd control, [15.100]
  duty to safeguard licensees and
      their property,
      [15.65]-[15.80]
  licensee's rights,
      [15.30]-[15.35]
  licensees, no duty to accept,
      [15.20]-[15.25]
  major events, [15.110]-[15.115]
  proprietors, rights and duties,
      [15.15]-[15.10]
  rights and duties of proprietors,
      [15.15]-[15.50]
  spectacle, rights of a proprietor
      over, [15.55]-[15.60],
      [15.110]
  street car racing, [15.115]
  ticket scalping, [15.43]-[15.45]
  torts and contract,
      [15.70]-[15.80]
  unauthorised advertising,
      [15.105]
  workplace health and safety,
      [15.90]

**Australia New Zealand Food
  Standards Code**,
  [14.25], [14.40]

**Australia New Zealand Food
  Standards Council**,
  [14.25], [14.35]

**Australian Competition and
  Consumer
  Commission (ACCC)**
  administration, [9.35]
  anti-competitive conduct,
      authorisation for, [9.285]
  Australian Competition
      Tribunal, [2.180]
  Australian Consumer Law,
      administration of, [9.30]
  functions, [2.180], [9.30]-[9.35]
  Trade Practices Act 1974 (Cth),
      administration of, [9.35]

Australian Consumer Law
  adventure tourism,
      [15.400]-[15.440]
  bait advertising, [9.150]
  coercion, [9.160]
  Competition and Consumer Act
      2010 (Cth), [9.40]
  conflict of laws, [9.235]
  consumer guarantees,
      [9.175]-[9.235]
  definitions, [9.45]
  enforcement and remedies,
      [9.60]-[9.65], [9.75],
      [9.85], [9.95], [9.195],
      [9.290]-[9.295]
  Fair Trading legislation, and,
      [9.100]
  false or misleading
      representation,
      [9.100]-[9.105]
  full price, statement of, [9.155]
  general conduct, [9.50]-[9.85]
  gift, offer of, [9.145]
  goods, consumer guarantees in
      the supply of,
      [9.175]-[9.180]
  harassment, [9.160]
  information standards, [9.215]
  international contracts,
      [9.225]-[9.235]
  legislative arrangements, [9.30]
  liability of manufacturers,
      [9.220]
  liability, product,
      [9.205]-[9.220]

Australian Consumer Law — *cont*
  manufacturers' liability, [9.220]
  misleading conduct re goods, [9.110]
  misleading conduct re services, [9.115]-[9.120]
  misleading or deceptive conduct, [9.50]-[9.55], [9.110]-[9.115]
  objectives, [9.30]
  overbooking, [9.165]
  payment without supply, acceptance of, [9.125]-[9.135]
  price, statement of full, [9.155]
  prize, offer of, [9.145]
  product liability, [9.205]-[9.220]
  reforms, [9.30]
  remedies, [9.60]-[9.65], [9.75], [9.85], [9.95], [9.195], [9.290]-[9.295]
  services, consumer guarantees in the supply of, [9.175], [9.185]-[9.205]
  specific unfair practices, [9.90]-[9.165]
  statutory consumer guarantees, [9.175]
  timetable, [9.30]
  Trade Practices Act 1974 (Cth) — *see* **Trade Practices Act 1974 (Cth)**
  unconscionable conduct, [9.50], [9.70]-[9.75]
  unfair contract terms, [9.50], [9.80]
  unfair practices, [9.90]-[9.165]
  Vienna Convention, [9.230]

Australian Federation of Travel Agents (AFTA)
  code of ethics, [11.370]-[11.380]
  objectives, [11.370]

Australian Hotels Association, [13.190]

Australian Youth Hostels Association (AYHA), [13.190]

B

Bailment, [13.115]

Beverage — *see* **Food and beverage**
Bills — *see also* **Statutes**
  committee stages, [3.45]
  drafting, [3.20]
  first reading, [3.35]
  original idea, [3.15]
  passage through parliament, [3.30]
  presentation, [3.25]
  Royal assent, [3.60]
  second reading, [3.40]
  third reading, [3.50]
  upper house, transmission to, [3.55]

Broker
  buyer for resale, [11.35]
  insurance, [7.110]-[7.115]
  travel agent acting as, [11.135], [11.265]-[11.275]

Buyer for resale
  agent, distinguished, [11.35]
  case studies, [11.285]-[11.305]
  travel agent acting as, [11.280]

C

Carrier — *see also* **Common carriers**
  common law, at, [12.10]
  definition, [12.15]
  fault of, [12.50]
  history of, [12.10]
  legislation, [12.65]-[12.100], [12.120]-[12.150]
  notice and receipt, [12.145]
  protection of, [12.140]
  Queensland legislation, [12.120]
  scope of legislation, [12.130]
  valuables, [12.135]

Casinos — *see also* **Gaming law**
  administration, [15.175]
  agreements, [15.175]
  Australian law and policy on, [15.145]
  benefits, [15.145]-[15.150]
  capacity, [15.165]
  community benefits levy, [15.155]
  control of, [15.175]
  costs, [15.145]-[15.150]
  customers and responsibility of Operators, [15.180]-[15.195]
  development, [15.165]
  fees, [15.175]
  gambler, problem, [15.200]
  gaming machines, [15.205]-[15.215]
  investment, [15.170]
  Kaldor Hicks criterion, [15.155]
  legislation, [15.145]
  levies, [15.175]
  licensing, [15.170]-[15.175]
  operation of, [15.175]
  Operators' responsibility to their customers, [15.180]-[15.195]
  Paretto criterion, [15.155]
  policy formulation, [15.155]-[15.160]
  problem gambler, [15.200]
  responsibility of Operators to their customers, [15.180]-[15.195]
  taxation, [15.170]
  tourists, for, [15.145], [15.155]

Child sex tourism
  offence, [6.85], [11.340]
  travel agents, responsibility, [11.340]

Civil Liability legislation
  adventure tourism, [15.445]-[15.465]
  breach of statutory duty, [5.175]
  contributory negligence, [5.155]
  dangerous recreational activities, [5.185]
  illegal enterprise, [5.165]
  intoxication, [14.325]
  nervous shock, [5.50]
  public authorities, [5.175]
  recreational activities, dangerous, [5.185]
  traveller accommodation, [13.60]
  vicarious liability, [5.100]
  voluntary assumption of risk, [5.150]

Civil trial
  costs, [10.120]
  method, [10.110]
  pleadings, [10.105]
  preliminary issues, [10.100]
  proceedings, [10.115]
  venue, [10.110]

Club licence, [14.170]

Codes of conduct
  Australian Federation of Travel Agents, [11.370], [11.380]
  tourism, travel and hospitality industries, [9.40]

Codes of practice
  occupational health and safety, [8.175]

Common carriers
  Australian Consumer Law, [12.65]-[12.95]

Common carriers — cont
  business travellers,
    [12.80]-[12.85]
  common law, [12.10]-[12.60]
  definition, [12.15]
  delay by, [12.30]
  deviation by, [12.30]
  exclusion or limitation of
    liability by, [12.60]
  history, [12.10]
  legislation, [12.65]-[12.100],
    [12.120]-[12.150]
  leisure travellers, [12.75]
  luggage, [12.40]-[12.50]
  passenger safety, [12.35]
  rights and duties,
    [12.20]-[12.50]
  safety of passengers, [12.35]
  special contracts, [12.60]
  statutes and convention,
    modification of, [12.100]
  statutory guarantees,
    [12.65]-[12.95]
  transit, [12.55]

Common law
  adversarial and inquisitorial
    process, [2.50]
  basis, [2.50], [2.95]
  colonial Australia, [2.45]
  damages for disappointment,
    [2.220]-[2.235]
  development, [2.50]
  exercise, [2.235]
  pleadings, [2.50]
  precedent — see **Precedent**
  statute, distinguished, [2.55]
  tort — see **Tort**

**Competition and Consumer
  Act 2010 (Cth)**,
    [9.240]-[9.290]
  anti-competitive practices,
    [9.250]
  authorisations, [9.285]
  cartel conduct, [9.245]
  enforcement and remedies,
    [9.290]-[9.295]
  exclusive dealing,
    [9.260]-[9.265]
  exemptions, [9.285]
  market power, misuse of,
    [9.255]
  mergers and acquisitions,
    [9.280]
  price fixing, [9.275]
  provisions, [9.240]
  remedies, [9.290]-[9.295]

Competition law
  anti-competitive practices,
    [9.250]
  Australian Competition and
    Consumer Commission,
    [9.285]

  authorisations, [9.285]
  cartel conduct, [9.245]
  cases, [9.265]
  Competition and Consumer Act
    2010 (Cth),
    [9.240]-[9.290]
  consumer protection, [9.20],
    [9.240]-[9.285]
  exclusive dealing,
    [9.260]-[9.265]
  exemptions, [9.285]
  market power, misuse of,
    [9.255]
  mergers and acquisitions,
    [9.280]
  price fixing, [9.275]

Conciliation, [10.40]

Consideration, [4.120]-[4.140]
  definition, [4.125]
  executed, [4.135]
  executory, [4.135]
  principles of, [4.130]
  values, [4.140]

Consumer claims courts
  role, [10.125]
  small claims jurisdiction,
    [10.130]-[10.155]

Consumer guarantees
  conflict of laws, [9.235]
  defective goods, [9.220]
  enforcement, [9.95], [9.195]
  exclusion, [9.200]
  goods, supply of,
    [9.175]-[9.180]
  information standards, [9.215]
  international contracts,
    [9.225]-[9.235]
  liability of manufacturers,
    [9.220]
  liability, product,
    [9.205]-[9.220]
  limitation, [9.200]
  manufacturers' liability, [9.220]
  product liability,
    [9.205]-[9.220]
  product safety, [9.210]
  remedies and enforcement,
    [9.95], [9.195]
  safety, [9.210]
  services, supply of, [9.175],
    [9.185]-[9.205]
  unfair practices, [9.90]-[9.165]
  Vienna Convention, [9.230]

Consumer protection
  Australian Consumer Law, —
    see **Australian
    Consumer Law**
  buyer beware maxim, [9.10]
  codes of conduct, [9.40]

  common law, [9.10]
  competition — see also
    Competition law,
    [9.240]-[9.285]
  Competition and Consumer Act
    2010 (Cth), [9.40]
  consumer guarantees,
    [9.175]-[9.235]
  contract, [4.170]-[4.180],
    [4.220], [4.275], [4.330],
    [4.390]
  definitions, [9.45]
  enforcement and remedies,
    [9.60]-[9.65], [9.75],
    [9.85], [9.95], [9.195],
    [9.290]-[9.295]
  exclusion clause, [4.275]
  Fair Trading legislation, [9.20],
    [9.35]-[9.40]
  general conduct, [9.50]-[9.85]
  goods, consumer guarantees in
    the supply of,
    [9.175]-[9.180]
  holidays, package,
    [9.300]-[9.365]
  implied term, [4.220]
  industry self-regulation, [9.40]
  information standards, [9.215]
  international contracts,
    [9.225]-[9.235]
  jurisdiction, [9.25]
  legislation overview,
    [9.15]-[9.20]
  liability of manufacturers,
    [9.220]
  liability, product,
    [9.205]-[9.220]
  manufacturers' liability, [9.220]
  misrepresentation,
    [4.170]-[4.180], [4.330]
  origin, [9.10]-[9.45]
  package holidays,
    [9.300]-[9.365]
  product liability,
    [9.205]-[9.220]
  product safety, [9.210]
  reforms, [9.30]
  remedies, [9.60]-[9.65], [9.75],
    [9.85], [9.95],
    [9.290]-[9.295]
  Sale of Goods legislation, [9.20]
  seller beware maxim, [9.15]
  services, consumer guarantees
    in the supply of, [9.175],
    [9.185]-[9.205]
  specific unfair practices,
    [9.90]-[9.165]

Trade Practices Act 1974 (Cth)
  — see **Trade
  Practices Act 1974
  (Cth)**
  unfair practices, [9.90]-[9.165]

Consumer protection legislation
Australian Consumer Law, — see **Australian Consumer Law**
civil remedies, [4.175]
damages, [4.175]
implied terms, [4.220]
misrepresentations, [4.175], [4.330]
rescission, [4.175]
unfair trading, [4.175]

Contract
acceptance, [4.80]-[4.115]
agent, liability of, [11.170]
anti-competitive, [9.250]
bilateral, [4.35]
breach of tort, overlap with, [5.10]
capacity to, [4.335]-[4.355]
commercial agreements, [4.155]
consideration, [4.120]-[4.140]
consumer protection legislation, [4.275]
damages, [4.400]-[4.440]
definition, [4.05]
domestic and social agreements, [4.150]
duress, [4.380]
employment — see **Employment contract**
exclusion clauses, [4.225]
exercise, [4.440]
express terms, [4.190]-[4.205]
formal, [4.20]
fraudulent misrepresentation, [4.170]
frustration, [4.375]
Himalaya clause, [4.395]
implied term, [4.190], [4.210]-[4.220]
injunction, [4.400], [4.420]
innocent misrepresentation, [4.170]
insurance — see **Insurance contract**
international, [9.225]-[9.235]
key elements, [4.40]
law, sources of, [4.10]
legal relations, intention to create, [4.145]
limitation clauses, [4.225]
mentally ill person, [4.355], [4.160]
minor — see **Minor**
misrepresentation — see **Misrepresentation**
mistake — see **Mistake**
negligent misrepresentation, [4.170]
offer — see **Offer**
parol evidence, [4.200]
previous dealings, [4.225], [4.235]
principal, liability of, [11.200]
privity of, [4.395]
reasonable notice, [4.240]-[4.270]
remedies for breach, [4.400]-[4.440]
representation, [4.170]-[4.185]
rescission, [4.400]-[4.405]
restitution, [4.400], [4.410]
simple, [4.25]
terms, [4.165]-[4.395]
types, [4.15]-[4.35]
unconscionability, [4.385]
undue influence, [4.380]
unenforceable, [4.285]
unilateral, [4.30]
validity, factors affecting, [4.280]
void, [4.295]
voidable, [4.290]

Costs of civil trial, [10.120]

COTIF Convention 1980, [12.295]

Courts
action, commencement of, [10.90]
appeal, avenues of, [10.90]
appellate jurisdiction, [2.100]
cross-vesting legislation, [2.190]
doctrine of precedent, [10.90]
federal system, [2.160]-[2.190]
hierarchy, [2.155]-[2.210]
jurisdiction, [10.80]-[10.90]
original jurisdiction, [2.100]

Creditor
agent, distinguished, [11.40]

Criminal law
arrest, [6.175]-[6.190]
classification of offences, [6.35]-[6.45]
codified jurisdictions, [6.15], [6.25]
common law jurisdictions, [6.20]
exercise, [6.205]
liability — see **Criminal liability**
offences — see **Offences**
preliminary hearing, [6.195]
procedure, [6.175]-[6.205]
proof, — see **Proof**
sources, [6.15]-[6.25]
standard of proof, [6.205]
tort, overlap with, [5.10], [6.10]
trial, [6.200]

Criminal liability
agent, of, [11.190]
defences to — see **Defences**
elements, [6.50]-[6.65]
gross negligence, [6.55]-[6.60]
intent to commit crime, [6.50]-[6.65]
principal of, [11.210]
strict liability, distinguished, [6.65]
wrongful act, [6.50]

Criminal trial, [2.205], [6.115], [6.170]-[6.205], [10.110]

Customary law
law, as source of, [2.45]
native title, recognition of, [2.65]

CVN Convention 1976, [12.430]

CVR Convention 1973, [12.220]

D

Damages
breach of contract, for, [4.425]-[4.440]
disappointment for, [2.220]-[2.235], [9.310]
heads of, [4.440]
mitigation of loss, [4.435]
package holidays, [9.310]
remoteness, [4.430]

Death
passengers, of — see **Passenger**

Deception
goods or services, obtaining by, [6.105]

Deceptive and misleading conduct, [4.175]

Defamation
defamatory statement, [5.130]
defences, [5.140]
elements of tort, [5.135]

Defences
anti-competitive practices, to, [9.285]
complete, [6.120]-[6.140]
criminal, [6.115]-[6.160]
diminished responsibility, [6.155]
insanity, [6.130]

549

Defences — *cont*
  intoxication, [6.150]
  mistake, [6.140]
  necessity, [6.135]
  negligence, [5.145]-[5.165]
  partial, [6.145]-[6.160]
  provocation, [6.160]
  self-defence, [6.125]
  statutory, [6.165]

Defences to negligence
  contributory negligence, [5.145], [5.155]
  illegal enterprise, [5.145], [5.165]
  ineviatble accident, [5.145], [5.160]
  onus of proof — *see* **Onus of proof**
  voluntary assumption of risk, [5.145]

Disciplinary procedure of liquor licensees — *see also* **Liquor licensing**
  appeal against determination, [14.240]
  disciplinary measures, [14.235]
  exercise, [14.240]
  grounds for disciplinary action, [14.230]
  inspection, [14.225]
  investigation, [14.225]

Discrimination in the workplace, [8.140]

Dispute resolution
  alternative, [10.10]-[10.75]
  arbitration, [10.60]-[10.75]
  arbitration after mediation, [10.65]
  case studies, [10.30], [10.55], [10.75]
  conciliation, [10.40]
  court, [10.80]-[10.120]
  exercise, [10.155]
  litigation method, [10.05]
  mediation, [10.35]-[10.55]
  methods, [10.05]-[10.75]
  negotiation, [10.15]-[10.30]
  Ombudsman's role, [10.45]
  "principled" negotiation, [10.20]
  processes, [10.10]-[10.75]
  small claims — *see* **Small claims**
  Travel Agent Commissioner, [11.365]
  trial — *see* **Trial**

District Court
  consumer claims' courts, [10.65], [10.125]-[10.155]
  jurisdiction, [2.205]
  powers, [2.205]

E

Ecotourism — *see also* **Sustainable tourismt**
  cultural heritage, [15.245]
  definition, [15.290]
  quality assurance, [15.345]
  sustainability, [15.300]
  World Heritage sites, in, [15.295]

Employee — *see also* **Employment contract**
  agent, distinguished, [11.20]
  attendance at workplace, [8.40]
  breach of contract, [8.90]-[8.95]
  compensation, [8.110]
  confidentiality after termination, [8.45]
  definition, [8.200]
  dismissal, [8.95]-[8.105]
  duties, [8.20]-[8.45]
  Fair Work legislation, [8.95]-[8.100], [8.110]-[8.125]
  faithful service, [8.25]
  misconduct, [8.95]
  reasonable directions, duty to obey, [8.35]
  re-employment, [8.110]
  reinstatement, [8.110]
  skill and care, [8.30]
  summary dismissal, [8.95]
  unfair dismissal, [8.100]
  unlawful dismissal, [8.100]
  wrongful dismissal, [8.105]

Employer
  definition, [8.100]
  duties, [8.20], [8.50]-[8.70]
  indemnification of employees, [8.70]
  occupational health and safety, [8.65], [8.205]-[8.215]
  paid leave, [8.60]
  wages, payment of, [8.55]
  work, obligation to provide, [8.50]

Employment
  agreement, [8.130]
  award, [8.125]
  contract — *see* **Employment contract**
  discrimination, [8.140]
  enterprise agreements, [8.130]
  equal opportunity, [8.145]
  Fair Work Act 2009 (Cth), [8.95]-[8.100], [8.110]-[8.125]
  Fair Work Australia, [8.100], [8.110]
  Hospitality Industry (General) Award 2010, [8.125]
  human rights, [8.135]
  modern award system, [8.100], [8.110], [8.125]-[8.130], [10.30]
  National Employment Standards, [8.100], [10.30]
  occupational health and safety, [8.160]-[8.235]
  reinstatement, [8.110]
  sexual harassment, [8.150]
  sources of law, [8.05]
  statutory intervention, [8.115]-[8.235]
  workers compensation, [8.70], [8.155]
  workplace — *see* **Workplace**

Employment contract
  breach of, [8.90]-[8.95]
  confidentiality after termination, [8.45]
  consequential termination, [8.85]
  contract for services, distinguished, [8.15]
  definition, [8.10]
  deliberate termination, [8.80]
  duties, [8.20]-[8.70]
  elements, [8.15]
  employee, duties of, [8.20]-[8.45]
  employer, duties of, [8.20], [8.50]-[8.70]
  general conditions, [8.10]
  independent contractor, distinguished, [8.15]
  key elements, [8.15]
  rights and duties, [8.20]-[8.70]
  statutory intervention, [8.115]-[8.235]
  termination, [8.75]-[8.110]
  unfair dismissal, [8.100]-[8.110]

Equal Employment Opportunity, [8.145]

Equity
  development, [2.60]
  law, as source of, [2.45]
  principles, [2.60]
  unconscionable conduct, [4.385]

Events — *see also* **Activities** — *see also* **Attractions**
  Australian Consumer Law, [15.85]

EventsActivitiesAttractions — *cont*
  Civil Liability legislation, [15.85]
  consumer protection, [15.40]
  contract, [15.70]-[15.80]
  criminal liability, [15.95]
  crowd control, [15.100]
  duty to safeguard licensees and their property, [15.65]-[15.80]
  licensee's rights, [15.30]-[15.35]
  licensees, no duty to accept, [15.20]-[15.25]
  major, [15.110]-[15.115]
  proprietors, rights and duties, [15.15]-[15.10]
  rights and duties of proprietors, [15.15]-[15.50]
  spectacle, rights of a proprietor over, [15.55]-[15.60], [15.110]
  sporting, [15.10], [15.45]-[15.60], [15.75]-[15.80]
  street car racing, [15.115]
  ticket scalping, [15.43]-[15.45]
  torts and contract, [15.70]-[15.80]
  unauthorised advertising, [15.105]
  workplace health and safety, [15.90]

Express terms, [4.190]-[4.205]

F

Fair Trading legislation
  administration, [9.35]
  codes of conduct, [9.40]
  consumer protection under, [9.20]
  overview, [9.20]

Fair Work Act 2009 (Cth), [8.95]-[8.100], [8.110]-[8.125]

Fair Work Australia, [8.100], [8.110]

False or misleading representation
  case study, [9.100]-[9.105]
  food labelling, [14.95]

Family Court of Australia, [2.170]

Federal Court of Australia, [2.165]

Federal Magistrates Court, [2.175]

Federal tribunals and commissions, [2.180]

Food and beverage — *see also* **Liquor licensing**
  administration of legislation, [14.75]
  contract law, remedies under, [14.80]
  contract terms, [14.85]
  co-operative scheme, [14.25]-[14.45]
  criminal liability, [14.115]
  definition, [14.50]
  development of law, [14.05]
  distribution, [13.160], [13.170]
  earliest law, [14.10]
  enforcement of legislation, [14.75]
  false representations, [14.95]
  Garibaldi metwurst case, [14.120]
  guarantees, statutory, [14.85]
  history, [14.10]
  hygiene, [14.70]
  international organisations, [14.15]
  labelling, [14.60]
  legislation, [14.25]-[14.75]
  national organisations, [14.20]
  organisations, [14.15]-[14.20]
  premises, [14.70]
  preparation, [14.50]
  product liability, [14.100]
  sale and preparation, [14.50]
  statutory guarantees, [14.85]
  tortious liability, [14.90]
  trade measurement, [14.65]
  workplace health and safety, [14.110]

Food legislation
  co-operative scheme, [14.25]-[14.45]
  definitions, [14.50]
  hygiene, [14.70]
  labelling, [14.60]
  premises, [14.70]
  preparation, [14.50]
  sale, [14.50]
  trade measurement, [14.65]

Food Standards Australia New Zealand (FSANZ), [14.25]-[14.30]

G

Gaming Law
  Australian law, [15.135]
  casinos — *see* **Casinos**
  definitions, [15.120]
  gambling policy, [15.140]
  gaming machines, [15.205]-[15.215]
  high rollers, [15.140]
  history, [15.125]-[15.130]
  poker machines, [15.140]
  problem gamblers, [15.200]

Gaming machines
  accounting, [15.210]
  administration, [15.210]
  community benefit levies, [15.205]
  definitions, [15.210]
  enforcement, [15.205]
  inspection, [15.210]
  legislation, [15.210]-[15.215]
  licences, [15.210]
  policy, [15.205]
  supervision, [15.210]

Goods — *see also* **Consumer guarantees**
  deception, obtaining by, [6.105]
  defective, [9.220]
  international sale of, [9.230]
  misleading conduct, [9.110]

Guests
  definition, [13.40]
  innkeepers, duties of, — *see* **Innkeepers**

H

Hearing
  preliminary, [6.195]
  small claims court, [10.150]

High Court of Australia, [2.160]

Highway, freedom of, [12.170]

Hire cars, [12.215]

Holiday rental
  definition, [13.155]
  growth, [13.155]

551

Holiday rental — *cont*
   internet, distribution via, [13.170]
   licensing intermediaries, [13.165]
   restrictions, few, [13.160]
   travel portals, [13.170]

Homicide offence, [6.75]

Hospitality industry — *see also* **Food and beverage**
   insurance, need for, [7.05]

Hotel licence, [14.170]

Hotel Motel and Accommodation Association (HMAA), [13.190]

I

Implied terms, [4.190], [4.210]-[4.220]

Independent contractor
   agent, distinguished, [11.25]
   employment contract, distinguished, [8.15]

Injunction, [4.420]

Injury to passengers — *see* **Passengers**

Inn, [13.30]

Innkeepers
   Australian Consumer Law, [13.125]
   bailment, [13.115]
   common law under, [13.10], [13.50]-[13.90]
   comparative table of legislation, [13.200]
   current position, [13.20]
   definitions, [13.35]
   duties, [13.40], [13.55]-[13.75]
   duty to receive and entertain guest, [13.55]
   exclusion of liability by, [13.100]-[13.110]
   guest, [13.40], [13.55]-[13.75]
   history of law, [13.10]
   infra hospitium, [13.95]
   inn, definition of, [13.30]
   international, [13.120]
   legislation, [13.120]-[13.150], [13.200]
   lien over property, [13.85]
   limitation of liability by, [13.100]-[13.110]
   lodger, [13.45]
   property, duty to safeguard guest's, [13.75]
   regulatory issues, [13.175]
   rights and duties at common law, [13.50]-[13.90]
   Rules of the House, right to set, [13.80]
   safety of guest, [13.60]
   South Australia, [13.135]
   special contracts, [13.100]-[13.110]
   statutory guarantees, [13.125]
   uniform legislation, need for, [13.150]
   Western Australia, [13.140]

Insanity
   criminal offence, defence to, [6.130]

Inspection,
   Licensing Authority, by, [11.495]

Insurance
   agent, [7.110]
   air carrier liability, [7.155]
   benefits, types of, [7.30]-[7.55]
   broker, [7.110]
   business interruption, [7.190]
   cancellation policy, [7.105]
   cash in transit, [7.180]
   commencement date, [7.90]
   commercial, [7.185]-[7.195]
   comprehensive motor vehicle, [7.170]
   contents of home and building, [7.165]
   contingency, [7.40]
   contract — *see* **Insurance contract**
   double, [7.55]
   exercise, [7.205]
   hospitality industry, need for, [7.05]
   indemnity, [7.30]-[7.55]
   insurable risk, types of, [7.120]-[7.195]
   intermediaries, [7.110]
   key person in commercial, [7.195]
   liability, [7.125]-[7.155]
   over insurance, [7.50]
   plate glass, [7.175]
   product liability, [7.140]
   professional indemnity, [7.130]
   property, [7.160]-[7.180]
   public liability, [7.135]
   renewal of policy, [7.100]
   subrogation, [7.60]
   third party motor vehicle, [7.150]
   tourism industry, need for, [7.05]
   travel, [7.05], [7.200]-[7.205]
   types, [7.120]-[7.195]
   under insurance, [7.45]
   workers compensation, [7.145]

Insurance contract
   acceptance, [7.75]
   consideration, [7.80]
   cover notes, [7.95]
   definitions, [7.15]
   distinguishing features, [7.15]
   duty of disclosure, [7.25]
   elements, [7.75]-[7.85]
   formation, [7.70]
   general principles, [7.65]-[7.195]
   indemnity principle, [7.30]-[7.55]
   insurable interest, [7.20]
   legal relations, intention to create, [7.85]
   nature, [7.25]-[7.60]
   offer, [7.75]
   principles, [7.65]-[7.195]
   sources of law, [7.10]
   subrogation, [7.60]
   timing, [7.90]
   uberrimae fidei, [7.25]

Intent
   criminal, [6.50]-[6.65]
   insurance, [7.85]
   legal relations, to create, [4.145]-[4.160], [7.85]
   legislative, [3.250]

International Air Transport Association (IATA)
   billing and settlement plan, [11.360]
   dispute resolution, [11.365]
   objectives, [11.350]
   Travel Agency Commission, [11.365]
   travel agent accreditation, [11.355]

International Hotel Association (IHA), [13.180]

International Youth Hostel Federation (IYHF), [13.185]

Internet
   travel distribution, [11.680]-[11.715]
   travel portals, [11.695]-[11.700]

Intoxication
   alcohol server liability, [14.280]

Intoxication — *cont*
  Civil Liability legislation, [14.325]
  criminal offence, defence to, [6.150]
  licensee's duty of care, [14.280]-[14.320]
  meaning, [14.250]
  responsibility for intoxicated guest, [14.280]-[14.320]

J

Judges, [2.75]

Judgment
  obiter dicta, [2.90]
  procedure, [2.80]
  ratio decidendi, [2.85]

Jurisdiction — *see also* **Courts**
  action, commencement of, [10.90]
  appeal, avenues of, [10.90]
  appellate, [2.100]
  coded, [6.15], [6.25]
  common law, [6.20]
  doctrine of precedent, [10.90]
  original, [2.100]

Justice
  law, morality and, tension between, [2.10], [2.35]

L

Law
  characteristics, [2.10]
  common — *see* **Common law**
  contract, [4.10]
  customary — *see* **Customary law**
  equity, [2.45], [2.60], [4.385]
  justice, morality and, tension between, [2.10], [2.35]
  legal positivism, [2.30]
  natural law, [2.25]
  origin, [2.15]
  role, [2.15]
  rule of, [2.40]
  sources, [2.45]
  statute — *see* **Statute**
  theories, [2.20]-[2.30]

Legal positivism, [2.30]

Licence
  gaming machines, for, [15.210]

liquor — *see* **Liquor licensing**
travel agent — *see* **Travel agency licensing**

Licensees — *see also* **Liquor licensing**
  case law, [14.270], [14.285]-[14.315]
  conduct of business, [14.210]-[14.215]
  disciplinary procedure, [14.225]-[14.240]
  general responsibilities, [14.215]
  intoxicated guests, responsibility for, [14.280]-[14.315]

Licensing Authority
  disciplinary procedure of liquor licensees, [14.225]-[14.240]
  inspection and investigation by, [11.495]

Lien
  carrier, of, over luggage, [12.50]
  innkeeper, of, over property, [13.85]
  luggage, over, [12.50]
  rail carrier, of, [12.290]
  road carrier, of, [12.210]

Liquor licensing — *see also* **Food and beverage** — *see also* **Licensees**
  alcohol servers' common law liability, [14.260]-[14.275]
  alcohol servers' statutory liability, [14.245]-[14.255]
  appeal, [14.205]
  application, [14.185]
  Civil Liability legislation, [14.325]
  conditions, [14.200]
  conduct of business, [14.210]-[14.215]
  decision, [14.195]
  definitions, [14.155]
  disciplinary procedure, [14.220]-[14.240]
  Dram Shop liability, [14.265]-[14.270]
  exemptions, [14.155]
  general responsibilities of licensee, [14.215]
  government revenue from liquor, [14.150]
  harm minimisation, [14.255]
  history, [14.135]

  intoxicated guests, responsibility for, [14.280]-[14.315]
  intoxication, meaning of, [14.250]
  investigation, [14.190]
  legislation, [14.140], [14.245]
  legislative history, [14.135]
  nature of, [14.160]-[14.165]
  objects of, [14.145]
  off licences, [14.170]
  on licences, [14.170]
  procedure, [14.175]-[14.205]
  reviews, [14.20]
  Rum Rebellion, [14.130]
  taxes on liquor, [14.155]
  statutory duty, [14.245], [14.150]
  types, [14.170]

Local Court — *see* **District Court** — *see* **Magistrates Court**

Lodger
  definition, [13.45]
  Australian Consumer Law, [12.65]-[12.90]

London Convention 1976, [12.375]-[12.410]

Luggage
  business traveller, [12.80]-[12.85]
  duty of carrier to accept, [12.40]
  leisure travellers, [12.75]
  lien of carrier over, [12.50]
  loss or damage to, [12.205], [12.285]
  rail transport, [12.285]
  responsibility for, [12.45]
  road transport, [12.205]
  statutory guarantees, [12.65]-[12.90]

M

Magistrates Court
  functions, [6.195]
  indictable offence, [6.195]
  jurisdiction, [2.210]
  powers, [2.210]

Mediation
  advantages, [10.50]
  case study, [10.55]
  conciliation, [10.40]
  definition, [10.35]
  features, [10.50]
  Ombudsman's role, [10.45]

Mediation — *cont*
what constitutes, [10.35]

Minor
contracts for necessaries, [4.345]
contracts of service, [4.350]
definition, [4.340]

Misconduct by employee, [8.95]

Misleading or deceptive misconduct
bait advertising, [9.150]
coercion, [9.160]
consumer protection, [9.55]-[9.65]
gift or prize, offer of, [9.145]
goods, [9.110]
harassment and coercion, [9.160]
overbooking, [9.165]
payment without supply, acceptance of, [9.125]-[9.135]
price, stated in full, [9.155]
prize, offer of, [9.145]
services, [9.115]-[9.120]

Misrepresentation
agent, by, [11.185]
consumer protection legislation, [4.330]
food labelling, [14.95]
fraudulent, [4.170], [4.305], [4.315]
innocent, [4.170], [4.305]-[4.310]
negligent, [4.170], [4.305], [4.320]
rescind, right to, [4.325]

Mistake
common, [4.360]
criminal offence, defence to, [6.140]
mutual, [4.360]
non est factum, [4.370]
unilateral, [4.360]-[4.365]

Morality
law, justice and, tension between, [2.10], [2.35]

N

Native title, [15.320]

Natural law, [2.20]-[2.25]

Necessity
criminal offence, defence to, [6.135]

Negligence
basis for action, [5.25]-[5.75]
breach of duty of care, [5.60]-[5.65]
causation, [5.70]
damage, [5.70]-[5.75]
defences to — *see* **Defences**
duty of care, [5.30]-[5.65]
elements of tort, [5.25]-[5.75]
employer and duty of care, [8.65]
exercise, [5.185]
gross — *see* **Criminal liability**
illegality, [5.55]
negligent misstatement, [5.80]-[5.95]
nervous shock, [5.50]
occupational health and safety, [8.205]
proof — *see* **Proof**
proximity, [5.45]
public authorities, [5.125]
reasonable foreseeability, [5.40]
remedy — *see* **Remedy**
remoteness of damage, [5.75]
res ipsa loquitur, [5.180]
standard of care, [5.65]
statutory duty, breach of, [5.175], [8.210]
tort reform, [5.185]
vicarious liability, [5.80], [5.100]-[5.120]

Negotiation
case study, [10.30]
definition, [10.15]
key features, [10.25]
"principle", [10.20]
what constitutes, [10.15]

Night club licence, [14.170]

Northern Territory Travel Industry Compensation Scheme, [11.625]

O

Occupational health and safety
accident prevention programs, [8.225]
codes of practice, [8.175], [8.235]
committees, [8.220]
definitions, [8.185]-[8.200]
duties imposed by legislation, [8.65], [8.205]-[8.215]
employee, definition, [8.200]
employer, definition, [8.195]
employer duties owed by, [8.65], [8.205]-[8.215]
enforcement, [8.230]
exercise, [8.235]
history, [8.160]
inspections and enforcement, [8.230]
International Labour Organisation, [8.170]
legislation, [8.65], [8.180], [8.205]-[8.215]
materials and substances, [8.215]
national standards, [8.175], [8.235]
organisations, [8.170]-[8.175]
particular industries, [8.215]
plant and equipment, [8.215]
premises, [8.215]
Safe Work Australia, [8.175]-[8.180]
specific health problems, [8.215]
state authorities, [8.175]
system of work, [8.215]
workplace, definition, [8.190]

Offences — *see also* **Defences**
anti-competitive practices, [9.250]
assault, [6.80]
child sex tourism, [6.85]
classification, [6.30]-[6.45]
conversion, [6.95]-[6.100]
deception, obtaining goods of services, [6.105]
defences, [6.115]-[6.165]
homicide, [6.75]
indictable, [6.35], [6.45]
misappropriation, [6.95]-[6.100]
person, against, [6.75]-[6.85]
property, against, [6.90]-[6.105]
secret commissions, [6.110]
stealing, [6.90]
summary, [6.45]
theft, [6.90]
travel agent, acting without licence, [11.390]

Offer — *see also* **Contract**
acceptance, [4.80]-[4.115]
communication of acceptance, [4.85]-[4.105]
counter offer, [4.70]
cross offer, [4.70]
definition, [4.45]
invitation to treat, [4.60]-[4.65]
mere supply of information, [4.70]
postal rule, [4.100]
revocation of acceptance, [4.115]
termination, [4.75]

Offer — *cont*
"to the world at large", [4.50]-[4.55]
unqualified, [4.110]

Onus of proof
civil proceedings, [10.110]
negligence, action for, [5.175]
strict liability, [6.65]

P

Package holidays
agency — *see* **Agency**
common law, [9.325]-[9.350]
damages for disappointment, [9.310]
definition, [9.305]
disappointment, damages for, [9.310]
European Community Directive, [9.355]-[9.360]
exercise, [9.365]
liability, [9.315]-[9.350]
responsibility, [9.315]-[9.350]
transactions involved in, [11.05]

Parliament
powers, [2.55]
sovereignty, [3.80]

Passenger
common carriers — *see* **Common carriers**
death or personal injury, [12.195], [12.275]
duty of carrier to accept, [12.25]
personal injury or death, [12.195], [12.275]
road transport — *see* **Road transport**
safety of, duty of carriers, [12.35]

Postal rule, [4.100]

Precedent
avoiding doctrine of, [2.130]-[2.150]
case law, [2.95]
doctrine of, [2.105]-[2.115]
doctrine of, avoiding, [2.130]-[2.150]
fact, distinguishing cases on, [2.135]
interpretation, [2.140]
jurisdiction, [10.90]
philosophy, [2.115]
rules of, [2.120]
social conditions, effect of, [2.145]

stare decisis, [2.110]
statutes, interpretation of, [3.235]
wrong decision, [2.150]

Premises
definition, [14.155]
food handling, for — *see* **Food and beverage**

Principal
agent's liability to, [11.160]
contract, liability of, [11.200]
criminal liability, [11.210]
definition, [11.10]
liability of, [11.195]-[11.210]
liability of agent to, [11.160]
tort, liability of, [11.205]
travel agent acting as, [11.280]-[11.305]

Privy Council, appeal to, [2.185]

Proof
breach of statutory duty, [5.175]
civil trial, [10.110]
criminal trial, [6.205]
negligence, action for, [5.175]-[5.180]
onus of, [5.175], [6.65], [10.110]
res ipsa loquitur, [5.180]

Provocation
criminal offence, defence to, [6.160]

R

Rail transport
administration, [12.235]-[12.245]
background, [12.230]
common carriers, liability of, [12.265]
COTIF Convention 1980, [12.295]
death or personal injury of passengers, [12.275]
delay, [12.280]
freedom on the railway, [12.250]
international, [12.235]
liability in, [12.265]-[12.290]
lien of carrier, [12.290]
luggage, loss or damage to, [12.285]
national and State, [12.240]
personal injury of passengers, [12.275]
public/private, [12.225]

railworthiness, [12.270]
regulation, [12.235]-[12.260]
revival of, in Australia, [12.245]
road, link with, [12.230]

Recreational activities
civil liability legislation, [15.460]
dangerous, [5.185], [15.460]

Regulations
statutes or acts, distinguished, [3.70]

Remedies
anti-competitive practices, [9.290]-[9.295]
contract, breach of, [4.400]-[4.440]
contract, misrepresentation in, [4.170]
damages, [4.425]-[4.440]
injunction, [4.420]
misrepresentation in contract, [4.170]
rescission, [4.405]
restitution, [4.410]
specific performance, [4.415]
unfair or wrongful dismissal, [8.100]-[8.105]

Rescission, [4.405]

Responsibility
diminished, defence to criminal offence, [6.155]

Restaurant licence, [14.170]

Restitution, [4.410]

Road transport
administration, [12.160]-[12.165]
common carriers, liability of, [12.185]
CVR Convention 1973, [12.220]
death or personal injury of passengers, [12.195]
delay, [12.200]
freedom on the railway, [12.170]
international, [12.160]
liability in, [12.185]-[12.215]
lien of road carrier, [12.210]
luggage, loss or damage to, [12.205]
national and State, [12.165]
personal injury of passengers, [12.195]
public/private, road, [12.175]
regulation, [12.160]-[12.180]
roadworthiness, [12.190]

Rule of law, [2.40]

Rum Rebellion, [14.130]

S

Safe Work Australia, [8.175]-[8.180]

Sale of Goods legislation, [9.20]

Sea transport
administration, [12.320]-[12.350]
admiralty law, [12.350]
Athens Convention 1974, [12.425]
background, [12.300]
charter vessels, [12.420]
common carriers, liability of, [12.335]
cruise shipping, [12.435]-[12.465]
CVN Convention 1976, [12.430]
freedom on the seas, [12.310]
history, [12.310]-[12.315]
international, [12.320], [12.425], [12.465]
law of the sea, [12.315]
liability in, [12.355]-[12.365]
limitation of liability, [12.365]-[12.410]
London Convention 1976, [12.375]-[12.410]
national and State, [12.325]
non-seagoing ships, unlimited liability for, [12.415]
public/private, road, [12.330]
registration of ships, [12.335]
regulation, [12.320]-[12.350]
seagoing ships, limitation of liability, [12.375]-[12.385]
seaworthiness, [12.360]
self-sail vessels, [12.420]
shipowners, policy to protect, [12.440]-[12.465]
SOLAS Convention 1974, [12.345]
Titanic, [12.305]
unlimited liability, [12.415]
valuable, exclusion of liability for, [12.370]

Self-defence
criminal offence, defence to, [6.125]

Self-regulation
codes of conduct, [11.380]

international organisations, [11.345]-[11.365]
national organisations, [11.370]-[11.380]

Services
consumer guarantees, supply of, [9.185]-[9.205]
contract for, [8.15]
deception, obtaining by, [6.105]
definition, [9.45]
enforcement, [9.195]
misleading conduct, [9.115]-[9.120]
remedies, [9.195]

Sexual harassment in the workplace, [8.150]

Small claims
definition, [10.135]
notice, [10.145]
parties, [10.140]

Small claims jurisdiction
appeal, [10.155]
establishment, [10.125]-[10.130]
hearing, [10.150]
order, [10.155]
parties, [10.140]

SOLAS Convention 1974, [12.345]

Specific performance, [4.415]

Sporting events — *see also* **Activities; Attractions**
Australian Consumer Law, [15.85]
Civil Liability legislation, [15.85]
consumer protection, [15.40]
contract, [15.70]-[15.80]
criminal liability, [15.95]
crowd control, [15.100]
duty to safeguard licensees and their property, [15.65]-[15.80]
licensee's rights, [15.30]-[15.35]
licensees, no duty to accept, [15.20]-[15.25]
major, [15.110]-[15.115]
proprietors, rights and duties, [15.15]-[15.10]
rights and duties of proprietors, [15.15]-[15.50]
spectacle, rights of a proprietor over, [15.55]-[15.60], [15.110]
street car racing, [15.115]
ticket scalping, [15.43]-[15.45]

torts and contract, [15.70]-[15.80]
unauthorised advertising, [15.105]
workplace health and safety, [15.90]

Standard of proof
civil trial, [10.95]-[10.120]
criminal trial, [6.170], [6.205]

Statutes — *see also* **Bills** — *see also* **Statutory interpretation**
Bills, procedural stages, [3.15]-[3.55]
colonial Australia, in, [2.45]
commencement, [3.65]
common law, distinguished, [2.55]
content and layout, [3.85]
delegated legislation, [3.260]
example, [3.85]
exercise, [3.150]-[3.155]
interpretation, [3.190]-[3.245]
proclamation, [3.65]
regulations, distinguished, [3.70]
retrospectivity, [3.75]

Statutory guarantees
adventure tourism, [15.410]
common carriers, [12.65]-[12.95]
food and beverage, [14.85]
innkeepers, [13.125]
luggage, [12.65]-[12.90]

Statutory interpretation
dictionaries, [3.190]
legislative intent, [3.190]
precedent — *see* **Precedent**
reading act as a whole, [3.245]
rules of, [3.160]-[3.185]
similar legislation, [3.230]
sources for, [3.145]
statutory intervention, [3.225]
target audience, [3.255]
text of statute, [3.95]-[3.140]

Supreme Court, [2.200]

Sustainable tourism
attractions and activities in sites, [15.305]
concept, [15.300]
ecotourism, [15.300]
education, [15.310]
local involvement, [15.315]
World Heritage, [15.290]-[15.295]

T

Theme parks — see **Attractions**

Tort
agent, tortious act by, [11.175]
breach of statutory duty, [5.175]
Civil Liability legislation, [5.10]
contract law, overlap with, [5.10]
criminal law, overlap with, [5.10]
defamation — see **Defamation**
definition, [5.05]
elements, [5.15]
evidential matters, [5.170]-[5.180]
intentional, distinguished, [5.20]
negligence — see **Negligence**
negligent misstatement, [5.85]-[5.95]
principal, liability of, [11.210]
public authorities, [5.125]
reform in Australia, [5.185]
res ipsa loquitur, [5.180]
specific torts, [5.25], [5.80]-[5.140]
unintentional, distinguished, [5.20]
vicarious liability, [5.100]-[5.120]

Tourism
adventure — see **Adventure tourism**
dangerous recreational activity and, [15.460]
defective goods and services, [9.10]
definition, [1.25]
difficulties, [15.510]
law and regulation, [1.30]
recreation and, [15.455]
regulation, [1.30]
regulatory compliance, [1.35]-[1.45]
sustainable, [15.285]-[15.320]
World Heritage sites, [15.290]-[15.295]

Trade Practices Act 1974 (Cth)
2010 reforms, [9.30]
administration, [9.35]
application of, [9.25]
Australian Consumer Law — see **Australian Consumer Law**
bait advertising, [9.150]
coercion, [9.160]
Competition and Consumer Act 2010 (Cth), [9.40]
consumer guarantees, [9.175]-[9.235]
consumer protection under, [9.20]
corporations, [9.25]
definitions, [9.45]
Fair Trading legislation, and, [9.20], [9.70]
false or misleading representation, [9.100]-[9.105]
full price, statement of, [9.155]
gift, offer of, [9.145]
goods, consumer guarantees in the supply of, [9.175]-[9.180]
harassment, [9.160]
jurisdiction, [9.25]
misleading conduct re goods, [9.110]
misleading conduct re services, [9.115]
misleading or deceptive conduct, [9.55], [9.110]-[9.115]
overbooking, [9.165]
payment without supply, acceptance of, [9.125]-[9.135]
price, statement of full, [9.155]
prize, offer of, [9.145]
reforms, [9.30]
Sale of Goods legislation, and, [9.20]
services, consumer guarantees in the supply of, [9.175], [9.185], [9.200]
unconscionable conduct, [9.70]
unfair practices, [9.90]-[9.165]

Trade Practices Amendment (Australian Consumer Law) Act (No.1) 2010 (Cth) — see **Australian Consumer Law**

Trade Practices Amendment (Australian Consumer Law) Act (No.2) 2010 (Cth) — see **Australian Consumer Law**

Transport
air — see **Air transport**
rail — see **Rail transport**
road — see **Road transport**
sea — see **Sea transport**

Travel
accommodation — see **Accommodation**
agent — see **Travel agent**
distribution, [11.690]-[11.715]
insurance, [7.200]-[7.205]
insurance regulations, [7.205]
prescribed contracts, [7.205]

Travel agency licensing
appeal, [11.445]-[11.450]
application, [11.405]-[11.410]
conditions, [11.430]-[11.435]
conduct of business, [11.455]-[11.480]
decision, criteria for, [11.420]-[11.425]
definitions, [11.390]-[11.395]
disciplinary procedure, [11.485]-[11.545]
disqualification, [11.470]-[11.475]
exemptions, [11.390], [11.400]
investigation, [11.415]
licensing procedure, [11.405]-[11.450]
revocation or restriction, [11.435]
undertaking, [11.540]
Uniform Scheme, [11.385]
unjust conduct, [11.535]-[11.545]

Travel agent
accounting, [11.630]
after sales service, [11.335]
agency law — see **Agency**
broker, acting as, [11.265]-[11.275]
business traveller, [12.80]-[12.85]
carriers, [11.660]
"carriers on business as a", definition, [11.395]-[11.400]
child sex tourism, [11.340]
client, relationship with, [11.225]-[11.245]
conduct of business, [11.455]-[11.480]
criminal liability and suppliers, [11.675]
disqualification, [11.470]
documentation, [11.330]
e-commerce, [11.695]-[11.700]
finance, [11.630]
hotels, [11.670]
insurance intermediaries, [7.115]
internet, impact on — see **Travel distribution**
legal relationships, [11.220]-[11.305]
leisure traveller, [12.75]

Travel agent — *cont*
  licensing — *see* **Travel agency licensing**
  management and supervision, [11.465]
  name and notice, [11.460]
  principal/buyer for resale, [11.280]
  reservations and documentation, [11.330]
  restraining order, [11.545]
  self-regulation, [11.345]-[11.380]
  suppliers, authority from, [11.315]
  tour operators, [11.665]
  transactions by, [11.310]-[11.335]
  travel portals, [11.695]-[11.700]
  travel suppliers, [11.660]-[11.675], [11.245]-[11.260]
  trust moneys, [11.645]-[11.655]
  undertaking, [11.540]
  unjust conduct and undertaking, [11.535]-[11.545]

Travel Agent Commissioner, [11.365]

Travel Compensation Fund
  administration, [11.555]
  appeal rights, [11.590]
  application, [11.565]-[11.570]
  claims entitlement, [11.600]
  claims procedure, [11.605]-[11.610]
  conditions, [11.585]
  decision on application, [11.580]
  establishment, [11.550]
  financial criteria, [11.635]-[11.640]
  initial application, [11.565]
  investigation, [11.575]
  participation, [11.560]-[11.595]
  purposes, [11.550]
  renewal of application, [11.570]
  subrogation, [11.615]
  trust moneys, [11.645]-[11.655]

Travel distribution
  e-commerce, [11.695]-[11.700]
  information and advice, [11.685]
  name, misuse of, [11.705]-[11.715]
  travel advisories, [11.690]
  travel portals, [11.695]

Traveller
  accommodation — *see* **Accommodation**
  business, [12.80]-[12.85]
  leisure, [12.75]

Trial
  civil, [10.105]-[10.120]
  criminal, [2.205], [6.115], [6.170]-[6.205], [10.110]

Tribunals
  federal, [2.180]
  small claims, [10.125]-[10.155]

Trustee and agent distinguished, [11.30]

U

Unconscionable conduct
  Australian Consumer Law, [9.70]
  consumer protection legislation, [4.390]
  contract, in, [4.385]
  equity considerations, [4.385]
  exclusion clause, [4.240]

Unfair trading, [4.175]

Uniform Scheme
  electronic communication, [4.105]
  food, regulation of sale of, [14.20]
  travel agency licensing, [11.385]-[11.390], [11.405]

Universal Federation of Travel Agents Association (UFTAA), [11.345]

Unjust conduct
  travel agent, [11.535]-[11.545]

V

Vicarious liability
  contract for services, [5.115]
  contract of service, [5.115]
  employment, acts done in the course of, [5.120], [8.70]
  independent contractor, distinguished, [5.115]
  master/servant relationship, [5.110]
  negligence, action for, [5.100]
  principal, of, [11.210]
  threshold questions, [5.105]

Vienna Convention
  sale of goods, international, [9.230]

W

Wagering contract, [15.120]

Warrant, arrest for, [6.185]

Words and phrases
  actus rea, [6.50]
  agency, [11.10]
  agent, [11.10]
  appeal court, [2.100]
  carries on a business as a travel agent, [11.395]
  caveat emptor, [9.10]
  caveat venditor, [9.15]
  committal proceeding, [6.195]
  common carrier, [12.15]
  common mistake, [4.360]
  consensus ad idem, [4.45]
  consideration, [4.125]
  contract, [4.05]
  court of first instance, [2.100]
  discrimination, [8.140]
  ecotourism, [15.290]
  ejusdem generis, [3.200]
  employee, [8.200]
  employer, [8.195]
  employment contract, [8.10]
  express term, [4.190]
  expressio unius est exclusio alterius, [3.210]
  food, [14.50]
  gaming contract, [15.120]
  golden rule, [3.175]
  guest, [13.40]
  implied term, [4.190]
  infra hospitium, [13.95]
  inn, [13.30]
  innkeeper, [13.35]
  insurance contract, [7.15]
  insurance intermediary, [7.110]
  jurisdiction, [10.85]
  liquor, [14.155]
  literal rule, [3.165]
  lodger, [13.45]
  luggage, [12.40]
  measurement, [14.65]
  mens rea, [6.50]
  minor, [4.340]
  mischeif rule, [3.180]
  mutual mistake, [4.360]
  non est factum, [4.370]
  noscitur a sociis, [3.205]
  obiter dicta, [2.90]
  offer, [4.45]
  package holiday, [9.305]
  pleading, [2.50]
  precedent, [2.95]
  premises, [14.155]
  ratio decidendi, [2.85]
  res ipsa loquitur, [5.180]
  services, [9.45]
  small claim, [10.135]
  stare decisis, [2.110]

Words and phrases — *cont*
  stipendiary magistrate, [2.210]
  sustainable tourism, [15.300]
  tort, [5.05]
  transit, [12.55]
  uberrimae fidei, [7.25]
  unilateral mistake, [4.365]
  unjust conduct, [11.535]
  wagering contracts, [15.120]
  workplace, [8.190]

Workers compensation
  employee's entitlements, [8.70], [8.155]
  liability insurance, [7.145]

Workplace
  accident prevention programs, [8.225]
  agreements, [8.130]
  committees, [8.220]
  definition, [8.190]
  employer's duties, [8.205]-[8.215]
  occupational health and safety, [8.160]-[8.235]

World Heritage — *see also* **Tourism**
  attractions and activities in sites, [15.305]
  Australian developments, [15.265]-[15.280]
  Australian sites, [15.230]
  cultural heritage, [15.245]
  history, [15.225]-[15.230]
  implementation, [15.325]-[15.350]
  laws, [15.340]
  local involvement, [15.315]
  management models, [15.330]
  management strategies, [15.335]
  native title, [15.320]
  natural heritage, [15.250]
  objectives, [15.255]-[15.230]
  organisations, [15.240]
  presenting sites, [15.260]
  recreational activities, [15.305]
  regulations, [15.340]
  sites, presenting, [15.260]
  sustainable tourism, [15.285]-[15.295]
  State party obligations, [15.255]
  tourism operators' accreditation, [15.345]
  UNESCO, [15.225], [15.235]-[15.260]
  World Heritage Convention, [15.235]-[15.260]

World Travel Agents Association Alliance (WTAA), [11.348]